STAR OCEAN®
THE LAST HOPE®
◇ INTERNATIONAL ◇

DATA EXPLANATION

Base Statistics: Illustrates the character's starting statistics. The values shown are an indicator of where the character's strengths lie. These stats increase as the character levels up. The nine stat types listed are:

	1	2	3	4	5	6	7	8	9
Base Statistics	HP	MP	ATK	DEF	HIT	GRD	INT	LUCK	Critical
	200	50	25	17	27	12	13	100	1.2

1 **HP:** The amount of hit points the character starts with. This number goes down as the character takes damage from enemies. Incapacitation occurs when this value reaches zero.

2 **MP:** The amount of magic points the character starts with. Symbols and special arts require a set amount of MP to use. Neither skill types can be used if this value reaches zero.

3 **ATK:** The base attack strength of the character's physical attacks. This value also affects the damage dealt by most special arts (with the exception of Lymle's special arts, which deal damage based on her INT).

4 **DEF:** The character's base defense rating. This value calculates the amount of HP damage received from enemy physical attacks. The higher the number, the less damage incurred.

5 **HIT:** The character's base hit rating. Dictates how easy it is for the character to attack through an enemy's defenses. Works directly with the enemy's GRD rating to calculate its probability of guarding your attack.

6 **GRD:** The character's base probability of guarding an incoming attack. This value is affected and modified by the enemy's HIT rating.

7 **INT:** The character's base intelligence. Directly affects the strength of symbology and some special arts. The higher the value, the stronger the symbology.

8 **LUCK:** Indicates how lucky the character is. Affects the rate at which characters score critical hits, and how often they are revived from incapacitation via Fury.

9 **Critical:** Shows the calculation used to modify the damage dealt during a critical hit. 1.2 is the lowest modifier, while 2.8 is the highest. Critical damage is calculated by multiplying the damage modifier with the normal damage dealt from the attack. Take note that this value does not appear in any in-game status screens.

Base Resistances: Details the base resistances for the character in question. The number shown is a percentage on how often the character is able to resist the ailment.

Base Resistances								
Poison	Stun	Freeze	Paralysis	Silence	Fog	Curse	Pumpkin	Void
0	0	20	0	0	0	0	0	0

MOVE SET TABLE NOTES

Each character's basic attacks are categorized as either "Long" or "Short" range. The player's distance from an enemy dictates which range they're at, changing the types of attacks at their disposal. Short range techniques can only be used when the player is very close to the enemy, while long range attacks are initiated when the player is well out of the monster's normal striking range. On the other hand, anti-air attacks are only initiated if an enemy is flying in the air within the specified range.

CHARACTER BLINDSIDE RANK

In an effort to quickly illustrate the usefulness of each character's Blindside, a letter-based ranking and a short description has been included with all of them. There are four grades in all, **A** being the best grade available, while **D** is the worst.

Name	Max Lv	Damage	MP Cost	CP Cost	Acquired	Notes
Rising Blade	10	ATK x260%~350%	8~12	2	Level 1	Attack with four rapid strikes, then launch the enemy skywards with a final rising thrust.
Stampede Slash	10	ATK x312%~436%	12~18	3	Level 10	Make a beeline for the enemy, slashing along the way.
Aura Spark	10	ATK x330%~380%	14~21	3	Level 23	Unleash a wave of focused energy with a downward swipe of the sword.
Mystic Cross	10	ATK x433%~766%	16~25	4	Level 39	Kick the enemy into the air, then jump up and run them through.
Cyclone Blade	10	ATK x300%~525%	16~25	4	Level 54	Spin upward with your sword, slashing repeatedly as you go.
Celestial Sword	10	ATK x400%~490%	18~27	5	Level 63	Spin jump to generate a huge energy sword, then strike the enemy three times.
Raging Strike	10	ATK x550%~650%	18~27	5	Level 80	Jump high into the air, then drive a high-speed downward kick into the enemy.
Scintillant Stream	10	ATK x816%~1120%	20~29	5	Skill Manual	Summon a sword of light in your left hand, then slash away fiercely with both swords.

1. **Name:** The label for the skill.

2. **Max Lv:** The maximum amount of skill levels the ability can be increased by. Skills with a 1 in this field cannot be leveled up. The number shown will always be 1 or 10. Leveling your skills up improves their effectiveness while also raising the MP needed to use them.

3. **Damage:** The amount of damage dealt by the attack. The number value shown is multiplied by a character's ATK or INT to get the final damage amount. Symbols use INT to calculate their damage, while special arts mostly use ATK, with the exception of Lymle who uses INT. Skills or symbols that inflict no damage have a "None" written here. Fields with two numbers represent the damage range between the level 1 and level 10 versions of the skill. For example, the damage calculation for Edge's Stampede Slash is listed as ATK x312%~436%. The first number, 312, is the level 1 strength of the skill, while the second number is the level 10 value.

4. **MP Cost:** The amount of MP required to use the skill. Two values are listed here if the skill's MP cost increases at higher levels, the first numbers being the level 1 MP cost, while the second is the MP requirement at level 10. For example, Edge's Stampede Slash has an initial MP cost of 12 at level 1, but then jumps to 18 MP when its skill level is increased to level 10.

5. **CP Cost:** The capacity points necessary to equip the skill in battle configuration.

6. **Acquired:** The method for obtaining the skill. Abilities with a "Level" value in this field require that the character reach the illustrated EXP level. Other techniques require the use of a Skill Manual to learn the ability. The necessary Skill Manual shares the same name as the ability. Refer to the item appendix for each manual's location.

7. **Notes:** Various bits of information about the skill that range from specific effect properties to info about the inputs needed to use it.

ELEMENT KEY

= EARTH   = FIRE   = THUNDER   = DARKNESS

= WATER   = WIND   = LIGHT

CHARACTER STAT COMPARISON

Though the majority of the following data is found in each individual character section, this is a quick comparison chart of the *Star Ocean* cast's statistics. Hopefully, this will illuminate the key differences between each character, as well as the areas they excel in the most. Areas highlighted in red designate an exceptionally high value.

Character	HP	MP	ATK	DEF	HIT	GRD	INT	LUCK	Critical
Edge	200	50	25	17	27	12	13	100	1.2
Reimi	167	41	17	20	28	13	5	140	2.8
Faize	172	66	16	21	23	14	10	90	1.2
Lymle	137	72	10	16	19	11	11	90	1.2
Bacchus	264	34	24	26	28	10	9	120	1.2
Meracle	185	37	31	14	25	13	9	80	1.2
Sarah	145	78	11	15	20	12	12	100	2.8
Myuria	158	69	14	16	21	11	11	90	1.2
Arumat	226	57	31	14	35	10	14	60	2.0

Characters

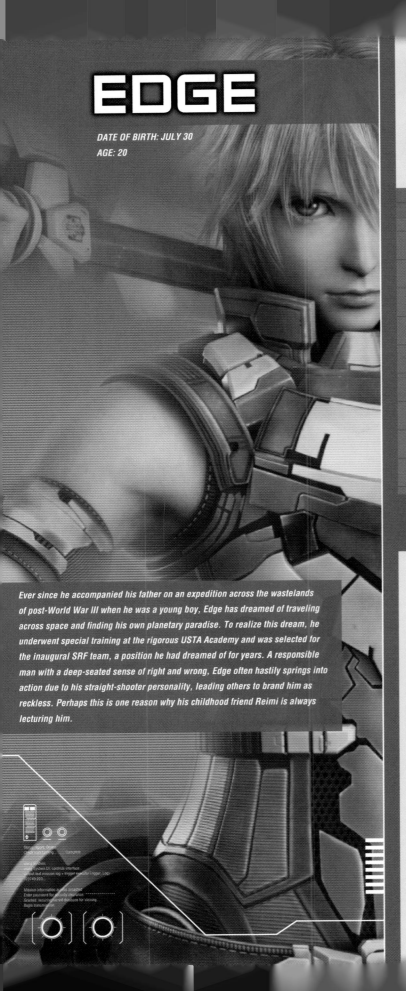

EDGE

DATE OF BIRTH: JULY 30
AGE: 20

Base Statistics

HP	MP	ATK	DEF	HIT	GRD	INT	LUCK	Critical
200	50	25	17	27	12	13	100	1.2

Base Resistances

Poison	Stun	Freeze	Paralysis	Silence	Fog	Curse	Pumpkin	Void
0	0	0	0	0	0	0	0	0

✣ MOVE SET

XBOX 360 VERSION

LONG RANGE (ATTACK)
Ⓐ

SHORT RANGE (ATTACK)
Ⓐ   ⒶⒶ   ⒶⒶⒶ

SHORT RANGE (DIRECTIONAL ATTACK)
🕹 + Ⓐ

ANTI-AIR ATTACK
Analog stick at neutral, then press
ⒶⒶⒶ against a flying enemy

JUMP Ⓑ

PS3 VERSION

LONG RANGE (ATTACK)
✕

SHORT RANGE (ATTACK)
✕   ✕✕   ✕✕✕

SHORT RANGE (DIRECTIONAL ATTACK)
L3 + ✕

ANTI-AIR ATTACK
Analog stick at neutral, then press
✕✕✕ against a flying enemy

JUMP ◎

BLINDSIDE – RANK C

Edge's Blindside causes him to swing behind the enemy in a wide arc. He's completely vulnerable to attack during this evasion, making it difficult to Blindside wide attacks with a large swinging range.

Ever since he accompanied his father on an expedition across the wastelands of post-World War III when he was a young boy, Edge has dreamed of traveling across space and finding his own planetary paradise. To realize this dream, he underwent special training at the rigorous USTA Academy and was selected for the inaugural SRF team, a position he had dreamed of for years. A responsible man with a deep-seated sense of right and wrong, Edge often hastily springs into action due to his straight-shooter personality, leading others to brand him as reckless. Perhaps this is one reason why his childhood friend Reimi is always lecturing him.

CHARACTER OVERVIEW

Edge's party role is to act as a well-rounded melee unit geared towards leadership. At higher levels, he has access to both damaging hand-to-hand combat abilities and a small variety of offensive and restorative symbols. This combination allows him to effectively attack from any position, and also act as a light support unit for

injured party members. Though ultimately weaker than Arumat and Meracle in the damage department, his main attack string is far more flexible then theirs, allowing for longer basic combos that don't require MP usage. His special arts are also quite potent, since they are an array of powerful short range skills that easily link together when used in combos. His final three special arts (the Celestial Sword, Raging Strike, and Scintillant Stream) are also ranked amongst the strongest skills available to any character.

Despite the symbols at his disposal, Edge's strongest assets are his short range capabilities. His flexible combos, high ATK rating, and relatively high DEF rating make him a powerful frontline brawler. When attacking, verify whether or not his short range string has connected (three taps of the attack button) before chaining into a fourth hit. This acts as a safety measure against defending enemies. If they happen to guard your attack, canceling into short-range directional attack may leave you open to counter attack. If his short range string hits, chain the third hit into the directional attack, then as he recovers from the uppercut, perform his three-hit anti-air combo (leave the analog stick at the neutral position, then tap the attack button three times) to juggle your airborne enemy. When MP is abundant, forgo the uppercut segment and chain the third hit of his short range combo into his Rising Blade or Stampede Slash. With the Chain Combos skill learned, additional special arts can be linked after either attack for even bigger damage. Learn this skill to quickly improve Edge's combo prowess (refer to his combo section for stronger combo examples).

TIPS & TACTICS

LEVEL 10 BERSERK + BLINDSIDES + ATK BOOST

The strongest position for a melee unit is behind an enemy after a Blindside. Make this position even more advantageous by equipping the **ATK Boost** skill and making frequent use of the **Berserk** skill. At level 10, Berserk nearly doubles your ATK rating, but comes with a high cost: characters with the Berserk status take double the damage they normally do. Don't be afraid to use it in certain situations though; its risk is negligible if you're fighting an enemy with attacks that are easy to dodge. Berserk is also useful for dealing high damage to an enemy whose focus is on a weaker party member. This switches its attention to you, which may leave you vulnerable to lethal damage, but it does keep the enemy from wrecking a vital member of your party. You're also a lot more capable of staying out of trouble than a computer controlled character is.

INFINITE COMBINATION

Edge's directional-attack uppercut launches enemies into the air, setting them up for follow-up strikes. It's possible to continuously launch the enemy with this same attack over and over again, effectively keeping it in a combo for an extended period of time. The enemy's only method of escape is to activate Rush Mode, which keeps it from being bumped into the air. Although this combo deals very little damage and leaves you very open to attack from alternate enemies, it still has its uses in one-on-one fights. If, for example, your opponent's Rush Gauge is almost full, use the uppercut combo to continuously hit them until they activate it. They'll still be in the sky when they enter Rush Mode, so end your assault and back away to safety.

EXAMPLE COMBOS

XBOX 360 VERSION

(A)(A)(A) ➡ ⬇️+(A), juggle with his anti-air (A)(A)(A)

(A)(A)(A) ➡ Stampede Slash ➡ Rising Blade ➡ Cyclone Blade ➡ Mystic Cross

(A)(A)(A) ➡ Stampede Slash ➡ Rising Blade ➡ Raging Strike ➡ Celestial Sword

(A)(A)(A) ➡ Rising Blade ➡ Raging Strike ➡ Scintillant Stream ➡ Celestial Sword

PS3 VERSION

✕✕✕ ➡ (L3)+✕, juggle with his anti-air ✕✕✕

✕✕✕ ➡ Stampede Slash ➡ Rising Blade ➡ Cyclone Blade ➡ Mystic Cross

✕✕✕ ➡ Stampede Slash ➡ Rising Blade ➡ Raging Strike ➡ Celestial Sword

✕✕✕ ➡ Rising Blade ➡ Raging Strike ➡ Scintillant Stream ➡ Celestial Sword

SKILLS

Field Skills

Name	Max Lv	MP Cost	Acquired	Notes
Smithery	10	--	Initially Available	Item Creation skill. Allows you to craft metallic weapons and armor. At higher levels, more types of items become available.
Anthropology	10	--	Skill Manual	Increases chance of earning items after defeating humanoid enemies. At higher levels, the effect increases. Once the skill is learned, its effect is always active.
Appetite	10	--	Skill Manual	Adds a bonus to the effect of HP recovery items. At higher skill levels, the effect increases. Once the skill is learned, its effect level is always active.
Chain Combos	10	--	Skill Manual	Allows you to assign multiple skills to a chain combo. At higher skill levels, the number of slots and the amount of damage dealt increases. Once the skill is learned, its effect is always active.
Sprinting	1	--	Initially Available	Allows you to run faster on the field for a limited distance. Press the ✕ or the ⬤ button while running to use.
Pickpocketing	10	--	Skill Manual	Allows you to steal items and Fol from others. At higher skill levels, the chance of success increases. To use this skill, press the (B) or ⬤ button while wearing the Bandit's Gloves. Be careful not to steal too much…

Symbols

Name	Max Lv	Damage	MP Cost	CP Cost	Acquired	Notes
Healing	10	--	6	--	Obtained after first entering the Alanaire Citadel.	HP recovery symbol. Recovers 31% of one ally's maximum HP at level 1. The HP healed increases to 40% at level 10.
Silence	10	--	22	--	Level 17	Support symbol. Places the target and nearby enemies in silence status, preventing them from using symbols. At higher skill levels, the chance of success increases.
Cure Condition	1	--	8	--	Level 30	Curative symbol. Purifies one ally of all status ailments.
Symbolic Weapon	10	--	17	--	Level 46	Support symbol. Allows one ally to absorb MP from the enemy with each attack. At higher skill levels, the effect duration increases.
Radiant Lancer	10	INT x169%~301%	5~14	2	Level 57	Attack symbol ⭕. At level 1, rains four spears of light down upon the enemy. At level 10, rains seven spears of light down upon the enemy.
Aurora Rings	10	INT x156%~260%	7~16	4	Level 70	Attack symbol ⭕. At level 1, erects three pillars of light, damaging any enemy that touches them. At level 10, erects six pillars of light.
Faerie Star	10	--	50	--	Skill Manual	HP recovery symbol. Summons a faerie to recover 81% of all allies' maximum HP at level 1. At level 10, it recovers 90% of their HP.

Special Arts

Name	Max Lv	Damage	MP Cost	CP Cost	Acquired	Notes
Rising Blade	10	ATK x260%~350%	8~12	2	Level 1	Attack with four rapid strikes, then launch the enemy skyward with a final rising thrust.
Stampede Slash	10	ATK x312%~436%	12~18	3	Level 10	Make a beeline for the enemy, slashing along the way.
Aura Spark	10	ATK x330%~380%	14~21	3	Level 23	Unleash a wave of focused energy with a downward swipe of the sword.
Mystic Cross	10	ATK x433%~766%	16~25	4	Level 39	Kick the enemy into the air, then jump up and run them through.
Cyclone Blade	10	ATK x300%~525%	16~25	4	Level 54	Spin upward with your sword, slashing repeatedly as you go.
Celestial Sword	10	ATK x400%~490%	18~27	5	Level 63	Spin jump to generate a huge energy sword, then strike the enemy three times.
Raging Strike	10	ATK x550%~650%	18~27	5	Level 80	Jump high into the air, then drive a high-speed kick downward onto the enemy.
Scintillant Stream	10	ATK x816%~1120%	20~29	5	Skill Manual	Summon a sword of light in your left hand, then slash away fiercely with both swords.

Battle Skills

Name	Max Lv	MP Cost	CP Cost	Acquired	Notes
ATK Boost	10	--	1	Skill Manual	Adds 10 to your ATK at level 1. The ATK boost granted increases as the skill's level increases (granting +1000 ATK at level 10). The effect is only active when set as a battle skill.
HP Boost	10	--	2	Skill Manual	Adds 100 to your maximum HP at level 1. At level 10, your maximum HP increases by 10000. The effect is only active when set as a battle skill.
MP Boost	10	--	2	Skill Manual	Adds 10 to your maximum MP at level 1. At level 10, your maximum MP increases by 1000. The effect is only active when set as a battle skill.
Critical Hit	10	--	1	Skill Manual	Allows you to perform critical hits outside of Rush Mode. At higher skill levels, the chance of success and the amount of damage dealt increases. The effect is only active when set as a battle skill.
No Guard	10	--	3	Skill Manual	Prevents you from being thrown off balance when taking damage of less than 1% of your maximum HP (at level 1). At level 10, the effect increases to 10%. The effect is only active when set as a battle skill.
First Aid	10	--	2	Skill Manual	When taking damage from an enemy, occasionally recovers 20% of damage taken as HP (at level 1). At level 10, 60% of the damage taken is converted. The effect is only active when set as a battle skill.
Auto Healing	10	--	1	Skill Manual	Gradually restores HP during battle. At higher skill levels, HP is restored more frequently. The effect is only active when set as a battle skill.
Stun	10	--	2	Skill Manual	Occasionally adds a stun effect when attacking enemies. At higher skill levels, the chance of success increases. The effect is only active when set as a battle skill.
Fury Boost	10	--	1	Skill Manual	Increases the chance of surviving via Fury when your HP hits 0. At higher skill levels, the effect increases. The effect is only active when set as a battle skill.
Taunt	1	1	--	Skill Manual	Attracts the attention of enemies, making them target you more often. Use this skill from the battle menu.
Berserk	10	8	--	Skill Manual	Boosts ATK by 40% for 30 seconds (at level 1), but doubles damage taken from attacks. At level 10 ATK is increased by 100%. Use this skill from the battle menu.
Convert	10	4	--	Skill Manual	Converts some HP to MP over a period of 30 seconds. At higher skill levels, the effect increases. Use this skill from the battle menu.

Transmission completed

Log of system using System UI; controls interface.
Output text mission log + trigger execute(Trigger_Log) 523749:223...

Sensing date: 3641 --
database 101 secured!

End of line

REIMI

DATE OF BIRTH: MARCH 28
AGE: 19

Reimi is a young woman from the Saionji family, one of the most prestigious families on Earth. Her parents serve as boardmembers of the Space Development Division of the USTA. Upon passing the USTA's examination, she was selected along with Edge as a member of the inaugural SRF team. A woman of both literary and martial talent, Reimi is always looking out for those around her. Her skill with the bow is second to none, having mastered both western and Asian forms of archery, and uses it as her weapon of choice in battle. She has been friends with Edge since childhood; she grew up with him like a sister, but her heartfelt concern for his well-being may suggest that a different sort of relationship may be blossoming.

Base Statistics

HP	MP	ATK	DEF	HIT	GRD	INT	LUCK	Critical
167	41	17	20	28	13	5	140	2.8

Base Resistances

Poison	Stun	Freeze	Paralysis	Silence	Fog	Curse	Pumpkin	Void
10	10	10	10	10	10	10	10	10

⚝ MOVE SET

XBOX 360 VERSION	PS3 VERSION
LONG RANGE (ATTACK)	**LONG RANGE (ATTACK)**
Ⓐ ⒶⒶ ⒶⒶⒶ	✕ ✕✕ ✕✕✕
SHORT RANGE (ATTACK)	**SHORT RANGE (ATTACK)**
Ⓐ	✕
SHORT RANGE (DIRECTIONAL ATTACK)	**SHORT RANGE (DIRECTIONAL ATTACK)**
ⓛ + Ⓐ	L3 + ✕
ANTI-AIR ATTACK	**ANTI-AIR ATTACK**
Analog stick at neutral, then press Ⓐ against a flying enemy	Analog stick at neutral, then press ✕ against a flying enemy
JUMP Ⓑ	**JUMP** ◉
JUMP ATTACK Ⓑ, then Ⓐ	**JUMP ATTACK** ◉, then ✕

BLINDSIDE – RANK B

When initiating a Blindside, Reimi leaps over the enemy to their backside. This generally clears most ground attacks as long as they have a thin horizontal range of effect. Attacks that tend to cover the sky may hit Reimi during her jump. Though useful as a means of opening the enemy up to short range attacks, Reimi's options at that distance are lacking. Instead, use Blindsides to confuse the enemy's targeting focus, which unveils the opportunity to run away to a safer distance.

CHARACTER OVERVIEW

Reimi's main objective is to inflict support damage from a distance. This role is highly important to both casters and the other melee units in your party, since her arrows can be focused on dangerous field enemies, occasionally interrupting them and canceling their actions. This strategy is further supplemented by her exceedingly high critical damage multiplier, which is the highest of any character type. It's best to focus your efforts on improving her critical hit rate, which not only helps her control the enemy's movements, but also skyrockets her damage output to extreme levels. This is done by giving her the **Critical Hit** skill or by simply equipping her with the many bow weapons that already come packed with a critical rate boost. If that wasn't enough, her **Focus** skill also boosts her critical rate at the cost of a mere 6 MP. Use this ability at the beginning of every fight to potentially inflict heavy damage.

Sadly, her high critical rate occasionally inflicts enough damage to draw enemies towards her. To avoid taking serious hurt when this happens, use a Blindside to force the attacker to lose sight of you. Rush Mode's No Guard attribute can be used to walk away from multi-hit combos or situations where you're surrounded. It's also worth equipping the **Energy Shield** skill to keep her safe when an adversary catches you off guard. The Darkblood Chainmail armor found in Tatroi's Colosseum nullifies HP damage 25% of the time, an effect that can boost Reimi's defense significantly if equipped with Energy Shield.

TIPS & TACTICS

JUMPING SNIPER

Reimi is the only character that can attack while jumping. This is useful for quickly moving away from enemies and immediately staging a counter attack, a tactic that can be done indefinitely to slowly kill foes early in the game. This in turn also makes her the perfect character for protecting the Bonus Board against foes that are good at smashing it. Keep in mind that this loses its effectiveness during the later portions of the game when enemies start to incorporate stronger symbols.

In addition to its defensive uses, her jumping attack can be performed *extremely* close to the ground to reduce its recovery period. If done as close to the ground as possible, its starting and recovery periods become much faster than that of her standard shots. It's so fast that she can even combo her jump shots repeatedly against larger enemies, who can't escape until they activate Rush Mode. Use this technique when MP isn't available to inflict moderate damage.

RAPID ARROW COMBINATIONS

As soon as they are available, it's highly recommended that you organize Reimi's Chain Combo set up to allow for repeated chains between the Hunter's Moon and Crimson Squall abilities. To do this, fill her Chain Combo 1 slots with Hunter's Moon, Crimson Squall, then Hunter's Moon again (Hunter's Moon ➡ Crimson Squall ➡ Hunter's Moon). In the Chain Combo 2 slots, equip two Crimson Squall skills, which can be chained into before or after her Hunter's Moon skill. Once it's set up, the idea is to chain between her skills in a loop-like fashion, like so: Crimson Squall ➡ Hunter's Moon ➡ Crimson Squall ➡ Hunter's Moon ➡ Crimson Squall. The beauty of this combination is that it rapidly builds Reimi's Rush Gauge while inflicting major damage. The damage dealt is increased substantially when this combo is performed with her critical boosting skills.

When the Savage Sparrows skill is available, it's worth setting up Chain Combos that consist of three back-to-back Savage Sparrows. Though slightly weaker than her Hunter's Moon loops, its faster attack speed and homing capabilities make it more flexible against multiple enemies.

BEAT MODE BURST: RUSH MODE VOLLEY

Reimi is very effective while in Rush Mode, which drastically increases her critical hit rate, reduces the MP cost of skills by 25%, and gives her a 5% ATK boost when she's using BEAT's "Burst" battle type. When Burst reaches rank 20, she gains the ability to build Rush Gauge while in Rush Mode. Rush Gauge is built by successfully hitting your foe with attacks, meaning the more attacks you hit with, the faster your Rush Gauge builds. Take advantage of this property by continuously chaining between her Hunter's Moon and Crimson Squall special arts, which hit numerous times, in order to rapidly build your Rush Gauge. This effectively keeps you in Rush Mode as long as you continue to attack. The sheer number of attacks released also raises the probability of scoring a critical hit. When combined with her **Focus, ATK Boost,** and **Critical Hit** skills, the critical damage dealt during this volley is astounding. Also, try using the **Berserk** skill with it, which doubles her ATK at the cost of a giant DEF penalty. This shouldn't be a problem as long as you keep your distance, though.

EXAMPLE COMBOS

XBOX 360 VERSION

Short range ⓛ+Ⓐ, wait a moment, neutral anti-air Ⓐ

Long range ⒶⒶⒶ ➡ Crimson Squall ➡ Hunter's Moon ➡ Crimson Squall ➡ Hunter's Moon ➡ Crimson Squall

Long range ⒶⒶⒶ ➡ Savage Sparrows ➡ Savage Sparrows ➡ Savage Sparrows

PS3 VERSION

Short range ⓛ + ✕, wait a moment, neutral anti-air ✕

Long range ✕✕✕ ➡ Crimson Squall ➡ Hunter's Moon ➡ Crimson Squall ➡ Hunter's Moon ➡ Crimson Squall

Long range ✕✕✕ ➡ Savage Sparrows ➡ Savage Sparrows ➡ Savage Sparrows

SKILLS

Field Skills

Name	Max Lv	MP Cost	Acquired	Notes
Cooking	10	--	Initially Available	Item Creation skill. Allows you to prepare food items. At higher skill levels, more types of items become available.
Botany	10	--	Skill Manual	Increases the chance of earning items after defeating plant enemies. At higher skill levels, the effect increases. Once the skill is learned, its effect is always active.
Chain Combos	10	--	Skill Manual	Allows you to assign multiple skills to a chain combo. At higher skill levels, the number of slots and the amount of damage dealt increases. Once the skill is learned, its effect is always active.
Harvesting	10	--	Initially Available	Allows you to harvest items at harvesting points. Press 🅑 or ⬤ at a harvesting point to use. At higher skill levels, the number of items you can harvest increases.

Special Arts

Name	Max Lv	Damage	MP Cost	CP Cost	Acquired	Notes
Sonic Thorn	10	ATK x210%~474%	8~12	2	Level 1	Fire a charged arrow that slices through everything in its path.
Seraphic Thunder	10	ATK x247%~262%	12~18	3	Level 14	Shoot an arrow into the air, causing lightning to rain down in the vicinity. At higher skill levels, the number of lightning bolts increases.
Crimson Squall	10	ATK x256%~464%	14~21	3	Level 28	Fire a charged arrow that erupts into a torrent of rapid-fire bolts. At higher skill levels, the number of bolts increases.
Chaotic Blossoms	10	ATK x300%~435%	16~25	3	Level 35	Close in on the enemy with a jump-kick, then launch a flurry of kicks that culminates with a crushing blow.
Hunter's Moon	10	ATK x250%~490%	16~25	4	Level 46	Fire a charged arrow that explodes into a sphere of smaller arrows that rain down upon the enemy.
Crescent Wings	10	ATK x300%~467%	18~27	3	Level 59	Fire an arrow adorned with wings of fury that cuts through any enemy it hits.
Heavenly Flight	10	ATK x280%~336%	18~27	4	Level 71	Fire a charged arrow that strikes down from above and explodes on impact, causing widespread damage.
Savage Sparrows	10	ATK x300%~510%	20~29	5	Skill Manual	Fire a string of charged arrows that home in on any enemies in the vicinity.

Battle Skills

Name	Max Lv	MP Cost	CP Cost	Acquired	Notes
ATK Boost	10	--	1	Skill Manual	Adds 10 to your ATK at level 1. The ATK boost granted increases as the skill's level increases (granting +1000 ATK at level 10). The effect is only active when set as a battle skill.
HP Boost	10	--	2	Skill Manual	Adds 100 to your maximum HP at level 1. At level 10, your maximum HP increases by 10000. The effect is only active when set as a battle skill.
MP Boost	10	--	2	Skill Manual	Adds 10 to your maximum MP at level 1. At level 10, your maximum MP increases by 1000. The effect is only active when set as a battle skill.
Energy Shield	10	--	1	Skill Manual	Occasionally nullifies physical attacks. At higher skill levels, the chance of success increases. The effect is only active when set as a battle skill.
Critical Hit	10	--	1	Skill Manual	Allows you to perform critical hits outside of Rush Mode. At higher skill levels, the chance of success and the amount of damage dealt increases. The effect is only active when set as a battle skill.
First Aid	10	--	2	Skill Manual	When taking damage from an enemy, occasionally recovers 20% of damage taken as HP (at level 1). At level 10, 60% of the damage taken is converted. The effect is only active when set as a battle skill.
Auto Healing	10	--	1	Skill Manual	Gradually restores HP during battle. At higher skill levels, HP is restored more frequently. The effect is only active when set as a battle skill.
Fury Boost	10	--	1	Skill Manual	Increases the chance of surviving via Fury when your HP hits 0. At higher skill levels, the effect increases. The effect is only active when set as a battle skill.
Rage	10	--	2	Skill Manual	Increases the chance of becoming enraged when an ally falls, and provides an ATK and INT bonus when enraged. At higher levels the effect increases. The effect is only active when set as a battle skill.
Taunt	1	1	--	Skill Manual	Attracts the attention of enemies, making them target you more often. Use this skill from the battle menu.
Berserk	10	8	--	Skill Manual	Boosts ATK by 40% for 30 seconds (at level 1), but doubles damage taken from attacks. At level 10, ATK is increased by 100%. Use this skill from the battle menu.
Focus	10	6	--	Skill Manual	Boosts HIT and critical hit chance for 30 seconds. At higher skill levels, the effect increases. Use this skill from the battle menu.

Transmission completed.

Log of system using System UI, conform interface
Output text release log - trigger execute(Trigger_Log)
657748.329

Serving data: 3841 -
database 764 second()

End of line.

FAIZE

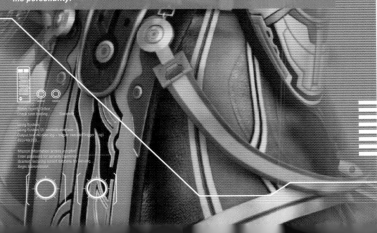

DATE OF BIRTH: FEBRUARY 3
AGE: 18

A young Eldarian, and the first being from another planet that Edge has ever met. His looks are indistinguishable from any Earthling. His somewhat large-looking ears are actually a type of Eldarian accessory. A stickler for politeness and harmony, Faize is capable of cool, calculated reasoning, and his engineering talents are vast enough that he designed the Sol (an Eldarian shuttlecraft) on his own. He can also use symbology, a form of magic-like power unavailable to Earthlings. Still, he was deeply moved upon meeting Edge, looking up to his swordsmanship skills and take-charge attitude. Seemingly quiet and calm, he is in fact easily surprised and emotionally swayed, revealing a pure, honest side to his personality.

Base Statistics

HP	MP	ATK	DEF	HIT	GRD	INT	LUCK	Critical
172	66	16	21	23	14	10	90	1.2

Base Resistances

Poison	Stun	Freeze	Paralysis	Silence	Fog	Curse	Pumpkin	Void
0	0	0	0	0	0	0	0	0

✿ MOVE SET

XBOX 360 VERSION

LONG RANGE (ATTACK)
Ⓐ

SHORT RANGE (ATTACK)
Ⓐ   ⒶⒶ   ⒶⒶⒶ

SHORT RANGE DIRECTIONAL ATTACK
🕹+Ⓐ

ANTI-AIR ATTACK
Analog stick at neutral, then press Ⓐ against a flying enemy

JUMP Ⓑ

XBOX 360 VERSION

LONG RANGE (ATTACK)
✕

SHORT RANGE (ATTACK)
✕   ✕✕   ✕✕✕

SHORT RANGE DIRECTIONAL ATTACK
L3 + ✕

ANTI-AIR ATTACK
Analog stick at neutral, then press ✕ against a flying enemy

JUMP ◉

BLINDSIDE – RANK C

Spinning his body while jumping, Faize swings to the enemy's rear with a twist. Slow-moving and awkward, Faize's Blindside presents frequent problems dodging attacks that many large enemies use. There are some benefits though, since the jumping segment of the evasion can avoid some ground attacks.

CHARACTER OVERVIEW

The kindhearted Faize is a hybrid of a frontline fighter and an offensive caster. His basic ATK stats and short range attack strings are much better than the typical symbologist, while his INT rating and list of symbols are certainly more potent than Edge's. His Terra Hammer, Dark Devourer, and Reaping Spark are amongst the strongest symbols encountered, and he has all of the necessary skills needed to boost their strength (**Mindflare**, **Enlighten**, **INT Boost**). Faize is fairly flexible in the right hands.

When you first acquire Faize, equip him with a Chain Combo that consists of Earth Glaive ➡ Earth Glaive, which is used to attack enemies from afar. When your level surpasses 21, change your Chain Combo setup to Stone Rain ➡ Earth Glaive or Ice Needles ➡ Earth Glaive. The Stone Rain combination works well against crowded groups of adversaries, while the Ice Needles variation should be used against those weak to the water element. Never approach an enemy unless it gives you a direct opening (like after initiating a recovery-heavy symbol). When that opening reveals itself, combo a standard attack (with the analog stick neutral) into a directional attack (pressing the analog stick towards the enemy).

As interesting as Faize's attack style is, his lack of focus in a particular area does him harm. Not having any special arts to use ultimately destroys the usefulness of his physical attacks, so it's necessary to fall back on his symbology. Since his INT rating is lower than the other casters available, and since he doesn't have access to the Fast Cast skill, there's simply no reason to pick him over a different symbologist. If that wasn't enough, Arumat, a similar melee unit/offensive caster, is strictly more effective than Faize despite their slight difference in play styles.

Since he's generally weaker than other characters, and since he takes an extended absence from the party later, it's recommended that you remove him from your ranks as soon as possible during your first play through the game. There's no reason to waste EXP points on a character that has a difficult time pulling his weight. If, however, you intend on using him regardless (or it's your second run through the game), focus your efforts on improving his symbology with **Mindflare**, **Enlighten**, **INT Boost**, and synthesized items that advance his INT. With the right equipment, Faize can act as a less-damaging, but far more resilient battle mage that's less prone to erratic deaths (due to his better defensive stats).

TIPS & TACTICS

SHATTER THEIR ICY SOULS

Faize is the first character to get ice symbols, which inflict the freeze ailment against enemies weak to the water element. Attacking an enemy while it is frozen occasionally results in a one-hit kill. Use the Scan Enemy skill to keep an eye out for enemies weak against water, and set up a Chain Combo that consists of Ice Needles ➡ Earth Glaive. The Earth Glaive follow-up is a quick means of potentially shattering frozen enemies, crushing their hopes of escape.

REAPING SPARK

The Reaping Spark symbol is arguably Faize's most interesting high-level attack symbol. It summons several floating balls of energy that rapidly hit enemies for several seconds. Its radius of effect is big enough to attack large groups of enemies at a time, and it's one of the few symbols of its strength level that can be added to a Chain Combo group. It's also considered to be a non-elemental symbol, which means that there is no risk of it being resisted. Organize a Chain Combo that consists of Reaping Spark ➡ Deep Freeze ➡ Extinction to score giant damage against adversaries caught in the spark's grasp. Much of his late-game attack strategy revolves around this symbol, so learn to use it effectively.

EXAMPLE COMBOS

XBOX 360 VERSION

Ⓐ (2-hits) ➡ 🔘+Ⓐ

Earth Glaive ➡ Earth Glaive

Stone Rain ➡ Earth Glaive

Shadow Needles ➡ Earth Glaive
➡ Earth Glaive

Reaping Spark ➡ Deep Freeze ➡
Extinction

Activate Terra Hammer from the
symbol menu, then chain Deep
Freeze ➡ Extinction

PS3 VERSION

❌ (2-hits) ➡ 🄻🄳 + ❌

Earth Glaive ➡ Earth Glaive

Stone Rain ➡ Earth Glaive

Shadow Needles ➡ Earth Glaive
➡ Earth Glaive

Reaping Spark ➡ Deep Freeze ➡
Extinction

Activate Terra Hammer from the
symbol menu, then chain Deep
Freeze ➡ Extinction

SKILLS

Field Skills

Name	Max Lv	MP Cost	Acquired	Notes
Alchemy	10	--	Initially Available	Item Creation skill. Allows you to forge metal into other materials. At higher skill levels, more types of items become available.
Entomology	10	--	Skill Manual	Increases the chance of earning items after defeating insect enemies. At higher skill levels, the effect increases. Once the skill is learned, its effect is always active.
Chain Combos	10	--	Skill Manual	Allows you to assign multiple skills to a chain combo. At higher skill levels, the number of slots and the amount of damage dealt increases. Once the skill is learned, its effect is always active.
Duplication	10	--	Skill Manual	Allows you to duplicate items using Magical Clay. At higher skill levels, the amount of clay needed decreases. Some items cannot be duplicated.

Symbols

Name	Max Lv	Damage	MP Cost	CP Cost	Acquired	Notes
Earth Glaive	10	INT x195%~260%	5~14	3	Level 1	Attack symbol ⬤. Blades of stone burst forth from under the enemy's feet.
Antidote	1	--	4	--	Level 6	Curative symbol. Purifies one ally of poison.
Ice Needles	10	INT x312%~532%	5~14	2	Level 12	Attack symbol ⬤. At level 1, launches six needles of ice at the enemy. At level 10, launches nine needles of ice.
Stone Rain	10	INT x195%~430%	7~16	4	Level 21	Attack symbol ⬤. Countless rocks rain down upon the enemy.
Shadow Needles	10	INT x162%~332%	5~14	2	Level 27	Attack symbol ⬤. At level 1, Launches five needles of darkness at the enemy from behind. At level 10, launches eight needles of darkness.
Enlighten	10	--	16	--	Level 34	Support symbol. Temporarily boosts one ally's INT by 30%. At higher skill levels, the effect duration increases.
Deep Freeze	10	INT x161%~281%	7~16	4	Level 41	Attack symbol ⬤. Cools the air surrounding the enemy, freezing them from the ground up.
Vampiric Blade	10	INT x41%~131%	10~19	4	Level 48	Attack symbol ⬤. Mows down the area surrounding the caster with dark blades that absorb MP.
Terra Hammer	10	INT x304%~672%	21~30	--	Level 55	Attack symbol ⬤. At level 1, digs up three giant boulders, then smashes them into the ground. At level 10, six giant boulders are dug up.
Dark Devourer	10	INT x375%~646%	21~30	--	Level 61	Attack symbol ⬤. Summons a creature from the netherworld and sends it to feast upon the enemy.
Reaping Spark	10	INT x163%~311%	10~19	5	Level 66	Attack symbol [non-elemental]. Creates four black spheres that slice up anything inside.
Extinction	10	INT x269%~399%	7~16	6	Level 73	Attack symbol [non-elemental]. Encases the enemy in a ball of light, then releases the energy inside in an explosive blast.
Divine Wave	10	INT x447%~616%	21~30	--	Skill Manual	Attack symbol [non-elemental]. Summons a wall of light around the caster, damaging nearby enemies.

Battle Skills

Name	Max Lv	MP Cost	CP Cost	Acquired	Notes
INT Boost	10	--	1	Skill Manual	Adds 10 to your INT at level 1. The INT boost granted increases as the skill's level increases (granting +1000 INT at level 10). The effect is only active when set as a battle skill.
HP Boost	10	--	2	Skill Manual	Adds 100 to your maximum HP at level 1. At level 10, your maximum HP increases by 10000. The effect is only active when set as a battle skill.
MP Boost	10	--	2	Skill Manual	Adds 10 to your maximum MP at level 1. At level 10, your maximum MP increases by 1000. The effect is only active when set as a battle skill.
No Guard	10	--	3	Skill Manual	Prevents you from being thrown off balance when taking damage of less than 1% of your maximum HP (at level 1). At level 10, the effect increases to 10%. The effect is only active when set as a battle skill.
First Aid	10	--	2	Skill Manual	When taking damage from an enemy, occasionally recovers 20% of damage taken as HP (at level 1). At level 10, 60% of the damage taken is converted. The effect is only active when set as a battle skill.
Auto Healing	10	--	1	Skill Manual	Gradually restores HP during battle. At higher skill levels, HP is restored more frequently. The effect is only active when set as a battle skill.
Stun	10	--	2	Skill Manual	Occasionally adds a stun effect when attacking enemies. At higher skill levels, the chance of success increases. The effect is only active when set as a battle skill.
Pride	10	--	--	Initially Available	Boosts status parameters when fighting weaker enemies. At higher skill levels, the effect increases. The effect is only active when set as a battle skill.
Fury Boost	10	--	1	Skill Manual	Increases the chance of surviving via Fury when your HP hits 0. At higher skill levels, the effect increases. The effect is only active when set as a battle skill.
Scan Enemy	1	1	--	Skill Manual	Allows you to view information on the targeted enemy. Use this skill from the battle menu.
Hide	1	1	--	Skill Manual	Diverts the attention of enemies, making them target you less often. Use this skill from the battle menu.
Mindflare	10	8	--	Skill Manual	Boosts INT by 40% for 30 seconds (at level 1), but triples MP costs. INT is boosted by 100% at level 10. Use this skill from the battle menu.
Convert	10	4	--	Skill Manual	Converts some HP to MP over a period of 30 seconds. At higher skill levels, the effect increases. Use this skill from the battle menu.

Transmission completed.

Log of system, using System UI: controls interface...
Output text:
relation log + trigger execute(Trigger_Log)
023749.123.

Securing data: 38%! — database 101 secured!

End of line

LYMLE

DATE OF BIRTH: JUNE 20
AGE: 15

A mysterious girl from Triom Village who is apparently 15 years old but doesn't look a day over six. Allegedly the greatest symbologist in the village, she draws symbol-like patterns on the walls all over town, though only she knows exactly what they do. She is generally an expressionless girl, and she rarely opens her heart to anyone, although she has taken a shine to both Edge and Reimi. Like any child, she has both an innocent personality and a penchant for getting in trouble, but because she never wears any of it on her face it has become a source of uneasiness for others. She can summon Cerberus with her symbology, causing the other villagers to fear her a bit. For some reason, she acts very cold and distant toward Faize.

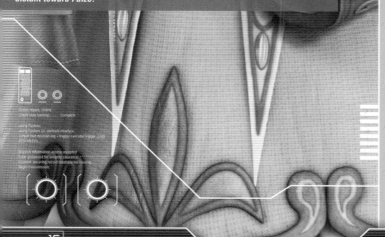

Base Statistics

HP	MP	ATK	DEF	HIT	GRD	INT	LUCK	Critical
137	72	10	16	19	11	11	90	1.2

Base Resistances

Poison	Stun	Freeze	Paralysis	Silence	Fog	Curse	Pumpkin	Void
0	0	20	0	0	0	0	0	0

❖ MOVE SET

XBOX 360 VERSION

LONG RANGE (ATTACK) Ⓐ

SHORT RANGE (ATTACK) Ⓐ

SHORT RANGE (DIRECTIONAL ATTACK)
+Ⓐ

ANTI-AIR ATTACK

Analog stick at neutral, then press Ⓐ against a flying enemy

ROLL Ⓑ

XBOX 360 VERSION

LONG RANGE (ATTACK) ✕

SHORT RANGE (ATTACK) ✕

SHORT RANGE (DIRECTIONAL ATTACK)
L3 + ✕

ANTI-AIR ATTACK

Analog stick at neutral, then press ✕ against a flying enemy

ROLL ◉

BLINDSIDE – RANK C

Similar to Edge's Blindside, Lymle rolls behind the foe in a wide arc. This occasionally causes her to run right into attacks with a wide area of effect, but it can get the job done.

CHARACTER OVERVIEW

Endowed with high intelligence and a wide array of symbols, Lymle is a primarily offensive symbologist. Her objective is to cast symbols against preoccupied enemies from a safe distance, healing party members as the need arises. Scanning adversaries and targeting their elemental weaknesses is an important aspect of this strategy. At lower levels, use the Fire Bolt, Lightning Blast, and Wind Blade symbols to cover a lot of the elemental weaknesses you might encounter. As her level raises and better abilities become available. The ultimate goal is to set up her Hound Grenade, a powerful Cerberus attack that can add major damage when chained into after symbols. Both the Tornado and the Volcanic Burst symbols can be used to set up a Hound Grenade for devastating results.

Use either the Tornado or Explosion abilities to control your adversary's movements. This can act as cover when performing follow-up actions or attacks. Tornado is the faster of the two, so use it to score quick damage when you see an opening, or as a means of covering healing symbols. Though slower, Explosion engulfs the majority of the field in flames, interrupting any monster that isn't in Rush Mode. If you see Explosion hit, follow-up with a long range symbol combo to score inescapable damage (like Tornado ➡ Hound Grenade).

Unfortunately, Lymle's symbol selection is weaker than Myuria's at high levels, a problem caused by their low damage output and lack of elemental variety. This makes her weak against monsters that are resistant to fire symbols, the dominant element in her symbol and special art list. Lymle's strengths over Myuria lie in her special arts, which act as fire-based symbology with a much faster casting time, and her debilitating Void and Silence symbols. These can be used to cripple enemies wielding strong symbols or bonus attributes. Use and abuse these symbols to roast the incoming opposition.

TIPS & TACTICS

FAST CAST + INT BOOST + MINDFLARE

Lymle's attack plan revolves around her attack symbols and special arts, which both deal damage based on her INT rating. It's best to increase her INT by investing points into her **INT Boost** and **Mindflare** skills (push both to level 10). Also, put points into the **Fast Cast** ability, a necessary supplement that speeds up her symbol casting time. Use Mindflare at the beginning of battle to boost her INT by 100%. This power up comes at the cost of triple the MP requirement for symbols and skills, but special items can be equipped to reduce the MP cost by a significant amount. With Mindflare, Fast Cast, and INT Boost activated, pummel your enemy with symbol combinations to take advantage of the boost (refer to her example combos).

SALAMANDERSTONE

Since the majority of Lymle's skills are fire-based, there's little reason not to improve their power. Synthesizing the Salamanderstone to Lymle's weapon of choice boosts the damage of fire symbols by 15%. However, there's no need to do this if you're using her Ruby Wand, Star Ruby Wand, or Blazing Wand, which already come with the same power-up.

EXAMPLE COMBOS

Scorching Star ➡ Hatchet Reel

Fire Bolt ➡ Thunder Blast ➡ Thunder Blast

Volcanic Burst ➡ Hound Grenade

Cast Explosion with the symbol menu, then chain Tornado ➡ Tornado ➡ Hound Grenade

Cast Explosion with the symbol menu, then chain Thunder Flare ➡ Thunder Flare

SKILLS

Field Skills				
Name	Max Lv	MP Cost	Acquired	Notes
Artistry	10	--	Initially Available	Item Creation skill. Allows you to create symbol cards and other symbology-related items. At higher skill levels, more types of items become available.
Parapsychology	10	--	Skill Manual	Increases the chance of earning items after defeating undead enemies. At higher skill levels, the effect increases. Once the skill is learned, its effect is always active.
Treasure Sense	1	--	Skill Manual	Displays the locations of treasure chests and harvesting points on the minimap. Once the skill is learned, its effect is always active.
Chain Combos	10	--	Skill Manual	Allows you to assign multiple skills to a chain combo. At higher skill levels, the number of slots and the amount of damage dealt increases. Once the skill is learned, its effect is always active.
Charge	10	--	Skill Manual	Allows you to use a Disintegration Stone to charge a Disintegration Ring. At level 1, one use adds two charges. At level 10, the ring is completely recharged.

Symbols

Name	Max Lv	Damage	MP Cost	CP Cost	Acquired	Notes
Fire Bolt	10	INT x117%~390%	5~14	2	Level 1	Attack symbol 🔥. At level 1, unleashes three enemy-seeking fireballs. At level 10, unleashes six fireballs.
Healing	10	--	6	--	Level 6	HP recovery symbol. Recovers 31% of one ally's maximum HP at level 1. The HP healed increases to 40% at level 10.
Wind Blade	10	INT x156%~358%	5~14	3	Level 13	Attack symbol 🌀. Fires swirling blades of wind at the enemy.
Faerie Healing	10	--	18	--	Level 21	HP recovery symbol. HP recovery symbol. Summons a faerie to recover at least 26% of all allies maximum HP (at level 1). At level 10, it recovers 35% of their HP.
Silence	10	--	22	--	Level 25	Support symbol. Places the target and nearby enemies in silence status, preventing them from using symbols. At higher skill levels, the chance of success increases.
Lightning Blast	10	INT x198%~418%	5~14	3	Level 28	Attack symbol ⚡. Hurls lightning bolts at the enemy.
Void	10	--	30	--	Level 36	Support symbol. Places the target and nearby enemies in void status, canceling all support effects. At higher skill levels, the chance of success increases.
Explosion	10	INT x272%~485%	21~30		Level 47	Attack symbol 🔥 Sets off a large explosion centered around the enemy.
Reflection	10	--	15	--	Level 51	Support symbol. Temporarily boosts one ally's elemental resistance by 3. At higher skill level, the effect duration increases.
Tornado	10	INT x250%~464%	7~16	5	Level 56	Attack symbol 🌀. Calls forth an enemy-seeking tornado that sweeps up any foe it touches.
Thunder Flare	10	INT x195%~374%	7~16	4	Level 65	Attack symbol ⚡. Summons a ball of lightning that envelops and damages the enemy.
Volcanic Burst	10	INT x433%~721%	10~19	5	Level 71	Attack symbol 🔥. Summons a swirling torrent of fire from beneath the enemy.
Faerie Star	10	--	50	--	Skill Manual	HP recovery symbol. Summons a faerie to recover 81% of all allies' maximum HP at level 1. At level 10, it recovers 90% of their HP.

Special Arts

Name	Max Lv	Damage	MP Cost	CP Cost	Acquired	Notes
Hatchet Reel	10	INT x300%~452%	8~12	2	Level 1	Summon Cerberus to perform a devastating spin attack on the enemy.
Scorching Star	10	INT x286%~342%	14~21	3	Level 18	Summon Cerberus to breathe a giant wave of fire that damages any enemies in the vicinity.
Hound Grenade	10	INT x400%~490%	18~27	4	Level 32	Summon Cerberus to chase after the enemy and set off an explosion.
Spiral Fang	10	INT x370%~510%	18~27	4	Level 41	Summon Cerberus to charge straight ahead in a swirling blaze of flame, knocking back any enemies in its path.
Trinity Blaze	10	INT x353%~520%	20~29	6	Skill Manual	Summon Cerberus, who generates an additional head on each shoulder and breathes three times the fire.

Battle Skills

Name	Max Lv	MP Cost	CP Cost	Acquired	Notes
INT Boost	10	--	1	Skill Manual	Adds 10 to your INT at level 1. The INT boost granted increases as the skill's level increases (granting +1000 INT at level 10). The effect is only active when set as a battle skill.
HP Boost	10	--	2	Skill Manual	Adds 100 to your maximum HP at level 1. At level 10, your maximum HP increases by 10000. The effect is only active when set as a battle skill.
MP Boost	10	--	2	Skill Manual	Adds 10 to your maximum MP at level 1. At level 10, your maximum MP increases by 1000. The effect is only active when set as a battle skill.
Fast Cast	10	--	2	Skill Manual	Reduces the amount of time it takes to cast a symbol. At higher skill levels, the effect increases. The effect is only active when set as a battle skill.
Energy Shield	10	--	1	Skill Manual	Occasionally nullifies physical attacks. At higher skill levels, the chance of success increases. The effect is only active when set as a battle skill.
First Aid	10	--	2	Skill Manual	When taking damage from an enemy, occasionally recovers 20% of damage taken as HP (at level 1). At level 10, 60% of the damage taken is converted. The effect is only active when set as a battle skill.
Auto Healing	10	--	1	Skill Manual	Gradually restores HP during battle. At higher skill levels, HP is restored more frequently. The effect is only active when set as a battle skill.
Fury Boost	10	--	1	Skill Manual	Increases the chance of surviving via Fury when your HP hits 0. At higher skill levels, the effect increases. The effect is only active when set as a battle skill.
Rage	10	--	2	Skill Manual	Increases the chance of becoming enraged when an ally falls, and provides an ATK and INT bonus when enraged. At higher levels, the effect increases. The effect is only active when set as a battle skill.
Elusion	10	--	--	Skill Manual	Allows you to run away from battles quickly. At higher levels, the time needed to escape decreases. The effect is only active when set as a battle skill.
Hide	1	1	--	Skill Manual	Diverts the attention of enemies, making them target you less often. Use this skill from the battle menu.
Mindflare	10	8	--	Skill Manual	Boosts INT by 40% for 30 seconds (at level 1), but triples MP costs. INT is boosted by 100% at level 10. Use this skill from the battle menu.

Transmission complete

Log of system using System UI: controls interface...
Output text mission log > trigger executeTrigger_Log> 823749.223...

Securing data: 3641:::
database 104 secured!

End of line

BACCHUS

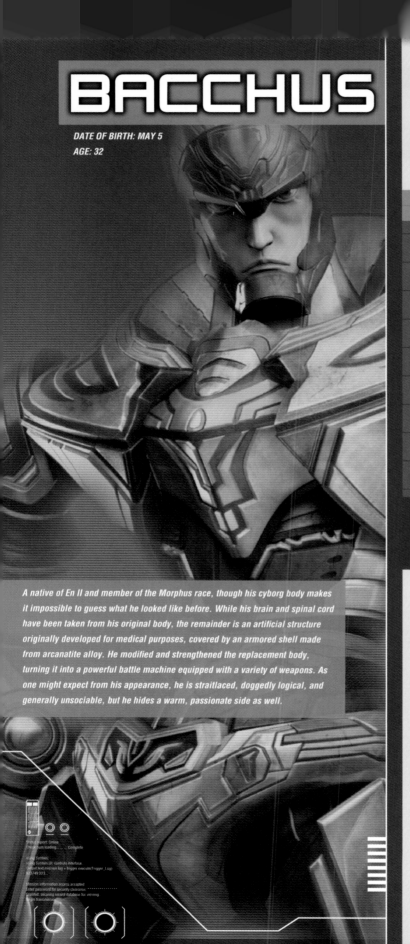

DATE OF BIRTH: MAY 5
AGE: 32

Base Statistics

HP	MP	ATK	DEF	HIT	GRD	INT	LUCK	Critical
264	34	24	26	28	10	9	120	1.2

Base Resistances

Poison	Stun	Freeze	Paralysis	Silence	Fog	Curse	Pumpkin	Void
20	0	0	0	0	0	0	0	0

⚘ MOVE SET

XBOX 360 VERSION	PS3 VERSION
LONG RANGE (ATTACK) Ⓐ	LONG RANGE (ATTACK) ✕
SHORT RANGE (ATTACK) Ⓐ	SHORT RANGE (ATTACK) ✕
SHORT RANGE (DIRECTIONAL ATTACK) ◉+ⒶⒶ	SHORT RANGE (DIRECTIONAL ATTACK) L3 + ✕✕
ANTI-AIR ATTACK Analog stick at neutral, then press Ⓐ against a flying enemy	ANTI-AIR ATTACK Analog stick at neutral, then press ✕ against a flying enemy
DASH Ⓑ	DASH ◯
DASH ATTACK Ⓑ, then ⒶⒶⒶ	DASH ATTACK ◯, then ✕✕✕

BLINDSIDE – RANK B

This maneuver rockets Bacchus into the sky for a surprise back attack. He's fairly vulnerable to fast attacks during the starting stages of the evasion, but very difficult to hit after he rockets into the sky.

A native of En II and member of the Morphus race, though his cyborg body makes it impossible to guess what he looked like before. While his brain and spinal cord have been taken from his original body, the remainder is an artificial structure originally developed for medical purposes, covered by an armored shell made from arcanatite alloy. He modified and strengthened the replacement body, turning it into a powerful battle machine equipped with a variety of weapons. As one might expect from his appearance, he is straitlaced, doggedly logical, and generally unsociable, but he hides a warm, passionate side as well.

CHARACTER OVERVIEW

Despite his size, Bacchus is one of the most mobile characters in *Star Ocean: The Last Hope*. His dash maneuver (executed with Ⓑ or ◯) quickly thrusts him across the ground, enabling him to dash around the field at blinding speeds. It's also possible to tap the attack button and fire off a barrage of stun-inducing gunshots while dashing. This attack can also be chained directly into a follow-up dash just as it starts to recover. Use this technique to target enemies and repeatedly dash left and right while pelting them with gunfire. As long as he continues to face his enemy after the dash, he can repeatedly chain his dashing shots together with little worry of ever being hit.

Bacchus's attacks also have an abnormally high chance of stunning their target. When combined with the high amount of attacks produced by chaining his dash attacks together, his ability to stun groups of adversaries is unmatched. Adding more impact to this potent runaway strategy, his **Emergency Repairs** battle skill instantly heals 55% of his HP at a mere 5 MP (assuming the skill is at level 10). This ability has no recovery period, so use it as often as you like to quickly restore his HP. Its lack of a cool down phase is particularly useful if he's taking damage from an enemy: activate Rush Mode and repeatedly use Emergency Repairs to turtle your way through an attack. When combined with his unmatched DEF rating, this gives Bacchus the edge he needs to survive almost any hazard.

If that wasn't enough, his seizure-inducing **Black Hole Sphere** is easily one of the most effective special arts available. It staggers all enemies within its blast radius while repeatedly inflicting damage to them. While they're being crushed by its gravitational pull, Bacchus and friends are free to attack with whatever they like *for nearly five seconds*. No one can keep enemies out of commission quite like Bacchus can.

TIPS & TACTICS

BLACK HOLE SPHERE AND YOU

Once you have it, Bacchus's attack plan should revolve around the Black Hole Sphere. As mentioned, it hits all enemies onscreen repeatedly for solid damage, while also leaving them immobile for almost five seconds. The damage dealt is based on Bacchus's ATK rating, so equip skills like **ATK Boost** and **Berserk** to boost its damage output. Though Berserk is risky because of its heavy defense penalty, the Black Hole continuously staggers enemies as it hits, usually leaving Bacchus safe from harm. The only exception is if your foe activates Rush Mode. Back away if this happens, to avoid punishment.

It's important to stage a follow-up attack once the Black Hole is released. When MP is low, start attacking your staggered adversaries with repeated dash attacks. If plenty of MP is available, chain the Black Hole Sphere directly into the Irradiation ability

to deal heavy damage. Setting up Chain Combos that consist of multiple loops between Black Hole Sphere, Irradiation, and then Black Hole Sphere again is an extremely powerful method of dealing heavy damage to everything on the field. You can replace Irradiation with the Justice Savior skill at later levels for a similarly devastating effect.

Transmission completed

Log of system: using System UI, controls interface.
Output text: interpolate log + trigger execute(Trigger_Log) @33749.225.

Securing data: 3841 database 191 secured*

End of line

RECOMMENDED BEAT MODE: BURST

The Black Hole Sphere attack loop builds Bacchus's Rush Gauge at an absurdly high rate. Utilizing Burst's rank 20 skill that allows Rush Gauge meter to be gained in Rush Mode, he can quickly fill his gauge to its maximum, activate Rush Mode, then repeatedly loop between Black Hole Sphere and Irradiation shots to stay in Rush Mode for as long as you have MP. Aside from the ability to absorb hits without being interrupted (which helps Bacchus absorb counter attacks during Black Hole loops), Rush Mode's small ATK and critical hit rate boost help improve the damage dealt by the Black Hole Sphere. The cost of using his special arts is also reduced by -25% while in Burst's Rush Mode, allowing for additional Black Holes Spheres.

EXAMPLE COMBOS

Anti-air attack (Ⓐ or ❌), then long-range attack (Ⓐ or ❌)

Galvanic Shock (3-hits) ➡ Galvanic Shock (3-hits) ➡ Galvanic Shock (3-hits) ➡ Galvanic Shock (3-hits) ➡ Galvanic Shock (3-hits) ➡ Galvanic Shock

Black Hole Sphere ➡ Irradiation ➡ Black Hole Sphere ➡ Irradiation ➡ Termination

Long-range attack (Ⓐ or ❌) ➡ Justice Savior ➡ Justice Savior ➡ Justice Savior

SKILLS

Field Skills

Name	Max Lv	MP Cost	Acquired	Notes
Engineering	10	--	Initially Available	Item Creation skill. Allows you to craft mechanical equipment and items such as bombs. At higher levels, more types of items become available.
Robotics	10	--	Initially Available	Increases the chance of earning items after defeating mechanical enemies. At higher skill levels, the effect increases. Once the skill is learned, its effect is always active.
Trap Evasion	10	--	Skill Manual	Reduces the amount of damage taken from traps on the field. At higher levels, the effect increases. Once the skill is learned, its effect is always active.
Chain Combos	10	--	Skill Manual	Allows you to assign multiple skills to a chain combo. At higher skill levels, the number of slots and the amount of damage dealt increases. Once the skill is learned, its effect is always active.
Mining	10	--	Initially Available	Allows you to mine ores at mining points. Press the 🅱 or ⬤ button at a mining point to use. At higher levels, the number of items you can mine increases.
Stealth	10	--	Initially Available	Allows you to hide from enemies on the field for a limited time. At higher levels, the duration of the stealth effect increases. If you touch an enemy, you'll enter into battle.

Special Arts

Name	Max Lv	Damage	MP Cost	CP Cost	Acquired	Notes
Force Breaker	10	ATK x216%~424%	6~8	3	Level 1	Launch a barrage of missiles from behind, exploding on contact and damaging any enemies in the vicinity.
Galvanic Shock	10	ATK x270%~752%	8~13	2	Level 16	Charge up both arms with electricity, then grab the enemy and shock them with a high-voltage burst.
Irradiation	10	ATK x316%~621%	10~15	4	Level 30	Lock on to the enemy and call in a massive laser attack from the skies.
Termination	10	ATK x428%~505%	11~18	3	Level 38	Rend the earth with a devastating chest beam, causing a shockwave.
Black Hole Sphere	10	ATK x200%~400%	11~18	4	Level 51	Generate a gravity field that immobilizes enemies in the vicinity.
Blessed Buster	10	ATK x454%~569%	13~19	5	Level 61	Tear enemies apart with a beam emitted by the Blessed Buster support mech.
Justice Savior	10	ATK x300%~570%	13~19	5	Level 73	Pepper the enemy with bullets fired by the Justice Savior support mech.
Godslayer	10	ATK x300%~600%	14~20	6	Skill Manual	Mow down the enemy with a chainsaw powered by the Godslayer support mech.

Battle Skills

Name	Max Lv	MP Cost	CP Cost	Acquired	Notes
ATK Boost	10	--	1	Skill Manual	Adds 10 to your ATK at level 1. The ATK boost granted increases as the skill's level increases (granting +1000 ATK at level 10). The effect is only active when set as a battle skill.
HP Boost	10	--	2	Skill Manual	Adds 100 to your maximum HP at level 1. At level 10, your maximum HP increases by 10000. The effect is only active when set as a battle skill.
MP Boost	10	--	2	Skill Manual	Adds 10 to your maximum MP at level 1. At level 10, your maximum MP increases by 1000. The effect is only active when set as a battle skill.
No Guard	10	--	3	Skill Manual	Prevents you from being thrown off balance when taking damage less than 1% of your maximum HP (at level 1). At level 10, the effect increases to 10%. The effect is only active when set as a battle skill.
First Aid	10	--	2	Skill Manual	When taking damage from an enemy, occasionally recovers 20% of damage taken as HP (at level 1). At level 10, 60% of the damage taken is converted. The effect is only active when set as a battle skill.
Auto Healing	10	--	1	Skill Manual	Gradually restores HP during battle. At higher skill levels, HP is restored more frequently. The effect is only active when set as a battle skill.
Fury Boost	10	--	1	Skill Manual	Increases the chance of surviving via Fury when your HP hits 0. At higher skill levels, the effect increases. The effect is only active when set as a battle skill.
Taunt	1	1	--	Skill Manual	Attracts the attention of enemies, making them target you more often. Use this skill from the battle menu.
Berserk	10	8	--	Skill Manual	Boosts ATK by 40% for 30 seconds (at level 1), but doubles the damage taken from attacks. At level 10 ATK is increased by 100%. Use this skill from the battle menu.
Scan Enemy	1	1	--	Skill Manual	Allows you to view information on the targeted enemy. Use this skill from the battle menu.
Convert	10	4	--	Skill Manual	Converts some HP to MP over a period of 30 seconds. At higher skill levels, the effect increases. Use this skill from the battle menu.
Emergency Repairs	10	5	--	Skill Manual	Recovers 30% of your maximum HP (at level 1). The effect increases to 55% at level 10. Use this skill from the battle menu.

Transmission completed

Log of system, using System UI, contrary interface.
Output text, mission log + trigger execute:Trigger_Log();
@53/68:223...

Securing data, 3841 —
distribute 591 secured?

End of line.

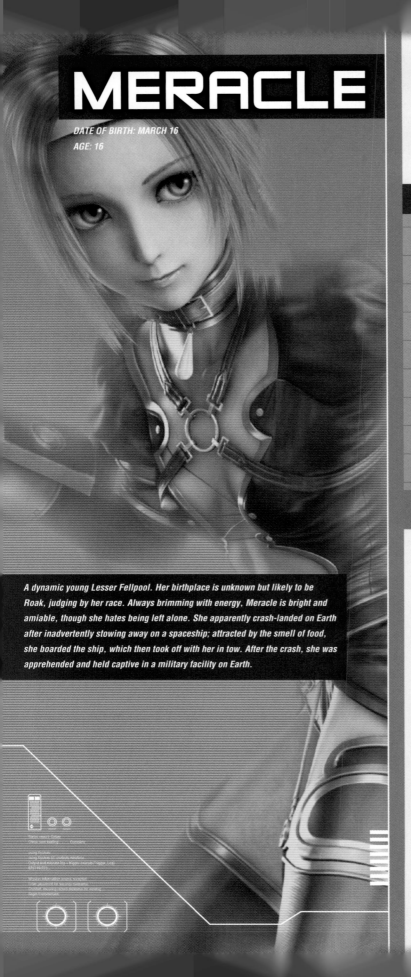

MERACLE

DATE OF BIRTH: MARCH 16
AGE: 16

A dynamic young Lesser Fellpool. Her birthplace is unknown but likely to be Roak, judging by her race. Always brimming with energy, Meracle is bright and amiable, though she hates being left alone. She apparently crash-landed on Earth after inadvertently stowing away on a spaceship; attracted by the smell of food, she boarded the ship, which then took off with her in tow. After the crash, she was apprehended and held captive in a military facility on Earth.

Base Statistics

HP	MP	ATK	DEF	HIT	GRD	INT	LUCK	Critical
185	37	31	14	25	13	9	80	1.2

Base Resistances

Poison	Stun	Freeze	Paralysis	Silence	Fog	Curse	Pumpkin	Void
0	0	0	0	0	0	0	0	0

✦ MOVE SET

XBOX 360 VERSION

LONG RANGE (ATTACK)
(A)   (A)(A)

SHORT RANGE (ATTACK)
(A)   (A)(A)

SHORT RANGE (DIRECTIONAL ATTACK)
(L)+(A)

ANTI-AIR ATTACK
Analog stick at neutral, then press (A) against a flying enemy

DASH (B)

BLINDSIDE – RANK A

Meracle rapidly dashes around the field during her Blindside, which is invulnerable during the majority of its movement. Highly effective at avoiding most attack types.

PS3 VERSION

LONG RANGE (ATTACK)
(X)   (X)(X)

SHORT RANGE (ATTACK)
(X)   (X)(X)

SHORT RANGE (DIRECTIONAL ATTACK)
(L3) + (X)

ANTI-AIR ATTACK
Analog stick at neutral, then press (X) against a flying enemy

DASH (◎)

CHARACTER OVERVIEW

The bird-loving Meracle is a melee unit with a focus on long combos and critical hits. Her high critical damage modifier meshes well with her powerful special arts, which raise the probability of scoring a critical hit because of the high number of blows they inflict. This strength can be enhanced further with the **Critical Hit** ability, or by using her **Focus** skill at the onset battle to temporarily increase her critical rate. Using these abilities, Meracle can crush a targeted foe in seconds.

Despite her status as a melee unit, Meracle's DEF and HP ratings are low, consequently making it risky for her to blindly rush into battle. She also has horrendous recovery periods on all of her attack combos and special arts. Compensate for this problem by attacking when your foe is recovering from a move, or after successfully using a Blindside. Isolating targets so you can perform uninterrupted combos against them is also helpful. Though skills like **HP Boost** and **First Aid** are also good for combating this problem, at least one of those slots should be reserved for **Critical Hit** or **ATK Boost** when they become available. Synthesis-strengthened armor and evasive play that revolves around Blindsides is usually the better route to take. Meracle has one of the better Blindside animations, which allows her to avoid attacks that other characters can't. There's no reason to stay married to any one set of skills or play styles though, you can always swap out abilities mid-battle to compensate for a variety of situations.

In regards to her offense, the final three attacks at the end of Meracle's short range string leave her very open when blocked. Instead of always committing to the combo, attack only a single time and verify whether her 2-hit scratch attack hits or not. If it hits, press Ⓐ or ❌ again to perform a follow-up combo that launches the enemy into the sky. Juggle your airborne foes with her anti-air attack just before they hit the ground (if performed close to the enemy, her anti-air attack hits twice instead of once). If MP is an abundant resource, forgo the launching flip kick and instead chain her first two short range hits into the Ripper Pounce. The Chain Combos skill can improve her combo potential by a staggering amount, so learn the skill as fast as possible. Refer to the example combos listed for tips on how to arrange your flurry of attacks.

Finally, use the Claws of Fury special art if you are ever surrounded by multiple enemies. This skill creates a shield of wind around Meracle that shreds adversaries encircling your position. Since her biggest concern is staying out of bad situations, this can help keep her from falling prey to sneak attacks. The Drill Spike skill is useful for the same reason. Not only can it damage long lines of enemies, but it generally flies Meracle through them to a safer position.

TIPS & TACTICS

CRITICAL MAYHEM

With **Critical Hit** and **Focus** being used, Meracle's combo damage puts Arumat to shame. At level 49, start setting up Chain Combo groups that allow you to string together one Ripper Pounce followed by four Somersault Smashes. Off of a successful Blindside, this combo absolutely eradicates an enemy's HP in no time flat.

You may opt to include nothing but the Drill Spike in your Chain Combo groups (up to 6) when Meracle reaches level 61. This skill dashes her across the screen at a high speed while hitting multiple times. If any of the Drill's hits connect as a critical, the damage dealt is sometimes four times that of normal. Because of this, chaining multiple Drill Spikes together erratically

deals huge damage to large enemies, enabling her to murder single monsters faster than almost any other character. Multiple Drill Spikes also work well against large groups of minor foes; though repeated Drill Spikes occasionally miss if their villainous bodies are small.

COMPENSATING FOR MERACLE'S POOR DEFENSE

The Darkblood Chainmail armor found in the Colosseum's shop nullifies HP Damage 25% of the time you take a hit. You can synthesize the Darkblood Chainmail with the Blue Talisman item to increase this rate by another 25%. In cases where you want to wear armor with a higher base DEF rating, the Darkblood Chainmail can be synthesized to the armor to add its nullification ability. For example, synthesizing the Darkblood Chainmail to the powerful Sorcerous Guard gives you a base 1651 DEF improvement, 15% immunity to status ailments, +80 GRD, *and* the HP damage nullification property. Use synthesis in this manner to help cover Meracle's weaknesses.

EXAMPLE COMBOS

XBOX 360 VERSION

Ⓐ Ⓐ, then juggle with a delayed anti-air Ⓐ

Ⓐ (2 hits) ➡ Ripper Pounce ➡ Comet Impact

Ⓐ (2 hits) ➡ Ripper Pounce ➡ Acrobatic Vault ➡ Ripper Pounce ➡ Comet Impact

Ⓐ (2 hits) ➡ Ripper Pounce ➡ Somersault Smash ➡ Acrobatic Vault ➡ Claws of Fury

Ⓐ (2 hits) ➡ Ripper Pounce ➡ Somersault Smash ➡ Somersault Smash ➡ Somersault Smash ➡ Claws of Fury

Ⓐ (2 hits) ➡ Drill Spike ➡ Drill Spike ➡ Drill Spike ➡ Drill Spike ➡ Drill Spike

PS3 VERSION

✕ ✕, then juggle with a delayed anti-air ✕

✕ (2 hits) ➡ Ripper Pounce ➡ Comet Impact

✕ (2 hits) ➡ Ripper Pounce ➡ Acrobatic Vault ➡ Ripper Pounce ➡ Comet Impact

✕ (2 hits) ➡ Ripper Pounce ➡ Somersault Smash ➡ Acrobatic Vault ➡ Claws of Fury

✕ (2 hits) ➡ Ripper Pounce ➡ Somersault Smash ➡ Somersault Smash ➡ Somersault Smash ➡ Claws of Fury

✕ (2 hits) ➡ Drill Spike ➡ Drill Spike ➡ Drill Spike ➡ Drill Spike ➡ Drill Spike

SKILLS

Field Skills

Name	Max Lv	MP Cost	Acquired	Notes
Crafting	10	--	Initially Available	Item Creation skill. Allows you to craft lightweight equipment and accessories. At higher skill levels, more types of items become available.
Ornithology	10	--	Skill Manual	Increases the chance of earning items after defeating avian enemies. At higher skill levels, the effect increases. Once the skill is learned, its effect is always active.
Appetite	10	--	Skill Manual	Adds a bonus to the effect of HP recovery items. At higher skill levels, the effect increases. Once the skill is learned, its effect level is always active.
Chain Combos	10	--	Skill Manual	Allows you to assign multiple skills to a chain combo. At higher skill levels, the number of slots and the amount of damage dealt increases. Once the skill is learned, its effect is always active.
Ocarina	1	1	Skill Manual	Allows you to attract nearby enemies by playing an alluring melody with the ocarina.

Special Arts

Name	Max Lv	Damage	MP Cost	CP Cost	Acquired	Notes
Ripper Pounce	10	ATK x310%~478%	8~12	2	Level 1	Scratch the enemy with feline obstinacy, shredding them to pieces.
Comet Impact	10	ATK x300%~650%	12~18	2	Level 11	Strike the enemy right where it hurts with a devastating wind-up punch.
Acrobatic Vault	10	ATK x360%~387%	14~21	3	Level 26	Launch a three-part kick combination that sends both you and the enemy sky-high.
Claws of Fury	10	ATK x360%~757%	16~25	5	Level 38	Unleash a lethal flurry of scratches, uppercuts, and straight punches.
Somersault Smash	10	ATK x304%~464%	16~25	3	Level 49	Roll forward, somersault kick the enemy into the air, then follow-up with a crushing heel kick.
Drill Spike	10	ATK x350%~560%	18~27	3	Level 61	Spin forward at high-speed, attacking any enemy in the way.
X Claw	10	ATK x440%~645%	18~27	4	Level 71	Jump up and slash your crossed arms downward, causing a shockwave underneath the enemy's feet.
Max Shockwave	10	ATK x560%~686%	20~29	6	Skill Manual	Summon a massive ball of energy and hurl at enemies, bowling them over as it surges past.

Battle Skills

Name	Max Lv	MP Cost	CP Cost	Acquired	Notes
ATK Boost	10	--	1	Skill Manual	Adds 10 to your ATK at level 1. The ATK boost granted increases as the skill's level increases (granting +1000 ATK at level 10). The effect is only active when set as a battle skill.
HP Boost	10	--	2	Skill Manual	Adds 100 to your maximum HP at level 1. At level 10, your maximum HP increases by 10000. The effect is only active when set as a battle skill.
MP Boost	10	--	2	Skill Manual	Adds 10 to your maximum MP at level 1. At level 10, your maximum MP increases by 1000. The effect is only active when set as a battle skill.
Critical Hit	10	--	1	Skill Manual	Allows you to perform critical hits outside of Rush Mode. At higher skill levels, the chance of success and the amount of damage dealt increases. The effect is only active when set as a battle skill.
No Guard	10	--	3	Skill Manual	Prevents you from being thrown off balance when taking damage less than 1% of your maximum HP (at level 1). At level 10, the effect increases to 10%. The effect is only active when set as a battle skill.
First Aid	10	--	2	Skill Manual	When taking damage from an enemy, occasionally recovers 20% of damage taken as HP (at level 1). At level 10, 60% of the damage taken is converted. The effect is only active when set as a battle skill.
Auto Healing	10	--	1	Skill Manual	Gradually restores HP during battle. At higher skill levels, HP is restored more frequently. The effect is only active when set as a battle skill.
Stun	10	--	2	Skill Manual	Occasionally adds a stun effect when attacking enemies. At higher skill levels, the chance of success increases. The effect is only active when set as a battle skill.
Fury Boost	10	--	1	Skill Manual	Increases the chance of surviving via Fury when your HP hits 0. At higher skill levels, the effect increases. The effect is only active when set as a battle skill.
Steal	10	--	1	Skill Manual	Occasionally steals an item when attacking enemies. At higher skill levels, the chance of success increases. The effect is only active when set as a battle skill.
Taunt	1	1	--	Skill Manual	Attracts the attention of enemies, making them target you more often. Use this skill from the battle menu.
Berserk	10	8	--	Skill Manual	Boosts ATK by 40% for 30 seconds (at level 1), but doubles the damage taken from attacks. At level 10, ATK is increased by 100%. Use this skill from the battle menu.
Focus	10	6	--	Skill Manual	Boosts HIT and critical chance for 30 seconds. At higher skill levels, the effect increases. Use this skill from the battle menu.

Transmission completed

Log of system:
using System.UI; controls
interface.
Output.text:
mission log + trigger
execute(Trigger_Log)
823749.223...

Securing data: 3841 :
database 101 secured!

End of line

MYURIA

DATE OF BIRTH: NOVEMBER 5
AGE: 22

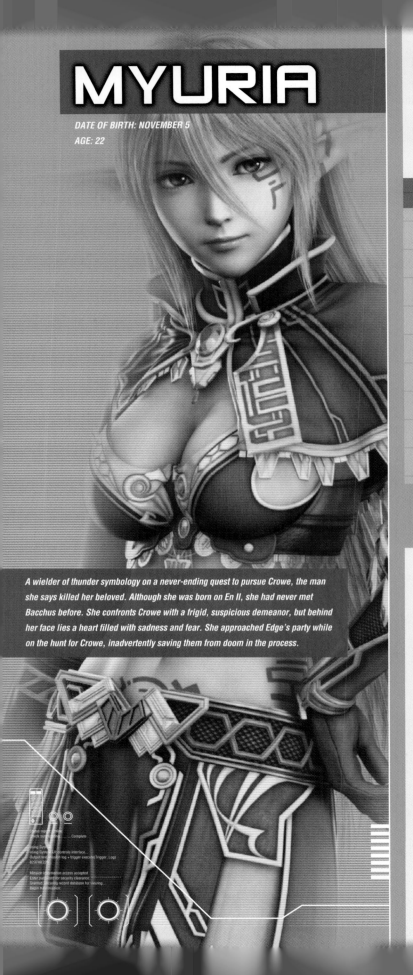

A wielder of thunder symbology on a never-ending quest to pursue Crowe, the man she says killed her beloved. Although she was born on En II, she had never met Bacchus before. She confronts Crowe with a frigid, suspicious demeanor, but behind her face lies a heart filled with sadness and fear. She approached Edge's party while on the hunt for Crowe, inadvertently saving them from doom in the process.

Base Statistics

HP	MP	ATK	DEF	HIT	GRD	INT	LUCK	Critical
158	69	14	16	21	11	11	90	1.2

Base Resistances

Poison	Stun	Freeze	Paralysis	Silence	Fog	Curse	Pumpkin	Void
0	0	0	0	0	0	0	0	0

⁘ MOVE SET

XBOX 360 VERSION	PS3 VERSION
LONG RANGE {ATTACK} Ⓐ	**LONG RANGE {ATTACK}** ✕
SHORT RANGE (ATTACK) Ⓐ ⒶⒶ ⒶⒶⒶ	**SHORT RANGE (ATTACK)** ✕ ✕✕ ✕✕✕
SHORT RANGE (DIRECTIONAL ATTACK) ⓛ+Ⓐ	**SHORT RANGE (DIRECTIONAL ATTACK)** L3 + ✕
ANTI-AIR ATTACK Analog stick at neutral, then press Ⓐ against a flying enemy	**ANTI-AIR ATTACK** Analog stick at neutral, then press ✕ against a flying enemy
JUMP Ⓑ	**JUMP** ◉

BLINDSIDE – RANK B

Myuria teleports behind her enemy in a dazzling fashion. Very effective at avoiding most attack types, though some awkwardly angled strikes can catch her before the teleport, or after she starts to recover from the movement.

CHARACTER OVERVIEW

Like Lymle, the beautiful Myuria is a support caster with a focus on attack symbology. Though lackluster at early levels, she eventually acquires a wide enough variety of both attack and support symbols to fill either a restorative or offensive role in your party. Symbology, like her Plasma Cyclone, inflicts heavy damage to multiple enemies on the field while also freeing her up to cast follow-up symbols. Her Arctic Impact and Divine Wave are also two of the most damaging attack symbols available to any character. She even comes packed with the Enlighten, Mindflare, and Fast Cast skills, which can all be stacked together to vastly improve the damage and speed of her symbols.

In addition to the above, the **Convert** skill is helpful for keeping Myuria's MP pool at its maximum during the early stages of the game. For 30 seconds, it rapidly converts your HP into MP, giving you a giant reserve for additional symbols when they're needed most. This is the perfect compliment to the Mindflare skill, which triples symbol MP costs for a massive INT increase. Convert becomes less useful as items that reduce MP costs become available, but it is useful during the earlier stages of the game as a last resort.

Despite her strengths, Myuria has nothing exceptionally powerful at her fingertips. Though her symbols are quite strong when backed by INT-boosting abilities, other characters can inflict the same amount of damage much faster at half the MP cost. The key to Myuria's success is the usage of both her restorative *and* attack symbols via the Fast Cast ability, which a support caster like Sarah doesn't have access to. The Faerie Star, a symbol acquired from a skill manual, can heal 90% of your entire party's HP almost instantly (assuming the skill is at level 10).

 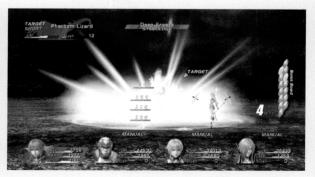

TIPS & TACTICS

FAST CAST + INT BOOST + ENLIGHTEN + MINDFLARE

It's highly recommended that you equip Myuria with both Level 10 **Fast Cast** and **INT Boost**. Both skills are essential to making the most out of Myuria's symbology. To boost her INT even further, cast both the Enlighten and Mindflare skills at the beginning of battle. Though costly, the tripled MP cost does very little to hurt Myuria, as combinations of synthesized items and monster jewels can reduce the base cost of symbols by almost 40%.

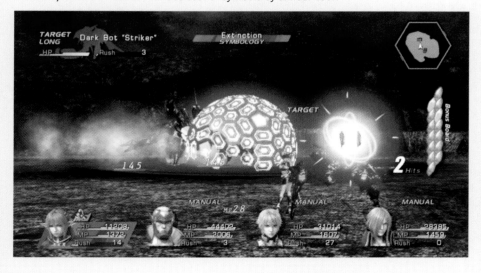

MP ABSORB

Myuria's directional attack (executed by pressing the analog stick towards an enemy while attacking) carries the unique ability to absorb MP when it hits. Though the amount drained is small, the attack comes in handy in emergency situations where MP and restorative items are low (admittedly a rare occurrence). A stylish way to land the attack is to chain into it off of the third hit of Myuria's short range string (three rapid attacks with the analog stick at neutral). This dazzling combo deals pitiful damage at best, but it should be just what she needs when her MP is low.

EXAMPLE COMBOS

XBOX 360 VERSION

Short range Ⓐ Ⓐ Ⓐ ➡ Ⓛ + Ⓐ

Long range Ⓐ ➡ Deep Freeze ➡ Lightning Blast ➡ Ice Needles

Cast Arctic Impact from the symbol menu, then perform a chain combo consisting of Deep Freeze ➡ Extinction ➡ Extinction

XBOX 360 VERSION

Short range ⓧ ⓧ ⓧ ➡ Ⓛ③ + ⓧ

Long range ⓧ ➡ Deep Freeze ➡ Lightning Blast ➡ Ice Needles

Cast Arctic Impact from the symbol menu, then perform a chain combo consisting of Deep Freeze ➡ Extinction ➡ Extinction

SKILLS

Field Skills				
Name	Max Lv	MP Cost	Acquired	Notes
Compounding	10	--	Initially Available	Item Creation skill. Allows you to create medicinal items. At higher skill levels, more types of items become available.
Demonology	10	--	Skill Manual	Increases the chance of earning items after defeating demon enemies. At higher skill levels, the effect increases. Once the skill is learned, its effect is always active.
Haggling	10	--	Skill Manual	Increases the amount of Fol received when selling items at shops by 5% over the original selling price at level 1. At level 10, the amount is increased by 30%.
Chain Combos	10	--	Skill Manual	Allows you to assign multiple skills to a chain combo. At higher skill levels, the number of slots and the amount of damage dealt increases. Once the skill is learned, its effect is always active.

Symbols

Name	Max Lv	Damage	MP Cost	CP Cost	Acquired	Notes
Healing	10	--	6	--	Level 1	HP recovery symbol. Recovers 31% of one ally's maximum HP at level 1. The HP healed increases to 40% at level 10.
Ice Needles	10	INT x312%~532%	5~14	2	Level 1	Attack symbol 🔵. At level 1, launches six needles of ice at the enemy. At level 10, nine needles of ice are launched.
Lightning Blast	10	INT x198%~418%	5~14	3	Level 1	Attack symbol 🔵. Hurls lightning bolts at the enemy.
Deep Freeze	10	INT x161%~281%	7~16	4	Level 12	Attack symbol 🔵. Cools the air surrounding the enemy, freezing them from the ground up.
Void	10	--	30	--	Level 17	Support symbol. Places the target and nearby enemies in void status, canceling all support effects. At higher skill levels, the chance of success increases.
Thunder Flare	10	INT x195%~374%	7~16	4	Level 23	Attack symbol 🔵. Summons a ball of lightning that envelops and damages the enemy.
Shadow Needles	10	INT x162%~332%	5~14	2	Level 35	Attack symbol ⚫. At level 1, launches five needles of darkness at the enemy from behind. At level 10, eight needles of darkness are launched.
Enlighten	10		16	--	Level 41	Support symbol. Temporarily boosts one ally's INT by 30%. At higher skill levels, the effect duration increases.
Faerie Healing	10	--	18	--	Level 47	HP recovery symbol. HP recovery symbol. Summons a faerie to recover at least 26% of all allies' maximum HP (at level 1). At level 10, it recovers 35% of their HP.
Reflection	10	--	15	--	Level 52	Support symbol. Temporarily boosts one ally's elemental resistance by 3. At higher levels, the effect duration increases.
Dark Devourer	10	INT x375%~646%	21~30	--	Level 56	Attack symbol ⚫. Summons a creature from the netherworld and sends it to feast upon the enemy.
Restoration	10	--	25	--	Level 61	Resurrection symbol. Revives an incapacitated ally with 22% of their maximum HP (at level 1). Revives allies with 40% of their HP at level 10.
Arctic Impact	10	INT x323%~430%	21~30	--	Level 67	Attack symbol 🔵. Encases the enemy in a giant pillar of ice, then shatters it to pieces.
Extinction	10	INT x269%~399%	7~16	6	Level 73	Attack symbol [non-elemental]. Encases the enemy in a ball of light, then releases the energy inside in an explosive blast.
Divine Wave	10	INT x447%~616%	21~30	--	Skill Manual	Attack symbol [non-elemental]. Summons a wall of light around the caster, damaging nearby enemies.
Plasma Cyclone	10	INT x355%~507%	21~30	--	Skill Manual	Attack symbol 🔵. Conjures up a storm of lightning bolts that streak across the battlefield.
Faerie Star	10	--	50	--	Skill Manual	HP recovery symbol. Summons a faerie to recover 81% of all allies' maximum HP at level 1. At level 10, it recovers 90% of their HP.

Battle Skills

Name	Max Lv	MP Cost	CP Cost	Acquired	Notes
INT Boost	10	--	1	Skill Manual	Adds 10 to your INT at level 1. The INT boost granted increases as the skill's level increases (granting +1000 INT at level 10). The effect is only active when set as a battle skill.
HP Boost	10	--	2	Skill Manual	Adds 100 to your maximum HP at level 1. At level 10, your maximum HP increases by 10000. The effect is only active when set as a battle skill.
MP Boost	10	--	2	Skill Manual	Adds 10 to your maximum MP at level 1. At level 10, your maximum MP increases by 1000. The effect is only active when set as a battle skill.
Fast Cast	10	--	2	Skill Manual	Reduces the amount of time it takes to cast a symbol. At higher skill levels, the effect increases. The effect is only active when set as a battle skill.
Energy Shield	10	--	1	Skill Manual	Occasionally nullifies physical attacks. At higher skill levels, the chance of success increases. The effect is only active when set as a battle skill.
First Aid	10	--	2	Skill Manual	When taking damage from an enemy, occasionally recovers 20% of damage taken as HP (at level 1). At level 10, 60% of the damage taken is converted. The effect is only active when set as a battle skill.
Auto Healing	10	--	1	Skill Manual	Gradually restores HP during battle. At higher skill levels, HP is restored more frequently. The effect is only active when set as a battle skill.
Pride	10	--	--	Initially Available	Boosts status parameters when fighting weaker enemies. At higher skill levels, the effect increases. The effect is only active when set as a battle skill.
Fury Boost	10	--	1	Skill Manual	Increases the chance of surviving via Fury when your HP hits 0. At higher skill levels, the effect increases. The effect is only active when set as a battle skill.
Rage	10	--	2	Skill Manual	Increases the chance of becoming enraged when an ally falls, and provides an ATK and INT bonus when enraged. At higher levels, the effect increases. The effect is only active when set as a battle skill.
Steal	10	--	1	Skill Manual	Occasionally steals an item when attacking enemies. At higher skill levels, the chance of success increases. The effect is only active when set as a battle skill.
Hide	1	1	--	Skill Manual	Diverts the attention of enemies, making them target you less often. Use this skill from the battle menu.
Mindflare	10	8	--	Skill Manual	Boosts INT by 40% for 30 seconds (at level 1), but triples MP costs. INT is boosted by 100% at level 10. Use this skill from the battle menu.
Convert	10	4	--	Skill Manual	Converts some HP to MP over a period of 30 seconds. At higher skill levels, the effect increases. Use this skill from the battle menu.

SARAH

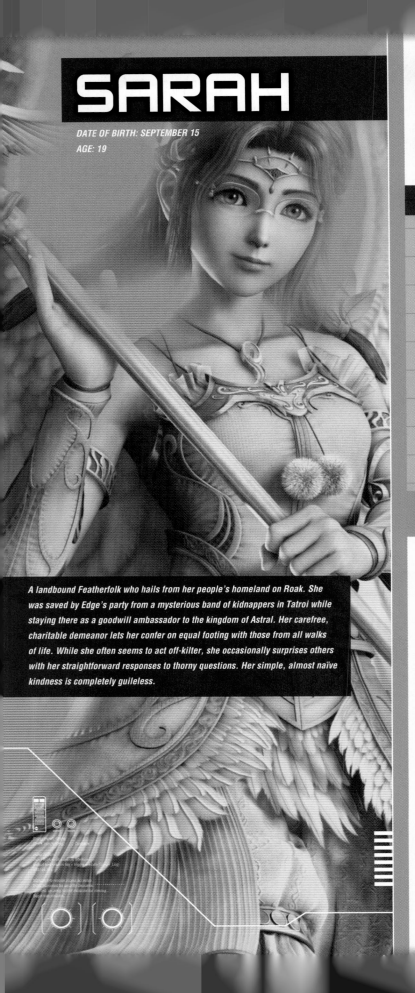

DATE OF BIRTH: SEPTEMBER 15
AGE: 19

Base Statistics

HP	MP	ATK	DEF	HIT	GRD	INT	LUCK	Critical
145	78	11	15	20	12	12	100	2.8

Base Resistances

Poison	Stun	Freeze	Paralysis	Silence	Fog	Curse	Pumpkin	Void
0	0	0	0	0	0	0	0	0

MOVE SET

XBOX 360 VERSION

LONG RANGE (ATTACK)
Ⓐ

SHORT RANGE (ATTACK)
Ⓐ   ⒶⒶ

SHORT RANGE DIRECTIONAL ATTACK
⬆+Ⓐ

ANTI-AIR ATTACK
Analog stick at neutral, then press Ⓐ against a flying enemy

JUMP   Ⓑ

PS3 VERSION

LONG RANGE (ATTACK)
✕

SHORT RANGE (ATTACK)
✕   ✕✕

SHORT RANGE DIRECTIONAL ATTACK
L3 + ✕

ANTI-AIR ATTACK
Analog stick at neutral, then press ✕ against a flying enemy

JUMP   ◉

BLINDSIDE – RANK C
Causes Sarah to fly behind the enemy. Her flight path is a little awkward, occasionally causing her to run into attacks with a high attack height.

A landbound Featherfolk who hails from her people's homeland on Roak. She was saved by Edge's party from a mysterious band of kidnappers in Tatroi while staying there as a goodwill ambassador to the kingdom of Astral. Her carefree, charitable demeanor lets her confer on equal footing with those from all walks of life. While she often seems to act off-kilter, she occasionally surprises others with her straightforward responses to thorny questions. Her simple, almost naïve kindness is completely guileless.

CHARACTER OVERVIEW

Angelic in every sense of the word, Sarah puts her heart and soul into keeping her allies healthy. Her selection of restorative symbols is unmatched, consisting of the potent Faerie Light, Faerie Star, and Resurrection symbols that act as the foundation to her restorative abilities. Though she has a number of offensive symbols at her disposal, her inability to learn the Fast Cast skill reduces their use to a single function: cover from enemy attack. Though unavailable to Sarah until she's level 74, the Tornado symbol is especially useful for keeping enemies at bay, since it travels slowly enough to give Sarah ample time to cast a follow-up symbol right behind it. This makes it far more difficult for a foe to approach Sarah when she's readying an action. Be careful when using this tactic though: damaging an enemy in any way may cause its rage to focus on her. Avoid this technique if your party members aren't dealing high amounts of damage.

If an enemy ever manages to slip past your defenses, use her directional attack to blow them away. You can even chain into the directional attack off of a short-range normal attack, or her two-hit launching combo, then juggle the falling enemy with the burst of wind. After knocking them to the far reaches of the battlefield, begin casting the symbol of your choice.

Sarah's biggest problem is the inability to use Fast Cast to improve her casting time. Adding insult to injury, the strongest healing symbol obtainable, Faerie Star, can be given to other party members who do have Fast Cast, like Myuria and Lymle. This essentially makes Sarah, a character that revolves around healing symbols, somewhat lacking during damage-heavy battles. This problem only comes up on occasion though, as Sarah's restorative abilities are still helpful during the main story arc. She is the only character that can cast Resurrection, a symbol that revives an ally from incapacitation with 100% of their HP.

The key to success is focusing on her status increasing symbols, which no other character has access to. Use Enshelter on characters like Meracle (who's weighed down by a weak defense), or utilize Enhance on offensive characters like Arumat, Edge, Reimi, or Bacchus. Angel Feather is designed to be a well-rounded enhancement, but its most valuable property is the +15% INT boost. Give it to any symbologist on your team for stronger attack symbols.

TIPS & TACTICS

BACCHUS AND SARAH, THE UNSTOPPABLE FORCE

Sarah works well in combination with Bacchus, who controls the field well enough to allow her to cast any support symbols she needs to. She can also improve Bacchus with ATK and DEF increasing symbology to make his Black Hole Sphere attack strategy even more potent. Cast Enhance on Bacchus to increase his damage output, or use Enshelter to boost his defense if he has Berserk activated. This same strategy can be applied to Reimi's powerful Rush Mode Chain Combo loops, which inflict horrific damage when backed by ATK enhancing symbols.

BUILDING AROUND A PLAY STYLE

If you aren't playing Sarah directly, equip her with the **HP Boost** and defensive skills like **Energy Shield** or **Auto Healing**. The last thing you want is your healer taking a fall. Also, remember to turn off any symbols you don't want her to use (via the symbol menu in battle). She'll often take on the role of a poor offensive caster if you don't. It's a good idea to turn off anything that isn't Faerie Light, Faerie Star, Resurrection, Cure Condition, Enhance, Enshelter, or Angel Feather.

If instead you like to personally control Sarah, keep Energy Shield on when taking a restorative role, then switch **INT Boost** in the rare instances where you have to go on the offensive. You can use **Mindflare** as well to further increase your INT just before making an attack. When attacking, strike with the Chain Combo Tornado ➡ Blast Hurricane or Aurora Rings ➡ Sunflare for big damage.

THE LONG ROAD TO VICTORY

If you have trouble winning a difficult battle through offensive means, try this: equip Sarah with MP regenerating items and factors so she has plenty of MP, and then field a party of aggressive characters (switch their Tactics to "Gang up on foes with full force"). Take control of Sarah and move her away from combat, then focus on casting symbols when your other party members need it most. This drags out boss fights because of the poor attack methods AI-driven characters use, but it almost certainly guarantees a win. Since symbols are the only threat if she's at the back of the battlefield, fortify this strategy by giving Sarah items that improve her elemental resistances.

Transmission completed

Log of system:
using System.UI; controls
interface...
Output text
mission log + trigger
execute(Trigger_Log)
§23749.223...

Securing data: 3841 --
database 101 secured!

End of line

EXAMPLE COMBOS

XBOX 360 VERSION

Short Range Ⓐ Ⓐ, juggle with neutral anti-air or
🎮+Ⓐ

Short Range Ⓐ, 🎮+Ⓐ

Short Range Ⓐ Ⓐ ➡ Tornado ➡ Blast Hurricane

Tornado ➡ Blast Hurricane

Aurora Rings ➡ Sunflare

PS3 VERSION

Short Range ✕ ✕, juggle with neutral
anti-air or L3 + ✕

Short Range ✕ , L3 + ✕

Short Range ✕ ✕ ➡ Tornado ➡
Blast Hurricane

Tornado ➡ Blast Hurricane

Aurora Rings ➡ Sunflare

SKILLS

Field Skills				
Name	Max Lv	MP Cost	Acquired	Notes
Synthesis	1	--	Initially Available	*Item Creation skill. Allows you to merge equipment with other items to synthesize even stronger equipment.*
Zoology	10	--	Skill Manual	*Increases the chance of earning items after defeating animal enemies. At higher skill levels, the effect increases. Once the skill is learned, its effect is always active.*
Chain Combos	10	--	Skill Manual	*Allows you to assign multiple skills to a chain combo. At higher skill levels, the number of slots and the amount of damage dealt increases. Once the skill is learned, its effect is always active.*
Augury	10	--	Skill Manual	*Allows you to listen to Eleyna's auguries anywhere you like. Auguries are special tips that come straight from Eleyna herself. There are 62 auguries in all, each appearing at random.*
Bunny Call	1	--	Skill Manual	*Allows you to summon a bunny to ride on the field. Requires Bunny Feed.*

Symbols

Name	Max Lv	Damage	MP Cost	CP Cost	Acquired	Notes
Healing	10	--	6	--	Level 1	HP recovery symbol. Recovers 31% of one ally's maximum HP (at level 1). The HP healed increases to 40% at level 10.
Cure Condition	1	--	8	--	Level 1	Curative symbol. Purifies one ally of all status ailments.
Wind Blade	10	INT x156%~358%	5~14	3	Level 1	Attack symbol. Fires swirling blades of wind at the enemy.
Lightning Blast	10	INT x198%~418%	5~14	3	Level 12	Attack symbol. Hurls lightning bolts at the enemy.
Radiant Lancer	10	INT x169%~301%	5~14	2	Level 25	Attack symbol. At level 1, rains four spears of light down upon the enemy. At level 10, rains seven spears of light down upon the enemy.
Faerie Healing	10	--	18	--	Level 32	HP recovery symbol. HP recovery symbol. Summons a faerie to recover at least 26% of all allies' maximum HP (at level 1). At level 10, it recovers 35% of their HP.
Enshelter	10	--	16	--	Level 35	Support symbol. Temporarily boosts one ally's DEF by 30%. At higher skill levels, the effect duration increases.
Restoration	10	--	25	--	Level 37	Resurrection symbol. Revives an incapacitated ally with 22% of their maximum HP (at level 1). Revives allies with 40% of their HP at level 10.
Enhance	10	--	18	--	Level 40	Support symbol. Temporarily boosts one ally's ATK by 30%. At higher skill levels, the effect duration increases.
Blast Hurricane	10	INT x225%~408%	10~19	4	Level 45	Attack symbol. Summons a great vortex that blows away any enemy caught in its grasp.
Ex Healing	10	--	10	--	Level 46	HP recovery symbol. Recovers at least 71% of one ally's HP (at level 1). Recovers 80% of their HP at level 10.
Sacred Pain	10	--	17	--	Level 48	Support symbol. Temporarily lowers one enemy's elemental resistance by 4. At higher skill levels, the effect duration increases.
Faerie Light	10	--	30	--	Level 51	HP recovery symbol. Summons a faerie to recover at least 51% of all allies' maximum HP (at level 1). Recovers 60% of their HP at level 10.
Aurora Rings	10	INT x156%~260%	7~16	4	Level 54	Attack symbol. At level 1, erects three pillars of light, damaging any enemy that touches them. At level 10, six pillars of light are erected.
Angel Feather	10	--	14	--	Level 59	Support symbol. Temporarily boosts one ally's ATK, INT, HIT, GRD, and DEF by 15%. At higher skill levels, the effect duration increases.
Thunder Flare	10	INT x195%~374%	7~16	4	Level 64	Attack symbol. Summons a ball of lightning that envelops and damages the enemy.
Resurrection	1	--	44	--	Level 69	Resurrection symbol. Revives an incapacitated ally with 100% of their maximum HP.
Tornado	10	INT x250%~464%	7~16	5	Level 74	Attack symbol. Calls forth an enemy-seeking tornado that sweeps up any foe it touches.
Sunflare	10	INT x478%~560%	10~19	7	Skill Manual	Attack symbol. Irradiates the enemy with a shower of light from above.
Faerie Star	10	--	50	--	Skill Manual	HP recovery symbol. Summons a faerie to recover 81% of all allies' maximum HP at level 1. At level 10, it recovers 90% of their HP.

Battle Skills

Name	Max Lv	MP Cost	CP Cost	Acquired	Notes
INT Boost	10	--	1	Skill Manual	Adds 10 to your INT at level 1. The INT boost granted increases as the skill's level increases (granting +1000 INT at level 10). The effect is only active when set as a battle skill.
HP Boost	10	--	2	Skill Manual	Adds 100 to your maximum HP at level 1. At level 10, your maximum HP increases by 10000. The effect is only active when set as a battle skill.
MP Boost	10	--	2	Skill Manual	Adds 10 to your maximum MP at level 1. At level 10, your maximum MP increases by 1000. The effect is only active when set as a battle skill.
Energy Shield	10	--	1	Skill Manual	Occasionally nullifies physical attacks. At higher skill levels, the chance of success increases. The effect is only active when set as a battle skill.
First Aid	10	--	2	Skill Manual	When taking damage from an enemy, occasionally recovers 20% of damage taken as HP (at level 1). At level 10, 60% of the damage taken is converted. The effect is only active when set as a battle skill.
Auto Healing	10	--	1	Skill Manual	Gradually restores HP during battle. At higher skill levels, HP is restored more frequently. The effect is only active when set as a battle skill.
Fury Boost	10	--	1	Initially Available	Increases the chance of surviving via Fury when your HP hits 0. At higher skill levels, the effect increases. The effect is only active when set as a battle skill.
Elusion	10	--	--	Skill Manual	Allows you to run away from battles quickly. At higher levels, the time needed to escape decreases. The effect is only active when set as a battle skill.
Focus	10	6	--	Skill Manual	Boosts HIT and critical chance for 30 seconds. At higher skill levels, the effect increases. Use this skill from the battle menu.
Hide	1	1	--	Skill Manual	Diverts the attention of enemies, making them target you less often. Use this skill from the battle menu.
Mindflare	10	8	--	Skill Manual	Boosts INT by 40% for 30 seconds (at level 1), but triples MP costs. INT is boosted by 100% at level 10. Use this skill from the battle menu.

ARUMAT

DATE OF BIRTH: APRIL 24
AGE: 26

Base Statistics								
HP	MP	ATK	DEF	HIT	GRD	INT	LUCK	Critical
226	57	31	14	35	10	14	60	2.0

Base Resistances								
Poison	Stun	Freeze	Paralysis	Silence	Fog	Curse	Pumpkin	Void
0	0	0	0	0	0	0	0	0

✦ MOVE SET

XBOX 360 VERSION

LONG RANGE (ATTACK)
Ⓐ

SHORT RANGE (ATTACK)
Ⓐ   ⒶⒶ   ⒶⒶⒶ

SHORT RANGE (DIRECTIONAL ATTACK)
⬆+Ⓐ

ANTI-AIR ATTACK
Analog stick at neutral, then press Ⓐ against a flying enemy

DASH   Ⓑ

PS3 VERSION

LONG RANGE (ATTACK)
✕

SHORT RANGE (ATTACK)
✕   ✕✕   ✕✕✕

SHORT RANGE (DIRECTIONAL ATTACK)
L3 + ✕

ANTI-AIR ATTACK
Analog stick at neutral, then press ✕ against a flying enemy

DASH   ◎

BLINDSIDE – RANK A
Arumat teleports to the enemy during his Blindside, making him almost completely invulnerable during the movement. Carries little risk against most attack types.

CHARACTER OVERVIEW

The cold and calculating Arumat is arguably the strongest melee unit on the team. His entire game plan is geared towards being an offensive monster at any distance, as he boasts both a giant ATK rating and comes loaded with a small selection of attack symbols. His attack strings are flexible, his special arts are damaging, and his Terra Hammer symbol is perfect for inflicting fatal damage to groups of enemies. Simply put, he's a beast!

Despite his array of symbols, short range is Arumat's primary position. His main short range string and the majority of his special arts have a wide area of effect, causing them to often hit foes approaching his sides. The third hit of his short range string also throws a projectile that returns to Arumat in a boomerang-like fashion. This interestingly makes it difficult for evil-doers to stage a counter attack even when the string is blocked. If this string hits, chain the third slash into his directional attack. If MP is available, ignore the directional attack and instead cancel into either his Unholy Maelstrom or Diabolic Edge.

An Eldarian soldier, blessed with extraordinary fighting ability even by Eldarian standards. A breakdown in the structure of his muscle cells has presented him with an ultimatum to give up his current body, or die an early death. Unsurprisingly, He has chosen to live out what time he has left as a fighter, partly as redemption for the men he has lost under his command. Unafraid of death, he lives a self-destructive life in his constant quest to push himself forward. Since meeting Crowe and Edge, however, he has begun to re-evaluate himself.

Take note that Arumat's DEF is relatively low, an attribute that doesn't work well with his aggressive nature. Though he does have a large enough pool of HP to make up for it, revolve the majority of your strategy around attacking during enemy recovery periods and using Blindsides. Arumat is especially effective when attacking after a Blindside, where his damaging combos come into play. Play it safe and never rush into the fray unless you're certain of the outcome.

If an enemy is too powerful to attack directly, move out to long range and use either Nether Strike or symbology. Nether Strike has the unique property of not being confined by an attack range; it can be done from any distance. Setup a Chain Combo group that consists of Nether Strike ➜ Earth Glaive to perform a cool 2-hit long range combo. If you aren't willing to invest the capacity points into Earth Glaive, Neither Strike ➜ Nether Strike works just as well. As long as the points are available, you can add even more Nether Strikes to your Chain Combo list for an even bigger amalgam of mayhem.

TIPS & TACTICS

LEVEL 10 BERSERK + CRITICAL HIT + ATK BOOST + BLINDSIDES = WIN

Invest SP into the **ATK Boost, Critical Hit,** and **Berserk** skills when they become available. Berserk comes packed with plenty of risk, but if used in the right situation, the payback is phenomenal. For example, activate Berserk against an enemy with attacks that are easy to dodge, and then use a Blindside against it. Berserk-boosted combos unleashed in this situation deal lethal damage. Also, try activating Berserk before chaining together multiple Nether Strikes. You can attack with Nether Strike from a safe distance, so Berserk's DEF penalty will hardly pose a threat.

If Berserk is too risky for you, stick with just ATK Boost and Critical Hit. Not only is Arumat's critical damage modifier exceedingly high, but many of his multi-hit special arts like the Diabolic Edge and Bloodstorm Revolution increase the probability of scoring a critical hit tenfold. His Aerial Gallows skill is also quite powerful if it happens to score a critical hit during its very last attack.

GROUP ERADICATION

Though his weak defense forces you to make more calculated attacks during boss fights, Arumat is second to only Bacchus when it comes to slaughtering groups of standard enemies. His Diabolic Edge and Bloodstorm Revolution special arts have an incredibly wide area of effect, enabling him to absolutely crush large groups of approaching monsters. Set up Chain Combo groups that consist of multiple uses of these skills to quickly rack up Bonus Board tiles in battle.

Transmission completed
Log of system, using System UI, controls interface,
Output text,
mission log + trigger execute(Trigger_Log)
825749.223.
Sensing data: 3841; database 101 secured!
End of line

EXAMPLE COMBOS

XBOX 360 VERSION

Short range Ⓐ Ⓐ Ⓐ ➡ 🔼 + Ⓐ

Long range Ⓐ, then juggle with neutral anti-air Ⓐ

Short range Ⓐ Ⓐ Ⓐ ➡ Unholy Maelstrom

Nether Strike ➡ Nether Strike ➡ Earth Glaive
(or Dragon Roar)

Short range Ⓐ Ⓐ Ⓐ ➡ Diabolic Edge ➡ Blood Storm
Revolution ➡ Aerial Gallows

Long range Ⓐ ➡ Nether Strike ➡ Earth Glaive

Short range Ⓐ Ⓐ Ⓐ ➡ Diabolic Edge ➡ Aerial Gallows ➡
Earth Glaive ➡ Dragon Roar

XBOX 360 VERSION

Short range ✕ ✕ ✕ ➡ L3 + ✕

Long range ✕, then juggle with neutral anti-air ✕

Short range ✕ ✕ ✕ ➡ Unholy Maelstrom

Nether Strike ➡ Nether Strike ➡ Earth Glaive
(or Dragon Roar)

Short range ✕ ✕ ✕ ➡ Diabolic Edge ➡ Blood
Storm Revolution ➡ Aerial Gallows

Long range ✕ ➡ Nether Strike ➡ Earth
Glaive

Short range ✕ ✕ ✕ ➡ Diabolic
Edge ➡ Aerial Gallows ➡ Earth
Glaive ➡ Dragon Roar

SKILLS

Field Skills				
Name	Max Lv	MP Cost	Acquired	Notes
Alchemy	10	--	Initially Available	Item Creation skill. Allows you to forge metal into other materials. At higher skill levels, more types of items become available.
Entomology	10	--	Skill Manual	Increases the chance of earning items after defeating insect enemies. At higher skill levels, the effect increases. Once the skill is learned, its effect is always active.
Chain Combos	10	--	Skill Manual	Allows you to assign multiple skills to a chain combo. At higher skill levels, the number of slots and the amount of damage dealt increases. Once the skill is learned, its effect is always active.
Duplication	10	--	Skill Manual	Allows you to duplicate items using Magical Clay. At higher skill levels, the amount of clay needed decreases. Some items cannot be duplicated.

Symbols

Name	Max Lv	Damage	MP Cost	CP Cost	Acquired	Notes
Earth Glaive	10	INT x195%~260%	5~14	3	Level 1	Attack symbol ⬤. Blades of stone burst forth from under the enemy's feet.
Fire Bolt	10	INT x117%~390%	5~14	2	Level 22	Attack symbol ⬤. At level 1, unleashes three enemy-seeking fireballs. At level 10, six balls of fire are unleashed.
Stone Rain	10	INT x195%~430%	7~16	4	Level 37	Attack symbol ⬤. Countless rocks rain down upon the enemy.
Explosion	10	INT x272%~485%	21~30	--	Level 58	Attack symbol ⬤. Sets off a large explosion centered around the enemy.
Terra Hammer	10	INT x304%~672%	21~30	--	Level 65	Attack symbol ⬤. At level 1, digs up three giant boulders and smashes them into the ground. At level 10, six giant boulders are dug up.

Special Arts

Name	Max Lv	Damage	MP Cost	CP Cost	Acquired	Notes
Unholy Maelstrom	10	ATK x250%~340%	8~12	3	Level 1	Generate a giant scythe, take a swing with it, then strike it into the ground.
Nether Strike	10	ATK x220%~476%	12~18	2	Level 11	Strike the ground to call up a pillar of fire, launching the enemy skyward.
Diabolic Edge	10	ATK x276%~402%	14~21	4	Level 29	Lunge forward with a five-hit spinning scythe attack.
Bloodstorm Revolution	10	ATK x379%~451%	16~25	4	Level 48	Spin your scythe vertically at high-speed, striking over and over as you rise into the air.
Aerial Gallows	10	ATK x330%~420%	18~27	5	Level 70	Attack with your scythe, then jump up and grab the enemy with it before slamming the villain to the ground.
Dragon Roar	10	ATK x450%~910%	20~29	6	Skill Manual	Strike down with your scythe and watch in glee as dragons pour forth along its tracks, attacking the target.

Battle Skills

Name	Max Lv	MP Cost	CP Cost	Acquired	Notes
ATK Boost	10	--	1	Skill Manual	Adds 10 to your ATK at level 1. The ATK boost granted increases as the skill's level increases (granting +1000 ATK at level 10). The effect is only active when set as a battle skill.
HP Boost	10	--	2	Skill Manual	Adds 100 to your maximum HP at level 1. At level 10, your maximum HP increases by 10000. The effect is only active when set as a battle skill.
MP Boost	10	--	2	Skill Manual	Adds 10 to your maximum MP at level 1. At level 10, your maximum MP increases by 1000. The effect is only active when set as a battle skill.
Critical Hit	10	--	1	Skill Manual	Allows you to perform critical hits outside of Rush Mode. At higher skill levels, the chance of success and the amount of damage dealt increases. The effect is only active when set as a battle skill.
No Guard	10	--	3	Skill Manual	Prevents you from being thrown off balance when taking damage less than 1% of your maximum HP (at level 1). At level, 10 the effect increases to 10%. The effect is only active when set as a battle skill.
First Aid	10	--	2	Skill Manual	When taking damage from an enemy, occasionally recovers 20% of damage taken as HP (at level 1). At level 10, 60% of the damage taken is converted. The effect is only active when set as a battle skill.
Auto Healing	10	--	1	Skill Manual	Gradually restores HP during battle. At higher skill levels, HP is restored more frequently. The effect is only active when set as a battle skill.
Stun	10	--	2	Skill Manual	Occasionally adds a stun effect when attacking enemies. At higher skill levels, the chance of success increases. The effect is only active when set as a battle skill.
Pride	10	--	0	Initially Available	Boosts status parameters when fighting weaker enemies. At higher skill levels, the effect increases. The effect is only active when set as a battle skill.
Fury Boost	10	--	1	Skill Manual	Increases the chance of surviving via Fury when your HP hits 0. At higher skill levels, the effect increases. The effect is only active when set as a battle skill.
Taunt	1	1	--	Skill Manual	Attracts the attention of enemies, making them target you more often. Use this skill from the battle menu.
Berserk	10	8	--	Skill Manual	Boosts ATK by 40% for 30 seconds (at level 1), but doubles the damage taken from attacks. At level 10 ATK is increased by 100%. Use this skill from the battle menu.
Scan Enemy	1	1	--	Skill Manual	Allows you to view information on the targeted enemy. Use this skill from the battle menu.
Convert	10	4	--	Skill Manual	Converts some HP to MP over a period of 30 seconds. At higher skill levels, the effect increases. Use this skill from the battle menu.

Transmission completed

Log of system, using System UI controls interface...
Output text mission log + trigger execute(Trigger_Log) 123749j223...

Securing data: 3641::- database 101 secured!

End of line

YOUR TRUSTY STARSHIP, THE SRF-003 CALNUS

In *Star Ocean: The Last Hope*, your quest will take you to new worlds and even new dimensions. Wherever you go, your base of operations is the starship Calnus, which holds all of the resources a team of adventurers could possibly need.

THE COMMAND CONSOLE

When you're ready to blast off, approach the central console on the Flight Deck to choose your destination. When enmeshed in a storyline objective, you may not be able to leave your current planet, but between quests, you can usually travel freely. There are plenty of new side quests, Private Actions, and item acquisition opportunities awaiting those who backtrack to previously visited worlds.

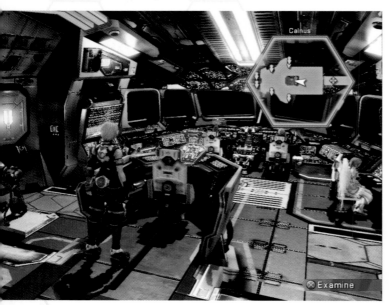

⊙ SAVE SPHERES

You can save your game at the glowing pink orbs found in both the Recreation Room and Edge's personal quarters. You get 20 save slots per storage device, so there's no excuse for not saving often!

CREW QUARTERS

The Calnus can host a crew of eight, with two characters assigned to each room. You can change your room assignment at any time by visiting the green computer screen across from the second-floor stairway, and you will also prompted to make assignments when new characters join later in the game. Characters gain affinity by sharing a room with each other (see the Private Actions section for more details).

Edge can sleep on his bunk at any time to completely refill the party's HP and MP, and to cure all status conditions. On long flights, you can choose to sleep until the next leg of the flight, or sleep until arrival. This allows you to skip Private Actions and hurry on to your next destination.

THE BATTLE SIMULATOR

The battle system in *Star Ocean: The Last Hope* can be tricky for new players to grasp. If you'd like to brush up on the basics or practice advanced moves like Blindsides and Rush Combos, visit the battle simulator in the room at the west end of the Calnus's second floor.

THE ITEM CREATION TERMINAL

Your guide through the Item Creation process is a colorful young lady named Welch. Visit her at the terminal in the meeting room, and she'll tell you everything you need to know about inventing recipes and creating items based on them. You can also pay social calls on Welch; visiting her at various points in the game triggers amusing event scenes. These are frequently unlocked after new characters join your party, so visit her soon after you recruit new personnel, but before the Calnus arrives at the next world.

S-, M-, AND L-SIZED OBJECT SPOTS

Later in the game, you can customize the Calnus with furnishings you find or create yourself. You can place S-sized objects on the desks in the Crew Quarters. These include devices like the Biorhythm Tester, which provides an analysis of each character's randomly fluctuating LUK stat, and the Aroma of Love, which increases the rate at which opposite-sex roommates acquire affinity for each other. You can place M-Sized Objects in the two slots near the entrance to the Flight Deck, as well as in the slot behind the terminal for the battle simulator. These include Healing Sheets that cure wounds, a Memory Plate to keep track of your accomplishments, and Gift Boxes that someone mysteriously refills with useful items. The only L-Sized Objects are Li'l Vending Machines that sell basic supplies and Item Creation ingredients and the Jukebox. You can place them in the northeast corner of the Recreation Room.

EDGE MAVERICK, INTERGALACTIC TREASURE HUNTER

It'll take more than a Workman's Blade and a pocket full of Blueberries to save the universe. In addition to the usual RPG staples of armaments, key items, and recovery items, Edge and his team require hundreds of different metals, textiles, and other materials to use as ingredients for Item Creation. Fortunately, there are plenty of ways to acquire the items you need.

 TREASURE CHESTS AND PODS

In addition to the items within, you earn a small amount of EXP and Party SP each time you successfully acquire an item from the universe's hundreds of scattered treasure chests and treasure pods. You'll also earn an Achievement or Trophy when you acquire 50% of the game's treasures, and another when you find them all. This should provide plenty of incentive to open every treasure chest, even when you aren't interested in the contents.

Note that you can't open a chest if you already have the maximum 20 units of the item it contains. When this happens, go to the item screen, select the item, and press the back button to discard one unit. You should then be able to open the chest and claim your EXP and Party SP.

Game Basics

HARVESTING AND MINING POINTS

You can also acquire items from nature, by foraging in the woods and mining rocky outcroppings. To harvest, you need Reimi in your party. You can use her Harvesting skill by pressing ● or ⓑ wherever you see green energy rising out of the earth. Only Bacchus knows the Mining skill, and you can use it by pressing ● or ⓑ when you see a yellow shimmer against a wall. Try to raise the level of the Harvesting and Mining skills as much and as early as possible, so that you can take a higher quantity of items out of each harvesting and mining point.

The contents of harvesting and mining points vary by region; you'll find tables for each area in the Walkthrough section that follows. (Note that some items on the harvesting and mining tables are rarer than others.) You'll reset all of a planet's harvesting and mining points whenever you return to the Calnus, allowing you to harvest and mine at the same points over and over again.

Not all harvesting and mining points appear on your map. Studious explorers may discover hidden harvesting points and mining points by pressing ✕ or Ⓐ at certain locations on the field.

MONSTER DROPS

Nearly all monsters carry items, and if you're lucky enough, they'll drop one when you defeat them. In the Walkthrough section, you'll find monster entries that look like this:

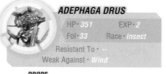

ADEPHAGA DRUS

HP · 351	EXP · 2
Fol · 33	Race · Insect

Resistant To · --
Weak Against · Wind

DROPS
Protection Seeds, Insect Leg, Insect Egg, Blueberries

The items listed under "drops" are in order of most rare to least; so while you are likely to win Blueberries from a pack of Adephaga Drus, you may need to fight scores of them before you ever win any Protection Seeds.

There are several ways to increase the odds of getting an item from a monster. Each character has a skill that increases the odds of winning items from a particular race of monsters. Since this monster is an insect, Faize's Entomology skill raises the odds of winning an item if you use him in combat. You can also raise the odds of getting items by triggering ambushes of multiple enemies (see "Engaging the Enemy" in this chapter for more details). Finally, you can equip the Steal battle skill, which gives characters a chance of swiping a monster's item each time they use a basic attack.

SHOPS AND VENDING MACHINES

There's no need to slaughter a herd of woodland creatures every time you need a Pie Crust or a handful of Rivets. Many goods can be purchased cheaply and at large quantities from shops and even your in-ship vending machines. The stock at shops and vending machines never changes, and they never run out of anything, so you can return whenever you need a rare ingredient or have finally saved up for that special weapon. You'll find full shop stock lists in both the Walkthrough and Items Appendix sections of this book.

PICKPOCKETING

At an early point in your quest, Edge can buy the Pickpocketing skill manual and the Bandit's Gloves accessory. By equipping the gloves and learning the skill, Edge gains the ability to pickpocket from human and feline characters with a tap of ● or ⓑ. (Shopkeepers are a frequent exception, since you can't always get around the counter to reach into their pockets.) Most characters hold a single item, while a few hold money (Fol) instead. You can only steal from each character once, but if you fail, you can keep trying until you succeed. Each character has a hidden pickpocket-resistance stat between 1 and 10, and if your level of Pickpocketing skill is higher than their level of resistance, you'll have a high chance of scoring the item. If it's lower, you'll most likely fail.

You can justify Pickpocketing to yourself ("One Fire Gem is a small price to pay for me saving your entire planet!"), but you can't justify it to your party. Whenever you attempt a pickpocket, there is a chance that one or more of your allies may notice, and their affinity for you will drop. You can read all about the affinity system in the Characters section, but suffice it to say that if you pickpocket a lot, it makes it difficult to get each character's special ending scene (and the corresponding Achievements or Trophies) at the end of the game. However, you can pick a few pockets without serious consequence.

PURSUING SIDE QUESTS AND SHOP ORDERS

Once you've proven your heroism, characters may ask for your help with more mundane matters. Delivering messages, fixing broken music boxes, and collecting bird droppings may not sound glamorous, but the rewards can be lucrative. All side quests are optional, but completing them is a good way to earn EXP, Party SP, (occasionally) rare item rewards and, ultimately, Achievements and Trophies. Completing quests often leads to additional quests from the same character, or a related one.

You'll find details about where and when you can accept side quests in both the Walkthrough and Side Quests Appendix sections of this book. Once accepted, a side quest is listed under the "Quests" section of your data menu. When you've satisfied the quest objective, an exclamation point appears by the name of the quest, signifying that you can now return to the person who gave you the quest and receive your reward. There are no time limits on completing quests, although certain game areas may become inaccessible during the course of the game, leaving you unable to complete quests that began there.

When you visit most item, material, and equipment shops, you can accept orders to deliver specific items to the shopkeeper. When you make the delivery, you'll receive the promised amount of Fol as well as additional EXP and Party SP rewards. Some requested items can be found at harvesting points, won from foes, or even bought at other shops. Others require you to gather ingredients and fire up the Item Creation terminal on the Calnus.

Once accepted, shop orders are added to your Quests menu, and are considered to be quests for the purposes of earning the Errand Boy, Potential Postman, and Dutiful Deliverer Achievements/Trophies.

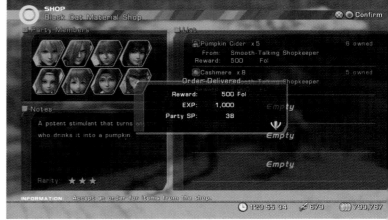

COLLECTIONS AND BATTLE TROPHIES

As your quest progresses, you'll discover all sorts of interesting things that your characters diligently record. Collections are saved on a separate file within your login, so a monster that you discover on one saved file is added to your collections data on every other saved file. When you begin a new game, you may either reset this file or transfer it over, so you are starting with all of your data from the previous game. There are several things to collect, and you'll unlock Achievements or Trophies as you reach certain benchmarks in each category. Additionally, the monster data you collect can be transformed into items with the aid of Monster Jewels.

SPACESHIPS AND WEAPONS

You'll collect spaceship data from terminals you find throughout your quest. Weapons data can be discovered from buying, finding, and making weapons for your characters, as well as from examining weapons lying on the ground, battling foes with unique weapons, or by speaking to characters who wield unique armaments.

BATTLE TROPHIES

A *Star Ocean* tradition, you unlock Battle Trophies by fulfilling various combat conditions for each of your characters, such as dealing certain amounts of damage, controlling them for certain lengths of time, using a fire-type symbol against a fire-weak foe, and so on. Some Battle Trophies must be stumbled across, while others are revealed in advance in the Battle Trophies Menu. When you hit certain Battle Trophy milestones for each character, you'll unlock bonuses like new combat voices, increased level caps, and even additional CP for equipping skills.

MONSTERS

If you fight a monster once, you'll unlock a data entry with its description and certain bits of information. Each time you battle that monster, the "% Analyzed" number rises, and when it hits 100%, you'll unlock the full entry. Once you unlock a full entry, you earn the right to turn that monster into a Monster Jewel (doing so requires blank Monster Jewels, which you can find or make throughout the game). Monster Jewels are Neck Accessories that provide stat boosts and penalties based on their monster of origin; see the Bestiary in this book to see what exactly each Monster Jewel does. Since you can transfer your data over when you begin a new game, the ability to make powerful Monster Jewels early on provides a boost on subsequent playthroughs.

ENGAGING THE ENEMY

When exploring field and dungeon areas, you'll find monsters roaming along with you. When Edge makes contact with one, your party of active characters is sent to a battlefield to fight that monster and its companions. The way in which you engage a foe can provide an advantage for one side or the other.

PREEMPTIVE ATTACKS

When Edge attacks an enemy from behind, you'll trigger a preemptive attack. You'll face fewer enemies, and they'll begin the battle with their backs turned towards your party.

SURPRISE ATTACKS

When an enemy attacks Edge from behind, it triggers a surprise attack. You'll face more monsters, you'll begin the battle surrounded, and the monsters have Rush Gauges that are partially full.

AMBUSHES

When you begin a battle with a monster while one or more other monster groups are only a few yards away, you'll provoke an ambush. After you defeat the first group of enemies, the second group immediately joins the battle. If there's a third enemy nearby, they'll join next. Ambushes are generally a good thing; the more ambushes you trigger, the higher your EXP bonus will be at the end of the fight (20% for one ambush, 50% for two, and so on, up to 200%). You'll also have

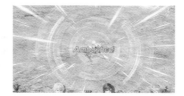

a higher chance of winning items from the enemies you defeat. Each ambush also earns you a green tile for your Bonus Board. (See "Building and Protecting your Bonus Board" in the next section.)

ON-FIELD EVASION SKILLS

When you're trying to avoid a fight, there are a few field skills that can help. Edge's Sprinting skill allows him to do a short, high-speed dash by tapping the ● or ✕, and Bacchus's Stealth skill (when selected from the skill menu) makes the party temporarily invisible. If you actually want to provoke your foes (say, to help engineer a multi-enemy ambush), Meracle's Ocarina skill is able to lure nearby foes to your position.

START WITH THE BASICS

You can practice *Star Ocean: The Last Hope*'s combat system at any time by selecting the battle simulator from the game's title screen or on the second-floor of the Calnus. The battle simulator does an excellent job of explaining the basics of combat and introducing advanced techniques like Blindsides and Chain Combos. Rather than repeat the same information, let's elaborate on a few of the finer points of combat in this section.

USING THE BATTLE MENU

One aspect of combat that the tutorial does not mention is the battle menu. At any point in battle, you can press 🔺 or Ⓨ to freeze the battle and bring up a ring-shaped menu. If you use 🎮 and 🎮 or the 🎮 and 🎮 (for 360) buttons to select another character, the battle remains frozen as you make a selection from that character's menu. (However, the character you choose will not be able to immediately use certain actions if he/she is already in the midst of some other action.) Many of the menu options are self-explanatory, but there are a few significant options that you may not immediately notice.

CHANGING YOUR SETUP

Choosing the setup menu allows you to rearrange your chain combos and equip different battle skills mid-combat. This is a great way to experiment with new skills or switch from single-enemy focused combos to wider-area ones when facing less favorable enemy odds.

If you press 🎮 and 🎮 or the 🎮 and 🎮 (for 360) buttons in the setup menu, you can pull up your equipment screen. The ability to change weapons mid-battle is invaluable when facing enemies with certain elemental weaknesses or resistances; for example, you can swap out the Flame Sword against a fire-resistant foe, or equip your Anti-Silence Amulet when facing foes that frequently inflict that condition.

TOGGLING OFF SYMBOLS

When you select the Symbology option, you'll pull up a list of your character's known symbols. As you might imagine, you can press ❌ or Ⓐ to order that character to cast a symbol, and again to confirm its target. You can also press ⬜ or ❌ on any symbol to toggle it off so that the computer AI will not cast it in combat. This allows you to shut off water-type symbols when battling water-resistant foes, or shut off all offensive symbols when you need your allies to focus on healing. You can toggle symbols back on in the Main Menu's Skills menu (under the Symbols sub-menu) or do it during your next fight. This sort of micromanagement is crucial for getting the most out of your AI companions.

CHANGING MEMBERS MID-FIGHT

Once you have five or more characters in your party, all characters beyond the first four in your roster remain waiting on a virtual bench for you to call them into battle. You can swap out a character whenever he or she is not in the midst of an action, even if that character has become incapacitated. Swapping out a fallen character for a fresh character is often easier than attempting a resurrection symbol or recovery item in the middle of battle. (However, once you swap out a character, you will not be able to make any other character swaps for a few seconds.) You'll also find that while you can't target characters on your bench, items and symbols that affect everyone affect them too, so a Resurrection Unit can resurrect them when they're dead, and a Faerie Light symbol can heal them even if they're not in play.

MORE ABOUT BLINDSIDES

Blindsides are the most reliable way of scoring a critical hits (and earning blue Bonus Board tiles), and are the only reliable way to reach the weak points of certain enemies. They also help you to elude the attention of an enemy that's targeting you, or break your own target lock so you can turn your blade on a different foe.

When you and an enemy are both targeting each other, you can charge a Blindside by holding down ● or Ⓑ. When the targeting icon (three yellow circle fragments) appear around your character, tilt the left stick in any direction. (If you charge for too long without executing the Blindside, your character becomes momentarily stunned.) Your character dives in whatever direction you tilt the stick, and then slips behind your foe. You can then attack for easy critical hits, and chain them into even more damaging special arts.

 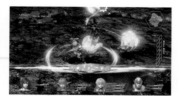

Blindsides won't always go as smoothly as they do in practice. If your target is in the midst of a move, it may hit you as you attempt to slip behind it. Or, another enemy could knock you out of your Blindside. As you level up BEAT:S, you'll earn bonuses (such as freezing nearby enemies) that help make it easier to pull off successful Blindsides. BEAT:S also eventually grants you the ability to do double Blindsides. Double Blindsides are useful against foes that can use Blindside counters. When an enemy is capable of countering your Blindside, the targeting icon that appears around your character is red instead of yellow. If you execute the Blindside while the targeting icon is flashing, your foe will be unable to counter. If not, an exclamation point will appear over the target's head instead of a question mark. You must then charge up and execute a second Blindside immediately, or you'll get nailed with a Bonus Board-smashing critical hit.

MORE ABOUT RUSH MODE

Whenever you deal damage, take damage, or hold ● or Ⓑ to build energy, you charge the Rush Gauge beneath your character's MP bar. When your bar is full, you can expend that energy in one of two ways:

ENTERING RUSH MODE

Press ● or ❌ to enter Rush Mode. Your character will flash white and the Rush Gauge will begin to deplete. Until it hits zero, you'll be faster, immune to enemy knockdowns, and have an increased chance of scoring critical hits. Entering Rush Mode is an effective defensive measure; if an enemy has you on the ropes, this action stops its attacks from juggling your character or knocking him around, allowing you to use your own combos without interruption. Setting your character to BEAT:B adds additional bonuses during Rush Mode, such as cheaper special arts and symbols, increased critical hit odds, and even the ability to replenish Rush Gauge energy while in Rush Mode.

USING RUSH COMBOS

To execute a Rush Combo, hold ● or ❌ and, before your character completes its Rush Mode animation, press L2 or R2 (🅻🆃 or 🆁🆃) to trigger a special art. If done correctly, you'll go to a special screen where your character faces off against his or her targeted enemy, and a button prompt then begins flashing. If you hit the button successfully, your nearest ally joins the combo with a special art of his/her own. If you both know the Chain Combos skill and have multiple special arts assigned to a Chain Combo, you can go and back forth until you've dished out an obscene amount of damage. Once the Rush Combo begins, there is nothing your target can do to defend or break out of it. Rush Combos are an extremely effective tactic against bosses, particularly late in the game when every character has full three-part Chain Combos configured, and can do perfect combos consistently. Rush Combos also allow you to put AI-controlled allies' full Rush Gauges to more effective use than the AI would; when an ally's Rush Gauge is full or nearly full, you can switch over to them, fire off a Rush Combo, and switch back to your preferred character.

BUILDING AND PROTECTING THE BONUS BOARD

The Bonus Board can be a great asset on your quest, since it provides the necessary EXP for leveling up quickly, gives an infinite source of HP and MP, and produces plenty of extra Party SP and Fol. There are four types of tiles you can earn, and each gives you a bonus at the end of every battle. Your Bonus Board has 14 slots in all.

Blue tiles provide a 10% EXP boost at the end of each fight. You earn them by killing foes with critical hits, which is easiest to do by using Blindsides against low-HP foes.

Yellow tiles provide a 10% increase in the amount of Fol you earn at the end of each fight. You earn them by killing multiple enemies with a single attack.

Red tiles restore 1% of each character's Max HP and Max MP at the end of each fight. You earn them by killing a monster exclusively with special arts and symbols.

Green tiles provide 1 additional Party SP at the end of each fight. You earn one each time you're ambushed.

Your Bonus Board breaks whenever the character you're controlling is hit with a critical hit or killed. When broken, you lose every tile that isn't adjacent to another tile of the same type, and half of the titles that are. Certain enemies excel at critical hits (an attribute you can view by scanning them with the Scan Enemy skill), and all enemies have a chance of scoring critical hits when they're in Rush Mode. When a character you control is about to be attacked by a monster in Rush Mode, you may want to use 🄻1 or 🅁1 or the 🄻🄱 🅁🄱 (for 360) buttons to switch to another character, particularly a ranged fighter who is unlikely to be targeted. (Your Bonus Board is not affected if one of the AI-controlled characters is killed or takes a critical hit.)

Your Bonus Board is not preserved when you save your game. You can save your game without losing it, but when you load the saved file, you begin with an empty Bonus Board.

DIFFICULTY LEVEL DIFFERENCES

When you start a new game, you'll have a choice between Earth Level (easy) and Galaxy Level (normal). If you beat Galaxy Mode, you'll unlock Universe Level (hard) and if you beat that, you'll unlock Chaos Level (very hard). The differences in difficulty modes mostly affect enemy stats. The only gameplay difference is that in Chaos Mode, certain targeting icons do not appear, giving you fewer clues about who is targeting whom and when you can execute Blindsides.

Earth Level
Enemy HP/MP x 0.7
Enemy ATK x 0.8
Enemy INT x 0.8
Enemy GRD x 0.8

Galaxy Level
Enemy HP/MP x 1.0
Enemy ATK x 1.0
Enemy INT x 1.0
Enemy GRD x 1.0

Universe Level
Enemy HP/MP x 1.3
Enemy ATK x 1.3
Enemy INT x 1.3
Enemy GRD x 1.3
Enemy Rush Gauge Increase Rate x 1.5

Chaos Level
Enemy HP/MP x 1.7
Enemy ATK x 1.7
Enemy INT x 1.7
Enemy GRD x 1.7
Enemy Rush Gauge Increase Rate x 2.0

EXCLUSIVE FEATURES IN THE PS3 VERSION

A few features have been added to the "International" version of Star Ocean 4 for the PlayStation 3. The Settings menu allows you to choose between Japanese and English voice tracks at any time you like. You can also switch the menu styles from "Modern" (the default) to "Classic," which offers a more colorful background and replaces all of the CGI-rendered images of the characters with hand-drawn artwork.

In combat, PS3 users can tap the START button to switch between enemy targets. (In the Xbox 360 version, players can choose a new target by running towards a monster and facing it for a few seconds.)

Finally, treasure placements and the item creation system have been rebalanced in the PS3 version. PS3 owners will find additional treasure chests that don't exist in the Xbox 360 version, as well as new treasures in old chests. These are typically ingredients that make creating new equipment through item creation easier. However, several higher-level item-creation recipes have been made more difficult in the PS3 version, which prevents players from creating certain powerful items early in the game.

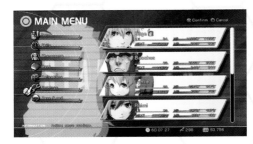

LEARNING, BOOSTING, AND USING SKILLS

A character is only as strong as his or her skills. Characters typically learn action skills by leveling up while other skills are mostly learned from skill manuals that are found in chests or purchased in skill shops. Skills in *Star Ocean: The Last Hope* break down into five general categories:

Action skills include special arts and symbols. Special arts are MP-consuming battle moves that can be arranged into combos and assigned to L2 or R2 (🅛 or 🅡). Symbols are the *Star Ocean* equivalent of spells, and can be cast from the Symbology menu in combat (some can also be cast from the field menu). Like special arts, many symbols can be assigned to trigger buttons for quick casting, but you can't really chain to them from normal attacks the way you can with special arts.

Field skills are skills that cannot be used in combat. They allow your character to dash, become invisible, pickpocket, harvest items, charge rings, and even duplicate items. They typically do not cost MP, but may have additional material costs.

Passive skills are a subset of field skills that are always on and do not need to be equipped. Skills like Zoology and Parapsychology that increase enemy item drops are passive skills, as are the Chain Combos skill, Item Creation skills, Haggling, and so on.

CONFIGURING YOUR SKILLS

To set up your action skills and battle skills, select Battle Config in the skills menu. At the start of the game, you have two slots for Chain Combos and two slots for battle skills. The Chain Combos passive skill will increase your chain combo slots, but there is no way to earn additional battle skill slots. Equipping skills to any slot costs CP, which you gain gradually over the course of the game. Prioritize your battle skills, and use high-CP skills sparingly in your Chain Combos.

Battle skills are among the most powerful skills in the game, offering such perks as massive stat boosts, automatic healing, and the ability to steal items or inflict status conditions upon your foes. The catch is that each character can only equip two battle skills at once. If a battle skill is not set into one of the two empty slots in the battle skills section of the Skill Config menu, it won't have any effect at all.

Battle menu skills are a subset of battle skill that can be used with the in-battle Skill Menu. They may or may not cost MP, and have effects like revealing enemy data, offering temporary stat boosts, or converting hit points into magic points. You do not need to equip these skills to use them, so they don't cost any CP.

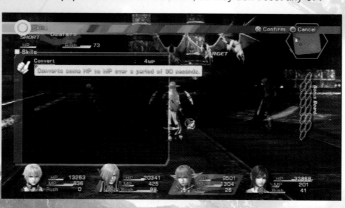

BOOSTING YOUR SKILLS

Most skills are learned at level 1 and attain their maximum potency at level 10. (A few skills, like Sprinting and Treasure Sense, cannot be leveled up at all.) There are two kinds of skill points you can spend to level up your skills: a character's individual SP, which is earned by gaining levels, and a party-wide pool of SP that is earned by opening chests, completing side quests, harvesting at harvesting points, and accomplishing other on-field actions. (You can also earn Party SP in combat if you have green Bonus Board tiles.) Earning Party SP from side quests such as fulfilling shop orders is a good way to strengthen your characters early in the game.

INCREASING YOUR PRIMARY STATS

Your character's base stats are based on a combination of his or her level, BEAT rank, and equipment. Characters can receive additional stat boosts from certain skills (like HP Boost and ATK Boost) and special abilities known as "factors" on their equipment. You can permanently increase a character's base stats by eating seeds, like Health Seeds, Protection Seeds, and Magic Seeds, which can be found on your quest, or generated by eating the Bizarre Fruit recovery item.

COOKING UP TEMPORARY BOOSTS

Several items provide temporary stat boosts. Special foods, typically cooked by Reimi, offer boosts of up to 50% to a single stat that can last for up to ten battles (or until the character is killed, whichever comes first). The ingredients for cooking items are relatively cheap and easy to find, so you should always be able to keep a variety of Reimi's concoctions on hand. However, each character can only have one

active food bonus at any given time; if a character eats a second meal, it replaces the effects of the first. Needless to say, DEF and ATK-boosting meals come in very handy before difficult boss fights.

You can also earn temporary stat boosts from items like Strength Potions, skills like Focus and Berserk, and symbols like Enhance and Enshelter. These last for only a set amount of time, and do not carry over from battle to battle (except in the case of multiple-battle ambushes). Counting both foods and temporary stat boosts, you cannot have more than four temporary stat-boosting effects active at once.

USING THE BEAT SYSTEM

Each character in your party can be assigned to one of three BEAT settings by selecting BEAT in the Characters menu. When a character is assigned to BEAT:B or BEAT:S, its BEAT type increases in ranks as you clear battles, eventually maxing out at rank 20 (there are no ranks to BEAT:N). As a general rule, your frontline fighters should be set to BEAT:S early in the game, while other characters should stick with BEAT:B. When fighting easier foes, you may want to switch your frontline fighters to BEAT:B so they can begin accumulating ranks in that as well.

BEAT:S (STRIKE)

BEAT:S offers boosts to the offensive ATK, INT, and HIT stats, and at higher ranks offers bonuses to make your Blindsides more powerful, more flexible, and easier to charge. Since your frontline fighters are typically doing most of the Blindsides, they'll want to focus on this setting.

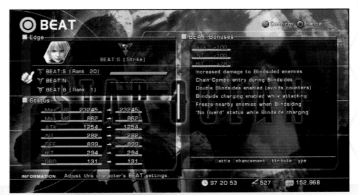

BEAT:B (BURST)

BEAT:B offers boosts to the defensive Max HP, DEF, and GRD stats, and at higher ranks offers bonuses to augment your abilities while in Rush Mode and make it easier to charge your Rush Gauge. As a general rule, AI-controlled characters should be set to BEAT:B, since they don't use Blindsides, are less skilled at defending themselves, and always use Rush Mode instead of Rush Combos. BEAT:B becomes the preferred choice for almost every character towards the end of the game, because the Max HP bonus of BEAT:B is based on a percentage of the character's Max HP (a 20% boost at rank 20), while all of the boosts from BEAT:S max out at +100, a negligible number when your stats are in the high thousands.

BEAT:N (NEUTRAL)

BEAT:N allows characters to reap the stat boosts from both of their current ranks in BEAT:B and BEAT:S, but not the special abilities. This is worth using only for bosses against whom both Blindsides and Rush Mode are irrelevant. (Against many bosses, it's preferable to use your Rush Gauge for Rush Combos.) Never leave a character on BEAT:N during normal battles, because sacrificing the ability to increase your BEAT:B and BEAT:S ranks leads to weaker characters in the long run.

PRIVATE ACTIONS AND THE AFFINITY SYSTEM

Throughout the game, several companions join Edge on his adventures, and the bonds between them strengthen as they get to know each other. This is reflected by a hidden stat known as "affinity" that each character has for each other character. There are several ways to raise or lower the affinity your characters share, most prominently by optional events known as Private Actions.

Private Actions mostly occur on the long flights when you travel to a new planet for the first time. These flights are broken up into legs, and in each leg you can trigger a Private Action by speaking to a certain character, or (in some cases) your choice of multiple characters. When the Private Action concludes, each character either gains or loses affinity for the other characters who appeared in the event, and you'll hear a musical tone that signifies that the flight has advance to the next leg. These in-flight Private Actions are entirely optional; you can blow them off by choosing to "Rest until arrival" in Edge's quarters. If you only want to blow off a specific leg, or you can't trigger a Private Action during that leg, you can instead choose "Rest" to advance to the next leg. You can see how close you are to your destination by checking the command console on the Flight Deck.

There are also Private Actions that occur while the Calnus is docked, and a few that occur outside of the Calnus. To trigger the latter type, you usually need to return to a previously visited location at a later point in the game. Some Private Actions won't trigger unless you've viewed some earlier Private Action, or you made the right choice of comments to a character during some other event. You can find detailed instructions on how to trigger each Private Action in this book's Walkthrough section.

At the end of the game, if the affinity Edge has for a character and the affinity that character has for Edge add up to a certain amount, you'll unlock that character's ending scene and a corresponding Achievement or Trophy. There are also a few Private Actions that wrap up character-specific subplots that you won't be able to see unless you already have a certain amount of affinity. Affinity does not affect any other aspect of the game. Outside of Edge, the only character relationship that unlocks anything (a single Private Action) is the relationship between Faize and Lymle.

Ways to Raise Affinity:

•*Seek out and trigger Private Actions with a character. (Note that a very few Private Actions have a negative affect on affinity.)*

•*Make the right choices when prompted for comment during Private Actions.*

•*Share a room with a character to gradually gain affinity for that character, and vice versa. (Note that many opposite-sex couples cannot share a room until they've earned a certain amount of affinity.) Gain even more affinity by setting furnishings like the Aroma of Love in the shared room. When sharing a room, you earn affinity based on your progress through the game's main quest, not the game clock. (So leaving your console on all night won't make Edge's roommate like him more.)*

•*Use Love Potion No. 256 on a character to make every other character gain affinity for him or her.*

Ways to Lower Affinity:

•*Trigger negative Private Actions (like peeping on Reimi in the shower) or say the wrong things during certain Private Actions.*

•*Get caught Pickpocketing. Your allies will not say or do anything differently when they catch Edge Pickpocketing, but their affinity stats fall all the same.*

•*Use the Super Aphrodisiac item on a character to make every other character lose affinity for him or her.*

•*Place Ominous Metal in a room shared by two characters to make them lose affinity for each other.*

ITEM CREATION

INVENTING AND ACQUIRING RECIPES

The Item Creation terminal in the Calnus allows you to make literally hundreds of items in the privacy of your own starship. But before you can make an item, you need a recipe. Some recipes are written on Recipe Memos that turn up in treasure chests or as rewards for side quests, but for the most part, you'll need to create them yourself.

THE RECIPE INVENTION PROCESS

Visit the Item Creation terminal and tell Welch that you want to "Invent new recipes." You'll then be able to arrange your party characters into "invention groups" of between one and three characters each. When you select START, your invention groups begin brainstorming ideas and, hopefully, inventing recipes. Every six seconds they spend forming ideas costs you one Party SP. There are three factors that determine what recipes you'll successfully invent:

ITEM CREATION SKILL LEVELS

Each character has a passive Item Creation skill like Smithery, Alchemy, or Cooking. Raising that skill increases the number of recipes you can invent; you'll never come up with a level 7 Engineering recipe if Bacchus doesn't have an Engineering skill of level 7 or higher. Resist the temptation to max out these skills early in the game; while you may get a jump on inventing the recipes, you won't find the ingredients to actually make them until much later.

INVENTION GROUP DYNAMICS

Many recipes can only be created by a certain combination of characters. For example, Reimi may not have the Smithery skill, but she knows a lot more about bows than Edge does. So for Edge to come up with a Smithery recipe for a bow, he'll need Reimi in his group. Lymle may be the only character who has the Artistry skill necessary to create symbol cards, but she can't make cards for symbols she doesn't personally know, unless another character can show her how. You can see which characters are required to make each recipe in the Recipes appendix at the back of this book.

SECONDARY ITEM CREATION SKILLS

This is where it gets a little tricky. While Edge may be the only character with the actual Smithery skill, every character has some aptitude for it. When you highlight a character in the recipe invention screen, you'll see scores for every Item Creation skill in the upper-right corner of the screen, as well as an eighth skill, "Sense," that exists only as a secondary skill. For example, the Smithery skill "Shell Armor" requires a total Smithery *score* of 15, which has nothing to do with Edge's level in the Smithery *skill*. Highlight Edge, and you'll see that his Smithery score is 10, which means you'll need to pair him with two other characters who have a combined Smithery score of at least 5. But that's not all; the Shell Armor also requires a Sense score of 13, so if you use Bacchus to reach the Smithery score of 15, his -8 score in Sense will keep you from success.

Trying every two- and three-person combination of eight characters would be time-consuming, so it's best that you approach recipe invention by first making a party that excels at each Item Creation skill; for example, Edge and the two characters with the highest Smithery scores. Then, for your next group, sacrifice your total Smithery score a little bit so you can have a high Smithery score with the highest possible *Sense* score. (Some recipes have high requirements in other secondary skills, but Sense is the most common.) Repeating this process for the other Item Creation arts should result in you learning the vast majority of recipes.

GATHERING INGREDIENTS AND MAKING ITEMS

Tell Welch you want to "Create items" and select an individual recipe to get to work. On the right side of the screen, you'll see a list of the necessary ingredients, showing both how many you have and how many you need. If you have enough ingredients to make at least one copy of the item, you'll be asked how many you wish to make. When making recovery items and other items that you want large quantities of, it's a good idea to make as many of them at a time as you can, because it increases the odds that you'll get lucky and make an extra item.

When all of a recipe's ingredients are commonly available at shops or freely found at harvesting and mining points, there's no reason to hesitate. However, when you're using exceptionally rare ingredients, like those found as rare monster drops or in treasure chests, don't burn your supply on a single recipe until you've made certain that you won't require that material in another, better recipe. The "Welch's Crafting Corner" sidebars in the Walkthrough section offer specific suggestions about where to acquire rare ingredients and what recipes to use them on.

IMPROVING YOUR GEAR THROUGH SYNTHESIS

Sarah's Synthesis skill is unique among the Item Creation skills in that it maxes out at level 1 and does not involve recipes at all. From the "Create Item" menu, select "Synthesis" to pull up a list of all of the weapons, armors, and accessories your party owns (not including those that are currently equipped by a character). Synthesis allows you to take any of those items and use a single ingredient in your inventory to boost its base stats or add special abilities known as "factors." You can use Synthesis on each item multiple times, although there are limits; rare items can typically be synthesized fewer times than common ones.

No item can have more than four factors. Some items add multiple factors when synthesized; for example, Sukiyaki offers both "ATK +50," which is a very good thing, and "ATK +2," which is a waste of a factor slot. You can cut off the lesser second factor of many items by adding them to items that already have three factors; in this case, only the ATK +50 would make the cut.

Once you've added factors to one piece of equipment, you can transfer those factors over to another piece of equipment by selecting the new item as the Base Item and the old item as the Additional Item. This is also a great way to circumvent the Synthesis Limits on items; if you attach all your desired factors to an older piece of equipment, transferring all of them to a newer item will only count as one Synthesis. The new item also gets stat boosts from the older item itself, with better equipment providing better boosts.

Many of the game's most easily acquired items can add useful factors to weapons via Synthesis, with the stat boosts from Reimi's cooked items being particularly potent. There's no reason to wait until you get the game's best items; it's cheap and easy to synthesize even items that you expect to replace soon.

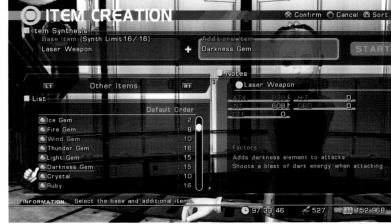

THE FUTURE OF MANKIND
WAITS IN THE STAR OCEAN

With the Earth's surface rendered uninhabitable by the missile volleys of World War III, humanity turned its eyes skyward. The ingenuity that was once channeled into weapons development was refocused on the space program, and with similar degrees of success. Within a generation, the Universal Science and Technology Administration spearheaded the invention of warp drive, the construction of a moonbase, and the assembly of a fleet of exploration starships.

Now it is time for the young crews of the Aquila, Balena, Calnus, Dentdelion, and Eremia to depart on their first major mission: To explore the Star Ocean, and find a new home for humanity.

SRF-003 CALNUS

THE MAIDEN FLIGHT OF THE CALNUS

You'll first meet Edge in the Crew Quarters of the SRF-003 Calnus, where he'll fire up the battle simulator for a bit of pre-mission training. You can return to this room at many points later in the game, and even access the battle simulator directly from the title screen, so don't feel like you have to master the entire combat system right now. For the moment, focus on the basic curriculum section and perhaps dabble a bit in Blindsides. Once you've mastered the fundamentals of combat, come back to learn the more advanced techniques.

After exiting the battle simulator and watching the cut scene, take a few moments to explore the Calnus. Save the game in Edge's room if you like, then descend to the lower decks by using one of the stairways marked with a blue plus icon on your map. When you reach the Flight Deck at the west end of the ship, sit down at your console at the front of the ship, or speak to Reimi to initiate the launch sequence.

ONE SMALL STEP ON AEOS . . .

The trip could have gone a whole lot more smoothly, but at least everyone has arrived on Planet Aeos in one piece. Wake up Reimi to trigger a cut scene, then leave the Flight Deck and take the passage to the south to exit the ship. So much for being the first to set foot on Aeos; the crews of the Balena and Dentdelion have beaten you to it.

Return to the Calnus, and inspect the terminals of the Flight Deck to find data entries for two ships in the SRF fleet. The data is recorded in the Spaceships section of your Collections menu, and if you manage to find data on all of the game's ships, you'll unlock the "Ship Savant" Trophy or Achievement for your efforts. You can also collect data on weapons, both your own and those used by other characters in the game.

Next speak to Van, who is standing outside of the Meeting Room, to earn Recipe Memo 05. Then, search the shelves in the storage area north of the Meeting Room to discover the data for the SRF-Issue F98 Assault Rifle.

Return to the landing site and seek out Rich, who is standing to the northwest of the save sphere. Rich gives you a Sniper's Bangle, which you can equip immediately by pulling up the main menu, selecting "Items," then "Equip Items," and setting it in Edge's Wrist Accessory slot.

Speak to Daniel, who is standing next to Rich, and then Andy, the next closest NPC. Once you've heard what they have to say, head towards the save sphere and speak with Reimi to trigger an event that ultimately ends in your first real battle. The pair of Adephaga monsters shouldn't give you too much trouble, and offer a good opportunity to practice the basics of combat. For example, the Adephaga telegraph their attacks by raising their front legs, giving you an opportunity to jump out of their attack range by pressing ● or Ⓑ and away on the left stick.

Planet Aeos

PLANET AEOS:
LANDING POINT

MAP TREASURES

1. Broken Metal Cutting Blade x 1
2. Blueberries x 3
3. Blackberries x 2
4. Iron x 1
5. Insect Egg x 2
6. Bigberries x 1
7. Wind Gem x 1
8. 103 Fol
9. Iron x 2
10. Insect Leg x 1, Warped Carapace x 1

LEGEND

 = SAVE SPHERE

 = PASSAGE

MONSTERS

 ADEPHAGA

| HP · *292* | EXP · *1* |
| Fol · *16* | Race · *Insect* |

Resistant To · --
Weak Against · *Wind*

DROPS
Protection Seeds, Insect Leg, Insect Egg, Blueberries

 ADEPHAGA DRUS

| HP · *351* | EXP · *2* |
| Fol · *33* | Race · *Insect* |

Resistant To · --
Weak Against · *Wind*

DROPS
Protection Seeds, Insect Leg, Insect Egg, Blueberries

 KILLER WASP

| HP · *228* | EXP · *1* |
| Fol · *33* | Race · *Insect* |

Resistant To · --
Weak Against · *Earth*

DROPS
Accuracy Seeds, Aquaberries, Blueberries

To Urd Falls Cave

To Calnus

HARVESTING POINT ITEMS

Aquaberries   Pickled Plum
Blueberries   Vegetables
Insect Egg   White Rice
Lemon

MINING POINT ITEMS

Iron
Silver

THE SEARCH FOR THE EREMIA

After defeating the pair of Adephaga, return to the Flight Deck and report to Captain Grafton. He'll ask Edge to scout out the Eremia, which crashed far to the north. Reimi insists on accompanying you. With her at your side, you can harvest items wherever you see glowing green energy rising from the ground. You'll also have a competent archer backing you up on the battlefield; press ⚫ or ⚫ (or ⬛ and ⬛) during combat if you want to take direct control of Reimi and leave Edge in the capable hands of the computer AI.

I said I wasn't letting you off, remember?

LOOTING THE LANDING POINT

The crew of the Dentdelion have succeeded in removing the debris that was blocking the passage to the north, but don't hurry off in that direction just yet; it's crawling with enemies. First, examine the unguarded chest and four glowing green pods to the northwest, which contain a useful assortment of recovery items. You also earn a few EXP (experience points) and Party SP (skill points that any character can use) each time you find some loot. Between those treasures and the harvesting point to the east of the save sphere, you can earn enough EXP to take Edge to level 2 before you face the Adephaga again.

While chests and pods are never refilled, harvesting points do grow back every time you return to your ship. Since this harvesting point is so close to the Calnus, you can harvest it as often as you like by repeatedly entering and exiting the ship. It's a great way to earn free EXP, rack up some Item Creation ingredients, and fill your inventory with HP-restoring Blueberries before you face the monsters in the northern part of the map.

DABBLING IN ITEM CREATION

After Edge's solo battle against the Adephaga, the crew of the Calnus finally gets the Item Creation terminal in the Calnus Meeting Room up and running. The only recipe you have at the moment is Van's Recipe Memo 05, which later makes a nifty Storm Blade for Edge once you assemble a Broken Metal Cutting Blade, Wind Gem, and Repair Kit. (The blade and gem can be found in nearby chests, but the Repair Kit won't turn up until the end of your adventures on Planet Aeos.) If you've earned any Party SP from enemy encounters or opening chests, you can select "Invent new recipes" and place Edge and Reimi in one of the four groups (either separately or together — it doesn't matter at this point) to start an invention session using Edge's Smithery skill and Reimi's Cooking skill. At level 1, all they'll come up with is the recipe for Pickled Plum Rice, which provides a 5% EXP boost for three consecutive battles and restores 5% of a character's HP. Of the three ingredients, White Rice and Pickled Plums can be found at nearby harvesting points, but Seaweed won't start turning up until the Urd Falls Cave.

SEARCH FOR A RIVER CROSSING

The wreckage of the spaceship Eremia is to the north, but a deep river blocks your progress in that direction. Instead, head east towards the Urd Falls Cave, which connects the Landing Point to the Northern Coast. Enemies grow tougher in the cave, and tougher still on the Northern Coast. Proceed slowly, earning EXP, items, and Bonus Board tiles before ducking back to Edge's room in the Calnus for an HP- and MP-recovering rest.

WORKING THE BONUS BOARD

You don't need to get fancy to best the Adephaga and Killer Wasps that patrol the Landing Point area, but you'll be richly rewarded if you do. When Edge has caught the attention of an enemy but isn't being actively attacked, hold ● or ⓑ to charge up energy until the aura around Edge glows blue. If the enemy who is targeting Edge is nearby, you can tilt the left stick in any direction to execute a Blindside. Edge then slips behind his target, and you may then tap ✖ or ⓐ to strike it in the back for easy critical hits. A successful Critical Finish (a kill with a critical hit) earns a blue tile for your Bonus Board, which provides a 10% EXP boost at the end of each battle. Your Bonus Board won't be cleared at the end of the fight, so that 10% EXP boost lasts until the Bonus Board is broken by an enemy that incapacitates or deals a critical hit to the current leader of the party. As long as you can stay alive and on your feet, you can keep piling on the tiles, potentially earning a 120% EXP bonus each battle! However, your Bonus Board cannot be saved at a save sphere, so if you load a saved game, you'll start with nothing.

Of course, there are other bonus tiles you might want to earn. The Killer Wasps present a good opportunity to take out a foe exclusively with special moves; make sure Reimi is targeting a different foe, then lay into an untouched wasp with repeated strikes from Edge's Rising Blade special art. If an enemy dies exclusively from special art damage, you'll earn a red tile, which recovers 1% of each character's HP and MP at the end of each fight. You can also earn a yellow tile (worth a 10% Fol boost) by killing two enemies with one attack, or a green tile (worth 1 additional party SP at the end of each fight) by getting in an ambush battle, which occurs when you enter combat with one foe while a second enemy is only a few steps away.

Any enemy can break your Bonus Board by scoring a critical hit to the leader. Certain enemies have a higher critical hit rate than others, however Rush Mode will highly increase that unit's chance of breaking the Bonus Board, which is indicated by a white glow around them. When a glowing foe comes at you, jump away or press ⬜ or ⬜ (or ⬜ and ⬜ in the Xbox 360 version) to switch to another character.

SPENDING YOUR SKILL POINTS

If you boost Reimi's Cooking skill to level 2, she can invent two new recipes. Ochazuke is an enhanced version of Pickled Plum Rice that requires Natural Water (which can be found in the Northern Coast), while Otherworldly Cuisine helps a character avoid enemy targeting, but cannot be created with the ingredients found on Planet Aeos. Since there isn't much point in making recipes for items you can't cook yet, you should probably invest Reimi's skill points (and most of your Party SP) into the Harvesting skill. Higher levels of Harvesting won't change the quality of the items you find at harvesting points, but it does increase the quantity. The more you boost it now, the more items you'll have to play with later.

If you boost Edge's Smithery skill to level 2 and put him in a group with Reimi, he comes up with the Iron Protector recipe. All this recipe requires is Reimi's current SRF Protector armor and four pieces of Iron, which can be found in treasure chests and pods in both the Landing Point and Urd Falls Cave areas. (Note: you'll need to unequip Reimi's SRF Protector before you can use it as an ingredient for the new item.)

You can also spend your SP to boost your combat skills, but do so sparingly — increasing a skill's power also increases its MP consumption.

PLANET AEOS:
PLANET AEOS: URD FALLS CAVE

 ## Map treasures

1. 203 Fol
2. Iron x 2
3. [Earth Barrier] Seasonings x 2, Warped Carapace x 1
4. [Earth Barrier] Attack Seeds x 1
5. Fresh Sage x 2
6. Blackberries x 2
7. Blueberries x 3

 ## Harvesting Point Items

Aquaberries	Insect Egg
Bizarre Fruit	Seaweed
Blackberries	Vegetables
Blueberries	White Rice

 ## Mining Point Items

Iron
Silver

Monsters

 **ADEPHAGA**
HP · 292 EXP · 1
Fol · 16 Race · Insect
Resistant To · --
Weak Against · Wind
DROPS
Protection Seeds, Insect Leg, Insect Egg Blueberries

 ADEPHAGA DRUS
HP · 351 EXP · 2
Fol · 33 Race · Insect
Resistant To · --
Weak Against · Wind
DROPS
Protection Seeds, Insect Leg, Insect Egg Blueberries

 **KILLER WASP**
HP · 228 EXP · 1
Fol · 33 Race · Insect
Resistant To · --
Weak Against · Earth
DROPS
Accuracy Seeds, Aquaberries, Blueberries

 GIANT BAT
HP · 259 EXP · 2
Fol · 25 Race · Bird
Resistant To · --
Weak Against · --
DROPS
Accuracy Seeds, Blackberries

 **GEREL**
HP · 327 EXP · 1
Fol · 27 Race · Plant
Resistant To · Wind
Weak Against · Earth
DROPS
Fresh Sage, Seaweed, Blackberries

Legend

 = PASSAGE
= INTERACTION POINT
= EARTH BARRIER

THE FOES THAT LURK BEHIND THE FALLS

Brace yourself for a fight when you step into the Urd Falls Cave, since an Adephaga is often waiting at the entrance. In addition to those familiar foes and the ever-annoying Killer Wasps, you'll begin encountering Giant Bat and Gerel enemies here. Of the two, Gerel are the more interesting, thanks to their ability to use the "Schism" special art to split into two foes whenever they are at the brink of death. If your party is hurting, never allow a seriously wounded Gerel to have a moment's respite, or the odds will suddenly become a whole lot worse.

To Northern Coast
To Northern Coast
To Landing Point

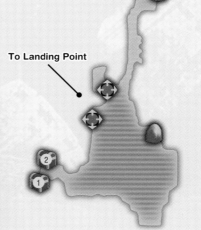

The Urd Falls Cave can be tough for inexperienced players, since the cave is thick with monsters and the thin passages don't allow a lot of room to dodge. More confident players can use this to their advantage by getting a Killer Wasp or Giant Bat to chase them, and then running at another foe. If the bat or wasp is right behind you when the first battle starts, it ambushes you as soon as the initial batch of enemies is slain. Having to fight two consecutive battles may sound like a bad thing, but the rewards are sweet: each ambush earns you a green Bonus Board tile (worth one additional Party SP per battle) and bonus EXP at the end of the fight.

WHEN EDGE FALLS, REIMI PERSEVERES

If you haven't tried playing as Reimi, the Urd Fall Caves are a good place to experiment. Reimi's auto-targeting bow is nice against quick-moving foes like Killer Wasps and Giant Bats, but it's her ability to fire it mid-jump that makes her such a powerful character. Against foes without ranged attacks, Reimi can turn losing battles around by jumping away from enemy attacks (by pressing ● or Ⓑ and away) and firing a shot at the peak of her jump (by pressing ✕ or Ⓐ). Switch to Reimi and use this tactic to stay alive whenever Edge becomes incapacitated in combat.

SECRETS OF THE URD FALLS CAVE

If you've been diligently gathering treasures, you'll find your fourth and fifth chunks of Iron in one of the pods in the southwest corner of the cave. These pieces give you everything you need to return to the Item Creation terminal at the Calnus and upgrade Reimi's SRF Protector to an Iron Protector. (If you don't have the recipe yet, upgrade Edge's Smithery skill to level 2 and put him in an invention group with Reimi.)

As you proceed north through the thin main passage of the cave, keep an eye out for mossy patches on the wall that surround a hole with a dim green glow at the center. Reach your hand in, and you can pull out a healing item: two Blueberries in the first hole, two Blackberries in the next, some Fresh Sage in the cavern down the right (east) fork, and Defense Seeds near treasure #6. Don't get greedy, though — if you reach into any hole a second time, you'll get a face full of searing steam. It only deals a few points of damage to your characters, but what about the damage it deals to your pride?

To reach your destination on the Northern Coast, you'll need to head west when the tunnel splits. But first, explore the passage to the east, where you'll find a dead-end cavern at the base of a ledge. In addition to a treasure hole and the cave's only harvesting point, you can trigger the game's first Private Action here, although you'll need to return for that later in the game (see page 70 for details).

Map Treasures

1. Natural Water x 2
2. Attack Seeds x 1
3. Wind Gem x 1
4. 81 Fol
5. Seaweed x 1, Warped Carapace x 1
6. Iron x 3
7. Fresh Sage x 2
8. Seaweed x 1
9. Bigberries x 1
10. Protection Seeds x 1
11. [Dark Barrier] 19,800 Fol

Harvesting Point Items

Blueberries
Defense Seeds
Fresh Sage
Insect Egg
Lemon
Pickled Plum
Seaweed
Vegetables

Mining Point Items

Iron
Silver

Monsters

ADEPHAGA DRUS

HP · 351	EXP · 2
Fol · 33	Race · Insect

Resistant To · --
Weak Against · Wind

DROPS
Protection Seeds, Insect Leg, Insect Egg
Blueberries

KILLER WASP

HP · 228	EXP · 1
Fol · 33	Race · Insect

Resistant To · --
Weak Against · Earth

DROPS
Accuracy Seeds, Aquaberries, Blueberries

GEREL

HP · 327	EXP · 1
Fol · 27	Race · Plant

Resistant To · Wind
Weak Against · Earth

DROPS
Fresh Sage, Seaweed, Blackberries

POLYPHAGA

HP · 447	EXP · 3
Fol · 58	Race · Insect

Resistant To · --
Weak Against · Earth

DROPS
Protection Seeds, Insect Leg, Insect Egg,
Fresh Sage, Iron

KILLER CHELAE

HP · 374	EXP · 4
Fol · 29	Race · Insect

Resistant To · Water
Weak Against · Thunder

DROPS
Fresh Sage, Warped Carapace, Seaweed,
White Rice

Legend

	=	SAVE SPHERE
	=	PASSAGE
	=	RECOVERY SPHERE
	=	SURVIVOR
	=	INTERACTION POINT

EXPLORE THE COASTAL HIGHLANDS

When you reach the Northern Coast, dash to the save sphere and preserve your hard-earned progress. Continue west to the green circle that appears on your map, and step into it for a complete HP and MP refill for your entire party. These recovery spheres can be used repeatedly, so this presents a good opportunity to rack up some red Bonus Board tiles by killing foes with Special Arts — you can burn through your entire MP bar in a single battle, then step back into the recovery sphere to get it all back. But you should devote most of your Bonus Bar to blue tiles, since their 10% EXP bonuses will better prepare you for the challenges ahead.

Before you jump down to the beach, you should do a lap of the highlands to hit the three harvesting points and pick up a chest or two. Along the way, you'll encounter giant cockroach-esque enemies called Polyphaga. They aren't much tougher than the Adephaga you've fought before (and offer triple the EXP), but watch out for the aggressive Bonus Board-smashing charges they sometimes use during Rush Mode. When you see their Rush Gauge (to the right of their HP) ticking towards 100, stay out of the way until their Rush Mode passes.

A PLEASANT STROLL ON THE SHORE

Use the recovery sphere and save sphere before you jump down the ledge to the beach, because there's no climbing back up. The yellow icon on your map directs you to your destination, the sole survivor of the Eremia. Walk along the water line, where the beach's treasure pods tend to be located, and make sure to battle at least one of the new crab-like Killer Chelae monsters for your monsters collection.

Heal up as soon as you spot the survivor lying on the beach. As soon as you approach him, you'll trigger a cut scene that ends with a boss attack. If you've cooked up any EXP-boosting foods, like the Pickled Plum Rice or Ochazuke, now would be a fine time for a meal.

BOSS

Armaros

HP · ?????	EXP · 40
Fol · 609	Race · Other
Resistant To · *Water, Wind*	
Weak Against · *Earth*	

DROPS
Warped Carapace

Break Through Armaros's Shell

The trick to defeating Armaros is smashing the rocky shell that protects the right side of its body. If there's a spray of rock shrapnel when you hit it, you're hitting the right place. As long as the shell is intact, no attack is able to do more than a few points of damage to Armaros, regardless of your characters' strength. But when the shell is gone, you can target the glowing white spot on the Armaros's side for triple-digit damage.

Take control of Reimi or Edge, and set Faize's tactics to "Fight freestyle without using MP!," so he'll help you strike the shell instead of interrupting your combos by juggling Armaros with his Earth Glaive symbol. Continuously circle around Armaros so you can strike from the shell side, which fortunately also keeps you out of range of most of its attacks. Whether the shell is intact or not, normal attacks tend to be more effective than Edge's Rising Blade special art, so stick with Edge's standard combos (executed by keeping the left stick in a neutral position as you attack with ⊗ or Ⓐ). When Armaros finally lifts the remnants of its shattered shell, its speed increases dramatically. The same tactics continue to be effective: circle and strike at the glowing white spot with standard combos. You can also speed things along by taking control of Faize and repeatedly hammering Armaros with the Earth Glaive symbol, since the boss is particularly weak to earth-type attacks.

Even if you master Armaros's pattern, your allies may not, and Armaros can dish out a lot of damage to low-level characters like Faize. Keep an eye on everyone's HP and use Blueberries when an ally drops below the halfway point — don't wait until they are near death. Armaros is very slow while its shell is intact, so you can avoid its deadliest attacks by running away and circling it from a distance whenever it enters Rush Mode. If everything goes horribly wrong, take control of Reimi and have her jump away while firing in mid-air for as long as it takes to bring down Armaros. The poor crustacean won't even be able to land a hit.

THE LONG WALK HOME

It's a long walk back to the Calnus, and there isn't so much as a single recovery sphere or save sphere on the way. That makes the journey a grueling one for parties who used up most of their resources in the Armaros fight, but fortunately, you now have a third man on the team to help even the odds. Give Faize free reign to fight all-out, using his Earth Glaive symbol to defeat foes from a safe distance. When he runs out of MP, he'll prove surprisingly useful in melee combat — his directional attack combo hits repeatedly and keeps foes locked in place, setting them up for other characters to slip in for the kill.

You can't go back the way you came, so continue east down the beach and enter the Urd Falls Cave through a new entrance to the north. From there, you can head south to the ledge marked with an exclamation point, and leap down to the chamber with the harvesting point. Once there, you can simply retrace your steps back to the Calnus, heading south at the first fork inside the cave. Just don't expect to find the ship exactly where you left it …

PLANET AEOS:
EXPLORATION BASE

MAP TREASURES

1. Lemon x 3
2. Blueberries x 2
3. 193 Fol
4. Skill Manual "Scan Enemy" x 1
5. Blueberries x 1, Blackberries x 1
6. Uncooked Pasta x 1, Olive Oil x 1

PICKPOCKETING

Exterior

a. Duncan, SRF-002 Crewman	Aquaberries x 1
b. Jakov, SRF-004 Crewman	Bigberries x 1
c. Jeter, SRF-004 Crewman	230 Fol
d. Ector, Eldarian Crewman	Aquaberries x 1

Interior

e. Bawles	1 Fol
f. Rose, SRF-002 Crewwoman	Fresh Sage x 1
g. Kaye, Eldarian Researcher	Monster Jewel x 1
h. Curious Eldarian	Bizarre Fruit x 1
i. Supreme Command Gaghan	Monster Jewel x 1
j. Chad, SRF-004 Crewman	Seaweed x 1
k. Commander Grafton	Natural Water x 1
l. Donald, SRF-002 Crewman	Blueberries x 1
m. Rose, Smiling Eldarian	10 Fol
n. Van	Pickled Plum x 1
o. Pazal, Eldarian Scientist	Seasonings x 1
p. David, SRF-002 Crewman	Olive Oil x 1
q. Lilia, Chief of Analysis	300 Fol
r. Airi, Eldarian Physician	Protection Seeds x 1
s. Alton, Eldarian Base Worker	Uncooked Pasta x 1

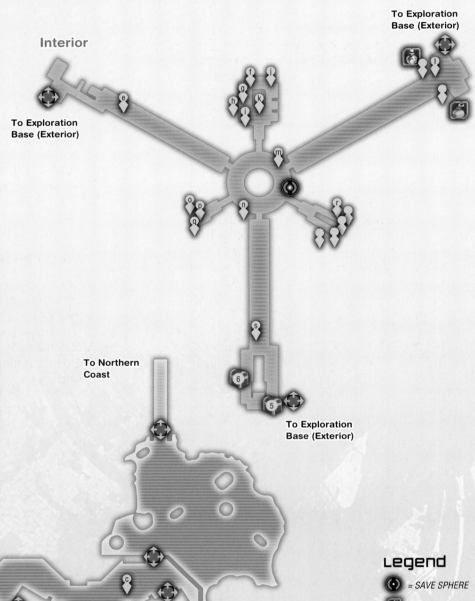

Interior

To Exploration
Base (Exterior)

To Exploration
Base (Exterior)

To Exploration
Base (Exterior)

To Northern
Coast

Exterior

Legend

⬡ = SAVE SPHERE

▣ = SHOP

✥ = PASSAGE

⬦ = NPC

THE WONDERS OF PREFABRICATION

The Eldarians don't mess around. Just when you think you're going to turn a corner and spot the Calnus, you find an entire military installation where your ship used to be. Look around a bit more, and you'll also discover a new bridge to the previously inaccessible western chunk of the Northern Coast, where that area's final three treasure chests await. (However, one of the chests is enveloped in dark energy, and cannot be opened until you acquire the Light Ring later in the game.)

Before you enter the base, do a lap around it and search out the four treasure chests that are hidden in the shadows of the surrounding crates. The best prize in the bunch is the skill manual in the chest near the Calnus's hangar, a one-shot item that can be used to permanently teach Faize the Scan Enemy skill. Scan Enemy allows you to instantly view the HP, resistances, and weaknesses of any monster in combat.

It takes no time to cast — you get the information as soon as you select it from the battle skill menu, so there are no drawbacks beyond the single-MP casting cost.

REPORT TO CAPTAIN GRAFTON

You'll find Captain Grafton and Faize's superior officer, Supreme Commander Gaghan, waiting in the communications room in the north wing of the base. They take the Meteorite Fragment you found on the beach and offer you Faize's services in return.

After your briefing, return to the communications room and search some of the empty terminals to unlock collections data on the SRF-002 Balena, SRF-004 Dentdelion, and SRF-005 Eremia spaceships (may they rest in peace). Your only assignment at the moment is to get some R&R, so step outside and see what else the base has to offer.

THE ALPHA AND OMEGA SHOPS

The pair of shops in the northeast wing of the base finally offers an opportunity to burn through some of the Fol that's been simmering in your pocket. Base Shop Omega has the most interesting stock, including an Eldarian Bow for Reimi, Silver Bangle accessories, and skill manuals that teach the arts of Anthropology (to Edge), Botany (to Reimi), Entomology (to Faize), and First Aid (to anyone). The science skills increase your drop rate when battling certain types of enemies, with Entomology being the most useful on this planet. First Aid is a healing skill that's extremely expensive, and will be trumped by superior skills in the future, but it provides a temporary boost for frontline fighters like Edge. Pick up one of each skill manual if you can afford it, and grab a Repair Kit while you're there — it's the last ingredient you need for the Storm Blade recipe.

Base Shop Alpha deals in basic supplies as well as cooking ingredients. If you have cash to spare, pick up a few of each ingredient. You probably don't have the recipes yet, but you may not be free to come back here when you do invent them.

You may notice that in addition to buying old items a la carte, each shop has a list of orders for specific items they want filled. You don't get huge amounts of money for fulfilling orders, but you do get large amounts of EXP and Party SP. Diligent harvesters may be able to part with some extra Lemons, Seaweed, Pickled Plums, and White Rice, but don't empty your inventory of any one item, or you could be left without an essential ingredient for a future recipe.

base shop: alpha - stock

Item	Type	Price
Blueberries	Usable Items	40
Blackberries	Usable Items	60
Aquaberries	Usable Items	30
Fresh Sage	Usable Items	150
Uncooked Pasta	Other Items	100
Raw Animal Meat	Other Items	60
Common Egg	Other Items	30
Vegetables	Other Items	60
Seasonings	Other Items	20
Olive Oil	Other Items	80

base shop: alpha - orders

White Rice x 3

Reward	Rarity	From
300	☆	Maria, SRF-004 Crewwoman

Pickled Plum x 5

Reward	Rarity	From
500	☆	Maria, SRF-004 Crewwoman

Seaweed x 5

Reward	Rarity	From
800	☆	Maria, SRF-004 Crewwoman

Gambleberries x 3

Reward	Rarity	From
800	☆☆☆	Maria, SRF-004 Crewwoman

base shop: omega - stock

Item	Type	Price
Eldarian Bow	Weapon	500
Silver Bangle	Wrist Accessory	800
Skill Manual "Anthropology"	Usable Items	800
Skill Manual "Botany"	Usable Items	900
Skill Manual "Entomology"	Usable Items	600
Skill Manual "First Aid"	Usable Items	2000
Repair Kit	Other Items	100

base shop: omega - orders

Iron x 5

Reward	Rarity	From
700	☆	Felius, Eldarian Clerk

Silver x 4

Reward	Rarity	From
700	☆	Felius, Eldarian Clerk

Lizardskin x 5

Reward	Rarity	From
900	☆	Felius, Eldarian Clerk

Lemon x 5

Reward	Rarity	From
300	☆☆	Felius, Eldarian Clerk

COMPLETING THE BASE TOUR

To trigger the next event, you merely need to leave the base and return. However, it may be wise to take your captain's advice and take a full tour of the base, as there are a few interesting things to find. In the sickbay (the southeast wing), you can rest up in a vacant medical unit, visit your wounded crewmates, and accept "The Missing Patient" quest from Airi, the physician on duty.

In the living quarters (the southern wing), you'll find a pair of treasure chests, and more medical pods that you can use for quick healing. The terminals in the center have collections data for the Eldarian Zagzagel, Sol, and Rednuht spaceships.

Finally, in the research and analysis laboratory (the southwest wing), Lila offers you the "Leg Collector" quest. Complete both this quest and the "Egg Collector" quest that follows, and you'll earn Recipe Memo 20 (Earth Armlet) as a reward. Don't get too excited, though — you won't be able to make the armlet until you get a character with the Crafting skill much later in the game.

EXPLORATION BASE QUESTS

THE MISSING PATIENT

REWARD: 10 EXP, 24 Party SP

Visit Airi in the sickbay, and she'll ask you to track down Rich, a patient who has gone AWOL. You'll find Rich in the exterior of the base, towards the hangar with the Calnus. Tell him about Airi, and he'll go straight back.

LEG COLLECTOR

REWARD: 20 EXP, 18 Party SP, Blueberries x 1

Lilia, the Chief of Analysis in the research lab, wants 10 Insect Legs. If you don't have enough on hand, purchase the "Entomology" skill for Faize and level it up as much as you can afford to. That helps increase your chances of winning Insect Legs by beating either type of Adephaga.

EGG COLLECTOR

REWARD: 30 EXP, 20 SP, Aquaberries x 1, Recipe Memo 20

When you bring Lilia her Insect Legs, she'll send you out again, this time in search of 8 Insect Eggs. If you don't already have them, continue battling Adephaga as well as searching harvesting points, where they turn up on occasion.

A BATTLEFIELD PROMOTION

Return to the communications room to speak to Supreme Commander Gaghan, then Captain Grafton. Grafton next leads your party to the newly refurbished Calnus. Congratulations, she's all yours!

Once your crew takes their positions, speak to Faize, who gives you a Monster Jewel. If you have collected the full 100% data on any monster in your collections data, you can use the Monster Jewel to make an accessory out of that monster. To do so, check the monsters section of your collections data, select a completed entry, and choose "Transfer to Monster Jewel." You'll get a preview of that Monster Jewel's special ability (but not its stat boosts), so check out all your options before you commit your one and only Monster Jewel (you'll get more in the future). Of all the monsters on Aeos, the +5 ATK boost and +100 Maximum HP boost of the Adephaga Drus is probably the best bet.

After speaking to Faize, approach the console at the center of the Flight Deck to choose your destination. But don't leave Aeos if you have unfinished business here, because once you are enmeshed in your next mission, it may be a while before you'll be able to return.

REIMI'S MYSTERIOUS FLOWERS

If you return to the Urd Falls Cave before you blast off, you can trigger the game's first Private Action. As old-school *Star Ocean* fans know, Private Actions are special events that allow you to permanently change the relationship between your hero and one of his allies. Say the right thing, and their affinity improves. Say the wrong thing, and it could take a dive. You'll need a certain amount of affinity with each character if you want to see their ending at the end of the game and earn the corresponding Achievement.

To trigger this event, head to the eastern cavern where the only harvesting point is located in the Urd Falls Cave. Examine the flower patch against the northern ledge (directly east of the exclamation point on your map) to begin a conversation that ends with one of three choices for Edge. Say "You're really beautiful, Reimi," and Reimi becomes understandably delighted. The other two options lower your affinity (with "They really are beautiful flowers" being particularly damaging).

CRAFTING WITH AN ELDARIAN TOUCH

Once you're back on the Calnus, you can finally make items again. After introducing Faize to Welch (a special Welch event that is triggered only during the flight to your next destination), add him to a group with Edge and Reimi to inspire all sorts of new Smithing recipes, including the Shell Armor and Hunting Bow. Remove Reimi from the group, and Edge should come up with the Iron Saber, a nice weapon upgrade for Faize. If you have Iron to spare, you can probably whip up the Shell Armor (Iron x 4, Warped Carapace x 2) right now. Don't forget to make the Storm Blade, now that you have that Repair Kit. (You *did* remember to buy one at the base, right?)

If Reimi's Cooking skill has reached level 3 or higher, she should come up with the recipe for Pasta Peperoncino and Caesar Salad. The pasta can be made entirely out of items that are for sale on the base (Uncooked Pasta, Seasonings, and Olive Oil) so pick up a few of each if you can afford to. A 30% DEF boost for 10 battles (as well as a one-shot restoration of 5% of your MP) makes Pasta Peperoncino the best meal yet.

Faize's Item Creation skill is Alchemy, which isn't worth much at this stage of the game. You'll have to boost it to level 3 before he comes up with his first recipe (for a Fortitude Potion), and it'll be a while before you find any of its ingredients.

PLANET lemuris:
TRIOM VILLAGE

Ghimdo's House

🎁 map treasures

1. Demon Amulet x 1
2. Blueberries x 2
3. [Ice Barrier] Recipe Memo 02 x 1,
[PS3-only] Earth Gem x 1

⚕ pickpocketing

a. Iron-Willed Man	Anti-Stun Amulet x 1
b. Minuit, Devout Man's Cat	Tasty Mushroom x 1
c. Devout Man	Vile Goop x 1
d. Obstinate Woman	Empty Bottle x 1
e. Spoiled Boy	Blueberries x 1
f. Shady Sorcerer	Alchemist's Water x 1
g. Faithful Elder	Sacrificial Doll x 1
h. Faithful Youth	Sacrificial Doll x 1
i. Lonely Young Girl	10 Fol
j. Chilly Old Crone	Hot Chocolate x 1
k. Big-Hearted Man	1 Fol

Residence

l. Ever-Smiling Old Woman	53 Fol
m. Clever Cat	Lizardskin x 1

Ghimdo's House

n. Ghimdo	780 Fol

To Thalia Plains

To Thalia Plains

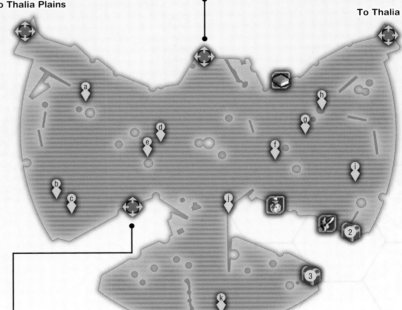

Legend

 = SAVE SPHERE

 = SHOP

 = PASSAGE

 = NPC

Residence

To Thalia Plains

Planet Lemuris

GETTING TO KNOW YOUR CREW

Once Faize has performed the calculations, go to the main console (Captain Grafton's old duty station) and set a course for the unexplored planet. Even at warp speed, it takes a while to get there, and the game has no less than five Private Actions cued up to help you pass the time. You can check your console after triggering each event to see how close you are to your destination.

To trigger the first event, speak to Reimi at her duty station. To trigger the second, visit your crew in the Recreation Room, where you'll find them chatting about Crowe. For the third, visit Reimi in her second-floor quarters, which are directly across the hall from your own. You don't have any choices to make in these first three events; just press ✕ or Ⓐ and let the bonding happen.

To trigger the fourth event, again visit your crew in the Recreation Room, where Reimi and Edge ask Faize to tell the sad story of the first contact between Earth and Eldaria. You have a choice of two responses: Faize likes you most if you man up and say "...I'm sorry that happened, Faize."

To trigger the next Private Action, leave the Recreation Room for a moment, and then return. You'll find Reimi and Faize hanging out again, discussing Eldarian swordsmanship. If you tell the story that begins with "Well, there was a bit of trauma I went through...", you'll win a few points with both now and pave the way for a follow-up Private Action that occurs after you land on Lemuris.

PRIVATE ACTIONS

THE SCOURGE OF BACCULUS

After the final Private Action, the Calnus drops out of warp to land on the unexplored planet. Speak to both members of your crew, then step outside and take your first breath of brisk Lemuris air. From the ship, head east through a tiny section of the Thalia Plains to reach the southern entrance to Triom Village, where a man named Ghimdo is waiting to meet you.

Ghimdo asks you to accompany his granddaughter, Lymle, as she heads northwest through the Thalia Plains to reach the oracle of the Alanaire Citadel. Before you take the first step of that journey, return to Ghimdo's house and grab a Demon Amulet from the treasure chest. The amulet offers its wearer a 20% chance of avoiding damage from demonic attacks, but since demons are so rare in these parts, the bigger perk is the +10 INT boost. Lymle is heavily focused on INT-based symbology attacks, so you should probably let her wear it.

There are two other chests in the village, although one is sealed under a thick sheet of ice. If those aren't enough freebies for you, talk to the Big-Hearted Man at the entrance to town, who gives you a couple sprigs of Basil, which can cure the paralysis condition. If you leave town and then return to speak to him again, he'll offer you a pair of Bigberries as well. If you really want to get greedy, you can even search the fields on either side of the village for Basil, Blueberries, and Blackberries.

You can rest for free and save your game at the residence in the southwest part of town.

The best buy at the weapon shop is a simple Bowstring, which allows Edge to complete the recipe that upgrades Reimi's current Eldarian Bow into a Hunting Bow. Edge's current Storm Blade is much stronger than the new Blessed 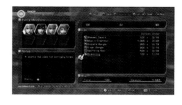 Sword, so unless you weren't able to make a Storm Blade, you can skip that one for now. You do need a Blessed Sword for a future recipe, so pick one up when you have Fol to burn.

 Finally, the general store offers plenty of ingredients for Reimi's recipes, as well as Fire Paint and Attack Cards that Lymle can use to whip up a few symbol cards (see Welch's Crafting Corner sidebar).

BARGAIN-HUNTING IN TRIOM

You wouldn't expect a rural town like Triom to offer a huge selection of high-level goods, but there are a few nice bargains in the local shops. At the skill shop, you'll find two new tomes that can be used to teach the Parapsychology and Elusion skills to Lymle. Neither skill is particularly essential at this point; Parapsychology increases the drop rate of undead foes (which are rare on Lemuris), and Elusion merely lets you escape from battle more easily. But if you haven't taught Reimi Botany yet, make sure to pick up that skill manual as soon as you can. You'll encounter plenty of plant-type enemies here, and they drop many of the ingredients that you'll need for Item Creation.

TIGER DOJO - STOCK

Item	Type	Price
Skill Manual "Botany"	Usable Items	900
Skill Manual "Parapsychology"	Usable Items	1000
Skill Manual "First Aid"	Usable Items	2000
Skill Manual "Elusion"	Usable Items	1000

REFLECTED MOON WEAPONS - STOCK

Item	Type	Price
Blessed Sword	Weapon	700
Mystic Chainmail	Armor	1000
Sniper's Bangle	Wrist Accessory	800
Silver Bangle	Wrist Accessory	800
Sacrificial Doll	Neck Accessory	500
Bowstring	Other Items	100

REFLECTED MOON WEAPONS - ORDERS

Flame Sword x 1

Reward	Rarity	From
600	☆☆☆	Taciturn Old Man

Hunting Bow x 1

Reward	Rarity	From
700	☆☆☆	Taciturn Old Man

Oyakodon x 2

Reward	Rarity	From
900	☆☆	Taciturn Old Man

CAN-CAN GENERAL GOODS - STOCK

Item	Type	Price	Item	Type	Price
Blueberries	Usable Items	40	Earth Paint	Other Items	80
Blackberries	Usable Items	60	Fire Paint	Other Items	80
Aquaberries	Usable Items	30	Attack Card	Other Items	60
Basil	Usable Items	30	Support Card	Other Items	40
Fresh Sage	Usable Items	150	Alchemist's Water	Other Items	300
Hot Chocolate	Usable Items	50	Vinegar	Other Items	40
Vile Goop	Usable Items	300	White Rice	Other Items	60
Ge Gen Tang	Other Items	400	Common Egg	Other Items	30
Empty Bottle	Other Items	40	Vegetables	Other Items	60
Natural Water	Other Items	120	Fresh Cream	Other Items	100
Magical Brush	Other Items	200	Pie Crusts	Other Items	60

CAN-CAN GENERAL GOODS - ORDERS

Custard Pie x 2

Reward	Rarity	From
700	☆☆☆	Lively Youth

Ginseng x 5

Reward	Rarity	From
400	☆☆☆	Lively Youth

Crystal x 1

Reward	Rarity	From
1,000	☆☆☆	Lively Youth

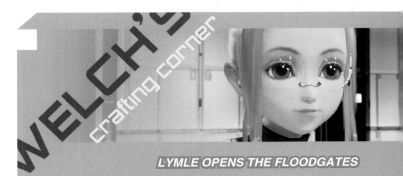

WELCH'S Crafting Corner

LYMLE OPENS THE FLOODGATES

With Lymle in the party, all sorts of new recipes are within your grasp. Putting her in a team with Edge and Faize (if their Smithery and Alchemy skills are at level 3 or higher) should inspire recipes for the Monster Jewel, Resistance Potion, and Flame Sword, the latter of which can be made with ingredients that are freely available on this planet. (The Blessed Sword can be purchased in Triom, and Fire Gems are dropped by upcoming Man-Eating Tree and Dragon Newt monsters.) Pair Lymle with Reimi, and you should be able to squeeze recipes for Lemon Juice (a healing item) and Oyakodon (an EXP booster) out of Reimi's level 3 Cooking skill.

If you bump up Lymle's Artistry skill to level 3, she'll begin cranking out recipes at a furious pace. Put her in invention groups with each party member, as well as by herself; every combination will inspire a unique recipe or two. All the recipes are for symbol cards, one-shot items that allow any character to cast a symbol. Most require only easily purchased paints and cards as ingredients, although the limited supply of paints at the Triom General Store unfortunately keeps you from making anything other than fire or earth-based cards at this point. This is not a problem, since fire symbol cards like Fire Bolt and Explosion you may want the most; roughly 80% of the monsters in Lemuris share a weakness to flame.

planet Lemuris:
THALIA PLAINS

 ## Map Treasures

1. Aquaberries x 3
2. Aquaberries x 1, Blackberries x 2
3. 255 Fol
4. Darkness Gem x 1
5. Blueberries x 2
6. Vile Goop x 2
7. Aquaberries x 2
8. Blackberries x 2
9. 401 Fol
10. Accuracy Seeds x 1
11. Monster Jewel x 1
12. Bizarre Fruit x 1
13. Skill Manual "Hide" x 1
14. [PS3 only] Fire Gem x 1

Harvesting Point Items

Bigberries
Common Egg
Gambleberries
Lemon
Nectar
Thornberries
Vegetables
White Rice

Mining Point Items

Crystal
Darkness Gem
Earth Gem
Fire Gem
Ice Gem
Mercury
Silver

Monsters

DRYAD

| HP · 341 | EXP · 5 |
| Fol · 49 | Race · Plant |

Resistant To · Earth
Weak Against · Fire

DROPS
Magic Seeds, Nectar, Wooden Stick, Blueberries

MIST GRAVE

| HP · 433 | EXP · 6 |
| Fol · 61 | Race · Plant |

Resistant To · Earth
Weak Against · Fire

DROPS
Tasty Mushroom, Basil, Tasty Mushroom?

LIZARD SOLDIER

| HP · 628 | EXP · 7 |
| Fol · 76 | Race · Animal |

Resistant To · --
Weak Against · Fire

DROPS
Lizardskin

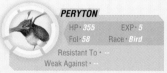

PERYTON

| HP · 355 | EXP · 5 |
| Fol · 58 | Race · Bird |

Resistant To · --
Weak Against · --

DROPS
Giant Bird Feather, Peryton Droppings, Common Egg

WISE LIZARDMAN

| HP · 628 | EXP · 9 |
| Fol · 68 | Race · Animal |

Resistant To · --
Weak Against · Fire

DROPS
Lizardskin, Attack Card, Support Card

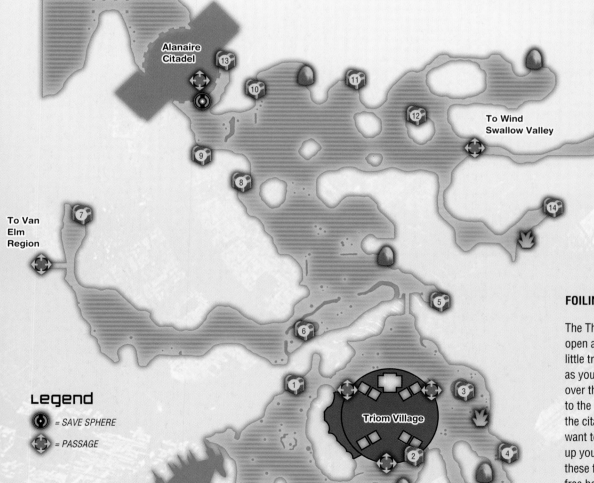

Alanaire Citadel

To Wind Swallow Valley

To Van Elm Region

Triom Village

Legend

◉ = SAVE SPHERE

✥ = PASSAGE

FOILING THE LOCAL FAUNA

The Thalia Plains is a vast and open area, so you should have little trouble dodging its monsters as you travel north to the bridge over the river, and then northwest to the citadel. But dodging foes in the citadel won't be easy, so you'll want to gather some EXP and build up your Bonus Board first. Battle these foes on your terms, with the free healing at Triom Village close at hand.

The deadliest of the bunch are the Mist Grave mushrooms, which spew out large clouds of pink spores that can paralyze anyone nearby. Paralysis leaves your characters unable to move or attack, and is *not* automatically healed at the end of the fight. Treat paralyzed characters with a dose of

Basil immediately, or better yet, head it off entirely. When you see a Mist Grave rub its head, you know the cloud is coming, so you have plenty of time to leap away or trigger a special art for a quick kill.

Some packs of Lizardmen include a Wise Lizardman symbologist guarded by a pack of Lizard Soldiers. The Wise Lizardman's symbols can be deadly, so you'll want to slip past the soldiers to strike this foe

directly. When the Wise Lizardman begins to cast a symbol, you can squash it by striking with a full combo, a launching attack, or most special arts.

A MEAGER HARVEST FOR ITEM HUNTERS

There are only two harvesting points in the entire Thalia Plains area, and the one to the northwest is so remote that it's quicker to skip it and instead travel repeatedly between your ship and the harvesting point east of Triom Village. Harvesters who are up for a little hike can cross the bridge over the river and head to the northwest corner of the map, where they'll find a bridge to the Van Elm Region of the planet. You won't be able to take more than a few steps before you find the path blocked by trees and boulders, but a small patch of grass contains a harvesting point where you'll find more exotic items than the ones available in Thalia Plains.

Most of the chests in the Thalia Plains merely contain basic supplies. (Of course, even the lowliest chest full of Aquaberries is worth visiting for the free EXP and Party SP you'll earn just for lifting the lid.) The best items all come at the end, including the Monster Jewel in chest 11, the Bizarre Fruit in chest 12, and the Hide skill manual in chest 13. The Bizarre Fruit is weak for a healing item, but after you eat it, you'll earn a seed that offers a permanent stat boost. Either Faize or Lymle can learn Hide, a battle skill that makes it harder for enemies to spot them in combat. (Like the Scan skill, you'll need to activate it manually in each battle.)

You can always use the Monster Jewel to whip up another Adephaga Drus Jewel, but the beasts of Lemuris offer plenty of interesting new options. The Dryad is the best choice of the enemies you've encountered so far, offering

stun resistance and a bit of in-battle HP regeneration. Later on, you'll encounter the Mana Yeti, who offers increased critical hit odds and resistance to the frozen condition, Horned Turtles who offer a whopping +40 GRD boost, and the Apprentice Scumbag, whose jewel boosts your post-battle Fol winnings by 15%.

MALE BONDING FOR FAIZE AND EDGE

Any time after you land on Lemuris, you can return to your ship to trigger a series of Private Actions between Edge and Faize. All of them take place in Faize's second-floor quarters, and the first two don't have any choices for you to make. Simply hear Faize out, and you'll rack up a few easy affinity points for both characters.

The third Private Action only occurs if you answered "Well, there was a bit of trauma I went through..." when Faize asked Edge why he used a sword during the flight to Lemuris. It begins with an apology from Faize, and then a choice of two responses for Edge. "Tell me something about yourself, then," helps receive the more interesting reply, but "There's nothing to apologize for" wins Edge more esteem from Faize (four affinity points instead of two).

PRIVATE ACTIONS

PLANET LEMURIS:
ALANAIRE CITADEL

 Map Treasures

1. Anti-Poison Amulet x 1
2. Shining Stone x 1
3. Skill Manual "Treasure Sense" x 1
4. [Ivy Barrier] Blue Talisman x 1
5. Shining Stone x 1
6. Guardian's Rapier x 1
7. Shining Stone x 1
8. Skill Manual "Focus" x 1
9. Shining Stone x 1
10. Guardian's Armor x 1
11. [Dark Barrier] Sacred Scepter x 1
12. Shining Stone x 1
13. [Light Barrier] Skill Manual "Trinity Blaze" x 1
14. [Ice Barrier] [PS3 only] Dragon Scale x 1, Fire Gem x 1

NOTE:

⬜ = Obelisk with Shining Stone

⬛ = Obelisk without Shining Stone

Legend

 = SAVE SPHERE

= PASSAGE

= RECOVERY SPHERE

= INTERACTION POINT

Monsters

THE GUARDIANS OF THE CITADEL

As soon as Edge reaches for the door of the Alanaire Citadel, he is enveloped by a white light that unlocks his latent powers of symbology. His first symbol is Healing, which comes in handy once you take a beating from the powerful monsters waiting inside.

The giant Stone Golems are the most intimidating, but their slow movement makes them highly susceptible to Blindsides. The weaker Kobolds actually pose a greater threat. They're fast and enjoy ganging up on a single target, so melee fighters who are trying to protect their Bonus Board need to continuously leap away from them to avoid being surrounded. If your character ends up facing a throng of Kobolds, or

you see one of them enter Rush Mode, press a bumper button to switch to a long-range character before your fighter succumbs to a Bonus Board-breaking beating.

THE WEST SIDE OF THE CITADEL

The Alanaire Citadel is full of blue obelisks, some of which have white stones set in them. When you examine an obelisk with a white stone, it rises up to create a bridge on the second floor of the citadel. An empty obelisk won't budge until you can activate it by finding a loose Shining Stone and setting it into the slot.

Activate the two obelisks on the ground floor of the west side of the map, and raid the treasure chests near them for an Anti-Poison Amulet and the first Shining Stone. If you're having trouble spotting the well-concealed chests, don't worry — finding loot is about to get a whole lot easier. Head up the stairway on the west side of the map, and activate the first of two obelisks to gain access to the treasure wing on the west side of the map. There you'll find the skill manual for Treasure Sense, a passive skill that makes all treasure chests, harvesting points, and mining points appear on your auto map. Teach it to Lymle (the only character who can learn it), and you'll never miss another treasure again!

Your newfound Treasure Sense leads you to a second Shining Stone, located in the room to the southwest. Rather than returning to the ground level to set the stones into the empty obelisks, continue up the stairs, activate a fourth pre-lit obelisk, and travel up to the second floor. If you've activated the four obelisks on the west side of the first floor, you should have no trouble traversing the network of catwalks to reach all of the treasures on the west side of the second floor. The loot includes a Guardian's Rapier for Faize, the Focus battle skill for Reimi, and another Shining Stone. Before you take the north staircase back down to the first floor, take the south staircase out to a dead-end chunk of the citadel's exterior, where you'll find the fourth Shining Stone. Heal up first, since you may face a double-enemy ambush as soon as you step outside.

THE EAST SIDE OF THE CITADEL

Set two of your Shining Stones into the obelisks on the east side of the ground floor, then set a third into the obelisk blocking the eastern staircase. Duck into the east treasure wing to grab a suit of Guardian's Armor for Faize or Edge, and activate the final first-floor obelisk (no stone required), which is blocking the stairway to the second floor.

On the second floor, you'll find a recovery sphere and, amidst the catwalks in the center of the citadel, a fifth Shining Stone. Head southwest from the final Shining Stone chest to a row of three obelisks, two of which require your remaining Shining Stones. The final upside-down obelisk is an elevator that takes you to the third floor, where you find a save sphere and the citadel's boss. You may want to backtrack to the recovery sphere before you ride it.

Dragon Newt

HP · 9563	EXP · 19
Fol · 176	Race · Demon
Resistant To · --	
Weak Against · --	

DROPS
Lizardskin, Fire Gem, Attack Card, Support Card

Avenge the Oracle

The Dragon Newt is a powerful foe with a quick-charging Rush Gauge that can keep him in Rush Mode for half of the fight. Even when he isn't in Rush Mode, nothing less than a Rush Combo, or a normal combo while you're in Rush Mode, can interrupt this creature while he's casting a symbol. The Dragon Newt is the first foe in the game who can counter Blindsides, and any attempt to use them in this battle will likely result in the destruction of your Bonus Board.

Rush Mode is important here, so it's preferable to use a character who is set to the Rush Mode-focused BEAT:B (the default setting for everyone except Edge), and who has earned enough ranks in it to collect a few good BEAT Bonuses. Reimi is likely to have the highest rank, which makes her the ideal choice. Set the tactics for Faize and Lymle to "Stay out of trouble!" so they'll spread out and focus on casting symbols, instead of rushing the Dragon Newt and allowing him to damage the whole party with his Sphere of Might special art. If Lymle has the Hide skill, have her use it for a bit of extra protection — she is your best healer, after all. (If Lymle hasn't learned the Healing symbol yet, you should return to the recovery sphere and battle enemies until she does.)

As Reimi, start the battle by triggering the Focus skill, then pluck away at the Dragon Newt with arrows when it's moving and special arts when it's not. (As always, you should switch to a jump-and-shoot evasion strategy if he sets his sights on Reimi.) When Reimi's Rush Gauge is full and the Dragon Newt is stationary, trigger a Rush Combo by holding down ⬜ or ✕, and then triggering a special art. Follow the on-screen button prompts to join the combo with other characters and dish out some seriously heavy damage.

PLANET LEMURIS:
WOODLEY VILLAGE

Map Treasures

1. Blackberries x 2
2. Curing Sheet x 1
3. Fresh Sage x 2
4. Anti-Stun Amulet x 1

Legend

 = SAVE SPHERE

 = SHOP

 = PASSAGE

 = NPC

Lutea's House

Thousand Gods General Store

Woodley Weapon Shop VIII

To Van Elm Region

To Van Elm Region

First Snow Inn

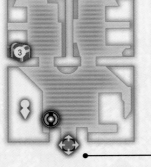

Pickpocketing

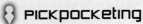

a. Village Weather Forecaster	Gambleberries x 1
b. Elmirre, Oracle Aspirant	Magic Bracelet x 1
c. Ultimate Master's Grandchild	Frozen Cider x 1
d. Nerve-Wracked Mother	Vinegar x 1
e. Hyperactive Kid	Attack Card x 1
f. Outdoor-Loving Cat	Basil x 1
g. Storehouse Worker	Ripe Berries x 1
h. Shy Boy	Hot Chocolate x 1
i. Accommodating Woman	642 Fol
j. Lutea	Fire Gem x 1
k. Lutea's Mother	Bigberries x 1
l. Foolhardy Girl	Lacquer x 1
m. Sir Francis, Curious Cat	Anti-Poison Amulet x 1

CURING BACCULUS, PLAN B

After defeating the Dragon Newt, head north to a balcony exit, and examine the strips of cloth marked with an exclamation point. Slide down after Reimi, and you'll find yourself just east of Woodley Village. Raid the chest near the citadel wall for the Chain Combos skill manual, which allows a character to use the Battle Config menu (under "Skills") to set two-part special art/symbology combos to the L2 and R2 skill (LT and RT for Xbox 360), but with only one copy of the book, you should give it to either Edge or Reimi, whoever you prefer to use most .

When you arrive in Woodley, head to the northwest building to find Lutea. She'll give you a Symbol Stone and send you to find the source of the bacculus disease. The party decides to consult with Ghimdo in Triom Village, but you'll have to ask around to figure out how to get there. The Village Weather Forecaster, who hangs out near the town's west entrance, helpfully spells it out for you. First, head to the southernmost tip of the Van Elm Region and pick a Faerie Orchid on the shore of Lake Aegis. That action removes the illusionary barriers that block the forest to the east, which connects to the bridge back to the Thalia Plains.

The Accommodating Woman in the southeast part of town gives you one free cup of Hot Chocolate, a consumable item that cures the frozen condition.

STOCK UP AT THE WOODLEY SHOPS

The Woodley shops are well-stocked with long-awaited ingredients, spicy new skills, and powerful weapon upgrades. You'll need to complete the Little Lost Girl quest (see Woodley Village Quests) before the clerk at the general store will do business with you, but you can visit the skill and weapon shops right off the bat.

At Three Leaf Books, you can pick up more copies of Skill Manual "Chain Combos," although they won't come cheap. On the other hand, Skill Manual "Pickpocketing" costs a mere 200 Fol, so you might as well pick that up. The only other new skill you can learn here is the attention-grabbing Taunt.

At the weapon shop, you can pick up the fire-element Torch Bow for Reimi and Flame Wand for Lymle. While the Torch Bow is statistically much weaker than the Hunting Bow, it is potentially more powerful here on Lemuris, where many foes are weak to fire and none are resistant. (Besides, you'll need it for a future recipe.) Would-be thieves can also buy Bandit's Gloves for Edge (see Adventures in Pickpocketing, in this portion of the walkthrough), one of a handful of good wrist accessories available here. Finally, if you need more Iron for your recipes, this is the only place on Lemuris where you can buy it.

The new items at the general store include Rich Cheese, the last ingredient Reimi needs to make MP cost-lowering Caesar Salad, the Special Warishita Sauce needed to cook EXP-boosting Oyakodon, and the missing Sharkskin that's been keeping you from making the Iron Saber. You'll also discover a few new paints for Lymle's Artistry projects, and cheap Rivets, which you should buy 20 of for future recipes.

The Curing Sheet located in chest #2 is the first available ship furnishing. Set it on one of the M-sized glowing blue squares in the Recreation Room, and you'll be able to cure any malady simply by walking over it.

THREE LEAF BOOKS - STOCK

Item	Type	Price
Skill Manual "Botany"	Usable Items	900
Skill Manual "Parapsychology"	Usable Items	1000
Skill Manual "Chain Combos"	Usable Items	3000
Skill Manual "Pickpocketing"	Usable Items	200
Skill Manual "First Aid"	Usable Items	2000
Skill Manual "Elusion"	Usable Items	1000
Skill Manual "Taunt"	Usable Items	800

THOUSAND GODS GENERAL STORE - STOCK

Item	Type	Price	Item	Type	Price
Blueberries	Usable Items	40	Mysterious Paint	Other Items	60
Blackberries	Usable Items	60	Support Card	Other Items	40
Mixed Syrup	Usable Items	100	Rivet	Other Items	20
Aquaberries	Usable Items	30	Alchemist's Water	Other Items	300
Basil	Usable Items	30			
Fresh Sage	Usable Items	150	Vinegar	Other Items	40
Hot Chocolate	Usable Items	50	White Rice	Other Items	60
Vile Goop	Usable Items	300	Raw Animal Meat	Other Items	60
Rich Cheese	Food	180			
Ge Gen Tang	Other Items	400	Raw Fish	Other Items	80
Sharkskin	Other Items	80	Common Egg	Other Items	30
Empty Bottle	Other Items	40	Vegetables	Other Items	60
Natural Water	Other Items	120	Olive Oil	Other Items	80
Magical Brush	Other Items	200	Special Warishita Sauce	Other Items	120
Earth Paint	Other Items	80			
Water Paint	Other Items	80	Fresh Cream	Other Items	100
Fire Paint	Other Items	80	Pie Crusts	Other Items	60

thousands god
general store - orders

Shortcake x 2

Reward	Rarity	From
800	☆☆	Harried Mother

Caterpillar Fungus x 2

Reward	Rarity	From
400	☆☆☆	Harried Mother

Mercury x 3

Reward	Rarity	From
600	☆☆	Harried Mother

woodley
weapon shop VIII - stock

Item	Type	Price
Blessed Sword	Weapon	700
Torch Bow	Weapon	800
Flame Wand	Weapon	1500
Mystic Chainmail	Armor	1000
Bandit's Gloves	Wrist Accessory	3300
Sniper's Bangle	Wrist Accessory	800
Silver Bangle	Wrist Accessory	800
Sacrificial Doll	Neck Accessory	500
Iron	Other Items	400
Bowstring	Other Items	100

woodley
weapon shop VIII - orders

Fire Gem x 4

Reward	Rarity	From
2,400	☆☆	Wise Old Woman

Wolf Fang x 3

Reward	Rarity	From
300	☆	Wise Old Woman

Lacquer x 5

Reward	Rarity	From
200	☆	Wise Old Woman

Iron Saber x 1

Reward	Rarity	From
600	☆☆	Wise Old Woman

⁘ WOODLEY VILLAGE QUESTS

TROUBLE AT THE GENERAL STORE

Speak to the clerk at the general store to accept a simple quest to find her missing daughter. Once that's finished, the daughter sends you on a follow-up quest to retrieve her cat.

THE LITTLE LOST GIRL

REWARD: 50 EXP, 8 Party SP

Reward: The "Foolhardy Girl" didn't get far — she's waiting at the west entrance to town. She'll return willingly after speaking with you, and you can collect the reward from her mother at the general store.

THE CURIOUS KITTY

REWARD: 50 EXP, 32 Party SP

Once she's safely back in the general store, speak to the Foolhardy Girl again. She'll ask you to find her cat, Sir Francis, who ran off into the Silent Forest. He isn't hard to find, since he is marked by an NPC icon on your map, but he's deep enough into the forest that you'll need the Faerie Orchid to reach him.

ADVENTURES IN PICKPOCKETING

If you teach Edge the Pickpocketing skill and equip him with the Bandit's Gloves, he'll have everything he needs to start picking pockets. With the gloves on, approach anyone in town (even felines) and press ● or Ⓑ to take a swipe at their pocket. Each character has a level of Pickpocketing resistance between 1 and 10, and you'll need to have Edge's Pickpocketing skill be equal to or higher than that number to have a good chance of success. You can attempt to pickpocket as often as you want, but each target has only a single item to steal.

Before you go too far to the dark side, know that there is a penalty for this sort of behavior: when your allies catch you stealing, you lose affinity points in their eyes. Each time you steal, each ally has roughly a 20-30% chance of noticing, so if you steal 10 times, expect to lose 2 or 3 points of affinity from each of your party members.

No one says anything at the time, but inveterate thieves later find out what their friends really think when they beat the game and don't get to see any of the special affinity-based endings (or earn the corresponding Trophies or Achievements). If you care about such things, try to pickpocket sparingly.

The most tempting item in Woodley is Lutea's Fire Gem, but you'll need to have your Pickpocketing skill up to level 4 to swipe it consistently. Elmirre's Magic Bracelet isn't bad, and the kid certainly deserves to lose it. But Elmirre's Pickpocketing resistance is a few notches higher, at level 6.

planet lemuris:
VAN ELM REGION

Map Treasures

1. Skill Manual "Chain Combos" x 1
2. Blueberries x 3
3. Bigberries x 1, Blueberries x 2
4. Vile Goop x 2
5. Aquaberries x 3
6. 51 Fol
7. Health Seeds x 1

Woodley Village

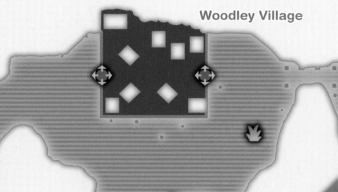

Alanaire Citadel

Legend

 = PASSAGE

 = INTERACTION POINT

To Thalia Plains

Harvesting Point Items

Bigberries	Lacquer
Bizarre Fruit	Lemon
Blackberries	Nectar
Caterpillar Fungus	Protection Seeds
Ebony	Ripe Berries
Gambleberries	Tasty Mushroom
Ginseng	Tasty Mushroom?
Fresh Sage	Wooden Stick

Mining Point Items

Crystal	Ice Gem
Darkness Gem	Mercury
Earth Gem	Silver
Fire Gem	

Monsters

APPRENTICE SCUMBAG
HP · 651　EXP · 13
Fol · 106　Race · Humanoid
Resistant To · —
Weak Against · —
DROPS
Support Card, Hot Chocolate, Special Warishita Sauce, Peryton Droppings, Tasty Mushroom?

GIANT FUNGUS
HP · 756　EXP · 8
Fol · 63　Race · Plant
Resistant To · Ice
Weak Against · Fire
DROPS
Tasty Mushroom, Basil, Tasty Mushroom?, Nectar

HORNED TURTLE
HP · 1124　EXP · 12
Fol · 96　Race · Animal
Resistant To · Ice
Weak Against · Fire
DROPS
Mercury, Raw Fish, Rotten Fish

KOBOLD
HP · 576　EXP · 5
Fol · 114　Race · Animal
Resistant To · Ice
Weak Against · —
DROPS
Attack Seeds, Raw Animal Meat, Hot Chocolate

MAN-EATING TREE
HP · 1082　EXP · 18
Fol · 83　Race · Plant
Resistant To · Earth
Weak Against · Fire
DROPS
Tasty Mushroom, Wooden Stick, Aquaberries, Blackberries, Fire Gem

MANA YETI
HP · 1291　EXP · 17
Fol · 86　Race · Animal
Resistant To · Ice
Weak Against · Fire
DROPS
Health Seeds, Ice Gem, Raw Animal Meat, Frozen Cider

MIST GRAVE
HP · 433　EXP · 6
Fol · 61　Race · Plant
Resistant To · Earth
Weak Against · Fire
DROPS
Health Seeds, Ice Gem, Raw Animal Meat, Frozen Cider

STONE GOLEM
HP · 1039　EXP · 13
Fol · 160　Race · Demon
Resistant To · Earth
Weak Against · Wind
DROPS
Iron, Crystal, Silver, Earth Gem

PICK AN ORCHID ON THE SOUTHERN SHORE

Head west from Woodley and follow the coast south to reach the tip of a peninsula where you'll find the one and only Faerie Orchid. You'll meet several new enemies on your journey, including powerful Mana Yetis that are best struck from a distance, and resilient Horned Turtles that won't go down easily unless you hit them with Blindsides, Rush Mode attacks, and special arts. Both of these new foes are weak to fire, so your new fire-type weapons and Lymle's fire-type symbols quickly prove their worth.

You'll encounter powerful Man-Eating Trees in the woods, and while they are slow, their large size makes them hard to avoid. In combat, it's easy to disrupt their symbols, but their melee attacks can tear a fighter to shreds and shatter the Bonus Board. They're particularly dangerous when two are close enough to double-team a single character, or when they're able to enter Rush Mode. If you are using a melee fighter at close range and they land a hit, immediately switch over to a long-range character. Not only does this protect your Bonus Board, but it allows you to cue up a good ranged symbol or special art to save your entangled fighter. As dangerous as Man-Eating Trees are, they're worth fighting to earn Fire Gems. If you have skill points to spare, you may want to boost Reimi's Botany to increase your odds of getting one.

Those hunting for a good Monster Jewel target should take special notice of the Apprentice Scumbags, spry little thieves who attempt to swipe a bit of Fol and dash away. If you can kill enough scumbags to fill up their monster data entry (around 34), you'll be able to make a Monster Jewel that earns you a 15% Fol bonus at the end of every battle.

The numerous harvest points here provide a great opportunity to pick up supplies, including rare Bizarre Fruits.

TRAVERSE THE SILENT FOREST

After grabbing the orchid, head north along the east wall until you find the entrance to the Silent Forest, which extends east to connect the Van Elm Region to the Thalia Plains. If you don't have the orchid in your possession, you'll find what appears to be an impassible blockade of boulders and trees at both the east and west ends of the forest, but possessing the orchid clears those illusions and allows you to cross.

If you're in the midst of The Curious Kitty quest, you'll find the missing cat in the heart of the forest. Talk to the cat to scoop him up, and then take him back to Woodley for your reward.

RETURN TO TRIOM VILLAGE

When you return to Triom Village, pay Ghimdo a visit. He'll point you towards the Wind Swallow Valley, which is east past the frozen lake in Thalia Plains, and give you the Fire Ring you need to cross it. Head outside, and look for the Shady Sorceress who hangs out to the southeast of his house. She'll charge up your Fire Ring for free this time, but she'll expect a payment of 800 Fol for the next recharge.

Turn your Fire Ring on the frozen chest in the southeast part of town, and you'll uncover Recipe Memo 02. Players of the PS3 version will also find a free Earth Gem in the box. Recipe Memo 02 allows you to upgrade Reimi's Torch Bow with two Earth Gems and two chunks of Iron. (Stone Golems occasionally drop Earth Gems, but you don't yet have the skill that increases the odds of getting one.) Even if you can't make the bow, now is a good time to return to the ship to reset all the harvesting points and possibly whip up Edge's Flame Sword.

If you're playing the PS3 version, there's one more frozen chest you can thaw. Return to the ground floor of the Alanaire Citadel and melt the barrier around the box on the east side of the round central room. It contains a Dragon Scale and a Fire Gem, two useful ingredients for item creation.

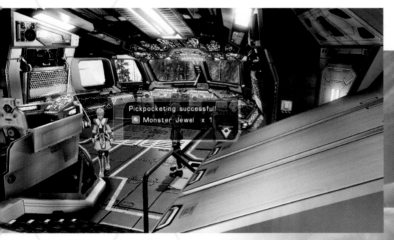

Once you return to the ship, you can turn your Pickpocketing skill against your own companions. Reimi and Lymle have junk (Blueberries and a Lemon, respectively), but Faize has been holding out on you — he has another Monster Jewel!

GETTING A JUMP ON LEVEL 4 RECIPES

Now that you can reach Woodley, there are a few new recipes that you can begin assembling ingredients for. Level your item-creation skills up to level 4, and pair everyone with Lymle to invent a few interesting new ideas. Reimi and Lymle should come up with the ideas for Hamburg Steak, Salt-Grilled Saury, and Custard Pie, all of which primarily require ingredients sold in Woodley or found at local harvesting points. Lymle and Faize can come up with the Strength Potion and a few new symbol cards that put Earth and Water Paint to good use, while Edge and Lymle should discover the recipe for Aqua Mail. Either Edge or Faize can equip the Aqua Mail, and its high level of water resistance eventually proves to be great for the challenges ahead. You can buy the required Iron and Rivets in Woodley, but the only way to get Ice Gems is to fight a whole lot of Mana Yetis and hope you get lucky.

Map treasures

1. [Ice Barrier] Blizzard Protector x 1
2. Blackberries x 2
3. [PS3-only] Aqua Robe x 1

Mining point items

Crystal
Darkness Gem
Earth Gem
Fire Gem

Ice Gem
Mercury
Silver

Monsters

DRAGON NEWT
HP · 1700	EXP · 19
Fol · 176	Race · Demon

Resistant To · --
Weak Against · --

DROPS
Lizardskin, Fire Gem, Attack Card, Support Card

HARPYIA
HP · 1220	EXP · 19
Fol · 85	Race · Bird

Resistant To · Wind
Weak Against · None

DROPS
Giant Bird Feather, Static Cider, Blackberries

LIZARD COMMANDER
HP · 1351	EXP · 15
Fol · 99	Race · Animal

Resistant To · --
Weak Against · Fire

DROPS
Lizardskin, Aquaberries

LIZARD SOLDIER
HP · 628	EXP · 7
Fol · 76	Race · Animal

Resistant To · --
Weak Against · Fire

DROPS
Lizardskin

SABER-TOOTHED TIGER
HP · 919	EXP · 6
Fol · 102	Race · Animal

Resistant To · Ice
Weak Against · Fire, Water

DROPS
Saber-Toothed Tiger Fang, Wolf Fang, Wolf Oil, Raw Animal Meat

WISE LIZARDMAN
HP · 628	EXP · 9
Fol · 68	Race · Animal

Resistant To · --
Weak Against · Fire

DROPS
Lizardskin, Attack Card, Support Card

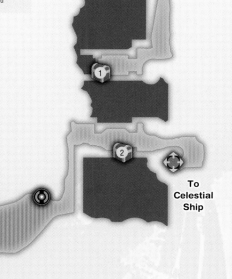

To Celestial Ship

To Celestial Ship

To Thalia Plains

Legend

⊙ = SAVE SPHERE

✥ = PASSAGE

⋮ TROPHY/ACHIEVEMENT HUNTING

Completists who are determined to earn all of the game's Trophies or Achievements must fulfill all of Triom's shop orders before battling the boss of this section of the game, as you are never given another opportunity to do so. Shop orders do contribute to the "Errand Boy," "Potential Postman," and "Dutiful Deliverer" Trophies and Achievements.

Map Treasures

1. Blueberries x 4, Bigberries x 1
2. [Ice Barrier] Skill Manual "HP Boost" x 1
3. Fainting Potion x 2
4. Cardianon Sword x 1
5. [Ivy Barrier] Immortal Smasher x 1
6. Bigberries x 2
7. Skill Manual "Critical Hit" x 1
8. [Ivy Barrier] Recipe Memo 25 x 1, Anti-Freezing Amulet x 1
9. Blackberries x 4
10. [Ice Barrier] Power Bracelet x 1
11. Fresh Sage x 2

Legend

 = SAVE SPHERE

= PASSAGE

 = RECOVERY SPHERE

 = INTERACTION POINT

NOTE

 = Plastic Explosives

| = Sealed Doors

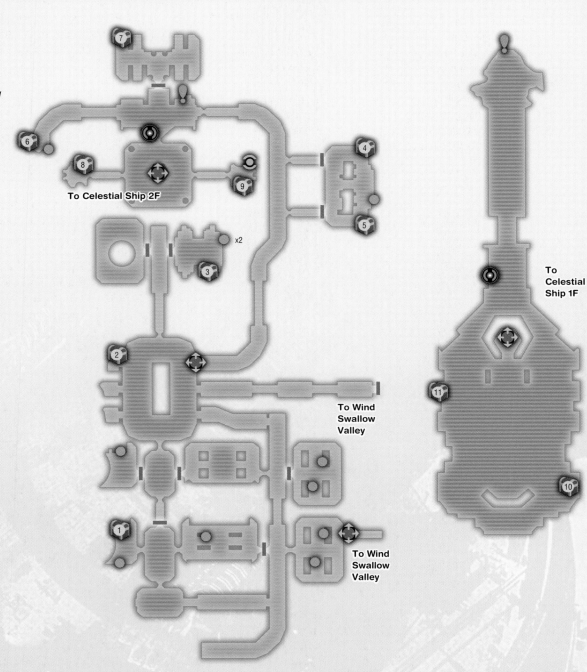

To Celestial Ship 2F

To Celestial Ship 1F

x2

To Wind Swallow Valley

To Wind Swallow Valley

CROSS WIND SWALLOW VALLEY

Head east across the frozen lake near Alanaire Citadel to reach the entrance to the tiny Wind Swallow Valley area. You'll find your path blocked by two massive ice boulders, but with your charged Fire Ring, you now have the power to liquify them by tapping ⊙ or Ⓑ. A third ice boulder conceals a mining spot and a chest that contains an Aqua Robe, which will provide a significant defensive boost for Lymle.

As you approach the Celestial Ship, you'll encounter two new enemies. Saber-Toothed Tigers aren't particularly difficult, but if you don't strike aggressively, they can

drag out the fight by howling for an endless stream of reinforcements. Harpyias are annoying because they can hover above the battlefield while they cast symbols. Their symbols can potentially break your Bonus Board, especially if they are in Rush Mode, so make sure that each Harpyia is being covered by a member of your party. Harpyia symbols are easy to disrupt; have Edge use a directional combo to uppercut them into the stratosphere.

BLAST A PATH THROUGH THE CELESTIAL SHIP

Inside the ship, you'll notice sparkling objects on some of the consoles. These are Plastic Explosives, which you can collect and set on the various sealed doors on the ship. You don't need to destroy every door to progress, but you should destroy as many as you can, as each is worth 40 EXP and 5 Party SP. There are exactly enough Plastic Explosives to destroy them all, but if you missed any Plastic Explosives during your search, you can

always leave the ship and re-enter to make the expended ones reappear.

After setting the explosives on a sealed door, you'll need to press ● or ⑧ to light it up with your Fire Ring. Step back quickly, or everyone will get hit for a sizable chunk of HP in the blast. However, if a door has electricity arcing through it, you won't need to use your Fire Ring to trigger the detonator. Just set the explosives on the door and get out of the way!

CLAIM THE TREASURES OF THE LOST CREW

Whoever they were, the crew of this ship had some really great stuff. Blast your way west from the entrance, collecting the first four Plastic Explosives and some healing supplies at chest #3. Then, head north to the ship's donut-shaped central hub, where you'll find a chest containing the HP Boost skill. Any member of your party can learn this self-explanatory skill, and this can be a difficult choice to make. Edge probably takes the brunt of the damage for the party, but symbol-users

like Lymle are more likely to have a Battle-Skills slot to spare. HP Boost is extremely expensive to level up, but the skill points you invest in it will pay off in the long run.

There are three passages on the east side of the hub. The upper passage leads to the command decks of the ship, and the lower passage leads to a room with two more sets of Plastic Explosives. Your auto-map makes it seem as though the central passage ends in a dead end, but at the eastern tip you'll find a door that can be blown open, which leads to the previously inaccessible chest #2 of Wind Swallow Valley. It contains the Blizzard Protector, an excellent piece of armor for Reimi.

There are two interesting treasures in the command decks of the ship. The Cardianon Sword in chest #6 isn't as good as Edge's Flame Sword, but if you haven't been able to make that yet, it's Edge's best option for the boss ahead. If you blast open the northernmost door, you'll find the Skill Manual "Critical Hit". This battle skill can be learned by either Edge or Reimi, and you should consider which character will benefit from it the

most. As a frontline fighter, Edge has a lot of battle skills to choose from, so he won't always have the open battle-skill slot necessary to equip Critical Hit. Reimi is much more likely to have a slot to spare.

THE LAST MOMENTS OF THE CELESTIAL SHIP

To find out what exactly is going on here; examine the console marked with a pink exclamation point on the ship's main deck. You'll discover a Cardianon Data Disc that gives you a glimpse of the crew's untimely demise, as well as the entry code to the door to the south.

When you open the door, your party ends up in a three-part ambush of Dragon Newt and Lizardman foes. Save your game first, and if you have any of Reimi's stat-boosting concoctions on hand, now would be a fine time to treat your party to a meal. Since

Check the terminal in the room with the recovery sphere to get the spaceship data for the Cardianon landing ship.

the effects last for at least three battles, they'll give you a boost for the ambush battle ahead, as well as the boss battle that follows. Don't hold anything back during the ambush, because there's a recovery sphere on the other side of the door. You'll definitely want to use it to heal up before you take the elevator to the upper deck of the ship, where — if you haven't already guessed — something far nastier awaits.

BOSS

Barachiel

HP · ???	EXP · 833
Fol · 2403	Race · Other
Resistant To · Earth, Ice	
Weak Against · Fire	

DROPS
Monster Jewel

A Beatdown for Barachiel

At the beginning of the Barachius battle, take control of Faize and press △ or Ⓨ to open the battle menu. Select Symbology, and use ▢ or ⊗ to set Faize's Ice Needles symbol to off. Barachiel is so resistant to water that Ice Needles actually heals him.

Fighting Barachiel at melee range is a losing proposition. Since Barachiel typically hovers above the battlefield, you'll be risking heavy damage for a chance at a single jumping strike that will barely nick his hide. So ignore Barachiel as long as he's airborne and have Edge focus on helping Lymle tend to the wounded. Try to stay directly behind Barachiel as much as possible, and when he drops to the surface to use one of his special attacks, hit him in the back with a Stampede Slash to Rising Blade combo.

The Stampede Slash alone should deal several hundred points of damage, and while Barachiel won't always stick around for the Rising Blade part, the move deals a ton of damage when you're lucky enough to land it. Since Barachiel is weak to fire, Edge's Flame Sword proves to be a godsend here.

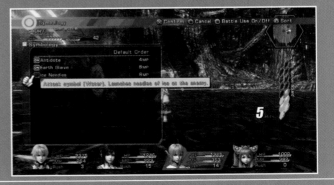

Your AI-controlled allies simply cannot be trusted to know when or where to target Barachiel, so all they'll ever really do is get in the way by wasting Barachiel's windows of vulnerability with underpowered attacks. Once the battle begins and your party is sufficiently spread out, you may find it easier to simply set Reimi and Faize to "Don't do anything" so they can't interfere. (Lymle's contributions will remain invaluable, although you should turn off her non-healing symbols.) Since Edge will be doing nearly all of the damage, you can really speed things along by giving him a Strength Potion (which Faize can make) or feeding him some ATK-boosting Hamburg Steak before the fight.

A SOLEMN FAREWELL TO LEMURIS

After defeating Barachiel, you'll have to hoof it back to Triom Village. But with all the Lizardmen and Dragon Newts out of the way, you won't have to deal with much opposition. The scene that awaits you in Triom is not a pretty one, but it points the way to your next objective. With all the shops closed, there isn't much to do in Triom, but you can visit the Shady Sorceress to get your Fire Ring recharged before you go. Then return to the Calnus, where you can now set a course for Cardianon!

AN OVERLY INTRUSIVE CHAT WITH COMMANDER GRAFTON

You don't need to return to Aeos to report your findings, but if you do go back, you can trigger a Private Action by speaking to Commander Grafton. He'll show more interest in your relationship with Reimi than your continuing mission, and presume that the pair of you are officially a couple. Edge and Reimi grow closer if you play along by saying "You knew, sir?" It only hardens Edge's heart if you deny it.

As long as you're back on Aeos, pick up any skill manuals and ingredients that you couldn't afford the first time, and rack up some easy Bonus Board tiles by taking down the local monsters. Completists should deliver as many Orders as they can, as the Exploration Base shops do not remain open for much longer.

cardianon mothership: DOCK

Map Treasures

Cardianon Mothership Dock
1. Defense Seeds x 1
2. Bigberries x 2

Cardianon Mothership 1F
3. Basil x 5
4. Defense Breaker x 2
5. Thunder Ring x 1
6. Fortitude Potion x 2
7. Blackberries x 3
8. Skill Manual "Taunt" x 1
9. Wisdom Bracelet x 1

Cardianon Mothership B1
10. Monster Jewel x 1
11. 1020 Fol
12. Skill Manual "Auto Healing" x 1
13. Skill Manual "Chain Combos" x 1
14. [Ice Barrier] Crystal x 1
15. Thunder Armlet x 1
16. Compact Freezing Bomb x 1

Cardianon Mothership B2
17. [Ice Barrier] Silver x 1
18. Universal Device x 1, Gunpowder x 1
19. Laser Oscillator x 1
20. Li'l Vending Machine No. 1 x 1

Monsters

 CARDIANON SOLDIER

HP · 1706	EXP · 19
Fol · 153	Race · Humanoid

Resistant To · --
Weak Against · --

DROPS
Strength Potion, Self-Destructor 3000, Gunpowder, Compact Silence Bomb

 DRAGON NEWT

HP · 1700	EXP · 19
Fol · 176	Race · Demon

Resistant To · --
Weak Against · --

DROPS
Lizardskin, Fire Gem, Attack Card, Support Card

 GUARD BOT "COMMANDO"

HP · 969	EXP · 19
Fol · 102	Race · Mech

Resistant To · Wind
Weak Against · Water, Thunder

DROPS
Compact Freezing Bomb, Universal Device, EM Bomb, Micro Circuit, Silver

 LIZARD SHAMAN

HP · 1382	EXP · 30
Fol · 148	Race · Animal

Resistant To · --
Weak Against · --

DROPS
Empty Bottle, Darkness Gem, Light Gem

 GUARD BOT "ASSAULTER"

HP · 1389	EXP · 23
Fol · 123	Race · Mech

Resistant To · Wind
Weak Against · Water, Thunder

DROPS
Compact Poison Bomb, Universal Device, EM Bomb, Micro Circuit, Quantum Processor

 LIZARD WARRIOR

HP · 1709	EXP · 39
Fol · 144	Race · Animal

Resistant To · Ice
Weak Against · None

DROPS
Iron, Frozen Cider

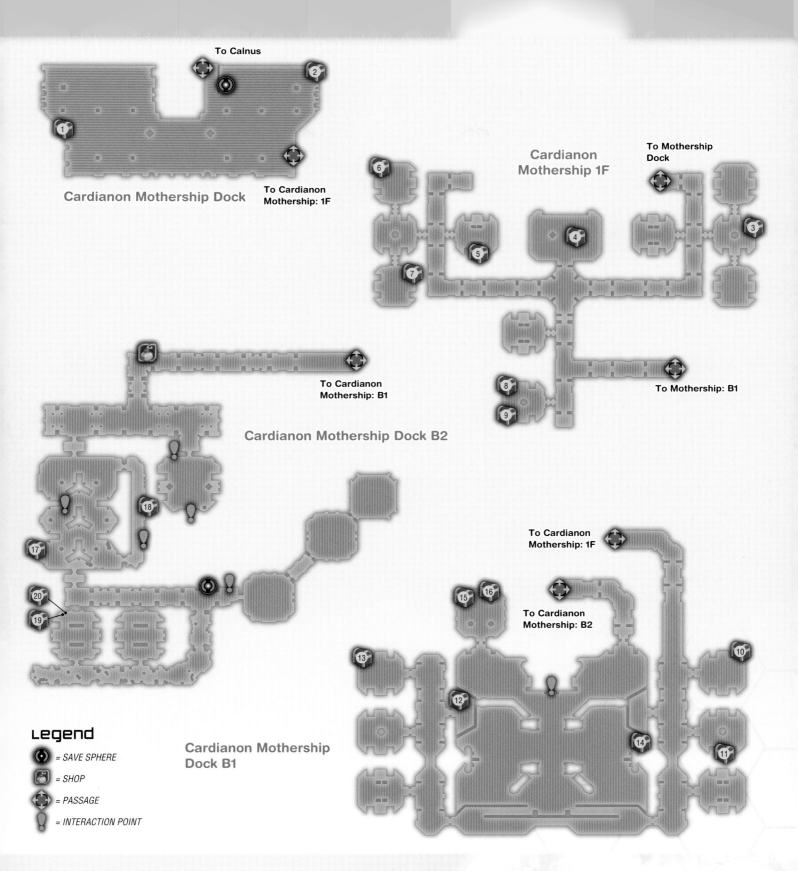

To Calnus

Cardianon Mothership Dock

To Cardianon Mothership: 1F

Cardianon Mothership 1F

To Mothership Dock

To Mothership: B1

To Cardianon Mothership: B1

Cardianon Mothership Dock B2

To Cardianon Mothership: 1F

To Cardianon Mothership: B2

Cardianon Mothership Dock B1

Legend

= SAVE SPHERE

= SHOP

= PASSAGE

= INTERACTION POINT

Cardianon Mothership

DOWNTIME ON THE FLIGHT TO CARDIANON

It's a long way to Cardianon, so you'll have plenty of time to bond with your crew. The Calnus won't reach its destination until you've triggered the six Private Actions listed below, in order. Before you land, make some time to visit Welch at the Item-Creation terminal. It doesn't count as a Private Action, but you can trigger an amusing new event scene. Begin the long trip with another report to the moonbase. Visit Reimi at her console to patch the non-interactive call through.

• The next Private Action also involves Reimi. Visit her in the Recreation Room, and you'll be prompted to guess what makes today special. Guess that it's her birthday, or Edge's stock will tumble in her eyes.

• After the Reimi events, visit the Meeting Room (where the Item Creation terminal is located) to trigger a special event with Lymle and Faize. Afterwards, Edge's opinion of Faize rises, and Lymle grows closer to both men.

• Exit to the Recreation Room, where it becomes abundantly clear to whom you need to speak with next.

• Reimi is your target once again. You can find her in the room with the battle simulator, reminiscing about the childhood she and Edge shared.

• Finally, join the entire party in the Recreation Room. Help yourself to a cookie — you're only moments away from Cardianon. Well, sort of.

PRIVATE ACTIONS

A WARM WELCOME FROM THE MOTHERSHIP CREW

As soon as you open the door on the Cardianon Mothership Dock, you'll be jumped by a pair of Cardianon Soldiers and their mechanized guard-bot companions. Since the healing facilities on your ship are so close, you can afford to go all out in this fight in an attempt to pick up a few Bonus Board tiles.

You'll see a lot of those guard bots in the decks ahead. They move extremely quickly on the field, so it isn't easy to run away from them. Either fight them one by one or round them up for a big multi-ambush battle. When battling a mixed group of bots, target the blue Assaulters first, since they are the more damaging of the two. The red Commando bots typically focus on stunning your characters to set them up for Assaulter attacks.

ZAP SECURITY LOCKS WITH THE THUNDER RING

Travel to the western wing of the mothership's first floor, where you'll find the Thunder Ring in chest #5. The Thunder Ring functions just like the Fire Ring you obtained on Lemuris, and can be used to overload a variety of Cardianon machines. You'll find your first target at the center of the map, where a security door automatically shuts when you approach it. Approach the control panel to the left, and give it a good zap to force open the door.

The Thunder Ring has only two charges, and the Shady Sorceress isn't around to fill it up for you. Fortunately, you don't need her; after the door lock explodes, you can refill your ring from the plasma that is left coursing through the conduit. You won't always have that opportunity, so fill up the ring while you can.

GATHER INTEL AT THE MOTHERSHIP'S COMMAND CENTER

The B1 floor of the mothership primarily consists of a large central room overlooked by two balconies. Before you head to that room's main terminal, pick out all the treasures from the rooms on the east and west wings, and on the west balcony. The best prize by far is Auto Healing, a continuous HP-recovery skill that can be learned by

any character in your party. It's good even for ranged fighters and symbol-users, since unlike First Aid, the character doesn't need to be under frequent attack to reap the rewards.

The terminal in the central room points your party towards its ultimate destination, and provides a code to unlock the door to the northeast. In the same room, you'll also find the collections data for the Cardianon Mothership, in the console at the opposite end of the room from chest 14. Grab the two treasures in the northwest room, then continue on to level B2.

AUTOMATED SHOPPING, CARDIANON STYLE

The Cardianon may be genocidal xenophobes, but even they know a good business opportunity when they see one. Your team can stock up on basic recovery supplies at the Compact Vendor Unit 003 on level B2, including Fresh Sage and party-healing Ripe Berries. You'll also find a variety of explosives for sale, but don't buy at these prices when you're

likely to find scores of explosives for free. Besides, there isn't any urgent need to stock up on new Gunpowder and Micro Circuit ingredients, as there will be several identical vending units to come.

compact vendor unit 003 - stock

Item	Type	Price
Blueberries	Usable Items	40
Blackberries	Usable Items	60
Ripe Berries	Usable Items	200
Basil	Usable Items	30
Fresh Sage	Usable Items	150
Compact Poison Bomb	Usable Items	800
Compact Stun Bomb	Usable Items	800
Compact Freezing Bomb	Usable Items	800
Compact Silence Bomb	Usable Items	700
Scrambling Unit	Usable Items	300
Gunpowder	Other Items	80
Micro Circuit	Other Items	400

WAKE THE COLDSLEEPERS

After hitting the vending unit, head west to a chilled room full of Cardianons and Lizardmen in coldsleep chambers. A Lizardman near the center of the room has a Cardianon ID Card that you'll need to progress further, but you won't be able to snap it off of his frozen corpse. Head through the eastern doors to find the temperature control unit, and give it a blast with your Thunder Ring. That'll thaw out the corpse, but it'll also awaken the sleepers, filling the room with Lizard Warriors.

Leave the room to the north, and head east to a computer room where you can register your new ID card. Then pass through the coldsleep area again, and save your game in the hallway to the south. Before you use your ID card on the nearby door, head south to the treasure room in the southwest part of the map. One of the treasures is a "Li'l Vending Machine" of your own, which you can install in the Recreation Room of the Calnus for future shopping convenience.

It's easy to score Blindsides against the straightforward Lizard Warriors, making the coldsleep area a great place to rack up blue tiles.

A LITTLE HELP FROM THE STEEL GIANT

Don't head through that ID-locked door until you're sure you've found all of the treasure chests on this floor and the previous floors. You won't ever have another chance to come back for chests that you may have missed.

After the event scene, Edge gets trapped in a room with his three companions. Speak to each in turn, telling them what they want to hear. (If you choose the wrong dialogue option, the whole conversation repeats until you get it right.) When everyone's mind is at ease, the steel giant bashes a hole through the wall to the Cardianon Mothership's Subterranean City.

Map Treasures

Biological Laboratory B1
1. Attack Bracelet x 1
2. Comet Robe x 1
3. Alchemist's Water x 3

Biological Laboratory 1F
4. Fresh Sage x 3

Biological Laboratory: Entrance
5. Cardianon Bow x 1

Cardianon Mothership: Subterranean City
6. Skill Manual "Rage" x 1
7. Dragonscale Armor x 1
8. EM Bomb x 4
9. [Ice Barrier] Icicle Rapier x 1

Legend

 = SHOP

 = PASSAGE

 = RECOVERY SPHERE

Monsters

CARDIANON SOLDIER
HP · 1706   EXP · 19
Fol · 153   Race · Humanoid
Resistant To · --
Weak Against · --
DROPS
Strength Potion, Self-Destructor 3000, Gunpowder, Compact Silence Bomb

LIZARD SHAMAN
HP · 1382   EXP · 30
Fol · 148   Race · Animal
Resistant To · --
Weak Against · --
DROPS
Empty Bottle, Darkness Gem, Light Gem

GUARD BOT "ASSAULTER"
HP · 1389   EXP · 23
Fol · 123   Race · Mech
Resistant To · Wind
Weak Against · Water, Thunder
DROPS
Compact Poison Bomb, Universal Device, EM Bomb, Micro Circuit, Quantum Processor

CARDIANON GENERAL
HP · 2048   EXP · 24
Fol · 164   Race · Humanoid
Resistant To · --
Weak Against · --
DROPS
Ripe Berries, Basil, EM Bomb, Barrier Spiritwater, Fortitude Potion

LIZARD WARRIOR
HP · 1709   EXP · 39
Fol · 144   Race · Animal
Resistant To · Ice
Weak Against · --
DROPS
Iron, Frozen Cider

ARMED DRAGON NEWT
HP · 2519   EXP · 68
Fol · 159   Race · Demon
Resistant To · --
Weak Against · --
DROPS
Basil, Berserker's Scarf, Mercury, Alchemist's Water

DRAGON NEWT
HP · 1700   EXP · 19
Fol · 176   Race · Demon
Resistant To · --
Weak Against · --
DROPS
Lizardskin, Fire Gem, Attack Card, Support Card

GUARD BOT "COMMANDO"
HP · 969   EXP · 19
Fol · 102   Race · Mech
Resistant To · Wind
Weak Against · Water, Thunder
DROPS
Compact Freezing Bomb, Universal Device, EM Bomb, Micro Circuit, Silver

ARMED DRAGOON
HP · 5215   EXP · 57
Fol · 270   Race · Mech
Resistant To · Wind
Weak Against · Water, Thunder
DROPS
Laser Oscillator, Compact Stun Bomb, Warning Brooch

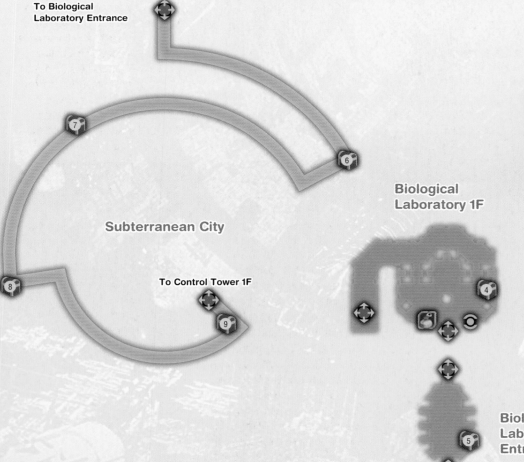

To Biological Laboratory Entrance

Biological Laboratory B1

Biological Laboratory 1F

Subterranean City

To Control Tower 1F

Biological Laboratory Entrance

ESCAPE FROM THE BIOLOGICAL LABORATORY

There's no going back, so march forward through the three tiny areas of the Biological Laboratory. The treasures start to get good here, with a Comet Robe for Lymle and a mighty Cardianon Bow for Reimi ranking among the best loot. Don't expect to take these items without a fight, though, as you'll be ambushed by four consecutive groups of foes as soon as you step through the door that connects the second and third map. Fortunately, there's a recovery sphere right before the door, so you can heal up beforehand and have your team go hog-wild with all their best special arts during the battle. Don't forget to return to the recovery sphere to recoup your MP afterward!

LYMLE'S THIRST FOR KNOWLEDGE

You'll find another vending unit in the Biological Laboratory 1F map. If you examine it, you'll discover that it sells the same stuff as the previous one. But if you examine it a second time, you'll trigger a Private Action between Edge, Lymle, and Bacchus that results in nice affinity boosts all around. Note that if you don't trigger it here, you can trigger the same event at the vending unit in the upcoming Control Tower.

Hmm... I don't get it. This is weird, 'kay? How can we buy things even though there's nobody here?

TAKING BACCHUS FOR A SPIN

There's quite a bit more to Bacchus than originally meets the eye. First things first: use his accumulated skill points to improve his Galvanic Shock and Force Breaker special arts, as well as his Robotics skill. If you have an extra Chain Combos manual on hand, teach it to Bacchus and set up a handy Galvanic Shock/Force Breaker combo that can launch foes and pelt them with missiles in mid-air.

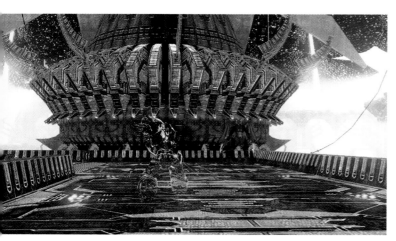

Among Bacchus's other skills are Mining, which allows you to extract ore from the glowing walls on Lemuris and Aeos, and Stealth, which allows you to become invisible and slip past your foes. You can use Stealth as much as you like (by selecting it from the skill menu) and there's really no downside to it, besides the missed combat rewards, of course. Stealth is especially useful when you're striving to avoid combat on your way to a save or recovery sphere.

Once Bacchus has had his skills upgraded and has been given some leftover accessories to equip, make him your leader and take him for a spin. His basic attack is simply to fire a single long-range shot, but if you get close to your target, you can do a thoroughly satisfying backhand-and-shoot combo. You'll also notice that ● or Ⓑ makes Bacchus slide instead of jump, and that while he's sliding (and *only* while he's sliding) he can fire a rapid sequence of shots that often leave foes stunned. If you're nimble enough, you can slide back and forth repeatedly until you land the stun. This technique even works against bosses!

Push on to the Control Tower. You'll exit the Biological Laboratory to find yourself in the heart of the Cardianon Mothership's Subterranean City. The path to the Control Tower is linear and quite thin, so you'll probably need to rely on Bacchus's Stealth skill if you want to avoid combat. Some battles are unavoidable, as the Cardianon troops attack from flying vessels at certain points on the map. Among the new foes are giant Armored Dragoons, who have a number of ways to smash your Bonus Board. As Edge, try to stay behind them, and switch to a ranged character when they enter Rush Mode.

On the bright side, the chests are full of powerful items, and a save sphere is just ahead...

cardianon mothership:
CONTROL TOWER

Monsters

CARDIANON SOLDIER
HP · 1706	EXP · 19
Fol · 153	Race · Humanoid

Resistant To · --
Weak Against · --

DROPS
Strength Potion, Self-Destructor 3000, Gunpowder, Compact Silence Bomb

CARDIANON GENERAL
HP · 2048	EXP · 24
Fol · 164	Race · Humanoid

Resistant To · --
Weak Against · --

DROPS
Ripe Berries, Basil, EM Bomb, Barrier Spiritwater, Fortitude Potion

LIZARD SHAMAN
HP · 1382	EXP · 30
Fol · 148	Race · Animal

Resistant To · --
Weak Against · --

DROPS
Empty Bottle, Darkness Gem, Light Gem

GUARD BOT "ASSAULTER"
HP · 1389	EXP · 23
Fol · 123	Race · Mech

Resistant To · Wind
Weak Against · Water, Thunder

DROPS
Compact Poison Bomb, Universal Device, EM Bomb, Micro Circuit, Quantum Processor

ARMED DRAGOON
HP · 5215	EXP · 57
Fol · 270	Race · Mech

Resistant To · Wind
Weak Against · Water, Thunder

DROPS
Laser Oscillator, Compact Stun Bomb, Warning Brooch

ARMED DRAGON NEWT
HP · 2519	EXP · 68
Fol · 159	Race · Demon

Resistant To · --
Weak Against · --

DROPS
Basil, Berserker's Scarf, Mercury, Alchemist's Water

DRAGON GENERAL
HP · 11157	EXP · 135
Fol · 191	Race · Demon

Resistant To · --
Weak Against · --

DROPS
Dragon Scale, Poison Cider

Map Treasures

Control Tower B1
1. Streaked Chainmail x 1
2. Compact Stun Bomb x 8
3. Skill Manual "Energy Shield" x 1

Control Tower B1

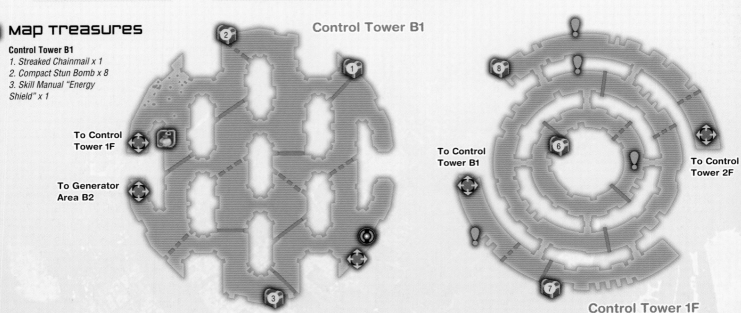

To Control Tower 1F

To Generator Area B2

Map Treasures

Generator Area B2
4. Sturdy Bracelet x 8
5. Poison Cider x 3

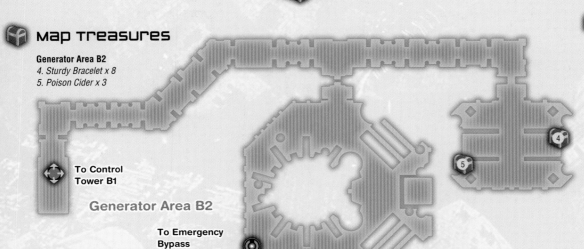

To Control Tower B1

Generator Area B2

To Emergency Bypass

To Control Tower B1

To Control Tower 2F

Control Tower 1F

Map Treasures

Control Tower 1F
6. Element Breaker x 3
7. Skill Manual "Stun" x 1
8. Booster Wand x 1

Legend

◈ = SAVE SPHERE

▣ = SHOP

✧ = PASSAGE

◎ = RECOVERY SPHERE

⬭ = INTERACTION POINT

Map Treasures

Control Tower 2F
9. Compact Poison Bomb x 4
10. [Ice Barrier] Skill Manual "Mindflare" x 1
11. Silvance x 1
12. Power Bracelet x 1

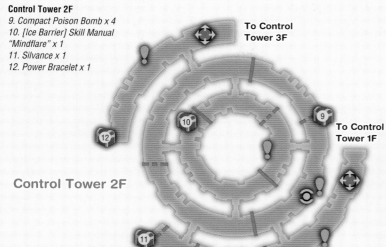

To Control Tower 3F

To Control Tower 1F

Control Tower 2F

Control Tower 55F

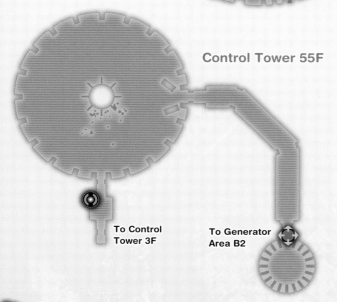

To Control Tower 3F

To Generator Area B2

Map Treasures

Control Tower 3F
13. Skill Manual "Fury Boost" x 1
14. Bronto Armor x 1
15. Riot Potion x 1, Anti-Paralysis Amulet x 1

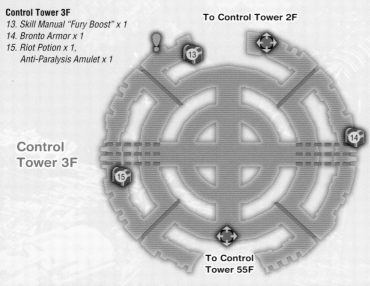

To Control Tower 2F

Control Tower 3F

To Control Tower 55F

THE MAZE OF ENERGY BARRIERS

Every floor of the Control Tower is protected by a maze of glowing red energy barriers. Monsters and guard bots can walk right through them, but if you so much as graze them, you'll get knocked back (potentially into an enemy surprise attack) and everyone in your party takes an amount of damage equal to 1% of their Max HP.

There are two types of energy barriers. Both flicker, but one type (marked by dotted red lines on the map) flickers off for a long enough period that you can run through it. There is no possible way to cross the barriers that are marked with solid red lines on the map.

To get the treasures in the B1 level of the Control Tower, you'll need to take a very roundabout route that begins by heading north from the entrance through the first flickering barriers and passing through two additional flickering barriers to the west. You can then head northeast to the first two treasure chests, or southeast

to the third. It's a hassle, but the one-two punch of Streaked Chainmail and the Energy Shield skill gives Reimi a significant boost on defense.

HIT THE GENERATOR AREA WHILE YOU CAN

There are two exits on the west side of the Control Tower's B1 level. Make sure to first take the one to the south, which leads to a small chunk of the Generator Area that contains two unguarded treasure chests. If you instead begin ascending through the tower, you never receive another good opportunity to come back for them.

EXPOSE THE HIDDEN BARRIERS

The twist in the next few levels of the Control Tower is that the energy barriers won't be visible until you use your Thunder Ring to destroy a steam vent in each of the floor's ring-shaped hallways. (The vents are marked with pink exclamation points.) As in the B1 level, you'll need to travel roundabout routes to reach the chests, but the contents are almost always worth the trouble.

If you have Bacchus in your party and a high level of Robotics skill, you should be racking up large quantities of bombs from the enemies on the mothership. Tossing EM Bombs is a great way to get damage in while the Dragon General is on a Rush Mode spree, and a blast from a Compact Poison Bomb is always a good way to start the fight.

THE LONG RIDE TO THE 55TH FLOOR

Level 3F is the easiest to navigate, thanks to a rotating central ring that is too low to be affected by the barriers above. Head west from the entrance to destroy the one and only steam vent, then pick up the final batch of treasure chests. The exit to the area is in the southern part of the map, where you'll find an elevator that takes you directly to the top floor of the tower. There, you'll find a save sphere and a very angry Cardianon leader.

You'll need to travel through the central ring of Level 1F to reach the chest with the Stun skill manual. Before you teach this to Edge, make sure he has an open Battle Skill slot. If not, you'd be better off teaching it to Faize or saving it for a future recruit.

BATTLING THE DRAGON GENERALS

The second floor of the Control Tower marks the debut of Dragon Generals, enemies that are so massive you have little hope of avoiding them. Dragon Generals have over 10,000 HP and are very good at breaking Bonus Boards, so you should take these fights seriously.

Despite their size, it's astonishingly easy to continuously juggle Dragon Generals with Edge's directional attack combo. Use this technique to  keep the dragons busy while Reimi and Bacchus pelt them in mid-air, but be prepared to run away or switch characters as soon as your target enters Rush Mode.

BOSS

Sahariel

HP · ???	EXP · 10003
Fol · 7711	Race · Animal

Resistant To · *Fire, Wind*
Weak Against · *Water, Thunder*

DROPS
--

Sahariel has a variety of attacks, and if he uses one that involves the guns on his back, hold your position and have Edge charge his Rush Gauge, use a Healing symbol on a wounded party member, or bring Basil to someone who's paralyzed. But if Sahariel rears up to attack instead, quickly hit the trigger for a Stampede Slash/Rising Blade combo to both dish out heavy damage and cancel the impending Voltage Blast. As soon as Sahariel falls back on all fours, use ⊚ or Ⓑ and push the stick away from the boss to back-leap far, far away, as he'll likely retaliate with a Bonus Board-smashing ground stomp.

Stick it to Sahariel

The trick to this fight is good positioning and careful timing. Control Edge, keeping him facing Sahariel and slightly to one side, at a distance roughly equivalent to the length of your foe's body. Like most of the previous bosses, there isn't much point in attacking Sahariel unless he exposes his weak spot, which is on his chest.

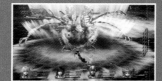

Even though Faize can cast symbols to exploit Sahariel's weaknesses, Lymle, Bacchus, and Reimi are the more useful allies here. Lymle's healing is essential, and the constant long-distance pot shots from Reimi and Bacchus can quickly fill up Sahariel's Rush Gauge. That may sound like a bad thing, but Sahariel uses the attacks that expose his weak point much more frequently when he's in Rush Mode. Note that when Sahariel is in Rush Mode, you will not be able to interrupt his attacks with a successful combo, so Edge may end up taking some damage himself.

ESCAPE THE CARDIANON MOTHERSHIP

After destroying Sahariel, you can take the elevator on the east side of the 55th floor down to the central part of the Generator Area. There, you'll find the button that is able to free the Calnus from its tractor beam, but don't press it until you're confident that you've claimed every treasure the Cardianon Mothership has to offer. Once you free the Calnus, there's no going back.

Your flight through the Emergency Bypass area isn't timed, but you'll need to hurry all the same. Press ⊚ or ✕ repeatedly to dash under the falling doors, because if you get stuck, the only way to open them again is to battle a few packs of Guard Bots.

SET A COURSE FOR EN II . . . EVENTUALLY

When everyone is safely back on the ship, speak to Bacchus, and he'll suggest you set a course for his home world of En II. But before you head in that direction, there are a few other options you may wish to pursue. For one thing, this is your last possible opportunity to fulfill the Orders from the shops on Aeos's Exploration Base, and retrieve the spaceship collections data from the terminals there (which now includes Calnus-II).

There are also a few good reasons to take a trip back to Lemuris. There you can have Bacchus mine up a few useful ingredients, and pursue some new side quests. If you burned through your last Fire Ring charge on the Cardianon Mothership, you definitely want to return to Lemuris's Shady Sorceress for a refill.

There's been a mass migration of villagers from Triom to Woodley, including the Shady Sorceress, so you'll have a long walk ahead of you. But it's well worth a trip to Woodley, as that's where all the action is (see New Quests in Woodley sidebar). You can also put Bacchus's Mining skill to good use by having him drill for gems and metals at the glowing yellow points in cliff walls. You can do the same thing on Planet Aeos, of course, but all the good stuff is found on Lemuris. Keep mining until you dig up at least a few Earth Gems and Crystals, which you'll want on hand for useful recipes you'll acquire in the near future. (An Earth Gem will also allow you to complete Reimi's Earthsoul Blow.)

Wherever you decide to go, you'll be prompted to make room assignments. You have a crew of five and only four rooms, so someone's got to share. This decision ultimately affects some of the game's dialogue and leads to a few exclusive Private Actions, and characters can gradually gain affinity for each other by sharing a room. (However, opposite-sex characters cannot be ordered to share a room unless they already have a considerable amount of affinity.) You can change room assignments at any time by selecting the room directory on the wall of the Crew Quarters hallway.

THE STUBBORN MATRIARCH

REWARD: 80 EXP, 40 Party SP

The Obstinate Woman in Woodley's First Snow Inn is concerned about her mother-in-law, who refused to join the evacuation from Triom. Return to Triom and say whatever you need to say to get the Chilly Old Crone to move to Woodley. Return to the Obstinate Woman for your reward, then speak to the Chilly Old Crone for an additional quest.

IN NEED OF NECTAR

REWARD: 100 EXP, 40 Party SP

The Storehouse Worker in the northern part of town needs 16 servings of Nectar for the coming winter. You can find plenty of Nectar at the harvesting points in the Thalia Plains and Van Elm Region, and earn them from defeating Dryads and other monsters.

OIL FOR THE COLD

REWARD: 80 EXP, 30 Party SP

The Chilly Old Crone has joined her family at Woodley's First Snow Inn, but she isn't happy about it. Help her deal with the cold by bringing her a dose of Wolf Oil. If you don't have any on hand, you can win some by battling Saber-Tooth Tigers in the Wind Swallow Valley.

IN SEARCH OF 'SHROOMS

REWARD: 120 EXP, 33 Party SP

The Storehouse Worker wants Tasty Mushrooms next, and getting 16 of them is a bit more of a challenge. They appear at Van Elm Region harvesting points, and are dropped by Giant Fungus and Man-Eating Tree monsters.

FANG FLUTE FABRICATION

REWARD: 800 EXP, 47 Party SP

The Lonely Young Girl in the southern part of town wants a Fang Flute, an item that you can only craft with the aid of a future party member. When you learn the recipe, make two flutes, and deliver them here to solve this quest and the one that follows it.

FURTHER FANG FLUTE FABRICATION

REWARD: 1,000 EXP, 50 Party SP

Leave the area and re-enter after delivering your first flute, and the Lovely Young Girl subsequently requests another. Good thing you thought to bring a spare!

Earth

BACCHUS'S ENGINEERING EFFORTS

When you're back on the Calnus, boost Bacchus's Engineering skill by a few levels, and put him to work. He mostly invents bombs like the ones you found so often on Cardianon, breakers that reduce a particular enemy stat, and recovery units that can cure the entire party of a status condition.

One-shot items are fine, but every now and then Bacchus can whip up something more interesting. He can make extremely powerful equipment for himself, like a Deadly Cannon and Fully-Tuned Plate, although the ingredients for those are far in the future. He can also make items needed in quests, like a Music Box that comes in handy in the next chapter of the game. Bacchus can also build ship furnishings, starting with a Biorhythm Tester that requires ingredients you already have on hand. Boost the Engineering skill to level 6 and pair Bacchus with Reimi and Faize to come up with the recipe.

DUELS ON THE BATTLEFIELD AND THE CHESS BOARD

Instead of impulsively triggering the first Private Action you see, make a full loop of the ship to see if you have any other options. And take a moment to introduce Bacchus to Welch in another bonus event at the Item-Creation terminal.

• The action kicks off with Reimi's traditional call to the moonbase from her Flight Deck console.

• When you leave the Flight Deck, you'll spot Bacchus playing chess in the Recreation Room. But if you continue on to the Crew Quarters, you'll find Lymle and Faize discussing something. You can only trigger one of the two events. If you choose Bacchus, he and Edge both raise their opinion of each other. If you choose Faize and Lymle, both grow closer to Edge, and Edge also grows closer to Lymle.

• To trigger the next event, visit the room north of the Meeting Room for the second part of Faize's training event. This one ends in a no-holds-barred training match between Faize and Edge, and while no one can actually die here, Faize will think nothing of destroying your Bonus Board if you aren't careful. Win or lose, both characters' opinion of the other rise, although the loser ends up thinking twice as much of the winner. If Faize emerges triumphant, it strengthens his relationship with Lymle as well.

• In the next part, you again have your choice of two events, but you can do both if you pursue them in the right order. Before you speak to Bacchus in his room, you have an opportunity to peep on Reimi in the women's bathroom without advancing the flight to the next leg. But you may not want to; while talking to Bacchus raises both characters' affinity, peeping on Reimi only causes her opinion of Edge to drop. So while Bacchus is the right tactical choice, watching a scantily clad Reimi fire her bow at Edge may be a more appealing option for some players.

• You'll only have one choice of Private Actions for the remainder of the voyage, with the next taking place in the Meeting Room. While the Private Action is triggered by speaking to Reimi, the result is a boost in Faize and Lymle's opinions of Edge, as well as his opinions of them.

• If you head upstairs, you can learn what Reimi has named your potted plants. That's not a Private Action, but you might be curious anyway. The actual Private Action is in the Recreation Room, where joining Lymle for "nappy time" results in Lymle and Faize taking the first rocky steps towards friendship.

• Join Bacchus at the chess table for the next event. If you chose to play chess with Bacchus during the second Private Action of this journey, you'll view the sequel to that event. If you didn't, you'll see the original chess event that you missed previously.

• For the final Private Action of the journey, visit Reimi in the room with the battle simulator. You have a choice of responses here, and both provide the same total amount of affinity. If you tell Reimi you'll "take her to the stars," it raises Edge's opinion of Reimi by 3, and her opinion of Edge by 1. The second choice has the opposite result, raising Reimi's opinion by 3, and Edge's by 1. But only the first choice will lead to an additional Private Action, which occurs in the very last section of the game. Whichever you choose, the event ends abruptly when the flight to En II takes an unexpected turn...

MAP TREASURES

1. Thornberries x 3
2. Red Herb x 2
3. Silver Amulet x 1
4. Blueberries x 4
5. Aquaberries x 2
6. Bigberries x 3
7. Fresh Sage x 2
8. Protection Seeds x 1

PICKPOCKETING

a. Ingratiating Cat	Intelligence Seeds
b. Klaus	Protection Seeds

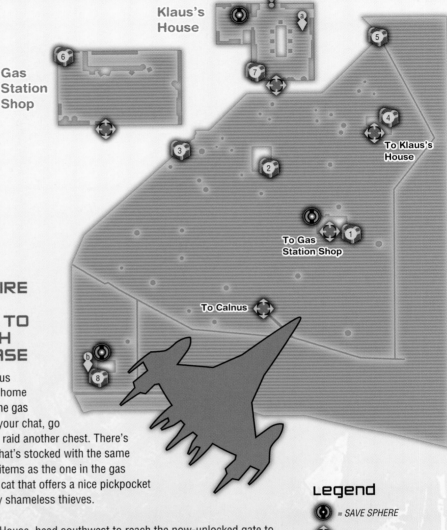

Klaus's House

Gas Station Shop

To Klaus's House

To Gas Station Shop

To Calnus

THE CALNUS'S SURPRISE DIVERSION

Your objective was En II, but now you've found yourself somewhere else entirely. Head north into the abandoned town to investigate, and you'll find your first clues in the Gas Station Shop. You'll automatically leave the building when a man named Klaus invites you to his home in the northeast, but you should head right back into the gas station. In addition to a chest full of Bigberries, you can repeatedly raid the fridge behind the bar to find an endless supply of Blackberries, Aquaberries, Mixed Syrup, and Fresh Sage.

CONSPIRE WITH KLAUS TO BREACH THE BASE

You'll find Klaus waiting in the home northeast of the gas station. After your chat, go back inside to raid another chest. There's also a fridge that's stocked with the same basic healing items as the one in the gas station, and a cat that offers a nice pickpocket target for truly shameless thieves.

From Klaus's House, head southwest to reach the now-unlocked gate to the west of the Calnus. Open the nearby chest, save your game, and pick up the phone to proceed. Once the entrance to the Military Facility rises, Klaus appears, giving you a fleeting chance to pick his pocket. Talk to him when you're ready to go inside.

Legend

= SAVE SPHERE

= PASSAGE

= NPC

= INTERACTION POINT

THE TECHNOLOGIES OF THE PAST

There are two Private Actions you can trigger in the Abandoned Town, and you'll want to do both before you proceed into the Military Facility. To trigger the first, examine the radio on the counter of the Gas Station Shop. That'll get Bacchus talking, and raise Edge's opinion of him.

The second Private Action is set in Klaus's house. Just examine the refrigerator to trigger an event that increases Edge's affinity for Faize and Lymle, and Faize's affinity for Edge.

PRIVATE ACTIONS

Monsters

BIGFOOT SAM

HP · 4030	EXP · 144
Fol · 134	Race · Mech

Resistant To · Thunder
Weak Against · Water

DROPS
Bigberries, Basil

LITTLE ALIEN

HP · 2267	EXP · 54
Fol · 81	Race · Humanoid

Resistant To · ---
Weak Against · ---

DROPS
Bizarre Fruit, Fresh Sage, Bigberries

SOLDIER ZOMBIE

HP · 3301	EXP · 76
Fol · 102	Race · Undead

Resistant To · ---
Weak Against · Fire

DROPS
Ripe Berries, Natto, Pickled Plum,
Gunpowder, Aquaberries

Map treasures

1. Aquaberries x 2
2. Skill Manual "Scan Enemy" x 1
3. [Ice Barrier] Compact Freezing Bomb x 3
4. Earth Ring x 1
5. Thornberries x 1, Blueberries x 1, Aquaberries x 1
6. Skill Manual "No Guard" x 1
7. Alien Arc x 1
8. Dragon Scale x 1, [PS3 only] Taffeta Ribbon x 1
9. Alien's Robe x 1
10. Foal Snaps x 1
11. Plasma Cannon x 1
12. Compact Stun Bomb x 2
13. Fresh Sage x 2
14. [Ice Barrier] Compact Freezing Bomb x 3

RALLY AT THE RECOVERY SPHERE

Talk to everyone in your holding cell, then talk to Faize again to put Klaus's plan in action. True to his word, Klaus opens the cell doors, freeing not only your party but a legion of secret government alien and bigfoot specimens. These are tough foes, so fire up Bacchus's Stealth and make your way to the cell with the recovery sphere to the southeast. Hold court there, clearing out a few enemies at a time before ducking back in for an HP and MP refill.

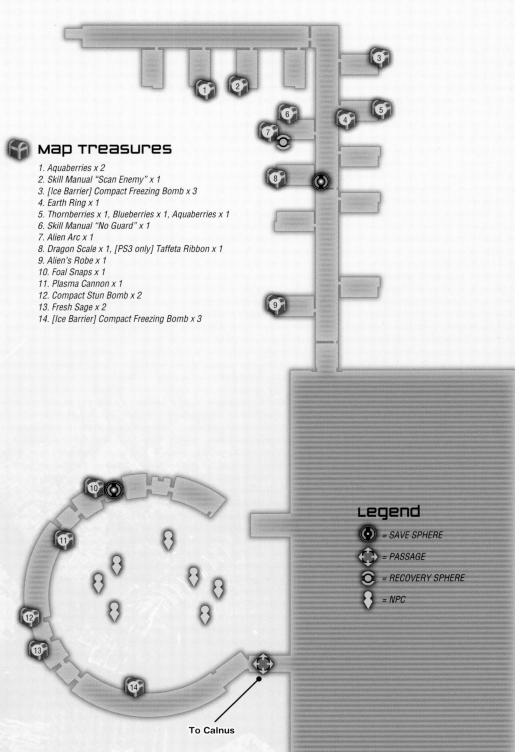

Legend

= SAVE SPHERE	
= PASSAGE	
= RECOVERY SPHERE	
= NPC	

To Calnus

The "No Guard" skill manual in that room is a strong skill for frontline fighters. The higher you jack it up, the more it protects your character from being knocked down by enemy attacks and having symbols and combos disrupted. At max level, a foe must deal damage equal to 10% or more of your health to knock you down, although getting there costs a fortune in SP.

Once you reach the recovery sphere, don't forget to backtrack for all the treasure chests. The highlight is the Earth Ring in Chest #4, although it's completely out of charges. But you'll have plenty of opportunities to get it charged before you need to use it.

PUTTING BIGFOOT SAM ON ICE

The Bigfoot Sams are hearty, powerful foes, but their weakness to the water element makes them very vulnerable to being frozen. Once frozen, you can shatter their 4,000+ HP with a single strike.

To exploit this weakness, begin each battle by having Faize cast Ice Needles, then take control of Edge to distract the target. (The Bigfoot Sams are quite skilled at countering spells with their long-range attack.) Once you get the Compact Freezing Bombs from chest 3, you'll be able to use those instead of relying entirely on Faize.

By combining Stun resistance with a Critical Hit boost, Bigfoot Sams make for an appealing Monster Jewel target. Keep fighting them until you earn the full monster collections data.

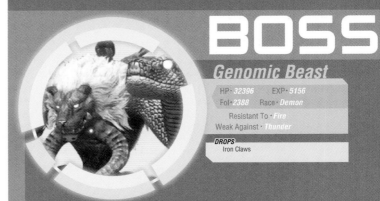

BOSS
Genomic Beast

HP · 32396	EXP · 5156
Fol · 2388	Race · Demon

Resistant To · **Fire**
Weak Against · **Thunder**

DROPS
Iron Claws

Rescue Meracle from the Genomic Beast

When you open the door by the save sphere, you'll find Meracle under attack by the massive Genomic Beast. Take him down, and you'll win your sixth party member.

Don't let the Genomic Beast's weakness to Thunder tempt you into taking control of Bacchus. Bacchus's Galvanic Shock special art is extraordinarily powerful here, but his height unfortunately results in him getting pummeled by the beast's fire spin attack. Edge, on the other hand, is short enough that the beast's arms go spinning right over his head, allowing you to continuously attack with standard combos or the Stampede Slash special art (when the Genomic Beast is spinning, you don't want to use moves like Rising Blade that cause you to jump).

Use Rush Mode combos to deal heavy damage to the Genomic Beast. You might even get lucky and get a free shot from Bacchus's Galvanic Shock.

A MIRACLE ON THE BATTLEFIELD

Meracle is a powerful and lightning-quick melee fighter, but with weak Defense and a low HP total, it can be tough to keep her alive. If you intend to use her in combat, give her all of the party's Defense and Health Seeds and any good defensive skills you have lying around, like HP Boost or First Aid. Equip her with Defense-boosting accessories, as well as the Iron Claws that the Genomic Beast dropped.

Meracle's combos offer some interesting options. The directional combo ends with a kick that can send even large monsters flying across the room, while the standard combo ends in a pop-up that sets the target up for further attacks. In terms of sheer damage-dealing potential, Meracle's Ripper Pounce special art is hard to beat. Its lengthy combo leaves her vulnerable to attacks from other enemies, so it's best used in one-on-one situations only — clear any potential interlopers away with directional combos or the Comet Impact special art.

One of Meracle's finest features is that she dashes from side to side when using a Blindside, avoiding a lot of the attacks that can disrupt other characters.

FLEE THE WRATH OF KEVIN

After exiting the Holding Area, you'll find yourself in yet another cell. Wake up Reimi and equip her with the Alien Arc bow. Speak to Faize, then Meracle, and Klaus will come to save you.

Be careful as you run through the thin doorways of the Experimental Area, as there may be monsters waiting to pounce just off to the sides. There are also plenty of treasure chests hidden in the corners, including a new weapon for Bacchus. When you finally reach the Calnus, you'll have no choice but to set a course for an emergency landing on Planet Roak.

planet roak:
NORTHEAST ASTRALIAN CONTINENT

 Map Treasures

1. Holy Water x 2
2. Blueberries x 3
3. Basil x 2
4. 2986 Fol
5. Riot Potion x 5
6. [PS3-only] Recipe Memo 17

 Mining Point Items

Silver
Gold
Thunder Gem

 Pickpocketing

| a. Autanim | 105 Fol |
| b. Patiently Waiting Girl | Natural Water x 1 |

Harvesting Point Items

Caterpillar Fungus
Lemon
Oak [PS3-only]
Red Herb
Vegetables
Wooden Stick

Legend

 = SAVE SPHERE

 = PASSAGE

= NPC

 = INTERACTION POINT

To Tatroi Area

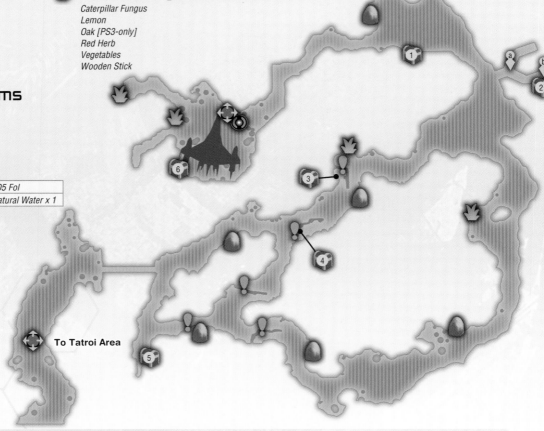

Monsters

HONEYBEE
HP · *2468*   EXP · *108*
Fol · *90*   Race · *Insect*
Resistant To · *--*
Weak Against · *Earth*

DROPS
Accuracy Seeds, Bee Stinger, Aquaberries

KOBOLD BANDIT
HP · *3084*   EXP · *162*
Fol · *189*   Race · *Animal*
Resistant To · *Fire*
Weak Against · *--*

DROPS
All-Purpose Ceramic

AXE BEAK
HP · *3393*   EXP · *189*
Fol · *151*   Race · *Bird*
Resistant To · *Wind*
Weak Against · *Earth*

DROPS
Rotten Fish, Basil, Giant Bird Feather,
Common Egg, Peryton Droppings

UNICORN WOLF
HP · *2776*   EXP · *108*
Fol · *111*   Race · *Animal*
Resistant To · *Fire*
Weak Against · *Water*

DROPS
Saber-Toothed Tiger Fang, Wolf Fang,
Blueberries

WAVING PINCERS
HP · *4510*   EXP · *162*
Fol · *163*   Race · *Insect*
Resistant To · *Water*
Weak Against · *Thunder*

DROPS
Protection Seeds, Rotten Fish, Warped
Carapace

BEACHCOMBING ON THE ASTRALIAN COAST

The new monsters in this area of Roak are not particularly difficult, but they can wear you down on the long walk from your ship to Roak's first village. Lower-level parties should spend some time sticking close to the ship and racking up blue Bonus Board tiles, which are very easy to get against straightforward, easily Blindsided foes like the Unicorn Wolf and Kobold Bandit.

The other reason to stick to the coast is wildlife spotting. Keep your eyes peeled for the blowhole-blast of a whale-like creature, the fish swimming near the docks, and the school of jellyfish that's perilously close to the beach. Beautiful!

When you travel towards the suspension bridge in the southwest part of the map, take the long way around by combing the beaches along the eastern coast. Here, you'll find little sparkling treasures that have been randomly washed up by the waves. You'll get a lot of common items, including Lemons and Wooden Sticks, but every now and then you'll find a Lesser Demon's Fetish or a precious chunk of Platinum.

Planet Roak

FOUR TICKETS TO EDGE'S PITY PARTY

Return to the Calnus any time between landing on Roak and visiting the third town (Tropp), and you'll be able to trigger four Private Actions in one fell swoop. In any order you like, speak to Lymle in the Recreation Room, Meracle in the Crew Quarters hallway, Bacchus in his quarters, and Reimi inside the room with the battle simulator. They may not succeed in pulling Edge out of his funk, but the interaction improves his opinion of each as well as Meracle's opinion of Edge. It isn't technically a Private Action, but if you turn on the Item Creation terminal, Welch also does her best to cheer Edge up!

PRIVATE ACTIONS

WELCH'S Crafting Corner

ARTS AND CRAFTS WITH MERACLE

Bring Meracle's Crafting skill up a few levels, put her in a group with Lymle and Reimi (your party's other top crafters), and they will invent dozens of new recipes. The fruits of Meracle's craft include the Fang Flute (needed for two quests on Woodley), armlets for nearly every element, and armors like Lymle's Protective Robe and Reimi's Lizard Guard. Swap Reimi out for Faize, and Meracle can learn how to craft a variety of amulets and magic wands (for Lymle). Meracle can also inspire new recipes for almost every Item Creation skill, so make sure to try her in a variety of different combinations.

While Meracle is able to come up with dozens of recipes, there aren't many good items you can make at this point in the game. One exception is the Anti-Pumpkin Amulet, a level 6 Crafting recipe. (If you're having trouble developing it, try pairing her with Lymle and Edge.) Its only ingredients are two pieces of Ebony, an Earth Gem, and three doses of the Pumpkin Extract sold by your ship's Li'l Vending Machine No. 1. The pumpkin condition is a rare one, but the +20 DEF boost is something Meracle can put to good use in any fight.

Players of the PS3 version should have found a chest with Recipe Memo 17 behind a tree near the Calnus's landing point. With a Crystal mined in Lemuris, the Taffeta Ribbon from Earth's Military Facility, and a piece of Oak found in nearby Roak harvesting points, you can put together a powerful new Crystal Wand for Lymle. (Players of the Xbox 360 version will find this recipe a bit later in the game.)

MAP TREASURES

1. Barrier Spiritwater x 1
2. Bunny Feed x 3
3. DANGER! DO NOT DRINK! x 3
4. Bellweather's Bow x 1, [PS3-only]
Dwarven Embroidery Thread x 1

MINING POINT ITEMS

Gold	Ruby
Iron	Silver
Light Gem	Thunder Gem
Platinum [PS3-only]	

HARVESTING POINT ITEMS

Blackberries	Red Seed
Blue Seed	Seasonings
Dendrobium	White Rice
Ebony	Wooden Stick

PICKPOCKETING

a. Fully-Prepared Man	Repair Kit x 1
b. Apprentice Tribesman	40 Fol
c. Hard-Working Tribesman	Bunny Feed x 1
d. Elder Tribesman	Magical Clay x 1
e. Friendly Tribeswoman	Sacrificial Doll x 1

*The characters listed above will not appear on your first visit to the Tatroi Area.

To Northeast Astralian Continent

Legend

 = PASSAGE

= NPC

Monsters

HONEYBEE

HP · 2468	EXP · 108
Fol · 90	Race · Insect

Resistant To · --
Weak Against · Earth

DROPS
Accuracy Seeds, Bee Stinger, Aquaberries

UNICORN WOLF

HP · 2776	EXP · 108
Fol · 111	Race · Animal

Resistant To · Fire
Weak Against · Water

DROPS
Saber-Toothed Tiger Fang, Wolf Fang, Blueberries

THIEVING SCUMBAG

HP · 3275	EXP · 163
Fol · 237	Race · Humanoid

Resistant To · --
Weak Against · --

DROPS
tri-Emblum, Hot Chocolate, Natto

KOBOLD BANDIT

HP · 3084	EXP · 162
Fol · 189	Race · Animal

Resistant To · Fire
Weak Against · --

DROPS
All-Purpose Ceramic

ALBERO DI ANIMA

HP · 6550	EXP · 354
Fol · 290	Race · Plant

Resistant To · Earth
Weak Against · Fire

DROPS
Bigberries, Aquaberries, Basil, Nectar

To Tatroi

To Astral Desert

Black Tribe Tent

TREAD CAREFULLY ON THE ROAD TO TATROI

You're almost to Tatroi, Roak's first village and the home of a long-awaited save sphere (at the inn). But as you cross the network of bridges that leads to the city gates, you must contend with two new enemies. Albero di Anima treefolk are extremely powerful and should be avoided entirely or fought from a safe distance with ranged characters. Thieving Scumbags can swipe a lot more Fol than the Apprentice Scumbags you fought on Lemuris, so you need to be vigilant about tracking down and slaying the ones that steal from you before they can escape with the loot.

Both new monsters offer great Monster Jewel opportunities. Like the Apprentice Scumbag, the Thieving Scumbag Monster Jewel offers a 15% Fol boost, and adds 30% immunity to the stun condition to sweeten the deal. The Albero di Anima jewel provides 30% immunity to both poison and paralysis, a bit of HP regeneration, and a solid DEF boost.

A BUNNY-CATCHING LESSON FROM THE BLACK TRIBE

When you reach the sandy patch at the south end of the Tatroi Area—head west to the entrance to Tatroi. You can't yet cross the desert to the south, nor can you find anyone near the tent outside of town. Walk down Tatroi's main street until you trigger the event that introduces Sarah. Return to the Tatroi Area, where you'll find a cluster of people around the large black tent.

Speak to the Fully-Prepared Man for a free Glowstick, then to the Apprentice Tribesman working on the east side of the tent. Ask them about the bunnies, and they'll send you to speak to the Tribe Elder at the entrance. Visit with him to trigger an event that teaches you everything you need to know about Bunnies, and a whole lot more. After the Friendly Tribeswoman hands you the Bunny Reins, repay her hospitality by heading inside the tent and swiping a Bellwether's Bow for Reimi. Players of the PS3 version will also find some Dwarven Embroidery Thread, which is a key ingredient in many of the robes that Meracle can create with her Crafting skill.

When you cross the bridge to the northeast to catch your first Bunny, the day's events soon take an unexpected turn. The Bunny must wait, as you suddenly have far more pressing matters to attend to.

PICKPOCKETING

a. Deeply-Sleeping Old Man	Super Aphrodisiac x 1
b. Gentle Old Woman	Fresh Sage x 1
c. Smooth-Talking Shopkeeper	Gold x 1
d. Fiercely Resolute Guard	Natto x 1
e. Cat-Loving Kid	Sweet Fruit x 1
f. Talking Cat	Holy Water x 1
g. Unlucky Old Woman	Vile Goop x 1
h. Fruit-Crazy Old Man	Thornberries x 1
i. Shadowy Dollmaker	Accuracy Seeds x 1
j. Potentially-Slacking Guard	Resistance Potion x 1
k. Relaxed Guard	Blueberries x 1
l. Impulsive Girl	Silk x 1
m. Cheerful Girl	Snakeskin x 1
n. Suspicious Psychokineticist	Disintegration Stone x 1
o. Veteran Guard	Resurrection Elixir x 1

p. Diligent Clerk	Ginseng x 1
q. Jarvis, Hot-Blooded Bouncer	Hyper Potion x 1

Gordeau's Spirits

r. Lazy Cat	Wool x 1
s. Sharp-Tongued Waitress	Aquaberries x 1

*You can pickpocket Vinegar from the Tavern Bartender only during "The Stray Carrot" quest. If you wish to do so, you must pickpocket before speaking to her.

East Part of Town

t. Dutiful Sailor	Coal x 1
u. Canal Barge Chief	Lemon x 1
v. Unsatisfied Guard	650 Fol
w. Envious Elder	Crystal x 1

Queen of Inventors' House

x. Jasmine, Queen of Inventors	Seasonings x 1

Mansion

y. Mischievous Woman	Fresh Cream x 1

MAP TREASURES

1. Blackberries x 2
2. Anti-Curse Amulet x 1
3. Bigberries x 2
4. [Ivy Barrier] Physical Stimulant x 3
5. Girl's Gift Box
6. Ripe Berries x 1
7. Aquaberries x 4
8. Recipe Memo 16 x 1
9. 12000 Fol

Legend

= SHOP

= PASSAGE

= NPC

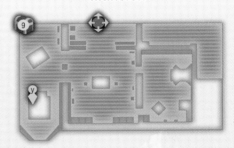

Mansion

Gordeau's Spirits

Queen of Inventors' House

Homespun Inn 1F

Homespun Inn 2F

To Mansion

To Queen of Inventor's House

To Gordeau's Spirits

To Astral City

To Tatroi Area

A QUICK TRIP THROUGH TATROI

You've only just arrived in Tatroi, and already you need to be on your way. After you rescue Sarah, meet the Black Tribe outside, and attempt to catch a Bunny, the canal barge that runs between Tatroi and Astral City becomes open for business. You can board it in the southeast part of town whenever you're ready to move on. Note that Edge won't let you leave Tatroi through any other exit.

While you are in town you can sign up for a few side quests, although neither can be pursued at this point. Speak to Fez at the Twin Books shop in the northwest corner of town, and he entrusts you with the "Missing Brother" quest. Then, the Dutiful Sailor in the east part of town asks for your help with "The Seafarer's Treasure" quest.

The Suspicious Psychokineticist can recharge any of your rings, including the new Earth Ring. However, you won't need to use it anytime soon.

NICE FINDS AT THE TATROI BAZAAR

Tatroi is full of shops, but the stock is mostly stuff that you have seen before. Diligent treasure hunters likely own every item for sale at Ed's Weapons, save for Edge's new Bastard Sword. But don't waste your money on that unless you're trying to complete the Weapons section of your Collections menu, as you'll find a much better sword before you ever have a chance to use it.

The only new skill at Fez's Books is Meracle's Ornithology (which raises the rate of item drops from Bird monsters), but they also have enough copies of the essential Skill Manual "Chain Combos" for the rest of your party. Don't miss the Tents available at Tools 'R' Us; they are pricy at 4,000 Fol, but the ability to completely refill the party's HP and MP anywhere on the field is absolutely invaluable.

Make sure to take a look at the Orders section of each shop, where you may be able to pick up easy EXP and Party SP by dipping into your on-hand stock of Red Herbs, Mixed Syrups, Thornberries, Ripe Berries, Holy Water, Gold, and Tasty Mushrooms. Put some of that money into buying a few each of every new ingredient for your item-creation endeavors. You'll want to stock up on Carbon Fiber and Aramid Fiber in particular, since they are used frequently in high-level recipes.

BLACK CAT MATERIAL SHOP - STOCK

Item	Type	Price	Item	Type	Price
Lacquer	Other Items	200	Handspun Thread	Other Items	100
Aramid Fiber	Other Items	800	Empty Bottle	Other Items	40
Carbon Fiber	Other Items	1,000	Rivet	Other Items	20
Fur Pelt	Other Items	2,000	Neck Chain	Other Items	80
Taffeta Ribbon	Other Items	200			

BLACK CAT MATERIAL SHOP - ORDERS

Holy Water x 4

Reward	Rarity	From
800	☆☆	Smooth-Talking Shopkeeper

Pumpkin Cider x 5

Reward	Rarity	From
500	☆☆☆	Smooth-Talking Shopkeeper

Silk x 10

Reward	Rarity	From
10,000	☆	Smooth-Talking Shopkeeper

Cashmere x 8

Reward	Rarity	From
7,000	☆☆	Smooth-Talking Shopkeeper

TOOLS 'R' US - STOCK

Item	Type	Price	Item	Type	Price
Tent	Usable Items	4,000	Light Paint	Other Items	100
Gunpowder	Other Items	80	Healing Paint	Other Items	80
Magical Brush	Other Items	200	Parchment	Other Items	400
Fire Paint	Other Items	80	Repair Kit	Other Items	100
Wind Paint	Other Items	80	Alchemist's Water	Other Items	300
Thunder Paint	Other Items	80			

TOOLS 'R' US - STOCK

Oak x 5

Reward	Rarity	From
700	☆	Percipient Elder

Anti-Silence Amulet x 1

Reward	Rarity	From
4,000	☆☆☆	Percipient Elder

Silver Amulet x 1

Reward	Rarity	From
1,200	☆☆	Percipient Elder

Fire Charm x 1

Reward	Rarity	From
2,000	☆☆☆	Percipient Elder

roomy foods - stock

Item	Type	Price
Rich Cheese	Food	180
Natural Water	Other Items	120
Vinegar	Other Items	40
Uncooked Pasta	Other Items	100
Raw Animal Meat	Other Items	60
Raw Fish	Other Items	80

Item	Type	Price
Common Egg	Other Items	30
Vegetables	Other Items	60
Seasonings	Other Items	20
Special Warishita Sauce	Other Items	120
Fresh Cream	Other Items	100

roomy foods - orders

Red Herb x 3

Reward	Rarity	From
300	☆	Peppita, Girl Who Loves to Help

Mixed Syrup x 5

Reward	Rarity	From
200	☆	Peppita, Girl Who Loves to Help

Pickled Pepper Potion x 10

Reward	Rarity	From
1,200	☆☆	Peppita, Girl Who Loves to Help

Caesar Salad x 3

Reward	Rarity	From
300	☆☆	Peppita, Girl Who Loves to Help

ed's weapons - stock

Item	Type	Price
Blessed Sword	Weapon	700
Silvance	Weapon	5,000
Bastard Sword	Weapon	11,000
Torch Bow	Weapon	800
Icicle Rapier	Weapon	4,000
Flame Wand	Weapon	1,500
Dragonscale Armor	Armor	3,500
Mystic Chainmail	Armor	1,000
Blizzard Protector	Armor	1,200
Comet Robe	Armor	2,400

ed's weapons - orders

Gold x 5

Reward	Rarity	From
7,000	☆	Knight-Obsessed Shopkeeper

Runic Metal x 2

Reward	Rarity	From
2,000	☆☆☆	Knight-Obsessed Shopkeeper

Venom Sword x 1

Reward	Rarity	From
1,500	☆☆☆	Knight-Obsessed Shopkeeper

Mithril x 1

Reward	Rarity	From
1,200	☆☆☆	Knight-Obsessed Shopkeeper

Nereidstone x 2

Reward	Rarity	From
6,000	☆☆☆☆	Knight-Obsessed Shopkeeper

good grocers - stock

Item	Type	Price
Blueberries	Usable Items	40
Bigberries	Usable Items	100
Blackberries	Usable Items	60
Aquaberries	Usable Items	30
Basil	Usable Items	30

Item	Type	Price
Fresh Sage	Usable Items	150
Hot Chocolate	Usable Items	50
Glowstick	Usable Items	90
Vile Goop	Usable Items	300
Pickled Plum	Food	20

good grocers - orders

Thornberries x 3

Reward	Rarity	From
100	☆	Cheerful Girl

Ripe Berries x 5

Reward	Rarity	From
200	☆☆	Cheerful Girl

Physical Stimulant x 3

Reward	Rarity	From
300	☆☆	Cheerful Girl

Tasty Mushroom x 8

Reward	Rarity	From
200	☆	Cheerful Girl

lovesong accessories - stock

Item	Type	Price
Bandit's Gloves	Wrist Accessory	3,300
Sniper's Bangle	Wrist Accessory	800
Silver Bangle	Wrist Accessory	800
Earth Armlet	Wrist Accessory	15,000

Item	Type	Price
Anti-Freezing Amulet	Neck Accessory	5,000
Sacrificial Doll	Neck Accessory	500
Warning Brooch	Neck Accessory	1,000

lovesong accessories - orders

Green Beryl x 3

Reward	Rarity	From
9,000	☆☆☆☆	Handmade Craftsman

Salamanderstone x 3

Reward	Rarity	From
26,000	☆☆☆☆	Handmade Craftsman

Shadestone x 2

Reward	Rarity	From
20,000	☆☆☆☆	Handmade Craftsman

Stallion Snaps x 1

Reward	Rarity	From
2,100	☆☆☆	Handmade Craftsman

fez's books - stock

Item	Type	Price
Skill Manual "Entomology"	Usable Items	600
Skill Manual "Ornithology"	Usable Items	1,100
Skill Manual "Chain Combos"	Usable Items	3,000
Skill Manual "First Aid"	Usable Items	2,000

Item	Type	Price
Skill Manual "Fury Boost"	Usable Items	4,000
Skill Manual "Elusion"	Usable Items	1,000
Skill Manual "Taunt"	Usable Items	800
Skill Manual "Hide"	Usable Items	1,200

MAP TREASURES

1. Monster Jewel x 1
2. Swept Hilt x 1
3. [Dark Barrier] Earthrock Mail x 1
4. Basil x 4
5. 8 Fol
6. Riot Potion x 2
7. Health Seeds x 1
8. Famed Sword "Veinslay" x 1

HARVESTING POINT ITEMS

Aquaberries
Bigberries
Blackberries
Blueberries
Lemon

LEGEND

 = SAVE SPHERE

 = SHOP

 = PASSAGE

 = NPC

The King's Inn 1F

The King's Inn 2F

To Tatroi

Residence

Mobius's
One-Stop
Shop 1F

Mobius's
One-Stop
Shop 2F

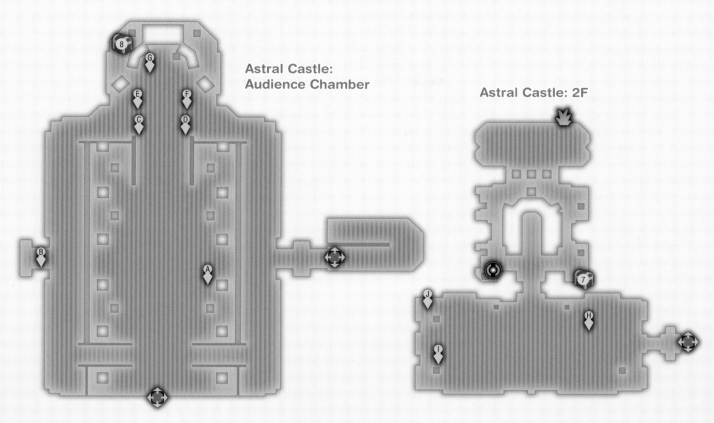

Astral Castle:
Audience Chamber

Astral Castle: 2F

PICKPOCKETING

a. Drooling Girl	Lemon x 1
b. Canal Barge Chief*	Lemon x 1
c. Woozy Man	Peryton Droppings x 1
d. Composed Knight	Tent x 1
e. Anessa the Tomboy	Sacrificial Doll x 1
f. Lias, Astralian Royal Knight	Astralian Emblem x 1
g. Ramrod-Stiff Knight	Empty Bottle x 1
h. Sickly Mother	Silver x 1
i. Terminally Shy Knight	Alchemist's Water x 1
j. Drowsy Old Woman	Resurrection Elixir x 1
k. Kind-Eyed Old Man	1000 Fol
l. Careless Shopkeeper	Warning Brooch x 1
m. Lively Girl	Giant Bird Feather x 1
n. Teary-Eyed Girl	Empty Bottle x 1
o. High-Spirited Girl	Aquaberries x 1
p. Madonna of the Greengrocers	Pie Crusts x 1
q. Heavily Made-Up Lady	Blueberries x 1
r. Man Who Appears to Be a Guard	1830 Fol
s. Fidgety Man	Common Egg x 1
t. Battle-Tested Soldier	Energy Bracelet x 1
u. Knight Whose Dream Was Fulfilled	Gambleberries x 1
v. Brand-New Guard	5 Fol
w. Guardsmanlike Guard	Astralian Emblem x 1

*This is the same character who appeared in Tatroi, and can only be pickpocketed once.

**You can pickpocket a Monster Jewel from Buster, Brawny Thug, who appears south of the barge after you defeat Black Eagle and stay at the inn.

Residence

x. Knight's Wife	Sacrificial Doll x 1

Mobius's One-Stop Shop

y. Jack-of-All-Trades	Alchemist's Water x 1

The King's Inn

z. Historic Old Man	Barrier Spiritwater x 1

Astral Castle: Audience Chamber

A. Unconditionally Obedient Knight	Thunder Gem x 1
B. Novice Knight	White Rice x 1
C. Serious Guard	200 Fol
D. Exceptionally Slow-Talking Guard	Mental Potion x 1
E. Guard Prone to Fantasizing	Miracle Pie x 1
F. Thoughtful Guard	Holy Water x 1
G. King of Astral	Ruby x 1

Astral Castle: 2F

H. Faithful Servant	Learning Gloves x 1
I. Shrewd Guard	Monster Jewel x 1
J. Overly-Cautious Knight	Pickled Plum x 1

*The characters listed above will not appear on your first visit to Astral Castle: 2F.

THE QUIET STREETS OF ASTRAL CITY

Astral City is full of people, but no one has much in the way of advice or quests to offer you. Speak to them all anyway, especially the knights, since simply viewing their weapons unlocks a few new entries in your collections data. Pickpocketers may want to snatch one of their Astralian Emblems, an accessory that offers a +25 Attack boost.

The two grocers don't sell much of anything that you haven't seen before, but there are a few good finds in Mobius's One-Stop Shop. You can buy Critical Hit skill manuals, a useful battle skill for fighters, and HP Boost skill manuals that provide an excellent long-term battle skill for any member of your party. You can also pick up a few staple ingredients like Silk and Wool, and buy 10 bolts of Silk to fill the order at Tatroi's Black Cat Material Shop. That transaction earns you a tidy profit of 6,000 Fol, 1,000 EXP, and 47 Party SP.

When you are done shopping at Mobius's, help yourself to a few free samples by picking up some dropped Fol at the base of the stairs and raiding the three chests on the second floor.

Mobius's one-stop shop - stock

Item	Type	Price
Anti-Paralysis Amulet	Neck Accessory	8,000
Sacrificial Doll	Neck Accessory	500
Warning Brooch	Neck Accessory	1,000
Tent	Usable Items	4,000
Skill Manual "HP Boost"	Usable Items	8,000
Skill Manual "Critical Hit"	Usable Items	4,400
Skill Manual "Fury Boost"	Usable Items	4,000
Skill Manual "Hide"	Usable Items	1,200
Iron	Other Items	400
Wool	Other Items	200
Silk	Other Items	400
Satin Ribbon	Other Items	400
Parchment	Other Items	400
Map of Astral	Other Items	1,000

Mobius's one-stop shop - orders

Coal x 10

Reward	Rarity	From
3,000	☆	Jack-of-All-Trades

Light Gem x 4

Reward	Rarity	From
8,000	☆☆	Jack-of-All-Trades

Ash x 3

Reward	Rarity	From
500	☆☆	Jack-of-All-Trades

Thunder Charm x 1

Reward	Rarity	From
2,000	☆☆☆	Jack-of-All-Trades

whole Heart foods - stock

Item	Type	Price
Pumpkin Extract	Usable Items	200
Sweet Fruit	Food	200
Natto	Food	300
Ge Gen Tang	Other Items	400
Natural Water	Other Items	120
Uncooked Pasta	Other Items	100
Raw Animal Meat	Other Items	60
Raw Fish	Other Items	80
Common Egg	Other Items	30
Vegetables	Other Items	60
Seasonings	Other Items	20
Special Warishita Sauce	Other Items	120
Fresh Cream	Other Items	100

whole Heart foods - orders

Poison Hemlock x 10

Reward	Rarity	From
3,000	☆☆	Madonna of the Greengrocers

Dendrobium x 2

Reward	Rarity	From
1,000	☆☆☆	Madonna of the Greengrocers

Curry Rice x 4

Reward	Rarity	From
500	☆☆	Madonna of the Greengrocers

Nectar x 8

Reward	Rarity	From
300	☆	Madonna of the Greengrocers

The Happy skip grocery - stock

Item	Type	Price
Blueberries	Usable Items	40
Bigberries	Usable Items	100
Blackberries	Usable Items	60
Aquaberries	Usable Items	30
Basil	Usable Items	30
Fresh Sage	Usable Items	150
Hot Chocolate	Usable Items	50
Glowstick	Usable Items	90
Vile Goop	Usable Items	300

The Happy skip grocery - orders

Red Seed x 5

Reward	Rarity	From
500	☆	High-Spirited Girl

Blue Seed x 5

Reward	Rarity	From
600	☆	High-Spirited Girl

Bizarre Fruit x 1

Reward	Rarity	From
2,000	☆☆	High-Spirited Girl

Perfect Berries x 4

Reward	Rarity	From
400	☆☆	High-Spirited Girl

AN AUDIENCE AT ASTRAL CASTLE

The king welcomes you warmly to his castle and sends you to wait on the second floor while the remedy is prepared. There, you find a treasure chest with Health Seeds, and a harvesting point that you can't harvest without Reimi. (Despite the message about "rare items," it contains mostly mundane recovery items, but the EXP bonus for harvesting it is unusually high.)

When you head downstairs to collect the remedy, you'll discover that it's been stolen by Black Eagle, the notorious bandit. Edge vows to catch Black Eagle and storms out of the castle, but you should storm right back in to search the chest behind the king's throne. The Famed Sword "Veinslay" is significantly stronger than any other weapon available to Edge at this point in the game.

BOSS

Black Eagle

HP · *37916*	EXP · *871*
Fol · *2,031*	Race · *Humanoid*
Resistant To · --	
Weak Against · --	

DROPS
Attack Seeds

The easiest way to beat Black Eagle is with a combination of Blindsides and Rush Mode combos. Begin by launching Black Eagle up with a directional combo, then reposition Edge and be ready for when he charges to unleash a Blindside. After you score with a Blindside, get in three good hits and then launch into your best special art combo to pile on the hurt. A few cycles of that should charge up Edge's Rush Gauge, allowing him to unleash a Rush Mode combo for a few thousand points of damage. (Just because Edge is alone doesn't mean that his Rush Mode combos are any less effective— he'll simply do all of the parts himself instead of passing it off to an ally.)

Facing Black Eagle in the Colosseum

No one in Astral City seems to know much, so hop a barge back to Tatroi. There, you'll find two witnesses who have seen Black Eagle: the Unlucky Old Woman south of the statue, and the Manly and Upright Warrior standing near the entrance to the colosseum. Only after you've spoken to both does the clerk allow you to enter the colosseum. Edge must now fight Black Eagle one-on-one, so make sure he's fully rested and his equipment is up to date before the battle begins.

UNFINISHED BUSINESS IN TATROI AND ASTRAL CITY

After your colosseum victory, tuck Reimi in for the night and head outside to get some fresh air. The next morning, Reimi rejoins you, and a new quest presents itself. Before you rush off to cross the Astral Desert south of Tatroi, you may want to spend some time accepting and completing the many new side quests that have opened up in Astral City and Tatroi.

If you want to get a jump on things, accept all of the Astral City quests, and pick up a Sweet Fruit in Astral City at the Whole Heart Foods shop. Head to Tatroi to finish the "Locked Out" and "The Stray Carrot" quests, and then accept all of the new quests available there. Raise your Entomology and Ornithology skills as much as you can and head back to the Calnus, battling Axe Beaks and Honeybees along the way. Take the coastal route so you can give the Sweet Fruit to the girl on the docks (finishing yet another quest), then grab the Seafarer's Treasure on the nearby beach. Visit the Calnus to fix the Music Box, then head on back to Tatroi and hit the newly reset harvesting and mining points on the way. You can finish all of the remaining quests when you reach Tropp.

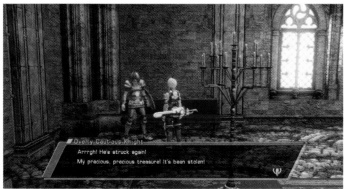

❖ QUESTS IN ASTRAL CITY

SIDE QUESTS

LOCKED OUT

REWARD: *300 EXP, 14 Party SP*

Speak to the Careless Shopkeeper near the fountain in the Astral City square. She hopes to reopen her shop, but can't find the keys, which she apparently lost at Gordeau's Spirits in Tatroi. Don't waste time searching the pub; just talk to the Tavern Bartender who is waiting outside of the door in Tatroi near the statue. Once you return the Weapon Shop Key, Treasure Hunter Weapons is once again open for business! The stock contains a Sylph's Saber weapon for Faize and Astral Armor for Faize and Edge.

MUSICAL MENDING

REWARD: *1,000 EXP, 45 Party SP, Recipe Memo 06*

The Teary-Eyed Girl outside The King's Inn has broken her music box. With Welch's help, it'll be easy to fix; the Music Box is a level 1 Engineering recipe (learned by pairing Bacchus and Meracle) requiring only the girl's Broken Music Box and a single Repair Kit. Repair Kits are sold at the Tool 'R' Us store in Tatroi for 100 fol.

THE LATEST BEAUTY FAD

REWARD: *1,000 EXP, 46 Party SP*

The Heavily Made-Up Lady north of the fountain wants ten Peryton Droppings, which can be earned by battling Axe Beak foes. Meracle's Ornithology skill makes winning them easier, so boost it up as much as you can. There's a good spot east of the bridge in the Northeast Astralian Continent where you can easily arrange an ambush of two or three Axe Beaks, which increases the odds of getting items to drop.

THE STRAY CARROT

REWARD: *1,200 EXP, 48 Party SP*

Talk to the Overly-Cautious Knight who appears in the second floor of Astral Castle after saving Reimi. He'll ask you to find his stolen… Carrot Doll?! Whatever!

You'll find it in the pub at Tatroi, in the pocket of the Manly and Upright Warrior. You'll need to equip Bandit's Gloves and have your Pickpocketing skill at level 6 or higher to snatch it.

TREASURE HUNTER WEAPONS - STOCK LIST

Item	Type	Price
Blessed Sword	Weapon	700
Bastard Sword	Weapon	11,000
Torch Bow	Weapon	800
Sylph's Saber	Weapon	19,800
Dragonscale Armor	Weapon	3,500
Bronto Armor	Armor	3,800
Astral Armor	Armor	6,000
Mystic Chainmail	Armor	1,000
Blizzard Protector	Armor	1,200
Streaked Chainmail	Armor	2,400

TREASURE HUNTER WEAPONS - ORDER LIST

Platinum x 4

Reward	Rarity	From
5,000	☆☆ *	Careless Shopkeeper

Meteorite x 2

Reward	Rarity	From
3,000	☆☆☆	Careless Shopkeeper

Ruby x 2

Reward	Rarity	From
4,000	☆☆	Careless Shopkeeper

Icecrusher Sword x 1

Reward	Rarity	From
3,000	☆☆	Careless Shopkeeper

⁙ QUESTS IN TATROI

MISSING BROTHER

REWARD: *300 EXP, 50 Party SP*

Fez, in the Twin Books skill shop, wants you to find his missing brother and deliver a note to him. You'll find him waiting at the docks in the city of Tropp, but he won't be able to find his way back until you're able to clear out all the Astral Desert quicksand by completing the two Sand Bird quests later in the game. When the quicksand is gone, he'll head straight back to Tatroi. There, he'll open his own counter in the Twin Books skill shop, and sell the rare skill manuals for HP Boost, MP Boost, No Guard, and Auto Healing.

THE SEAFARER'S TREASURE

REWARD: *400 EXP, 22 Party SP, Seafarer's Harpoon*

The Dutiful Sailor in the east part of town lost an Old Pendant at sea and hopes that it has since washed up on the shore. You'll find it in the Northeast Astralian Continent, on the beach closest to the Calnus. Your reward for returning it is the Seafarer's Harpoon, a weapon for a future party member.

CRAZY FOR GRAPE JUICE

REWARD: *800 EXP, 50 Party SP*

The Fruit-Crazy Old Man south of Tatroi's central statue wants to special order some grape juice from Tropp. You'll find the juice dealer in Tropp's Weapon Shop, and he'll sell you a bottle for 300 Fol. Bring it back to claim your reward.

THE SHODDY DOLL

REWARD: *400 EXP, 42 Party SP*

Speak to the Shadowy Dollmaker southwest of the statue, and he'll give you a Wooden Doll to deliver to an inn patron in Tropp. The woman you bring it to won't be happy, but you'll receive your reward when you return to the Dollmaker all the same. He'll then offer you the "In Search of Anessa" quest.

IN SEARCH OF ANESSA

REWARD: *800 EXP, 38 Party SP*

When you complete "The Shoddy Doll" quest, the Shadowy Dollmaker offers this follow-up quest. The girl you're looking for is Anessa the Tomboy, hanging out by the lamppost northeast of the barge in Astral City.

❖ QUESTS IN TATROI

THE FIRST ERRAND

REWARD: 150 EXP, 30 Party SP, Ultimate Bomb x 2

At her Tatroi home, Jasmine, Queen of Inventors sends you on a series of item-gathering errands. To finish the first one, bring her ten pieces of Fresh Sage. You'll find your reward in the open chest behind you.

THE SECOND ERRAND

REWARD: 300 EXP, 32 Party SP, HP Absorption Unit x 4

After completing the first task, speak to Jasmine for your next mission: gather nine Bee Stingers. The Entomology skill should make it easier to squeeze them out of the local Honeybees.

THE THIRD ERRAND

REWARD: 600 EXP, 32 Party SP, Time Stopper x 1

For the final errand (for a while, at least), Jasmine merely wants 13 pieces of Wool. You can purchase them at Mobius's One-Stop Shop in Astral City for a total cost of 2,600 Fol.

chaz's books - stock list

Item	Type	Price
Skill Manual "Anthropology"	Usable Items	800
Skill Manual "Botany"	Usable Items	900
Skill Manual "Parapsychology"	Usable Items	1,000
Skill Manual "HP Boost"	Usable Items	8,000
Skill Manual "MP Boost"	Usable Items	8,000
Skill Manual "No Guard"	Usable Items	3,000
Skill Manual "Auto Healing"	Usable Items	4,200

❖ QUESTS IN NORTHEAST ASTRALIAN CONTINENT

FOOD RUN

REWARD: 600 EXP, 42 Party SP, Recipe Memo 19

After curing Reimi and speaking to the cat-girl near the arch between central and eastern Tatroi, return to the Patiently Waiting Girl on the docks near the Calnus. She desperately desires a Sweet Fruit, which is sold at the food shop in Astral City. When you bring her one, she rewards you with the recipe for the Wisdom Bracelet.

MAP TREASURES

1. Silver Chalice x 1
2. Fainting Potion x 2
3. Attack Seeds x 1
4. Defense Seeds x 1
5. Bandit's Gloves x 1
6. 9856 Fol

MINING POINT ITEMS

Iron	Salamanderstone
Light Gem	Silver
Platinum	Sylphstone
Ruby	

HARVESTING POINT ITEMS

Bizarre Fruit	Seasonings
Poison Hemlock	Thornberries

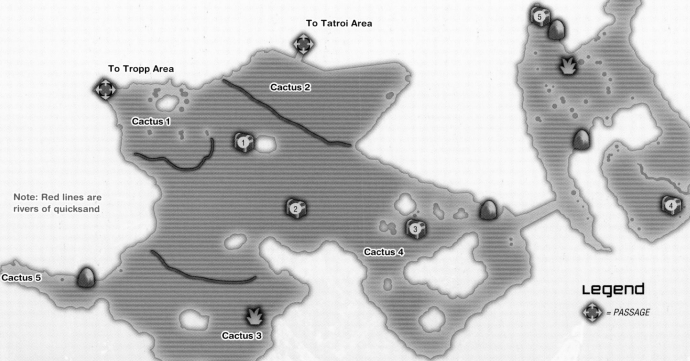

To Tatroi Area

To Tropp Area

Cactus 2

Cactus 1

Note: Red lines are
rivers of quicksand

Cactus 5

Cactus 4

Cactus 3

Legend

= PASSAGE

MONSTERS

HONEYBEE
HP · 2460   EXP · 108
Fol · 90   Race · Insect
Resistant To · --
Weak Against · Earth
DROPS
Accuracy Seeds, Bee Stinger, Aquaberries

KOBOLD BANDIT
HP · 3084   EXP · 162
Fol · 189   Race · Animal
Resistant To · Fire
Weak Against · --
DROPS
All-Purpose Ceramic

DESERT OGRE
HP · 7205   EXP · 409
Fol · 949   Race · Animal
Resistant To · Wind
Weak Against · Earth
DROPS
Attack Seeds, Bigberries

UNICORN WOLF
HP · 2776   EXP · 108
Fol · 111   Race · Animal
Resistant To · Fire
Weak Against · Water
DROPS
Saber-Toothed Tiger Fang, Wolf Fang,
Blueberries

SKELETON ARMOR
HP · 3930   EXP · 236
Fol · 179   Race · Undead
Resistant To · --
Weak Against · Fire, Light
DROPS
Defense Seeds, Vile Goop, Solid Protector

THIEVING SCUMBAG
HP · 3275   EXP · 163
Fol · 237   Race · Humanoid
Resistant To · --
Weak Against · --
DROPS
tri-Emblum, Hot Chocolate, Natto

CROSSING THE DEADLY SANDS ON BUNNYBACK

The entrance to the Astral Desert is in the southwest corner of the Tatroi Area, but you won't get anywhere near Tropp without a Bunny. If you attempt to cross the flowing quicksand on foot, you'll sink into it and reappear at the entrance of the area. You'll need a big fluffy Bunny to stay afloat.

Cross the bridge north towards the central part of the Tatroi Area, and hunt down the giant pink Bunny. Circle behind it and press ✖ or Ⓐ to hop on. You can hop off with ⬤ or Ⓑ, but the Bunny runs away, forcing you to catch a new one.

While on a Bunny, you won't be able to enter the menu or use Reimi and Bacchus's Harvesting and Mining skills. You can still open treasure chests and pick up glowing white items with ✖ or Ⓐ, although positioning the Bunny in front of them can be a challenge. When you encounter an enemy, battles unfold as normal, and you'll still be riding a Bunny when you return to the field.

The chest at the oasis holds something cool: a Silver Chalice that acts as a bottomless Blueberry, recharging after every fifth fight. (Not that Blueberries are in short supply or anything…)

TWO PATHS THROUGH THE ASTRAL DESERT

There are many rivers of quicksand in the Astral Desert, but only the first one completely blocks your path. Once you cross it, you'll have a choice to make: continue hopping west to Tropp, or ditch the Bunny and cross the desert on foot. Going on foot allows you to extract several rare and valuable items from the harvesting and mining points, including soon-to-be-valuable Sylphstone and Salamanderstone. However, hoofing it makes monsters harder to avoid and forces you to take a detour through the Cave to the Purgatorium in order to reach Tropp.

If you choose to explore on foot, make sure to scour the coastline for the white sparkles of washed-up items. They are the same things that wash up on the Northeast Astralian Continent, but another chance to find Platinum is always welcome.

⁜ ASTRAL DESERT QUEST

SIDE QUESTS

THE UNOFFICIAL CACTUS RESCUE QUEST

REWARD: *Potent Attack Seeds x 1, Intelligence Seeds x 2, Potent Health Seeds x 1, and Magic Seeds x 2*

Rescuing the dying cacti of the Astral Desert doesn't go into your quest log or count towards the quest-related achievements, but it nevertheless reaps you some nice rewards. When you reach Tropp, speak to the Curious Youth (who should be the person closest to the entrance), and he'll give you an Empty Bucket. Grab a Bunny in the Tropp Area and hop back to the desert, where you can fill the bucket at either of the two freshwater oases. (You can both fill the bucket and use it while on the Bunny, so don't ditch your ride.)

A full bucket can water a single cactus, but the watering won't take unless you visit the cacti in a precise order. Begin with the cactus nearest to the entrance to the Tropp Area. Once rejuvenated, its arms point to the next cactus. Fill up the bucket again, cross the quicksand, and save cactus #2. Once again, the cactus points to your next target. When all five cacti have been rejuvenated, the final one rains a treasure trove of seeds on you: one Potent Attack Seeds, two Intelligence Seeds, one Potent Health Seeds, and two Magic Seeds. Not a bad day's work!

MAP TREASURES

Tropp Area
1. Magic Capacitor x 1
2. Bigberries x 3
3. Holy Water x 1
4. 4445 Fol
5. Resurrection Elixir x 1
6. [Ice Barrier] Barrier Spiritwater x 1

HARVESTING POINT ITEMS

Tropp Area
Ash
Blue Seed
Dendrobium
Ebony
Fresh Sage
Lemon
Oak
Red Seed

MINING POINT ITEMS

Tropp Area
Gold
Iron
Light Gem
Ruby
Salamanderstone
Silver
Thunder Gem

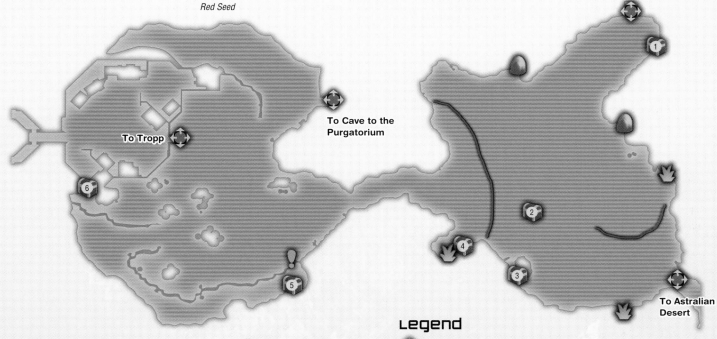

To Cave to the Purgatorium

To Cave to the Purgatorium

To Tropp

To Astralian Desert

To Purgatorium Area

Legend

 = PASSAGE

 = INTERACTION POINT

To Tropp Area

To Tropp Area

MAP TREASURES

Cave to the Purgatorium
7. Health Seeds x 1
8. Basil x 2
9. Riot Potion x 3

HARVESTING POINT ITEMS

Cave to the Purgatorium
Caterpillar Fungus
Ebony
Fresh Sage
Magic Seeds
Poison Hemlock
White Rice

MINING POINT ITEMS

Cave to the Purgatorium
Coal
Shadestone
Silver
Sylphstone
Thunder Gem

Monsters

WAVING PINCERS
HP · 4510   EXP · 162
Fol · 163   Race · Insect
Resistant To · Water
Weak Against · Thunder

DROPS
Protection Seeds, Rotten Fish, Warped Carapace

ALBERO DI ANIMA
HP · 6550   EXP · 354
Fol · 290   Race · Plant
Resistant To · Earth
Weak Against · Fire

DROPS
Bigberries, Aquaberries, Basil, Nectar

AXE BEAK
HP · 3393   EXP · 189
Fol · 151   Race · Bird
Resistant To · Wind
Weak Against · Earth

DROPS
Rotten Fish, Basil, Giant Bird Feather, Common Egg, Peryton Droppings

VOMITING GEL
HP · 5119   EXP · 183
Fol · 248   Race · Plant
Resistant To · Water
Weak Against · Earth

DROPS
Natto, Vile Goop, Blackberries, Glowstick

SKELETON ARMOR
HP · 3930   EXP · 236
Fol · 179   Race · Undead
Resistant To · --
Weak Against · Fire, Light

DROPS
Defense Seeds, Vile Goop, Solid Protector

CORPSE BAT
HP · 3890   EXP · 97
Fol · 165   Race · Bird
Resistant To · --
Weak Against · Fire

DROPS
Protection Seeds, Raw Animal Meat, Lizardskin

DESERT OGRE
HP · 7205   EXP · 409
Fol · 949   Race · Animal
Resistant To · Wind
Weak Against · Earth

DROPS
Attack Seeds, Bigberries

HARPY
HP · 4090   EXP · 226
Fol · 304   Race · Bird
Resistant To · Wind
Weak Against · Thunder

DROPS
Cashmere, Glowstick, Common Egg, Silk

THIEVING SCUMBAG
HP · 3275   EXP · 163
Fol · 237   Race · Humanoid
Resistant To · --
Weak Against · --

DROPS
tri-Emblum, Hot Chocolate, Natto

MANDRAGORA
HP · 4648   EXP · 187
Fol · 241   Race · Plant
Resistant To · Earth
Weak Against · Fire

DROPS
Faerie Embroidery Thread, Nectar, Dwarven Embroidery Thread, Mixed Syrup

HOP-HOP-HOPPING TO THE CITY OF TROPP

If you kept your Bunny, you can leap right over the river of quicksand that splits the Tropp Area's dune-filled east from its coastal west. Collecting the area's treasures should be a breeze, until you need to ditch your Bunny to use the Fire Ring on Chest #6. You can always catch another nearby, in the lightly wooded area south of Tropp.

Even on Bunny-back, it can be hard to avoid new enemies like the symbol-using Harpies and wide-stomping Mandragora. If you're hurting, head straight for Tropp, where you can heal and save at an inn, and buy new weapons and skills. However, there isn't much happening in Tropp, plot-wise; you'll need to visit the Purgatorium to advance the story.

TRAVERSING THE CAVE TO THE PURGATORIUM

If you ditched your Bunny in the Astral Desert, you won't be able to cross the quicksand in the eastern side of the Tropp Area, and instead you must make your way towards the northern cave. The Cave to the Purgatorium connects both halves of the Tropp Area, as well as the Purgatorium Area to the north. The game's next plot point occurs at the Purgatorium but, if you want to heal and buy equipment first, travel west to exit the cave near Tropp's main gates.

There are a few interesting items to find in the cave, including the first appearance of Coal at mining points. You can turn Coal and Iron into Steel with a simple Smithery recipe, and use that to finish the recipe for Faize's Elastic Rapier, among others. You can also snag Crimson Fireflies by running up to the glowing red dots flying around the cave passages and pressing ✖ or Ⓐ to swipe one.

The cave also presents a few new perils in the form of Vomiting Gel and Corpse Bat enemies. Both are capable of slowing down your offense by inflicting your fighters with the fog condition.
You can wait until the end of the battle when the fog clears automatically or, if the situation is dire, clear it mid-battle with a Glowstick.

Map Treasures

Tropp Area
1. Fresh Sage x 2
2. Recipe Memo 09 x 1
3. Resurrection Elixir x 1

Legend

 = SAVE SPHERE

 = PASSAGE

 = INTERACTION POINT

Harvesting Point Items

Lemon
Poison Hemlock
Ripe Berries
Seasonings
Thornberries
White Rice

Mining Point Items

Aluminum
Coal [PS3-only]
Iron
Light Gem
Shadestone
Thunder Gem

To Purgatorium: 1F

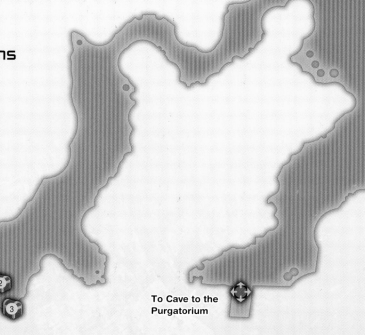

To Cave to the Purgatorium

A PEEK AT THE PURGATORIUM

To find your first real clue about Sarah's disappearance, take the Cave to the Purgatorium north to the Purgatorium Area. This small area is home to new Spirit Priest enemies, as well as mining points that offer your first chance to dig up Aluminum. Don't miss the beautiful cove to the west, where you'll find picturesque schools of jellyfish and a chest containing Recipe Memo 09 (Mental Potion).

Monsters

THIEVING SCUMBAG
HP · **3275**	EXP · **163**
Fol · **237**	Race · **Humanoid**

Resistant To · --
Weak Against · --

DROPS
tri-Emblum, Hot Chocolate, Natto

MANDRAGORA
HP · **4648**	EXP · **187**
Fol · **241**	Race · **Plant**

Resistant To · **Earth**
Weak Against · **Fire**

DROPS
Faerie Embroidery Thread, Nectar, Dwarven Embroidery Thread, Mixed Syrup

SYDONAIST ALPHA
HP · **2513**	EXP · **114**
Fol · **117**	Race · **Humanoid**

Resistant To · --
Weak Against · --

DROPS
Cloudy Cider, Aquaberries, DANGER! DO NOT DRINK!, Static Cider

HARPY
HP · **4090**	EXP · **226**
Fol · **304**	Race · **Bird**

Resistant To · **Wind**
Weak Against · **Thunder**

DROPS
Cashmere, Glowstick, Common Egg, Silk

SPIRIT PRIEST
HP · **3230**	EXP · **228**
Fol · **304**	Race · **Humanoid**

Resistant To · --
Weak Against · --

DROPS
Lezard's Flask, Glowstick, Pumpkin Extract, Healing Card, Pumpkin Cider

SYDONAIST BETA
HP · **2513**	EXP · **125**
Fol · **141**	Race · **Humanoid**

Resistant To · --
Weak Against · --

DROPS
Intelligence Seeds, Aquaberries, Healing Card, Poison Cider, Frozen Cider

Sydonaist Alpha and Beta will not appear on the first visit to the Purgatorium Area.

When you enter the Purgatorium, you'll find one of Sarah's feathers, but no means to proceed deeper into the structure. Meracle suggests you talk to Eleyna in Tropp, and while Eleyna may not have been home previously, she'll be expecting you now. If you haven't visited Tropp, take the Cave to the Purgatorium's west exit to arrive just east of its gates.

More info about the Purgatorium is revealed in full in a few pages, but those who just can't wait to explore can raid the three accessible chests to uncover the skill manuals for the Trap Evasion and Steal skills, as well as a three-pack of Wide-Range EM Bombs.

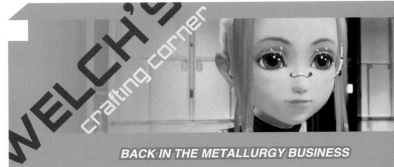

WELCH'S crafting corner

BACK IN THE METALLURGY BUSINESS

Between the Aluminum in the Purgatorium Area and the Coal in the Cave to the Purgatorium, you finally have the materials you need to start making weapons again. Reimi's Composite Bow is a top choice; it's a level 6 Smithery recipe that can be developed by Reimi, Edge, and Meracle. The recipe upgrades the Alien Arc bow, and requires only a single piece of Aluminum, as well as the Carbon Fiber (3 pieces) and Aramid Fiber (2 pieces) sold in Tatroi.

Many mid-level recipes require Steel, which isn't ever found in the wild. If you haven't created the recipe for Steel yet, pair Edge with Myuria and they'll whip it up. Steel requires a mix of Iron and Coal, the latter of which can be found at mining points in the Cave to the Purgatorium and (in the PS3 version) the Purgatorium Area. Edge's Venom Sword (a level 3 Smithery recipe) requires one piece of Aluminum and 3 pieces of Steel, which means you need to gather six pieces of Coal to make the Steel. Faize's Elastic Rapier (a level 4 Smithery recipe) also requires three pieces of Steel, so you'll probably have to pick one or the other; both provide roughly equivalent boosts over your current weapons.

Windswept Inn: 1F

Morgan's Weapons

Windswept Inn: 2F

To Eleyna's House

To Tropp Area

Legend

- = SAVE SPHERE
- = SHOP
- = PASSAGE
- = NPC

Map Treasures

1. [Dark Barrier] Skill Manual "Augury" x 1
2. [Dark Barrier] Anti-Fog Amulet x 1
3. Bizarre Fruit x 1
4. Stamina Pie x 2

Pickpocketing

a. Curious Youth	Mixed Syrup x 1
b. Haughty Girl	Mixed Syrup x 1
c. Tough-Talking Girl	Shadestone x 1
d. Retired Explorer	Gambleberries x 1
e. Quick-Fleeing Man	Speed Pie x 1
f. Yawning Girl	Sushi x 1
g. Overweight Woman	Sweet Fruit x 1
h. Man Who's All Talk	Pickled Pepper Potion x 1
i. Li'l Pumpkin	Pumpkin Extract x 1
j. Chaz	80 Fol
k. Sharp Cat	Strength Potion x 1
l. Sprightly Old Man	Bunny Feed x 1

Windswept Inn

m. Pathologically Petulant Woman	Fire Paint x 1

Morgan's Weapons

n. Out-of-Work Sailor	Anti-Paralysis Amulet x 1

Eleyna's Hideout (not Shown on Map)

o. Eleyna	Disintegration Stone x 1

*The above area cannot be accessed until after completing certain game events.

A FLURRY OF QUESTS, OLD AND NEW

You'll be hit by both updates to old quests and several new side quest opportunities as soon as you step through the arch to the City of Tropp. The Curious Youth who's waiting near the gate gives you an Empty Bucket so you can begin the unofficial cactus-rescue quest (see the Astral Desert section). But if you talk to him again, he'll eat your Note from Fez, messing up "The Missing Brother" quest (even though it has nothing to do with him). If you lose the note, you'll have to go back to Tatroi to get a new one. You can find the missing brother on the docks in the west part of town, although he won't be in any hurry to go home.

The youth ate the note from Fez!

The next two young women you encounter both have quests for you: "A Symbol of Bravery" and "Grooming is Essential." A woman a short distance to the north offers a third, called "Otherworldly Diet." Bring the Wooden Doll to the woman in the inn, and you can not only progress "The Shoddy Doll" quest, but also trigger the start of the new "The Second Doll" quest.

Finally, visit the weapon shop, where the Out-of-Work Sailor sells you the Famous Grape Juice for 300 Fol, allowing you to complete the "Crazy for Grape Juice" quest. You can visit him later to buy a bottle for yourself (it restores 70% of a character's HP). More details on each of the new quests can be found below.

GIFTS AND GUIDANCE FROM ELEYNA

Eleyna's house is in the northeast part of town. But as soon as you open the door, a series of events unfold that end with your party in an underground hideout near the Tropp Area's northern beach.

After Eleyna collapses, examine her body to get the collections entry for her Maiden's Staff. You can also pickpocket her Disintegration Stone, if that's how you roll! To wake her, speak to Reimi, Faize, and Reimi again. Eleyna then provides your party with a Lamp of Guidance that allows you to unlock the Purgatorium doors. But that isn't Eleyna's only gift; Myuria is waiting outside, ready to join your party at last.

HITTING THE SHOPS OF TROPP

Tropp only has two stores, but they both have some welcome finds. At Morgan's Weapons, you can pick up Vermilion Claws for Meracle and a Wand of Wonder for Lymle, and both should provide a significant boost over their current weapons. The Volcanic Chainmail should make for a nice armor upgrade for both Reimi and Meracle.

Morgan's Weapons may not have anything for Myuria, but Rascal's Guild has plenty of nice skills for your newest recruit. Start with Demonology, her exclusive monster-drop booster. Then, pick up the powerful new Convert skill, which allows her to drain her HP to refill her MP. That combos nicely with skills like Auto Healing and HP Boost, which are also available here. It's possible for Faize, Edge, and Bacchus to learn Convert as well, and Meracle and Edge can find a new skill in the form of Appetite. Appetite isn't very good, but it won't waste a skill slot and is pretty cheap to level up, so you might as well get it for both.

MORGAN'S WEAPONS - STOCK LIST

Item	Type	Price
Silvance	Weapon	5,000
Icicle Rapier	Weapon	4,000
Sylph's Saber	Weapon	19,800
Wand of Wonder	Weapon	5,800
Vermilion Claws	Weapon	5,800
Bronto Armor	Armor	3,800
Streaked Chainmail	Armor	2,400
Volcanic Chainmail	Armor	7,700
Comet Robe	Armor	2,400
Blueberries	Usable Items	40
Red Herb	Usable Items	100

MORGAN'S WEAPONS - ORDERS

Aluminum x 5

Reward	Rarity	From
1,300	☆	Sharp-Eyed Man

Thunder Gem x 5

Reward	Rarity	From
9,000	☆☆	Sharp-Eyed Man

Sylphstone x 3

Reward	Rarity	From
18,000	☆☆☆☆	Sharp-Eyed Man

Composite Bow x 1

Reward	Rarity	From
2,000	☆☆☆	Sharp-Eyed Man

Ruby Wand x 1

Reward	Rarity	From
2,000	☆☆	Sharp-Eyed Man

rascal's Guild - stock

Item	Type	Price
Skill Manual "Anthropology"	Usable Items	800
Skill Manual "Botany"	Usable Items	900
Skill Manual "Entomology"	Usable Items	600
Skill Manual "Parapsychology"	Usable Items	1,000
Skill Manual "Ornithology"	Usable Items	1,100
Skill Manual "Demonology"	Usable Items	2,200
Skill Manual "Appetite"	Usable Items	1,800
Skill Manual "Chain Combos"	Usable Items	3,000
Skill Manual "HP Boost"	Usable Items	8,000

Item	Type	Price
Skill Manual "Critical Hit"	Usable Items	4,400
Skill Manual "First Aid"	Usable Items	2,000
Skill Manual "Auto Healing"	Usable Items	4,200
Skill Manual "Stun"	Usable Items	3,500
Skill Manual "Fury Boost"	Usable Items	4,000
Skill Manual "Elusion"	Usable Items	1,000
Skill Manual "Taunt"	Usable Items	800
Skill Manual "Convert"	Usable Items	2,500
Skill Manual "Hide"	Usable Items	1,200

⁛ QUESTS IN TROPP

A SYMBOL OF BRAVERY

REWARD: 100 EXP, 40 Party SP, Scumbag Slayer x 1

The Tough-Talking Girl in Tropp's central square needs a Purgatorium Stone to win the respect of her peers. You'll find it on the Purgatorium's first floor; walk straight up the stairs from the entrance and it should be to your left at the end of the staircase.

GROOMING IS ESSENTIAL

REWARD: 2,000 EXP, 36 Party SP, Recipe Memo 22

The Haughty Girl speaking to the Tough-Talking Girl wants something too. Her Feathered Comb is a level 2 Crafting recipe invented by Meracle, Myuria and Lymle. It requires four Giant Bird Feathers and a splash of Lacquer. Make one for her, and she'll reward you with a ton of EXP and the recipe for the Anti-Fog Amulet.

OTHERWORLDLY DIET

REWARD: 900 EXP, 50 Party SP

The woman north of the inn is going on a diet, and wants Reimi to cook her something special. The key world is "Otherworldly," which should point you to three servings of Reimi's Otherworldly Cuisine recipe. You'll need to rack up plenty of Insect Legs, Insect Eggs, and Rotten Fish from monster drops, but you can buy Vinegar in Tatroi if you're short on that.

THE SECOND DOLL

REWARD: 1,000 EXP, 46 Party SP, Magical Clay x 2

The Pathologically Petulant Woman in the Windswept Inn spits upon your Wooden Doll, and offers you the "Second Doll" quest instead. When you

go back to the Shadowy Dollmaker in Tatroi, he won't begin work on the doll until you complete his new "In Search of Anessa" quest. After bringing Anessa home, briefly visit another game area (such as the east side of Tatroi), and when you return he'll have completed the Exquisite Wooden Doll.

MYURIA THE INTRACTABLE

If you're thinking of taking a trip back to the Calnus, now would be a fine time to do it. You can report your side quest progress at Tatroi, whip up that Music Box, Feathered Comb, Otherworldly Cuisine, and make a few new items for personal use. You'll also be able to invent many new recipes by adding Myuria to your Invention Groups and resetting all the harvesting and mining points will give you another chance to get Aluminum and Coal.

Returning to the Calnus also lets you trigger a Private Action with a very brief window of availability. You'll find Bacchus and Myuria hanging out together in one of the Crew Quarters rooms, and if you join the conversation, Edge grows closer to both characters, and Bacchus raises his opinion of Edge. This Private Action is also a prerequisite for earning one of the secret endings, and if you don't trigger it before you complete the Purgatorium, you'll never have another opportunity.

Planet ROAK: THE PURGATORIUM

Map Treasures

Purgatorium: 1F
1. Skill Manual "Trap Evasion" x 1
2. Skill Manual "Steal" x 1
3. Wide-Range EM Bomb x 3
4. Flare Robe x 1
5. Poison Relief Unit x 2
6. [Fire Barrier] Lightning Sword x 1

Note:

 = shadow barriers

= light crystals

 = statues

Legend

 = PASSAGE

To Purgatorium: B1

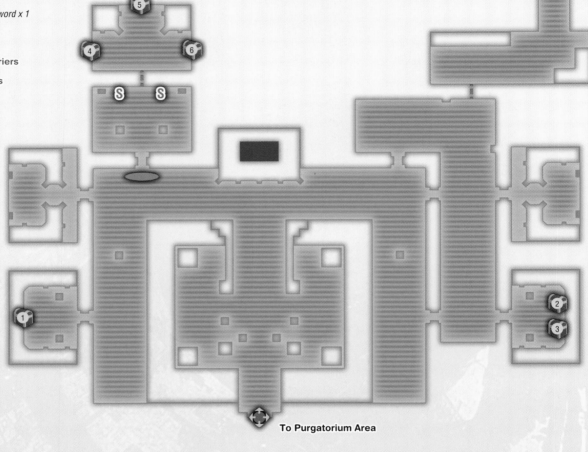

To Purgatorium Area

Monsters

CORPSE BAT		
HP · 3890	EXP · 97	
Fol · 165	Race · Bird	

Resistant To · --
Weak Against · Fire

DROPS
Protection Seeds, Raw Animal Meat, Lizardskin

SYDONAIST ALPHA		
HP · 2513	EXP · 114	
Fol · 117	Race · Humanoid	

Resistant To · --
Weak Against · --

DROPS
Cloudy Cider, Aquaberries, DANGER! DO NOT DRINK!, Static Cider

FIRE CORPSE		
HP · 5527	EXP · 214	
Fol · 156	Race · Undead	

Resistant To · Fire
Weak Against · Water

DROPS
Fire Gem, Holy Water

SUCCUBUS		
HP · 4523	EXP · 863	
Fol · 299	Race · Demon	

Resistant To · --
Weak Against · --

DROPS
Manacloth, Velvet Ribbon, Silent Cider

SPIRIT PRIEST		
HP · 3230	EXP · 228	
Fol · 304	Race · Humanoid	

Resistant To · --
Weak Against · --

DROPS
Lezard's Flask, Glowstick, Pumpkin Extract, Healing Card, Pumpkin Cider

SYDONAIST BETA		
HP · 2513	EXP · 125	
Fol · 141	Race · Humanoid	

Resistant To · --
Weak Against · --

DROPS
Intelligence Seeds, Aquaberries, Healing Card, Poison Cider, Frozen Cider

MAGE CHIMERA		
HP · 9646	EXP · 576	
Fol · 532	Race · Demon	

Resistant To · Earth
Weak Against · Wind

DROPS
Snakeskin, Aquaberries, Raw Animal Meat, Lizardskin

132

Map Treasures

Purgatorium: B1
7. [Ivy Barrier] Recipe Memo 24 x 1
8. Holy Water x 3
9. Bow of Wisdom x 1
10. Runic Metal x 3, Bracteate x 1, Quantum Processor x 1, Fire Gem x 4

Note:

⬭ = shadow barriers

◆ = light crystals

Ⓢ = statues

Legend

✦ = PASSAGE

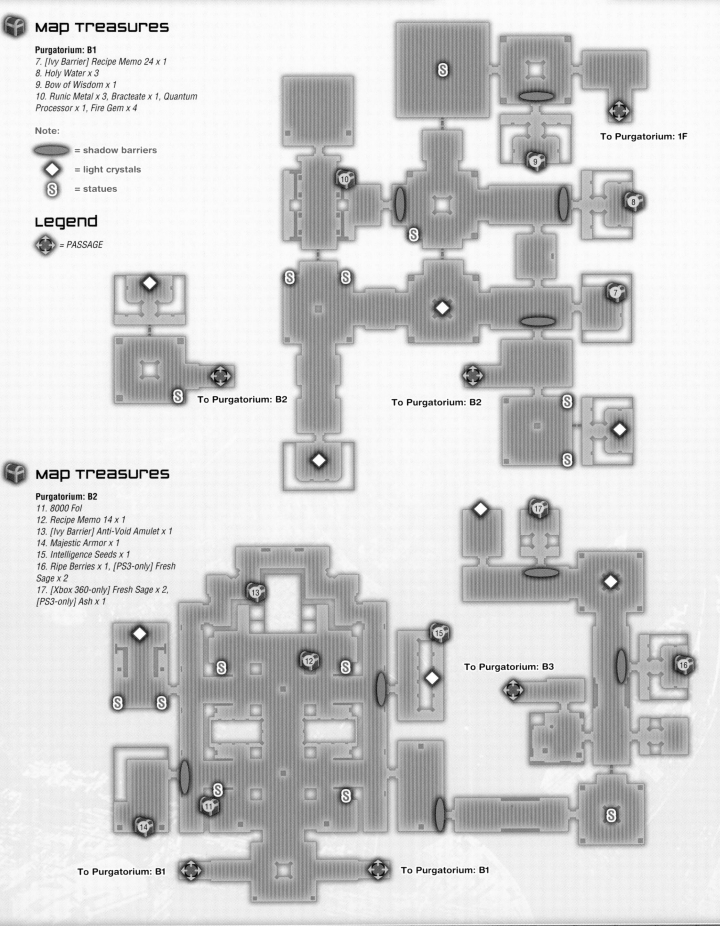

To Purgatorium: 1F

To Purgatorium: B2

To Purgatorium: B2

Map Treasures

Purgatorium: B2
11. 8000 Fol
12. Recipe Memo 14 x 1
13. [Ivy Barrier] Anti-Void Amulet x 1
14. Majestic Armor x 1
15. Intelligence Seeds x 1
16. Ripe Berries x 1, [PS3-only] Fresh Sage x 2
17. [Xbox 360-only] Fresh Sage x 2, [PS3-only] Ash x 1

To Purgatorium: B3

To Purgatorium: B1

To Purgatorium: B1

MAP TREASURES

Purgatorium: B3

18. *Skill Manual "Focus" x 1*
19. *Ancient Cannon x 1*
20. *Micro Hadron Collider x 1, [PS3-only]*
Wind Gem x 1
21. *Sylphide's Mail x 1*
22. *Folklore Plate x 1*

Note:

 = shadow barriers

 = light crystals

 = statues

Legend

 = *SAVE SPHERE*

= *PASSAGE*

= *RECOVERY SPHERE*

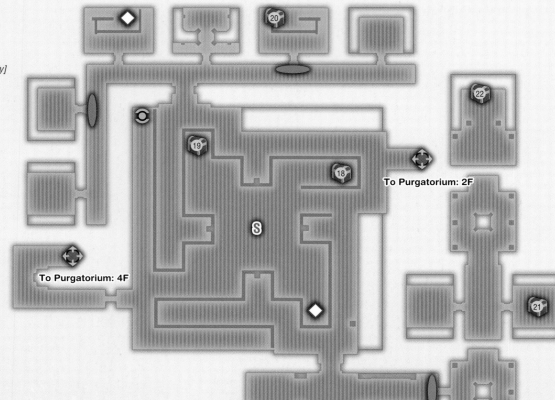

To Purgatorium: 2F

To Purgatorium: 4F

 MAP TREASURES

Purgatorium: B4

23. *[Light Barrier] [X360-only] Skill Manual "Savage Sparrows" x 1, [PS3-only] Skill Manual "Sunflare" x1*

To Purgatorium: 3F

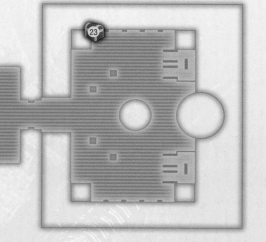

LIGHTING A PATH TO THE PURGATORIUM BASEMENT

Climb the staircase at the entrance to the Purgatorium, and find the shining Purgatorium Stone (needed for the "A Symbol of Bravery" side quest) just to your left when you near the Muah statues. You'll also find treasure rooms in the southwest and southeast corners of this floor, with the Skill Manual "Steal" being the best item in the bunch. When set as a battle skill, Steal allows Edge or Meracle to knock items out of monsters with standard attacks, making it a must for those pursuing side quests and difficult Item Creation recipes. Don't waste your skill points on Trap Evasion, which does nothing at this point in the game.

You'll notice a single unlit firepot in the northeast corner of the ground floor. Slide your Lamp of Guidance into it, opening the door to the lower floor. Since you don't have a way to cleanse the door of the shadow barrier to the northwest, you'll have to come back for the remaining three chests later.

HEEDING THE STATUES' COMMANDS

The B1 level of the Purgatorium is filled with unlit firepots, but if you light them willy-nilly, all you'll get is a surprise attack from a Flame Corpse. Look to the statue of a man with a glowing axe, which can always be found near unlit firepots. His ax points to the one you need to light, and when you light it, he turns to point to the next. When all the pots have been lit in the order dictated by the statue, the path appears.

Things get a little trickier in the third statue-puzzle room, where there are two statues pointing the way. You'll have to triangulate their directions to figure out which pot to light. For example, if one is pointing to the middle while another points south, you'll need to light the southwest pot.

THE FOUL QUEENS OF THE PURGATORIUM

You'll face a mostly new menagerie of foes in the Purgatorium, consisting of everything from giant chimeras to diminutive priests. Many fight with status conditions, including the Mage Chimera, which can transform a character into a pumpkin that can do little but roll away for the remainder of the status effect.

The Mage Chimera is splashy, but it's the Succubus that is the deadliest foe. In addition to her own fatal charms, the Succubus empowers every other enemy on the battlefield with her sheer presence. Eliminate her quickly with a barrage of special arts and symbols, then pick off the other foes at your leisure. When battling the Fire Corpses that are her frequent companions, it's a good idea to take control of your symbol-users directly, so you can make sure they are fighting with powerful water-type symbols or at least refraining from restoring the Fire Corpse's health with fire-type symbols.

While it may be tempting to flee whenever you see a Succubus, those who stick it out and fight them regularly can earn the ability to make an excellent Monster Jewel. The jewel offers significant ATK, DEF, and Max MP boosts.

BOSS

Guardian Beast

HP · *55733*   EXP · *5,940*
Fol · *4,626*   Race · *Demon*

Resistant To · *Light*
Weak Against · *Water, Fire, Thunder, Dark*

DROPS
Lezard's Flask

Winning the Light Ring from the Guardian Beast

The path unlocked by the pair of statues leads north to a room guarded by a powerful Guardian Beast. If your party is in bad shape, pitch a Tent before you open the door, as the battle begins as soon as the beast lays eyes on your party.

The Guardian Beast is a straightforward foe with a lot of hit points, but little in the way of unusual attacks. Use symbol-users to exploit its elemental weaknesses while you keep it on the ropes with constant strikes from Meracle or Edge. When it enters Rush Mode, try to strike at it from the side, which gives you some protection from its powerful leaps and lunges. This is a battle of endurance, so make sure your healers have plenty of MP to keep the attackers going. When the Guardian Beast finally falls, it transforms into a Light Ring that can penetrate the shadow barriers sometimes found over doors and chests.

BANISHING THE SHADOW BARRIERS

The good news: your Light Ring comes fully loaded. The bad news: it can only hold a single charge. You can refill your ring by draining the large white crystals found in the Purgatorium, but if you don't open the doors in a specific order, you could run out of light sources. This isn't the big deal it may seem to be; if you leave the Purgatorium and reenter, all of the light crystals will be fully recharged. So feel free to ignore the door to the B2 level and focus on opening the chests: the Bow of Wisdom on this floor and the Flare Robe in the first floor's treasure room definitely make the rest of the Purgatorium a little bit easier.

If you're determined to clear the Purgatorium in one pass, open the shadow barrier to the southeast first. This action gives you access to two more light crystals and allows you to reach the next floor down.

CLEARING THE B2 STATUE CHAMBER

The entire west side of the B2 map is a single platform where four statues look over ten different firepots. It's very easy to be misled by the layout of this room, particularly when the statues point towards the pots in the center. Before you light a pot, stand by it and rotate the camera until you've confirmed that every statue is pointing your way. When all the firepots have been lit in the correct order, stairs appear to the lower part of the level. If you haven't tapped the last level-B1 light crystal by taking the stairs to the southwest, do that now so you'll have enough light to both open the door to chest 14 (which contains the excellent Majestic Armor for Edge or Faize) and the door to the southeast section of the map.

In the southeast section, you'll encounter what seems to be a standard statue puzzle. However, once you light the first firepot, the statue quickly reveals the order of the three remaining firepots and then shuts itself down. Make sure your camera is pointing at the statue so you don't miss the first steps of the sequence.

DRAINING THE B3 WATERWAYS

At the center of the B3-level of the Purgatorium, you'll find a single statue that points to the eight firepots around it. The twist here is that at times the statue seems to point to already lit pots, which indicates that it's actually pointing

towards distant pots in the hallways to the north or south. There should never be more than one unlit pot in any one direction, so once you know that the pots could be in the hallways, you shouldn't have much trouble completing the sequence and draining the water from both the large central room and a few smaller rooms to the north.

When the water recedes, you'll reveal a recovery sphere, two chests (one of which holds a new Bacchus weapon), some light crystals, and the stairway to the Purgatorium's final floor. However, you will not reveal any way to access the southeast wing of this floor; to get past the ivy on the door, you'll need to come back with the Wind Ring later in the game.

BOSS

Tamiel

HP · **59099**	EXP · **4,778**
Fol · **14,129**	Race · **Other**

Resistant To · *Fire, Darkness*
Weak Against · *Water, Thunder*

DROPS
Fanatic's Staff

Thwarting Tamiel's Ambitions

After saving at the level-B4 save sphere, heal up and dine on a few of Reimi's finest entrees. As soon as you step through the door, you'll be attacked by a quartet of Sydonaists that quickly give way to an ambush by six more, and then a second Ambush by Tamiel himself. Tamiel can continue to summon Sydonaists throughout the battle, and killing them should always be priority one; it'll be hard to win if you are fighting off status conditions and your symbol-users are constantly being interfered with. If you do end up poisoned, cure it immediately, since it can take a toll in this long battle.

Unlike other bosses, Tamiel is vulnerable to juggles, stuns, and other side effects of Edge and Meracle's special arts combos. Early on, gang up on him with both characters and flip between them so you can take control of their individual Rush Modes whenever possible. Pile on the special art combo damage, and you should be able to keep Tamiel from doing much damage. Don't worry about MP; the Convert skill should ensure that Edge never runs out of it.

As he gets weaker, Tamiel becomes more aggressive. When he starts using his devastating Rage Reflection special art to cleave through your heroes with a pink energy blade, you'll have to rethink your strategy. Swap out

close-range fighters like Meracle and Faize for ranged fighters and symbol-users, and make sure everyone stays separated. Have Edge focus on clearing out the Sydonaists, and when Tamiel is the only foe on the board, try to attack him from behind, where it is easier to evade the Rage Reflection beam.

MAP TREASURES

1. Saber-Toothed Tiger Fang x 1
2. Skill Manual "Berserk" x 1
3. Bunny Feed x 2

Legend

= SAVE SPHERE

= PASSAGE

= NPC

PICKPOCKETING

Colosseum

a. Diligent Clerk	Ginseng x 1
b. Totally Buff Guy	Health Seeds x 1
c. Mentally-Focusing Warrior	Natural Water x 1
d. Aimless Man	Gunpowder x 1
e. Torte, Hard-Working Girl	Rich Cheese x 1
f. Jack, Nonchalantly Threatening Bouncer	Blackberries x 1
g. Battle Starved Woman	Caterpillar Fungus x 1
h. Daniel, Self-Confident Bouncer	Peryton Droppings x 1

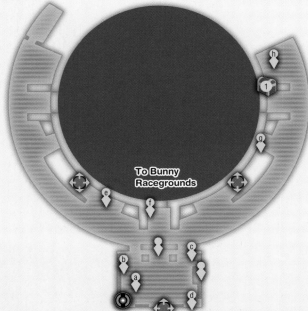

To Bunny
Racegrounds

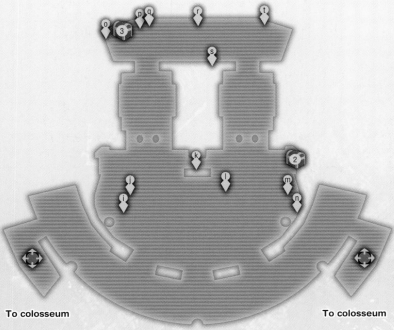

To colosseum

To colosseum

PICKPOCKETING

Bunny Racegrounds

i. Excited Man	Strength Potion x 1
j. Analytical Man	Alchemist's Water x 1
k. Bunny Race Clerk	Pickled Plum x 1
l. Bunny Lover	Nectar x 1
m. Lost Bunny	Magic Seeds x 1
n. Chatty Bunny Trainer	Bunny Feed x 1
o. Research-Obsessed Man	Super Aphrodisiac x 1
p. Boy Spectator	Empty Bottle x 1
q. Woman Spectator	Empty Bottle x 1
r. Ravenous Girl	Sushi x 1
s. Macho Man	Poison Cider x 1
t. Purebred Breeder	Perfect Berries x 1

THE SCENIC ROUTE BACK TO THE CALNUS

On your way out of the Purgatorium, charge up your Light Ring if there are any untapped light crystals left. If not, step back in and find a crystal for a free recharge after leaving the building—it's more convenient than returning to Tatroi and paying 3,000 Fol to the Suspicious Psychokineticist.

When you step outside, Welch calls to summon you back to the Calnus. There's no need to go rushing back, since there is plenty left to do on Roak.

While you won't be able to catch up to Sarah, you can use your new Light Ring to open three dark energy-sealed chests, complete several new quests in Tropp, and complete a series of quests that eventually lead to the reopening of the Tatroi colosseum. But since Roak isn't about to self-destruct like your last two destinations, you're free to continue on with your quest and return for the side quests later.

The dark energy-sealed chest in the northeast part of Tropp contains the rare Augury skill manual, although you don't yet have a character who can learn it. The other sealed chest, in the northern back alley, contains an Anti-Fog Amulet and, in the PS3 version, a Dragon Scale used in high-level recipes.

NEW LIFE, NEW CLOTHES

REWARD: 777 EXP, 37 Party SP

The Ex-Cultist at the entrance to Tropp wants to go straight, but he needs new clothes before anyone will take him seriously. You can make him a Traveler's Cloak, a level 1 Crafting recipe, out of 4 bolts of Wool (sold in Astral City) and five spools of Handspun Thread (sold in Tatroi). Bring him the cloak, and he'll give you "The Mapless Traveler" quest.

THE MAPLESS TRAVELER

REWARD: 123 EXP, 37 Party SP

The Ex-Cultist (now known as "Ruddle the Traveler") needs a map to find Tatroi. You'll find the Map of Astral at Mobius's One-Stop Shop in Astral City, but each copy sets you back 1,000 Fol. You're gonna want to buy two maps, because…

RUDDLE STRIKES AGAIN

REWARD: 456 EXP, 38 Party SP

After delivering the first map, leave Tropp and return. You'll find a befuddled Ruddle on the docks, where he'll promptly lose the first map. Give him the re-placement and send him on his way. Once you've completed the two Sand Bird quests, he will find Tatroi, where he'll set up a shop with a small selection of miscellaneous goods.

REBOUND QUEEN

REWARD: 1,100 EXP, 52 Party SP

If you fulfilled the "Otherworldy Diet" quest and at least two in-game hours have passed, the Dieting Woman has a new request for Reimi: bring her a fattening plate of Pasta Bolognese. If you've been back to Woodley recently, you should have been given Recipe Memo 07 by Lutea's Mother; if not, you'll have to go there to get it, as Reimi cannot invent the recipe herself. All the ingredients are available in Tatroi.

WHODUNIT?

REWARD: 1,300 EXP, 39 Party SP

The Absolutely Hysterical Woman in the Tropp Inn (formerly known as the Pathologically Petulant Woman, from the "Shoddy Doll" and "Second Doll" quests) has had her precious Gorgeous Gem stolen. You'll find the culprit wearing ex-cultist garb in the Twin Books store in Tatroi. Pick the pocket of the Bashful Man to liberate the gem and bring it back to its rightful owner.

DESERT DILEMMA

REWARD: 600 EXP, 40 Party SP

A Retired Explorer hangs out west of Tropp's central square. He'll send you to fight the great Sand Bird, which is somehow connected to the rivers of quicksand. You'll find the Sand Bird in the Astral Desert, usually flying around the tall sand dune south of the central oasis. When battling it, use skills like Edge's Mystic Cross to keep it juggled in the air while Bacchus and Reimi blast it. When the Sand Bird enters Rush Mode, have Edge back up and cast healing symbols on your party instead of engaging the bird while it's strongest.

THE SAND BIRD STRIKES BACK

REWARD: 1,200 EXP, 50 Party SP, Skill Manual "Ocarina"

You'll next encounter the Retired Explorer in the Astral Desert, on the south bank of the oasis. Apparently the Sand Bird has survived, and the explorer wants you to finish it off for good. Chase down the Sand Bird and take it down a second time. Upon its defeat, the quicksand in the deserts dries up, allowing you to finally complete quests like "The Missing Brother." As for this quest, speak to the Retired Explorer at the oasis, and then track him down in Tatroi's inn to get your reward.

SAND BIRD	
HP · 94798	EXP · 6,384
Fol · 15,893	Race · Bird
Resistant To · Earth, Wind	
Weak Against · --	

DROPS
Bracteate

Ruddle's Place - Stock

Item	Type	Price
Sylph's Saber	Weapon	19,800
Resurrection Elixir	Usable Items	2,000
Skill Manual "Energy Shield"	Usable Items	3,000
Skill Manual "Convert"	Usable Items	2,500
Sweet Fruit	Food	200
Quantum Processor	Other Items	1,600
Laser Oscillator	Other Items	3,000
Bunny Feed	Other Items	80

Ruddle's Place - Orders

Caterpillar Fungus x 2

Reward	Rarity	From
5,000	☆☆☆	Ruddle the Traveler

Lizard Guard x 1

Reward	Rarity	From
3,000	☆☆	Ruddle the Traveler

Water Armlet x 1

Reward	Rarity	From
2,500	☆☆☆	Ruddle the Traveler

Mental Potion x 1

Reward	Rarity	From
400	☆☆	Ruddle the Traveler

RE-OPENING THE TATROI COLOSSEUM

When you visit Tatroi after completing the Purgatorium, you'll be able to engage in a pair of quests—"Where's the Receptionist?" and "Sore Throat Soother" (see quest list for details)—which result in the colosseum opening for regular business. Once you have earned access to the colosseum, you'll be able to earn Fight Coins by climbing the leaderboards in one-on-one or team-vs-team battles, and by racing bunnies at the underground Bunny Track. (It's not a good idea to pursue the colosseum's Survival Mode at this point, since you might be brutally pummeled by much higher-level teams.) The Fight Coins you earn can be spent on a variety of exclusive weapons, armaments, and Item Creation ingredients. Reopening the colosseum also allows you to engage in a few new side quests.

Before you begin to climb your way up the colosseum ranks, have the Suspicious Psychokineticist recharge your Light Ring and use it to open the dark-energy-sealed chest in Astral City's southwest Residence. The Earthrock Mail armor inside should make surviving the colosseum a little bit easier. Make sure to recharge your Light Ring again before you return to the Calnus, so you'll also be able to open a dark energy chest on Planet Aeos.

Fight Coin Exchange - Stock

Item	Type	Price
Ripe Berries	Usable Items	20
Monster Jewel	Other Items	200
Dragon Scale	Other Items	300
Wild Arc	Weapon	1,500
Mithril Rapier	Weapon	1,900
Crested Spear	Weapon	2,200
Mithril Sword	Weapon	2,500
Dragon Claws	Weapon	2,800
Earthcrest Guard	Armor	3,200
Crystal Armor	Armor	3,900
Mystic Robe	Armor	4,200
Inferno Sickle	Weapon	9,000
Darkblood Chainmail	Armor	11,000
Dark Elf's Robe	Armor	12,000

WHERE'S THE RECEPTIONIST?

REWARD: 330 EXP, 30 Party SP

Speak to the Diligent Clerk who guards the entrance to the colosseum, and she'll send you to search for the building's missing receptionist, Lucy. You'll find her tending to her ailing mother on the second floor of Mobius's One-Stop Shop in Astral City. To claim your reward, return to the Diligent Clerk (who will be inside of the colosseum) after completing the "Sore Throat Soother" quest.

SORE THROAT SOOTHER

REWARD: 400 EXP, 22 Party SP

Lucy doesn't want to leave her ailing mother's side, so it's up to you to come up with a cure. Fortunately, the remedy is a simple Red Herb, which you probably already have in your inventory. If not, you can find one at Northeast Astralian Continent harvesting points or buy one in Tropp. One Red Herb is all it takes to get the colosseum running again!

NO WAY HOME

REWARD: 800 EXP, 49 Party SP, Blueberry Tart x 3

In Astral City, the Woozy Man near the canal barge needs a shot of Lemon Juice to cure his seasickness. Lemon Juice is a simple Reimi/ Lymle Cooking recipe with easily available ingredients; you can find Lemons at almost any harvesting point (or washed up on the beach), and Natural Water can be purchased at Astral City's Whole Heart Foods.

LISTLESS BUNNY

REWARD: 555 EXP, 30 Party SP, Lost Bunny

The Chatty Bunny Trainer in the Bunny Racegrounds is having trouble keeping her Bunny fed. Bring her one of the Stamina Pies you found in Tropp's Windswept Inn, and she'll let you keep the Bunny. Now you can enter it in the races!

PUFFY'S DEBUT

REWARD: 200 EXP, 31 Party SP

The Mischievous Woman in Tatroi's Northeast Mansion has a job for you: enter the colosseum and throw a solo match against her daughter, Puffy. Speak to Lucy at the colosseum Reception Desk, and you'll find that the match has already been arranged. It's a solo battle, so send someone low on HP, like Myuria. (Puffy's mercenary is a terrible fighter, so taking a dive is harder than it sounds.) Remove your armor to lower your defense, and choose the strategic item set before entering the arena. Use the two Gambleberries immediately; with some luck, this will automatically incapacitate your character. Failing that, use Myuria's Convert skill to lower her HP.

PUFFY'S RAGE

REWARD: 400 EXP, 34 Party SP

After reporting to the Mischievous Woman and earning your "reward," leave the Mansion and reenter. You'll find Puffy arguing with her mom, and she'll demand that you fight her for real. Return to the colosseum, this time for a team match against Miss Puffy's Lullaby, a powerful team of foes. Have both Myuria and Lymle on your team to take out the hearty Lovely Rock foes with symbols, after your conventional fighters kill her Lovely Scumbags. Once you win, return to the Mansion to collect another humble reward.

PUFFY'S REVENGE

REWARD: 800 EXP, 36 Party SP

Leave the Mansion and return again to provoke Puffy's next angry outburst. Once again, she'll challenge you to a colosseum battle with a team of hired guns. Use the same symbol-focused team, as most of her hirelings are very resistant to damage from physical attacks. Return to the Mansion for your usual EXP boost from the Mischievous Woman.

MAP TREASURES

Astral Caves: B2 (North)
8. Fresh Sage x 2
9. Ripe Berries x 1, Blueberries x 2
10. Fainting Potion x 1
11. [X360-only]
    Basil x 3,
    [PS3-only]
    [Dark Barrier]
    Bracteate x 1

MINING POINT ITEMS

Aluminum   Light Gem
Coal   Runic Metal
Crystal   Shadestone
Green Beryl   Thunder Gem

PICKPOCKETING

a. Ralph, Slow-Motion Knight	Natto x 1
b. Tony, Wandering Knight	Glowstick x 1
c. Lewis, Knight Near Death	Sacrificial Doll x 1
d. Wystal, Knight Corporal	Raw Animal Meat x 1
e. Richard, Faultless Knight	Skill Manual "Chain Combos" x 1

Note:
✕ = cave-ins
◎ = boulders

MAP TREASURES

Astral Caves: B1
1. Holy Water x 3,
   [PS3-only] Resurrection Elixir x 1
2. Health Seeds x 1
3. Skill Manual "Mindflare" x 1
4. Barrier Spiritwater x 1
5. [X360-only] Resurrection Elixir x 1
   [PS3-only] [Dark Barrier] Bracteate x 1
6. Crystal x 1
7. 7200 Fol

To Astral Caves: B1

To Astral Caves: B3

To Astral Caves: B3

To Astral City

To Astral Caves: B2

To Tatroi

MAP TREASURES

Astral Caves: B2 (South)
14. Riot Potion x 1
15. Blackberries x 3, [PS3-only] Basil x 3
16. [X360-only] Recipe Memo 17 x 1,
    [PS3-only] Bracteate x 1
17. 10,008 Fol
18. Physical Stimulant x 2, DANGER! DO NOT DRINK! x 3

Map Treasures

Astral Caves: B3
12. [Light Barrier] Burning Claws x 1
13. Attack Seeds x 1, [PS3-only]
    Bracteate x 1

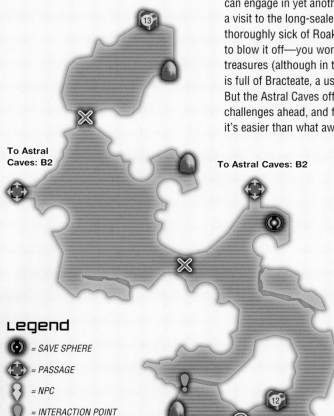

To Astral
Caves: B2

To Astral Caves: B2

Legend

 = SAVE SPHERE

 = PASSAGE

 = NPC

 = INTERACTION POINT

Monsters

VOMITING GEL
HP · 5119   EXP · 183
Fol · 248   Race · Plant
Resistant To · Water
Weak Against · Earth, Fire
DROPS
Natto, Vile Goop, Blackberries, Glowstick

ICE CORPSE
HP · 11674   EXP · 448
Fol · 257   Race · Undead
Resistant To · Water
Weak Against · Fire
DROPS
Dwarven Embroidery Thread, Holy Water, Cursed Cider, Frozen Cider

CORPSE BAT
HP · 3890   EXP · 97
Fol · 165   Race · Bird
Resistant To · --
Weak Against · Fire
DROPS
Protection Seeds, Raw Animal Meat, Lizardskin

SUCCUBUS
HP · 4523   EXP · 863
Fol · 299   Race · Demon
Resistant To · --
Weak Against · --
DROPS
Manacloth, Velvet Ribbon, Muting Cider

MAGE CHIMERA
HP · 9646   EXP · 576
Fol · 532   Race · Demon
Resistant To · Earth
Weak Against · Wind
DROPS
Snakeskin, Aquaberries, Raw Animal Meat, Lizardskin

ROCK HERMIT
HP · 9474   EXP · 600
Fol · 993   Race · Demon
Resistant To · Earth
Weak Against · Wind
DROPS
Mystery Box, Thunder Gem

HANG A U-TURN AND RETURN TO ROAK

Back on the Calnus, set a course for Planet Aeos to trigger an event in which Sarah reveals herself and officially joins your party. After clearing a series of the Private Actions (see the next section for details) and landing on Aeos, step off the ship to take a quick look around. You can then hop right back onto the Calnus and return to Roak where you can engage in yet another series of quests, including a visit to the long-sealed Astral Caves. If you are thoroughly sick of Roak at this point, you can feel free to blow it off—you won't miss any particularly great treasures (although in the PS3 version, the dungeon is full of Bracteate, a useful item creation ingredient). But the Astral Caves offer good experience for the challenges ahead, and from a difficulty perspective, it's easier than what awaits you on Aeos.

WELCH'S crafting corner

SYNTHESIZING WITH SARAH

Sarah's item-creation skill is called Synthesis, and it's already maxed out at level 1. Unlike other item-creation skills, Synthesis doesn't use recipes at all. Instead, it allows you to take any weapon, armor, or accessory you already own and enhance it with factors and stat boosts generated by other items. Synthesis never fails, and you can use it repeatedly on the same item, although no item can have more than four factors. It consumes only a single ingredient, and many of the best Synthesis ingredients are easy to acquire. In short, there's no reason to wait until you get each character's best gear; you should synthesize every new armament, and do so repeatedly.

When synthesizing weapons, a few ingredients to look out for include Snakeskin, which can add a 20% Fol bonus, Riot Potions, which reduce MP costs, Crystal, which increases your odds of scoring a critical hit, various bombs, which boost damage and add a chance of afflicting a status condition, and elemental stones (like Salamanderstone and Sylphstone) that offer damage boosts to specific elemental types. Reimi's foods often offer permanent stat boosts that correspond to their temporary effect when eaten, including EXP and Fol boosts.

When synthesizing armor, ciders and units can add limited immunity to negative status conditions, potions can have powerful effects like the Fainting Potion's +80 GRD bonus, and foods can offer a significant DEF boost or, in the case of Natto, a 15% immunity for all status conditions. When synthesizing accessories, you'll find that you can't improve your monster jewels, which is unfortunate. However, your other accessories can acquire powerful effects from potions, such as a +20 Def boost from a Fortitude Potion, and from symbol cards, such as across-the-board stat boosts from the Symbol Card "Angel Feather" + .

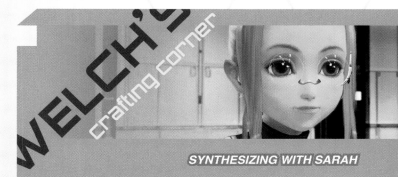

MOONLIGHT FOR THE ASTRAL KNIGHTS

Return to Astral City and speak to Lias of the Astral Knights, at his post just north of where you step off the canal barge. If Sarah is in your party, he'll offer you the "Ogre Battling" quest. To complete it, you'll need to hunt down and kill 30 of the Desert Ogres that can be found roaming the Astral Desert and Tropp Area. If you lose track, you can open your Quests list from the Data menu, and an exclamation point will pop up by the name of the quest when you've killed enough.

Report your success to Lias, and he'll propose a much more interesting quest, titled "Rumble in the Caves." The Astral City entrance to the Astral Caves has been opened, and you're now free to poke around inside as you search for the source of the tremors.

DODGE THE LEVEL-B1 CAVE-INS

A series of sudden cave-ins block what appear to be passable routes in the Astral Caves—these are marked with an  on the provided maps. There's no way around those, so you'll need to find another route. Other routes are blocked by large boulders that do not appear on the game's auto-map—these are marked with an ◉ on this guide's maps. That type of blockade finally provides an opportunity to have some fun with your Earth Ring, which can melt them the way the Fire Ring melted ice.

If your Earth Ring hasn't been charged yet, visit the Suspicious Psychokineticist in Tatroi to get it filled. If you're playing the PS3 version, you'll want to get your Light Ring charged as well, since two of the chests have been sealed with Dark Barriers in this version of the game. You don't need to use the Earth Ring to get through the Astral Caves, but you do need it to get all the treasures. You'll also need to use it to save Ralph (marked with an "a" on the map), who has been trapped by a dissolvable boulder. Melt it to earn his gratitude as well as some EXP and Party SP.

When a cave-in falls southwest of Ralph, it seems to block the only path to level B2. But if you climb the stairs just to the southeast, you can actually step on the fallen boulder to cross over to the other side.

PUTTING THE HURT ON ROCK HERMITS

Rock Hermits are easily the toughest normal monsters you'll encounter in the Astral Caves. Normal attacks barely nick their hides, and even symbols that exploit their weakness to wind aren't particularly effective. But while they're tough against normal attacks, critical hits still can deal heavy damage to Rock Hermits. Start each battle by wiping out their Corpse Bat companions before they can curse you, then turn on the Rock Hermits with Blindsides and flurries of Rush Mode attacks. If you have more than two symbol-users on the field, swap one out for another fighter so you can keep the Rock Hermits under constant pressure. Your allies' standard combos may not do any real damage, but they can still cancel the Hermits' endless stream of Stone Rain symbols.

A KEEPSAKE FROM A FALLEN HERO

Level B2 is strewn with massive webs that can slow your progress to a crawl. If you encounter any monsters near the webs, take them out so they won't be able to snare you in surprise attacks.

In the center of the first web, you encounter Lewis, a fallen knight who can't hold on any longer. He'll give you his Knight's Bangle and ask you to deliver it to his wife in a side quest entitled "A Cherished Bangle."

When you near the exit of this floor, you'll trigger an event in which Lymle is threatened by an Ice Corpse. As soon as the event scene ends, prepare to be rushed by a Mage Chimera.

SAVE AND HEAL BEFORE THE BOSS'S AMBUSH

When you reach level B3, save your game and proceed south to the treasure chests and mining points. Jump down a level at the pink exclamation point, and you'll find yourself on the bank of an underground river. Examine it for a full HP and MP refill.

A cave-in has blocked the path to the west, but it's also dropped a perfectly round boulder near the edge of the raised ledge just south of the save sphere. Climb up on the ledge and step onto the boulder to send it smashing through the blockade. When you step over the blockade's rubble, you'll end up in a battle with the Cave Guardian. So if you want to do a little prep work (like changing your fighters to BEAT:B), do it now!

BOSS

Cave Guardian

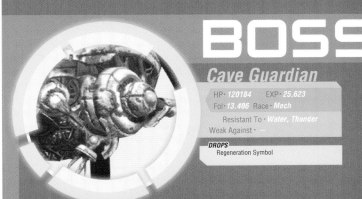

HP · *120184*   EXP · *25,623*
Fol · *13.406*   Race · *Mech*
Resistant To · *Water, Thunder*
Weak Against · *--*

DROPS
Regeneration Symbol

Crush the Cave Guardian

The ideal party here is a melee fighter like Edge or Meracle set to BEAT:B, Reimi and Bacchus for back-up, and Sarah for healing. The Cave Guardian's attacks are difficult to dodge, so don't bother trying, and instead just pound on the beast with chained special arts. The Cave Guardian is too big of a target to miss, and its propensity for falling down ensures that you land nearly every hit of even three-part combos.

When the Cave Guardian enters Rush Mode, back up and fight a little more conservatively, using your combos to retaliate after one of its own attacks. The boss has a lot of HP to cut

through, so be vigilant about watching your allies' Rush Gauges and taking control of whoever is near their max, so you can have them trigger a devastating Rush Mode combo.

REAP THE REWARDS OF YOUR HEROISM

You'll need to do a similar boulder-rolling trick to blast open the path to the final treasure chest on level B3. Then, take the stairs up to the southern part of level B2, where you can roll another boulder straight through the sealed gate to the city of Tatroi. Now you're just a barge ride away from collecting rewards from Lias and the Knight's Wife.

NEW QUESTS IN TATROI AND ASTRAL CITY

SIDE QUESTS

OGRE BATTLING

REWARD: *400 EXP, 56 Party SP, Astralian Emblem x 1*

After Sarah joins your party, speak to the Astralian Royal Knight Lias in Astral City, just northeast of the canal barge. He'll ask you to hunt down and kill 30 of the Desert Ogres that roam the Astral Desert and Tropp Area.

RUMBLE IN THE CAVES

REWARD: *1,000 EXP, 80 Party SP, Recipe Memo 21*

After completing the "Ogre Battling" quest, Lias next asks you to get to the bottom of the earthquakes in the Astral Caves. All the details for this lengthy quest are in the main text of this section.

A CHERISHED BANGLE

REWARD: *500 EXP, 32 Party SP*

You'll encounter Lewis in the center of the first web on level B2 of the Astral Caves. Lewis's final wish is that you deliver his Knight's Bangle to his wife, who lives in the Residence in the southwest corner of Astral City.

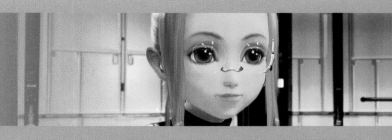

Sarah may not have a recipe-generating skill of her own, but she can come up with plenty of ideas for the rest of your party. If you aren't yet level 10 in all of your Crafting skills, now would be a good time to start working your way up to the highest-level recipes. If you can max out Bacchus's Engineering skill, he can collaborate

with Sarah and Edge on the recipe for Li'l Vending Machine No. 2, which makes Item Creation a lot easier by increasing the number of items you can buy on the Calnus. The vending machine is made of pretty common ingredients, with the only rare one being the Scrambling Unit. However, you should already have the recipe for that, as well as all the ingredients you need to make it.

Sarah can inspire hundreds of new recipes, including scores of symbol cards (with various combinations of Lymle, Faize, and Myuria), a few new weapons with Edge, and a wide selection of pies with Reimi. Not only are pies essential for building up your

Bunny in the colosseum's Bunny Racegrounds, but also many of them are useful for your party as well; the Stamina Pie is particularly strong, which revives a character with 90% of their HP and MP.

Sarah can join Meracle in developing the HP-regenerating Healing Band accessory, a level 7 Crafting recipe. The MP equivalent is the level 8 Regeneration Symbol, which requires Lymle, Meracle. and someone else to push them over a total of 20 in Crafting. Both are fine accessories to use as a base for Sarah's Synthesis skill.

Finally, Sarah and Myuria can collaborate on two items that help you win affinity points from your party. Give a shot of Love Potion No. 256 (a level 7 Compounding recipe) to any character in your party, and all other characters raise their opinion of that character. Frequent pickpocketers definitely want to douse Edge in buckets of the stuff. The Aroma of Love (a level 3 Compounding recipe) is a ship furnishing that you can set in any character's room to double the rate by which that person gains affinity for others. Just don't get these legitimate aphrodisiacs confused with the so-called Super Aphrodisiac, which actually lowers the entire party's opinion of the character who uses it.

The Bracteate won in the Sand Bird battles and found throughout the Astral Caves (in the PS3 version) allows you to finish Reimi's Mystic Bow and make Slayer's Bangles. Slayer's Bangles add an extra hit to melee combos, making them an exceptional accessory for

If you stuck around on Roak to finish up the side quests, you should have found a Saber-Toothed Tiger Fang (in the colosseum), which now allows you to make the Wildfang Staff.

melee fighters. To make it, you'll need Meracle's Crafting skill at level 9 or higher; pair her with Edge and Lymle to learn the recipe.

Map Treasures

1. Defense Seeds x 1

Monsters

ADEPHAGA VENOM

HP · 6370	EXP · 467
Fol · 224	Race · Insect

Resistant To · --
Weak Against · Wind

DROPS
Fresh Sage, Aquaberries, Insect Egg

ADEPHAGA MILIES

HP · 8214	EXP · 431
Fol · 155	Race · Insect

Resistant To · --
Weak Against · Wind

DROPS
Light Gem, Insect Egg, Blueberries, Fresh Sage

VAMPIRE BAT

HP · 6345	EXP · 236
Fol · 105	Race · Bird

Resistant To · --
Weak Against · Light

DROPS
Biocloth, Blackberries, Bigberries

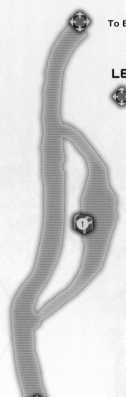

To Base Area

Legend

 = PASSAGE

To Southern Beaches

SLEEPING WITH MERACLE AND OTHER SECRET PRIVATE ACTIONS

And finally, you're off to Planet Aeos. This flight is where the Private Action situation begins to get complicated, with hard-to-find hidden Private Actions that appear as alternatives to the default set. One of the events requires Lymle and Faize to be sharing a room, so pair them up if you can. But if Lymle and Faize don't have enough affinity for each other already, they'll refuse to be roommates.

• Trigger the first event by speaking to Lymle in the Recreation Room. This one boosts both Lymle and Meracle's opinion of Edge, as well as Edge's opinion of Lymle. But his affinity for Meracle subsequently drops a bit.

• For the next Private Action, you can either speak to Reimi and Myuria in the Recreation Room, or speak to Bacchus in his own quarters. There's more total affinity gained by speaking to the girls, since it raises Edge's opinion of both, and Reimi's opinion of Edge.

• Your next choice is between Meracle and the ever-squabbling duo of Lymle and Faize. Speak to Meracle in her room to receive an affinity boost for both Meracle and Edge. Or, speak to Lymle in the Recreation Room for an event that boosts Edge's affinity for Reimi and Faize, and Faize's for Edge. The Lymle and Faize event is a prerequisite for one of the game's hidden endings; you will have another opportunity to view the Meracle event later.

• You could trigger one of a number of events on the next leg of the flight. In the Recreation Room, you'll find Bacchus waiting for a game of chess, unless you've already viewed both of Bacchus's chess-related Private Actions. If you have, it will be a new event with Reimi instead. If Faize and Lymle are sharing a room, you'll have a second option for an event that takes place in their shared room. That event is a wash in terms of affinity, but it is a prerequisite for one of the game's hidden endings. (If you miss it now, you can also trigger it after you land on Planet Aeos.)

• For the next Private Action, speaking to Meracle in the Recreation Room seems to be your only option. But there's a secret Private Action you can trigger if you go to your bed and choose "Rest" instead. Like the Recreation Room event, the bedroom event earns you a few points with Meracle, but this one also costs you a few points with Reimi. Luckily, you can make them back—and then some—by choosing the follow-up Reimi event on the next leg. Save your game before you make the choice, because they're both must-see events for Meracle fans.

• If you did the event in Edge's bedroom, you can now trigger that follow-up event by talking to Reimi near the battle simulator. Otherwise, your only option is to go to the Recreation Room and speak with Myuria, Lymle, and Meracle. You'll have three choices of responses here. Choose "they look really cute," and you'll win points with both Lymle and Meracle (slightly more with Lymle). Choose "they look really beautiful," and you'll also win points with Lymle and Meracle, but slightly more with Meracle. Choose "They can't hold a candle to you, Myuria" and, of course, you'll lose points with both. But you'll gain points with Myuria, which isn't easy to do.

• If you did the Reimi event in the previous leg, you can do the Myuria/Lymle/Meracle event in the next one. If not, this becomes a free leg with no Private Actions, and you'll need to go to your room and rest to advance it. The next leg is also a free one, although if you repeatedly open the men's bathroom door, you might find something interesting… (The toilet scene may occur at any point after Bacchus joins your party.)

PRIVATE ACTIONS

Return to Planet Aeos

A GRIM HOMECOMING ON PLANET AEOS

The Exploration Base lies in ruins, and its staff is nowhere to be found. A new stairway extends south to an empty beach, where you'll find the entrance to a short Undersea Tunnel that connects to the Southern Reaches.

If you're willing to take a quick detour, you can pick up a few new items by heading north from the base to the Northern Coast, and making a loop through the Urd Falls Cave. First, you can use your Light Ring to open

the dark energy-sealed chest north of the base and liberate its 19,800 Fol. Then, you can hop down to the coast and enter the Urd Falls Cave, where your Earth Ring allows you to clear the cave-in that blocks the final two treasure pods. But their contents—Seasonings, a Warped Carapace, and Attack Seeds—are barely worth the trouble.

ALWAYS TIME FOR R&R ON THE CALNUS

You just completed many Private Actions, but you can do a whole bunch more after you set down on Planet Aeos. Return to your ship at any point before the Phantom battle of the Southern Reaches to trigger the following four-part series.

• Trigger the first event by visiting Faize in the storage room north of the Meeting Room (with the Item Creation terminal). This event strains the bond between Edge and Faize, but inexplicably, it boosts Edge's opinion of Lymle.

• After that, you'll have an opportunity to pick up one of two events you may have missed earlier. If Faize and Lymle are sharing a room, and you haven't yet seen the event where Lymle pulled a prank on a sleeping Faize, then you can view that event now. If you didn't speak to Meracle in her bedroom on the third leg of the flight over, that too becomes an option. If you've seen both, you can skip to the next phase.

• Your next choice is between Sarah and Meracle. You'll find Sarah in the Recreation Room, and Meracle in the storage room south of the Item Creation terminal. Both events boost the chosen woman's opinion of Edge, and his of her.

• For the final event of the sequence, visit Meracle in her room. After her lengthy story, Edge gets quizzed on the details. Select "A town with a colosseum," or both characters' opinion of each other sadly take a hit.

TRAVERSE THE UNDERSEA TUNNEL

You'll find the entrance to the Undersea Tunnel on the beach area south of the ruined base. The map is a simple one, with only a single fork. The area's lone treasure chest is halfway down the left path.

The enemies you'll encounter are similar to the ones you've fought elsewhere on the planet, but both the Adephaga Venom and Vampire Bat have toxic attacks that can poison every character who doesn't have some form of protection. Synthesizing anti-poison factors onto your weapons may not save anyone's lives, but it really does head off a lot of tiresome poison-curing.

SOUTHERN REACHES

Map Treasures

1. Aquaberries x 7
2. Monster Jewel x 1
3. Cursed Cider x 3, Vile Goop x 2
4. [Dark Barrier] Light Charm x 1
5. Recipe Memo 29 x 1
6. 35,003 Fol
7. Glowstick x 4
8. Bigberries x 3, Blackberries x 1
9. [Ice Barrier] Regeneration Symbol x 1
10. Steel x 2
11. [PS3-only] Biocloth x 2

To Undersea Tunnel

Shortcut to Base Area

To Miga Insect Warren

Monsters

ADEPHAGA VENOM
| HP · 6370 | EXP · 467 |
| Fol · 224 | Race · *Insect* |

Resistant To · --
Weak Against · *Wind*

DROPS
Fresh Sage, Aquaberries, Insect Egg

STINGER
| HP · 6698 | EXP · 266 |
| Fol · 128 | Race · *Insect* |

Resistant To · --
Weak Against · *Earth*

DROPS
Bigberries, Aquaberries, Bee Stinger

LAMIA RADIX
| HP · 6738 | EXP · 512 |
| Fol · 160 | Race · *Plant* |

Resistant To · *Earth*
Weak Against · *Fire*

DROPS
Ripe Berries, Glowstick, Nectar

HORNED TORTOISE
| HP · 9165 | EXP · 1,477 |
| Fol · 361 | Race · *Animal* |

Resistant To · --
Weak Against · *Ice*

DROPS
Defense Seeds, Red Herbs

Legend

 = SAVE SPHERE

 = PASSAGE

 = RECOVERY SPHERE

 = INTERACTION POINT

Harvesting Point Items

Aquaberries	Gambleberries
Bigberries	Ginseng
Blackberries	Insect Egg
Blue Seed	Red Seed
Cane	Ripe Berries
Fresh Sage	Thornberries

Mining Point Items

Disintegration Stone
Earth Gem
Gold
Iron
Light Gem
Magical Clay

PROCEED SOUTH TO THE PHANTOM VESSEL

The Southern Reaches are a vast loop, with the path from the Undersea Tunnel forking at a short distant to the south. If you head east, you encounter a giant wall of rock that you can liquidate with your Earth Ring. It blocks a one-way passage back to the north that allows you to return to the Base Area without having to deal with the monsters of the Undersea Tunnel.

The path to the southwest leads past several harvesting and mining points before leading you to a save and recovery sphere just before the Phantom vessel. You couldn't ask for a bigger hint than that; heal, save, spend your skill points, arrange your party, eat plenty of Reimi's stat-boosting meals, and do everything else you need to do to ready your party for the longest brawl they've ever endured.

Oh, and at the risk of revealing a minor spoiler... if Faize has any top-notch armor or accessories that you'd rather not lose, now might be a good time to take them away from him.

SURVIVE THE EIGHT-STAGE PHANTOM AMBUSH

On paper, phantoms may not seem to be the deadliest of foes. But what the stats don't show is their high levels of resistance to both physical and magical attacks, as well as the abilities of Phantom Leaders to buff their troops with significant ATK and DEF bonuses. When multiple leaders are on the field, even high-level characters may find that their standard attacks are doing only single-digit damage!

As soon as one phantom squad is destroyed, another soon enters in an ambush. The battles get progressively tougher as the number of enemies increases, and as the ratio of leaders to soldiers grows. In each new wave, have your best character (almost certainly Edge) isolate the leader by looking for their distinctive helmets. Hit them with normal attacks to lock on, and then employ special arts to knock them down or pop them up; that combo gives you the opening you need to charge up for a Blindside, which is able to bypass the enemies' damage resistances.

Your Rush Gauge thankfully grows quickly, and you should always use it for a Rush Gauge combo. The ideal companions are Meracle and two symbol-users. Sarah is the best healer, but if you came straight here after recruiting her, she may be too low-level to survive. Fortunately, Myuria and Lymle make for competent replacements.

If a character dies near the start of a battle, don't bother trying to resurrect them, as your foes are so aggressive that they can usually disrupt symbols and often disrupt even recovery items. Instead, swap out the fallen character's body for a fresh fighter, and swap it back in for a Resurrection symbol or some Fresh Sage when only one enemy remains. Needless to say, this is also when you should be doing the bulk of your healing.

PHANTOM LEADER
HP · *5476*   EXP · *470*
Fol · *232*   Race · *Humanoid*
Resistant To · --
Weak Against · *Dark*
DROPS
Darkness Gem, Glowstick, Wide-Range EM Bomb, Self-Destructor 3000

PHANTOM SOLDIER
HP · *4648*   EXP · *374*
Fol · *168*   Race · *Humanoid*
Resistant To · --
Weak Against · *Dark*
DROPS
Healing Card+, Compact Stun Bomb, Self-Destructor 3000

THE GRIM REAPER OF THE BATTLEFIELD

Faize may be gone, but you've received a far superior replacement. When configured correctly, Arumat may well be the strongest character in your party. The Critical Hit skill is ideal for him, because his critical hits do nearly triple damage. His standard attacks are a little slow but hit repeatedly, and the kick-to-the-ribs he uses against fallen foes is a lot of fun. Arumat doesn't have the intelligence to get much out of his symbols, but his special arts are amazing.

A Diabolic Edge-to-Nether Strike combo does the job of Edge's ever-useful Stampede Slash with a lot more power and a wider attack range, and Unholy Maelstrom is a fantastic crowd-control skill that excels at earning Multi-Enemy finishes. If you jack up Arumat's MP Boost skill and use his special arts to rack up red Bonus Board tiles, you can turn Arumat into a perpetual motion killing machine.

WINNING ARUMAT'S RESPECT

After Arumat joins your party, you can trigger a new Private Action when you return to the Calnus. You'll have an opportunity to trigger it on the first leg of your next flight, but doing it now allows you to pursue some other event at that point, so affinity-seekers shouldn't miss the opportunity.

You'll find Arumat hanging out near the battle simulator, where he'll challenge Edge to a duel. If you win, Arumat's respect for Edge raises, and vice versa. If you lose or refuse, Arumat's respect for Edge falls.

Arumat is a powerhouse, but this should be an easy fight for Edge to win. Edge's sword is much faster than Arumat's scythe, so you can get in with a Stampede Slash before Arumat can ready his blade. Continue to combo off that first attack, bouncing him up with Mystic Cross, nailing him with a Rising Blade when he lands, and so on. When Arumat enters Rush Mode, back off and only strike when he gives you a clear opening.

PRIVATE ACTIONS

COMPLETE THE LOOP OF THE SOUTHERN REACHES

From the save and recovery spheres, continue your counter-clockwise loop around the Southern Reaches. Keep hitting those harvesting points, as they're the easiest way to get rare Canes, which are key ingredients in some of the game's highest-level weapon recipes.

In the northeast corner of the map, you'll discover the cave where Arumat believes you'll find the Grigori. There's a recovery sphere just outside, and a save sphere on the first floor.

MAP TREASURES

Miga Insect Warren: B2
1. Blackberries x 4, Basil x 2
2. Potent Accuracy Seeds x 1
3. Aluminum x 2

MAP TREASURES

Miga Insect Warren: B2 (Exit Passage)
14. Broken Metal Cutting Blade x 1

Note:

✕ = indestructable barrier

◎ = destructable barrier

S#a = Sinkhole entrance

S#b = Sinkhole exit

To Miga Insect Warren: B3

To Miga Insect Warren: B2

To Miga Insect Warren: B2

S1a

To Southern Reaches

To Miga Insect Warren: B3

S2a

To Miga Insect Warren: B1

S1b

To Miga Insect Warren: B1

Mining Point Items

Darkness Gem	Green Beryl
Earth Gem	Light Gem
Gnomestone	Magical Clay
Gold	Meteorite

Legend

◈ = SAVE SPHERE

✛ = PASSAGE

⬮ = INTERACTION POINT

Monsters

ADEPHAGA VENOM
HP · 6370	EXP · 467
Fol · 224	Race · *Insect*

Resistant To · --
Weak Against · *Wind*

DROPS
Fresh Sage, Aquaberries, Insect Egg

ADEPHAGA MILIES
HP · 8214	EXP · 431
Fol · 155	Race · *Insect*

Resistant To · --
Weak Against · *Wind*

DROPS
Light Gem, Insect Egg, Blueberries, Fresh Sage

VAMPIRE BAT
HP · 6345	EXP · 236
Fol · 105	Race · *Bird*

Resistant To · --
Weak Against · *Light*

DROPS
Biocloth, Blackberries, Bigberries

LAMIA RADIX
HP · 6738	EXP · 512
Fol · 160	Race · *Plant*

Resistant To · *Earth*
Weak Against · *Fire*

DROPS
Ripe Berries, Glowstick, Nectar

POLYPHAGA DRUS
HP · 7255	EXP · 1,030
Fol · 415	Race · *Insect*

Resistant To · --
Weak Against · *Earth*

DROPS
Health Seeds, Red Herb, Thornberries

DERMOPTERA
HP · 8707	EXP · 475
Fol · 311	Race · *Insect*

Resistant To · --
Weak Against · *Earth*

DROPS
Magick Emblem, Aquaberries, Basil, Earth Gem

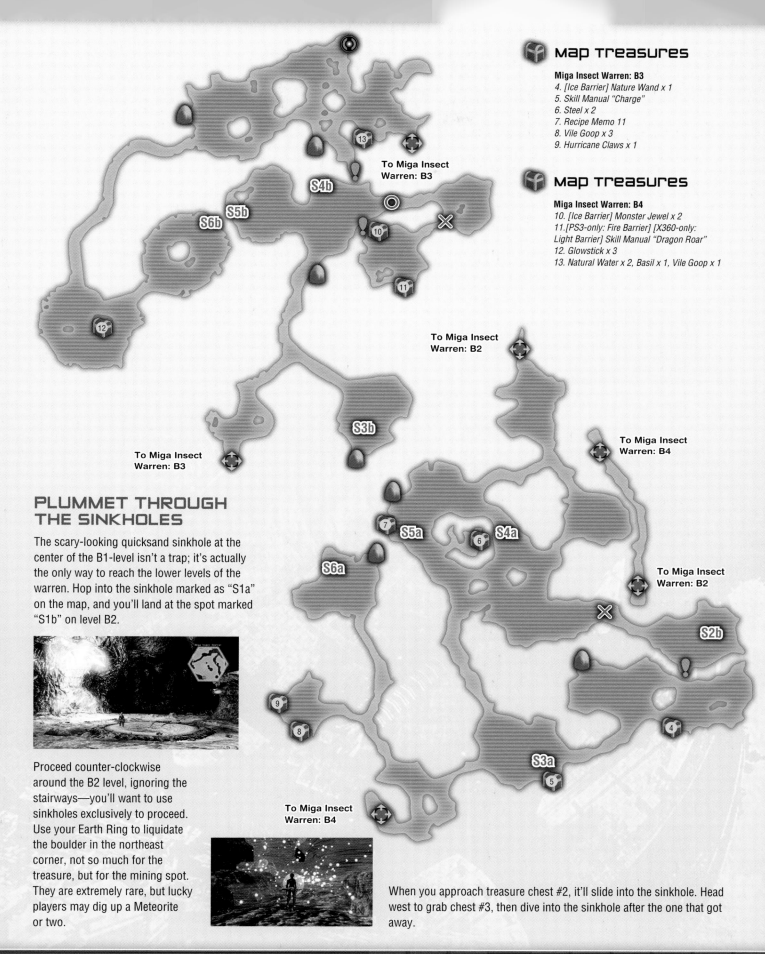

MAP TREASURES

Miga Insect Warren: B3
4. [Ice Barrier] Nature Wand x 1
5. Skill Manual "Charge"
6. Steel x 2
7. Recipe Memo 11
8. Vile Goop x 3
9. Hurricane Claws x 1

MAP TREASURES

Miga Insect Warren: B4
10. [Ice Barrier] Monster Jewel x 2
11. [PS3-only: Fire Barrier] [X360-only: Light Barrier] Skill Manual "Dragon Roar"
12. Glowstick x 3
13. Natural Water x 2, Basil x 1, Vile Goop x 1

To Miga Insect Warren: B3

To Miga Insect Warren: B2

To Miga Insect Warren: B4

To Miga Insect Warren: B3

To Miga Insect Warren: B2

To Miga Insect Warren: B4

PLUMMET THROUGH THE SINKHOLES

The scary-looking quicksand sinkhole at the center of the B1-level isn't a trap; it's actually the only way to reach the lower levels of the warren. Hop into the sinkhole marked as "S1a" on the map, and you'll land at the spot marked "S1b" on level B2.

Proceed counter-clockwise around the B2 level, ignoring the stairways—you'll want to use sinkholes exclusively to proceed. Use your Earth Ring to liquidate the boulder in the northeast corner, not so much for the treasure, but for the mining spot. They are extremely rare, but lucky players may dig up a Meteorite or two.

When you approach treasure chest #2, it'll slide into the sinkhole. Head west to grab chest #3, then dive into the sinkhole after the one that got away.

PUT THE SHADY SORCERESS OUT OF BUSINESS

From the point where you land at level B3, you can only head south; the route to the west is blocked by a boulder that can only be destroyed when you approach it from the west side. Instead, dive down at the exclamation point to

grab the Nature Wand out of chest #4. If your Flame Ring is empty, don't worry about it. Just keep going to chest #5, and dive into sinkhole S3a after it. When you open the chest up, you'll find the Charge skill for Lymle. This skill transforms a Disintegration Stone (which you probably have plenty of) into two charges for any disintegration ring. Having the ability to refill your own rings makes it a whole lot easier to

open whichever dark-energy chest on Planet Aeos you weren't able to open earlier (there's one in the Southern Reaches, and one north of the base).

NAVIGATE THE SINKHOLES TO REACH THE BOSS

After grabbing the Charge skill manual, head west to the staircase to return to level B3. Grab chest #6 to the north, then follow chest #7 (which contains the Recipe Memo for a Light Charm) down a sinkhole to level B4. Melt the ice blockade to the east of where you landed, then examine the solid wall that appears to be an open passage on your map. No need to use a ring, as a Polyphaga Drus is happy to tear the wall down for you.

After collecting the Monster Jewels from the frozen chest, take the stairs back up to level B3, and this time head northwest to sinkhole S6a. This is the only sinkhole that can take you to the northwest region of level B4, which is home to the final two chests and the dungeon boss. As you approach the save sphere, make sure to stick close to

the northern wall, and save your progress at the save sphere *before* you approach chest #13. The boss won't let you reach that chest without a fight.

BOSS

Armaros Manifest

HP· ?????	EXP· 34,147
Fol·34,302	Race· Other
Resistant To · Earth	
Weak Against · Wind	

DROPS
Monster Jewel

Destroy the Insect Queen Grigori

Before you depart the save sphere, set Edge to BEAT:S and feed him Reimi's finest ATK-boosting meal. If you've made a Slayer's Bangle (which adds a hit to a fighter's basic combo), make sure Edge is wearing it. If you don't have the No Guard skill equipped and maxed out… well, there's simply no excuse for that. Never de-equip No Guard!

The ideal back-up team for this difficult fight is Sarah and Lymle for healing and Bacchus just because he's so resilient. If you have any accessories that protect against the silence condition, no matter how weak, equip them to your symbol users. You should probably set everyone except Edge to "Stay Out of Trouble" so the boss's attention will stay focused on Edge, allowing him to continuously Blindside it. Those who don't mind doing a lot of mid-battle tinkering can switch everyone to "Fight freestyle with full force!" when the Dermoptera are around, as their added power is definitely welcome.

Begin the battle by wiping out the Dermoptera, and whenever the boss summons a new batch, drop whatever you're doing and wipe them out immediately. Not only do their attacks keep your healers on the ropes, but their Silence symbols cripple your characters and force you to burn through your supply of Red Herbs.

When you are alone with Armaros Manifest, have Sarah cast Enhance and Enshelter on Edge. Then, take control of Edge and pummel the boss until she turns her attention his way (indicated by the red arrow). Her weak point is the Grigori on her tail, but she never lowers it voluntarily, so you'll need to rely on Blindsides to hit it. Wait until the boss has finished an attack, then charge in and execute a Blindside from right between the boss's mandibles. (If the boss switches to ground-pounding mandible attacks, back up and wait for it to switch tactics, as it usually uses that attack several times in a row.)

When the coast is clear, fire up a Blindside, hit four times with your Slayer's Bangle-enhanced standard combo, and then fire off your longest special arts chain. If that causes a stun, repeat the process. Pulling off the Blindside isn't always easy, but when you score a hit, you can easily chain it into tens of thousands of points of damage.

COZYING UP TO YOUR NEW RECRUITS

After defeating the Armaros Manifest and taking the shortcut back to the Calnus, it is finally time to make the long-delayed trip to En II. But as Bacchus warns you, the flight does take "a significant amount of time." There are nine legs to this journey, but you can do as many as thirteen Private Actions, since not every Private Action causes the game to advance to the next leg.

• As you leave the Flight Deck, you'll run into Sarah in the Recreation Room. Go ahead and speak to her (earning a small affinity bonus for both characters), since this event is a freebie that won't end the leg. After that, there are two possible events. If you didn't duel with Arumat back on Planet Aeos, you'll find him waiting at the battle simulator to challenge you to a fight. Otherwise, set things up so that Edge and Reimi are sharing a room, then rest for the leg. If you remembered Reimi's birthday way back on the flight to Cardianon, and you're sharing a room with her now, you can trigger a special event.

• If you haven't yet seen Meracle's ocarina event, you'll have a choice to make. Option one is to view that event now, by speaking to Meracle in the room with the battle simulator. Their conversation raises Edge's opinion of Meracle by 2 points, and hers of him by 3. Option two is to speak to Reimi and Lymle in the Recreation Room, which raises Edge's opinion of Lymle by 2 points, and both Reimi and Lymle's opinion of Edge by 2 points. The latter event is a prerequisite for one of the hidden endings.

• If you haven't seen Sarah's pratfalls on the Recreation Room treadmill yet, you'll have a second chance to see that event on the third leg of the flight. Your other option is to chat with Arumat in his bedroom, but this event is only available if you beat him in the duel earlier.

• Once again, talking to Sarah does not advance the day. Meet her in her bedroom and listen to her dream. When she asks if you think it will come true, you can answer "No Way" for a slight affinity boost, or tell her it sounds plausible to unlock a future chain of Private Actions. You can then finish off the day by visiting Arumat and Meracle in the storage area south of the Meeting Room. This event will raise Edge's opinion of Arumat more than it lowers Arumat's opinion of Edge.

• Speak to Reimi and Arumat in the Recreation Room. When Arumat asks you about your relationship with Crowe, declare that he's a rival (the second option) for the best results.

• The next leg begins with another freebie event. Speak to Bacchus in his room for an easy affinity boost that can lead to future Private Actions with Arumat. Then, visit the battle simulator room for a rare opportunity to win some points with Myuria.

• If you spoke to Bacchus in the previous leg, you can visit Arumat in his room for a free event. Then, finish the leg by speaking with Sarah and Lymle in the battle simulator room.

• Sarah, Myuria, and Meracle are gathered in the Recreation Room for the next leg's only event. You'll gain points with Myuria and Sarah, but drop a few notches in Meracle's eyes. Sounds like a fair trade. Besides, you can win back Meracle's heart in a follow-up event on En II.

• To trigger the final event of the flight, head upstairs to the restrooms. This one costs you three affinity points with Reimi, while ultimately netting you only a single point with Sarah. You may be tempted to blow this one off (by sleeping during the leg), but you may need that point with Sarah, and can almost certainly afford to lose a few with Reimi.

Map Treasures

1. Void Recovery Unit x 2, Potent Intelligence Seeds x 1
2. [Ice Barrier] Health Seeds x 1, Bunny Feed x 1, Ripe Berries x 2
3. Recipe Memo 18 x 1
4. Physical Stimulant x 2, Skill Manual "Emergency Repairs" x 1

Pickpocketing

Central Control Room

a. Smiling Woman	Sweet Fruit x 1
b. Hopeful Man	Ash x 1
c. Traffic-Control Woman	Manacloth x 1

Monitor Room A

d. Giotto	Monster Jewel x 1

Monitor Room B

e. Operator	17,000 Fol
f. Orwen, Dutiful Warrior	Fire Gem x 1

Monitor Room C

g. Impassioned Symbologist	Magic Seeds x 1

To Central Control Room

To Calnus

Monitor Room B

Monitor Room A

Monitor Room C

To Docks

Legend

= SAVE SPHERE

= PASSAGE

= NPC

= INTERACTION POINT

AN AUDIENCE WITH THE ENIGMATIC EX

Although a friendly voice greets you to En II, don't expect a welcoming committee. You'll have to walk from the Dock to the Central Control Room, ride a moving platform to the elevator, and then descend to Monitor Room A to finally get some answers. After meeting Giotto, speak to the glowing white orb and ask it questions from the menu to unlock new options. Once you've asked all of the available questions, your party rejoins you, and your new objective becomes clear.

While in the area, make sure to speak to the people in the Central Control Room, so you can collect the weapons data for the NDS002 Symbolic Rod and ND003 Handblaster. You can add a bunch of spaceship data to your collections file by stopping off at Monitor Room B and examining the four spinning…well, whatever those are. They hold the specs for the Rednuht, Morphus battleship, Morphus exploration craft, Morphus escape pod, Cardianon battlecraft, and Calnus (USTA transport).

COLLECT A QUEST FROM BARAGO

Your meeting with Ex ended with a bit of breaking news: a Grigori has landed at the Sanctuary in En II. All the transporters to the area are offline, so the only route left is the Old Road to the Sanctuary, selectable from the Central Control Room's main elevator.

Don't worry, you don't have to do any fighting before loading up on new gear at Centropolis. For now, simply pop onto the Old Road and head southeast in search of a man named Barago, Keeper of Past Knowledge. He'll tip you off that the Wind Ring is somewhere in Centropolis, and suggest you talk to the chief of the Flora/Fauna Laboratory for more information. You can return here to reach the Sanctuary after completing "The Wind Ring" quest in Centropolis.

LADIES' NIGHT ON THE CALNUS

Back at the Calnus, you can view a new series of Private Actions at any point before you defeat the Grigori and report your victory to Ex. If you missed certain Private Actions earlier in the game (such as Edge's attempt to console Myuria in the battle simulation room), you may get a second chance to view them before the new events, listed below, will occur.

• For the first new event, speak to Myuria and Meracle at the bar in the Recreation Room. This event repairs the damage dealt to the Edge-Meracle relationship by the second-to-last Private Action on the flight over.

• Next, speak to Myuria on the Recreation Room couch for a rare opportunity to bond with your most elusive companion.

• Finally, meet Reimi in her quarters for a quick conversation. Then, follow her to the battle simulator room to do a bit of stargazing and learn about her future dreams.

En II

Map Treasures

1. Health Seeds x 1, Magic Seeds x 1
2. Bizarre Fruit x 1
3. [Ivy Barrier] Secret Diary x 1
4. 19,000 Fol
5. Perfect Berries x 2
6. Holy Water x 4
7. Recipe Memo 23 x 1

Pickpocketing

a. Insomniac Man	Compact Silence Bomb x 1
b. Viola, Awakened Master	Magic Capacitor x 1
c. Skittish Cat	Raw Fish x 1
d. Girl Who Sings from the Heart	Faerie of Wisdom x 1
e. Katrina, Believer in Fate	Gambleberries x 1
f. Jessica, Praying Woman	Demon Amulet x 1
g. Jealous Wife	Lesser Demon's Fetish x 1
h. Unyielding Man	MP Absorption Unit x 1
i. Depressed Man	DANGER! DO NOT DRINK! x 1
j. Determined Warrior	Sacrificial Doll x 1

Transport Room

k. Transport Controller	Resistance Potion x 1

Capsule Resort

l. Modest Woman	Holy Water x 1
m. Psychic Girl	Citrine x 1

Shopping Mall

n. Free-Spirited Woman	1001 Fol
o. Fanatic Cat	Greater Demon's Fetish x 1
p. Philosophical Man	Parchment x 1
q. Magical Chef	Fresh Sage x 1

Flora/Fauna Laboratory

r. Young-at-Heart Researcher	Secret Memo x 1

Legend

 = SAVE SPHERE

 = SHOP

 = PASSAGE

 = NPC

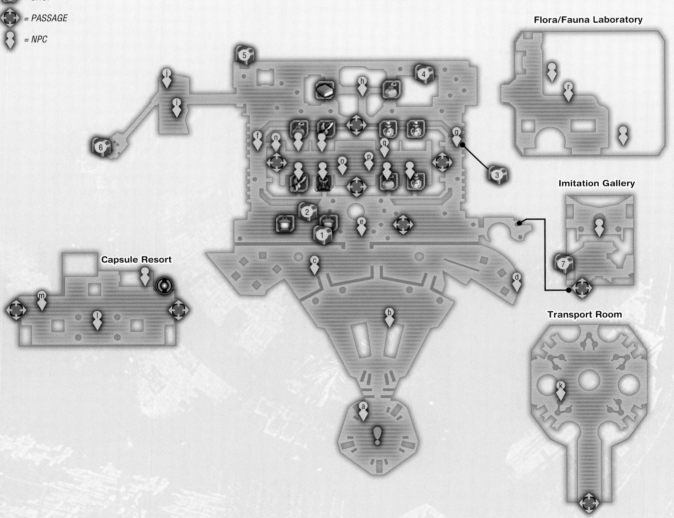

Flora/Fauna Laboratory

Imitation Gallery

Capsule Resort

Transport Room

UNEARTH THE WIND RING

To follow up on "The Wind Ring" quest, you can speak to the chief of the Flora/Fauna lab in the northeast corner of Centropolis, or go straight to the northwest graveyard. Amidst the headstones, a visitor soon informs you that the ring was buried, and you'll find the spot at the northernmost grave in the second row. There, you'll turn up a riddle that speaks of an "unyielding gravekeeper," referring to the tree in the upper part of the graveyard. Examine it to find the Wind Ring.

If you chat a bit with Myuria's friend Katrina, she'll give you a Funereal Bouquet and the recipe to make more. See the next chapter for details on how to use Funereal Bouquets to unlock Private Actions.

The Psychic Girl in the hotel can refill your rings. Your Wind Ring comes fully charged, but you'll also need a blast or two from your Earth and Fire Rings in the Old Road to the Sanctuary.

You can put the Wind Ring to work immediately by solving the "Unopenable Chest" quest offered by the Jealous Wife in the northeast part of town. That's only the first of several side quests in Centropolis; you can pick up another at the park near the skill shop, a pair of quests in the Shopping Mall, and one more quest (as well as a dozen exotic orders) in the Flora/Fauna Laboratory.

QUESTS IN EN II

THE WIND RING

REWARD: 1,000 EXP, 23 Party SP

Barago, Keeper of Past Knowledge is waiting near the entrance of the Old Road to the Sanctuary, where he'll ask you to get the Wind Ring from the cemetery in Centropolis. Read the grave with the pink exclamation point, and solve its riddle by examining the nearby tree. Report back to Barago for your reward.

THE UNOPENABLE CHEST

REWARD: 1,800 EXP, 45 Party SP, Echo Machine

The Jealous Wife standing near chest #3 desperately wants to get into her husband's ivy-sealed chest. Give it a blast from the Wind Ring, and hand her the Secret Diary inside. Your reward includes the Echo Machine ship's furnishing, which causes sound effects to echo in whichever room it's placed.

A DISTINGUISHED RARITY

REWARD: 2,400 EXP, 60 Party SP, Angelstone x 1

In the north part of town, the Unyielding Man wants to see a vase with true artistic merit. The solution to this quest is right in the title; of the four vases you can make with the Crafting skill, the Japonesque Vase is the one with the highest rarity. Pick up a Mental Stimulant at the Shopping Mall, and use it to whip up a vase on the Calnus.

GUITAR MAKER

REWARD: 3,600 EXP, 45 Party SP

The Free-Spirited Woman in the northwest corner of the Shopping Mall wants to break into music, but needs a guitar. Meracle can make the recipe with companions who add up to at least a 15 Crafting score and a 10 Sense score. The only rare ingredients are the Guitar Parts sold right here in the mall (you only need one).

WHERE'S THE RECIPE?

REWARD: 1,500 EXP, 41 Party SP, Recipe Memo 08

The Magical Chef in the shopping mall has lost the shopping list for her top-secret Mille-feuille. Strap on those Bandit's Gloves; you'll

find the Secret Memo in the pocket of her husband, the Young-at-Heart Researcher in the Flora/Fauna Laboratory. Return it for the reward, a copy of the recipe, and to re-open the chef's Magical Foods shop.

THE ELUSIVE FEMALE FIREFLY

REWARD: 3,000 EXP, 49 Party SP, Shortcake x 1

The Young-at-Heart Researcher in the Flora/Fauna Laboratory is looking for a female Crimson Firefly. If you have a pocket full of them already, he'll sift through them in search of one. If not, you'll have to go catch the glowing red fireflies that float around in Roak's Cave to the Purgatorium. Females are rare and occur at random, so you may have to catch a lot of them before you get lucky.

LOOK BEYOND THE EN II SHOPPING MALL

Don't blow all your money at Red Claw Weapons and D. Fense's Defensive Tools in the Shopping Mall, as Centropolis has another hidden armament shop in the grassy area to the southeast. It's called the Imitation Gallery, and it sells high-quality armor for the ladies in your party, as well as the Mighty Varigear for Bacchus. Xbox 360 owners should be wary about buying the Grim Reaper scythe, because you can probably make a better one with Item Creation (see Welch's Crafting Corner for details). But players of the PS3 version may want to pick it up. Myuria's Mysterious Scepter is a lousy buy for everyone, since you'll find a rough equivalent, the Raven Staff at the Old Road to the Sanctuary.

Don't miss the two other shops found outside of the mall; they sell a few ingredients at the Flora/Fauna Laboratory, and have a great selection of skill manuals at Green's Skill Guild. New skills include Sarah's Zoology and the must-buy Fast Cast for Myuria and Lymle.

IMITATION GALLERY - STOCK

Item	Type	Price
Mysterious Scepter	Weapon	48,000
Grim Reaper	Weapon	39,000
Holy Chainmail	Armor	58,000
Mighty Varigear	Armor	41,000
Sorceress's Robe	Armor	32,000
Sighting Unit	Other Items	500
Bunny Feed	Other Items	80

IMITATION GALLERY - ORDERS

Otherworldly Cuisine x 3

Reward	Rarity	From
5,000	☆	Shifty Guy

Mystery Box x 2

Reward	Rarity	From
10	☆☆	Shifty Guy

tri-Emblem x 9

Reward	Rarity	From
2,700	☆	Shifty Guy

GREEN'S SKILL GUILD - STOCK

Item	Type	Price
Skill Manual "Anthropology"	Usable Items	800
Skill Manual "Botany"	Usable Items	900
Skill Manual "Entomology"	Usable Items	600
Skill Manual "Parapsychology"	Usable Items	1,000
Skill Manual "Ornithology"	Usable Items	1,100
Skill Manual "Demonology"	Usable Items	2,200
Skill Manual "Zoology"	Usable Items	1,500
Skill Manual "Appetite"	Usable Items	1,800
Skill Manual "Chain Combos"	Usable Items	3,000
Skill Manual "HP Boost"	Usable Items	8,000
Skill Manual "MP Boost"	Usable Items	8,000
Skill Manual "Fast Cast"	Usable Items	8,000
Skill Manual "Critical Hit"	Usable Items	4,400
Skill Manual "No Guard"	Usable Items	3,000
Skill Manual "First Aid"	Usable Items	2,000
Skill Manual "Auto Healing"	Usable Items	4,200
Skill Manual "Stun"	Usable Items	3,500
Skill Manual "Fury Boost"	Usable Items	4,000
Skill Manual "Elusion"	Usable Items	1,000
Skill Manual "Rage"	Usable Items	3,000
Skill Manual "Steal"	Usable Items	19,800
Skill Manual "Taunt"	Usable Items	800
Skill Manual "Berserk"	Usable Items	2,500
Skill Manual "Scan Enemy"	Usable Items	1,500
Skill Manual "Convert"	Usable Items	2,500
Skill Manual "Hide"	Usable Items	1,200
Skill Manual "Mindflare"	Usable Items	3,000

FRONT DESK - STOCK

Item	Type	Price
Thornberries	Usable Items	100
Basil	Usable Items	30
Red Herb	Usable Items	100
Pumpkin Extract	Usable Items	200
Seaweed	Food	30

FRONT DESK - ORDERS

Bee Stinger x 15

Reward	Rarity	From
1,000	☆	Nimahl, Flora/Fauna Laboratory Chief

Saber-Toothed Tiger Fang x 15

Reward	Rarity	From
4,000	☆☆	Nimahl, Flora/Fauna Laboratory Chief

Peryton Droppings x 15

Reward	Rarity	From
300	☆	Nimahl, Flora/Fauna Laboratory Chief

Insect Egg x 15

Reward	Rarity	From
500	☆	Nimahl, Flora/Fauna Laboratory Chief

Tasty Mushroom? X 15

Reward	Rarity	From
600	☆	Nimahl, Flora/Fauna Laboratory Chief

Vile Goop x 15

Reward	Rarity	From
500	☆☆	Nimahl, Flora/Fauna Laboratory Chief

Rotten Fish x 15

Reward	Rarity	From
1,000	☆☆	Nimahl, Flora/Fauna Laboratory Chief

Sandfish x 1

Reward	Rarity	From
9,000	☆☆☆	Nimahl, Flora/Fauna Laboratory Chief

Raw Fish x 15

Reward	Rarity	From
1,000	☆	Nimahl, Flora/Fauna Laboratory Chief

Wolf Oil x 15

Reward	Rarity	From
600	☆	Nimahl, Flora/Fauna Laboratory Chief

meltina Jewelers - stock

Item	Type	Price
Magic Bracelet	Wrist Accessory	900
Stallion Snaps	Wrist Accessory	3,000
Fire Armlet	Wrist Accessory	15,000
Wind Armlet	Wrist Accessory	15,000
Earth Armlet	Wrist Accessory	15,000
Water Armlet	Wrist Accessory	15,000
Thunder Amulet	Wrist Accessory	15,000
Anti-Poison Amulet	Neck Accessory	8,000
Anti-Stun Amulet	Neck Accessory	4,000
Anti-Silence Amulet	Neck Accessory	4,000
Anti-Pumpkin Amulet	Neck Accessory	5,000
Raven Amulet	Neck Accessory	4,000
Green Talisman	Neck Accessory	4,800
Earth Charm	Neck Accessory	9,000
Water Charm	Neck Accessory	9,000
Fire Charm	Neck Accessory	9,000
Wind Charm	Neck Accessory	9,000
Thunder Charm	Neck Accessory	9,000

meltina Jewelers - stock

Slayer's Bangle x 2

Reward	Rarity	From
10,000	☆☆☆☆☆	Dazzling Woman

Darkness Scarf x 3

Reward	Rarity	From
30,000	☆☆	Dazzling Woman

Anti-Curse Amulet x 3

Reward	Rarity	From
12,000	☆☆☆☆	Dazzling Woman

Demon Amulet x 3

Reward	Rarity	From
2,000	☆☆☆	Dazzling Woman

Light Charm x 2

Reward	Rarity	From
6,000	☆☆☆☆	Dazzling Woman

silkworm's retro shop - stock

Item	Type	Price
Blessed Sword	Weapon	700
Silvance	Weapon	5,000
Bastard Sword	Weapon	11,000
Eldarian Bow	Weapon	500
Torch Bow	Weapon	800
Alien Arc	Weapon	5,400
Icicle Rapier	Weapon	4,000
Flame Wand	Weapon	1,500
Wand of Wonder	Weapon	5,800
Vermilion Claws	Weapon	5,800
Dragonscale Armor	Armor	3,500
Bronto Armor	Armor	3,800
Mystic Chainmail	Armor	1,000
Blizzard Protector	Armor	1,200
Streaked Chainmail	Armor	2,400
Aqua Robe	Armor	800
Comet Robe	Armor	2,400
Bandit's Gloves	Wrist Accessory	3,300
Sniper's Bangle	Wrist Accessory	800
Silver Bangle	Wrist Accessory	800
Sacrificial Doll	Neck Accessory	500
Warning Brooch	Neck Accessory	1,000
Alchemist's Water	Other Items	300

silkworm's retro shop - orders

Earthsoul Bow x 1

Reward	Rarity	From
3,000	☆☆☆	Hardcore Collector

Rune Wand x 1

Reward	Rarity	From
12,000	☆☆☆	Hardcore Collector

Staff of Freezing x 2

Reward	Rarity	From
30,000	☆☆☆	Hardcore Collector

Shell Armor x 2

Reward	Rarity	From
800	☆☆	Hardcore Collector

Iron Protector x 3

Reward	Rarity	From
500	☆☆	Hardcore Collector

Protective Robe x 2

Reward	Rarity	From
9,000	☆☆☆	Hardcore Collector

Sturdy Bracelet x 10

Reward	Rarity	From
12,000	☆	Hardcore Collector

red claw weapons - stock

Item	Type	Price
Observer's Sword	Weapon	36,000
Saint's Bow	Weapon	33,000
Sylph's Saber	Weapon	19,800
Booster Wand	Weapon	3,000
Plasma Cannon	Weapon	4,000
TO8 Lightning Cannon	Weapon	36,000
Slasher Claws	Weapon	48,000
Observer's Spear	Weapon	51,000

red claw weapons - orders

Spirit Bow "Darkstriker" x 1

Reward	Rarity	From
20,000	☆☆☆☆☆	Man Who Knows Too Much

Wand of Resonance x 1

Reward	Rarity	From
30,000	☆☆☆	Man Who Knows Too Much

Dragoon Blaster x 1

Reward	Rarity	From
25,000	☆☆☆☆	Man Who Knows Too Much

Sacred Spear x 1

Reward	Rarity	From
30,000	☆☆☆	Man Who Knows Too Much

Quadplex Scythe x 1

Reward	Rarity	From
40,000	☆☆☆	Man Who Knows Too Much

D. Fense's defensive tools - stock

Item	Type	Price
Astral Armor	Armor	6,000
Majestic Armor	Armor	8,000
Earthrock Mail	Armor	10,800
Duel Armor	Armor	36,000
Volcanic Chainmail	Armor	7,700
Star Protector	Armor	34,500
Alien's Robe	Armor	3,300
Flare Robe	Armor	10,000
Feathered Robe	Armor	12,000

D. Fense's defensive tools - orders

Ogre's Armor x 2

Reward	Rarity	From
12,000	☆☆☆	Armor Shopkeeper

Dragon Guard x 1

Reward	Rarity	From
11,000	☆☆☆	Armor Shopkeeper

Mithril Protector x 1

Reward	Rarity	From
15,000	☆☆☆	Armor Shopkeeper

Fully-Tuned Plate x 1

Reward	Rarity	From
15,000	☆☆☆	Armor Shopkeeper

Earthen Robe x 2

Reward	Rarity	From
20,000	☆☆☆☆	Armor Shopkeeper

masterful materials - stock

Item	Type	Price	Item	Type	Price
Tent	Usable Items	4,000	Dark Paint	Other Items	100
Ash	Other Items	800	Nil Paint	Other Items	160
Cashmere	Other Items	600	Healing Paint	Other Items	80
Velvet Ribbon	Other Items	800	Mysterious Paint	Other Items	60
Dwarven Embroidery Thread	Other Items	400	Attack Card	Other Items	60
All-Purpose Ceramic	Other Items	2,400	Attack Card+	Other Items	400
Magical Brush	Other Items	200	Healing Card	Other Items	60
Earth Paint	Other Items	80	Healing Card+	Other Items	400
Water Paint	Other Items	80	Support Card	Other Items	40
Fire Paint	Other Items	80	Support Card+	Other Items	300
Wind paint	Other Items	80	Parchment	Other Items	400
Thunder Paint	Other Items	80	Fine Parchment	Other Items	600
Light Paint	Other Items	100	Repair Kit	Other Items	100
			Swept Hilt	Other Items	200
			Guitar Parts	Other Items	200

masterful materials - orders

Fur Pelt x 6

Reward	Rarity	From
11,000	☆☆	Creative Warrior

Manacloth x 1

Reward	Rarity	From
2,000	☆☆☆	Creative Warrior

Mana Ribbon x 2

Reward	Rarity	From
1,000	☆☆☆☆	Creative Warrior

Citrine x 2

Reward	Rarity	From
9,900	☆☆☆☆	Creative Warrior

Faerie Embroidery Thread x 4

Reward	Rarity	From
3,000	☆☆☆☆	Creative Warrior

MIN-MIN'S REJUVENATION SHOP - STOCK

Item	Type	Price
Blueberries	Usable Items	40
Bigberries	Usable Items	100
Blackberries	Usable Items	60
Mixed Syrup	Usable Items	100
Perfect Berries	Usable Items	1,200
Physical Stimulant	Usable Items	800
Mental Stimulant	Usable Items	1,000
Aquaberries	Usable Items	30

Item	Type	Price
Basil	Usable Items	30
Fresh Sage	Usable Items	150
Hot Chocolate	Usable Items	50
Red Herb	Usable Items	100
Glowstick	Usable Items	90
Holy Water	Usable Items	120
Resurrection Elixir	Usable Items	2,000

MIN-MIN'S REJUVENATION SHOP - ORDERS

Super Aphrodisiac x 6

Reward	Rarity	From
10,000	☆☆	Soothing Girl

Growth Stimulant Ampule x 3

Reward	Rarity	From
6,000	☆☆☆	Soothing Girl

Hyper Potion x 5

Reward	Rarity	From
1,000	☆☆	Soothing Girl

Love Potion No. 256 x 5

Reward	Rarity	From
11,000	☆☆	Soothing Girl

Symbol Card "Healing"+ x 8

Reward	Rarity	From
10,000	☆☆☆☆	Soothing Girl

Symbol Card "Ex Healing"+ x 6

Reward	Rarity	From
12,000	☆☆☆☆	Soothing Girl

Symbol Card "Faerie Healing"+ x 6

Reward	Rarity	From
12,000	☆☆☆☆	Soothing Girl

Symbol Card "Faerie Light"+ x 4

Reward	Rarity	From
16,000	☆☆☆☆	Soothing Girl

Symbol Card "Antidote" x 10

Reward	Rarity	From
1,000	☆☆☆	Soothing Girl

Symbol Card "Cure Condition" x 5

Reward	Rarity	From
2,000	☆☆☆	Soothing Girl

Symbol Card "Restoration"+ x 5

Reward	Rarity	From
3,000	☆☆☆☆	Soothing Girl

FLAMING FIST EXPLOSIVES - STOCK

Item	Type	Price
Poison Relief Unit	Usable Items	300
Melting Unit	Usable Items	500
Mobilization Unit	Usable Items	300
Speech Restoration Unit	Usable Items	1,000
Vision Enhancement Unit	Usable Items	900
Dispelling Unit	Usable Items	1,200
Intelligence Breaker	Usable Items	500
Defense Breaker	Usable Items	400
EM Bomb	Usable Items	400
Wide-Range EM Bomb	Usable Items	1,200
Compact Poison Bomb	Usable Items	800
Compact Stun Bomb	Usable Items	800
Compact Freezing Bomb	Usable Items	800
Compact Silence Bomb	Usable Items	700
Scrambling Unit	Usable Items	300
Rivet	Other Items	20
Magic Capacitor	Other Items	800
Universal Device	Other Items	100
Micro Circuit	Other Items	400
Micro Hadron Collider	Other Items	3,200
Laser Oscillator	Other Items	3,000
Mystery Electronic Circuit	Other Items	1,300
Mystery Mobile Frame	Other Items	1,800

flaming fist explosives - orders

Plastic Explosive x 15

Reward	Rarity	From
3,000	☆☆	Symbologist Woman

Intensified Gunpowder x 12

Reward	Rarity	From
2,000	☆☆	Symbologist Woman

Disintegration Stone x 8

Reward	Rarity	From
5,000	☆☆☆	Symbologist Woman

Steel x 4

Reward	Rarity	From
2,000	☆☆	Symbologist Woman

Element Breaker x 10

Reward	Rarity	From
1,200	☆☆	Symbologist Woman

magical foods - stock

Item	Type	Price
Riot Potion	Usable Items	600
Fainting Potion	Usable Items	200
Natto	Food	300
Natural Water	Other Items	120
Vinegar	Other Items	40
White Rice	Other Items	60
Uncooked Pasta	Other Items	100
Common Egg	Other Items	30
Vegetables	Other Items	60
Seasonings	Other Items	20
Olive Oil	Other Items	80
Special Warishita Sauce	Other Items	120
Fresh Cream	Other Items	100
Pie Crusts	Other Items	60

magical foods - orders

Raw Animal Meat x 14

Reward	Rarity	From
500	☆	Magical Chef

Dragonblood Crystal x 1

Reward	Rarity	From
6,000	☆☆☆☆	Magical Chef

Sharkskin x 12

Reward	Rarity	From
800	☆	Magical Chef

Hamburg Steak x 4

Reward	Rarity	From
800	☆☆	Magical Chef

WELCH'S crafting corner

ARUMAT P. THANATOS, WEAPON DESIGNER EXTRAORDINAIRE

Arumat may have the same Alchemy skill that Faize did, but don't assume that he'll inspire the same recipes in others. When paired with Edge or Bacchus, Arumat is able to come up with many of the game's best Smithery and Engineering recipes, and can inspire a few new recipes with Lymle, Meracle, and Myuria as well. The majority of these recipes require very rare gems or metals, but with the ingredients sold on En II, you can complete a few of them, as well as a bunch of old recipes that were missing one key ingredient.

In the Xbox 360 version, the Laser Oscillators and All-Purpose Ceramics that are available in the Shopping Mall allow you to complete two powerful recipes. Those ingredients are all you need to make Arumat's powerful Laser Scythe, which outclasses anything you can buy for him at this point. Also, a team of Bacchus (with Engineering at level 10), Arumat and Sarah can whip up a recipe for a super-tough Laser Suit that any party member can wear. In addition to Laser Oscillators, the recipe requires a few Gnomestones (which you probably mined in the Miga Insect Warren) and an Aurora Rings+ Symbol Card (Which requires six bottles of Light Paint and a piece of Fine Parchment).

However, in Star Ocean International for the PS3, both of these recipes have become more difficult. The Laser Scythe now requires two pieces of Citrine, while the Laser Suit requires four pieces of Thorstone instead of the Gnomestones. Both of these rare minerals can be mined in the Sanctuary area to come. At least PS3 owners can still whip up a music-playing Jukebox for their ship; the recipe requires two Micro Circuits, a Laser Oscillator, and four pieces of Ebony in either version of the game. And while it's nowhere near as powerful as the Laser Suit, PS3 owners can make a powerful suit of Ogre's Armor for Edge or Arumat if they have 12 pieces of Steel on hand.

Many of the recipes Arumat inspires are legendary weapons that appear only as "???????????" when invented. These aren't necessarily the game's best weapons, but they're very strong. In the Xbox 360 version of the game, you can make the first one: Reimi's legendary Spirit Bow "Darkstriker," a level-9 Smithery recipe developed by Edge, Reimi, and Arumat. The recipe requires Darkness Gems (mined throughout Lemuris) as well as the Aramid Fiber and Carbon Fiber sold in Tatroi. Sadly, PS3 users are out of luck again, as the Star Ocean International version of this recipe also requires a Darkness Charm, which can only be made with a Recipe Memo acquired on the game's final planet.

Map Treasures

1. Poison Relief Unit x 3
2. Ebony x 1
3. [Ivy Barrier] Skill Manual "Bunny Call" x 1
4. Skill Manual "Focus" x 1
5. Recipe Memo 15 x 1
6. [Light Barrier] Skill Manual "Godslayer" x 1
7. 30,003 Fol
8. Skill Manual "Haggling" x 1
9. [Ice Barrier] Raven Staff x 1
10. [Dark Barrier] Recipe Memo 03 x 1
11. Disintegration Stone x 1
12. Bracteate x 1

Pickpocketing

a. Barago, Keeper of Past Knowledge	Natto x 1

Monsters

STROPER

HP · 13649	EXP · 629
Fol · 263	Race · Plant

Resistant To · Water
Weak Against · Fire

DROPS
Intelligence Seeds, Aquaberries, Basil

CURSED HORROR

HP · 12242	EXP · 842
Fol · 171	Race · Undead

Resistant To · Dark
Weak Against · Light

DROPS
Faerie Embroidery Thread, Red Herb, Lesser Demon's Fetish, Shadow Rose, Alchemist's Cloak

METAL GOLEM

HP · 15581	EXP · 1,474
Fol · 2,351	Race · Mech

Resistant To · Earth
Weak Against · Thunder

DROPS
Bracteate, Void Recovery Unit

LIGHTNING CORPSE

HP · 10651	EXP · 943
Fol · 269	Race · Undead

Resistant To · Thunder
Weak Against · Water

DROPS
Thorstone, Disintegration Stone, Thunder Paint, Thunder Gem

MASTER WIZARD

HP · 11524	EXP · 1,375
Fol · 270	Race · Undead

Resistant To · --
Weak Against · --

DROPS
Dragonblood Crystal, Hot Chocolate, Mana Ribbon, Manacloth, Fine Parchment

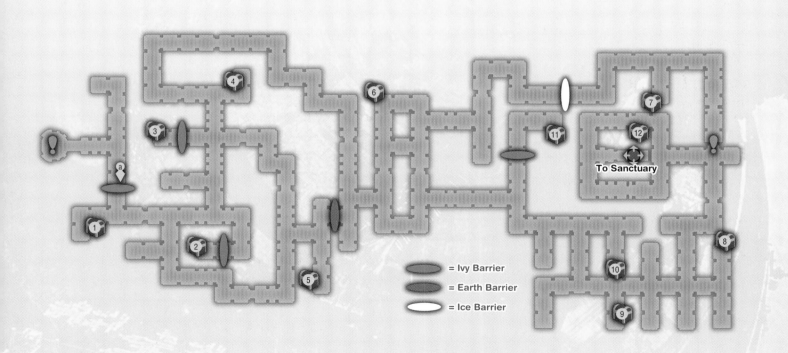

To Sanctuary

= Ivy Barrier

= Earth Barrier

= Ice Barrier

HUNT DOWN THE OLD ROAD SKILL MANUALS

The Old Road to the Sanctuary is a straightforward, single-floor maze. The only potential hitch is the ivy, ice, and earth barriers that block some of the chests, so you'll want to make sure you have at least a few charges in each of your rings. To get through the maze quickly, follow the chests in numerical order, dropping down the ledge after you claim chest #7 and making another loop around the Sanctuary exit. There's a save sphere right at the entrance to the Sanctuary, so if you're hurting, stop in to save your game before claiming chests 8 through 11.

Besides Recipe Memo 03 (for Sarah's Sacred Spear), the most interesting items here are the Bunny Call and Haggling skill manuals. Bunny Call allows Sarah to summon a Bunny on any field area, but not in dungeons like this one. Haggling won't lower the prices of the items you buy, but it does slightly raise the resale value of the items you sell.

CORPSE-ROBBING THE UNDEAD

The monsters of the Old Road to the Sanctuary hold a few rare items, including Shadow Roses, Dragonblood Crystals, and Mana Ribbons. The Cursed Horrors and Mana Wizards that hold the good stuff are both undead, so make sure Lymle has full mastery of the Parapsychology skill.

Neither foe is particularly dangerous, since both rely on symbols that can be disrupted by an aggressive frontline offense. It's the company they keep that may get you into trouble; the explosive bursts of electricity from their frequent Lightning Corpse companions can easily paralyze half your party, especially when you have multiple melee fighters on the board. Take the Lightning Corpses out first, and be quick with the Basil so you can get your fighters back on line before they are swamped by Cursed Horrors.

EN II: SANCTUARY

Map Treasures

1. Recipe Memo 28 x 1
2. Holy Chainmail x 1
3. Biocloth x 2
4. Memorial Plate x 1

Legend

 = SAVE SPHERE

 = PASSAGE

◎ = RECOVERY SPHERE

⚱ = NPC

Harvesting Point Items

Bigberries	Perfect Berries
Blueberries	Ripe Berries
Blue Rose	Shadow Rose
Fresh Sage	Thornberries
Oak	

Mining Point Items

Angelstone	Nereidstone
Disintegration Stone	Ruby
Gnomestone	Silver
Magical Clay	Thorstone
Meteorite	Wind Gem
Mithril	

To Old Road to the Sanctuary

Monsters

CURSED HORROR
HP · 12242	EXP · 842
Fol · 171	Race · Undead

Resistant To · Dark
Weak Against · Light

DROPS
Faerie Embroidery Thread, Red Herb, Lesser Demon's Fetish, Shadow Rose, Alchemist's Cloak

MASTER WIZARD
HP · 11524	EXP · 1,375
Fol · 270	Race · Undead

Resistant To · --
Weak Against · --

DROPS
Dragonblood Crystal, Hot Chocolate, Mana Ribbon, Manacloth, Fine Parchment

ANCIENT CHIMERA
HP · 21955	EXP · 2,040
Fol · 804	Race · Demon

Resistant To · Fire, Wind
Weak Against · Earth, Water

DROPS
Cane, Basil, Ebony, Snakeskin

EARLY PSYNARD
HP · 25237	EXP · 4,500
Fol · 419	Race · Bird

Resistant To · Fire
Weak Against · Water

DROPS
Psynard Egg, Holy Water, Barrier Spiritwater, Giant Bird Feather

SEARCH THE SANCTUARY BEFORE FACING THE GRIGORI

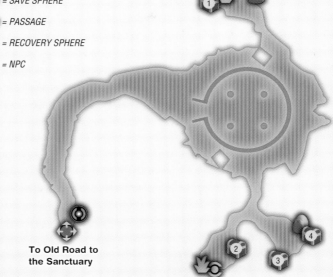

En II's precious sacred gems must look out for themselves for a while, because there's no way you and your team are rushing straight at the boss without clearing a path to the recovery sphere first. You'll find it to the south from the Grigori, near a chest that contains a suit of Holy Chainmail for Reimi or Meracle. None of the other chests can help with the battle ahead, but fighting the local monsters, collecting treasure, and hitting the harvesting and mining points is a good way to level up.

Don't get cocky when dealing with the Early Psynards, who can quickly send you to an early grave if you allow them to repeatedly use their devastating Plasma Cyclone symbols. When facing these flaming raptors, swap out anyone who is able to cast fire-type symbols (they just can't hold back!) and swap in aggressive fighters like Edge, Arumat, and Meracle. Use special arts like Mystic Cross and Acrobatic Vault as soon as the Psynards begin the casting process.

The Memorial Plate in the southeast chest is the final ingredient for the Memory Plate, a level 8 Smithery Recipe. This ship furnishing records all sorts of interesting gameplay data.

Search around the walls in the southwest and southeast nooks of the Sanctuary to reveal hidden harvesting points and mining points.

Kokabiel

HP · ???	EXP · 63,166
Fol · 30,712	Race · Other

Resistant To · *Earth, Ice, Fire, Wind, Thunder, Light*

Weak Against · *Dark*

DROPS
Potent Magic Seeds

BOSS

Kokabiel Spawn

HP · ???	EXP · 0
Fol · 15	Race · Other

Resistant To · *Earth, Ice, Fire, Wind, Thunder, Light*

Weak Against · *Dark*

DROPS
--

Crush Kokabiel and Slaughter its Spawn

The ideal party for this battle is Arumat, Edge, and Reimi, all set to "Gang up on foes with full force!" Fill out your party with Sarah for buff symbols and healing, and if that's not enough to keep your party alive, swap out Reimi for Lymle so you'll have a back-up healer. Don't try to battle Kokabiel with symbols, since even dark-type ones deal negligible amounts of damage.

Kokabiel is initially accompanied by 16 Kokabiel Spawn, grouped in clusters of four. You can destroy 12 of the spawn with minimal amounts of damage, while the other four are completely immune to all forms of attack. When you kill all but the four indestructible ones, Kokabiel then pulls them towards himself and regenerates his fallen spawn in a giant ball of light. This is your opportunity to go hog-wild on Kokabiel, damaging him heavily and destroying many of the spawn as soon as they're regenerated. You'll want to play as Arumat, whose wide strikes make it easy to hit the evasive Kokabiel Spawn, and whose Critical Hit skill helps ramp up the damage to Kokabiel itself.

Most of Kokabiel's attacks involve the spawn, so destroying them weakens him on both offense and defense. But every now and then, Kokabiel decides to get a little more personally involved, dishing out a long combo with a green energy blade. This combo deals devastating amounts of damage but is slow enough that you can dodge it by continuously leaping out of the way.

There's no need to bother with anything fancy in this fight; Blindsides aren't worth the bother, and Rush Mode combos typically won't do much damage. Just focus on staying alive as you repeat the cycle of culling the Kokabiel Spawn and unloading your special arts combos on Kokabiel's light bubble.

THE TRIALS OF THE SANCTUARY

You'll be returned to Centropolis as soon as Kokabiel falls. Don't worry about any unclaimed treasures, since you can now return directly to the Sanctuary whenever you like by using a portal in Centropolis's Transport Room. This makes it relatively easy to farm the harvesting and mining points in the Sanctuary. Players who intend to complete all the remaining Private Actions must make several trips until they find enough Blue Roses and Dendrobium to make seven more Funereal Bouquets. You'll also want to speak to the four sacred gems at the shrine in the center of the Sanctuary, which offer a challenging series of trials with exceptional rewards.

All of that is optional, of course, as are the two new Private Actions in Centropolis. When you're ready to move on to the game's final challenges, take the elevator to Monitor Room A for a second chat with "Ex." Then, return to the Calnus and set a course for Nox Obscurus.

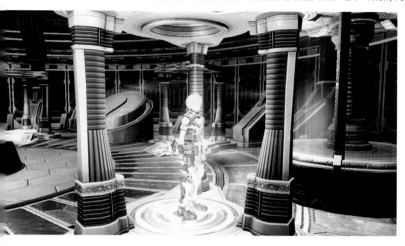

QUIET HOMECOMINGS FOR YOUR MORPHUS FRIENDS

After rescuing the Sanctuary, Myuria and Bacchus finally have a bit of time to catch up on personal business. Myuria lives in the apartment building west of the Shopping Mall, while Bacchus lives in the building to the east. Simply examine the buildings' front doors to trigger the events.

• After Myuria reminisces about her lost love, she'll ask Edge how he intends to propose. You'll gain affinity from any of the choices, but you'll gain the most by selecting "I'd probably hide a letter in a gift I gave her."

• The Bacchus event is a follow-up to the long-ago event in which he first told Edge about his wife, so if you blew that one off, you won't be able to see its sequel here. Once again, you'll have three choices. If you urge Bacchus to see his wife, his opinion of Edge will drop. Instead, simply say, "It's a really nice building."

✦ THE TRIALS OF THE SACRED GEMS

Each of the four Sacred Gems in the heart of the Sanctuary has a side quest to offer. The Trials of Courage and Might are the easiest to complete, and offer spectacular rewards. The Greater Sacrificial Doll is one of the game's best accessories, and the high-ATK, high-INT Laser Weapon can be used by anyone in your party, outpacing all but the best weapons of Lymle, Sarah, and Myuria. The Trial of Love is barely worth the trouble,although Achievement hunters do need to finish it, and the Chalice of Love prize makes for a good Synthesis ingredient (providing a 3% bonus to HP and MP in a single factor). The Trial of Wisdom is well worth the lengthy diversion, as its Skill Manual "Faerie Star" reward offers access to the strongest recovery symbol in the game.

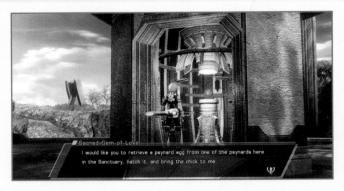

THE TRIAL OF LOVE

REWARD: *4,000 EXP, 40 Party SP, Chalice of Love*

The Sacred Gem of Love (red) wants you to win a Psynard Egg from one of the local Early Psynard monsters, hatch it, and bring the chick to the Sanctuary. Psynard Eggs are a very rare drop, so max out Meracle's Ornithology skill and have her equip the Steal battle skill to raise your odds of winning one. Bring the egg to Nimahl in the Flora/Fauna Laboratory, where you'll receive Recipe Memo 30, a Compounding recipe that allows you to make a Growth Stimulant Ampule out of common ingredients. Bring the completed ampule to Nimahl, and he'll hatch the chick for you. Return to the sacred gem for your reward.

THE TRIAL OF COURAGE

REWARD: *4,000 EXP, 40 Party SP, Greater Sacrificial Doll*

Heal up and save before you speak to the Sacred Gem of Courage (blue), as you'll be plunged into a lengthy battle as soon as you accept its quest. The battle is a four-part ambush, featuring new foes that are minor variations on enemies you've fought in the past. If you can handle the Sanctuary's Early Psynards and Ancient Chimeras, you should be able to handle these foes. Make sure to heal at the end of each ambush, when only a single foe remains.

THE TRIAL OF WISDOM

REWARD: *4,000 EXP, 40 Party SP, Skill Manual "Faerie Star"*

The Sacred Gem of Wisdom (green) gives you a Cryptograph and asks you to follow its hints on an intergalactic treasure hunt. Cryptograph 1 points you to a thin icy path in the northeast corner of Lemuris's Thalia Plains. Cryptograph 2 directs you to a swampy patch of Aeos's Southern Reaches, and Cryptograph 3 sends you to a pillar outside of the eastern Cave to the Purgatorium entrance in the Tropp Area. (You'll find more specific details in the next section.)

THE TRIAL OF MIGHT

REWARD: *4,000 EXP, 40 Party SP, Laser Weapon*

As with the Trial of Courage, the Sacred Gem of Might (white) plunges you into a battle as soon as you accept its quest. The Vigorous Beast you'll face is vulnerable to symbols of all types except earth and dark, so you'll want a party heavy on symbol-users. You should play as your best fighter, keeping the beast juggled with special arts combos that make it a sitting duck for your friends' symbols.

Map Treasures

1. Void Recovery Unit x 3, Fresh Sage x 1
2. Hot Chocolate x 2
3. Manacloth x 1
4. 68,000 Fol
5. Recipe Memo 12 x 1
6. Insect Egg x 2
7. [Dark Barrier] Darkness Charm x 1
9. Vile Goop x 4
10. [PS3-only] Mana Ribbons x 2

Harvesting Point Items

Basil	Insect Egg
Bigberries	Red Herb
Fresh Sage	Ripe Berries
Ginseng	Thornberries

Mining Point Items

Coal	Mercury
Darkness Gem	Mithril
Disintegration Stone	Ruby
Green Beryl	Runic Metal

Pickpocketing

a. Extremely Prudent Woman	Support Card x 1
b. Trembling Girl	Magic Seeds x 1
c. Self-Suggesting Warrior	Hyper Potion x 1
d. Vigorous Warrior	Dragonblood Crystal x 1
e. Morale-Boosting Warrior	Ripe Berries x 1
f. Louvre, Healing Symbol Master	Healing Paint x 1

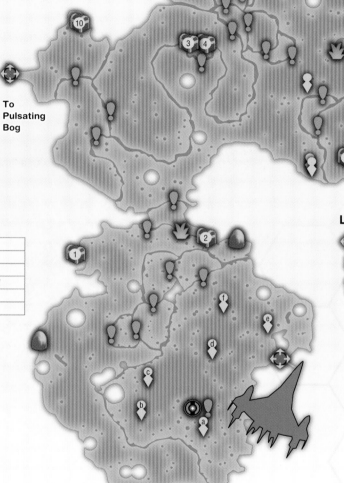

To Pulsating Bog

To Pulsating Bog

Legend

= PASSAGE

= NPC

= INTERACTION POINT

Nox Obscurus

Monsters

PHANTOM BEETLE

HP · *19384* EXP · *1,643*
Fol · *311* Race · *Insect*

Resistant To · *Dark*
Weak Against · *Earth*

DROPS
Biocloth, Insect Leg, Thornberries

PHANTOM CHIMERA

HP · *23609* EXP · *3,486*
Fol · *965* Race · *Demon*

Resistant To · *Dark*
Weak Against · *Earth*

DROPS
Bizarre Fruit, Red Herb, Holy Water, Snakeskin

SOUL REAPER

HP · *20017* EXP · *1,419*
Fol · *2,572* Race · *Undead*

Resistant To · *Dark*
Weak Against · *Light*

DROPS
Lezard's Flask, Runic Metal, Attack Card

DARK PANZER

HP · *20017* EXP · *1,878*
Fol · *386* Race · *Humanoid*

Resistant To · *Dark*
Weak Against · --

DROPS
Mercury, Blackberries, Thornberries

DARK SOLDIER

HP · *17893* EXP · *1,598*
Fol · *280* Race · *Humanoid*

Resistant To · *Dark*
Weak Against · --

DROPS
Shadestone, Blackberries, Bracteate

PHANTOM LIZARD

HP · *17893* EXP · *2,215*
Fol · *467* Race · *Animal*

Resistant To · *Dark*
Weak Against · --

DROPS
Physical Stimulant, Fresh Sage, Bigberries

LITTLE PHANTOM

HP · *19384* EXP · *3,930*
Fol · *311* Race · *Humanoid*

Resistant To · *Dark*
Weak Against · --

DROPS
Intelligence Seeds, Hot Chocolate, Red Herb, Silent Cider, Alien's Robe

---

THE AMPLE RESOURCES OF NOX OBSCURUS

With a name like Ravine of Extinction, this region of Nox Obscurus probably won't be a resort community anytime soon. However, you couldn't ask for more amenities: the Calnus is there, and while it isn't going anywhere, you're free to use all of its facilities, craft items with Welch, and rest in its rooms. A nearby healer will also heal you for free.

Perhaps the best resource of all is the transporter that the Morphus have kindly installed in the southern part of the map. The transporter can take you directly to any city on any planet that Edge hasn't accidentally obliterated.

As you might have guessed, you're nearing the end of the game, so now is the time to return to Lemuris, Aeos, Roak, and En II to finish up old quests, trigger a few new quests, view a final batch of Private Actions, and collect the loot from all of those ivy-sealed chests that confounded you so long ago. Of course, all of those tasks are optional, but if you want to get the best pre-boss gear and an affinity boost for each of your allies, you won't want to miss this opportunity.

GREET THE NEW ORACLE OF LEMURIS (OPTIONAL)

For your questing convenience, it's easiest to tackle the planets in Trial-of-Wisdom order. If you haven't visited Lemuris in a while, you'll find that a lot has changed: the Alanaire Citadel is open again, with Lutea as the Oracle. Meracle can translate for all of the cats in Woodley, and one of them helpfully points you to a hidden cache that contains 22,222 Fol. You can now accept the "A Cherished Keepsake" quest, and finish up "Fang Flute Fabrication" and "Further Fang Flute Fabrication" while you're in town. If you haven't spoken to Lutea's mom lately, do so now to get Recipe Memo 07.

From Woodley, head east to the north entrance of the Alanaire Citadel, which has been repaired by the townsfolk. Make your way to the top, pausing to hit the ivy-sealed chest and dark energy-sealed chest along the way. In the PS3 version, the ivy-sealed chest contains a Sacred Scepter for Myuria, while the dark energy-sealed chest contains a damage-nullifying Blue Talisman accessory. In the Xbox 360 version, the contents are reversed, with the Sacred Scepter in the dark-energy chest.

When you get to the top, speak with Lutea to trigger a Lymle Private Action and earn the weapons data for the Oracle's Staff. Exit to the icy balcony to the north and come back to trigger a second Lymle Private Action. After two game hours have passed, you can return to Lutea to accept the "Lutea's Secret Stones" quest.

SAY HELLO TO LUTEA AND GOODBYE TO GHIMDO

After hearing Lutea's first story about Lymle's early years, exit to the balcony, and then go speak to Lutea again to trigger a second Private Action. Both of her stories slightly boost Edge's Affinity with Lymle.

For another affinity boost, you can trigger the first of eight funeral Private Actions. Viewing each event costs you a Funereal Bouquet, so if you don't intend to mass-produce bouquets, you may want to save your free one for a Private Action on Nox Obscurus that directly impacts the game's ending. But if you're willing to burn one on Lymle, bring her to Triom and examine Ghimdo's grave.

PRIVATE ACTIONS

NEW QUESTS ON LEMURIS

SIDE QUESTS

A CHERISHED KEEPSAKE
REWARD: 100 EXP, 20 Party SP, Skill Manual "Chain Combos" x 1

The boy in the Woodley inn has lost a cherished keepsake, and thinks that a cat is to blame. Have Meracle translate for the cat in the item shop (assuming you rescued it already during the side quest "The Curious Kitty"), and it will give you the Oracle's Charm. Return it to earn another copy of the ever-useful Chain Combos skill.

WOOD FOR THE HEARTH
REWARD: 140 EXP, 20 Party SP, Attack Seeds x 1

The Accommodating Woman in the southeast part of town needs 10 Wooden Sticks for her fire. Wooden Sticks are a common find at Van Elm Region harvesting points, and are also dropped by Dryads and Man-Eating Trees.

LUTEA'S SECRET STONE
REWARD: 2,000 EXP, 99 Party SP, Lutea's Sacred Stone

Lutea challenges Lymle to bring her a Salamanderstone, Gnomestone, Sylphstone, Nereidstone, Thorstone, Angelstone, and Shadestone. Salamanderstone and Sylphstone can be mined in the Astral Desert, while Gnomestone, Nereidstone, Thorstone, and Angelstone are all found in the mining points within En II's Sanctuary. Shadestone can be mined in the Astral Desert and the Cave to the Purgatorium. It hurts to hand over such precious ingredients, but the reward is worth it: Lutea's Sacred Stone is a neck accessory that provides the same 15% damage-negation as the Blue Talisman, but also tacks on across-the-board stat and elemental boosts when worn by Lymle. Synthesize it ad nauseam—Lymle's not going to find anything better.

HUNT FOR TREASURE IN LEMURIS'S ICY EAST (OPTIONAL)

Players in the midst of the Sanctuary's Trial of Wisdom quest should leave the Alanaire Citadel through its original south exit, then head east along the northern wall to find a thin snowy valley where a white sparkle marks the second Cryptograph.

While in the neighborhood, cut through Wind Swallow Valley to pay a visit to the celestial ship. There, you'll find two ivy-sealed chests and little in the

way of enemies to guard them. The loot includes Bacchus's Immortal Smasher, an Anti-Freezing Amulet, and Recipe Memo 25, which reveals all you need to know to make more Blue Talismans.

PAY YOUR RESPECTS TO PLANET AEOS'S FALLEN (OPTIONAL)

You can find transfer symbols (which function the same as the Nox Obscurus transporter) just outside of Triom and Woodley. Use either one to reach Planet Aeos, where you can locate the next Cryptograph and lay flowers at two different memorial spots.

The third Cryptograph is in a small, swampy area on the west side of the Southern Reaches, just north of where you fought the Phantoms.

MAKESHIFT MEMORIALS ON PLANET AEOS

A pink exclamation point marks the spot in the Exploration Base rubble where Edge and Reimi can pay tribute to Captain Grafton and their other fallen comrades. This Private Action simply raises Edge's opinion of Reimi, who may already be your closest friend. So if you're being stingy

with the flowers, sorry Captain— your death just isn't bouquet-worthy.

Those who do have bouquets to spare will surely want to use one on Arumat. To trigger his funeral event, traverse the Undersea Tunnel to reach the Southern Reaches, and head to the open shoreline south of the entrance (but north of where you fought the phantoms). You'll notice some spaceship debris has landed here, which Arumat identifies as being from an Eldarian evacuation vessel. Lay down a bouquet and gain affinity from Arumat's relatively warm words.

PRIVATE ACTIONS

UNSEAL THE PURGATORIUM'S IVY PASSAGE (OPTIONAL)

Transport yourself to Tropp, and pay Lady Eleyna a visit. She'll demand you complete the "It Came from the Vent" quest, and then trigger a pair of Private Actions for Meracle. You can see a third Private Action on the docks in Tropp.

Head east through the Tropp Area, towards the far entrance to the Cave to the Purgatorium. If you've been following the Trial of Wisdom, you should see the sparkle of the Philosopher's Tome at the base of a pillar at the desert's edge. Continue through the cave to the Purgatorium, where you'll find ivy-bound chests on level B1 (containing Recipe Memo 24) and B2 (an Anti-Void Amulet). But the good stuff is on level B3, where using the Wind Ring to clear an ivy-bound wall allows you into the previously inaccessible southeast wing. You then must clear two statue puzzles, and in both the statues quickly point out the order of all remaining firepots as soon as you light the first one. The first statue opens a passage to a light crystal to the south, where you can charge your Light Ring. Use that on a shadow barrier to reach the first chest, which contains Sylphide's Mail for Edge. The chest to the north holds a suit of Folklore Plate for Bacchus.

LADY ELEYNA AND HER FELINE FRIEND

After completing the "It Came from the Vent" quest (see below), return to Lady Eleyna to trigger the first of three Meracle-focused Private Actions. If you're willing to spend a Funereal Bouquet on Meracle, leave Eleyna's hideout and return to speak with her yet again.

Meracle's third Private Action is set on Tropp's northern dock, but you won't trigger it unless you already have a considerable amount of affinity with Meracle. (Note that this is the only condition to seeing it; it isn't dependent on the previous two Eleyna-related Private Actions.) If you don't trigger the cutscene, you'll need to slather on the Love Potion No. 256 and give the Pickpocketing a rest.

PRIVATE ACTIONS

LEAD SARAH ON A TRIP DOWN MEMORY LANE (OPTIONAL)

Now make your way back to Tatroi, where you'll find three doses of Physical Stimulant in the ivy-bound chest outside of the colosseum. Then visit Jasmine, Queen of Inventors to complete her final pair of errands and win Recipe Memo 01 (Edge's Arcana Sword). You can visit Astral Castle to trigger Sarah's Funereal Bouquet Private Action, or lead her back to the Calnus's landing spot in the Northeast Astralian Continent for a bit of flight practice.

❖ NEW QUESTS ON ROAK

IT CAME FROM THE VENT

REWARD: *600 EXP, 38 Party SP, Recipe Memo 13*

A monster is blocking the air vent to Eleyna's secret hideout, and she wants you to kill it. The blocked air vent is directly above the hideout, on the edge of the cliff. Follow the cliff's edge until it meets the ground, then get on top of the cliff. Follow the same edge back to the north until you see a Vomiting Gel on a stone chimney, and defeat it in combat. A grateful Eleyna then gives you the recipe for a Healing Sheet you can roll out on the Calnus.

THE FOURTH ERRAND

REWARD: *1,200 EXP, 34 Party SP, Silent Talisman*

Jasmine wants 20 units of Intensified Gunpowder, which you can make with a level 4 Compounding recipe. Mine for the Thunder Gems in the Astral Desert and Tatroi Area, and buy the Gunpowder in Tatroi or, better yet, from your ship's Li'l Vending Machine No. 2.

THE FIFTH ERRAND

REWARD: *2,400 EXP, 36 Party SP, Recipe Memo 01*

After you deliver the Intensified Gunpowder, Jasmine makes her final request: 12 Giant Bird Feathers. You can get these from local Axe Beaks, or you may already have them on hand. Delivering them finally satisfies Jasmine for good, earning you Recipe Memo 01 as severance.

THE CLUELESS EMISSARY OF THE FEATHERFOLK

Sarah's Funereal Bouquet event is a fun one: speak to the king of Astral Castle with a bouquet in your inventory to make Sarah recall an important errand.

To trigger Sarah's other Private Action, you'll need to return to the place where the Calnus used to dock in the Northeast Astralian Continent. This is the sequel to the treadmill event on the Calnus, which you had several chances to see earlier in the game. If you blew it off, don't bother making the long hike.

TAKE CARE OF UNFINISHED BUSINESS IN EN II (OPTIONAL)

You're close to completing your tour of the galaxy on En II, where you can return the Philosopher's Tome at the Sanctuary to receive your reward for the Trial of Wisdom quest. You can use the Skill Manual "Faerie Star" to teach the game's best mass-healing symbol to Edge, Lymle, Myuria, or Sarah. Sarah's already a pretty strong healer, so you should probably teach it to Lymle or Myuria to spread the wealth around.

The Computers in Monitor Room B have now been updated with a ton of new spaceship data files, giving you the opportunity to add the Zamzagiel, Dominion, Calnus-III, Aquila-B, Phantom craft [SRF Style], and USTA warship to your collections. You can now also view the Funereal Bouquet events for Bacchus and Myuria.

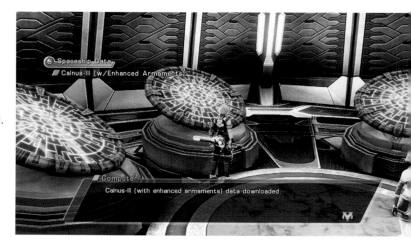

THE MORPHUS MEMORIAL SERVICES

Myuria's Funereal Bouquet event is right where you'd expect it to be: at Lucien's grave beneath the tree in the Centropolis cemetery. Myuria can be stingy with the affinity, so it's probably a good idea to whip up a bouquet for this one.

It's unlikely that you'll need to raise your affinity with Bacchus, but if you want to see  his event, return to the Docks where the Calnus used to be. Head down the dead-end passageway in the northwest corner of the map to remind Bacchus of the heavy losses suffered by the Morphus fleet.

Don't blunder into the gray gas jets that dot the ravine. Instead of the usual 1% of HP damage, these toxic fumes can poison half your party.

TRAVERSE THE HARSH LANDSCAPE OF NOX OBSCURUS

And now, you're back! Say goodbye to the pristine snow of Lemuris and the clear waters of Roak, and say hello to the toxic wasteland of Nox Obscurus. When you're ready to get your feet dirty, head north to the series of pink exclamation points that mark the places where you can hop down to the ravine basin. As soon as you take that first leap, you'll be attacked by an army of Dark Soldiers, which are among the most difficult enemies in the area. Single out the Dark Panzers that are the leaders of the group and take them out as quickly as possible to negate the bonuses they grant to their foot soldiers. The enemies in the basin aren't much more pleasant, with

Soul Reapers that cause nasty status conditions with their every strike, and dark, tiny Little Phantoms that are difficult to spot against Nox Obscurus's black soil.

In the ravine basin, head north to the next exclamation point, where you'll find giant bubbles rising out of a swamp. The only way to get on top of the ledge is to hitch a ride; stand near the point where the last bubble emerged and wait for another one to rise beneath you. When the bubble is roughly 20 feet over the ledge with Edge inside, press Ⓐ to leap out of it. If you leap too soon or too late, you'll fall back and have to wait for the next one to form. Riding bubbles in the ravine's southernmost swamp is the only way to return to the plateau with the Calnus and transporter.

ATTAINING CLOSURE WITH YOUR CREW

When you visit the cabin of the grounded Calnus, you can trigger a final series of Private Actions. However, none of these events can occur unless you already have a substantial amount of affinity with each crew member. If any of the Private Actions fail to trigger, it's a safe bet that you won't be seeing that character's ending unless you can inflate your affinity with heavy doses of Love Potion No. 256. (Note that the final Private Actions for Meracle and Sarah occur in Tropp and the Northeast Astralian Continent, respectively; see earlier in this section for details.)

If you've seen all of the prerequisite events (and you should have, if you've been following this guide), you'll find Myuria at the Recreation Room bar, Lymle and Cerberus in the storage room north of the Item Creation terminal, Bacchus in the 2F Hallway, Arumat in his quarters, and Reimi in the battle simulator room. Only the Reimi event has a secondary condition: way back on the flight from the Cardianon Mothership, you have to have told Reimi that you promised to "show her the stars."

Map Treasures

1. Disintegration Stone x 2
2. Monster Jewel x 2
3. Nightmare Wand x 1
4. Ripe Berries x 2
5. Blueberries x 19
6. Magic Seeds x 1, Fresh Sage x 2

Pickpocketing

a. Orwen, Dutiful Warrior	Fire Gem x 1

Harvesting Point Items

Ash	Fresh Sage
Basil	Poison Hemlock
Bigberries	Thornberries
Blackberries	

Mining Point Items

Coal	Mercury
Crystal Skull	Mithril
Darkness Gem	Runic Metal
Disintegration Stone	Star Ruby

Monsters

PHANTOM CHIMERA
HP · 23609 · EXP · 3,486
Fol · 965 · Race · Demon
Resistant To · Dark
Weak Against · Earth

DROPS
Bizarre Fruit, Red Herb, Holy Water, Snakeskin

CHAOTIC LEADER
HP · 21557 · EXP · 1,878
Fol · 386 · Race · Undead
Resistant To · Dark
Weak Against · Fire

DROPS
Attack Seeds, Aquaberries, Vile Goop, DANGER! DO NOT DRINK!

SOUL REAPER
HP · 20017 · EXP · 1,419
Fol · 2,572 · Race · Undead
Resistant To · Dark
Weak Against · Light

DROPS
Lezard's Flask, Runic Metal, Attack Card

DARK MATERIAL
HP · 28593 · EXP · 2,230
Fol · 646 · Race · Demon
Resistant To · Dark
Weak Against · Light

DROPS
Crystal Skull, Glowstick, Cloudy Cider, Darkness Gem, Shadestone

PHANTOM LIZARD
HP · 17893 · EXP · 2,215
Fol · 467 · Race · Animal
Resistant To · Dark
Weak Against · --

DROPS
Physical Stimulant, Fresh Sage, Bigberries

LITTLE PHANTOM
HP · 19384 · EXP · 3,930
Fol · 311 · Race · Humanoid
Resistant To · Dark
Weak Against · --

DROPS
Intelligence Seeds, Hot Chocolate, Red Herb, Silent Cider, Alien's Robe

Legend

 = SAVE SPHERE

 = PASSAGE

 = RECOVERY SPHERE

 = NPC

 = INTERACTION POINT

To Ravine of Extinction

To Ravine of Extinction

To Halls of Termination

HOLD THE NORTHERN RIDGE AGAINST THE PHANTOMS

Enter the Pulsating Bog from the northeast entrance, and head directly northwest to find the only rising bubble that can take you up to the top of the ridge. There, you'll find the only new armament on the fields of Nox Obscurus: Lymle's Nightmare Wand. You'll also find a recovery sphere, which gives you an opportunity to earn blue and red Bonus Board tiles by emptying your MP pools as you fight every enemy on the

ridge. When you have had your fill of fighting, drop down to the bog and make your way southwest through the area.

THE TWO SURVIVORS OF THE MORPHUS OFFENSIVE

Ever since you left the Calnus's plateau, the NPC map icons have lead you to nothing but dead bodies. You'll finally find a pair of survivors just outside of the entrance to the Halls of Termination, although neither is long for this world. Orwen, Dutiful Warrior entrusts you with "The Last Letter" side quest, while Lenore, Dying Symbologist offers to use the last of her strength to recharge one of your rings. It's the Earth Ring that you'll need most in the area ahead, but you should charge it yourself if you have the skill and Disintegration Stones to spare. If you let Lenore do it, it serves as her last act on this cruel, cruel world.

❖ THE MOST DEPRESSING SIDE QUEST EVER   **SIDE QUESTS**

THE LAST LETTER

REWARD: 3,000 EXP, 50 Party SP

A dying Orwen entrusts you with the "Letter from Orwen," asking you to find his wife, Jessica, on En II. Take the transporter back to En II, and ask around in the Monitor Rooms. You'll learn that Jessica has herself hopped a ship to Nox Obscurus, and hasn't been heard from since. Return to Orwen, where you'll see that Jessica has already discovered her husband. Give her the letter to earn your reward.

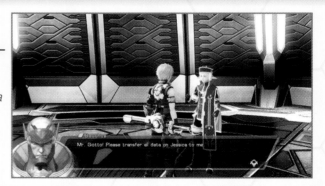

MAP TREASURES

1. Bizarre Fruit x 1
2. 53 Fol
3. Mental Stimulant x 3
4. Manacloth x 2
5. Health Seeds x 1
6. Disintegration Stone x 2
7. [Light Barrier] Skill Manual "Plasma Cyclone"
8. Dragon Scale x 1

HARVESTING POINT ITEMS

Ash	Health Seeds
Basil	Basil
Bigberries	Blackberries
Blackberries	Ripe Berries
Cane	Thornberries

MINING POINT ITEMS

Crystal Skull	Runic Metal
Darkness Gem	Shadestone
Disintegration Stone	Star Ruby
Mithril	Star Sapphire

MONSTERS

DARK RAPTOR
HP · 28593	EXP · 2,115
Fol · 331	Race · Humanoid

Resistant To · Dark
Weak Against · Light

DROPS
Disintegration Stone, Cardianon Sword, Basil, Static Cider

DARK BOT "STRIKER"
HP · 15885	EXP · 1,538
Fol · 497	Race · Demon

Resistant To · Dark
Weak Against · Light

DROPS
MP Absorption Unit, Poison Relief Unit, Scrambling Unit

PHANTOM DRAGOON
HP · 37159	EXP · 7,448
Fol · 819	Race · Mech

Resistant To · Wind, Thunder
Weak Against · Water

DROPS
Symbol Booster, Cardianon Bow, Rivet

CHAOTIC LEADER
HP · 21557	EXP · 1,878
Fol · 386	Race · Undead

Resistant To · Dark
Weak Against · Fire

DROPS
Attack Seeds, Aquaberries, Vile Goop, DANGER! DO NOT DRINK!

PHANTOM DRAGON NEWT
HP · 25069	EXP · 3,279
Fol · 887	Race · Demon

Resistant To · --
Weak Against · --

DROPS
Red Dragon Scale, Dragon Scale

DARK MATERIAL
HP · 28593	EXP · 2,230
Fol · 646	Race · Demon

Resistant To · Dark
Weak Against · Light

DROPS
Crystal Skull, Glowstick, Cloudy Cider, Darkness Gem, Shadestone

Legend

◎ = SAVE SPHERE

✦ = PASSAGE

❗ = INTERACTION POINT

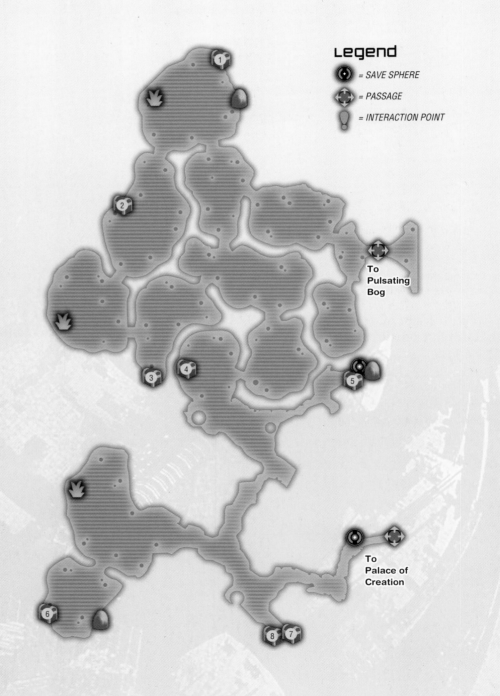

To Pulsating Bog

To Palace of Creation

DESTROY THE SILENT CRYSTALS

Glowing crystals that cast wide circles of dark energy obstruct the trail through the Halls of Termination. If you end up in a battle within a crystal's energy field, you'll discover that all of your skills, symbols, and special arts have been sealed away, leaving you with standard attacks

and items as your only defense against some very powerful foes. To proceed safely, lure enemies out of the circle, where you can more effectively defeat them, then approach the crystal and disintegrate it with your Earth Ring. Don't attempt to sneak up to the crystals with Bacchus's Stealth ability, or you'll be in for a nasty surprise.

A CHOICE BETWEEN DISCRETION AND VALOR

If you're determined to begin your assault on the Palace of Creation, you'll find the entrance at the end of this map. But if you don't feel

well prepared for the tougher challenges ahead, you should search the Halls of Termination for rare ingredients (see sidebar below) and then make your way back to the Calnus to craft new and better gear.

THE FINAL FUNERAL

If you still have a Funereal Bouquet, you can trigger the game's final Private Action at the end of the Halls of Termination. Laying flowers at the remains of Crowe's ship inspires a poignant speech from Edge and earns him a few last affinity points from Reimi. More importantly, it unlocks a new scene after the ending credit roll, which is worth a Trophy/Achievement.

PRIVATE ACTIONS

WELCH'S crafting corner

INGREDIENT HUNTING IN THE HALLS OF TERMINATION

As you near the end of the game, there are only a handful of missing ingredients that are keeping you from making the game's best items. The big culprits are Moonstones and the Philosopher's Stone, which show up in almost every high-level recipe and yet remain impossible to find. Sigh.

However, there are a few rare ingredients on Nox Obscurus that expand your Item Creation options. Star Rubies, Star Sapphires, and Crystal Skulls can be mined occasionally in the Pulsating Bog and more frequently in the Halls of Termination. Those who are willing to put even more effort into their Item Creation endeavors can farm the Halls of Termination for two rare monster drops: the Phantom Dragon Newt's Red Dragon Scale and the Phantom Dragoon's Symbol Booster.

Star Sapphires allow you to make Arumat's Quadplex Scythe and attack-negating Blue Talismans. In the PS3 version, a Star Sapphire will also allow you to complete Bacchus's Fully-Tuned Plate armor (the sapphire isn't necessary in the Xbox 360 version). You can use Star Rubies to make Lymle's fire-boosting Star Ruby Wand and magic-negating Red Talismans. Pick up a Symbol Booster, and you can turn your Star Sapphires into Lymle's Wand of Resonance (which thoroughly trumps the Star Ruby Wand) or Myuria's mighty Calamity Staff (which also requires a single Crystal Skull). A few Red Dragon Scales allow you to whip up Meracle's Bigfoot's Claws or a suit of Dragon Mail armor. Finally, in the PS3 version, a Crystal Skull will also allow you to complete the recipe for Sarah's Sacred Spear. (No Crystal Skull is required in the Xbox 360 version.)

If you've earned Recipe Memo 01 by completing Jasmine's series of quests in Tatroi, you should now have enough Meteorites to complete Edge's Arcana Sword. Don't forget to make a bunch of Resurrection Units (in the Compounding recipes section), which eventually prove useful in the difficult boss fights ahead.

Map Treasures

Area 1
1. Physical Stimulant x 4
2. Aquaberries x 4, Tent x 1
3. 81,000 Fol
4. Dragon Scale x 2

Area 2
1. [Ice Barrier] Sea Serpent Harpoon x 1
2. Scrambling Unit x 3
3. Attack Seeds x 1, Health Seeds x 1
4. 15 Fol
5. Frozen Cider x 2, Poison Cider x 1, Silent Cider x 2, Pumpkin Cider x 1, DANGER! DO NOT DRINK! x 1
6. Bizarre Fruit x2, [PS3-only] Thornberries x 1
7. Vile Goop x 3
8. Monster Jewel x 1, Fresh Sage x 4
9. Fresh Sage x 3

Area 3
1. [Ice Barrier] Magic Seeds x1
2. Mental Stimulant x 3, Ripe Berries x 1
3. Mercury x 1
4. Mithril x 1
5. 108,000 Fol
6. Disintegration Stone x 2
7. Parchment x 9
8. Meteorite x 1
9. Thunderbolt Gear x 1

Area 4
1. Vulcan Discharger x 1
2. Darkness Gem x 2
3. Monster Jewel x 1, Tent x 1
4. [Ivy Barrier] [PS3-only] Star Sapphire x 1

Area 5
1. Bracteate x 2
2. Shadestone x 1
3. Skill Manual "ATK Boost" x 1

Area 6
1. [Fire Barrier] Intelligence Seeds x 1
2. [Dark Barrier] Holy Sword "Farewell" x 1
3. Pumpkin Extract x 3, Resurrection Elixir x 2
4. Rivet x 1
5. [Ice Barrier] [X360-only] Red Dragon Scale x 1, [PS3-only] Red Dragon Scale x 2
6. [Ivy Barrier] Recipe Memo 10 x 1
7. Mithril x 1
8. Dullahan's Armor x 1
9. Meteorite x 1

Area 7
1. Fresh Sage x4, [PS3-only] Blackberries x 12
2. Manacloth x 1
3. [X360-only] Blackberries x 12, Thornberries x 1, [PS3-only] Dragonblood Crystal x 1

Legend

 = SAVE SPHERE

 = PASSAGE

= RECOVERY SPHERE

 = INTERACTION POINT

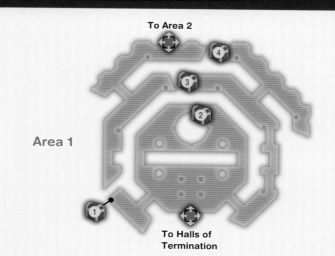

To Area 2

Area 1

To Halls of Termination

Note: Special icon is warp gate. Each warp gate connects to the warp gate it's pointing towards.

Area 2

To Area 3

To Area 1

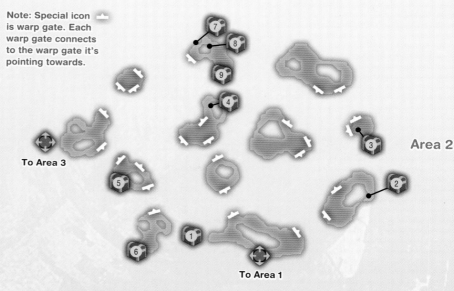

To Area 4

To Area 2

Area 3

To Area 5

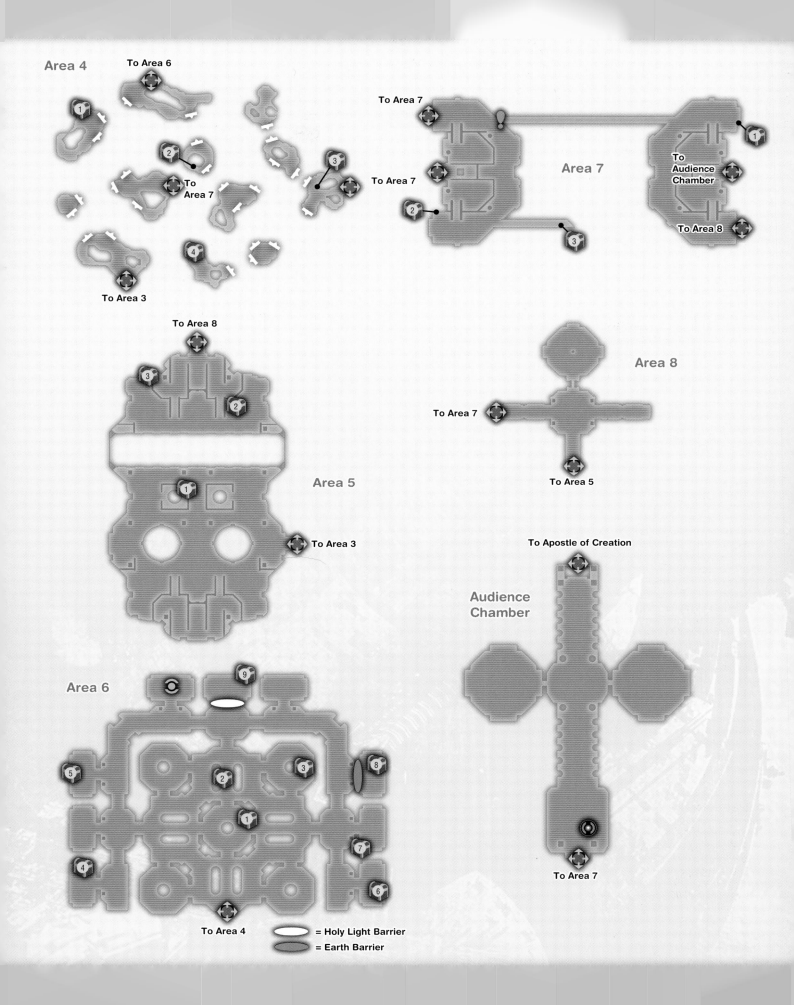

Area 4

To Area 6

1

2

3

To Area 7

4

To Area 3

To Area 7

To Area 7

2

3

Area 7

1

To Audience Chamber

To Area 8

To Area 8

3

2

1

To Area 3

Area 5

Area 8

To Area 7

To Area 5

To Apostle of Creation

Audience Chamber

Area 6

9

5

2

3

8

1

4

7

6

To Area 4

To Area 7

= Holy Light Barrier

= Earth Barrier

monsters

PHANTOM LIZARD
HP · 17893   EXP · 2,215
Fol · 467   Race · Animal
Resistant To · Dark
Weak Against · --
DROPS
Physical Stimulant, Fresh Sage, Bigberries

PHANTOM DRAGON NEWT
HP · 25069   EXP · 3,279
Fol · 887   Race · Demon
Resistant To · --
Weak Against · --
DROPS
Red Dragon Scale, Dragon Scale

DARK APE
HP · 30967   EXP · 3,137
Fol · 443   Race · Animal
Resistant To · Dark
Weak Against · --
DROPS
Health Seeds, Hot Chocolate, Frozen Cider, Bigberries

DARK CLOWN
HP · 25673   EXP · 2,609
Fol · 1,163   Race · Demon
Resistant To · --
Weak Against · --
DROPS
Dragonblood Crystal, Pumpkin Extract, Pumpkin Cider

DARK RAPTOR
HP · 28593   EXP · 2,115
Fol · 331   Race · Humanoid
Resistant To · Dark
Weak Against · Light
DROPS
Disintegration Stone, Cardianon Sword, Basil, Static Cider

CHAOTIC CELL
HP · 18920   EXP · 1,551
Fol · 396   Race · Plant
Resistant To · Fire
Weak Against · Thunder
DROPS
Accuracy Seeds, Aquaberries, Basil, Vile Goop, Poison Cider

DARK BISHOP
HP · 21614   EXP · 1,895
Fol · 456   Race · Humanoid
Resistant To · Dark
Weak Against · --
DROPS
Mental Stimulant, Pumpkin Extract, Parchment

FORSAKEN BEAST
HP · 59815   EXP · 14,617
Fol · 3,404   Race · Demon
Resistant To · Dark
Weak Against · Light
DROPS
Star Sapphire, Star Ruby, Shadestone

CHAOTIC LEADER
HP · 21557   EXP · 1,878
Fol · 386   Race · Undead
Resistant To · Dark
Weak Against · Fire
DROPS
Attack Seeds, Aquaberries, Vile Goop, DANGER! DO NOT DRINK!

LAVA GOLEM
HP · 48224   EXP · 2,952
Fol · 6,482   Race · Demon
Resistant To · Fire
Weak Against · Water
DROPS
Meteorite, Mithril, Coal

NECROMANCER
HP · 33386   EXP · 2,776
Fol · 378   Race · Undead
Resistant To · Dark
Weak Against · --
DROPS
Biocloth, Hot Chocolate, Holy Water, Void Recovery Unit

RESTART THE FLOW OF TIME IN AREA 1

A strange temporal phenomenon has frozen the first area of the Palace of Creation, stilling all movement and transforming monsters into statues. You can still open treasure chests, although a frozen golem is blocking the path to the first one. For now, loot chests #2-4, then return to the lower of the two eastern catwalks. There, you'll find what appears to be a small platform at the end of a pendulum. Like turning the hands of a clock, putting Edge's weight on the platform both restarts time and swings the pendulum across to the west side of the map. Before you make your way to the door to Area 2, swing back across to the east side so you can reach the newly accessible chest #1.

 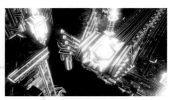

If you have to fight the Lava Golem for the chest, and you have a Bonus Board to protect, don't even try engaging the Lava Golem at close range. Take control of Myuria and have her blast it with Deep Freeze symbols from a safe distance.

WARP ACROSS AREA 2'S METEOR FIELD

You'll be in for a surprising change of scenery when you step through the door to Area 2, and a pair of Phantoms seems very happy to take advantage of that by launching an ambush. Get used to it; the tiny planetoids that compose this area don't leave much room for maneuvering, and the sudden transition from warp gate to warp gate allows foes to strike while you're still recovering your bearings. Using Bacchus's Stealth skill may not allow you to avoid all of the monsters, but it does make it a whole lot easier to prevent ambushes and surprise attacks.

From the entrance to the area, head to your right and use the chain of glowing warp gates to reach chests #2 and #3 on the east side of the map. Then, backtrack to the first planetoid and use the western series of warp gates to collect the remaining chests and reach the entrance to Area 3.

CUT THROUGH AREA 3 TO REACH THE HEART OF THE PALACE

Area 3 is a straightforward map with plenty of treasure chests and wide hallways that make it easy to avoid monsters. None of the loot here is all that great; the only item you can put to immediate use is Bacchus's

Thunderbolt Gear in the northwest-corner room. (And that isn't really any better than the Fully-Tuned Plate you may have already whipped up on the Calnus.)

From this map, you can exit north to Area 4 or west to Area 5. Don't let the numbers fool you—it's quickest to go to Area 5 first. Area 5 is another frozen room, and to get things moving again, you'll need to climb the stairs at the south end and melt the ice around the pendulum platform. Take that for a ride to the north end of the map, where you'll find the Skill Manual "ATK Boost," the only truly great treasure in the Palace of Creation. Teach ATK Boost to a fighter, max it up (it's much cheaper than the other

boost skills), and equip it to a battle-skill slot for a *1,000 point* ATK boost. Consider this choice carefully, because whoever gets it is going to your most powerful character for a good long time.

DISCOVER THE SECRET OF THE SERPENT STAFF

Leave Area 5 to the north and you'll find yourself in the tiny Area 8. Continue north, using your newly ATK-Boosted warrior to cut through a Forsaken Beast that would otherwise have been a considerable challenge. Examine the statue, and then study its reflection in one of the mirrors to the north. That action allows you to return to the statue and claim the Serpent Staff for your own.

Before you return to Area 3, head west to Area 7, another frozen room. All of the stairways on this map subsequently collapse under Edge's weight, so from this entrance, all you can do is grab the contents of Chest #1.

USE THE STAFF TO REACTIVATE THE AREA 7 PENDULUM

Go back the way you came, taking the south exit of Area 8 and riding the pendulum across Area 5 to return to Area 3. This time, leave through the north exit to Area 4. Area 4 is another planetoid maze, with

the only twist being that the warp gates won't appear until you step within a few feet of them.

From the entrance, warp north to the nearest gate to Area 7. Once again, all the staircases in the frozen room collapse when you step on them, so all you can do is claim the remaining pair of chests.

Back out in Area 4, warp one planetoid to the northwest to find a new weapon for Bacchus, and then warp to the northeast to find the entrance to Area 6. Area 6 is a dead-end treasure room that holds a new weapon for Edge and new armor for either Edge or Arumat, but the greatest treasure of all is a long-awaited recovery sphere. Don't think you can reach it easily, however; you'll have to face Dark Clowns that can cast powerful symbols, steamroll foes for thousands of points of damage, and throw condition-inflicting confetti. Make them your priority targets, because they're the deadliest foes in the Palace of Creation.

Once Area 6 has been thoroughly looted (save for the chests that require the Water and Darkness Rings, of course), return to Area 4. Warp your way to chests #2 and #3, and then head to Area 7 via the easternmost warp gate. As soon as you step through the gate, your Serpent Staff comes alive to destroy the shackles on the pendulum, allowing you to swing across to the Audience Chamber. There, you'll find a save sphere and the door to the first boss of Nox Obscurus.

BOSS

Apostle of Creation

HP • ???	EXP • 63,052
Fol • 7,984	Race • Other
Resistant To • Dark	
Weak Against • Light	

DROPS
--

Bring Destruction to the Apostle of Creation

To keep your party spaced out, you'll want to face the Apostle of Creation with a single frontline fighter backed up by three long-range characters: Sarah (with all of her non-healing, non-enhancement symbols turned off), either Reimi or Bacchus, and Myuria or Lymle. Everyone should probably be set to BEAT:N, because at this point, good stats are more important than anything else. Obviously, this would be a fine time to feed everyone meals from Reimi's catering cart.

The Apostle of Creation is a tentative fighter, but when he does strike, his attacks can be devastating. Fortunately, he usually telegraphs them with a line of dialogue that gives you plenty of time to get out of the way. When you hear "witness the quintessence of my catastrophic powers," leap far away to get out of range of his powerful circular strike. But when you hear "away with your pointless ostentation," you know he'll be attacking straight ahead, and a simple leap to either side can get you out of the way and in position to retaliate. Always attack the apostle with your longest special arts combos so you can keep him on the ropes as long as possible, buying time for your symbol users to do their thing.

As he gets weaker, he'll become more aggressive, warping around the battlefield to attack characters at random. He'll also add a new wide-area attack, heralded by the phrase "be destroyed." If you leap away, you'll have time to dodge the deadly energy fields, but your allies are rarely so lucky. Be ready to throw down a Fresh Sage or Resurrection Elixir on Sarah before you charge back into the fray.

REUNITE WITH OLD FIENDS IN AN ALTERNATE DIMENSION

You didn't really think it would be that easy, did you? The apostle next plunges you into an alternate dimension populated by all of the Grigori you've defeated before: Sahariel, Barachiel, Armaros Manifest, and Kokabiel. They're stronger than they used to be, but significantly easier than the Apostle of Creation was, and still every bit as vulnerable to the strategies you used to beat them the first time. This area is a battle of endurance, so make sure to keep your characters' MP up with skills like Convert and items that offer MP regeneration; you'll need to use symbols for most of your healing so you can save your best items for the final battle.

There's no map for this area, so pick a direction—either to Edge's left or Edge's right—and follow the rim of the path on that side. Either route should lead you to two of the four bosses, with Sahariel and Barachiel along the left rim, and Armaros Manifest and Kokabiel along the right. It's actually possible to avoid all of the boss encounters, although it isn't easy. The trick is to hug the wall closely and move towards the bright white light in the distance at all times. Whenever your path forks, switch sides and hug the wall on the opposite side while continuing to move towards the bright white light. Whether you successfully avoid the bosses or not, the glowing white light eventually leads you to the game's final boss.

BOSS

Satanail

HP · ???	EXP · 0
Fol · 0	Race · Other
Resistant To · Dark	
Weak Against · Light	

DROPS
--

Hammer Down Satanail

In the first phase of the final battle, Satanail protects himself with a shield of four colored orbs. When he spins the shield, whatever color is on the bottom determines the attacks available to him. Most of the attacks are similar, but the yellow orb's unique ability to inflict status conditions makes it particularly annoying. Be ready with recovery items and Cure Condition symbols whenever it rolls around.

The bottom orb is the only one thing that can be successfully targeted by your fighters, and it can only be hit from head on. Keep your allies on the "Gang up on foes with full force!" tactic so they'll follow your lead and attack the crystal instead of striking at Satanail. When everyone's lining up to hit the orbs, they'll

be very vulnerable to counterattacks, so choose your party on the basis of the fighters who are most likely to survive a constant stream of physical punishment; probably Edge, Bacchus, and Arumat, unless you've given your best defensive gear to Meracle. (Of course, you'll always want Sarah in the fourth slot for healing.)

When the orb shield is destroyed, you'll need to shake up your roster. Satanail frequently uses a spin attack that can heavily damage everyone near him, so a spread-out party is essential.

That means one fighter, Sarah, and two ranged attackers or symbol-users. Well-equipped parties with levels around 55 or higher can win most quickly with Lymle and Myuria, but weaker parties may need to field Bacchus in place of their weakest symbol-user to stay alive.

Satanail has a ton of hit points, so taking control of your frontline fighter and making sure he's always using his most effective special arts combos is the quickest way to bring this long battle to a conclusion. But if you're having trouble surviving, you should take control of Sarah instead. That way, you can use Restoration on dead characters immediately, use the right healing symbol at the right time, and put the Enshelter, Enhance, and Angel Feather enhancement symbols to good use on the rare occasions when you have a bit of breathing room. Since

Satanail can now be hit from any angle, and any form of attack, your NPC allies should be capable of putting on a competent offense. Their inability to use special arts combos leads to a much longer fight, but with Sarah always casting the right symbol at the right time, even underpowered parties should eventually be able to eke out a victory.

THE DARK RING

RESUME YOUR QUEST AFTER THE CREDITS ROLL

Choose to save your game when prompted during the ending, and load up that file when you are ready to continue your quest. You'll resume from the Palace of Creation save sphere, but with all of the EXP and Fol you earned in the game's final battles. Chronologically, you'll still be where you were when you first made this save file, before you defeated the Apostle of Creation and Satanail. (So you can beat the game again if you want to unlock additional endings.)

The only difference is that the two sealed doors on the east and west sides of the Palace of Creation's Audience Chamber are now open. To the east, you'll find a one-way transfer symbol to the Calnus. To the west, you'll find the powerful Undying Dragon. This dragon holds the Darkness Ring, and slaying it is the first step of *Star Ocean: The Last Hope*'s post-ending content.

THE NINE BONUS ENDINGS OF *STAR OCEAN 4*

After defeating the boss, you'll view the game's lengthy ending, followed by up to seven brief ending vignettes, one for each of Edge's comrades. After the credits roll, you can view up to two bonus epilogues. You'll earn a 10-point Achievement or Bronze Trophy for each scene you unlocked.

Your comrades' endings are based entirely on affinity. If a character's affinity for Edge and Edge's affinity for that character combine to reach a preset value, you'll earn the ending. If you rarely pickpocket and are diligent about viewing each of the game's Private Actions, it is possible to unlock all seven endings in a single playthrough. Those who pickpocket more regularly consequently must use several doses of Love Potion No. 256 to repair the damage. Arumat is the hardest character to unlock, so you'll want to make sure he's Edge's roommate from the moment he joins your party. Myuria and Sarah are a little tricky, so you'll want to prioritize their Private Actions whenever you have a choice. Winning affinity with Reimi, Bacchus, Lymle, and Meracle should be easy for attentive players.

To unlock Crowe's epilogue, you need to earn the endings for Reimi, Meracle, and Sarah, and to have completed the following four specific Private Actions:

• On the fifth leg of the flight to Cardianon, speak to Reimi in the battle-simulator room. (This is the only Private Action option for that leg of the flight.)

• After recruiting Myuria but before you complete the Purgatorium, return to the Calnus and speak to Bacchus and Myuria in the Crew Quarters.

• During the flight to En II and also while docked on En II, you're given several opportunities to trigger a Private Action between Edge, Arumat, and Reimi in which Arumat asks about your relationship with Crowe. You must tell Arumat that Crowe is either your best friend or rival.

• Place a Funereal Bouquet near the remains of Crowe's ship in the Halls of Termination (near the entrance to the Palace of Creation) on Nox Obscurus.

To unlock Faize's epilogue, you must trigger the following eight Private Actions over the course of the game:

• On the third leg of the flight from Lemuris to Cardianon, view Faize's first training event in the storage area north of the Meeting Room.

• On the fifth leg of the flight from the Cardianon Mothership to the alternate Earth, trigger the event at the Item Creation terminal that ends with an accidental kiss between Lymle and Faize.

• On the next leg of the same flight, speak with Lymle in the Recreation Room.

• On the third leg of the flight from Planet Roak to Planet Aeos, skip the Meracle event and speak to Lymle in the Recreation Room instead.

• The next Private Action requires that Faize and Lymle be roommates. Speak to them in their shared room on either the fourth leg of the flight from Roak to Planet Aeos, or after triggering the angry-Faize training event while docked on Planet Aeos.

• On the second leg of the flight from Planet Aeos to En II, have some cookies with Lymle and Reimi in the Recreation Room.

• On the seventh leg of the flight from Planet Aeos to En II, speak to Sarah and Lymle in the room with the battle simulator.

• Finally, while docked on Nox Obscuris, speak with Lymle in the storage area north of the Meeting Room. To trigger this Private Action, Lymle needs to have a good amount of affinity for Edge and Faize, and vice versa.

If the epilogue doesn't provide enough closure for you, try replaying the game. At the point at which Arumat joins you, players with a cleared game file are given the option to keep Faize in their party instead of adding Arumat. This doesn't change the game's story —Arumat still appears in the event scenes.

Post-Ending Content

BOSS

Undying Dragon

HP · *1896572*   EXP · *41,365*
Fol · *31,189*   Race · *Demon*

Resistant To · *Fire*
Weak Against · *Water*

DROPS
Darkness Ring

Bring Death to the Undying Dragon

The Undying Dragon has an obscene amount of hit points, but should be much easier to defeat than Satanail was. As a creature vulnerable to all forms of juggles and knockbacks, it's easy to keep bouncing it off the tip of Edge or Arumat's blade while Reimi, Bacchus, and Myuria pelt it from a distance. When the Undying Dragon enters Rush Mode, the tables will turn. The dragon's ability to leap up and land with earthquake-level force makes it dangerous to be anywhere near it, so leap away as soon as it enters Rush Mode or launches itself into the air. Switch from fighter to fighter until you find the character with the fullest Rush Gauge, and fill it up with a few long-distance pot shots so you can unload a Rush Combo on the beast from a nice safe distance. Repeat, repeat, and repeat again… eventually, you'll bring the Undying Dragon down.

TRACK DOWN THE HOLY LIGHT CHESTS

Before you use the Darkness Ring to open the door to the Cave of the Seven Stars, it's a good idea to open the rest of the light-sealed chests that have been scattered throughout the universe. These chests primarily contain exclusive special arts and symbol skills, one for each member of your party. (The skills for Edge, Sarah, and Meracle are still to come.) Here's a quick list of holy light-sealed chests to jog your memory:

- You'll find Skill Manual "Trinity Blaze" (for Lymle) at the balcony on the top floor of the Alanaire Citadel.

- On the bottom floor of the Purgatorium (where you fough Tamiel), you'll find Reimi's Skill Manual "Savage Sparrows" in the Xbox 360 version, and Sarah's Skill Manual "Sunflare" in the PS3 version.

- A set of Meracle's Burning Claws can be found in the sealed chest on level B3 of the Astral Caves (easily reached from the Tatroi entrance).

- Arumat's Skill Manual "Dragon Roar" is on the B4 level (east side) of Planet Aeos's Miga Insect Warrens.

- The light-sealed chest on En II's Old Road to the Sanctuary contains Bacchus's Skill Manual "Godslayer."

- Myuria's Skill Manual "Plasma Cyclone" is in Nox Obscurus's Halls of Termination, near the entrance to the Palace of Creation.

- Completists seeking to open 100% of the chests must use the Darkness Ring to open the light barrier in Area 6 of the Palace of Creation, although the chest beyond the barrier holds only a single Meteorite.

BREAK THE SEAL ON THE COLOSSEUM DOOR

There's one light barrier left to clear, and that's in the colosseum. If you enter the colosseum and go left, passing the stairs to the Bunny Racegrounds, you should see a mysterious white pattern against the wall. Blast it with the Darkness Ring to reveal a stairway that leads to a glowing green transport symbol. Save your game and heal up, because in terms of combat difficulty, the upcoming Cave of the Seven Stars puts the Palace of Creation to shame.

Map Treasures

Cave of the Seven Stars: B1
1. Aquaberries x 2
2. Platinum x 1
3. Bracteate x 1
4. Cane x 1
5. Stone Fragment x 1

Cave of the Seven Stars: B2
1. Ripe Berries x 1
2. [Dark Barrier] Evil Spirit's Bow x 1
3. Stone Fragment x 1
4. Moonstone x 1
5. Gnomestone x 1
6. Stone Fragment x 1

Cave of the Seven Stars: B3
1. Disintegration Stone x 2
2. Stone Fragment x 1
3. 180,000 Fol
4. Gold x 4
5. [Ice Barrier] Stone Fragment x 1
6. [Ivy Barrier] Sylphstone x 2

Exit

Elevator

B2

Legend

= PASSAGE

= NPC

= INTERACTION POINT

Note:

= sliding block which can only be moved by examining the yellow side.

Exit

Elevator

B1

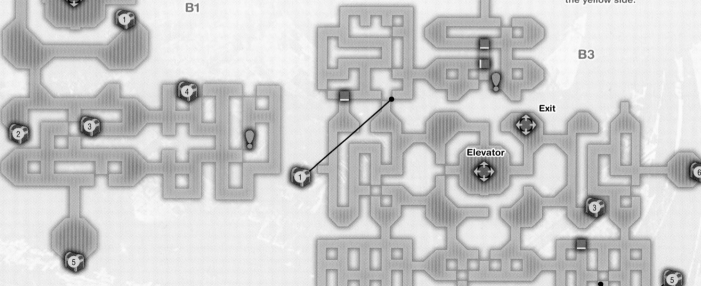

B3

Exit

Elevator

monsters

GUST HORNET
HP · 95807   EXP · 4,193
Fol · 382   Race · Insect
Resistant To · --
Weak Against · Earth

DROPS
Anti-Poison Amulet, Aquaberries, Darkness Gem

WINGED NIGHTMARE
HP · 97913   EXP · 7,151
Fol · 630   Race · Bird
Resistant To · Wind
Weak Against · Fire

DROPS
Gnomestone, Red Herb, Cashmere

CRATER PERYTON
HP · 109943   EXP · 6,579
Fol · 532   Race · Bird
Resistant To · Wind
Weak Against · Earth

DROPS
Sylphstone, Basil, Peryton Droppings, Bunny Feed

GUIAFAIRO
HP · 104435   EXP · 4,657
Fol · 385   Race · Bird
Resistant To · --
Weak Against · --

DROPS
Anti-Fog Amulet, Glowstick, Barrier, Spiritwater

BONE KNIGHT
HP · 94685   EXP · 6,695
Fol · 443   Race · Undead
Resistant To · Dark
Weak Against · Fire, Light

DROPS
Bracteate, Hyper Potion, Magical Clay

TREANT
HP · 166288   EXP · 25,960
Fol · 871   Race · Plant
Resistant To · Earth
Weak Against · Fire

DROPS
Cane, Red Herb, Pumpkin Extract

LEONBLADE
HP · 116146   EXP · 4,967
Fol · 441   Race · Demon
Resistant To · --
Weak Against · --

DROPS
Protection Seeds, Saber-Toothed Tiger Fang, Gambleberries, Bigberries

SEARCH THE MAZES FOR STONE FRAGMENTS

Each floor of the Cave of the Seven Stars is a winding maze that contains both a glowing star (marked with an exclamation point) and at least one Stone Fragment in a treasure chest. At this point, there's nothing you can do with the stars, so focus on hunting down the fragments, which can be set into the patterned walls surrounding the elevator to unlock lower floors. If you want to return to the surface, the transfer symbols located on every floor can take you directly to the entrance, and you can use the elevators to quickly resume your progress when you return.

Before you head into the caves, enroll in a few colosseum bouts or head out into the wilds of the Tatroi Area to slaughter for blue and red Bonus Board tiles.

The enemies in even the first floor of the cave are brutally difficult, but they offer rich rewards in terms of EXP. In the early floors, avoid the Gust Hornets if possible, since they are particularly good at destroying your Bonus Board. Bone Knights are the easiest foes to defeat, and their vulnerability to Blindsides offers a relatively easy opportunity to earn blue tiles. Pick fights with them every chance you get.

BOSS

Temple Guardian

HP · *958949*	EXP · *110,000*
Fol · *3,270*	Race · *Mech*

Resistant To · *Water*

Weak Against · *Thunder*

DROPS
Basil, Void Recovery Unit, Poison Relief Unit

Overthrow Level B1's Temple Guardian

You'll rarely reach a Stone Fragment without a fight, and the one in chest #5 of the first map is no exception. In the Cave of the Seven Stars, you should always steel yourself for a boss battle before you step into the octagonal rooms that sit outside the main mazes.

The boss of level B1 is the Temple Guardian, a more aggressive version of the Cave Guardian you fought in the Astral Caves. This one uses its spin-around tail whip much more frequently (it telegraphs the move by turning its back to its targeted enemy), which makes battling it difficult at close range. Bench your frontline fighters and have Bacchus and Reimi lead the offense with backup from Myuria and Sarah. By now, Bacchus should have the phenomenal Black Hole Sphere special art, which is easy

to build powerful Chain Combos out of. With unlimited HP from the Emergency Repairs skill and unlimited MP from the Convert skill, Bacchus can take on the guardian almost single-handedly, just so long as he has a healer to resurrect him when things go wrong.

FINALLY, SOME DECENT LOOT ON LEVEL B2

Level B2 introduces powerful new Treant foes, which can block the mazes' thin passageways entirely, forcing you into difficult fights. Take out their frequent Gust Hornet companions first, then put the AI in charge of your frontline fighters while you cast symbols or use ranged attacks to protect what's left of your Bonus Board.

At least level B2 offers some rich rewards for your challenges. The dark energy-sealed chest #2 has a powerful new bow for Reimi, and in chest #5 you'll finally find a long-awaited Moonstone, one of the key ingredients of the game's best recipes. Don't use it in a recipe yet! It may be a very long time before you find another Moonstone, so you'll want to use the upcoming Duplication skill to make copies of it first.

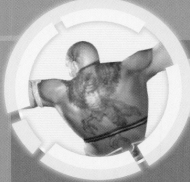

BOSS

Blue Eagle Ranger

HP · 916237 EXP · 40,000
Fol · 3,364 Race · Humanoid
Resistant To · Water
Weak Against · Fire

DROPS
Ice Gem

White Eagle Ranger

HP · 839884 EXP · 40,000
Fol · 3,364 Race · Humanoid
Resistant To · Light
Weak Against · Dark

DROPS
Light Gem

Black Eagle Ranger

HP · 839884 EXP · 40,000
Fol · 3,364 Race · Humanoid
Resistant To · Dark
Weak Against · Light

DROPS
tri-Emblum

Red Eagle Ranger

HP · 763531 EXP · 40,000
Fol · 3,364 Race · Humanoid
Resistant To · Fire
Weak Against · Water

DROPS
Fire Gem

Eradicate Level B2's Black Eagle Clones

The Temple Guardian was a pushover compared to what's waiting for you in the boss room of level B2. You'll have to face four clones of Black Eagle at once, and each has nearly a million HP.

The White and Red Eagle Rangers are the bosses of the group, providing DEF and ATK boosts, respectively. The White Eagle Ranger is the #1 target, so make sure to isolate his white shirt and strike directly at him. The Eagle Rangers dart around the battlefield like hummingbirds, so lock on to the White Eagle Ranger with an early flurry of violence so you can follow him around the battlefield. If you lock on to the wrong Eagle Ranger, you'll have to switch out your character or execute a Blindside to lose him. Once the White Eagle Ranger falls, turn your sights to the red one. When he falls, the two-to-one odds should give you some breathing room. Considering switching to Lymle to incinerate the fire-weak Blue Eagle Ranger, which allows you to bypass his 15% physical damage resistance. (The Black Eagle Ranger has no special properties.)

In the chaos of the early four-on-four fight, it's hard to pull off Resurrection and Healing spells consistently. Myuria can do it with the Fast Cast skill, but you should replace Sarah with a third fighter and rely on items for most of your healing and resurrection.

BOSS

Sahariel Shtayim

HP · ?????	EXP · 160.000
Fol · 41,400	Race · Other

Resistant To · *Fire, Wind*
Weak Against · *Water, Thunder*

DROPS
Drops:
--

Slaughter Sahariel Shtayim on Level B3

Level B3 is an uneventful floor, with no new enemies or interesting treasures. The only new twist comes from the giant blocks that obstruct your progress, and that can only be cleared by examining the glowing runes that appear on one of their four sides.

The boss of the floor is Sahariel Shtayim, who strikes in the northern treasure room. This new version of Sahariel has a few new attacks, but you can defeat him the same way you always have. Simply stand in front and slightly to the side of Sahariel, waiting patiently for him to rear back and use an attack that reveals the eye on his chest. When he does, pound him with the longest chain combo of special arts you can muster. Since you only need a single fighter, you're free to triple up on healers: with Sarah, Myuria and Lymle all backing you up, Sahariel Shtayim has little hope of victory.

Map Treasures

Cave of the Seven Stars: B4
1. [Light Barrier] (X360-only) Skill Manual 'Sunflare' x 1, (PS3-only) Skill Manual "Max Shockwave"
2. Stone Fragment x 1
3. Basil x 2
4. Green Beryl x 1
5. Stone Fragment x 1
6. [Fire Barrier] Bizzare Fruit x 1
7. Stone Fragment x 1
8. Poison Relief Unit x 2
9. Stone Fragment x 1

Monsters

TREANT
HP · 166288   EXP · 25,980
Fol · 871   Race · Plant
Resistant To · Earth
Weak Against · Fire

DROPS
Cane, Red Herb, Pumpkin Extract

LEONBLADE
HP · 116146   EXP · 4,967
Fol · 441   Race · Demon
Resistant To · --
Weak Against · --

DROPS
Protection Seeds, Saber-Toothed Tiger Fang, Gambleberries, Bigberries

GUIAFAIRO
HP · 104,435   EXP · 4,657
Fol · 385   Race · Bird
Resistant To · --
Weak Against · Weak

DROPS
Anti-Fog Amulet, Glowstick, Barrier Spiritwater

QUEEN MANDRAGORA
HP · 141851   EXP · 7,758
Fol · 431   Race · Plant
Resistant To · Earth
Weak Against · Fire

DROPS
Shadow Rose, Basil, Nectar, Ripe Berries

FLYING ICE
HP · 145584   EXP · 8,695
Fol · 9,752   Race · Demon
Resistant To · Water
Weak Against · Fire

DROPS
Nereidstone, Gold, Platinum

SYDONAIST DELTA
HP · 99261   EXP · 4,678
Fol · 542   Race · Humanoid
Resistant To · --
Weak Against · --

DROPS
Sacrificial Doll, Aquaberries, Holy Water

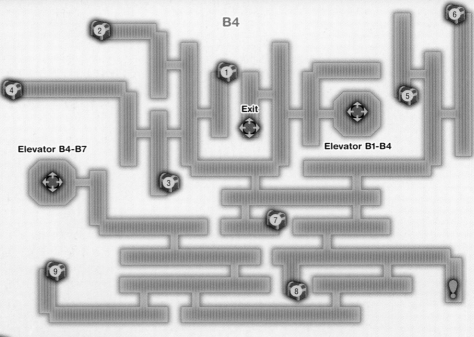

B4

Map Treasures

Cave of the Seven Stars: B5
1. Unicorn Lance x 1
2. Stone Fragment x 1
3. [Dark Barrier] Shadow Rose x 1
4. Fresh Sage x 3
5. [Fire Barrier](PS3-only) Gold Chalice x 1
6. Stone Fragment x 1

Legend

 = PASSAGE

= INTERACTION POINT

Note:
= sliding block which can only be moved by examining the yellow side.

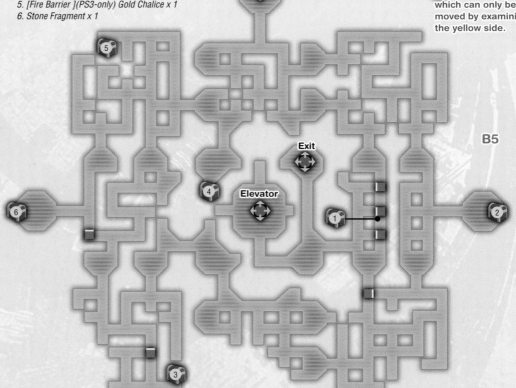

B5

THE CONNECTING PIECE BETWEEN WEST AND EAST

The mystical elevator hits its bottom at level B4, where you'll need to transfer to a new elevator on the west side of the map in order to reach the lower floors of the Cave of the Seven Stars. This map has a simpler layout than the other floors in the cave, so it's relatively easy to hunt down and claim its nine treasure chests, which include another character's ultimate skill: Sarah's Sunflare in the Xbox 360 version, and Meracle's Max Shockwave in the PS3 version.

Several new enemies make their debut on this map, with the Sydonaist Deltas being the most potentially dangerous. They attack in large groups that allow them to gang up on their targets, and they can strike at even distant characters with their hard-to-see throwing knives. When you can't avoid a fight with them, use a party of hearty warriors and rely on items instead of easily disrupted symbols for healing and resurrection.

While this floor's new foes offer plenty of peril, they also offer a great opportunity. The Treants have abandoned their usual Gust Hornet companions, and now mostly fight alone. Battling these slow-moving foes is a cinch with an army of symbol-users and a lone fighter to keep the Treants distracted. With a few blue tiles, you can easily earn 70,000 from each Treant you destroy.

BLAZE A CIRCUITOUS TRAIL AROUND LEVEL B5

The route through level B5 is a little more confusing than it appears on the automap, thanks to the block south of chest #1 that can only be cleared from the east side. After you move the blocks obstructing the first chest (which contains Sarah's excellent Unicorn Lance), you'll have to head north and work your way through the passages north of the exit in order to loop around to the east side of the block. You can then proceed clockwise through the level, ending at the boss that guards chest #6.

BOSS

Shadow Reimi
HP· *299388* EXP· *70,000*
Fol· *3,530* Race· *Other*
Resistant To · --
Weak Against · --
DROPS
--

Shadow Arumat
HP· *411658* EXP· *70,000*
Fol· *3,530* Race· *Other*
Resistant To · --
Weak Against · --
DROPS
--

Shadow Sarah
HP· *299388* EXP· *70,000*
Fol· *3,530* Race· *Other*
Resistant To · --
Weak Against · --
DROPS
--

Destroy Your Deadly Doppelgängers

The bosses of this floor bear a striking resemblance to Sarah, Arumat, and Reimi. Shadow Sarah seems a heck of a lot stronger than the real one, since she can cast symbols with zero casting time. Make her your priority target, hammering her at melee range to ensure she never gets a chance to cast anything. The ideal character is one with the No Guard skill, as Reimi often peppers the battlefield with arrows, and you don't want a stray shot messing up your combos. Back up your fighter with companions that can cast symbols or attack from long range, and that are set to "Stay out of trouble." (When your AI-controlled characters challenge Shadow Arumat at close range, it never ends well.)

The next target is the ruthless and deadly Shadow Arumat. The best character to use against him is Meracle, who can strike quickly and consistently enough to keep the slower Arumat on the ropes. With him out of the way, finishing off Shadow Reimi should be a breeze.

the cave of the seven stars:
B6-B7 / INNER SANCTUM

Map Treasures

Cave of the Seven Stars: B6
1. Stone Fragment x 1
2. [Light Barrier] Skill Manual "Scintillant Stream" x 1
3. Stone Fragment x 1
4. Stone Fragment x 1

Note:

 = sliding block which can only be moved by examining the yellow side.

B6

Exit

Elevator

Monsters

SYDONAIST GAMMA

HP · 115380   EXP · 4,923
Fol · 545   Race · Humanoid
Resistant To · --
Weak Against · --
DROPS
Healing Band, Aquaberries, Holy Water, Neck Chain

SYDONAIST DELTA

HP · 99261   EXP · 4,678
Fol · 542   Race · Humanoid
Resistant To · --
Weak Against · --
DROPS
Sacrificial Doll, Aquaberries, Holy Water

MOONLIGHT LADY

HP · 142527   EXP · 10,218
Fol · 27   Race · Demon
Resistant To · Dark
Weak Against · Light
DROPS
Mana Ribbon, Glowstick, Mental Potion

SPRIGGAN

HP · 145920   EXP · 8,900
Fol · 832   Race · Demon
Resistant To · --
Weak Against · --
DROPS
Anti-Freezing Amulet, Hot Chocolate, Bigberries

SPIRIT ARCHBISHOP

HP · 137436   EXP · 8,616
Fol · 729   Race · Humanoid
Resistant To · --
Weak Against · --
DROPS
Symbol Booster, Pumpkin Extract, Faerie Embroidery Thread

METAL SCUMBAG

HP · 149913   EXP · 82,184
Fol · 558   Race · Mechanical
Resistant To · --
Weak Against · --
DROPS
Thorstone, Hot Chocolate, Void Recovery Unit, Self-Destructor 3000

HADES CRAB

HP · 186754   EXP · 27,738
Fol · 733   Race · Insect
Resistant To · Water, Dark
Weak Against · Thunder
DROPS
Green Beryl, Vile Goop, Runic Metal

FACE DEADLY FOES IN LEVEL B6'S LABYRINTH

The Cave of the Seven Stars gets extremely challenging on level B6, where powerful new enemies roam an especially confusing maze. The deadliest of the bunch is the Moonlight Lady, an enhanced version of the Purgatorium's Succubus that boosts the DEF of her combat allies by 300%. When there are multiple Moonlight Ladies on the battlefield, nothing less than a critical hit is going to register. They are easy to Blindside, but with over 140,000 HP to cut through, you'll need to be able to follow that up with normal attacks enhanced by the Critical Hit skill, the Focus skill, or weapons with Critical Hit-boosting factors (which are added via Synthesis with Crystals and other items). Metal Scumbags are another noteworthy foe, mostly for the 80,000+ EXP they're worth. However, you'll need to be extremely aggressive to kill them before they can flee the battlefield.

Map Treasures

Cave of the Seven Stars: B7
1. Skill Manual "Duplication" x 1
2. Star Dipper x 1
3. Thorstone x 1
4. Seven Star Cloak x 1
5. Void Recovery Unit x 3

Legend

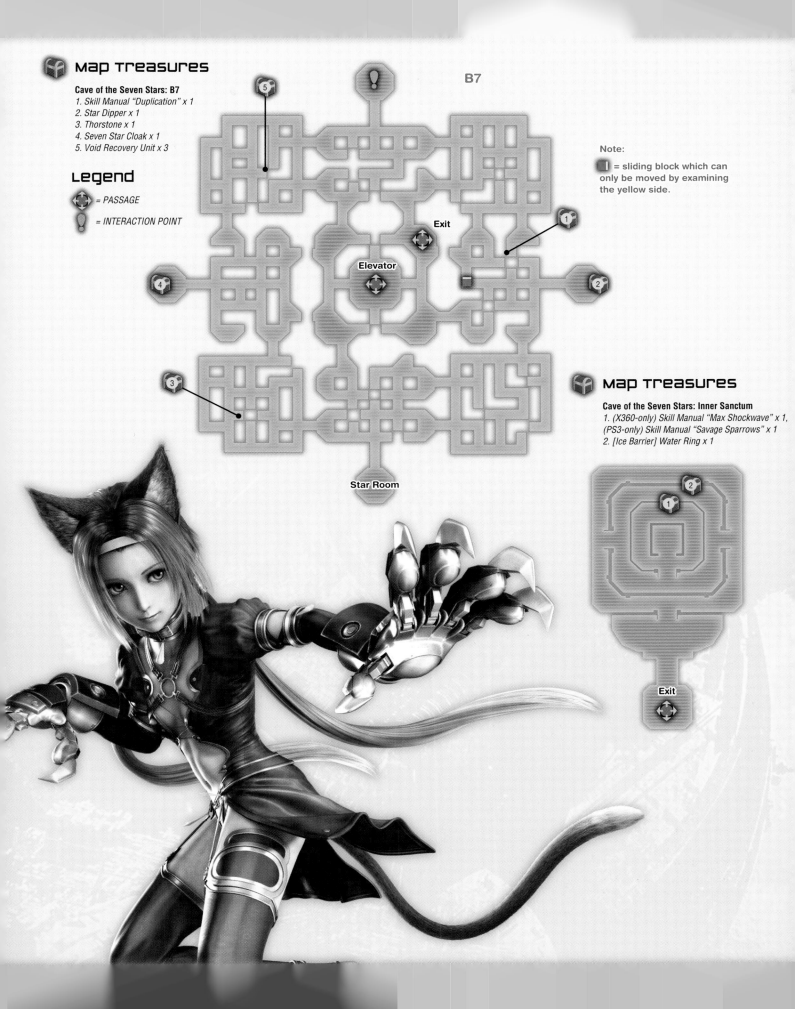

= PASSAGE

= INTERACTION POINT

B7

Note:

= sliding block which can only be moved by examining the yellow side.

Exit

Elevator

Star Room

Map Treasures

Cave of the Seven Stars: Inner Sanctum
1. (X360-only) Skill Manual "Max Shockwave" x 1, (PS3-only) Skill Manual "Savage Sparrows" x 1
2. [Ice Barrier] Water Ring x 1

Exit

All but one of the paths through level B6 are obstructed by moving blocks with control runes on sides you can't reach. From the elevator, head southwest to reach chest #1, which is guarded by the Custom Newt and Custom Dragoon. Then make your way back to the elevator and head

north towards chest #2 in the northwest. From there, you can make your way clockwise around the floor, ending with a second boss fight at chest #4, this time against the powerful Wrathful Tamiel.

BOSS

Custom Newt

HP · 1128848   EXP · 115,000
Fol · 3,739   Race · Demon

Resistant To · --
Weak Against · --

DROPS
--

Custom Dragoon

HP · 1015963   EXP · 115,000
Fol · 3,739   Race · Mech

Resistant To · --
Weak Against · --

DROPS
--

Crush the Custom Newt and Custom Dragoon

Take control of your favorite frontline fighter and round out your team with three ranged characters. Go after the Custom Newt first, and rely on Blindsides and Rush Mode combos rather than trading blows with the powerful fighter.

When the Custom Newt falls, swap out your fighter for a fourth ranged attacker or symbol-user. Keep a safe distance from the Custom Dragoon at all times, as you blast it with special arts chain combos.

BOSS

Wrathful Tamiel

HP · **1505869** EXP · **210,000**
Fol · **51,750** Race · **Humanoid**

Resistant To · *Fire, Dark*
Weak Against · *Water, Thunder*

DROPS
--

Fight Wrathful Tamiel for the Final Fragment

Outside of the final boss, Wrathful Tamiel is the toughest foe you'll face in the Cave of the Seven Stars. His Sydonaist henchmen are a threat all by themselves, and he respawns new batches almost as soon as the first ones are killed. Tamiel himself is extraordinarily powerful, and only the heartiest of characters can survive a lashing from his Rage Reflection special art.

Take control of either Sarah or Myuria and focus on healing, buffing, and raising your fallen. Fill your other slots with your best crowd

control party: Arumat, Meracle and Bacchus should do the job nicely. Whenever you have a bit of breathing room (say, while your healer is casting a symbol), pop over to Bacchus and have him use a combo that begins with the Black Hole Sphere special art. That's a great way to pull your enemies in for some damage and to set them up for a beating from Arumat.

When nearly all of the Sydonaists have been slain, you may want to switch Meracle out for another healer so that Arumat has more backup as he goes head-to-head with Tamiel. Even with the constant healing, Arumat is likely to take a beating, but you can turn that damage into powerful Rush Mode combos. The opportunity to tackle Tamiel solo won't last long, and you'll need to swap a healer back out for Meracle and return to crowd control mode when the new batch of Sydonaists arrive.

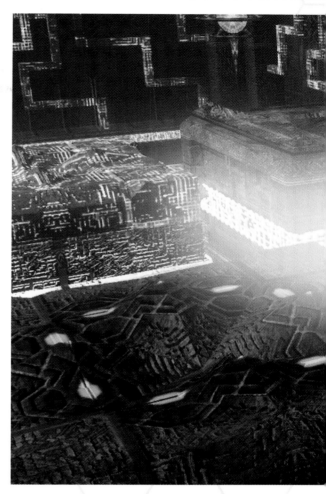

REAP INFINITE REWARDS ON LEVEL B7

The first chest of level B7 contains the invaluable Skill Manual "Duplication," an Arumat skill that allows you to turn Magical Clay into copies of almost any item you own. (Exceptions include key items and equipment that has been modified through Synthesis.) Try to max out Duplication by the time you reach chest #4, which contains the Seven Star Cloak that can be worn by Myuria, Sarah, and Lymle. There's no need to play favorites; just fire up the Duplication skill, select the cloak, and for the price of six pieces of Magical Clay each (at max level), you can make copies for everyone. You can also copy your super-rare chunk of Moonstone for only one piece of clay per copy!

BOSS

Barachiel Fallen

HP · ?????? EXP · 260,000
Fol · 16,221 Race · Other
Resistant To · Earth, Water
Weak Against · Fire

DROPS
--

Win the Star Dipper from Barachiel Fallen

To clear level B7 in a single loop, you'll need to head east from the elevator and then north, U-turning down to chest #1. Clear the floor's lone moving block, and then continue to collect the treasures in numerical order. The only boss you'll face is Barachiel Fallen, a more powerful version of good old Barachiel from way back in the

celestial ship. As before, you'll want to shut off your characters' water-type symbols, and field a couple of healers to keep Edge alive as he goes about doing the real work: pounding Barachiel with lengthy chain combos whenever he drops to the ground and exposes his eye.

GATHER THE SEVEN STARS TO OPEN THE PORTAL

Instead of the usual Stone Fragment, Barachiel Fallen guards a Star Dipper that finally allows you to collect the stars from each floor of the cave. Take the elevator to each previous floor, make your way to the spot marked by the pink exclamation point, and examine the star to send it straight to the level B7 star room. When all seven stars are present and accounted for, the room transforms into a portal that takes you directly to the cave's Inner Sanctum. There, you'll find the Water Ring, the final Skill Manual (for Meracle in the Xbox 360 version or Reimi in the PS3 version), and the legendary superboss, Gabriel Celeste.

GEARING UP TO TAKE DOWN GABRIEL CELESTE

With a Moonstone and the ability to copy it with the Duplication skill, you can now make all but the very best of the game's recipes. The Moonstone weapons are Edge's Moonstone Sword (which requires 3 Moonstones) and Bacchus's Photonic Blaster (which requires 4). You can also make Valiant Mail armor, which requires 3 Moonstones and 4 Red Dragon Scales (which can be copied for 3 pieces of Magical Clay a piece). Both Arumat and Edge can wear the Valiant Mail, so you'll want to dig up an additional 9 pieces of Magical Clay to make a copy of the armor itself.

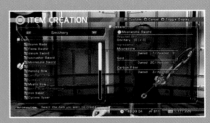

Everyone has good armor but poor Meracle and Reimi, who haven't had an upgrade in a long time. You can fight for suits of Darkblood Chainmail at the Colosseum, or you can just make them Laser Suits, which have better base stats but weaker factors.

When it's time to hit the Synthesis machine, don't give anyone factors that add an element to their weapons, as that action makes them useless against Gabriel Celeste. If you want to tune your weapons for the fight, use items like DANGER! DO NOT DRINK! or Compact Stun Bombs to add the stun effect to their attacks, and employ Crystals to raise their critical hit chances. (This guide's suggested offense revolves around Bacchus and Reimi, so those modifications are most important for his Photonic Blaster and her Evil Spirit's Bow.)

You can mine for Magical Clay by either making a loop of the Southern Reaches and Miga Insect Warren on Planet Aeos, or warping to the Sanctuary at En II. There's no need to return to the Calnus to reset mining points; simply warping to another destination does the trick.

BOSS

Gabriel Celeste

HP · ?????? EXP · *400,000*
Fol · *3,776* Race · *Other*
Resistant To · *Earth, Water, Fire, Wind, Thunder, Light, Dark*
Weak Against · --

DROPS
Gabriel Celeste's Feather

Fight for Your Life against Gabriel Celeste

Gabriel Celeste is an extremely difficult foe, even for parties with levels approaching triple digits. But with a bit of preparation and a great deal of patience, even lower-level parties can emerge triumphant.

Gabriel Celeste is immune to every elemental type, so any character who wields a weapon with an elemental factor is unfortunately rendered useless. This is particularly important for Bacchus, whose last two weapons both had elemental properties. If you hope to use him (and you should, since he's strong here), you'll need to return to the Calnus to make his Photonic Blaster.

Since Gabriel Celeste has the No Guard skill, it's extremely difficult to fight him at close range. Since you can't stagger or juggle Gabriel, he can disrupt your combos and turn the tables on your fighters at any point. For that reason, one good idea is to field a team of Reimi, Bacchus, Sarah,

and Myuria. Prepare Reimi with chain combos that are effective against a single target, like Crescent Wings-Hunter's Moon-Savage Sparrows. Turn off all Myuria and Sarah's symbols except for ones that heal or enhance stats. Myuria can still deal some damage with the Extinction symbol, and though you want her focused on healing, assigning that to one of the shoulder buttons allows her to launch Rush Mode combos.

Reimi's special arts tend to be quicker and more effective than Bacchus's, and she can up her damage-dealing potential with the Focus skill, so you should control her for most of the fight. Use your combo repeatedly from a safe distance, until Gabriel Celeste starts chasing after Reimi. Then, run in circles around the battlefield until Gabriel gives up; there's almost nothing he can do to Reimi while she's running (moving in a circle causes even his projectiles to miss), and you'll buy Myuria and Sarah plenty of time to heal and cast stat-boosting symbols while you're leading the chase. When Gabriel gives up, have Reimi return to her special arts combos. Keep an eye on everyone's Rush Gauge so you can trigger plenty of Rush Mode combos as well, which are the most effective way of damaging Gabriel.

As Gabriel weakens, he relys more and more on attacks that deal massive amounts of damage to everyone near him. Glance at the battlefield map from time to time to make sure your party isn't clustered in one location, and start moving characters around if they are. Resurrection Units are invaluable here, since you'll often need to resurrect two or three characters at once. If you win, you can return here for a rematch (and a chance to win another Gabriel Celeste's Feather) whenever you like.

DOUSE THE FLAMING TREASURE CHESTS

You can now use your Water Ring to douse the flames on three underwhelming treasures: Edge's already-obsolete Lightning Sword in the Purgatorium, Intelligence Seeds in Area 7 of the Palace of Creation, and a Bizarre Fruit in level B4 of the Cave of the Seven Stars. Don't eat those seeds—you should save them for Synthesis when you're able to make the game's best weapons. (You can also harvest Bizarre Seeds easily in Lemuris's Van Elm Region.)

Monsters 1F+

ADEPHAGA PROX
HP · 228692 EXP · 7,345
Fol · 3,752 Race · Insect
Resistant To · --
Weak Against · Wind

DROPS
Geostone, Insect Leg, Bigberries

TRINITY TUSK
HP · 297160 EXP · 49,980
Fol · 1,259 Race · Demon
Resistant To · Earth, Fire, Wind
Weak Against · Water

DROPS
Geostone, Salamanderstone, Sylphstone, Snakeskin

JADE GOLEM
HP · 314299 EXP · 19,652
Fol · 19,000 Race · Demon
Resistant To · Thunder
Weak Against · Earth

DROPS
Geostone, Shadestone, Darkness Gem, Moonstone, Disintegration Stone

MYCONID
HP · 235841 EXP · 11,996
Fol · 629 Race · Plant
Resistant To · Earth, Water
Weak Against · Fire

DROPS
Geostone, Tasty Mushroom, Tasty Mushroom?

ACID GEREL
HP · 246264 EXP · 10,292
Fol · 627 Race · Plant
Resistant To · Dark
Weak Against · Fire

DROPS
Geostone, Red Herb, Vile Goop

MISFORTUNER
HP · 232835 EXP · 10,368
Fol · 631 Race · Undead
Resistant To · Dark
Weak Against · Light

DROPS
Geostone, Greater Demon's Fetish, Lesser Demon's Fetish

KOBOLD RANGER
HP · 234537 EXP · 10,292
Fol · 627 Race · Animal
Resistant To · --
Weak Against · --

DROPS
Geostone, Tent, Fresh Sage

Monsters 6F+

GHOSTKEEPER
HP · 200527 EXP · 14,780
Fol · 959 Race · Undead
Resistant To · Dark, Earth, Water, Fire, Wind,
Weak Against · Thunder, Light

DROPS
Geostone, Disintegration Stone, Parchment, Fine Parchment

ARCH SPELLMASTER
HP · 244732 EXP · 14,666
Fol · 953 Race · Undead
Resistant To · Earth, Water, Fire, Wind, Thunder, Light, Dark
Weak Against · --

DROPS
Geostone, Cane, Ash

ANTLERED TORTOISE
HP · 247795 EXP · 14,723
Fol · 956 Race · Animal
Resistant To · Earth, Fire, Wind, Thunder, Light, Dark
Weak Against · Water

DROPS
Geostone, Warped Carapace, Raw Fish

Monsters 11F+

AUGMENTOID
HP · 253623 EXP · 10,216
Fol · 923 Race · Undead
Resistant To · --
Weak Against · --

DROPS
Geostone, Aquaberries, Pickled Plum Rice

LITTLE MUTANT
HP · 241596 EXP · 8,999
Fol · 585 Race · Demon
Resistant To · --
Weak Against · --

DROPS
Geostone, Micro Heavy Ion Collider, Mixed Syrup

DAMASCUS FORT
HP · 282245 EXP · 66,470
Fol · 1,254 Race · Demon
Resistant To · Earth, Water, Fire, Wind, Thunder, Light, Dark
Weak Against · --

DROPS
Geostone, Philosopher's Stone, Alchemist's Water, Disintegration Stone

Monsters 16F+

LIZARD TYRANT
HP · 262513 EXP · 17,610
Fol · 2,133 Race · Animal
Resistant To · --
Weak Against · Water

DROPS
Geostone, Lizardskin, Dragon Scale

GRIM REAPER
HP · 286203 EXP · 12,644
Fol · 660 Race · Undead
Resistant To · Dark
Weak Against · Light

DROPS
Geostone, Philosopher's Stone, Bracteate

DOMINATOR DRAGON
HP · 477858 EXP · 41,197
Fol · 2,528 Race · Demon
Resistant To · Water
Weak Against · Fire

DROPS
Valkyrie's Garb, Geostone, Dragonblood Crystal, Dragon God Scale

BLOODTAIL
HP · 259550 EXP · 10,634
Fol · 645 Race · Insect
Resistant To · Earth
Weak Against · Wind

DROPS
Geostone, Insect Egg, Caterpillar Fungus, Disintegration Stone

HELL CLOWN
HP · 271404 EXP · 17,679
Fol · 978 Race · Demon
Resistant To · --
Weak Against · --

DROPS
Bizarre Fruit, Pumpkin Extract, Common Egg, Pie Crusts

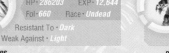

HAVE BARAGO GUIDE YOU TO THE WANDERING DUNGEON

After clearing the Cave of the Seven Stars, you'll be allowed to enter the Wandering Dungeon that is *Star Ocean: The Last Hope*'s ultimate

challenge. To find it, take the elevator in En II to the Old Road to the Sanctuary. Speak to Barago, Keeper of Past Knowledge, and he'll guide you to the entrance.

The Wandering Dungeon consists of an infinite number of randomly generated floors that hold randomly placed treasure pods. To advance through the dungeon, you need to locate the red-and-white obelisk on each floor, and fulfill the objective it assigns to you. Odd-numbered floors have randomly determined objectives, while even-numbered floors require you to collect a Seraphic Doll by defeating preset bosses. The dungeon's ultimate boss is the Ethereal Queen, said to be the most

powerful being in the galaxy. She waits for you on the 20th floor. (The 21st floor and beyond merely repeat the treasure tables and bosses of the 19th and 20th floors.)

There are no save spheres or recovery spheres in the Wandering Dungeon. Every floor has an exit that can take you back to the Old Road to the Sanctuary, but when you re-enter the dungeon, you'll be at a new randomly generated first floor. You'll have to fight all the bosses again, and your supply of Geostones and Seraphic Dolls will be reset to zero.

RARE TREASURES OF THE WANDERING DUNGEON

Most of the Wandering Dungeon's treasure pods hold common ingredients that are of little use to you, but if you're diligent about treasure-hunting, you'll find that each floor (from 3F on) has one or two exclusive items hidden in its random-treasure pool. Many of the exclusive finds are high-quality items that you'll want to equip immediately; others are mere curiosities for your Collections data, like a new saber for Faize. Note that there is only a small chance that any given treasure will actually appear

on its listed floor; these items appear so rarely that you may need to challenge the Wandering Dungeon several times before you're able to find them all.

Floor	Wandering Dungeon-Exclusive Item
3F	Plate of the Lost Monarch
4F	Artifact Bow
5F	Plate of the Lost Monarch
6F	Artifact Bow
7F	Blazing Wand
7F	Infinity Saber
8F	Blazing Wand
9F	Li'l Vending Machine No. 3
9F	Trident Harpoon
10F	Hidden Claws "Crimson Falcons"
11F	Absolute Protector
11F	Infinity Saber
12F	Hidden Claws "Crimson Falcons"
13F	Absolute Protector
13F	Trident Harpoon
14F	Blood Scepter
15F	Blood Scepter
16F	Absolute Protector
16F	Ultimate Cannon
17F	Demon Sword "Levantine"
18F	Ultimate Cannon
19F	Demon Sword "Levantine"

LEVELING UP IN THE EARLY FLOORS

In the halls of the Wandering Dungeon, all monsters are represented as a black, shambling zombie-like creatures. They're easy to avoid, but if you hope to beat the dungeon's later bosses, you'll want to fight as many as you can to raise your character levels into the 150+ range.

With a little bit of preparation, you can level up rapidly in the Wandering Dungeon. Before you talk to Barago, set all of your allies to "Don't do anything" and use Blindsides to slaughter monsters for blue tiles in the Old Road to the Sanctuary. Use Synthesis to slather your weapons with Curry Rice for an additional 20% bonus, and when battling in the Wandering Dungeon, try to arrange each room's monsters into three-monster ambush battles, which earn you another 50% bonus on top of that. When you have a Bonus Board to protect, control a symbol-user who battles far from the front lines so you can protect your tiles for as long as possible.

THE OBJECTIVES OF THE ODD-NUMBERED FLOORS

In each of the odd-numbered floors, the obelisk presents you with one of three challenges:

• "Bring to us X Geostones." Geostones are key items that are found in the treasure pods of the Wandering Dungeon and dropped by most of the local monsters. The obelisk typically demands a number between 8

and 18, and when it's at the high end, you may need to spend a great deal of time attacking with the Steal skill and arranging foes into three-part battles to raise your odds of winning Geostones.

• "Destroy the abhorrent crystals." On floors with this objective, you'll find colored crystals scattered throughout the level. Track them down and destroy them with your various Disintegration Rings. Never

enter the Wandering Dungeon without 20 Disintegration Stones, because this objective can drain your rings quickly (particularly the single-charge Light Ring).

• "Defeat our assassins." Always heal up before you approach an obelisk, as this objective is immediately followed by a battle with a random number of

ambushes. Pray for this one; you can earn EXP totals in the millions if you survive.

PAY FOR PRESENTS AT SANTA'S MERCANTILE

On the higher floors of the dungeon (roughly 8F or above), you may run into a randomly appearing shopkeeper named Santa, Mercantilean. With a treasure-laden sleigh and red hat, Santa has carefully modeled himself after his namesake, with one glaring exception: his presents aren't free…or even remotely affordable.

Many of them aren't that good, either. While his armaments tend to have one extremely high stat, they have huge penalties in other stats. Once you begin to find Philosopher's Stones (on 11F and up), you'll be able to make more reliable gear than many of the items he sells. Still, there are definitely exceptions.

tri-Emblems are the game's best accessories, bar none. They double the speed at which your Rush Gauge charges, add two (!) attacks to

every combo, reduce MP costs by 15%, and grant full immunity to paralysis. They also boost every stat by 100-200 points. Buy as many as you can afford.

Divine Wand "Empyreal Reverie" is a nice upgrade for Lymle, especially since you can't make anything better without first defeating the Ethereal Queen. Arumat's best Item Creation weapon is earth-type and therefore worthless against many of the dungeon's most difficult bosses, so equipping him with Conqueror Scythe "Asura Vajra" and Battle Armor "God of Hellfire" (which is the only way to compensate for the Conqueror Scythe's deep DEF penalty) makes sense for the battles ahead, even if it does reduce his HIT to 0. Bacchus's best Item Creation weapon isn't dragged down by an elemental type, but the combination of Ogre Cannon "Legion's Howl" and Electroshock Gear "War Deity" does offer better stats in most categories.

The Santa Maria - Stock

Item	Type	Price
Binding Sword "Shiho Murasame"	Weapon	1,200,000
Fierce Bow "Reppu Shingetsu"	Weapon	980,000
Sky Sword "Ama-no-Murakumo"	Weapon	1,500,000
Nightmare Wand	Weapon	30,000
Divine Wand "Empyreal Reverie"	Weapon	2,000,000
Ogre Cannon "Legion's Howl"	Weapon	1,000,000
Conqueror Scythe "Asura Vajra"	Weapon	1,200,000
Battle Armor "God of Hellfire"	Armor	800,000
Electroshock Gear "War Deity"	Armor	1,300,000
tri-Emblem	Neck Accessory	2,000,000
Skill Manual "ATK Boost"	Usable Items	6,000
Skill Manual "INT Boost"	Usable Items	6,000
Skill Manual "Divine Wave"	Usable Items	1,000,000
Natto	Food	300
Disintegration Stone	Other Items	30,000
Aramid Fiber	Other Items	800
Carbon Fiber	Other Items	1,000
Rivet	Other Items	20
Laser Oscillator	Other Items	3,000
Sighting Unit	Other Items	500
Mystery Electronic Circuit	Other Items	1,300

The Santa Maria - Orders

Attack Seeds x 1

Reward	Rarity	From
2	☆☆☆☆	Santa, Mercantilean

Intelligence Seeds x 1

Reward	Rarity	From
2	☆☆☆☆	Santa, Mercantilean

Defense Seeds x 1

Reward	Rarity	From
5	☆☆☆☆	Santa, Mercantilean

Accuracy Seeds x 1

Reward	Rarity	From
1	☆☆☆☆	Santa, Mercantilean

Protection Seeds x 1

Reward	Rarity	From
3	☆☆☆☆	Santa, Mercantilean

Health Seeds x 1

Reward	Rarity	From
10	☆☆☆☆	Santa, Mercantilean

Magic Seeds x 1

Reward	Rarity	From
5	☆☆☆☆	Santa, Mercantilean

Fermented Sushi x 10

Reward	Rarity	From
2,000	☆☆☆	Santa, Mercantilean

WELCH'S Crafting Corner

CRAFTING WITH PHILOSOPHER'S STONES

You'll earn your first Philosopher's Stones from the Damascus Fort monsters that begin appearing on Level 11F of the Wandering Dungeon, and they'll drop more frequently once Grim Reapers are added to the mix on level 16F. Harvest as many Philosopher's Stones as you can, because at 11 Magical Clays apiece, they're prohibitively expensive to Duplicate.

Each Philosopher's Stone you find allows you to finish another top-class recipe: Edge's Imperial Sword (the untitled level 10 Smithery recipe), Reimi's Mediumistic Bow, Sarah's Victory Lance (the untitled level 9 Smithery Recipe, which also requires Gabriel Celeste's Feather), Arumat's Quake Scythe, Myuria's Wizard Staff, and Bacchus's Override Gear "Omega" and Symbol Cannon "Tempest" (the untitled level 8 Engineering recipe). If you have any Philosopher's Stones to spare, you can use them in Synthesis to add 3% MP regeneration to armor (or 2% to accessories).

Another important Wandering Dungeon monster is the Dominator Dragon, which is the only source of Dragon God Scales. You'll need two of these to make a Virtuous Robe, the best armor for your symbol-users. (Once you've made one robe, you can copy it with only 7 pieces of Magical Clay.) If you're extremely lucky, you may score an even rarer Valkyrie's Garb drop from the Dominator Dragon. You won't earn the recipe for the Valkyrie's Garb until after you defeat the Ethereal Queen (Barago gives it to you), and since it requires both Gabriel Celeste's Feather and the Ethereal Queen's Feather, it's extremely difficult to make. Earning a freebie from the Dominator Dragon is the game's luckiest drop.

Now that you can make, find, or buy all but two pieces of equipment (Meracle's Rumble Claws and Lymle's untitled Ancient Sage's Wand, both of which require an Ethereal Queen's Feather), you should have a good idea of what gear you're going to take against the Ethereal Queen and the other bosses of the Wandering Dungeon. Take that gear and pull out all the stops on the item Synthesis menu, which means using Health Seeds, Intelligence Seeds, and the like to give your equipment stat

boosts that are much more significant than the ones your character would earn by eating them instead. If you don't have any leftover seeds in your inventory, repeatedly warping to Woodley on Lemuris and searching all of the Van Elm Region harvesting points is a good way to build a supply of seed-generating Bizarre Fruits.

Prehistoric Psynard

HP · *1504988* EXP · *230,000*
Fol · *20,047* Race · *Bird*

Resistant To · *Earth, Water, Fire, Wind, Thunder, Light, Dark*

Weak Against · *--*

DROPS
Seraphic Doll

Level 2F Boss: Prehistoric Psynard

The first boss should pose little threat to players who have bested the far tougher Gabriel Celeste. As in that battle, you'll need to stick with fighters whose weapons have no elemental type and symbol-users who have only their recovery spells turned on. Fight aggressively, relying on your symbol-users to heal the wounded. If you're controlling a frontline fighter, have it leap away as soon as the Psynard begins doing its tremor-causing cannonball drop. If you're hit by the first tremor, it becomes almost impossible to escape the subsequent ones, unless you're using the No Guard skill. Hit a bumper button to protect your Bonus Board and take control of a healer, so you can promptly revive the fallen fighter.

BOSS

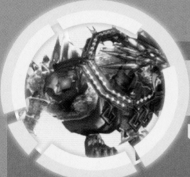

Ring Beast

HP · *1582849* EXP · *260,000*
Fol · *12,164* Race · *Demon*

Resistant To · *Light*

Weak Against · *Dark*

DROPS
Seraphic Doll

Level 4F Boss: Ring Beast

Do your best to survive the Ring Beast's pounces while you kill off its Lizard Tyrant henchmen. The Ring Beast's deadliest attacks—its pounce and energy beam—have long ranges but can typically only hit targets that it's facing. Using a long-range character (such as Myuria, repeatedly casting Deep Freeze on the Lizard Tyrants) gives you a better perspective on the battlefield and makes it easier to dodge. When you're alone with the beast, any character can put on an effective offense, provided he/she avoids striking it straight ahead. Use mostly symbol-users and ranged fighters to ensure your party spreads out, depriving the Ring Beast of opportunities to fell two characters with one hit.

BOSS

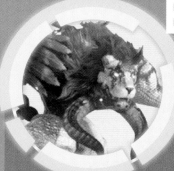

Chimera Beast

HP · *1994019*	EXP · *290,000*
Fol · *8,195*	Race · *Demon*
Resistant To · *Earth*	
Weak Against · *--*	

DROPS
Seraphic Doll

Level 6F Boss: Chimera Beast

Begin with an aggressive party that can take out the Arch Spellmasters as quickly as possible. Then, switch out your fallen characters and extra frontline fighters for a trio of symbol-users. In order to hold the Chimera Beast's attention, use only a single warrior. Arumat is a fine choice.

Keep the Chimera Beast juggled up in the air until it's about to enter Rush Mode, then leap out of the way. The enraged Chimera Beast then chases your warrior, but does not have any effective way of hitting you while you run.

BOSS

Imperfect Armaros

HP · *?????*	EXP · *330,000*
Fol · *8,276*	Race · *Other*
Resistant To · *Water, Wind*	
Weak Against · *Earth*	

DROPS
Seraphic Doll

Level 8F Boss: Imperfect Armaros

This battle can be a frustrating one, not because it's particularly hard, but because it drags on for an unusually long time. No matter how often you hit the Imperfect Armaros's shell, it doesn't even seem to shatter, which means you'll need to beat this boss with attacks that do only a fraction of their usual damage. Force Sarah to use symbols like Enhance on your primary fighter, and set up lengthy combos of low-CP moves so you can jump from one three-part combo to the next and end with a full 280% damage bonus.

BOSS

Armaros Manifest II

HP · ?????	EXP · 340,000
Fol · 12529	Race · Other

Resistant To · Earth
Weak Against · Wind

DROPS
Seraphic Doll

BOSS

Runaway Dragon

HP · 3836566	EXP · 16,852
Fol · 390,000	Race · Demon

Resistant To · Fire, Wind, Thunder
Weak Against · Earth, Water

DROPS
Seraphic Doll

Level 10F Boss: Armaros Manifest II

Though he comes at only the halfway point, Armaros Manifest II may be the second most challenging boss in the Wandering Dungeon. Begin the battle by wiping out the deadly Bloodtails, and be ready to switch back to Bloodtail control when Armaros Manifest II lays a new brood. If you're having trouble breaking out of your target-lock on the boss, switch out your fighter for a new character who is free to hunt down the vile spawn.

The boss's Toxic Breath makes it difficult to strike at it from close range and survive. When it begins to constantly spew gas in the latter half of the fight, switch to Reimi or Bacchus, who can charge and execute a Blindside from farther away, and leap over the gas plumes when they strike.

Level 12F Boss: Runaway Dragon

The Runaway Dragon is similar to the Undying Dragon you fought for the Dark Ring. Its most dangerous attack is a tremor-inducing cannonball drop, which can keep close-range fighters perpetually on the ropes. So deploy only your heartiest one, and count on Myuria and Sarah to keep him alive. In the meantime, take control of Reimi and blast the Runaway Dragon with lengthy combos from a distance. While your frontline fighter keeps the dragon occupied, Reimi can finish the fight.

BOSS

Kokabiel Risen

HP · ?????	EXP · 439,972
Fol · 42,480	Race · Other

Resistant To · *Earth, Water, Fire, Wind, Thunder, Light*
Weak Against · *Dark*

DROPS
Seraphic Doll

Level 14F Boss: Kokabiel Risen

Outside of its boosted stats, Kokabiel Risen seems to be the exact same boss you fought at the Sanctuary. Keep your symbol-users focused on healing and use wide-area special arts like Arumat's Nether Strike and Bacchus's Black Hole Sphere to wipe out the destructible Kokabiel Risen Spawn. Kokabiel Risen next calls the indestructible spawn back to himself and heals them in a giant light bubble, giving you an opportunity to unload with your most powerful special arts combos.

BOSS

Shadow Edge

HP · 919735	EXP · 160,000
Fol · 21,406	Race · Other

Resistant To · --
Weak Against · --

DROPS
Seraphic Doll

Shadow Bacchus

HP · 1104061	EXP · 160,000
Fol · 21,406	Race · Other

Resistant To · --
Weak Against · --

DROPS
--

Shadow Myuria

HP · 601969	EXP · 160,000
Fol · 21,406	Race · Other

Resistant To · --
Weak Against · --

DROPS
--

Level 16F Boss: Shadow Team II

If the Cave of the Seven Stars left you wondering what happened to your other characters' doppelgängers, you'll find the answer in the upper floors of the Wandering Dungeon. This time, Myuria is your priority target, and you should field an aggressive team that can keep Bacchus and Edge busy while you personally destroy her. With 2:1 odds in your favor, it should be safe to bring in symbol-users for support when you turn to finish off Edge and Bacchus.

Shadow Lymle

HP · 617138 EXP · 190,000
Fol · 21,716 Race · Other

Resistant To · --

Weak Against · --

DROPS
Seraphic Doll

BOSS

Shadow Meracle

HP · 837654 EXP · 190,000
Fol · 21,716 Race · Other

Resistant To · --

Weak Against · --

DROPS
--

Shadow Faize

HP · 771174 EXP · 190,000
Fol · 21,716 Race · Other

Resistant To · --

Weak Against · --

DROPS
--

Level 18F Boss: Shadow Team III

The final shadow trio packs a brutal offensive punch, especially from Lymle's special arts. She may pick off a character with an early combo, but you can make that her last with an aggressive counterattack and a good Rush Mode combo. Take out the weaker Faize next, who has trouble defending himself at close range. Since close range is exactly where Meracle excels, finish her off with long-range special arts and Rush Mode combos.

THE QUEEN IS DEAD, LONG LIVE THE QUEEN

After the battle, the Ethereal Queen gives you the Ethereal Queen's Feather. You can also collect Recipe Memo 04 (Valkyrie's Garb) from Barago at the dungeon's entrance, and Recipe Memo 27 (tri-Emblem) from Santa, Mercantilean, if you can find him again.

If you want to win another feather and you have the strength to keep fighting, head back to the 20F obelisk and continue on to level 21 (which is, as far as items and monsters go, a repeat of level 19). The Wandering Dungeon continues for as long as you like, with the Ethereal Queen as the boss of every even-numbered level.

BOSS

Ethereal Queen

HP · **?????**   EXP · **900,000**
Fol · **4,449**   Race · **Other**
Resistant To · *Earth, Water, Fire, Wind, Thunder, Light, Dark*
Weak Against · ---

DROPS
Seraphic Doll

Level 20F Boss: Ethereal Queen

The Ethereal Queen lacks the No Guard skill, so you can battle her effectively at close range. A good party might consist of a melee fighter, a ranged fighter, and healers Sarah and Myuria. The Ethereal Queen frequently uses the Divine Wave symbol in an attempt to knock your fighter away, but if you trigger your Rush Mode when she uses it, you'll be able to stay on your feet and continue to dish out damage.

The trouble comes when the Ethereal Queen falls below a certain level of HP and begins using a new move called Supernova, which pretty much just kills anyone caught within an extraordinarily wide blast radius. You do get plenty of time to get out of the way: the Ethereal Queen says "Cease to be," the Supernova move name appears on the screen, and then the clouds of destruction spread out from the Ethereal Queen's position. Though your character can read these signs and escape the death cloud, your AI-controlled allies cannot.

To ensure a safe recovery from the Supernova, position Sarah in one corner of the battlefield and Myuria in another, with both set to "Stay out of trouble." (Sarah is pretty good about staying put, but for some reason, AI-controlled Myuria just can't resist charging into the fray from time to time, so you'll need to watch out for that.) Leave offense in the hands of your AI-controlled fighters while you focus on minimizing the damage from Supernovas. Make good use of the battlefield map to make sure your healers are in their corners and that the fighters haven't lead the Ethereal Queen towards one of them. When that happens, take control of the healer who's nearest to the Ethereal Queen and start moving her to another corner. If a healer does get caught in a Supernova blast, revive her immediately, and then have both healers aid your fighters. In addition to providing healing services, be ready to throw some MP-recovery items to your fighters, who may end up having their MP drained by the Ethereal Queen.

It may take your fighters a while to finish the job (they are dead half of the time, after all), but as long as you can keep the Supernovas

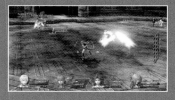

from snaring more than two characters at a time, you should be able to keep the battle going for as long as it takes.

The search for habitable planets comes with both rewards and heavy responsibilities. The souls Edge comes in contact with often need a special kind of assistance, the kind that only he and a group of space explorers can offer. Though the fear of harmful interference may cause him to ignore a cry for help, his empathy for the weak ultimately leads him towards necessary tasks. Welcome to the Quest Appendix, a culmination of all you need to know about the various errands to undertake. Though detailed descriptions on how to complete quests are found in the walkthrough, this section is designed to act as a quick reference for players focused on completing unfinished quests. Please refer to the walkthrough when looking for detailed explanations on how to complete special dungeons or battles associated with quests.

DATA EXPLANATION

1 How to Obtain: Details the means of starting the quest. Includes locations, NPC names, and any additional things that need to be triggered to obtain it.

2 Battle Reward: The EXP, SP, and item rewards obtained after completing a quest-related battle. Only a small number of quests have this field.

3 Quest Reward: The EXP, SP, and item rewards obtained after completing a quest. All quests award EXP and Party SP after their completion, while items are only awarded in specific cases.

4 Items: Lists any specific items needed to complete the quest. The amount of the item needed appears next to its name.

5 Description: An explanation on how to complete the acquired quest.

❖ PUFFY'S DEBUT

Obtained:
After the "Where's the Receptionist?" quest has been completed, speak to the Mischievous Woman living within the giant mansion in Tatroi.
2 **BATTLE REWARD**: 25 EXP, 28 FOL
3 **QUEST REWARD**: 200 EXP, 31 PARTY SP

4
This noble woman's daughter, Puffy, wants her colosseum fighting team to finally win a match. Your job is to challenge them and purposely lose. Proceed over to the colosseum and accept the fight from the front desk. Winning the colosseum battle has no effect on the quest; you can challenge  Puffy's team and defeat them as many times as you like before finally losing to them. Since the contender is extremely weak in comparison to your party, remove your armor to increase the damage they deal to your fighter. When the battle has been lost, return to Puffy's mother for your reward. **5**

PLANET AEOS
EXPLORATION BASE

❖ THE MISSING PATIENT

Obtained:
At the Exploration Base, speak to Airi, the Eldarian Physician.
QUEST REWARD: 10 EXP, 24 PARTY SP, AND A GENTLE KISS...

Airi, the on-duty sickbay doctor, needs you to find a missing patient. He's found within the outer wall of the northwest corner of Exploration Base, near the Calnus. Speak to Rich and select the top dialogue option.

✨ LEG COLLECTOR

Obtained:

At the Exploration Base, speak to Lilia, the Chief of Analysis.

QUEST REWARD: 20 EXP, 18 PARTY SP, BLUEBERRY X 1

Items: Insect Legs x 10

Collect 10 **Insect Legs** and bring them back to Lilia. The legs are dropped from defeated Adephaga and Adephaga Drus monsters. Use the Entomology skill found in Exploration Base's shops to improve the Adephaga's drop rate.

✨ EGG COLLECTOR

Obtained:

At the Exploration Base, speak to Lilia, the Chief of Analysis after the "Leg Collector" quest is completed.

QUEST REWARD: 30 EXP, 20 PARTY SP, AQUABERRIES X 1, RECIPE MEMO 20

Items: Insect Egg x 8

Lilia needs you to collect eight **Insect Eggs**, which are found at harvesting points and off of defeated Adephaga monsters. Use Entomology to improve the chances of insects dropping the egg.

PLANET LEMURIS
WOODLEY

✨ THE LOST LITTLE GIRL

Obtained:

Speak to the owner of the Thousand Gods General Store in Woodley.

QUEST REWARD: 50 EXP, 8 PARTY SP

The owner of the Thousand Gods Store is unable to open shop until her worries are put to rest. Find her missing daughter and bring her home. You'll find her standing near Woodley's west entrance. Speak to her before returning to her mother.

✨ THE CURIOUS KITTY

Obtained:

After "The Lost Little Girl" has been completed, speak to the Foolhardy Girl in the Thousand Gods General Store.

QUEST REWARD: 50 EXP, 32 PARTY SP

Items: Curious Cat x 1

A young girl can't find her cat, Sir Francis. He's sitting next to a giant rock plateau within the Silent Forest on Lemuris. You need the **Faerie Orchid,** an item obtained in the southern reaches of Woodley Area (near a big lake), to remove the false stone boulder blocking the path to him.

✨ IN NEED OF NECTAR

Obtained:

After visiting the Cardianon Mothership, return to Woodley and speak to the Storehouse Worker.

QUEST REWARD: 100 EXP, 40 PARTY SP

Items: Nectar x 16

The Storehouse Worker in Woodley is worried about the town's food shortage. Move out to the warmer Van Elm Region or Thalia Plains and slay the Nectar-dropping **Dryads,** an enemy often paired with Man-Eating Trees. Return to the worker with 16 Nectar items to receive your prize. Nectar can also be found at Van Elm Region and Thalia Plains harvesting points.

✨ IN SEARCH OF 'SHROOMS

Obtained:

Automatically starts after completing the "In Need of Nectar" quest.

QUEST REWARD: 120 EXP, 33 PARTY SP

Items: Tasty Mushroom x 16

Woodley is in need of Tasty Mushrooms, an item dropped by the **Giant Fungus** and Mist Grave monsters. Tasty Mushrooms are also found through harvest points in the Van Elm Region.

Quest Appendix

❖ FANG FLUTE FABRICATION

Obtained:
After visiting the Cardianon Mothership, return to Woodley and speak to the Lonely Young Girl. Take note that this quest cannot be completed until Meracle joins your party.

QUEST REWARD: 800 EXP, 47 PARTY SP

Items: Fang Flute x 1

This little girl wants her broken flute repaired. Launch the Item Creation interface and form an invention group with Meracle and Lymle. If Meracle's "Crafting" skill is level three or higher, she will invent the Fang Flute recipe. To create the item, obtain **Wolf Fangs** from the Saber-Toothed Tigers in the Wind Swallow Valley area, and **Lacquer** from harvesting points on Lemuris.

❖ FURTHER FANG FLUTE FABRICATION

Obtained:
After completing the "Fang Flute Fabrication" quest, talk to the Lonely Young Girl (leave and reenter town).

QUEST REWARD: 1,000 EXP, 50 PARTY SP

Items: Fang Flute x 1

The Lonely Young Girl wants a second **Fang Flute** for her new friend. Make another flute using the same materials as before, then bring it back to the girl.

❖ WOOD FOR THE HEARTH

Obtained:
Once Sarah has joined your party, return to Woodley and speak to the Accommodating Woman.

QUEST REWARD: 140 EXP, 20 PARTY SP, ATTACK SEEDS X 1

Items: Wooden Stick x 10

Woodley's Accommodating Woman needs wood to build a fire. To obtain the Wooden Stick item, hunt **Man-Eating Trees** in the Van Elm Region. Sticks are also found at local harvesting points. Bring 10 Wooden Sticks back to the woman for your reward.

❖ A CHERISHED KEEPSAKE

Obtained:
Once Sarah has joined your party, return to Woodley and speak to the Spoiled Boy in the town inn.

QUEST REWARD: 100 EXP, 20 PARTY SP, SKILL MANUAL "CHAIN COMBOS" X 1

Items: Oracle's Charm x 1

The boy's dropped charm was picked up by a cat in Triom. Don't go looking around out there, though; stay in Woodley and proceed over to the Thousand Gods General Store. Speak to **Sir Francis, Curious Cat** to obtain the missing charm. Bring it back to the boy when ready.

❖ THE STUBBORN MATRIARCH

Obtained:
After visiting the Cardianon Mothership, return to Woodley and speak to the Obstinate Woman in the town inn.

QUEST REWARD: 80 EXP, 40 PARTY SP

A woman's mother-in-law refuses to move to Woodley after Triom's demise. Go to Triom and convince the woman to join her family (select the top dialogue option when it appears). Proceed back to Woodley and speak to the Obstinate Woman again.

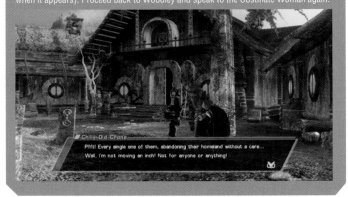

❖ OIL FOR THE COLD

Obtained:
After "The Stubborn Old Matriarch" is completed, speak to the Chilly Old Crone at Woodley's inn twice.

QUEST REWARD: 80 EXP, 30 PARTY SP

Items: Wolf Oil x 1

Granny needs Wolf Oil to keep herself warm. Slay **Saber-Toothed Tigers** in the Wind Swallow Valley until one drops the oil. When you have it, return to the old woman to complete the quest.

LUTEA'S SECRET STONES

Obtained:
After Sarah joins your party, travel to the top of the Alanaire Citadel to find Lutea. To receive this quest, two Personal Action events regarding Lymle must be triggered. Speak to Lutea once to trigger the first PA, and then again after leaving and reentering the room to trigger the second. After the events have finished, the quest only appears after two games hours have passed.

QUEST REWARD: 2,000 EXP, 99 PARTY SP, LUTEA'S SACRED STONE

Items: Salamanderstone x 1, Gnomestone x 1, Sylphstone x 1, etc.

Lutea is asking Lymle to collect the following stones: Salamanderstone, Gnomestone, Sylphstone, Nereidstone, Thorstone, Angelstone, and Shadestone. Salamanderstone and Sylphstone can be acquired at mining points on Roak (Astral Desert), while Gnomestone, Nereidstone, Thorstone, and Angelstone are found in the mining points within En II's **Sanctuary**. The final stone type, Shadestone, is commonly found in mining points within the **Astral Cave** or the **Cave to the Purgatorium**. When you've obtained the necessary items, return to Lutea and select the top option once prompted.

PLANET ROAK
ASTRALIAN CONTINENT

FOOD RUN

Obtained:
After the Black Eagle event, speak to the Impulsive Girl sitting on the crates near the statue in Tatroi, then visit the Patiently Waiting Girl at the abandoned dock (east of the Calnus' landing space).

QUEST REWARD: 600 EXP, 42 PARTY SP, RECIPE MEMO 19

Items: Sweet Fruit x 1

This lovely feline is waiting for her friend to return with food. Go to Tatroi and talk to the Impulsive Girl, who's sitting on top of a stack of crates (near the epic statue at the center of town). You'll receive the **Sweet Fruit** item in return. Bring it back to the girl at the dock to complete the quest.

TATROI

THE SEAFARER'S TREASURE

Obtained:
Speak to the Dutiful Sailor in Tatroi.

QUEST REWARD: 400 EXP, 22 PARTY SP, SEAFARER'S HARPOON

Items: Old Pendant x 1

Find the man's missing pendant. It's sitting along the very first beach you come to after first landing on Roak (it's sparkling at shore). Obtain the item and return it to the Dutiful Sailor for your reward.

MISSING BROTHER

Obtained:
Speak to the shop keeper at Fez's Books, a store in Tatroi.

QUEST REWARD: 300 EXP, 50 PARTY SP

Item: Note from Fez x 1

Chaz, Fez's brother, has disappeared. He asks you to find his sibling and give him a special letter (**Note from Fez**). Chaz is in Tropp, a town reached by crossing Astral Desert with a bunny. Find him at the edge of the town dock. Once you've handed the letter over to him, Chaz expresses his concern with the quicksand blocking his path home. Complete the "Desert Dilemma" and "The Sand Bird Strikes Back" quests to clear the way for Chaz's return. Once home, he'll open Chaz's Books directly next to his brother.

Take caution when first entering Tropp with Fez's letter. Speaking to the boy near the town's entrance (the **Curious Youth**) twice causes him to eat the note. Losing the note in this manner forces you to return to Fez's shop to receive another one. You should avoid this situation if you can, though it is amusing to see a boy eat paper…

WHERE'S THE RECEPTIONIST?

Obtained:
Speak to the Diligent Clerk standing outside of Tatroi's colosseum (after rescuing Sarah from the Purgatorium).
QUEST REWARD: 330 EXP, 30 PARTY SP, OPENS THE COLOSSEUM

The colosseum's clerk needs the desk receptionist to return to work. Travel to **Astral City** and enter **Mobius's One-Stop Shop**. Lucy, the receptionist, is visiting her sick mother on the second floor. Speak to her to pick up the **Sore Throat Soother** quest. Complete the quest and return to the newly reopened colosseum, then speak to the Diligent Clerk for your reward.

SORE THROAT SOOTHER

Obtained:
Speak to Lucy during the "Where's the Receptionist?" quest.
QUEST REWARD: 400 EXP, 22 PARTY SP

Items: Red Herb x 1

Lucy needs a **Red Herb** to help heal her mother's throat. Red Herbs are found in harvesting points throughout the Northeast Astralian Continent area. Bring an herb back to Lucy to complete the quest. Head out to the colosseum afterwards and speak to the Diligent Clerk to finish off the "Where's the Receptionist?" quest.

THE SHODDY DOLL

Obtained:
Speak to the Shadowy Dollmaker in Tatroi (after the Black Eagle event).
QUEST REWARD: 400 EXP, 42 PARTY SP

Items: Wooden Doll x 1

A shady dollmaker wants you to deliver a **Wooden Doll** to a client in Tropp. Hand the doll over to the woman standing in the back of Tropp's inn. Refusing to take such a ragged doll, she asks you to return the item back to the maker, demanding that he make a better one.

THE SECOND DOLL

Obtained:
Give the Pathologically Petulant Woman the Wooden Doll.
QUEST REWARD: 1,000 EXP, 46 PARTY SP, MAGICAL CLAY X 2

Items: Exquisite Wooden Doll x 1

Unhappy with the doll she received, the angry client is demanding a new one. Return to the Shadowy Dollmaker in Tatroi. Complete the "In Search of Anessa" quest to trigger the next event. Go back to the dollmaker after leaving the town and re-entering in order to receive the finished doll. Take the **Exquisite Wooden Doll** back to the woman in Tropp for your reward.

IN SEARCH OF ANESSA

Obtained:
Speak to the Shadowy Dollmaker in Tatroi once "The Second Doll" quest has been obtained.
QUEST REWARD: 800 EXP, 38 PARTY SP

The dollmaker's poor work is the result of his worry for his missing daughter. To find her, travel to Astral City and speak to Anessa the Tomboy, the little girl standing by a lamppost staring at nearby knights. Return back to Tatroi and speak to her father to end the quest.

CRAZY FOR GRAPE JUICE

Obtained:
After the Black Eagle event has finished (and Reimi has rejoined your party), speak to the Fruit-Crazy Old Man in Tatroi (he's standing next to the giant statue).
QUEST REWARD: 800 EXP, 50 PARTY SP

Items: Famous Grape Juice x 1

This old man wants to taste his favorite grape juice again. Make your way out to Tropp and enter the Morgan's Weapons shop. Talk to the Out-of-Work Sailor inside to get the **Famous Grape Juice** item.

❖ LISTLESS BUNNY

Obtained:
After completing the "Where's the Receptionist?" quest, speak to the Chatty Bunny Trainer in the Bunny Racegrounds.
QUEST REWARD: 555 EXP, 30 PARTY SP, AND A BUNNY

Items: Stamina Pie x 1

A woman has found a stray bunny in need of food. Come back to her with a Stamina Pie, an item found within a box in **Tropp's Inn**. You can also make it with Item Creation; just start a invention session with Reimi and Sarah (if Reimi's Cooking skill is level 7 or higher). After the bunny has been fed, you're asked to take permanent care of him. You now have a bunny of your own to use in races!

❖ PUFFY'S DEBUT

Obtained:
After the "Where's the Receptionist?" quest has been completed, speak to the Mischievous Woman living within the giant mansion in Tatroi.
BATTLE REWARD: (OPTIONAL VICTORY) 25 EXP, 28 FOL
QUEST REWARD: 200 EXP, 31 PARTY SP

This noble woman's daughter, Puffy, wants her colosseum fighting team to finally win a match. Your job is to challenge them and purposely lose. Proceed over to the colosseum and accept the fight from the front desk. Winning the colosseum battle has no effect on the quest; you can challenge Puffy's team and defeat them as many times as you like before finally losing to them. Since the contender is extremely weak in comparison to your party, remove your armor to increase the damage they deal to your fighter, then choose the strategic item set and use the gambleberries during battle. With some luck, this could automatically incapacitate your fighter. When the battle has been lost, return to Puffy's mother for your reward.

❖ PUFFY'S RAGE

Obtained:
After completing "Puffy's Debut," exit then reenter the Tatroi mansion and speak to the Mischievous Woman again.
BATTLE REWARD: 4,186 EXP, 1,688 FOL
QUEST REWARD: 400 EXP, 34 PARTY SP

Puffy is aware of the fall you took against her colosseum team. Unhappy with the outcome, she has challenged Edge's team to a rematch. Make your way to the colosseum and defeat her fighting team. There's no penalty for losing, so challenge the team as many times as you need to.

❖ PUFFY'S REVENGE

Obtained:
After completing "Puffy's Rage," exit then re-enter the Tatroi mansion and speak to Puffy.
BATTLE REWARD: 5,903 EXP, 1,927 FOL
QUEST REWARD: 800 EXP, 36 PARTY SP

Miss Puffy is at it again. Unhappy with her loss to your powerful team, she challenges you again to another match. Accept her challenge and defeat the enemy party waiting at the colosseum. As before, there's no penalty for losing the fight, so fight until victory is achieved. Return to her after their defeat to complete the quest.

❖ THE FIRST ERRAND

Obtained:
Speak to the Queen of Inventors in Tatroi after the Black Eagle event.
QUEST REWARD: 150 EXP, 30 PARTY SP, ULTIMATE BOMB X 2

Items: Fresh Sage x 10

Fetch 10 pieces of Fresh Sage from the **Good Grocers** store in town, and then return to the inventor. Your reward is sitting in the open box next to her desk.

❖ THE SECOND ERRAND

Obtained:
After "The First Errand" has been completed, speak to the Queen of Inventors in Tatroi.
QUEST REWARD: 300 EXP, 32 PARTY SP, HP ABSORPTION UNIT X 4

Items: Bee Stingers x 9

Obtain 9 Bee Stingers from the **Honeybees** in the fields just outside of Tatroi. Bring the stingers back to Jasmine for your reward.

❖ THE THIRD ERRAND

Obtained:
After "The Second Errand" has been completed, speak to the Queen of Inventors in Tatroi.
QUEST REWARD: 600 EXP, 32 PARTY SP, TIME STOPPER

Items: Wool x 13

The incredible Jasmine is in need of Wool for her next endeavor. Buy 13 bushels of it in **Mobius's One-Stop Shop,** a store found in Astral City. Bring it back to Jasmine for your reward.

❖ THE FOURTH ERRAND

Obtained:
Talk to Jasmine, Queen of Inventors after defeating the Armaros Manifest and completing the side quest "The Third Errand".
QUEST REWARD: 1,200 EXP, 34 PARTY SP, SILENT TALISMAN

Items: Intensified Gunpowder x 20

Our favorite inventor, Jasmine, needs 20 increments of Intensified Gunpowder. This recipe is invented through Item Creation, by forming an invention group with Myuria and Sarah. Myuria's Compounding skill must be level 4 or higher. To make it, buy Gunpowder at the Tools 'R' Us store in Tatroi, and obtain Thunder Gems from any mining point on Roak's main fields (try Astral Desert and the Tatroi Area). Unfortunately, 20 increments of Gunpowder are needed just to make five batches of Intensified Gunpowder, and you can only carry 20 of any item. If you don't yet have the Gunpowder-selling Li'l Vending Machine No. 2 in your ship (the vending machine is a level 10 Engineering recipe created by Bacchus, Edge and Sara), you'll have to make four painful trips from Tatroi back to the Calnus just to make all of the Intensified Gunpowder you need. Anything for science, right?

❖ THE FIFTH ERRAND

Obtained:
Talk to Jasmine, Queen of Inventors after completing the "The Fourth Errand" quest.
QUEST REWARD: 2,400 EXP, 36 PARTY SP, RECIPE MEMO 01

Items: Giant Bird Feather x 12

Jasmine's final request is for 12 Giant Bird Feathers, an item dropped off of the local **Axe Beaks** (They're located on Planet Roak: Astralian Continent). Use Meracle and her Ornithology skill to improve the drop rate. When you have the feathers, proceed back to Jasmine.

ASTRAL CITY

❖ MUSICAL MENDING

Obtained:
Speak to the Teary-Eyed Girl in Astral City. You'll find her outside of the town inn (available after the Black Eagle event).
QUEST REWARD: 1,000 EXP, 45 PARTY SP, RECIPE MEMO 06

Items: Music Box x 1

Bacchus has offered to fix a little girl's broken music box. To do so, make a new Music Box via Item Creation. Form an invention group with Bacchus and Meracle. Besides the **Broken Music Box** that the girl gives you, you'll need one **Repair Kit**, available in the Tool 'R' Us store in Tatroi (buy it for 100 Fol).

❖ LOCKED OUT

Obtained:
Speak to the Careless Shopkeeper in Astral City (available after the Black Eagle event).
QUEST REWARD: 300 EXP, 14 PARTY SP, OPENS THE TREASURE HUNTER WEAPONS STORE.

Items: Weapon Shop Key x 1

The drunken shopkeeper of Astral City's weapon store has lost her shop key. Travel to Tatroi and speak to the Tavern Bartender standing outside of the town bar. Bring the **Weapon Shop Key** back to the careless shopkeeper for your reward.

❖ THE LATEST BEAUTY FAD

Obtained:
Speak to the Heavily Made-Up Lady in Astral City (available after the Black Eagle event).
QUEST REWARD: 1,000 EXP, 46 PARTY SP

Items: Peryton Droppings x 10

The makeup-saturated woman near Astral City's item shops is looking for the secret to beautiful skin. Bring the old woman 10 Peryton Droppings, an item found off of defeated **Axe Beaks**.

Once the quest is completed, head out to Tropp and speak to Tepeki, the owner of the Rascal's Guild shop, for an amusing ending to this story. This is completely optional, so don't break your back heading out there.

❖ NO WAY HOME

Obtained:
Speak to the Woozy Man in Astral City (after rescuing Sarah from the Purgatorium).
QUEST REWARD: 800 EXP, 49 PARTY SP, BLUEBERRY TART x 3

Items: Lemon Juice x 1

This sickly guy needs Lemon Juice to quench his thirst. The item can only be made through Item Creation. Form an invention group that consists of only Reimi and Lymle. Once you have the recipe, obtain the **Natural Water** ingredient from Whole Heart Foods in Astral City, and **Lemons** from harvesting points on Roak.

❖ OGRE BATTLING

Obtained:
Once you've landed on Aeos (just after Sarah has joined your party), return to Roak and speak to Astralian Royal Knight Lias in Astral City.
QUEST REWARD: 400 EXP, 56 PARTY SP, ASTRALIAN EMBLEM

Defeat thirty **Desert Ogres** to prove your strength to Lias. They are often found wandering aimlessly in the Astral Desert and Tropp Area. Use the "# Defeated" field in the monster Collection menu to keep track of your kill count. The Desert Ogre is the 47th monster on the list. Desert Ogres defeated before accepting the quest do not count, so make sure to check the "# Defeated" field before you start.

❖ RUMBLE IN THE CAVES

Obtained:
Speak to the Astralian Royal Knight Lias after completing the "Ogre Battling" quest.
QUEST REWARD: 2,000 EXP, 80 PARTY SP, RECIPE MEMO 21

Lias speaks of a monster trapped in Astral Caves that's causing the earthquakes in the area. Concerned with the damage the beast is causing, he asks you to proceed into Astral Caves to slay the monster. The cave entrance is located at the east end of Astral City. Once you've defeated the **Cave Guardian** there, go back to Astral City and speak to Lias.

❖ A CHERISHED BANGLE

Obtained:
In Astral Caves, speak to Lewis, Knight Near Death.
QUEST REWARD: 500 EXP, 32 PARTY SP

Items: Knight's Bangle x 1

The Astral knight Lewis is dying, asking you to take his bangle to his beloved wife in Astral City. Enter the house on the west side of town and speak to the Knight's Wife. A strangely amusing scene occurs after handing over the bangle.

❖ THE STRAY CARROT

Obtained:
Speak to the Overly-Cautious Knight in Astral Castle (available after the Black Eagle event).
QUEST REWARD: 1,200 EXP, 48 PARTY SP

Items: Carrot Doll x 1

A bandit has run off with this knight's Carrot Doll. Head out to the pub in Tatroi and use Pickpocketing on the **Manly and Upright Warrior**. Once the Carrot Doll is acquired, go back to Astral Castle and return the doll to its owner.

TROPP

❖ OTHERWORLDLY DIET

Obtained:
Speak to the Overweight Woman in Tropp.
QUEST REWARD: 900 EXP, 50 PARTY SP

Items: Otherworldly Cuisine x 3

This deliciously strange woman is looking for three otherworldly meals that disgust her. Make sure Reimi's Cooking skill is at least level 2 or higher, then use the Item Creation terminal. If the recipe isn't already available to make, put Reimi in an invention group by herself and she should come up with it shortly. The dish itself requires four ingredients: Insect Legs (dropped from most insects), Insect Eggs (also dropped from insects), Rotten Fish (dropped by Waving Pincers), and Vinegar (buy it at Roomy Foods in Tatroi).

❖ THE REBOUND QUEEN

Obtained:
After completing the "Otherworldly Diet" quest, wait two hours, and then speak to the Dieting Woman.
QUEST REWARD: 1,100 EXP, 52 PARTY SP

Item: Pasta Bolognese x 1

The dieting Tropp citizen has given up. Enter Item Creation and make the **Pasta Bolognese** dish, a recipe obtained from **Lutea's mother** in **Woodley** (speak to her to receive **Recipe Memo 07**). Once you have it, you can acquire all of the ingredients needed to make the recipe at **Roomy Foods** in Tatroi. Pick up **Uncooked Pasta, Raw Animal Meat, Vegetables**, and **Rich Cheese**.

GROOMING IS ESSENTIAL

Obtained:
Speak to the Haughty Girl in Tropp town.
QUEST REWARD: 2,000 EXP, 36 PARTY SP, RECIPE MEMO 22

Items: Feathered Comb x 1

Make a Feathered Comb for her, a low-level item fashioned through Item Creation. To obtain this recipe, form an invention group with Meracle, Myuria and Reimi whith Meracle's Crafting skill at level two or higher.

A SYMBOL OF BRAVERY

Obtained:
Speak to the Tough-Talking Girl in Tropp.
QUEST REWARD: 100 EXP, 40 PARTY SP, SCUMBAG SLAYER

Items: Purgatorium Stone x 1

Ignoring the entire point of the contest, this sneaky feline is looking for an easy way out of the competition. Her friends are asking her to get a special stone from the Purgatorium to show she ventured there. Get the stone for her, which is located in the Purgatorium's very first room. Look for a shiny object to your left after climbing the first set of stairs.

NEW LIFE, NEW CLOTHES

Obtained:
Speak to the Ex-Cultist in Tropp after rescuing Sarah from the Purgatorium.
QUEST REWARD: 777 EXP, 37 PARTY SP

Items: Traveler's Cloak x 1

The Ex-Cultist is in need of new clothes. Make a Traveler's Cloak for him, a low-level item created through Crafting. Form an invention group with Meracle and Lymle to obtain the recipe.

THE MAPLESS TRAVELER

Obtained:
Complete the "New Life, New Clothes" quest.
QUEST REWARD: 123 EXP, 37 PARTY SP

Items: Map of Astral x 1

The newly dressed Ex-Cultist needs a map of Astral. Go to **Mobius's One-Stop Shop** in Astral City and buy the **Map of Astral** there. Bring it back to the traveler for your reward.

RUDDLE STRIKES AGAIN

Obtained:
After completing the "The Mapless Traveler" quest, exit the area and reenter, then speak to Ruddle at Tropp's dock.
QUEST REWARD: 456 EXP, 38 PARTY SP

Items: Map of Astral x 1

Poor, hopeless Ruddle has lost his map. Head back to **Mobius's One-Stop Shop** in Astral City and obtain a second **Map of Astral**. Return to Tropp with the item to finish the scenario. With Ruddle prepped and ready to go, his new shop (Ruddle's Place) opens in Tatroi once the "Desert Dilemma" and

"The Sand Bird Strikes Back" quests are also completed. Stop by and pay him a visit.

WHODUNIT?

Obtained:
Speak to the Art-Loving Woman in Tropp's inn after finishing "The Second Doll" quest (can only be started after saving Sarah from the Purgatorium).
QUEST REWARD: 1,300 EXP, 39 PARTY SP

Items: Gorgeous Gem x 1

A beautiful gem has been stolen by an ex-Sydonai cultist. The culprit is hiding in **Fez's Books**, a shop in Tatroi. Use the Pickpocketing ability on the Bashful Man to take back the **Gorgeous Gem**. He'll confess once you have the item. Return to Tropp and speak to the woman for your reward.

DESERT DILEMMA

Obtained:
Speak to the Retired Explorer in Tropp (after saving Sarah from the Purgatorium).
BATTLE REWARD: 6,384 EXP, 15,893 FOL, BRACTEATE X 1
QUEST REWARD: 600 EXP, 40 PARTY SP

An old explorer in Tropp says a monster called the **Sand Bird** is causing the quicksand in the Astral Desert area. Find the bird flying just south of the oasis near the exit to Tatroi. Slay the creature and report back to the old man. After he disappears, leave Tropp and proceed to Astral Desert again. The Retired Explorer is standing by the oasis near the Tatroi exit. Speak to him to open up "The Sand Bird Strikes Back" quest.

THE SAND BIRD STRIKES BACK

Obtained:
Speak to the Retired Explorer in Astral Desert after the "Desert Dilemma" is completed. He's found standing next to the oasis near the Tatroi exit.
BATTLE REWARD: 6,384 EXP, 15,893 FOL, BRACTEATE X 1
QUEST REWARD: 1,200 EXP, 50 PARTY SP, SKILL MANUAL "OCARINA"

It looks like the Sand Bird never croaked, despite the beating it took from your party. Run out and give the persistent bird a thorough bashing. It's found just south of the old man's position. Report back to the Retired Explorer once you've defeated it. When he takes his leave, go to Tatroi and head to the inn. Talk to the old explorer one last time to complete the quest.

IT CAME FROM THE VENT

Obtained:
After defeating the Armaros Manifest, speak to Lady Eleyna in her secret hideout.
BATTLE REWARD: 1,098 EXP, 1,488 FOL, VILE GOOP X 1
QUEST REWARD: 600 EXP, 38 PARTY SP, RECIPE MEMO 13

The air in Eleyna's hideout is getting stuffy, caused by a monster blocking her chimney. The chimney is directly above the hideout, on the edge of the cliff. Exit Eleyna's hideout and follow the cliff's edge southeast until it meets the ground. Get on top of the cliff, following the same edge back north until you see a green **Vomiting Gel** monster. Make contact with the creature and defeat it in battle. Return to Eleyna to complete the mission.

With this quest finished, exit and reenter Eleyna's abode to catch a special Private Action event concerning Meracle.

EN II

THE UNOPENABLE CHEST

Obtained:
Speak to the Jealous Wife located in En II's Centropolis.
QUEST REWARD: 1,800 EXP, 45 PARTY SP, ECHO MACHINE

Items: Secret Diary x 1

The Jealous Wife wants you to open the yellow chest beside her. The Wind Ring is needed to unlock it. This item is obtained during "The Wind Ring" quest (acquired from **Barago** at the beginning of the **Old Road to the Sanctuary**). Once the ring is in your possession, use it to unseal the glowing box. Give the Secret Diary inside the box to the Jealous Wife.

THE ELUSIVE FEMALE FIREFLY

Obtained:
Speak to the Young-at-Heart Researcher located in the Flora/Fauna Laboratory in Centropolis.
QUEST REWARD: 3,000 EXP, 49 PARTY SP, SHORTCAKE X 1

Items: Crimson Firefly x 1

The Morphus researcher is hoping to find the female version of a Crimson Firefly, an extreme rarity. The creature is found inside the **Cave to the Purgatorium** on Roak. Stand next to a shining red light in the cave and examine it to pick one up. It's entirely random whether the firefly given to the researcher is female or not, so obtain as many flies as possible before returning to En II.

A DISTINGUISHED RARITY

Obtained:
Speak to the Unyielding Man located in En II's Centropolis.
QUEST REWARD: 2,400 EXP, 60 PARTY SP, ANGELSTONE X 1

Item: Japonesque Vase x 1

A pretentious critic wants you to create an artful vase. There are four different vases you can make: the Vivid Vase, Coquettish Vase, Traditional Vase, and a Japonesque Vase. The vase he wants is the **Japonesque Vase**, which completes the quest once you've given it to him. Discover this level 4 Crafting recipe with an invention group containing Arumat, Sarah and Meracle. Having any of the other vases in your inventory sends him into a rage, causing him to appraise and then destroy each of them until he finally gets to the vase he wants. (You'll still want to make the other vases at some point, in order to unlock the "World's Biggest Welch Fan" Trophy/Achievement.)

GUITAR MAKER

Obtained:
Speak to the Free-Spirited Woman located in the Centropolis Shopping Mall on En II.
QUEST REWARD: 3,600 EXP, 45 PARTY SP

Items: Small Guitar x 1

This hippy friend needs a guitar. Enter the Item Creation menu and create an invention group with Meracle, a total Crafting score of at least 15, and a total Sense score of at least 10. You should eventually obtain the **Small Guitar** recipe. Pick up ingredients like **Guitar Parts** at the Masterful Materials store in the Centropolis mall. **Steel** and **Ebony** can only be found via Mining and Harvesting. Fly out to either Lemuris or Roak to find these materials.

✣ WHERE'S THE RECIPE?

Obtained:
Speak to the Magical Chef located in the Centropolis Shopping Mall on En II.
QUEST REWARD: 1,500 EXP, 41 PARTY SP, RECIPE MEMO 08

Items: Secret Memo x 1

Dazzled by the possibility of a new dessert, Reimi agrees to help the Magical Chef find her missing recipe. The chef's husband, the **Young-at-Heart Researcher**, is holding the item in the Centropolis research lab. Use the Pickpocketing ability to steal the item from him. It's difficult to steal, so raise your Pickpocketing skill level to 10. Return to the chef once you have the recipe. Not only does she give you the recipe for her dessert in return, but she also opens up her Magical Foods shop.

✣ THE WIND RING

Obtained:
Speak to Barago, Keeper of Past Knowledge in the Old Road to the Sanctuary (En II).
QUEST REWARD: 1,000 EXP, 23 PARTY SP

Items: Wind Ring x 1

The **Wind Ring** is needed to tear down the vines within the Old Road to the Sanctuary. Speak to Nimahl at the Flora/Fauna Laboratory, who informs you that the ring has been buried in the **Centropolis Graveyard**. Proceed to the graveyard in the northwest corner of town and examine the grave marked with a pink exclamation point on the map. A note is attached to the grave, which says the ring has been left in the hands of an "unyielding gravekeeper." The note is referring to the only tree in the graveyard, which sits at the top of the nearby staircase. Stand at the base of the tree and examine it to obtain the ring.

✣ TRIAL OF MIGHT

Obtained:
Examine the glowing white console in En II's Sanctuary, where Kokabiel was defeated.
BATTLE REWARD: 24,834 EXP, 25,275 FOL, LEZARD'S FLASK X 1
QUEST REWARD: 4,000 EXP, 40 PARTY SP, LASER WEAPON

The Sacred Gem of Might asks you to undertake The Trial of Might. This is a mini-boss battle against the **Vigorous Beast**, a blue lion similar to the Guardian Beast you encountered in the Purgatorium. Defeat the monster to obtain the Laser Weapon, a powerful weapon that any character can equip.

✣ TRIAL OF LOVE

Obtained:
Examine the glowing red console in En II's Sanctuary after Kokabiel is defeated.
QUEST REWARD: 4,000 EXP, 40 PARTY SP, CHALICE OF LOVE

Items: Psynard Chick x 1

The Gem of Love asks you to obtain a **Psynard Egg** from one of the Early Psynards in the Sanctuary. The egg is an extremely rare item dropped after the bird's defeat, so make use of Meracle's Ornithology and Steal abilities to improve the drop rate. To hatch the egg, head to En II's Centropolis and go to the **Flora/Fauna Laboratory**. Speak to Nimahl at the front desk. She'll give you **Recipe Memo 30**, which is needed to create the **Growth Stimulant Ampule** used to help the chick grow. The ingredients for the recipe are Ginseng (found at harvesting points on Aeos: Southern Reaches), Caterpillar Fungus (obtained at harvesting points in the Van Elm Region on Roak), and the Empty Bottle (obtained at the Black Cat Material Shop on Roak). When you have the items you need, make the ampule in Item Creation and give it to Nimahl. After she hatches the Psynard Chick into being, return to the Sacred Gem of Love to complete the quest.

✣ TRIAL OF COURAGE

Obtained:
Examine the glowing blue console in En II's Sanctuary, where Kokabiel was defeated.
QUEST REWARD: 4,000 EXP, 40 PARTY SP, GREATER SACRIFICIAL DOLL

The trial given by the Sacred Gem of Courage consists of several back-to-back battles against numerous enemy types. The end result is a life-draining endurance test that seems scary at first, but simply requires that you keep your party members from being surrounded. Complete the string of battles to obtain the Greater Sacrificial Doll.

☆ TRIAL OF WISDOM

Obtained:
Examine the glowing green console in En II's Sanctuary after Kokabiel is defeated.
QUEST REWARD: 4,000 EXP, 40 PARTY SP, SKILL MANUAL "FAERIE STAR"

Items: Philosopher's Tome x 1

The Sacred Gem of Wisdom gives you the Cryptograph 1 item and asks you to find the Philosopher's Tome. To obtain it, you must find Cryptographs 2 and 3, which contain clues that shall lead you towards your goal.

The clue written on Cryptograph 1 speaks of a "cleft in an argent land." This is referring to the Thalia Plains on **Lemuris**. The Cryptograph is lying in the snow in the narrowest path by the ice lake, on the north edge of the map and east of the citadel(look for a shining light).

Cryptograph 2 reads that the next item is located in "A fosse within an azure forest." Fly out to **Aeos** and enter the **Southern Reaches** section of the planet. Travel south, passing the first small swamp and the beach, until you reach the second swampy area in the jungle with water on the floor. There's a big mossy boulder in the middle of the water near here. Look for a shining light in the water around the south side of the boulder. Examine it to find Cryptograph 3.

The text on the third Cryptograph says to look for "An ancient pillar amid a sea of dust." Travel to **Roak** and enter the Tropp Area. Make your way to the pillars just outside of the eastern mouth of the cave to the Purgatorium. Examine the glimmer of light next to the pillar to the west to obtain the Philosopher's Tome. With the tome in hand, go back to the green gem in the Sanctuary. Speak to it to obtain the Faerie Star spell, one of the most useful restorative abilities in the game.

☆ THE LAST LETTER

Obtained:
In the Pulsating Bog on Nox Obscurus, speak to Orwen, Dutiful Warrior.
QUEST REWARD: 3,000 EXP, 50 PARTY SP

Items: Letter from Orwen x 1

With his final breath, Orwen asks you to deliver a letter to a woman named Jessica. Proceed to En II and speak to **Giotto** in **Monitor Room A**. He reveals that Jessica has taken a ship out to the frontlines of the battle on Nox Obscurus. Return to Nox Obscurus and proceed back to the position where Orwen was originally found. Examine the new body lying next to him to find Jessica...

DATA EXPLANATION

① **Item Creation:** Whether or not the item can be made with Item Creation. Shows the type and level of skill needed to invent the recipe. For armor, the portraits of the characters able to equip the armor are displayed in full color underneath this bar.

② **Statistics:** The character attributes the item improves. The statistics improved are as follows:

ATK: The attack rating of the item. This value combines with the character's base ATK rating to increase it. Helps determine the amount of damage dealt by the character's attacks.

INT: The intelligence rating of the item. This value combines with the character's base INT rating to increase it. This field determines the amount of damage dealt by the character's symbols.

DEF: The defense rating of the item. This value combines with the character's base DEF rating to increase it. Determines how resilient a character is to enemy attack.

HIT: The hit rating of the item. This value combines with the character's base HIT rating to increase it. Determines how easy it is for a character to smash through the enemy's defenses.

GRD: The item's guard rating. This value combines with the character's base GRD rating to increase it. Determines how often the character guards attacks.

Elemental Resistance: How the item affects the character's elemental defense. Elements with a negative number show a weakened defense against that element, while positive numbers show an improvement.

③ **Effect:** The latent special effects a weapon may have. These vary anywhere between basic stat increases to the ability to shoot flames when attacking.

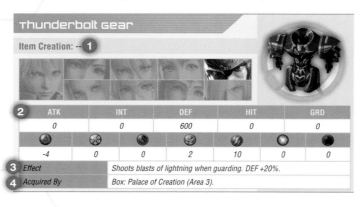

④ **Acquired By:** How the item is obtained. Items obtainable without using Item Creation are listed with six category headers: Shops, Box, Monster, Quest, Mining, Harvest, and Pickpocket. The Shops header indicates that the item may be purchased at certain shops, and is followed by a list of shops which sell that item. The Box header notates that the item is found in a treasure chest or pod within the specified area. Monster notates that the item is found by defeating a specific enemy. The Quest header signifies that the item appears only during a specific quest. As you may have guessed, the Mining and Harvest headers show that the item is acquired from mining and harvesting points within the specified area. The Pickpocket header is only used for items that cannot be easily found without pickpocketing certain NPCs.

WEAPONS

SWORDS (EDGE)

workman's blade

Item Creation: --

ATK	INT	DEF	HIT	GRD
22	0	0	0	0

Effect	--
Acquired By	Automatically obtained during first event on planet Aeos.

silvance

Item Creation: --

ATK	INT	DEF	HIT	GRD
103	0	2	0	0

Effect	--
Acquired By	Box: Cardianon Mothership (Control Tower, 2F). Shops: Ed's Weapons, Morgan's Weapons, Silkworm's Retro Shop.

storm blade

Item Creation: Smithery (Lv 1)

ATK	INT	DEF	HIT	GRD
44	0	0	0	0

Effect	Adds wind element to attacks.
Acquired By	Item Creation only (Recipe Memo 05).

venom sword

Item Creation: Smithery (Lv 3)

ATK	INT	DEF	HIT	GRD
231	0	0	0	0

Effect	Adds poison effect to attacks.
Acquired By	Item Creation only.

blessed sword

Item Creation: --

ATK	INT	DEF	HIT	GRD
36	0	0	0	0

Effect	--
Acquired By	Shops: Reflected Moon Weapons, Woodley Weapon Shop VIII, Ed's Weapons, Treasure Hunter Weapons, Silkworm's Retro Shop.

bastard sword

Item Creation: --

ATK	INT	DEF	HIT	GRD
198	0	0	0	0

Effect	--
Acquired By	Shops: Ed's Weapons, Treasure Hunter Weapons, Silkworm's Retro Shop.

flame sword

Item Creation: Smithery (Lv1)

ATK	INT	DEF	HIT	GRD
78	0	0	0	0

Effect	--
Acquired By	Item Creation only.

icecrusher sword

Item Creation: Smithery (Lv 5)

ATK	INT	DEF	HIT	GRD
291	0	0	0	0

Effect	Adds water element to attacks. Shoots a blast of ice when attacking.
Acquired By	Item Creation only.

cardianon sword

Item Creation: --

ATK	INT	DEF	HIT	GRD
60	0	0	0	0

Effect	--
Acquired By	Box: Celestial Ship 1F North.

famed sword "veinslay"

Item Creation: --

ATK	INT	DEF	HIT	GRD
220	0	0	0	0

Effect	HIT +60
Acquired By	Box: Astral Castle Audience Chamber, behind the king's throne.

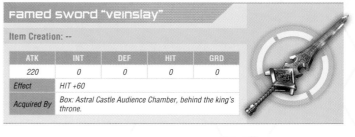
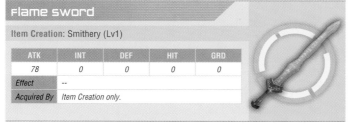
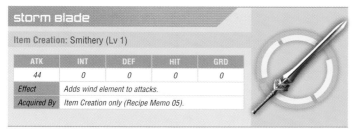

Items

Mithril sword

Item Creation: --

ATK	INT	DEF	HIT	GRD
590	0	0	0	0

Effect	--
Acquired By	Shops: Colosseum Fight Coin Exchange.

observer's sword

Item Creation: --

ATK	INT	DEF	HIT	GRD
522	0	0	0	0

Effect	--
Acquired By	Shops: Red Claw Weapons.

Arcana sword

Item Creation: Smithery (Lv 8)

ATK	INT	DEF	HIT	GRD
750	0	0	0	0

Effect	MP Cost -10% in battle.
Acquired By	Item Creation only (Recipe Memo 01).

Holy sword "Farewell"

Item Creation: --

ATK	INT	DEF	HIT	GRD
650	0	0	0	0

Effect	Adds light element to attacks. Shoots a blast of light when attacking.
Acquired By	Box: Palace of Creation (Area 6).

Lightning sword

Item Creation: --

ATK	INT	DEF	HIT	GRD
2100	0	0	0	0

Effect	Adds thunder element to attacks. Shoots a blast of lightning when attacking.
Acquired By	Box: Purgatorium (B1).

moonstone sword

Item Creation: Smithery (Lv 9)

ATK	INT	DEF	HIT	GRD
2860	108	0	0	0

Effect	Adds silence effect to attacks.
Acquired By	Item Creation only.

Demon sword "Levantine"

Item Creation: --

ATK	INT	DEF	HIT	GRD
3500	0	-514	-319	0

Effect	Shoots blasts of dark energy when attacking.
Acquired By	Box: Wandering Dungeon (17F, 19F).

imperial sword

Item Creation: --

ATK	INT	DEF	HIT	GRD
4400	0	0	0	0

Effect	--
Acquired By	Item Creation only.

Binding sword "shiho murasame"

Item Creation: --

ATK	INT	DEF	HIT	GRD
5999	999	-1999	-999	-999

Effect	--
Acquired By	Shops: The Santa Maria.

BOWS (REIMI)

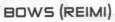

short bow

Item Creation: --

ATK	INT	DEF	HIT	GRD
19	0	0	0	0

Effect	--
Acquired By	Initially equipped to Reimi.

Eldarian bow

Item Creation: --

ATK	INT	DEF	HIT	GRD
35	0	0	10	0

Effect	Increases critical hit chance.
Acquired By	Shops: Base Shop: Omega, Silkworm's Retro Shop.

Torch bow

Item Creation: --

ATK	INT	DEF	HIT	GRD
47	0	0	0	0

Effect	Adds fire element to attacks.
Acquired By	Shops: Woodley Weapon Shop VIII, Ed's Weapons, Treasure Hunter Weapons, Silk Worm's Retro Shop.

Hunting Bow

Item Creation: Smithery (Lv 2)

ATK	INT	DEF	HIT	GRD
81	0	0	0	0

Effect	Increases critical hit chance.
Acquired By	Item Creation only.

Mystic Bow

Item Creation: Smithery (Lv 7)

ATK	INT	DEF	HIT	GRD
303	0	0	0	0

Effect	--
Acquired By	Item Creation only.

Earthsoul Bow

Item Creation: Smithery (Lv 4)

ATK	INT	DEF	HIT	GRD
89	0	5	0	0

Effect	Adds earth element to attacks.
Acquired By	Item Creation only (Recipe Memo 02).

Bow of Wisdom

Item Creation: --

ATK	INT	DEF	HIT	GRD
230	30	0	0	0

Effect	Increases critical hit chance.
Acquired By	Box: Purgatorium (B1).

Cardianon Bow

Item Creation: --

ATK	INT	DEF	HIT	GRD
101	0	0	0	0

Effect	+20% damage to humanoids.
Acquired By	Box: Cardianon Mothership (Biological Laboratory Entrance).

Wild Arc

Item Creation: --

ATK	INT	DEF	HIT	GRD
445	0	0	0	10

Effect	--
Acquired By	Shops: Colosseum Fight Coin Exchange.

Alien Arc

Item Creation: --

ATK	INT	DEF	HIT	GRD
118	0	0	0	0

Effect	Adds light element to attacks. Shoots a blast of light when attacking.
Acquired By	Box: Alternate Earth (Military Facility).

Spirit Bow "Darkstriker"

Item Creation: Smithery (Lv 9)

ATK	INT	DEF	HIT	GRD
685	22	0	0	0

Effect	Adds darkness element to attacks. +20% damage to undead.
Acquired By	Item Creation only.

Composite Bow

Item Creation: Smithery (Lv 6)

ATK	INT	DEF	HIT	GRD
194	0	0	0	0

Effect	Increases critical hit chance. HIT +3%.
Acquired By	Item Creation only.

Saint's Bow

Item Creation: --

ATK	INT	DEF	HIT	GRD
502	0	0	0	0

Effect	Adds light element to attacks.
Acquired By	Shops: Red Claw Weapons.

Bellwether's Bow

Item Creation: --

ATK	INT	DEF	HIT	GRD
155	0	0	0	0

Effect	+20% damage to birds. +20% damage to animals.
Acquired By	Box: Within the Black Tribe Tent on Roak.

Homing Arc

Item Creation: Engineering (Lv 7)

ATK	INT	DEF	HIT	GRD
594	0	0	30	0

Effect	HIT +10%.
Acquired By	Item Creation only.

EVIL SPIRIT'S BOW

Item Creation: --

ATK	INT	DEF	HIT	GRD
1857	0	0	0	0

Effect	Adds curse effect to attacks.
Acquired By	Box: Cave of the Seven Stars (B2).

ARTIFACT BOW

Item Creation: --

ATK	INT	DEF	HIT	GRD
2684	200	0	0	0

Effect	--
Acquired By	Box: Wandering Dungeon (4F, 6F).

FIERCE BOW "REPPU SHINGETSU"

Item Creation: --

ATK	INT	DEF	HIT	GRD
2999	0	0	0	0

Effect	Adds wind element to attacks.
Acquired By	Shops: The Santa Maria.

MEDIUMISTIC BOW

Item Creation: Smithery (Lv 9)

ATK	INT	DEF	HIT	GRD
4100	0	0	0	0

Effect	Increases critical hit chance.
Acquired By	Item Creation only.

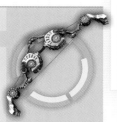

RAPIERS (FAIZE)

ELDARIAN RAPIER

Item Creation: --

ATK	INT	DEF	HIT	GRD
22	10	0	0	0

Effect	--
Acquired By	Initially equipped to Faize.

GUARDIAN'S RAPIER

Item Creation: --

ATK	INT	DEF	HIT	GRD
40	13	0	0	10

Effect	INT +10
Acquired By	Box: Alanaire Citadel, 1F.

IRON SABER

Item Creation: Smithery (Lv 2)

ATK	INT	DEF	HIT	GRD
75	20	0	0	0

Effect	Increases critical hit chance.
Acquired By	Item Creation only.

ICICLE RAPIER

Item Creation: --

ATK	INT	DEF	HIT	GRD
78	23	0	0	0

Effect	Adds water element to attacks.
Acquired By	Box: Cardianon Mothership Subterranean City.

ELASTIC RAPIER

Item Creation: Smithery (Lv 4)

ATK	INT	DEF	HIT	GRD
194	30	0	0	0

Effect	Adds stun effect to attacks.
Acquired By	Item Creation only.

RUNE SABER

Item Creation: Smithery (Lv 6)

ATK	INT	DEF	HIT	GRD
164	63	0	0	0

Effect	+15% damage for earth symbols.
Acquired By	Item Creation only.

MITHRIL RAPIER

Item Creation: --

ATK	INT	DEF	HIT	GRD
440	333	0	0	0

Effect	ATK +7%
Acquired By	Shops: Colosseum Fight Coin Exchange.

SYLPH'S SABER

Item Creation: --

ATK	INT	DEF	HIT	GRD
170	48	0	40	0

Effect	Adds wind element to attacks. Shoots a blast of wind when attacking.
Acquired By	Shops: Ruddle's Place, Treasure Hunter Weapons, Morgan's Weapons, Red Claw Weapons.

infinity saber

Item Creation: --

ATK	INT	DEF	HIT	GRD
2550	2388	0	0	0

Effect	Adds stun effect to attacks.
Acquired By	Box: Wandering Dungeon (7F, 11F).

ruby wand

Item Creation: Crafting (Lv 3)

ATK	INT	DEF	HIT	GRD
99	78	0	0	5

Effect	+15% damage for fire symbols.
Acquired By	Item Creation only.

sky sword "ama-no-murakumo"

Item Creation: --

ATK	INT	DEF	HIT	GRD
4999	3199	-1999	-999	-999

Effect	--
Acquired By	Shops: The Santa Maria.

wand of wonder

Item Creation: --

ATK	INT	DEF	HIT	GRD
120	85	0	0	0

Effect	--
Acquired By	Shops: Morgan's Weapons, Silkworm's Retro Shops.

onyx saber

Item Creation: Smithery (Lv 8)

ATK	INT	DEF	HIT	GRD
3600	3814	0	0	0

Effect	Adds darkness element to attacks.
Acquired By	Item Creation only.

rune wand

Item Creation: Crafting (Lv 5)

ATK	INT	DEF	HIT	GRD
30	118	0	0	0

Effect	Shoots a blast of mystic energy when attacking. INT +20.
Acquired By	Item Creation only.

WANDS (LYMLE)

candy wand

Item Creation: --

ATK	INT	DEF	HIT	GRD
17	12	0	0	0

Effect	--
Acquired By	Initially equipped to Lymle.

crystal wand

Item Creation: Crafting (Lv 6)

ATK	INT	DEF	HIT	GRD
165	70	0	0	0

Effect	Increases critical hit chance.
Acquired By	Item Creation only (Recipe Memo 17).

flame wand

Item Creation: --

ATK	INT	DEF	HIT	GRD
30	20	0	0	0

Effect	Adds fire element to attacks. Shoots a blast of fire when attacking.
Acquired By	Shops: Woodley Weapon Shop VIII, Ed's Weapons, Silkworm's Retro Shop.

nature wand

Item Creation: --

ATK	INT	DEF	HIT	GRD
192	141	10	0	0

Effect	--
Acquired By	Box: Miga Insect Warren B3.

booster wand

Item Creation: --

ATK	INT	DEF	HIT	GRD
60	34	0	0	0

Effect	--
Acquired By	Box: Cardianon Mothership Control Tower 1F.

star ruby wand

Item Creation: Crafting (Lv 7)

ATK	INT	DEF	HIT	GRD
280	270	0	0	0

Effect	+15% for fire symbols.
Acquired By	Item Creation only (Recipe Memo 18).

Nightmare Wand

Item Creation: --

ATK	INT	DEF	HIT	GRD
401	356	0	0	0

Effect	Adds darkness element to attacks.
Acquired By	Box: Nox Obscurus (Pulsating Bog). Shops: The Santa Maria.

Wand of Resonance

Item Creation: Crafting (Lv 8)

ATK	INT	DEF	HIT	GRD
460	512	0	0	0

Effect	INT +7%. MP cost -10% in battle.
Acquired By	Item Creation only.

Blazing Wand

Item Creation: --

ATK	INT	DEF	HIT	GRD
1163	2588	0	0	0

Effect	Adds fire element to attacks. +15% damage to fire symbols. Shoots a blast of fire when attacking.
Acquired By	Box: Wandering Dungeon (7F, 8F).

Divine Wand "Empyreal Reverie"

Item Creation: --

ATK	INT	DEF	HIT	GRD
1499	3399	0	0	0

Effect	INT +10. MP cost -20% in battle.
Acquired By	Shops: The Santa Maria.

Ancient Sage's Wand

Item Creation: Crafting (Lv 10)

ATK	INT	DEF	HIT	GRD
1311	4100	0	0	0

Effect	20% damage to undead.
Acquired By	Item Creation only.

CANNONS (BACCHUS)

Maser Cannon

Item Creation: --

ATK	INT	DEF	HIT	GRD
110	0	0	10	0

Effect	--
Acquired By	Initially equipped to Bacchus.

Plasma Cannon

Item Creation: --

ATK	INT	DEF	HIT	GRD
145	0	0	0	0

Effect	Adds thunder element to attacks.
Acquired By	Box: Alternate Earth (Military Facility).

Ancient Cannon

Item Creation: --

ATK	INT	DEF	HIT	GRD
249	80	0	0	0

Effect	--
Acquired By	Box: Purgatorium (B3).

Deadly Cannon

Item Creation: Engineering (Lv 4)

ATK	INT	DEF	HIT	GRD
308	0	0	30	0

Effect	Increases critical hit chance. Shoots a blast of mystic energy when attacking.
Acquired By	Item Creation only.

T08 Lightning Cannon

Item Creation: --

ATK	INT	DEF	HIT	GRD
523	0	0	0	0

Effect	Adds thunder element to attacks.
Acquired By	Shops: Red Claw Weapons.

Dragoon Blaster

Item Creation: Engineering (Lv 6)

ATK	INT	DEF	HIT	GRD
621	0	0	0	0

Effect	+20% damage to demons.
Acquired By	Item Creation only.

Immortal Smasher

Item Creation: --

ATK	INT	DEF	HIT	GRD
550	0	0	0	0

Effect	Adds darkness element to attacks. Shoots a blast of dark energy when attacking.
Acquired By	Box: Celestial Ship 1F North.

vulcan discharger

Item Creation: --

ATK	INT	DEF	HIT	GRD
930	0	0	0	0
Effect	Adds thunder element to attacks.			
Acquired By	Box: Palace of Creation (Area 4).			

vermillion claws

Item Creation: --

ATK	INT	DEF	HIT	GRD
231	0	0	0	0
Effect	--			
Acquired By	Shops: Morgan's Weapons, Silkworm's Retro Shop.			

photonic blaster

Item Creation: Engineering (Lv 10)

ATK	INT	DEF	HIT	GRD
1710	0	0	0	0
Effect	20% damage to mechs.			
Acquired By	Item Creation only.			

ocean claws

Item Creation: Crafting (Lv 4)

ATK	INT	DEF	HIT	GRD
458	0	0	0	0
Effect	Adds water element to attacks. Shoots a blast of ice when attacking.			
Acquired By	Item Creation only.			

ultimate cannon

Item Creation: --

ATK	INT	DEF	HIT	GRD
3100	0	-300	0	0
Effect	Shoots blasts of mystic energy when attacking. Increases critical hit chance.			
Acquired By	Box: Wandering Dungeon (16F, 18F).			

dragon claws

Item Creation: --

ATK	INT	DEF	HIT	GRD
610	53	0	0	0
Effect	Increases critical hit chance. +20% damage to demons.			
Acquired By	Shops: Colosseum Fight Coin Exchange.			

ogre cannon "legion's how!"

Item Creation: --

ATK	INT	DEF	HIT	GRD
5999	999	-1999	999	0
Effect	HP damage +10%. Adds stun effect to attacks.			
Acquired By	Shops: The Santa Maria.			

hurricane claws

Item Creation: --

ATK	INT	DEF	HIT	GRD
378	0	0	0	0
Effect	Adds wind element to attacks.			
Acquired By	Box: Miga Insect Warren B3.			

symbol cannon "tempest"

Item Creation: Engineering (Lv 8)

ATK	INT	DEF	HIT	GRD
4092	0	0	0	0
Effect	--			
Acquired By	Item Creation only.			

slasher claws

Item Creation: --

ATK	INT	DEF	HIT	GRD
540	0	0	0	0
Effect	--			
Acquired By	Shops: Red Claw Weapons.			

CLAWS (MERACLE)

iron claws

Item Creation: --

ATK	INT	DEF	HIT	GRD
170	0	0	0	0
Effect	--			
Acquired By	Initially equipped to Meracle.			

bigfoot's claws

Item Creation: Crafting (Lv 6)

ATK	INT	DEF	HIT	GRD
1330	0	0	-30	30
Effect	Adds stun effect to attacks.			
Acquired By	Item Creation only.			

burning claws

Item Creation: --

ATK	INT	DEF	HIT	GRD
1933	0	0	0	0

Effect	Adds fire element to attacks. ATK +3%.
Acquired By	Box: Astral Caves(B3).

hidden claws "crimson falcons"

Item Creation: --

ATK	INT	DEF	HIT	GRD
4999	0	0	0	0

Effect	Increases critical hit chance. +20% damage to animals.
Acquired By	Box: Wandering Dungeon (10F, 12F).

rumble claws

Item Creation: Crafting (Lv 9)

ATK	INT	DEF	HIT	GRD
5200	0	0	40	0

Effect	Shoots blasts of fire while attacking. HP damage +10%.
Acquired By	Item Creation only.

SPEARS (SARAH)

ceremonial spear

Item Creation: --

ATK	INT	DEF	HIT	GRD
183	84	0	0	5

Effect	--
Acquired By	Initially equipped to Sarah.

seafarer's harpoon

Item Creation: --

ATK	INT	DEF	HIT	GRD
222	90	0	20	0

Effect	Increases critical hit chance.
Acquired By	Quest: Complete "The Seafarer's Treasure" quest.

crested spear

Item Creation: --

ATK	INT	DEF	HIT	GRD
541	338	0	0	0

Effect	ATK +10
Acquired By	Shops: Colosseum Fight Coin Exchange.

cyclone spear

Item Creation: Smithery (Lv 3)

ATK	INT	DEF	HIT	GRD
301	139	0	0	0

Effect	Shoots a blast of wind when attacking. Adds wind element to attacks.
Acquired By	Item Creation only.

judgment spear

Item Creation: Smithery (Lv 5)

ATK	INT	DEF	HIT	GRD
407	254	0	0	0

Effect	Increases critical hit chance. HP damage +5%.
Acquired By	Item Creation only.

observer's spear

Item Creation: --

ATK	INT	DEF	HIT	GRD
423	281	5	0	0

Effect	--
Acquired By	Shops: Red Claw Weapons.

sacred spear

Item Creation: Smithery (Lv 7)

ATK	INT	DEF	HIT	GRD
860	604	0	0	0

Effect	Shoots a blast of light when attacking. Adds light element to attacks.
Acquired By	Item Creation only (Recipe Memo 03).

sea serpent harpoon

Item Creation: --

ATK	INT	DEF	HIT	GRD
740	465	0	40	0

Effect	Adds water element to attacks. Adds frozen effect to attacks.
Acquired By	Box: Palace of Creation (Area 2).

unicorn lance

Item Creation: --

ATK	INT	DEF	HIT	GRD
1386	1569	0	0	0

Effect	+20% damage to animals. Adds fog effect to attacks.
Acquired By	Box: Cave of the Seven Stars (B5).

Trident Harpoon

Item Creation: --

ATK	INT	DEF	HIT	GRD
1781	2497	0	77	0

Effect	--
Acquired By	Box: Wandering Dungeon (9F, 13F).

Wildfang Staff

Item Creation: Crafting (Lv 5)

ATK	INT	DEF	HIT	GRD
229	94	0	0	0

Effect	Increases critical hit chance. HP Damage +5%.
Acquired By	Item Creation only.

Victory Lance

Item Creation: Smithery (Lv 9)

ATK	INT	DEF	HIT	GRD
2206	3599	0	0	0

Effect	Shoots blasts of wind when attacking. Adds wind element to attacks.
Acquired By	Item Creation only.

Mysterious Scepter

Item Creation: --

ATK	INT	DEF	HIT	GRD
320	224	0	0	0

Effect	MP Damage +10%.
Acquired By	Shops: Imitation Gallery.

STAVES (MYURIA)

Symbol Staff

Item Creation: --

ATK	INT	DEF	HIT	GRD
130	74	0	0	0

Effect	--
Acquired By	Initially equipped to Myuria.

Raven Staff

Item Creation: --

ATK	INT	DEF	HIT	GRD
289	241	0	0	30

Effect	Adds darkness element to attacks. +20% damage to birds.
Acquired By	Box: Old Road to the Sanctuary (En II).

Fanatic's Staff

Item Creation: --

ATK	INT	DEF	HIT	GRD
195	114	0	-40	0

Effect	Adds darkness element to attacks. Adds curse effect to attacks. Causes attacks to damage allies as well.
Acquired By	Monster: Tamiel.

Calamity Staff

Item Creation: Crafting (Lv 8)

ATK	INT	DEF	HIT	GRD
576	642	0	0	0

Effect	MP cost -10% in battle. INT +3%.
Acquired By	Item Creation only.

Staff of Freezing

Item Creation: Crafting (Lv 4)

ATK	INT	DEF	HIT	GRD
187	146	0	0	0

Effect	Adds water element to attacks. Shoots a blast of ice when attacking.
Acquired By	Item Creation only.

Blood Scepter

Item Creation: --

ATK	INT	DEF	HIT	GRD
1017	2556	0	0	0

Effect	Adds water element to attacks. Shoots blasts of ice when attacking.
Acquired By	Box: Wandering Dungeon (14F, 15F).

Sacred Scepter

Item Creation: --

ATK	INT	DEF	HIT	GRD
165	116	0	0	0

Effect	Adds light element to attacks.
Acquired By	Box: Alanaire Citadel 2F.

Wizard's Staff

Item Creation: Crafting (Lv 10)

ATK	INT	DEF	HIT	GRD
1815	3630	0	0	0

Effect	INT +7%.
Acquired By	Item Creation only.

SCYTHES (ARUMAT)

eldarian scythe

Item Creation: --

ATK	INT	DEF	HIT	GRD
518	0	0	0	0

Effect	--
Acquired By	Initially equipped to Arumat.

inferno sickle

Item Creation: --

ATK	INT	DEF	HIT	GRD
670	0	0	0	0

Effect	Adds fire element to attacks. Shoots blasts of fire when attacking. ATK +18%
Acquired By	Shops: Colosseum Fight Coin Exchange.

laser scythe

Item Creation: Engineering (Lv 7)

ATK	INT	DEF	HIT	GRD
830	0	0	30	30

Effect	Increases critical hit chance. ATK +3%.
Acquired By	Item Creation only.

grim reaper

Item Creation: --

ATK	INT	DEF	HIT	GRD
600	0	0	0	0

Effect	Adds darkness element to attacks.
Acquired By	Shops: Imitation Gallery.

quadplex scythe

Item Creation: Engineering (Lv 8)

ATK	INT	DEF	HIT	GRD
920	0	-20	50	0

Effect	ATK +7%. +20% damage to birds.
Acquired By	Item Creation only.

conqueror scythe "asura vajra"

Item Creation: --

ATK	INT	DEF	HIT	GRD
6499	999	-1999	-999	-999

Effect	+20% damage to humanoids.
Acquired By	Shops: The Santa Maria.

quake scythe

Item Creation: Engineering (Lv 10)

ATK	INT	DEF	HIT	GRD
5414	0	0	-100	0

Effect	Adds earth element to attacks. Shoots blasts of earth when attacking.
Acquired By	Item Creation only.

OTHER WEAPONS (ALL)

scumbag slayer

Item Creation: Smithery (Lv 1)

ATK	INT	DEF	HIT	GRD
1	0	0	0	0

Effect	ATK -60%, INT -60%. Instantly kills scumbags 20% of the time.
Acquired By	Quest: Complete the "A Symbol of Bravery" quest. May also be made through Item Creation.

laser weapon

Item Creation: --

ATK	INT	DEF	HIT	GRD
900	600	0	0	0

Effect	--
Acquired By	Quest: Complete the "Trial of Might" quest.

ARMOR

SRF Armor

Item Creation: --

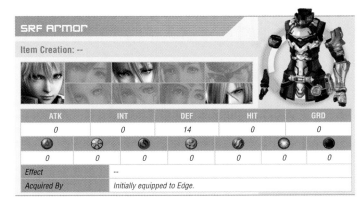

ATK	INT	DEF	HIT	GRD
0	0	14	0	0

0	0	0	0	0	0	0

Effect	--
Acquired By	Initially equipped to Edge.

Aqua Mail

Item Creation: Smithery (Lv 4)

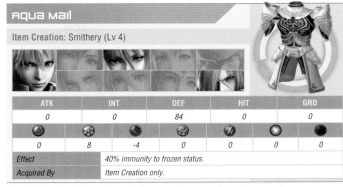

ATK	INT	DEF	HIT	GRD
0	0	84	0	0

0	8	-4	0	0	0	0

Effect	40% immunity to frozen status.
Acquired By	Item Creation only.

Eldarian Armor

Item Creation: --

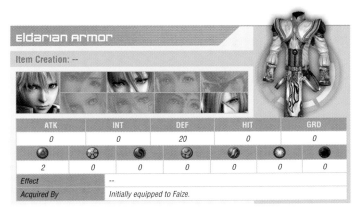

ATK	INT	DEF	HIT	GRD
0	0	20	0	0

2	0	0	0	0	0	0

Effect	--
Acquired By	Initially equipped to Faize.

Dragonscale Armor

Item Creation: --

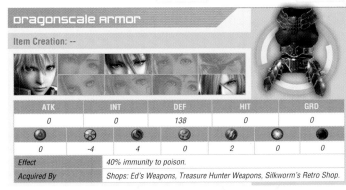

ATK	INT	DEF	HIT	GRD
0	0	138	0	0

0	-4	4	0	2	0	0

Effect	40% immunity to poison.
Acquired By	Shops: Ed's Weapons, Treasure Hunter Weapons, Silkworm's Retro Shop.

Shell Armor

Item Creation: Smithery (Lv 1)

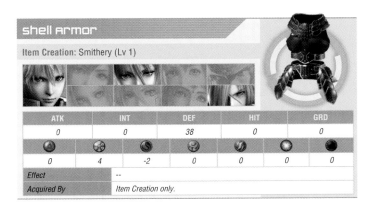

ATK	INT	DEF	HIT	GRD
0	0	38	0	0

0	4	-2	0	0	0	0

Effect	--
Acquired By	Item Creation only.

Bronto Armor

Item Creation: --

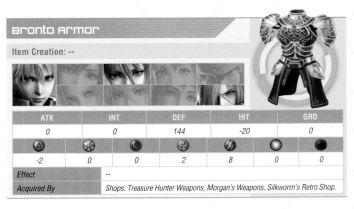

ATK	INT	DEF	HIT	GRD
0	0	144	-20	0

-2	0	0	2	8	0	0

Effect	--
Acquired By	Shops: Treasure Hunter Weapons, Morgan's Weapons, Silkworm's Retro Shop.

Guardian's Armor

Item Creation: --

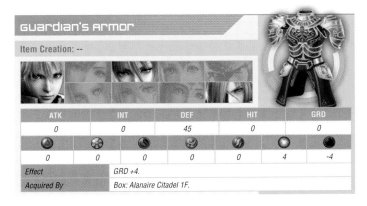

ATK	INT	DEF	HIT	GRD
0	0	45	0	0

0	0	0	0	0	4	-4

Effect	GRD +4.
Acquired By	Box: Alanaire Citadel 1F.

Astral Armor

Item Creation: --

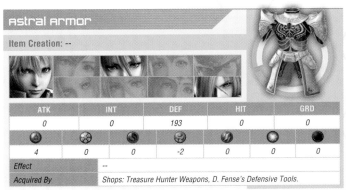

ATK	INT	DEF	HIT	GRD
0	0	193	0	0

4	0	0	-2	0	0	0

Effect	--
Acquired By	Shops: Treasure Hunter Weapons, D. Fense's Defensive Tools.

Flame Rune Mail

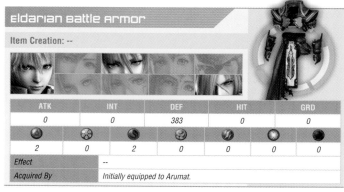

Item Creation: Smithery (Lv 6)

ATK	INT	DEF	HIT	GRD
0	0	302	0	0

0	-4	8	0	0	0	0

Effect	--
Acquired By	Item Creation only.

Eldarian Battle Armor

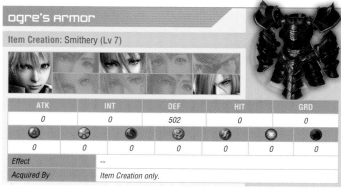

Item Creation: --

ATK	INT	DEF	HIT	GRD
0	0	383	0	0

2	0	2	0	0	0	0

Effect	--
Acquired By	Initially equipped to Arumat.

Majestic Armor

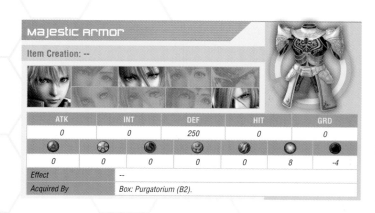

Item Creation: --

ATK	INT	DEF	HIT	GRD
0	0	250	0	0

0	0	0	0	0	8	-4

Effect	--
Acquired By	Box: Purgatorium (B2).

Ogre's Armor

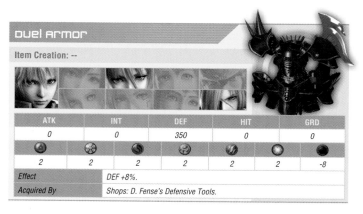

Item Creation: Smithery (Lv 7)

ATK	INT	DEF	HIT	GRD
0	0	502	0	0

0	0	0	0	0	0	0

Effect	--
Acquired By	Item Creation only.

Crystal Armor

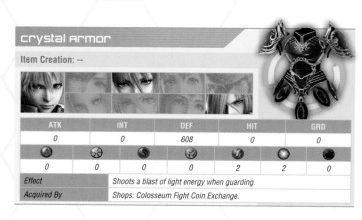

Item Creation: --

ATK	INT	DEF	HIT	GRD
0	0	608	0	0

0	0	0	0	2	2	0

Effect	Shoots a blast of light energy when guarding.
Acquired By	Shops: Colosseum Fight Coin Exchange.

Duel Armor

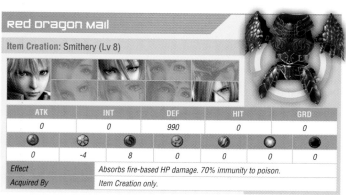

Item Creation: --

ATK	INT	DEF	HIT	GRD
0	0	350	0	0

2	2	2	2	2	2	-8

Effect	DEF +8%.
Acquired By	Shops: D. Fense's Defensive Tools.

Earthrock Mail

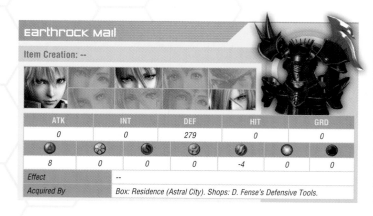

Item Creation: --

ATK	INT	DEF	HIT	GRD
0	0	279	0	0

8	0	0	0	-4	0	0

Effect	--
Acquired By	Box: Residence (Astral City). Shops: D. Fense's Defensive Tools.

Red Dragon Mail

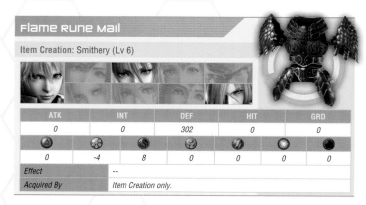

Item Creation: Smithery (Lv 8)

ATK	INT	DEF	HIT	GRD
0	0	990	0	0

0	-4	8	0	0	0	0

Effect	Absorbs fire-based HP damage. 70% immunity to poison.
Acquired By	Item Creation only.

Dullahan's Armor

Item Creation: --

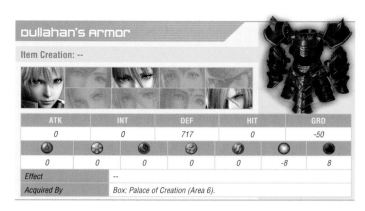

ATK	INT	DEF	HIT	GRD
0	0	717	0	-50

0	0	0	0	0	-8	8

Effect	--
Acquired By	Box: Palace of Creation (Area 6).

Universal Armor

Item Creation: Smithery (Lv 10)

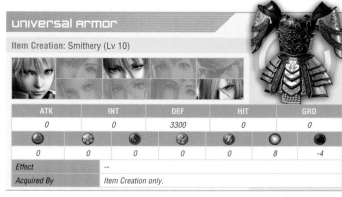

ATK	INT	DEF	HIT	GRD
0	0	3300	0	0

0	0	0	0	0	8	-4

Effect	--
Acquired By	Item Creation only.

Sylphide's Mail

Item Creation: --

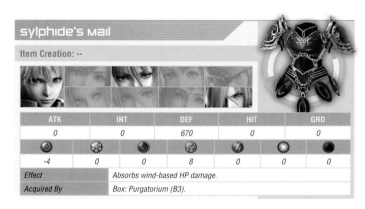

ATK	INT	DEF	HIT	GRD
0	0	670	0	0

-4	0	0	8	0	0	0

Effect	Absorbs wind-based HP damage.
Acquired By	Box: Purgatorium (B3).

SRF Protector

Item Creation: --

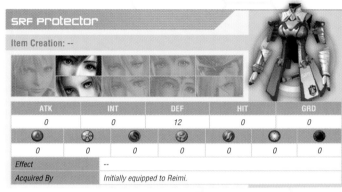

ATK	INT	DEF	HIT	GRD
0	0	12	0	0

0	0	0	0	0	0	0

Effect	--
Acquired By	Initially equipped to Reimi.

Valiant Mail

Item Creation: Smithery (Lv 9)

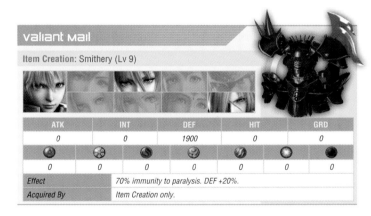

ATK	INT	DEF	HIT	GRD
0	0	1900	0	0

0	0	0	0	0	0	0

Effect	70% immunity to paralysis. DEF +20%.
Acquired By	Item Creation only.

Iron Protector

Item Creation: Smithery (Lv 2)

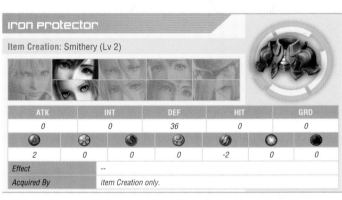

ATK	INT	DEF	HIT	GRD
0	0	36	0	0

2	0	0	0	-2	0	0

Effect	--
Acquired By	Item Creation only.

Battle Armor "God of Hellfire"

Item Creation: --

ATK	INT	DEF	HIT	GRD
-999	-999	4999	-999	999

2	2	2	2	2	-8	-8

Effect	--
Acquired By	Shops: The Santa Maria.

Mystic Chainmail

Item Creation: --

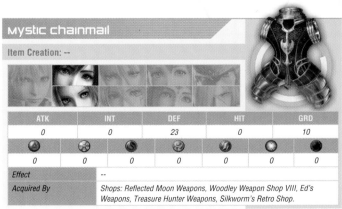

ATK	INT	DEF	HIT	GRD
0	0	23	0	10

0	0	0	0	0	0	0

Effect	--
Acquired By	Shops: Reflected Moon Weapons, Woodley Weapon Shop VIII, Ed's Weapons, Treasure Hunter Weapons, Silkworm's Retro Shop.

blizzard protector

Item Creation: --

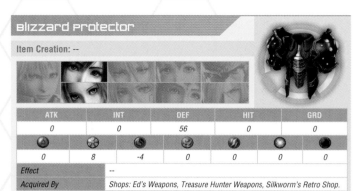

ATK	INT	DEF	HIT	GRD
0	0	56	0	0

0	8	-4	0	0	0	0

Effect	--
Acquired By	Shops: Ed's Weapons, Treasure Hunter Weapons, Silkworm's Retro Shop.

volcanic chainmail

Item Creation: --

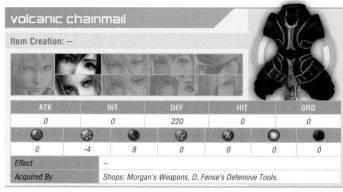

ATK	INT	DEF	HIT	GRD
0	0	220	0	0

0	-4	8	0	0	0	0

Effect	--
Acquired By	Shops: Morgan's Weapons, D. Fense's Defensive Tools.

streaked chainmail

Item Creation: --

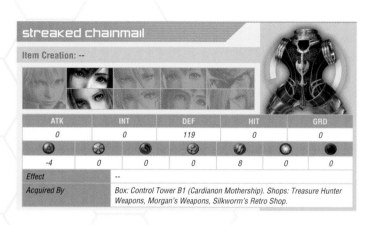

ATK	INT	DEF	HIT	GRD
0	0	119	0	0

-4	0	0	0	8	0	0

Effect	--
Acquired By	Box: Control Tower B1 (Cardianon Mothership). Shops: Treasure Hunter Weapons, Morgan's Weapons, Silkworm's Retro Shop.

dragon guard

Item Creation: Crafting (Lv 7)

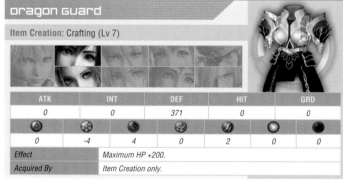

ATK	INT	DEF	HIT	GRD
0	0	371	0	0

0	-4	4	0	2	0	0

Effect	Maximum HP +200.
Acquired By	Item Creation only.

solid protector

Item Creation: --

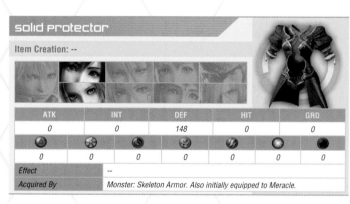

ATK	INT	DEF	HIT	GRD
0	0	148	0	0

0	0	0	0	0	0	0

Effect	--
Acquired By	Monster: Skeleton Armor. Also initially equipped to Meracle.

earthcrest guard

Item Creation: --

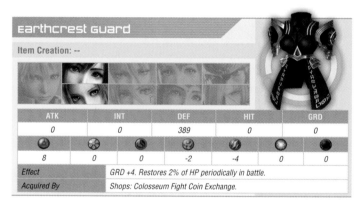

ATK	INT	DEF	HIT	GRD
0	0	389	0	0

8	0	0	-2	-4	0	0

Effect	GRD +4. Restores 2% of HP periodically in battle.
Acquired By	Shops: Colosseum Fight Coin Exchange.

lizard guard

Item Creation: Crafting (Lv 5)

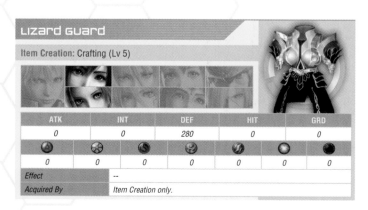

ATK	INT	DEF	HIT	GRD
0	0	280	0	0

0	0	0	0	0	0	0

Effect	--
Acquired By	Item Creation only.

star protector

Item Creation: --

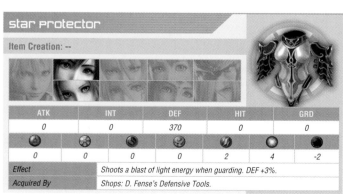

ATK	INT	DEF	HIT	GRD
0	0	370	0	0

0	0	0	0	2	4	-2

Effect	Shoots a blast of light energy when guarding. DEF +3%.
Acquired By	Shops: D. Fense's Defensive Tools.

Mithril Protector

Item Creation: Engineering (Lv 7)

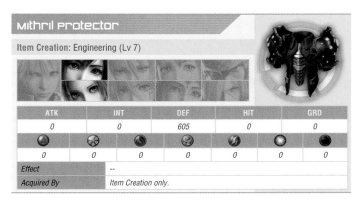

ATK	INT	DEF	HIT	GRD		
0	0	605	0	0		
0	0	0	0	0	0	0

Effect	--
Acquired By	Item Creation only.

Absolute Protector

Item Creation: --

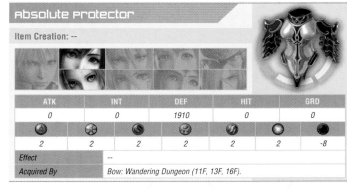

ATK	INT	DEF	HIT	GRD		
0	0	1910	0	0		
2	2	2	2	2	2	-8

Effect	--
Acquired By	Bow: Wandering Dungeon (11F, 13F, 16F).

Holy Chainmail

Item Creation: --

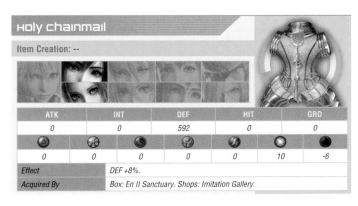

ATK	INT	DEF	HIT	GRD		
0	0	592	0	0		
0	0	0	0	0	10	-6

Effect	DEF +8%.
Acquired By	Box: En II Sanctuary. Shops: Imitation Gallery.

Varigear

Item Creation: --

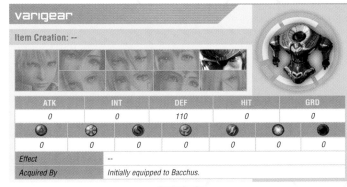

ATK	INT	DEF	HIT	GRD		
0	0	110	0	0		
0	0	0	0	0	0	0

Effect	--
Acquired By	Initially equipped to Bacchus.

Darkblood Chainmail

Item Creation: --

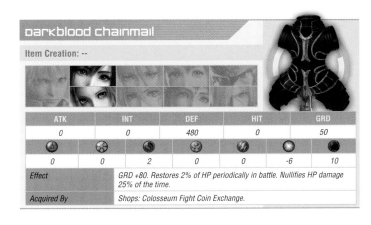

ATK	INT	DEF	HIT	GRD		
0	0	480	0	50		
0	0	2	0	0	-6	10

Effect	GRD +80. Restores 2% of HP periodically in battle. Nullifies HP damage 25% of the time.
Acquired By	Shops: Colosseum Fight Coin Exchange.

Folklore Plate

Item Creation: --

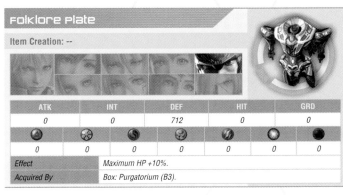

ATK	INT	DEF	HIT	GRD		
0	0	712	0	0		
0	0	0	0	0	0	0

Effect	Maximum HP +10%.
Acquired By	Box: Purgatorium (B3).

Sorcerous Guard

Item Creation: Crafting (Lv 9)

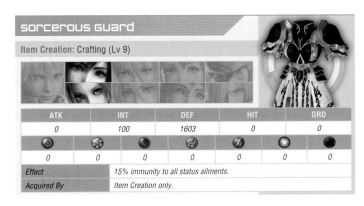

ATK	INT	DEF	HIT	GRD		
0	100	1603	0	0		
0	0	0	0	0	0	0

Effect	15% immunity to all status ailments.
Acquired By	Item Creation only.

Volcanic Gear

Item Creation: Engineering (Lv 4)

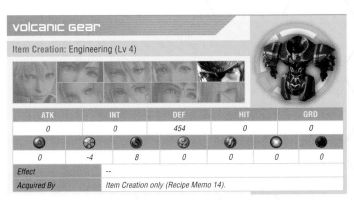

ATK	INT	DEF	HIT	GRD		
0	0	454	0	0		
0	-4	8	0	0	0	0

Effect	--
Acquired By	Item Creation only (Recipe Memo 14).

Mighty Varigear

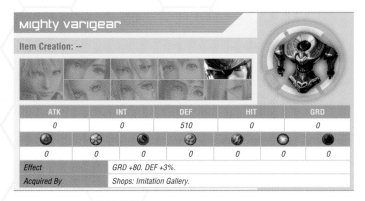

Item Creation: --

ATK	INT	DEF	HIT	GRD
0	0	510	0	0

0	0	0	0	0	0	0

Effect	GRD +80. DEF +3%.
Acquired By	Shops: Imitation Gallery.

Electroshock Gear "War Deity"

Item Creation: --

ATK	INT	DEF	HIT	GRD
-999	-999	4999	-999	0

-8	0	0	4	8	0	0

Effect	Absorbs thunder-based HP damage.
Acquired By	Shops: The Santa Maria.

Fully-Tuned Plate

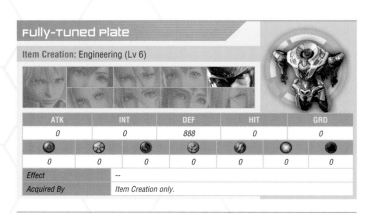

Item Creation: Engineering (Lv 6)

ATK	INT	DEF	HIT	GRD
0	0	888	0	0

0	0	0	0	0	0	0

Effect	--
Acquired By	Item Creation only.

Override Gear "Omega"

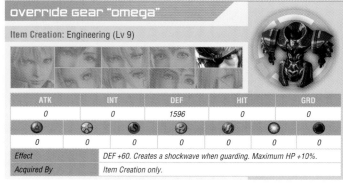

Item Creation: Engineering (Lv 9)

ATK	INT	DEF	HIT	GRD
0	0	1596	0	0

0	0	0	0	0	0	0

Effect	DEF +60. Creates a shockwave when guarding. Maximum HP +10%.
Acquired By	Item Creation only.

Thunderbolt Gear

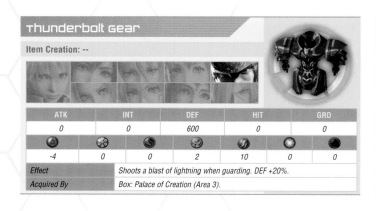

Item Creation: --

ATK	INT	DEF	HIT	GRD
0	0	600	0	0

-4	0	0	2	10	0	0

Effect	Shoots a blast of lightning when guarding. DEF +20%.
Acquired By	Box: Palace of Creation (Area 3).

Symbologist's Robe

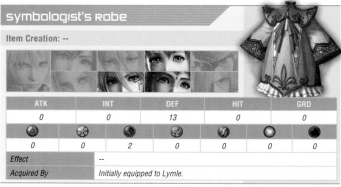

Item Creation: --

ATK	INT	DEF	HIT	GRD
0	0	13	0	0

0	0	2	0	0	0	0

Effect	--
Acquired By	Initially equipped to Lymle.

Plate of the Lost Monarch

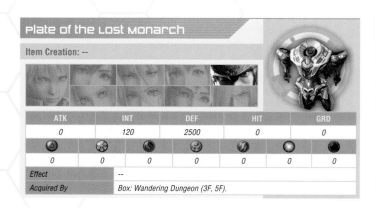

Item Creation: --

ATK	INT	DEF	HIT	GRD
0	120	2500	0	0

0	0	0	0	0	0	0

Effect	--
Acquired By	Box: Wandering Dungeon (3F, 5F).

Aqua Robe

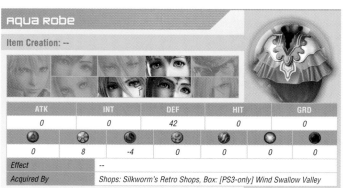

Item Creation: --

ATK	INT	DEF	HIT	GRD
0	0	42	0	0

0	8	-4	0	0	0	0

Effect	--
Acquired By	Shops: Silkworm's Retro Shops, Box: [PS3-only] Wind Swallow Valley

Comet Robe

Item Creation: --

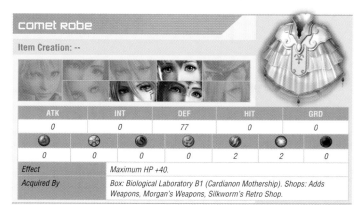

ATK	INT	DEF	HIT	GRD		
0	0	77	0	0		
0	0	0	0	2	2	0

Effect	Maximum HP +40.
Acquired By	Box: Biological Laboratory B1 (Cardianon Mothership). Shops: Adds Weapons, Morgan's Weapons, Silkworm's Retro Shop.

Alchemist's Cloak

Item Creation: --

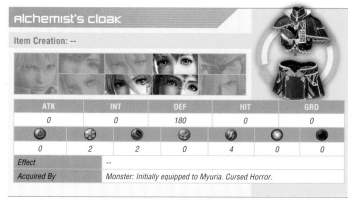

ATK	INT	DEF	HIT	GRD		
0	0	180	0	0		
0	2	2	0	4	0	0

Effect	--
Acquired By	Monster: Initially equipped to Myuria. Cursed Horror.

Alien's Robe

Item Creation: --

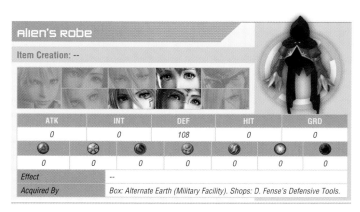

ATK	INT	DEF	HIT	GRD		
0	0	108	0	0		
0	0	0	0	0	0	0

Effect	--
Acquired By	Box: Alternate Earth (Military Facility). Shops: D. Fense's Defensive Tools.

Flare Robe

Item Creation: --

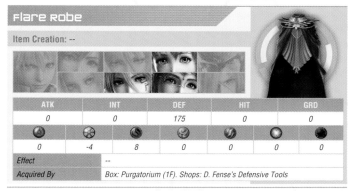

ATK	INT	DEF	HIT	GRD		
0	0	175	0	0		
0	-4	8	0	0	0	0

Effect	--
Acquired By	Box: Purgatorium (1F). Shops: D. Fense's Defensive Tools

Traveler's Cloak

Item Creation: Crafting (Lv 1)

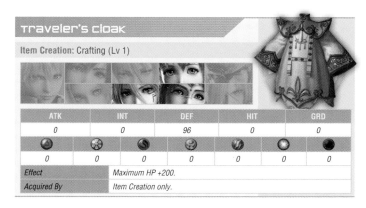

ATK	INT	DEF	HIT	GRD		
0	0	96	0	0		
0	0	0	0	0	0	0

Effect	Maximum HP +200.
Acquired By	Item Creation only.

Mirage Robe

Item Creation: Crafting (Lv 4)

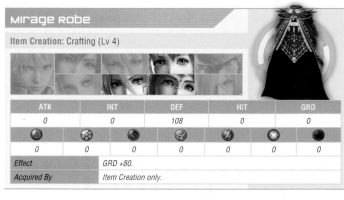

ATK	INT	DEF	HIT	GRD		
0	0	108	0	0		
0	0	0	0	0	0	0

Effect	GRD +80.
Acquired By	Item Creation only.

Protective Robe

Item Creation: Crafting (Lv 3)

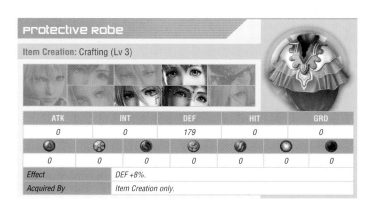

ATK	INT	DEF	HIT	GRD		
0	0	179	0	0		
0	0	0	0	0	0	0

Effect	DEF +8%.
Acquired By	Item Creation only.

Feathered Robe

Item Creation: --

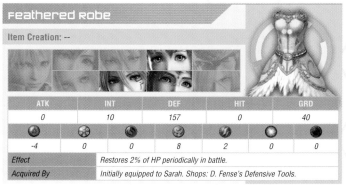

ATK	INT	DEF	HIT	GRD		
0	10	157	0	40		
-4	0	0	8	2	0	0

Effect	Restores 2% of HP periodically in battle.
Acquired By	Initially equipped to Sarah. Shops: D. Fense's Defensive Tools.

MYSTIC ROBE

Item Creation: --

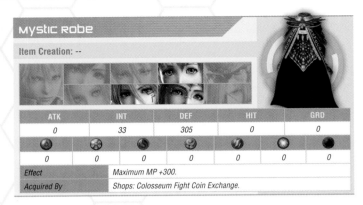

ATK	INT	DEF	HIT	GRD
0	33	305	0	0

0	0	0	0	0	0	0

Effect	Maximum MP +300.
Acquired By	Shops: Colosseum Fight Coin Exchange.

DARK ELF'S ROBE

Item Creation: --

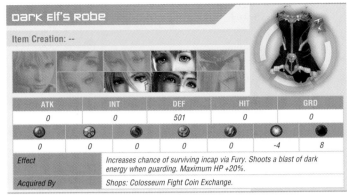

ATK	INT	DEF	HIT	GRD
0	0	501	0	0

0	0	0	0	0	-4	8

Effect	Increases chance of surviving incap via Fury. Shoots a blast of dark energy when guarding. Maximum HP +20%.
Acquired By	Shops: Colosseum Fight Coin Exchange.

EARTHEN ROBE

Item Creation: Crafting (Lv 6)

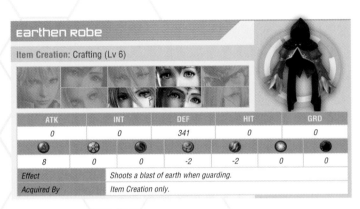

ATK	INT	DEF	HIT	GRD
0	0	341	0	0

8	0	0	-2	-2	0	0

Effect	Shoots a blast of earth when guarding.
Acquired By	Item Creation only.

SEVEN STAR CLOAK

Item Creation: --

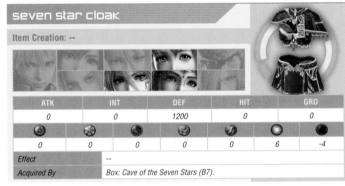

ATK	INT	DEF	HIT	GRD
0	0	1200	0	0

0	0	0	0	0	6	-4

Effect	--
Acquired By	Box: Cave of the Seven Stars (B7).

SORCERESS'S ROBE

Item Creation: --

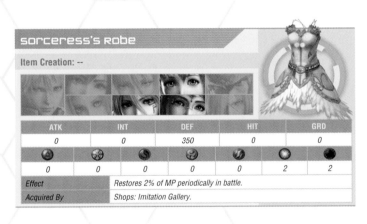

ATK	INT	DEF	HIT	GRD
0	0	350	0	0

0	0	0	0	0	2	2

Effect	Restores 2% of MP periodically in battle.
Acquired By	Shops: Imitation Gallery.

VIRTUOUS ROBE

Item Creation: Crafting (Lv 8)

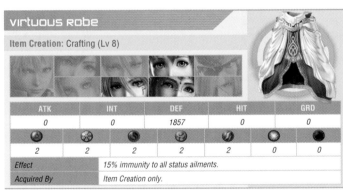

ATK	INT	DEF	HIT	GRD
0	0	1857	0	0

2	2	2	2	2	0	0

Effect	15% immunity to all status ailments.
Acquired By	Item Creation only.

LUSTROUS ROBE

Item Creation: Crafting (Lv 7)

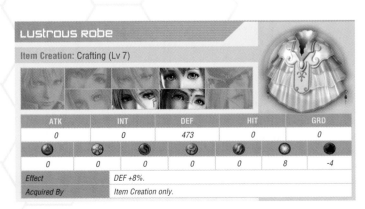

ATK	INT	DEF	HIT	GRD
0	0	473	0	0

0	0	0	0	0	8	-4

Effect	DEF +8%.
Acquired By	Item Creation only.

LASER SUIT

Item Creation: Engineering (Lv 10)

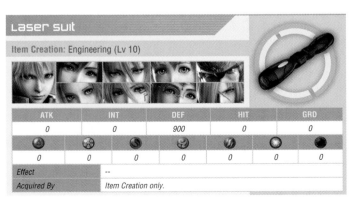

ATK	INT	DEF	HIT	GRD
0	0	900	0	0

0	0	0	0	0	0	0

Effect	--
Acquired By	Item Creation only.

valkyrie's garb

Item Creation: Smithery (Lv 10)

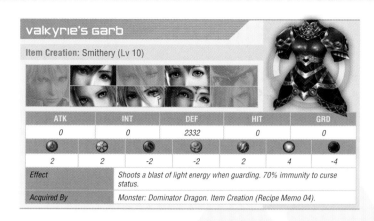

ATK	INT	DEF	HIT	GRD
0	0	2332	0	0

2	2	-2	-2	2	4	-4

Effect	Shoots a blast of light energy when guarding. 70% immunity to curse status.
Acquired By	Monster: Dominator Dragon. Item Creation (Recipe Memo 04).

WRIST ACCESSORIES

astralian emblem

Item Creation: --

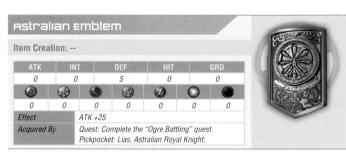

ATK	INT	DEF	HIT	GRD
0	0	5	0	0

0	0	0	0	0	0	0

Effect	ATK +25
Acquired By	Quest: Complete the "Ogre Battling" quest. Pickpocket: Lias, Astralian Royal Knight.

magic bracelet

Item Creation: Crafting (Lv 4)

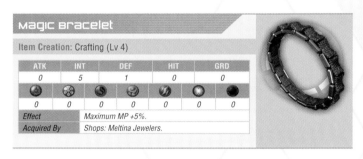

ATK	INT	DEF	HIT	GRD
0	5	1	0	0

0	0	0	0	0	0	0

Effect	Maximum MP +5%.
Acquired By	Shops: Meltina Jewelers.

bandit's glove

Item Creation: --

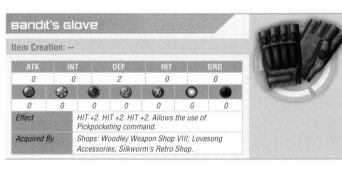

ATK	INT	DEF	HIT	GRD
0	0	2	0	0

0	0	0	0	0	0	0

Effect	HIT +2. HIT +2. HIT +2. Allows the use of Pickpocketing command.
Acquired By	Shops: Woodley Weapon Shop VIII, Lovesong Accessories, Silkworm's Retro Shop.

power bracelet

Item Creation: Crafting (Lv 4)

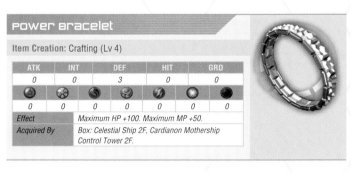

ATK	INT	DEF	HIT	GRD
0	0	3	0	0

0	0	0	0	0	0	0

Effect	Maximum HP +100. Maximum MP +50.
Acquired By	Box: Celestial Ship 2F, Cardianon Mothership Control Tower 2F.

energy bracelet

Item Creation: Crafting (Lv 2)

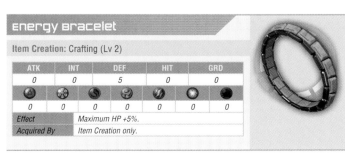

ATK	INT	DEF	HIT	GRD
0	0	5	0	0

0	0	0	0	0	0	0

Effect	Maximum HP +5%.
Acquired By	Item Creation only.

wisdom bracelet

Item Creation: Crafting (Lv 7)

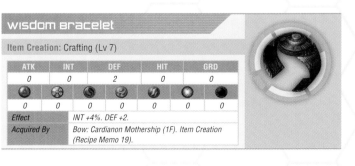

ATK	INT	DEF	HIT	GRD
0	0	2	0	0

0	0	0	0	0	0	0

Effect	INT +4%. DEF +2.
Acquired By	Bow: Cardianon Mothership (1F). Item Creation (Recipe Memo 19).

Attack Bracelet

Item Creation: Crafting (Lv 7)

ATK	INT	DEF	HIT	GRD
10	0	2	0	0

0	0	0	0	0	0	0

Effect	ATK +4%.
Acquired By	Box: Cardianon Mothership (Biological Laboratory B1).

Sturdy Bracelet

Item Creation: Crafting (Lv 3)

ATK	INT	DEF	HIT	GRD
0	0	10	0	0

0	0	0	0	0	0	0

Effect	DEF +5%.
Acquired By	Box: Cardianon Mothership (Generator Area B2).

Sniper's Bangle

Item Creation: --

ATK	INT	DEF	HIT	GRD
0	0	2	10	0

0	0	0	0	0	0	0

Effect	HIT +6%.
Acquired By	Shops: Reflected Moon Weapons, Woodley Weapon Shop VIII, Lovesong Accessories, Silkworm's Retro Shop.

Slayer's Bangle

Item Creation: Crafting (Lv 9)

ATK	INT	DEF	HIT	GRD
0	0	2	0	0

0	0	0	0	0	0	0

Effect	Adds one hit chance per attack.
Acquired By	Item Creation only.

Silver Bangle

Item Creation: --

ATK	INT	DEF	HIT	GRD
0	0	5	0	2

0	0	0	0	0	0	0

Effect	DEF + 10.
Acquired By	Shops: Base Shop: Omega, Reflected Moon Weapons, Woodley Weapon Shop VIII, Lovesong Accessories, Silkworm's Retro Shop.

Light Scarf

Item Creation: Crafting (Lv 5)

ATK	INT	DEF	HIT	GRD
0	1	2	0	2

0	0	0	0	0	4	-4

Effect	Restores 1% of light-based damage as MP.
Acquired By	Item Creation only.

Darkness Scarf

Item Creation: Crafting (Lv 5)

ATK	INT	DEF	HIT	GRD
1	0	2	0	2

0	0	0	0	0	-4	4

Effect	Restores 1% of darkness-based damage as MP.
Acquired By	Item Creation only.

Berserker's Scarf

Item Creation: Crafting (Lv 3)

ATK	INT	DEF	HIT	GRD
0	0	-30	0	0

0	0	2	0	0	0	0

Effect	Causes attacks to damage allies as well. ATK +4%
Acquired By	Item Creation only.

Healing Band

Item Creation: Crafting (Lv 7)

ATK	INT	DEF	HIT	GRD
0	0	10	0	0

0	2	0	0	0	0	0

Effect	Restores 2% of HP periodically in battle.
Acquired By	Item Creation only.

Faerie Band

Item Creation: Crafting (Lv 8)

ATK	INT	DEF	HIT	GRD
0	3	8	0	0

0	0	0	2	0	0	0

Effect	Restores 2% of MP periodically in battle.
Acquired By	Item Creation only.

Learning Gloves

Item Creation: Crafting (Lv 9)

ATK	INT	DEF	HIT	GRD
0	0	1	0	0

0	0	0	0	0	0	0

Effect	ATK -20%. +10% EXP after each battle.
Acquired By	Pickpocket: Faithful Servant in Astral Castle.

Foal Snaps

Item Creation: Crafting (Lv 8)

ATK	INT	DEF	HIT	GRD
0	0	-30	0	0

0	0	0	0	0	0	0

Effect	INT -20%. +15% Fol after each battle.
Acquired By	Box: Alternate Earth (Military Facility).

stallion snaps

Item Creation: Crafting (Lv 7)

ATK	INT	DEF	HIT	GRD
0	0	2	-20	30

●	●	●	●	●	●	●
0	0	0	0	0	0	0

Effect	Rush Gauge charge rate +2.
Acquired By	Shops: Meltina Jewelers.

fire armlet

Item Creation: Crafting (Lv 3)

ATK	INT	DEF	HIT	GRD
0	2	1	0	0

●	●	●	●	●	●	●
0	0	6	0	0	0	0

Effect	Nullifies fire symbols 20% of the time.
Acquired By	Shops: Meltina Jewelers.

wind armlet

Item Creation: Crafting (Lv 4)

ATK	INT	DEF	HIT	GRD
0	2	1	0	0

●	●	●	●	●	●	●
0	0	0	6	0	0	0

Effect	Nullifies wind symbols 20% of the time.
Acquired By	Shops: Meltina Jewelers.

earth armlet

Item Creation: Crafting (Lv 3)

ATK	INT	DEF	HIT	GRD
0	2	1	0	0

●	●	●	●	●	●	●
6	0	0	0	0	0	0

Effect	Nullifies earth symbols 20% of the time.
Acquired By	Shops: Meltina Jewelers.

water armlet

Item Creation: Crafting (Lv 4)

ATK	INT	DEF	HIT	GRD
0	2	1	0	0

●	●	●	●	●	●	●
0	6	0	0	0	0	0

Effect	Nullifies water symbols 20% of the time.
Acquired By	Shops: Meltina Jewelers.

thunder armlet

Item Creation: Crafting (Lv 3)

ATK	INT	DEF	HIT	GRD
0	2	1	0	0

●	●	●	●	●	●	●
0	0	0	0	6	0	0

Effect	Nullifies thunder symbols 20% of the time.
Acquired By	Shops: Meltina Jewelers.

tri-emblem

Item Creation: Crafting (Lv 10)

ATK	INT	DEF	HIT	GRD
200	200	100	100	100

●	●	●	●	●	●	●
0	0	0	0	0	0	0

Effect	Rush Gauge charge rate +3. Grants immunity to paralysis. MP cost -15% in battle. Adds two hit chances per attack.
Acquired By	Shops: The Santa Maria. Item Creation (Recipe Memo 27)

tri-emblum

Item Creation: --

ATK	INT	DEF	HIT	GRD
2	2	1	1	1

●	●	●	●	●	●	●
0	0	0	0	0	0	0

Effect	HIT +2.
Acquired By	Monster: Thieving Scumbag, Black Eagle Ranger.

NECK ACCESSORIES

anti-poison amulet

Item Creation: Crafting (Lv 7)

ATK	INT	DEF	HIT	GRD
0	0	10	0	0

●	●	●	●	●	●	●
0	0	0	0	0	0	0

Effect	Grants immunity to poison.
Acquired By	Shops: Meltina Jewelers.

anti-stun amulet

Item Creation: Crafting (Lv 5)

ATK	INT	DEF	HIT	GRD
0	0	8	0	0

●	●	●	●	●	●	●
0	0	0	0	0	0	0

Effect	Grants immunity to stun status.
Acquired By	Box: Lemuris (Woodley Weapon Shop VIII). Shops: Meltina Jewelers. Item Creation (Recipe Memo 21).

anti-freezing amulet

Item Creation: Crafting (Lv 6)

ATK	INT	DEF	HIT	GRD
0	0	10	0	0

●	●	●	●	●	●	●
0	0	0	0	0	0	0

Effect	Grants immunity to stun status.
Acquired By	Box: Celestial Ship 1F North. Shops: Lovesong Accessories.

Anti-Paralysis Amulet

Item Creation: Crafting (Lv 7)

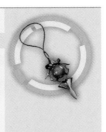

ATK	INT	DEF	HIT	GRD
0	0	10	0	0

0	0	0	0	0	0	0

Effect	Grants immunity to paralysis.
Acquired By	Box: Cardianon Mothership (Control Tower 3F). Shops: Mobius's One-Stop Shop.

Anti-Silence Amulet

Item Creation: Crafting (Lv 5)

ATK	INT	DEF	HIT	GRD
0	5	10	0	0

0	0	0	0	0	0	0

Effect	Grants immunity to silence.
Acquired By	Shops: Meltina Jewelers.

Anti-Fog Amulet

Item Creation: Crafting (Lv 5)

ATK	INT	DEF	HIT	GRD
0	0	20	0	0

0	0	0	0	0	0	0

Effect	Grants immunity to fog status.
Acquired By	Darkness Box: Tropp. item Creation (Recipe Memo 22).

Anti-Curse Amulet

Item Creation: Crafting (Lv 6)

ATK	INT	DEF	HIT	GRD
0	0	10	0	0

0	0	0	0	0	0	0

Effect	Grants immunity to curse status.
Acquired By	Box: Tatroi. item Creation (Recipe Memo 23).

Anti-Pumpkin Amulet

Item Creation: Crafting (Lv 6)

ATK	INT	DEF	HIT	GRD
0	0	20	0	0

0	0	0	0	0	0	0

Effect	Grants immunity to pumpkin status.
Acquired By	Shops: Meltina Jewelers.

Anti-Void Amulet

Item Creation: Crafting (Lv 8)

ATK	INT	DEF	HIT	GRD
0	0	10	0	0

0	0	0	0	0	0	0

Effect	Grants immunity to void status.
Acquired By	Box: Purgatorium (B2). item Creation (Recipe Memo 24).

Battler Amulet

Item Creation: Crafting (Lv 7)

ATK	INT	DEF	HIT	GRD
12	0	5	0	0

0	0	0	0	0	0	0

Effect	Nullifies damage from humanoids 20% of the time.
Acquired By	Item Creation only.

Demon Amulet

Item Creation: Crafting (Lv 6)

ATK	INT	DEF	HIT	GRD
0	10	5	0	0

0	0	0	0	0	0	0

Effect	Nullifies damage from demons 20% of the time.
Acquired By	Box: Lemuris (Ghimdo's House in Triom Village).

Raven Amulet

Item Creation: Crafting (Lv 6)

ATK	INT	DEF	HIT	GRD
0	0	5	0	10

0	0	0	0	0	0	0

Effect	Nullifies damage from birds 20% of the time.
Acquired By	Shops: Meltina Jewelers.

Silver Amulet

Item Creation: Crafting (Lv 7)

ATK	INT	DEF	HIT	GRD
0	0	5	0	0

0	0	0	0	0	0	0

Effect	Nullifies damage from undead 20% of the time.
Acquired By	Box: Earth (Abandoned Town).

Sacrificial Doll

Item Creation: --

ATK	INT	DEF	HIT	GRD
0	0	1	0	0

1	1	1	1	1	1	1

Effect	Automatically revives from incap, then vanishes.
Acquired By	Box: Wandering Dungeon. Shops: Reflected Moon Weapons, Woodley Weapon Shop VIII.

Greater Sacrificial Doll

Item Creation: --

ATK	INT	DEF	HIT	GRD
0	0	30	0	0

1	1	1	1	1	1	1

Effect	Automatically revives from incap once per battle.
Acquired By	Complete the "Trial of Courage" quest.

oracle's charm

Item Creation: --

ATK	INT	DEF	HIT	GRD
0	20	4	0	0

0	0	0	0	0	2	0

Effect	INT +1. 30% immunity to frozen status.
Acquired By	Quest: Complete the Curious Kitty quest. Trigger the Cherished Keepsake quest. Talk to the Spoiled Boy in Woodley Inn. Talk to Sir Francis in Thousand Gods General Store.

Lutea's sacred stone

Item Creation: --

ATK	INT	DEF	HIT	GRD
0	0	1	0	0

1	1	1	1	1	1	1

Effect	INT +46, DEF +31, and GRD +30 (for Lymle only). Nullifies HP damage 15% of the time.
Acquired By	Complete the "Lutea's Sacred Stones" quest.

warning brooch

Item Creation: --

ATK	INT	DEF	HIT	GRD
0	0	8	0	0

0	0	0	0	0	0	0

Effect	GRD +2. Prevents surprise attacks.
Acquired By	Shops: Lovesong Accessories, Mobius's One-Stop Shop, Silkworm's Retro Shop. Monster: Armed Dragoon.

silent talisman

Item Creation: --

ATK	INT	DEF	HIT	GRD
0	0	1	0	0

0	2	0	0	0	0	0

Effect	DEF +2. Silences all sound.
Acquired By	Quest: Complete "The Fourth Errand" quest.

magick emblem

Item Creation: --

ATK	INT	DEF	HIT	GRD
0	0	2	0	0

0	0	1	0	1	0	0

Effect	Maximum HP -20%. Maximum MP +10%
Acquired By	Monster: Dermoptera.

solo champion medal

Item Creation: --

ATK	INT	DEF	HIT	GRD
20	0	132	0	0

0	0	0	0	0	0	0

Effect	Rush Gauge charge rate +2. ATK +10%. Grants immunity to poison. Nullifies HP damage 15% of the time.
Acquired By	Obtained after completing "Solo" mode in colosseum.

Team champion medal

Item Creation: --

ATK	INT	DEF	HIT	GRD
0	80	108	0	0

0	0	0	0	0	2	0

Effect	Nullifies MP damage 15% of the time. Adds one hit chance per attack. MP cost -5% in battle. Nullifies light symbols 20% of the time.
Acquired By	Obtained after completing "Team" mode in colosseum.

Bunny champion medal

Item Creation: --

ATK	INT	DEF	HIT	GRD
0	0	99	60	0

2	0	0	0	0	0	0

Effect	Nullifies damage from animals 20% of the time. Creates a shockwave when guarding. 20% immunity to all status ailments. Increases chance of surviving incap via Fury.
Acquired By	Win the 100cc Bunny Race!

Green Talisman

Item Creation: Crafting (Lv 6)

ATK	INT	DEF	HIT	GRD
0	0	15	0	0

0	0	0	0	0	0	0

Effect	Increases chance of surviving incap via Fury.
Acquired By	Shops: Meltina Jewelers. Box: Wandering Dungeon.

Red Talisman

Item Creation: Crafting (Lv 6)

ATK	INT	DEF	HIT	GRD
0	11	25	0	0

0	0	0	0	0	0	0

Effect	Nullifies MP damage 15% of the time.
Acquired By	Box: Wandering Dungeon.

Blue Talisman

Item Creation: Crafting (Lv 4)

ATK	INT	DEF	HIT	GRD
0	3	5	0	0

0	0	0	0	0	0	0

Effect	Nullifies HP damage 15% of the time.
Acquired By	Box: Alanaire Citadel 1F. Item Creation (Recipe Memo 25).

Regeneration symbol

Item Creation: Crafting (Lv 8)

ATK	INT	DEF	HIT	GRD
0	10	2	0	0

0	0	0	0	0	0	0

Effect	Restores 2% of MP periodically in battle.
Acquired By	Monster: Cave Guardian. Ice Box: Planet Aeos (Southern Reaches).

earth charm

Item Creation: Artistry (Lv 4)

ATK	INT	DEF	HIT	GRD
0	0	7	0	5

🜨	🜨	🜨	🜨	🜨	🜨	🜨
4	0	0	0	0	0	0

Effect	Shoots a blast of earth when guarding. Nullifies earth symbols 20% of the time.
Acquired By	Shops: Meltina Jewelers.

thunder charm

Item Creation: Artistry (Lv 4)

ATK	INT	DEF	HIT	GRD
0	0	7	0	5

🜨	🜨	🜨	🜨	🜨	🜨	🜨
0	0	0	0	4	0	0

Effect	Shoots a blast of thunder when guarding. Nullifies thunder symbols 20% of the time.
Acquired By	Shops: Meltina Jewelers.

water charm

Item Creation: Artistry (Lv 6)

ATK	INT	DEF	HIT	GRD
0	0	7	0	5

🜨	🜨	🜨	🜨	🜨	🜨	🜨
0	4	0	0	0	0	0

Effect	Shoots a blast of water when guarding. Nullifies water symbols 20% of the time.
Acquired By	Shops: Meltina Jewelers.

light charm

Item Creation: Artistry (Lv 8)

ATK	INT	DEF	HIT	GRD
0	0	3	0	5

🜨	🜨	🜨	🜨	🜨	🜨	🜨
0	0	0	0	0	4	0

Effect	Shoots a blast of light when guarding. Nullifies light symbols 20% of the time.
Acquired By	Box: Aeos (Southern Reaches). Item Creation (Recipe Memo 11).

fire charm

Item Creation: Artistry (Lv 4)

ATK	INT	DEF	HIT	GRD
0	0	7	0	5

🜨	🜨	🜨	🜨	🜨	🜨	🜨
0	0	4	0	0	0	0

Effect	Shoots a blast of fire when guarding. Nullifies fire symbols 20% of the time.
Acquired By	Shops: Meltina Jewelers.

darkness charm

Item Creation: Artistry (Lv 5)

ATK	INT	DEF	HIT	GRD
0	0	3	0	5

🜨	🜨	🜨	🜨	🜨	🜨	🜨
0	0	0	0	0	0	4

Effect	Shoots a blast of dark when guarding. Nullifies dark symbols 20% of the time.
Acquired By	Box: Ravines of Extinction (Nox Obscurus). Item Creation (Recipe Memo 12).

wind charm

Item Creation: Artistry (Lv 5)

ATK	INT	DEF	HIT	GRD
0	0	7	0	5

🜨	🜨	🜨	🜨	🜨	🜨	🜨
0	0	0	4	0	0	0

Effect	Shoots a blast of wind when guarding. Nullifies wind symbols 20% of the time.
Acquired By	Shops: Meltina Jewelers.

USABLE ITEMS

Name	Item Creation	Effect	Acquired By
Blueberries	--	Restores 40% of HP.	Shops: Base Shop: Alpha, Can-Can General Goods, Thousand Gods General Store, Compact Vendor Unit 003, Compact Vendor Unit 025, Compact Vendor Unit 050, Good Grocers, The Happy Skip Grocery, Morgan's Weapons, Min Min's Rejuvenation Shop.
Bigberries	--	Restores 70% of HP.	Shops: Good Grocers, The Happy Skip Grocery, Min Min's Rejuvenation Shop.
Blackberries	--	Restores 40% of MP.	Shops: Base Shop: Alpha, Can-Can General Goods, Thousand Gods General Store, Compact Vendor Unit 003, Compact Vendor Unit 025, Compact Vendor Unit 050, Good Grocers, The Happy Skip Grocery, Min Min's Rejuvenation Shop.
Thornberries	--	Restores 50% of HP, sometimes causes poison.	Shops: Flora/Fauna Laboratory. Harvest: Aeos (Southern Reaches), Nox Obscurus (Pulsating Bog, Halls of Termination).
Mixed Syrup	Compounding (Lv 1)	Restores 20% of HP/MP.	Shops: Thousand Gods General Store, Min Min's Rejuvenation Shop.
Bizarre Fruit	--	Restores 5% of HP/MP. Generates a seed when used.	Box: Tropp, Nox Obscurus, Palace of Creation (Area 2), Cave of the Seven Stars (B4).
Ripe Berries	Compounding (Lv 3)	Restores 30% of HP (party).	Shops: Compact Vendor Unit 003, Compact Vendor Unit 025, Compact Vendor Unit 050, Colosseum Fight Coin Exchange.
Perfect Berries	Compounding (Lv 5)	Restores 50% of HP (party).	Shops: Min Min's Rejuvenation Shop.
Physical Stimulant	Compounding (Lv 5)	Restores 100% of HP.	Box: Astral Caves. Shops: Min Min's Rejuvenation Shop.

Name	Item Creation	Effect	Acquired By
Mental Stimulant	Compounding (Lv 6)	Restores 70% of MP.	Shops: Min Min's Rejuvenation Shop. Speak to Katrina, Believer in Fate on En II. Item Creation (Recipe Memo 28).
Gambleberries	Compounding (Lv 2)	Restores all HP or causes incapacitation.	Harvest: Lemuris (Thalia Plains, Van Elm Region), Aeos (Southern Reaches).
Aquaberries	--	Cures poison.	Shops: Base Shop: Alpha, CanCan General Goods, Thousand Gods General Store, Good Grocers, The Happy Skip Grocery, Min Min's Rejuvenation Shop.
Basil	--	Cures paralysis.	Shops: CanCan General Goods, Thousand Gods General Store, Compact Vendor Unit 003, Compact Vendor Unit 025, Compact Vendor Unit 050, Good Grocers, The Happy Skip Grocery, Front Desk, Min Min's Rejuvenation Shop.
Fresh Sage	--	Revives from incap and restores 30% HP/MP.	Shops: Base Shop: Alpha, Can-Can General Goods, Thousand Gods General Store, Compact Vendor Unit 003, Compact Vendor Unit 025, Compact Vendor Unit 050, Good Grocers, The Happy Skip Grocery, Min Min's Rejuvenation Shop.
Hot Chocolate	--	Cures frozen status.	Shops: Can-Can General Goods, Thousand Gods General Store, Good Grocers, The Happy Skip Grocery, Min Min's Rejuvenation Shop.
Red Herb	--	Cures silence.	Shops: Morgan's Weapons, Front Desk, Min Min's Rejuvenation Shop.
Glowstick	--	Cures fog status.	Shops: Good Grocers, The Happy Skip Grocery, Min Min's Rejuvenation Shop.
Pumpkin Extract	--	Cures pumpkin status.	Shops: Whole Heart Foods, Front Desk.
Holy Water	Alchemy (Lv 2)	Cures curse status.	Shops: Min Min's Rejuvenation Shop.
Void Recovery Unit	Engineering (Lv 6)	Cures void status.	Box: En II (Central Control Room), Nox Obscurus (Ravine of Extinction). Monster: Metal Golem, Necromancer. Item Creation (recipe Memo 15).
Poison Relief Unit	Engineering (Lv 5)	Cures poison (party).	Shops: Flaming Fist Explosives.
Melting Unit	Engineering (Lv 3)	Cures frozen status (party).	Shops: Flaming Fist Explosives.
Mobilization Unit	Engineering (Lv 4)	Cures paralysis (party).	Shops: Flaming Fist Explosives.
Speech Restoration Unit	Engineering (Lv 4)	Cures silence (party).	Shops: Flaming Fist Explosives.
Vision Enhancement Unit	Engineering (Lv 3)	Cures fog status (party).	Shops: Flaming Fist Explosives.
Dispelling Unit	Engineering (Lv 5)	Cures curse status (party).	Shops: Flaming Fist Explosives.
Resurrection Elixir	Compounding (Lv 6)	Revives from incap and restores 60% HP/MP.	Shops: Ruddle's Place, Min Min's Rejuvenation Shop.
Resurrection Unit	Compounding (Lv 8)	Revives from incap and restores 50% HP/MP (party).	Item Creation only.
Resistance Potion	Alchemy (Lv 1)	Elemental resistance +3 for 60 seconds.	Box: Centropolis (Transport Room).
Strength Potion	Alchemy (Lv 4)	ATK +20% for 60 seconds.	Item Creation only.
Mental Potion	Alchemy (Lv 4)	INT +20% for 60 seconds.	Item Creation (Recipe Memo 09).
Fortitude Potion	Alchemy (Lv 3)	DEF +30% for 60 seconds.	Box: Cardianon Mothership (1F).
Hyper Potion	Alchemy (Lv 5)	All parameters +15% for 60 seconds.	Item Creation only.
Pickled Pepper Potion	Cooking (Lv 3)	Grants Berserk status for 60 seconds.	Box: Wandering Dungeon.
Vile Goop	Alchemy (Lv 5)	Grants Symbolic Weapon status for 60 seconds.	Shops: Can-Can General Goods, Thousand Gods General Store, Good Grocers, The Happy Skip Grocery.
Riot Potion	Compounding (Lv 4)	Symbols cost 0 MP for 60 seconds.	Shops: Magical Foods.
Fainting Potion	Compounding (Lv 4)	Invincible but can't act for 60 seconds.	Shops: Magical Foods.
DANGER! DO NOT DRINK!	Compounding (Lv 1)	Sets drinker's HP to 1.	Box: Tatroi Area. Monster: Skeleton Warrior, Sydonaist Base Shop: Alpha, Chaotic Leader.
Poison Cider	Compounding (Lv 1)	Places drinker in poison status.	Box: Cardianon Mothership (Generator Area B2), Palace of Creation (Area 2). Monster: Dragon General, Sydonaist Beta.
Frozen Cider	Compounding (Lv 1)	Places drinker in frozen status.	Box: Palace of Creation (Area 2). Monster: Mist Grave, Mana Yeti, Lizard Warrior, Sydonaist Beta, Ice Corpse.
Static Cider	Compounding (Lv 1)	Places drinker in paralyzed status.	Monster: Harpyia, Sydonaist Base Shop: Alpha, Dark Raptor.
Silent Cider	Compounding (Lv 1)	Places drinker in silence status.	Box: Palace of Creation (Area 2). Monster: Succubus, Little Aliens.
Cloudy Cider	Compounding (Lv 1)	Places drinker in fog status.	Monster: Sydonaist Base Shop: Alpha, Dark Material.
Cursed Cider	Compounding (Lv 1)	Places drinker in curse status.	Box: Aeos (Southern Reaches). Monster: Ice Corpse. Item Creation (Recipe Memo 29).
Pumpkin Cider	Compounding (Lv 1)	Places drinker in pumpkin status.	Box: Palace of Creation (Area 2). Monster: Spirit Priest, Dark Clown.
Element Breaker	Engineering (Lv 6)	Enemy elemental resistance -4 for 60 seconds. 90 HP damage to target and nearby enemies.	Box: Cardianon Mothership (Control Tower 1F).
Attack Breaker	Engineering (Lv 5)	Enemy ATK -30% for 60 seconds. 90 HP damage to target and nearby enemies.	Item Creation only.

Name	Item Creation	Effect	Acquired By
Intelligence Breaker	Engineering (Lv 5)	Enemy INT -30% for 60 seconds. 90 HP damage to target and nearby enemies.	Shops: Flaming Fist Explosives.
Defense Breaker	Engineering (Lv 3)	Enemy DEF -40% for 60 seconds. 90 HP damage to target and nearby enemies.	Shops: Flaming Fist Explosives.
Ultimate Bomb	--	Detonates a wide-area explosion in one minute.	Quest: Complete "The First Errand" quest.
EM Bomb	Engineering (Lv 2)	2500 HP Damage to target and nearby enemies.	Monster: Cardianon General, Guard Bot "Assaulter", Guard Bot "Commando".
Wide-Range EM Bomb	Engineering (Lv 5)	2000 HP wide-area damage.	Shops: Flaming Fist Explosives. Item Creation (Recipe Memo 16).
Self-Destructor 3000	Engineering (Lv 1)	Causes the user to self-destruct.	Monster: Cardianon Soldier, Phantom Leader, Phantom Soldier.
Compact Poison Bomb	Engineering (Lv 4)	Poisons an enemy. 90 HP damage to target and nearby enemies.	Shops: Compact Vending Unit 003, Compact Vending Unit 025, Compact Vending Unit 050, Flaming Fist Explosives.
Compact Stun Bomb	Engineering (Lv 3)	Stuns an enemy. 90 HP damage to target and nearby enemies.	Shops: Compact Vending Unit 003, Compact Vending Unit 025, Compact Vending Unit 050, Flaming Fist Explosives.
Compact Freezing Bomb	Engineering (Lv 4)	Freezes an enemy. 90 HP damage to target and nearby enemies.	Shops: Compact Vending Unit 003, Compact Vending Unit 025, Compact Vending Unit 050, Flaming Fist Explosives.
Compact Silence Bomb	Engineering (Lv 2)	Silences an enemy. 90 HP damage to target and nearby enemies.	Shops: Compact Vending Unit 003, Compact Vending Unit 025, Compact Vending Unit 050, Flaming Fist Explosives.
Lesser Demon's Fetish	Artistry (Lv 4)	Curses an enemy. 90 HP damage to target and nearby enemies.	Monster: Cursed Horror.
Deluxe Poison Bomb	Engineering (Lv 6)	Poisons enemies in a wide area. 700 HP wide-area damage.	Item Creation only.
Deluxe Stun Bomb	Engineering (Lv 5)	Stuns enemies in a wide area. 700 HP wide-area damage.	Item Creation only.
Deluxe Freezing Bomb	Engineering (Lv 6)	Freezes enemies in a wide area. 700 HP wide-area damage.	Item Creation only.
Deluxe Silence Bomb	Engineering (Lv 4)	Silence enemies in a wide area. 700 HP wide-area damage.	Item Creation only.
Greater Demon's Fetish	Artistry (Lv 8)	Curses enemies in a wide area. 700 HP wide-area damage.	Item Creation only.
Time Stopper	Engineering	All time stops for one second.	Quest: Complete "The Third Errand" quest.
HP Absorption Unit	Engineering (Lv 7)	Absorbs HP from an enemy.	Quest: Complete "The Second Errand" quest.
MP Absorption Unit	Engineering (Lv 8)	Absorbs MP from an enemy.	Item Creation only.
Scrambling Unit	Engineering (Lv 2)	Allows instant escape from battles.	Shops: Compact Vending Unit 003, Compact Vending Unit 025, Compact Vending Unit 050, Flaming Fist Explosives.
Super Aphrodisiac	Compounding (Lv 5)	...Makes the user look bad to others.	Item Creation only.
Love Potion No. 256	Compounding (Lv 7)	Makes the user look good to others.	Item Creation only.
Silver Chalice	--	Restores 30% HP [usable once every five battles].	Box: Roak (Astral Desert).
Gold Chalice	--	Restores 30% MP [usable once every five battles].	Fire Box: Cave of the Seven Stars (B5).
Chalice of Love	--	Revives from incap [usable once every five battles].	Quest: Complete the "Trial of Love" quest.
Tent	--	Restores 100% of HP/MP (party).	Shops: Tools 'R' Us, Mobius's Anything Stop Shops, Masterful Materials.
Symbol Card "Earth Glaive"	Artistry (Lv 2)	Casts Earth Glaive at level 5.	Item Creation only.
Symbol Card "Earth Glaive" +	Artistry (Lv 5)	Casts Earth Glaive at level 10.	Item Creation only.
Symbol Card "Stone Rain"	Artistry (Lv 4)	Casts Stone Rain at level 5.	Item Creation only.
Symbol Card "Stone Rain" +	Artistry (Lv 7)	Casts Stone Rain at level 10.	Item Creation only.
Symbol Card "Terra Hammer"	Artistry (Lv 6)	Casts Terra Hammer at level 5.	Item Creation only.
Symbol Card "Terra Hammer " +	Artistry (Lv 9)	Casts Terra Hammer at level 10.	Item Creation only.
Symbol Card "Ice Needles"	Artistry (Lv 2)	Casts Ice Needles at level 5.	Item Creation only.
Symbol Card "Ice Needles" +	Artistry (Lv 5)	Casts Ice Needles at level 10.	Item Creation only.

Name	Item Creation	Effect	Acquired By
Symbol Card "Deep Freeze"	Artistry (Lv 4)	Casts Deep Freeze at level 5.	Item Creation only.
Symbol Card "Deep Freeze" +	Artistry (Lv 7)	Casts Deep Freeze at level 10.	Item Creation only.
Symbol Card "Arctic Impact"	Artistry (Lv 6)	Casts Arctic Impact at level 5.	Item Creation only.
Symbol Card "Arctic Impact" +	Artistry (Lv 9)	Casts Arctic Impact at level 10.	Item Creation only.
Symbol Card "Fire Bolt"	Artistry (Lv 1)	Casts Fire Bolt at level 5.	Item Creation only.
Symbol Card "Fire Bolt" +	Artistry (Lv 4)	Casts Fire Bolt at level 10.	Item Creation only.
Symbol Card "Explosion"	Artistry (Lv 3)	Casts Explosion at level 5.	Item Creation only.
Symbol Card "Explosion" +	Artistry (Lv 6)	Casts Explosion at level 10.	Item Creation only.
Symbol Card "Volcanic Burst"	Artistry (Lv 5)	Casts Volcanic Burst at level 5.	Item Creation only.
Symbol Card "Volcanic Burst" +	Artistry (Lv 8)	Casts Volcanic Burst at level 10.	Item Creation only.
Symbol Card "Wind Blade"	Artistry (Lv 1)	Casts Wind Blade at level 5.	Item Creation only.
Symbol Card "Wind Blade" +	Artistry (Lv 4)	Casts Wind Blade at level 10.	Item Creation only.
Symbol Card "Blast Hurricane"	Artistry (Lv 3)	Casts Blast Hurricane at level 5.	Item Creation only.
Symbol Card "Blast Hurricane" +	Artistry (Lv 6)	Casts Blast Hurricane at level 10.	Item Creation only.
Symbol Card "Tornado"	Artistry (Lv 5)	Casts Tornado at level 5.	Item Creation only.
Symbol Card "Tornado" +	Artistry (Lv 8)	Casts Tornado at level 10.	Item Creation only.
Symbol Card "Lightning Blast"	Artistry (Lv 1)	Casts Lightning Blast at level 5.	Item Creation only.
Symbol Card "Lightning Blast" +	Artistry (Lv 4)	Casts Lightning Blast at level 10.	Item Creation only.
Symbol Card "Thunder Flare"	Artistry (Lv 3)	Casts Thunder Flare at level 5.	Item Creation only.
Symbol Card "Thunder Flare" +	Artistry (Lv 6)	Casts Thunder Flare at level 10.	Item Creation only.
Symbol Card "Plasma Cyclone"	Artistry (Lv 5)	Casts Plasma Cyclone at level 5.	Item Creation only.
Symbol Card "Plasma Cyclone" +	Artistry (Lv 8)	Casts Plasma Cyclone at level 10.	Item Creation only.
Symbol Card "Radiant Lancer"	Artistry (Lv 2)	Casts Radiant Lancer at level 5.	Item Creation only.
Symbol Card "Radiant Lancer" +	Artistry (Lv 5)	Casts Radiant Lancer at level 10.	Item Creation only.
Symbol Card "Sunflare"	Artistry (Lv 4)	Casts Sunflare at level 5.	Item Creation only.
Symbol Card "Sunflare" +	Artistry (Lv 7)	Casts Sunflare at level 10.	Item Creation only.
Symbol Card "Aurora Rings"	Artistry (Lv 6)	Casts Aurora Rings at level 5.	Item Creation only.
Symbol Card "Aurora Rings" +	Artistry (Lv 9)	Casts Aurora Rings at level 10.	Item Creation only.
Symbol Card "Shadow Needles"	Artistry (Lv 2)	Casts Shadow Needles at level 5.	Item Creation only.
Symbol Card "Shadow Needles" +	Artistry (Lv 5)	Casts Shadow Needles at level 10.	Item Creation only.
Symbol Card "Vampiric Blade"	Artistry (Lv 4)	Casts Vampiric Blade at level 5.	Item Creation only.
Symbol Card "Vampiric Blade" +	Artistry (Lv 7)	Casts Vampiric Blade at level 10.	Item Creation only.
Symbol Card "Dark Devourer"	Artistry (Lv 6)	Casts Dark Devourer at level 5.	Item Creation only.
Symbol Card "Dark Devourer" +	Artistry (Lv 9)	Casts Dark Devourer at level 10.	Item Creation only.

Name	Item Creation	Effect	Acquired By
Symbol Card "Divine Wave"	Artistry (Lv 8)	Casts Divine Wave at level 5.	Item Creation only.
Symbol Card "Divine Wave" +	Artistry (Lv 10)	Casts Divine Wave at level 10.	Item Creation only.
Symbol Card "Extinction"	Artistry (Lv 7)	Casts Extinction at level 5.	Item Creation only.
Symbol Card "Extinction" +	Artistry (Lv 9)	Casts Extinction at level 10.	Item Creation only.
Symbol Card "Reaping Spark"	Artistry (Lv 7)	Casts Reaping Spark at level 5.	Item Creation only.
Symbol Card "Reaping Spark" +	Artistry (Lv 9)	Casts Reaping Spark at level 10.	Item Creation only.
Symbol Card "Healing"	Artistry (Lv 2)	Casts Healing at level 5.	Item Creation only.
Symbol Card "Healing" +	Artistry (Lv 5)	Casts Healing at level 10.	Item Creation only.
Symbol Card "Ex Healing"	Artistry (Lv 4)	Casts Ex Healing at level 5.	Item Creation only.
Symbol Card "Ex Healing" +	Artistry (Lv 7)	Casts Ex Healing at level 10.	Item Creation only.
Symbol Card "Faerie Healing"	Artistry (Lv 5)	Casts Faerie Healing at level 5.	Item Creation only.
Symbol Card "Faerie Healing" +	Artistry (Lv 8)	Casts Faerie Healing at level 10.	Item Creation only.
Symbol Card "Faerie Light"	Artistry (Lv 7)	Casts Faerie Light at level 5.	Item Creation only.
Symbol Card "Faerie Light " +	Artistry (Lv 10)	Casts Faerie Light at level 10.	Item Creation only.
Symbol Card "Antidote"	Artistry (Lv 3)	Casts Antidote.	Item Creation only.
Symbol Card "Cure Condition"	Artistry (Lv 7)	Casts Cure Condition.	Item Creation only.
Symbol Card "Restoration"	Artistry (Lv 6)	Casts Restoration at level 5.	Item Creation only.
Symbol Card "Restoration" +	Artistry (Lv 9)	Casts Restoration at level 10.	Item Creation only.
Symbol Card "Resurrection"	Artistry (Lv 10)	Casts Resurrection.	Item Creation only.
Symbol Card "Enhance"	Artistry (Lv 4)	Casts Enhance at level 5.	Item Creation only.
Symbol Card "Enhance" +	Artistry (Lv 6)	Casts Enhance at level 10.	Item Creation only.
Symbol Card "Enlighten"	Artistry (Lv 4)	Casts Enlighten at level 5.	Item Creation only.
Symbol Card "Enlighten" +	Artistry (Lv 6)	Casts Enlighten at level 10.	Item Creation only.
Symbol Card "Angel Feather"	Artistry (Lv 5)	Casts Angel Feather at level 5.	Item Creation only.
Symbol Card "Angel Feather" +	Artistry (Lv 8)	Casts Angel Feather at level 10.	Item Creation only.
Symbol Card "Enshelter"	Artistry (Lv 4)	Casts Enshelter at level 5.	Item Creation only.
Symbol Card "Enshelter" +	Artistry (Lv 6)	Casts Enshelter at level 10.	Item Creation only.
Symbol Card "Reflection"	Artistry (Lv 5)	Casts Reflection at level 5.	Item Creation only.
Symbol Card "Reflection" +	Artistry (Lv 7)	Casts Reflection at level 10.	Item Creation only.
Symbol Card "Sacred Pain"	Artistry (Lv 3)	Casts Sacred Pain at level 5.	Item Creation only.
Symbol Card "Sacred Pain" +	Artistry (Lv 6)	Casts Sacred Pain at level 10.	Item Creation only.
Symbol Card "Silence"	Artistry (Lv 2)	Casts Silence at level 5.	Item Creation only.
Symbol Card "Silence" +	Artistry (Lv 5)	Casts Silence at level 10.	Item Creation only.
Symbol Card "Void"	Artistry (Lv 6)	Casts Void at level 5.	Item Creation only.
Symbol Card "Void" +	Artistry (Lv 9)	Casts Void at level 10.	Item Creation only.
Symbol Card "Symbolic Weapon"	Artistry (Lv 5)	Casts Symbolic Weapon at level 5.	Item Creation only.
Symbol Card "Symbolic Weapon" +	Artistry (Lv 9)	Casts Symbolic Weapon at level 10.	Item Creation only.

SKILL MANUALS
(USABLE ITEMS CONTINUED)

Name	Useable By	Acquired By
Skill Manual "Faerie Star"	Edge, Lymle, Sarah, Myuria	Complete the "Trial of Wisdom" quest.
Skill Manual "Anthropology"	Edge	Shops: Chaz's Books, Rascal's Guild, Green's Skill Guild.
Skill Manual "Botany"	Reimi	Shops: Chaz's Books, Stinker's 's Guild, Green's Skill Guild.
Skill Manual "Entomology"	Faize, Arumat	Shops: Fez's Books, Rascal's Guild, Green's Skill Guild.
Skill Manual "Parapsychology"	Lymle	Shops: Chaz's Books, Rascal's Guild, Green's Skill Guild.
Skill Manual "Ornithology"	Meracle	Shops: Fez's Books, Rascal's Guild, Green's Skill Guild.
Skill Manual "Demonology"	Myuria	Shops: Rascal's Guild, Green's Skill Guild.
Skill Manual "Zoology"	Sarah	Shops: Green's Skill Guild.
Skill Manual "Treasure Sense"	Lymle	Box: Alanaire Citadel.
Skill Manual "Appetite"	Edge, Meracle	Shops: Rascal's Guild.
Skill Manual "Haggling"	Myuria	Box: En II (Old Road to the Sanctuary).
Skill Manual "Trap Evasion"	Arumat	Box: Purgatorium.
Skill Manual "Chain Combos"	All	Shops: Fez's Books, Three Leaf Books.
Skill Manual "Duplication"	Faize, Arumat	Box: Cave of the Seven Stars (B7).
Skill Manual "Augury"	Sarah	Box: Roak (Tropp).
Skill Manual "Pickpocketing"	Edge	Shops: Three Leaf Books.
Skill Manual "Ocarina"	Meracle	Complete "The Sand Bird Strikes Back" quest.
Skill Manual "Bunny Call"	Sarah	Box: En II (Old Road to the Sanctuary).
Skill Manual "Charge"	Lymle	Bow: Miga Insect Warren (B3).
Skill Manual "ATK Boost"	Edge, Reimi, Bacchus, Meracle, Arumat	Box: Palace of Creation (Area 5). Shops: The Santa Maria.
Skill Manual "INT Boost"	Faize, Lymle, Sarah, Myuria	Box: Wandering Dungeon. Shops: The Santa Maria.
Skill Manual "HP Boost"	All	Shops: Chaz's Books, Mobius's One-Stop Shops, Rascal's Guild, Green's Skill Guild.
Skill Manual "MP Boost"	All	Shops: Chaz's Books, Green's Skill Guild.
Skill Manual "Fast Cast"	Lymle, Myuria	Shops: Green's Skill Guild.
Skill Manual "Energy Shield"	Reimi, Lymle, Sarah, Myuria	Box: Cardianon Mothership: Control Tower
Skill Manual "Critical Hit"	Edge, Reimi, Meracle, Arumat	Shops: Mobius's One-Stop Shops, Rascal's Guild, Green's Skill Guild.
Skill Manual "No Guard"	Edge, Faize, Bacchus, Meracle, Arumat	Shops: Chaz's Books, Green's Skill Guild.
Skill Manual "First Aid"	All	Shops: Fez's Books, Rascal's Guild, Green's Skill Guild.
Skill Manual "Auto Healing"	All	Shops: Chaz's Books, Rascal's Guild, Green's Skill Guild.
Skill Manual "Stun"	Edge, Meracle, Arumat	Shops: Rascal's Guild, Green's Skill Guild.
Skill Manual "Fury Boost"	All	Shops: Fez's Books, Mobius's One-Stop Shops, Rascal's Guild, Green's Skill Guild.
Skill Manual "Elusion"	Lymle, Sarah	Shops: Fez's Books, Rascal's Guild, Green's Skill Guild.
Skill Manual "Rage"	Lymle, Myuria	Shops: Green's Skill Guild.
Skill Manual "Steal"	Meracle, Myuria	Box: Purgatorium.
Skill Manual "Taunt"	Edge, Reimi, Bacchus, Meracle, Arumat	Shops: Fez's Books, Rascal's Guild, Green's Skill Guild.
Skill Manual "Berserk"	Edge, Reimi, Bacchus, Meracle, Arumat	Shops: Green's Skill Guild.
Skill Manual "Focus"	Reimi, Meracle, Sarah	Box: Alanaire Citadel, The Purgatorium, Old Road to the Sanctuary.
Skill Manual "Scan Enemy"	Faize, Bacchus, Arumat	Box: Exploration Base, Alternate Earth.
Skill Manual "Convert"	Edge, Faize, Bacchus, Myuria, Arumat	Shops: Rascal's Place, Rascal's Guild, Green's Skill Guild.
Skill Manual "Emergency Repairs"	Bacchus	Box: En II.
Skill Manual "Hide"	All	Shops: Fez's Books, Mobius's One-Stop Shops, Rascal's Guild, Green's Skill Guild.
Skill Manual "Mindflare"	Faize, Lymle, Sarah, Myuria	Box: Cardianon Mothership: Control Tower, Astral Caves.
Skill Manual "Scintillant Stream"	Edge	Box: Cave of the Seven Stars (B6).
Skill Manual "Savage Sparrows"	Reimi	Box: [X360 version] Purgatorium B4, [PS3 version] Cave of the Seven Stars (Inner Sanctum)
Skill Manual "Divine Wave"	Faize	Shops: The Santa Maria.
Skill Manual "Trinity Blaze"	Lymle	Box: Alanaire Citadel.
Skill Manual "Godslayer"	Bacchus	Box: Old Road to the Sanctuary.
Skill Manual "Max Shockwave"	Meracle	Box: [X360 version] Cave of the Seven Stars (Inner Sanctum), [PS3 version] Cave of the Seven Stars (B4)
Skill Manual "Plasma Cyclone"	Myuria	Nox Obscurus's Hall of Termination, near the entrance to the Palace of Creation.
Skill Manual "Sunflare"	Sarah	Box: [X360 version] Cave of the Seven Stars (B4), [PS3 version] Purgatorium B4
Skill Manual "Dragon Roar"	Arumat	Box: Miga Insect Warren (B4).

FOOD

Name	Item Creation	Effect	Acquired By
Pickled Plum Rice	Cooking (Lv 1)	+5% EXP for three battles. Restores 5% of HP.	Item Creation only.
Ochazuke	Cooking (Lv 2)	+10% EXP for three battles. Restores 5% of HP.	Item Creation only.
Oyakodon	Cooking (Lv 3)	+20% EXP for three battles. Restores 5% of HP.	Item Creation only.
Curry Rice	Cooking (Lv 4)	+5% EXP for three battles. Restores 20% of HP.	Item Creation only.
Pasta Peperoncino	Cooking (Lv 3)	DEF +30% for 10 battles. Restores 5% of MP.	Item Creation only.
Pasta Bolognese	Cooking (Lv 5)	DEF +30% for 10 battles. Restores 20% of MP.	Item Creation only.
Pasta Genovese	Cooking (Lv 7)	DEF +50% for 10 battles. Restores 20% of MP.	Item Creation only.
Hamburg Steak	Cooking (Lv 4)	ATK +20% for five battles. Restores 5% of HP.	Item Creation only.
Beef Steak	Cooking (Lv 7)	ATK +30% for five battles. Restores 5% of HP.	Item Creation only.
Sukiyaki	Cooking (Lv 10)	ATK +30% for five battles. Restores 20% of HP.	Item Creation only.
Salt-Grilled Saury	Cooking (Lv 4)	INT +20% for five battles. Restores 5% of MP.	Item Creation only.
Salmon Meuniere	Cooking (Lv 6)	INT +20% for five battles. Restores 20% of MP.	Item Creation only.
Swordfish Piccata	Cooking (Lv 8)	INT +30% for five battles. Restores 5% of MP.	Item Creation only.
Sushi	Cooking (Lv 9)	INT +30% for five battles. Restores 20% of MP.	Item Creation only.
Nectar	--	Restores 5% of MP.	Monster: Dryad, Giant Fungus, Albero di Anima, Mandragora, Lamia Radix. Harvest: Lemuris (Thalia Plains, Van Elm Region).
Tasty Mushroom	--	Restores 20% of HP.	Monster: Giant Fungus, Man-Eating Tree. Harvest: Lemuris (Van Elm Region).
Tasty Mushroom?	--	Restores 50% of HP, sometimes causes poison.	Monster: Apprentice Scumbag, Giant Fungus. Harvest: Lemuris (Van Elm Region).
Famous Grape Juice	--	Restores 70% of HP.	Quest: Complete the "Crazy for Grape Juice" quest.
Sweet Fruit	--	Restores 100% of HP.	Shops: Whole Heart Foods, Ruddle's Place.
Lemon	--	Restores 20% of HP. Restores 5% of MP.	Harvest: Aeos (Landing Point, Northern Coast, Exploration Base), Lemuris (Thalia Plains, Van Elm Region), Roak (Astralian Continent, Astral Castle, Tropp Area, Cave to the Purgatorium).
Pickled Plum	--	Restores 20% of HP/MP.	Shops: Good Grocers. Monster: Soldier Zombie. Harvest: Aeos (Landing Point, Northern Coast).
Seaweed	--	Restores 5% of MP.	Shops: Flora/Fauna Laboratory. Box: Aeos (Northern Coast). Monster: Gerel, Killer Chelae. Harvest: Aeos (Urd Falls Cave, Northern Coast).
Lemon Juice	Cooking (Lv 1)	Restores 40% of HP. Restores 20% of MP.	Item Creation only.
Caesar Salad	Cooking (Lv 3)	MP cost -30% for 10 battles. Restores 5% of HP.	Item Creation only.
Ratatouille	Cooking (Lv 8)	MP cost -30% for 10 battles. Restores 20% of HP.	Item Creation only.
Vegetable Stir-fry	Cooking (Lv 10)	MP cost -30% for 10 battles. Restores 40% of HP.	Item Creation only.
Rich Cheese	--	+20% Fol for three battles. Restores 5% of MP.	Shops: Thousand Gods General Store, Roomy Foods.
Custard Pie	Cooking (Lv 4)	+20% Fol for three battles. Restores 20% of MP.	Item Creation only.
Shortcake	Cooking (Lv 5)	+30% Fol for three battles. Restores 5% of MP.	Quest: Complete "The Elusive Female Firefly" quest.
Blueberry Tart	Cooking (Lv 6)	+30% Fol for three battles. Restores 20% of MP.	Item Creation only.
Mille-feuille	Cooking (Lv 8)	+40% Fol for three battles. Restores 20% of MP.	Item Creation (Recipe Memo 08).
Natto	--	Cures all status ailments.	Shops: Whole Heart Foods, Magical Foods, The Santa Maria. Monster: Soldier Zombie, Thieving Scumbag, Vomiting Gel.
Rotten Fish	--	Restores 50% of HP, sometimes causes poison.	Monster: Skeleton Soldier, Horned Turtle, Waving Pincers.
Otherworldly Cuisine	Cooking (Lv 2)	Prevents enemy targeting for 10 battles.	Item Creation only.
Fermented Sushi	Cooking (Lv 7)	Elemental resistances +3 for five battles.	Item Creation only.
Attack Seeds	--	ATK +4 [permanent].	Box: Aeos (Urd Falls Cave, Northern Coast). Monster: Kobold, Desert Ogre.
Defense Seeds	--	DEF +4 [permanent].	Box: Cardianon Mothership (dock), Roak (Astral Desert). Harvest: Aeos (Northern Coast). Monster: Horned Tortoise, Skeleton Armor.
Accuracy Seeds	--	HIT +4 [permanent].	Box: Lemuris (Thalia Plains). Monster: Killer Wasp, Honeybee, Giant Bat, Chaotic Cell.
Protection Seeds	--	GRD +4 [permanent].	Harvest: Woodley Area.
Intelligence Seeds	--	INT +4 [permanent].	Monster: Sydonaist Beta, Stroper.
Health Seeds	--	Maximum HP +50 [permanent].	Box: Nox Obscurus, Astral Castle.
Magic Seeds	--	Maximum MP +30 [permanent].	Box: Palace of Creation (Area 3).
Potent Attack Seeds	Compounding (Lv 10)	ATK +10 [permanent].	Item Creation only.
Potent Defense Seeds	Compounding (Lv 9)	DEF +10 [permanent].	Item Creation only.
Potent Accuracy Seeds	Compounding (Lv 9)	HIT +10 [permanent].	Box: Miga Insect Warren B2.
Potent Protection Seeds	Compounding (Lv 9)	GRD +10 [permanent].	Item Creation only.
Potent Intelligence Seeds	Compounding (Lv 10)	INT +10 [permanent].	Box: En II (Central Control Room).
Potent Health Seeds	Compounding (Lv 10)	Maximum HP +200 [permanent].	Item Creation only.
Potent Magic Seeds	Compounding (Lv 10)	Maximum MP +100 [permanent].	Monster: Kokabiel.
Stamina Pie	Cooking (Lv 7)	Revives from incap and restores 90% HP/MP.	Box: Roak (Tropp).
Speed Pie	Cooking (Lv 8)	Restores 70% of HP.	Item Creation only.
Acceleration Pie	Cooking (Lv 8)	Restores 20% of MP.	Item Creation only.
Miracle Pie	Cooking (Lv 10)	Cures all status ailments.	Item Creation only.

OTHER ITEMS

Name	Item Creation	Use	Acquired By
Iron	--	IC Component	Shops: Woodley Weapon Shop VIII, Mobius's One-Stop Shop.
Silver	--	IC Component	Mining: Aeos (Landing Point, Urd Falls Cave, Northern Coast), Roak (Astralian Continent, Tatroi Area, Astral Desert, Tropp Area), En II (Sanctuary). Monster: Guard Bot "Commando".
Gold	Alchemy (Lv 2)	IC Component	Roak: Roak (Astralian Continent, Tatroi Area, Tropp Area), Aeos (Southern Reaches, Miga Insect Warren).
Mercury	--	IC Component	Mining: Lemuris (Thalia Plains, Van Elm Region, Celestial Ship), Nox Obscurus (Ravine of Extinction, Pulsating Bog). Monster: Horned Turtle, Armed Dragon Newt, Dark Panzer.
Steel	Smithery (Lv 3)	IC Component	Box: Wandering Dungeon.
Platinum	Alchemy (Lv 4)	IC Component	Box: Cave of the Seven Stars (B1). Mining: Astral Desert, Tatroi Area (PS3 only).
Coal	--	IC Component	Mining: Cave to the Purgatorium, Astral Caves, Purgatorium Area (PS3 only).
Aluminum	Alchemy (Lv 2)	IC Component	Mining: Roak (Purgatorium Area, Astral Caves).
Runic Metal	--	IC Component	Monster: Soul Reaper. Mining: Astral Caves, Nox Obscurus (Ravine of Extinction, Pulsating Bog, Halls of Termination).
Mithril	Alchemy (Lv 9)	IC Component	Mining: En II (Sanctuary), Nox Obscurus (Ravine of Extinction, Pulsating Bog, Halls of Termination).
Meteorite	Alchemy (Lv 8)	IC Component	Box: Palace of Creation (Area 3 and Area 6). Mining: Miga Insect Warren, Palace of Creation (Area 3). Monster: Lava Golem. Item Creation (Recipe Memo 10).
Moonstone	--	IC Component	Box: Cave of the Seven Stars (B2). Monster: Jade Golem.
Earth Gem	--	IC Component	Mining: Lemuris (Thalia Plains, Van Elm Region, Wind Swallow Valley), Aeos (Southern Reaches, Miga Insect Warren). Monster: Stone Golem. Box: Triom Village (PS3 only).
Ice Gem	--	IC Component	Mining: Lemuris (Thalia Plains, Van Elm Region, Wind Swallow Valley). Monster: Mist Grave, Man Yeti.
Fire Gem	--	IC Component	Mining: Lemuris. Box: Alanaire Citadel 1F (PS3 only), Thalia Plains (PS3 only)
Wind Gem	--	IC Component	Box: Aeos (Landing Point, Northern Coast), Purgatorium (B3) (PS3 only). Mining: En II (Sanctuary).
Thunder Gem	--	IC Component	Mining: Roak (Astralian Continent, Tatroi Area, Tropp Area, Purgatorium Area, Astral Caves). Monster: Lightning Corpse, Rock Hermit.
Light Gem	--	IC Component	Mining: Roak (Tatroi Area, Astral Desert, Purgatorium Area, Astral Caves), Aeos (Southern Reaches, Miga Insect Warren). Monster: Lizard Shaman, Adephaga Milies.
Darkness Gem	--	IC Component	Mining: Lemuris (Thalia Plains, Van Elm Region, Wind Swallow Valley), Nox Obscurus (Ravine of Extinction, Pulsating Bog, Halls of Termination). Monster: Skeleton Warrior, Lizard Shaman, Dark Material.
Crystal	--	IC Component	Mining: Lemuris (Thalia Plains, Van Elm Region, Wind Swallow Valley), Roak (Astral Caves). Monster: Stone Golem.
Ruby	--	IC Component	Mining: Roak (Tatroi Area, Astral Desert, Tropp Area), En II (Sanctuary), Nox Obscurus (Ravine of Extinction).
Green Beryl	--	IC Component	Box: Cave of the Seven Stars (B4). Mining: Roak (Astral Caves), Aeos (Miga Insect Warren), Nox Obscurus (Ravine of Extinction). Monster: Hades Crab.
Gnomestone	Alchemy (Lv 6)	IC Component	Mining: Aeos (Miga Insect Warren), En II (Sanctuary). Box: Cave of the Seven Stars (B2). Monster: Winged Nightmare.
Nereidstone	Alchemy (Lv 7)	IC Component	Mining: En II (Sanctuary). Monster: Flying Ice.
Salamanderstone	Alchemy (Lv 7)	IC Component	Mining: Roak (Astral Desert, Tropp Area). Monster: Trinity Tusk.
Sylphstone	Alchemy (Lv 6)	IC Component	Box: Cave of the Seven Stars (B3). Mining: Roak (Astral Desert, Cave to the Purgatorium). Monster: Trinity Tusk.
Thorstone	Alchemy (Lv 7)	IC Component	Mining: En II (Sanctuary). Box: Cave of the Seven Stars (B7). Monster: Metal Scumbag.
Angelstone	Alchemy (Lv 9)	IC Component	Quest: Complete the "A Distinguished Rarity" quest. Mining: En II (Sanctuary).
Shadestone	Alchemy (Lv 9)	IC Component	Box: Palace of Creation (Area 5). Mining: Roak (Astral Caves, Cave to the Purgatorium), Nox Obscurus (Ravine of Extinction, Halls of Termination). Monster: Dark Soldier, Forsaken Beast, Dark Material.
Citrine	--	IC Component	Mining: En II (Sanctuary).
Star Ruby	--	IC Component	Mining: Nox Obscurus (Pulsating Bog). Monster: Forsaken Beast.
Star Sapphire	--	IC Component	Box: Palace of Creation (Area 6) (PS3 only). Mining: Nox Obscurus (Halls of Termination). Monster: Forsaken Beast.
Philosopher's Stone	--	IC Component	Monster: Damascus Fort, Grim Reaper.
Magical Clay	--	Catalyst for "Duplication" skill.	Mining: Aeos (Southern Reaches, Miga Insect Warren), En II (Sanctuary). Monster: Bone Knight.
Disintegration Stone	--	Catalyst for "Charge" skill.	Mining: En II (Sanctuary), Aeos (Southern Reaches). Monster: Lightning Corpse.
Lacquer	--	IC Component	Shops: Black Cat Material Shop. Harvest: Lemuris (Van Elm Region).
Wooden Stick	--	IC Component	Harvest: Lemuris (Van Elm Region), Aeos (Astralian Continent, Tatroi Area). Monster: Dryad, Man-Eating Tree.
Ebony	--	IC Component	Harvest: Lemuris (Van Elm Region), Roak (Tatroi Area).
Oak	--	IC Component	Harvest: Roak (Tropp Area), En II (Sanctuary). Box: Wandering Dungeon.
Ash	--	IC Component	Box: Purgatorium (B3) (PS3 only). Harvest: Roak (Tropp Area), Nox Obscurus (Pulsating Bog, Halls of Termination). Shops: Masterful Materials.
Cane	--	IC Component	Mining: Aeos (Southern Reaches), En II (Sanctuary), Nox Obscurus (Halls of Termination). Box: Cave of the Seven Stars (B1).
Blue Rose	--	IC Component	Harvest: En II (Sanctuary).
Shadow Rose	--	IC Component	Harvest: En II (Sanctuary). Monster: Cursed Horror. Box: Cave of the Seven Stars (B5).
Dendrobium	--	IC Component	Harvest: Roak (Tatroi Area, Tropp Area).
Funereal Bouquet	Crafting (Lv 6)	IC Component	Speak to Katrina, Believer in Fate on En II. Item Creation (Recipe Memo 26).
Red Seed	--	IC Component	Harvest: Roak (Tatroi Area), Aeos (Southern Reaches).
Blue Seed	--	IC Component	Harvest: Roak (Tatroi Area), Aeos (Southern Reaches).
Ge Gen Tang	--	IC Component	Shops: Can-Can General Goods, Thousand Gods General Store, Whole Heart Foods.
Ginseng	--	IC Component	Harvest: Lemuris (Van Elm Region), Aeos (Southern Reaches), Nox Obscurus (Ravine of Extinction).
Poison Hemlock	--	IC Component	Harvest: Roak (Astral Desert, Cave to the Purgatorium).

Caterpillar Fungus	--	IC Component	Harvest: Lemuris (Van Elm Region), Roak (Astralian Continent, Cave to the Purgatorium).
Aramid Fiber	--	IC Component	Shops: Black Cat Material Shop, The Santa Maria.
Carbon Fiber	--	IC Component	Shops: Black Cat Material Shop, The Santa Maria.
Wool	--	IC Component	Shops: Mobius's One-Stop Shop.
Silk	--	IC Component	Shops: Mobius's One-Stop Shop. Monster: Harpy.
Cashmere	--	IC Component	Shops: Masterful Materials. Monster: Harpy.
Manacloth	--	IC Component	Monster: Master Wizard, Succubus.
Fur Pelt	--	IC Component	Shops: Black Cat Material Shop.
Biocloth	--	IC Component	Box: Aeos (Southern Reaches) (PS3 only), En II (Sanctuary), Monster: Vampire Bat, Phantom Beetle, Necromancer.
Taffeta Ribbon	--	IC Component	Shops: Black Cat Material Shop. Box: Alternate Earth (Military Facility) (PS3 only), Shops: Black Cat Material Shop
Satin Ribbon	--	IC Component	Shops: Mobius's One-Stop Shop.
Velvet Ribbon	--	IC Component	Shops: Masterful Materials.
Mana Ribbon	--	IC Component	Box: Ravine of Extinction (PS3 only). Monster: Master Wizard.
Handspun Thread	--	IC Component	Shops: Black Cat Material Shop.
Dwarven Embroidery Thread	--	IC Component	Box: Wandering Dungeon. Shops: Masterful Materials. Monster: Mandragora, Ice Corpse.
Faerie Embroidery Thread	--	IC Component	Monster: Cursed Horror.
Sharkskin	--	IC Component	Shops: Thousand Gods General Store.
Lizardskin	--	IC Component	Monster: Dragon Newt, Lizard Commander, Lizard Soldier, Wise Lizardman, Corpse Bat, Mage Chimera.
Snakeskin	--	IC Component	Monster: Trinity Tusk.
Insect Leg	--	IC Component	Monster: Adephaga, Adephaga Drus, Polyphaga, Phantom Beetle, Adephaga Prox.
Insect Egg	--	IC Component	Monster: Adephaga, Adephaga Drus, Polyphaga, Bloodtail.
Bee Stinger	--	IC Component	Monster: Honeybee, Stinger,
Warped Carapace	--	IC Component	Monster: Killer Chelae, Armaros, Waving Pincers.
Peryton Droppings	--	IC Component	Monster: Peryton, Apprentice Scumbag, Axe Beak.
Wolf Fang	--	IC Component	Monster: Saber-Toothed Tiger, Unicorn Wolf.
Wolf Oil	--	IC Component	Monster: Saber-Toothed Tiger.
Saber-Toothed Tiger Fang	--	IC Component	Box: Tatroi Colosseum. Monster: Saber-Toothed Tiger.
Giant Bird Feather	--	IC Component	Monster: Peryton, Harpyia, Axe Beak, Early Psynard.
Dragon Scale	--	IC Component	Box: Alanaire Citadel (1F) (PS3 only), Tropp (PS3 only), Earth (Military Facility), Nox Obscurus (Halls of Termination, Palace of Creation). Shops: Colosseum Fight Coin Exchange. Monster: Dragon General, Phantom Dragon Newt.
Red Dragon Scale	--	IC Component	Ice Box: Palace of Creation (Area 6). Monster: Phantom Dragon Newt.
Dragon God Scale	--	IC Component	Monster: Dominator Dragon.
Dragonblood Crystal	--	IC Component	Box: Palace of Creation (Area 7) (PS3 only). Monster: Dark Clown, Master Wizard, Dominator Dragon.
Sandfish	--	IC Component	Found near any oasis in Astral Desert.
Crimson Firefly	--	IC Component	Found in the Cave to the Purgatorium.
Psynard Egg	--	IC Component	Monster: Early Psynard.
Barrier Spiritwater	--	IC Component	Box: Roak (Tatroi Area, Tropp Area, Astral Caves). Monster: Cardianon General, Early Psynard.
All-Purpose Ceramic	--	IC Component	Shops: Masterful Materials. Box: Wandering Dungeon
Bracteate	--	IC Component	Box: Purgatorium (B1), Astral Caves (PS3 only), Old Road to the Sanctuary, Palace of Creation, Cave of the Seven Stars. Monster: Metal Golem, Dark Soldier.
Crystal Skull	--	IC Component	Mining: Nox Obscurus.
Gunpowder	--	IC Component	Shops: Tools 'R' Us, Lil Vending Machine No. 2.
Intensified Gunpowder	Compounding (Lv 4)	IC Component	Item Creation only.
Empty Bottle	--	IC Component	Shops: Can-Can General Goods, Thousand Gods General Store, Black Cat Material Shop,
Natural Water	--	IC Component	Shops: Can-Can General Goods, Thousand Gods General Store, Roomy Foods, Whole Heart Foods, Magical Foods.
Magical Brush	--	IC Component	Shops: Masterful Materials.
Earth Paint	--	IC Component	Shops: Can-Can General Goods, Thousand Gods General Store, Masterful Materials.
Water Paint	--	IC Component	Shops: Thousand Gods General Store, Masterful Materials.
Fire Paint	--	IC Component	Shops: Can-Can General Goods, Thousand Gods General Store, Tool 'R' Us, Masterful Materials.
Wind Paint	--	IC Component	Shops: Tool 'R' Us, Masterful Materials.
Thunder Paint	--	IC Component	Shops: Tool 'R' Us, Masterful Materials.
Light Paint	--	IC Component	Shops: Tool 'R' Us, Masterful Materials.
Dark Paint	--	IC Component	Shops: Masterful Materials.
Nil Paint	--	IC Component	Shops: Masterful Materials.
Healing Paint	--	IC Component	Shops: Tool 'R' Us, Masterful Materials.
Mysterious Paint	--	IC Component	Shops: Thousand God General Store, Masterful Materials.
Attack Card	--	IC Component	Shops: Can-Can General Goods, Masterful Materials.
Attack Card +	--	IC Component	Shops: Masterful Materials.
Healing Card	--	IC Component	Shops: Masterful Materials. Box: Wandering Dungeon.
Healing Card +	--	IC Component	Shops: Masterful Materials.

Support Card	--	IC Component	Shops: Can-Can General Goods, Thousand Gods General Store, Masterful Materials.
Support Card +	--	IC Component	Shops: Masterful Materials.
Parchment	--	IC Component	Box: Palace of Creation (Area 3).
Fine Parchment	--	IC Component	Monster: Master Wizard.
Broken Metal Cutting Blade	--	IC Component	Box: Miga Insect Warren.
Repair Kit	--	IC Component	Shops: Base Shop: Omega, Tools 'R' Us, Masterful Materials.
Rivet	--	IC Component	Box: Palace of Creation (Area 6)
Bowstring	--	IC Component	Shops: Reflected Moon Weapons, Woodley Weapon Shop VIII.
Swept Hilt	--	IC Component	Box: Astral City. Shops: Masterful Materials.
Neck Chain	--	IC Component	Shops: Black Cat Material Shops. Lil Vending Machine No. 2.
Broken Music Box	--	IC Component	Quest: Obtained after starting the "Music Mending" quest.
Music Box	Engineering (Lv 1)	IC Component	Item Creation only.
Guitar Parts	--	IC Component	Shops: Masterful Materials.
Small Guitar	Crafting (Lv 3)	IC Component	Item Creation only.
Mystery Box	--	IC Component	Monster: Rock Hermit.
Memorial Plate	--	IC Component	Box: En II (Sanctuary).
Magic Capacitor	--	IC Component	Box: Roak (Tropp Area). Shops: Flaming Fist Explosives.
Symbol Booster	--	IC Component	Box: Wandering Dungeon. Monster: Phantom Dragoon, Spirit Archbishop.
Universal Device	--	IC Component	Shops: Flaming Fist Explosives.
Micro Circuit	--	IC Component	Shops: Compact Vendor Unit 003, Compact Vendor Unit 025, Compact Vendor Unit 050, Flaming Fist Explosives.
Quantum Processor	--	IC Component	Shops: Ruddle's Place.
Micro Hadron Collider	--	IC Component	Shops: Flaming Fist Explosives.
Micro Heavy Ion Collider	--	IC Component	Monster: Little Mutant.
Laser Oscillator	--	IC Component	Shops: Ruddle's Place.
Sighting Unit	--	IC Component	Shops: Imitation Gallery.
Mystery Electronic Circuit	--	IC Component	Shops: Flaming Fist Explosives.
Mystery Mobile Frame	--	IC Component	Shops: Flaming Fist Explosives.
Alchemist's Water	--	IC Component	Shops: Can-Can General Goods, Thousand Gods General Store, Tool 'R' Us, Silkworm's Retro Shop.
Lezard's Flask	--	IC Component	Monster: Guardian Beast, Soul Reaper, Spirit Priest.
Plastic Explosives	--	IC Component	Found in shining points within the celestial ship.
Bunny Feed	--	IC Component	Shops: Ruddle's Place, Imitation Gallery. Box: Wandering Dungeon.
Japonesque Vase	Crafting (Lv 4)	IC Component	Item Creation only.
Vivid Vase	Crafting (Lv 4)	IC Component	Item Creation only.
Coquettish Vase	Crafting (Lv 4)	IC Component	Item Creation only.
Traditional Vase	Crafting (Lv 4)	IC Component	Item Creation only.
Growth Stimulant Ampule	Compounding (Lv 2)	IC Component	Item Creation only (Recipe Memo 29).
Faerie of Aggression	Alchemy (Lv 10)	IC Component	Box: Wandering Dungeon.
Faerie of Wisdom	Alchemy (Lv 10)	IC Component	Box: Wandering Dungeon.
Faerie of Fortification	Alchemy (Lv 9)	IC Component	Box: Wandering Dungeon.
Faerie of Accuracy	Alchemy (Lv 7)	IC Component	Box: Wandering Dungeon.
Faerie of Protection	Alchemy (Lv 7)	IC Component	Box: Wandering Dungeon.
Fang Flute	Crafting (Lv 3)	IC Component	Item Creation only.
Feathered Comb	Crafting (Lv 2)	IC Component	Item Creation only.
Gabriel Celeste's Feather	--	IC Component	Defeat Gabriel Celeste, the boss of the Cave of the Seven Stars.
Ethereal Queen's Feather	--	IC Component	Defeat the Ethereal Queen, the boss of the Wandering Dungeon.
Vinegar	--	IC Component	Shops: Can-Can General Goods, Thousand Gods General Store, Roomy Foods, Magical Foods.
White Rice	--	IC Component	Harvest: Lemuris
Uncooked Pasta	--	IC Component	Shops: Base Shop: Alpha, Roomy Foods, Whole Heart Foods, Magical Foods.
Raw Animal Meat	--	IC Component	Shops: Base Shop: Alpha, Thousand Gods General Store, Roomy Foods, Whole Heart Foods.
Raw Fish	--	IC Component	Shops: Thousand Gods General Store, Roomy Foods, Whole Heart Foods.
Common Egg	--	IC Component	Harvest: Lemuris. Shops: Can-Can General Goods, Thousand Gods General Store, Roomy Foods, Whole Heart Foods, Magical Foods.
Vegetables	--	IC Component	Shops: Base Shop: Alpha, Can-Can General Goods, Thousand Gods General Store, Roomy Foods, Whole Heart Foods, Magical Foods.
Seasonings	--	IC Component	Shops: Base Shop: Alpha, Roomy Foods, Whole Heart Foods, Magical Foods.
Olive Oil	--	IC Component	Shops: Base Shop: Alpha, Magical Foods.
Special Warishita Sauce	--	IC Component	Shops: Roomy Foods, Whole Heart Foods.

Fresh Cream	--	IC Component	Shops: Can-Can General Goods, Thousand Gods General Store, Roomy Foods, Whole Heart Foods, Magical Foods.
Pie Crusts	--	IC Component	Shops: Can-Can General Goods, Thousand Gods General Store, Magical Foods.
Monster Jewel	Alchemy (Lv 3)	May be fused with monster data to gain special properties. Acts as a Neck Accessory when given data.	Box: Lemuris (Thalia Plains), Nox Obscurus, Palace of Creation (Area 2), Palace of Creation (Area 4), Wandering Dungeon. Shops: Colosseum Fight Coin Exchange.
Recipe Memo 01	--	Recipe	Complete "The Fifth Errand" quest.
Recipe Memo 02	--	Recipe	Ice Box: Lemuris (Triom Village)
Recipe Memo 03	--	Recipe	Box: Old Road to the Sanctuary (En II)
Recipe Memo 04	--	Recipe	After defeating the Ethereal Queen in the Wandering Dungeon, speak to Barago in the Old Road to the Sanctuary.
Recipe Memo 05	--	Recipe	Speak to Van after crash landing on Aeos for the first time.
Recipe Memo 06	--	Recipe	Complete the "Music Mending" quest.
Recipe Memo 07	--	Recipe	On Lemuris, speak to Lutea's mother after completing the Celestial Ship scenario.
Recipe Memo 08	--	Recipe	Quest: Complete the "Where's the Recipe?" quest.
Recipe Memo 09	--	Recipe	Box: Roak (Purgatorium Area).
Recipe Memo 10	--	Recipe	Box: Palace of Creation (Area 6).
Recipe Memo 11	--	Recipe	Box: Miga Insect Warren.
Recipe Memo 12	--	Recipe	Box: Nox Obscurus: Ravine of Extinction.
Recipe Memo 13	--	Recipe	Quest: Complete the "It Came From the Vent" quest.
Recipe Memo 14	--	Recipe	Box: Purgatorium.
Recipe Memo 15	--	Recipe	Box: Old Road to the Sanctuary (En II).
Recipe Memo 16	--	Recipe	Box: Tatroi, inside Queen of Inventors house.
Recipe Memo 17	--	Recipe	Box: Northeast Astralian Continent (PS3 only), Astral Caves (X360 only)
Recipe Memo 18	--	Recipe	Box: En II.
Recipe Memo 19	--	Recipe	Quest: Complete the "Food Run" quest.
Recipe Memo 20	--	Recipe	Quest: Complete the "Egg Collector" quest.
Recipe Memo 21	--	Recipe	Quest: Complete the "Rumble in the Caves" quest.
Recipe Memo 22	--	Recipe	Quest: Complete the "Grooming is Essential" quest.
Recipe Memo 23	--	Recipe	Box: En II Imitation Gallery (Centropolis).
Recipe Memo 24	--	Recipe	Ivy Box: Purgatorium.
Recipe memo 25	--	Recipe	Box: celestial ship.
Recipe Memo 26	--	Recipe	Speak to Katrina, Believer in Fate on En II.
Recipe Memo 27	--	Recipe	Collected from Santa, the Mercantilean after defeating the Ethereal Queen in the Wandering Dungeon.
Recipe Memo 28	--	Recipe	Box: En II (Sanctuary).
Recipe Memo 29	--	Recipe	Box: Aeos (Southern Reaches).
Recipe Memo 30	--	Recipe	Quest: Obtained during the "Trial of Love" quest.
Secret Memo	--	Recipe	Use Pickpocketing on the Young-at-Heart Researcher found on En II (Centropolis).
Map of Astral	--	Map	Shops: Mobius's One-Stop Shop.
Echo Machine	--	Ship Furnishing (S). A device that can control the echo effects heard nearby. Can be switched on and off.	Quest: Complete "The Unopenable Box" quest.
Boy's Gift Box	Crafting (Lv 9)	Ship Furnishing (M). A mysterious box; leave it out, and someone comes and places a present inside.	Item Creation only.
Girl's Gift Box	--	Ship Furnishing (M). A mysterious box; leave it out, and someone comes and places a present inside.	Box: Tatroi.
Li'l Vending Machine No. 1	--	Ship Furnishing (L). A handy vending machine for buying and selling items at any time.	Box: Cardianon Mothership (B2).
Li'l Vending Machine No. 2	Engineering (Lv 10)	Ship Furnishing (L). A handy vending machine for buying and selling items at any time.	Item Creation only.
Li'l Vending Machine No. 3	--	Ship Furnishing (L). A handy vending machine for buying and selling items at any time.	Box: Wandering Dungeon (9F).
Biorhythm Tester	Engineering (Lv 6)	Ship Furnishing (S). A gadget that measures everyone's biorhythms.	Item Creation only.
Aroma of Love	Compounding (Lv)	Ship Furnishing (S). A perfume with a dangerous scent that causes those who catch a whiff to fall madly in love.	Item Creation only.
Mood Stone	Alchemy (Lv 8)	Ship Furnishing (S). A stone designed to make those in its vicinity feel a bit more cheerful.	Item Creation only.
Bunny Plush	Crafting (Lv 7)	Ship Furnishing (S). A stuffed animal that's so adorable, it makes everyone around it smile.	Item Creation only.
Ominous Metal	Alchemy (Lv 6)	Ship Furnishing (S). A loathsome stone that gives everyone around it the creeps.	Item Creation only.
Healing Sheet	--	Ship Furnishing (M). Restores the HP of those who stand on it.	Item Creation (Recipe Memo 13).
Curing Sheet	--	Ship Furnishing (M). A sheet with a curing symbol on it. Cures the illnesses of those who stand on it.	Box: Lemuris (Woodley Village).
Memory Plate	Smithery (Lv 8)	Ship Furnishing (M). A special plate used to store records of past accomplishments.	Item Creation only.
Jukebox	Engineering (Lv 9)	Ship Furnishing (L). A music player for listening to songs you've unlocked.	Item Creation only.

VALUABLES

Name	Acquired By
Knight's Bangle	Quest: Start the "A Cherished Bangle" quest.
Old Pendant	Quest: Obtained during "The Seafarer's Treasure" quest.
Meteorite Fragment	Found after defeating Armaros on Aeos.
Symbol Stone	Obtained from Lutea when first entering Woodley.
Cardianon Data Disc	Found on the Cardianon Mothership.
Bunny Reins	Speak to Roak tribeswoman (just outside of Tatroi).
Lamp of Guidance	Obtained from Lady Eleyna just before entering the Purgatorium.
Curious Cat	Quest: Obtained during "The Curious Kitty" quest.
Gorgeous Gem	Quest: Obtained during the "Whodunit?" quest.
Wooden Doll	Quest: Start "The Shoddy Doll" quest.
Exquisite Wooden Doll	Quest: Obtained during "The Second Doll" quest.
Note from Fez	Quest: Start "Missing Brother" quest.
Weapon Shops Key	Quest: Obtained during the "Locked Out" quest.
Purgatorium Stone	Quest: Obtained during the "A Symbol of Bravery" quest.
Secret Diary	Quest: Obtained during "The Unopenable Chest" quest.
Cryptograph 1	Quest: Obtained after starting the "Trial of Wisdom" quest.
Cryptograph 2	Quest: Found on Lemuris during the "Trial of Wisdom" quest.
Cryptograph 3	Quest: Found on Aeos during the "Trial of Wisdom" quest.
Philosopher's Tome	Quest: Found on Roak during the "Trial of Wisdom" quest.
Psynard Chick	Quest: Obtained during the "Trial of Love" quest.
Letter from Orwen	Quest: Obtained after starting "The Last Letter" quest.
Earth Ring	Box: Earth (Military Facility).
Water Ring	Ice Box: Cave of the Seven Stars (Inner Sanctum)
Fire Ring	Received from Ghimdo after the Alanaire Citadel scenario.
Wind Ring	Quest: Obtained during the "Wind Ring" quest.
Thunder Ring	Box: Cardianon Mothership {F1}.

Name	Acquired By
Light Ring	Monster: Guardian Beast.
Darkness Ring	Monster: Undying Dragon (can only be fought after completing the game once).
Cardianon ID Card	Acquired from the Cardianon Mothership.
Cardianon ID Card +	Acquired from the Cardianon Mothership.
Shining Stone	Found throughout Alanaire Citadel.
Faerie Orchid	Found in the Woodley Area on Roak (next to giant lake).
Empty Bucket	Speak to the Curious Youth in Tropp.
Bucket of Water	Use Empty Bucket item near an oasis in Astral Desert.
Serpent Staff	Box: Palace of Creation (Area 8). Look into the mirrors in the room to see the staff's reflection, then examine the statue holding the staff.
Stone Fragment	Box: Cave of the Seven Stars (B1, B2, B3, B4, B5, B6, and B7).
Star of Reason	Found in the Cave of the Seven Stars (B1). Must have the Star Dipper item to acquire it.
Star of Life	Found in the Cave of the Seven Stars (B2). Must have the Star Dipper item to acquire it.
Star of Being	Found in the Cave of the Seven Stars (B3). Must have the Star Dipper item to acquire it.
Star of Fortune	Found in the Cave of the Seven Stars (B4). Must have the Star Dipper item to acquire it.
Star of Justice	Found in the Cave of the Seven Stars (B5). Must have the Star Dipper item to acquire it.
Star of Faith	Found in the Cave of the Seven Stars (B6). Must have the Star Dipper item to acquire it.
Star of Ruin	Found in the Cave of the Seven Stars (B7). Must have the stars of Faith, Justice, Fortune, Being, Life, and Reason for it to appear.
Star Dipper	Box: Cave of the Seven Stars (B7).
Geostone	Box: Wandering Dungeon. Monster: All Wandering Dungeon enemies.
Seraphic Doll	Defeat the Prehistoric Psynard in the Wandering Dungeon.
Carrot Doll	Use Pickpocketing on the Manly And Upright Warrior in Tatroi's pub.

The super-fantastic Welch is the supervisor for Item Creation, the act of forging weapons, food, and the other oddities used on your adventure. Using Welch's superb direction, only the shiniest and tastiest of items are built, which rank amongst the most useful items acquirable. Item creation is your ticket to good health and incredible equipment, so it's only fitting to include plenty of related data on the subject. Found here is a full list of the recipes that are possible to make, along with the methods needed to invent them. This section includes the ingredients you'll need to make each item, and it's designed to be used in combination with the **Items Section** to find all of the components you'll ever need.

Each table is organized by the Item Creation category where each recipe appears. These categories are associated with the field skills individual characters use to invent new items. Carefully look over the Data Explanation below before getting started; it should provide additional insight on the various labels associated with Item Creation.

❖ DUPLICATION

At the cost of Magical Clay, Arumat's Duplication ability enables him to carbon copy the item of your choice. This is exceedingly useful for the obvious reason of duplicating powerful equipment, and to multiply the resources needed to create new wares with Item Creation. Instead of fighting the Ethereal Queen multiple times to get her feather, just duplicate the item. Getting Magical Clay is a far easier task than beating the Queen multiple times.

DATA EXPLANATION

1 Recipe: The name of the recipe in question.

2 S. Lvl: This value represents the level of the type of field skill needed to invent the recipe. All field skills are associated with the character that has the skill (Smithery = Edge, Cooking = Reimi, Faize & Arumat = Alchemy, Lymle = Artistry, Bacchus = Engineering, Meracle = Crafting, Sarah = Synthesis, and Myuria = Compounding). This column is not referring to IC skills of the same name.

3 Item Creation Skills (Smith, Cook, Alch, etc): The total number of points needed from individual IC skill types to invent the recipe. Despite the misleading skill level associated with every recipe, all inventions require a specific number of points from many different IC skill types to make an appearance. For example, the Icecrusher Sword requires a total of 9 skill points from the Alchemy category, 4 from Artistry, and 10 from Synthesis, while still requiring the base level 5 Smithery field skill level. The points needed to satisfy these conditions are obtained from all characters within an invention group. A "-" appears when a skill has no involvement with the recipe. The IC skill names in each column have been shortened to the following: Smith = Smithery, Cook = Cooking, Alch = Alchemy, Art = Artistry, Engine = Engineering, Craft = Crafting, Sense = Sense, and Comp = Compounding.

4 Additional Flags: Includes any characters that *must* be involved with the invention group for the recipe to be created. Recipes that don't require at least one character are found via a Recipe Memo. The needed memo appears in this column whenever this is the case.

5 Ingredients: The type and amount of each ingredient needed to make the item. The items listed are only involved with the actual creation of the item, and not the invention of the recipe associated with it. Ingredients are found from mining points, harvesting points, monsters, and treasure boxes.

Ingredients listed in blue text are required only in *Star Ocean: The Last Hope* for the PlayStation 3. Ingredients listed in green text are required only in *Star Ocean: The Last Hope* for the Xbox 360.

Artistry

Recipe	S. Lvl	Smith	Cook	Alch	Art	Engine	Craft	Comp	Sense	Additional Flags	Ingredients
Earth Charm	4	--	--	9	1	--	--	2	--	Lymle	Fine Parchment x 2, Magical Brush x 1, Earth Gem x 4
Water Charm	6	--	--	--	9	--	--	12	9	Lymle	Fine Parchment x 2, Magical Brush x 1, Ice Gem x 4
Fire Charm	4	--	--	7	10	--	--	6	6	Lymle	Fine Parchment x 2, Magical Brush x 1, Fire Gem x 4

smithery

Recipe	S. Lvl	Smith	Cook	Alch	Art	Engine	Craft	Comp	Sense	Additional Flags	Ingredients
Storm Blade	1	--	--	--	--	--	--	--	--	Recipe Memo 05	Broken Metal Cutting Blade x 1, Repair Kit x 1, Wind Gem x 1
Flame Sword	1	5	--	12	--	--	3	--	11	Edge	Blessed Sword x 1, Fire Gem x 2
Venom Sword	3	15	--	--	--	--	8	--	6	Edge	Steel x 3, Aluminum x 1, Carbon Fiber x 1, Poison Hemlock x 2
Icecrusher Sword	5	--	--	9	4	--	--	--	10	Edge	Runic Metal x 2, Bracteate x 1, Ash x 1, Ice Gem x 3
Arcana Sword	8	--	--	--	--	--	--	--	--	Recipe Memo 01	Meteorite x 2, Gold x 1, Carbon Fiber x 1
Moonstone Sword	9	9	--	--	--	--	--	12	1	Edge	Moonstone x 3, Gold x 1, Carbon Fiber x 2
Imperial Sword	10	20	--	12	--	10	--	8	2	Edge	Moonstone x 4, Gold x 2, Platinum x 1, Carbon Fiber x 2, Philosopher's Stone x 1
Hunting Bow	2	11	--	--	--	--	--	--	10	Edge, Reimi	Eldarian Bow x 1, Bowstring x 1, Iron x 2
Earthsoul Bow	4	--	--	--	--	--	--	--	--	Recipe Memo 02	Torch Bow x 1, Earth Gem x 2, Iron x 2
Composite Bow	6	16	--	--	--	--	10	--	7	Edge, Reimi	Carbon Fiber x 3, Aluminum x 1, Aramid Fiber x 2, [PS3-only] Alien Arc x 1
Mystic Bow	7	9	--	--	2	8	--	10	11	Edge, Reimi, Myuria	Runic Metal x 2, Bracteate x 1, Ash x 2, Aramid Fiber x 1
Spirit Bow "Darkstriker"	9	17	1	6	--	10	--	6	2	Edge, Reimi, Arumat	Carbon Fiber x 4, All-Purpose Ceramic x 3, Aramid Fiber x 2, Darkness Gem x 6, [PS3-only] Darkness Charm x 1
Mediumistic Bow	9	4	9	--	9	--	11	3	16	Edge, Reimi	Carbon Fiber x 2, Moonstone x 2, Aramid Fiber x 2, Sighting Unit x 1, Philosopher's Stone x 1
Iron Saber	2	10	--	8	--	1	--	--	9	Edge, Faize	Iron x 3, Silver x 1, Sharkskin x 2
Elastic Saber	4	19	--	4	--	12	6	--	2	Edge, Faize	Steel x 3, Silver x 1, Carbon Fiber x 2, Swept Hilt x 1
Rune Saber	6	12	4	4	--	12	--	--	9	Edge, Faize	Runic Metal x 2, Bracteate x 2, Ash x 1, Swept Hilt x 1
Onyx Saber	8	7	1	8	--	2	--	1	13	Edge, Faize	Moonstone x 2, Gold x 1, Swept Hilt x 1, Philosopher's Stone x 1, Darkness Gem x 4
Cyclone Spear	3	3	--	--	3	--	6	3	10	Edge, Sarah	Runic Metal x 3, Bracteate x 2, Ash x 3, Wind Gem x 8
Judgment Spear	5	1	--	--	--	3	--	11	7	Edge, Sarah, Arumat	All-Purpose Ceramic x 4, Carbon Fiber x 4, [PS3-only] Angelstone x 1
Sacred Spear	7	--	--	--	--	--	--	--	--	Recipe Memo 03	Meteorite x 2, Carbon Fiber x 4, Angelstone x 2, [PS3-only] Crystal Skull x 1
Victory Lance	9	1	--	--	--	1	--	11	7	Edge, Sarah	Moonstone x 2, Carbon Fiber x 4, Philosopher's Stone x 1, Sylphstone x 1, Gabriel Celeste's Feather x 1
Scumbag Slayer	1	8	--	--	--	5	5	--	--	Edge, Meracle	Meteorite x 1, Swept Hilt x 1, Mana Ribbon x 1, Wooden Stick x 2
Shell Armor	1	15	--	6	--	9	1	--	13	Edge	Iron x 4, Warped Carapace x 2
Aqua Mail	4	1	--	1	3	--	--	4	10	Edge	Iron x 4, Rivet x 8, Ice Gem x 2
Flame Rune Mail	6	8	--	--	--	4	3	--	--	Edge, Lymle	Runic Metal x 3, Bracteate x 2, Rivet x 8, Fire Gem x 8
Ogre's Armor	7	9	--	4	--	3	--	6	--	Edge, Arumat	All--Purpose Ceramic x 2, Rivet x 8, Gold x 1, Aluminum x 1, Steel x 12
Red Dragon Mail	8	9	--	4	--	3	--	8	2	Edge, Arumat	Meteorite x 4, Rivet x 12, Red Dragon Scale x 2
Valiant Mail	9	9	--	5	--	3	--	11	2	Edge, Arumat	Moonstone x 3, Rivet x 12, Red Dragon Scale x 4
Universal Armor	10	14	--	14	--	16	--	18	2	Edge	Moonstone x 4, Rivet x 12, Dragon God Scale x 2, Philosopher's Stone x 1, Gabriel Celeste's Feather x 1
Iron Protector	2	5	--	--	--	3	--	--	2	Edge, Reimi	Iron x 4, SRF Protector x 1
Valkyrie's Garb	10	--	--	--	--	--	--	--	--	Recipe Memo 04	Gabriel Celeste's Feather x 1, Ethereal Queen's Feather x 1, Moonstone x 1, Philosopher's Stone x 1, Dragonblood Crystal x 2
Steel	3	8	--	4	--	4	--	2	--	Edge	Iron x 4, Coal x 2
Memory Plate	8	--	--	--	--	--	--	--	--	Edge, Bacchus	Memorial Plate x 1, Magical Brush x 3

cooking

Recipe	S. Lvl	Smith	Cook	Alch	Art	Engine	Craft	Comp	Sense	Additional Flags	Ingredients
Pickled Pepper Potion	3	--	--	--	--	--	--	--	--	Recipe Memo 06	Seasonings x 1, Vinegar x 1, Empty Bottle x 1
Pickled Plum Rice	1	--	5	--	--	--	--	--	--	Reimi	White Rice x 1, Pickled Plum x 1, Seaweed x 1
Ochazuke	2	--	10	--	--	--	--	--	--	Reimi	White Rice x 1, Pickled Plum x 1, Seaweed x 1, Natural Water x 1
Oyakodon	3	--	11	--	--	--	--	4	3	Reimi	White Rice x 2, Raw Animal Meat x 1, Common Egg x 1, Special Warishita Sauce x 1
Curry Rice	4	--	12	--	4	--	--	-9	7	Reimi, Meracle	White Rice x 2, Raw Animal Meat x 1, Vegetables x 1, Seasonings x 1
Pasta Peperoncino	3	--	5	--	--	--	--	--	--	Reimi	Uncooked Pasta x 1, Seasonings x 1, Olive Oil x 1
Pasta Bolognese	5	--	--	--	--	--	--	--	--	Recipe Memo 07	Uncooked Pasta x 1, Raw Animal Meat x 1, Vegetables x 1, Rich Cheese x 1
Pasta Genovese	7	--	13	--	--	--	8	--	2	Reimi	Uncooked Pasta x 1, Seasonings x 1, Blue Seed x 2, Olive Oil x 1, Rich Cheese x 1
Hamburg Steak	4	--	10	--	--	--	--	--	6	Reimi	Raw Animal Meat x 2, Vegetables x 1, Common Egg x 1, Seasonings x 1
Beef Steak	7	--	17	--	--	--	--	--	2	Reimi, Meracle	Raw Animal Meat x 2, Vegetables x 1, Seasonings x 1
Sukiyaki	10	--	9	--	--	--	--	--	10	Reimi, Sarah	Raw Animal Meat x 2, Vegetables x 1, Special Warishita Sauce x 1
Salt-Grilled Saury	4	--	11	--	7	--	--	--	--	Reimi	Raw Fish x 1, Vegetables x 1
Salmon Meuniere	6	--	12	--	--	--	9	--	5	Reimi, Meracle	Raw Fish x 1, Olive Oil x 1, Lemon x 1
Swordfish Piccata	8	--	9	--	9	--	--	1	10	Reimi, Sarah	Raw Fish x 1, Common Egg x 1, Rich Cheese x 1
Sushi	9	--	10	--	12	--	--	3	11	Reimi, Sarah	White Rice, x 2, Vinegar x 1, Raw Fish x 1
Lemon Juice	1	--	6	--	11	--	9	0	8	Reimi, Lymle	Lemon x 1, Natural Water x 1
Caesar Salad	3	--	11	--	--	--	--	--	1	Reimi	Vegetables x 2, Olive Oil x 1, Lemon x 1, Rich Cheese x 1
Ratatouille	8	--	13	--	--	--	--	--	2	Reimi, Meracle	Vegetables x 3, Olive Oil x 2
Vegetable Stir-fry	10	--	9	--	--	--	--	--	5	Reimi, Sarah	Raw Animal Meat x 1, Vegetables x 2, Seasonings x 1
Stamina Pie	7	--	6	--	7	--	9	--	5	Reimi, Sarah	Pie Crusts x 2, Raw Animal Meat x 2
Speed Pie	8	--	9	--	7	--	5	--	3	Reimi, Sarah	Pie Crusts x 2, Lemon x 1, Fresh Cream x 1
Acceleration Pie	8	--	6	--	9	--	5	--	3	Reimi, Sarah	Pie Crusts x 2, Sweet Fruit x 3
Miracle Pie	10	--	9	--	9	--	9	--	10	Reimi, Sarah	Pie Crusts x 2, Common Egg x 1, Vegetables x 1, Rich Cheese x 1
Custard Pie	4	--	11	--	7	--	--	--	8	Reimi	Pie Crusts x 1, Fresh Cream x 1
Shortcake	5	--	6	--	--	--	--	--	9	Reimi	Common Egg x 1, Fresh Cream x 2, Blueberries x 1
Blueberry Tart	6	--	15	--	10	--	9	-9	8	Reimi, Meracle	Common Egg x 1, Fresh Cream x 1, Blueberries x 4
Mille-feuille	8	--	--	--	--	--	--	--	--	Recipe Memo 08	Pie Crusts x 3, Fresh Cream x 1, Sweet Fruit x 1
Otherworldly Cuisine	2	--	10	--	--	--	--	--	3	Reimi	Insect Leg x 2, Insect Egg x 4, Rotten Fishx 1, Vinegar x 2
Fermented Sushi	7	--	12	--	9	--	--	--	5	Reimi, Meracle	White Rice x 2, Raw Fish x 2

Item Creation

Alchemy

Recipe	S. Lvl	Smith	Cook	Alch	Art	Engine	Craft	Comp	Sense	Additional Flags	Ingredients
Holy Water	2	--	3	4	--	--	--	--	--	Meracle	Natural Water x 1, Empty Bottle x 1, Light Gem x 1
Resistance Potion	1	--	--	10	--	--	--	--	2	--	Ge Gen Tang x 1, Light Gem x 1, Darkness Gem x 1, Empty Bottle x 1
Strength Potion	4	--	--	10	--	--	--	--	5	--	Ginseng x 1, Fire Gem x 1, Empty Bottle x 1
Mental Potion	4	--	--	--	--	--	--	--	--	Recipe Memo 09	Ge Gen Tang x 1, Ice Gem x 1, Empty Bottle x 1
Fortitude Potion	3	--	--	10	--	--	--	--	5	--	Caterpillar Fungus x 1, Earth Gem x 1, Empty Bottle x 1
Hyper Potion	5	4	--	14	--	--	--	6	7	Myuria	Earth Gem x 1, Ice Gem x 1, Fire Gem x 1, Wind Gem x 1, Empty Bottle x 1
Vile Goop	5	--	--	10	--	--	--	6	5	Arumat	Natto x 1, Darkness Gem x 2
Platinum	4	2	--	10	--	1	--	8	--	Myuria	Gold x 3, Silver x 3, Alchemist's Water x 1
Aluminum	2	2	--	10	--	--	--	10	--	Myuria	Iron x 4, Alchemist's Water x 1
Silver	1	2	--	10	--	6	--	--	--	Bacchus	Mercury x 2, Alchemist's Water x 1
Mithril	9	4	--	10	--	7	--	2	--	--	Platinum x 8, Alchemist's Water x 2, Symbol Card "Angel Feather" x 1
Gold	2	2	--	10	--	6	--	2	--	Bacchus	Silver x 2, Alchemist's Water x 1
Meteorite	8	--	--	--	--	--	--	--	--	Recipe Memo 10	Runic Metal x 4, Lezard's Flask x 1
Angelstone	9	--	--	13	--	--	--	2	3	Lymle	Mithril x 1, Light Gem x 4, Lezard's Flask x 1
Gnomestone	6	--	--	10	--	--	--	2	--	Lymle	Mithril x 1, Earth Gem x 4, Lezard's Flask x 1
Nereidstone	7	--	--	10	--	--	--	2	--	Lymle	Mithril x 1, Ice Gem x 4, Lezard's Flask x 1
Salamanderstone	7	--	--	10	--	--	--	2	--	Lymle	Mithril x 1, Fire Gem x 4, Lezard's Flask x 1
Sylphstone	6	--	--	10	--	--	--	2	--	Lymle	Mithril x 1, Wind Gem x 4, Lezard's Flask x 1
Thorstone	7	--	--	10	--	--	--	2	--	Lymle	Mithril x 1, Thunder Gem x 4, Lezard's Flask x 1
Shadestone	9	--	--	13	--	--	--	2	3	Lymle	Mithril x 1, Darkness Gem x 4, Lezard's Flask x 1.
Faerie of Aggression	10	2	--	17	4	--	--	--	--	--	Attack Seeds x 1, Sacrificial Doll x 1, Mercury x 2, Lezard's Flask x 1
Faerie of Wisdom	10	5	--	17	4	--	--	--	--	--	Intelligence Seeds x 1, Sacrificial Doll x 1, Mercury x 2, Lezard's Flask x 1
Faerie of Fortification	9	--	--	17	4	--	--	4	11	--	Defense Seeds x 1, Sacrificial Doll x 1, Mercury x 2, Lezard's Flask x 1
Faerie of Accuracy	7	2	--	17	4	--	4	--	--	--	Accuracy Seeds x 1, Sacrificial Doll x 1, Mercury x 2, Lezard's Flask x 1
Faerie of Protection	7	--	--	17	4	--	--	4	11	--	Protection Seeds x 1, Sacrificial Doll x 1, Mercury x 2, Lezard's Flask x 1
Monster Jewel	3	--	--	17	--	--	--	--	--	--	Crystal x 1, Mercury x 2, Alchemist's Water x 4
Mood Stone	8	7	--	10	--	--	--	--	--	--	Meteorite x 2, Light Gem x 8
Ominous Metal	6	7	--	10	--	--	2	--	--	--	Runic Metal x 2, Darkness Gem x 9

Artistry

Recipe	S. Lvl	Smith	Cook	Alch	Art	Engine	Craft	Comp	Sense	Additional Flags	Ingredients
Earth Charm	4	--	--	9	1	--	--	2	--	Lymle	Parchment x 2, Magical Brush x 1, Earth Gem x 4
Water Charm	6	--	--	--	9	--	--	12	9	Lymle	Parchment x 2, Magical Brush x 1, Ice Gem x 4
Fire Charm	4	--	--	7	10	--	--	6	6	Lymle	Parchment x 2, Magical Brush x 1, Fire Gem x 4
Wind Charm	5	--	--	--	11	--	--	--	8	Lymle, Sarah	Parchment x 2, Magical Brush x 1, Wind Gem x 4
Thunder Charm	4	--	--	--	9	--	--	12	9	Lymle, Myuria	Parchment x 2, Magical Brush x 1, Thunder Gem x 4
Light Charm	8	--	--	--	--	--	--	--	--	Recipe Memo 11	Parchment x 2, Magical Brush x 1, Light Gem x 5
Darkness Charm	5	--	--	--	--	--	--	--	--	Recipe Memo 12	Parchment x 2, Magical Brush x 1, Darkness Gem x 5
Lesser Demon's Fetish	4	--	--	--	1	--	--	10	--	Lymle	Parchment x 1, Dark Paint x 2
Greater Demon's Fetish	8	--	--	--	8	--	--	11	3	Lymle	Parchment x 1, Dark Paint x 4, Dragonblood Crystal x 1
Symbol Card "Earth Glaive"	2	--	--	11	7	--	--	--	--	Lymle	Earth Paint x 2, Attack Card x 1
Symbol Card "Earth Glaive" +	5	--	7	9	10	--	11	--	10	Lymle	Earth Paint x 4, Attack Card + x 1
Symbol Card "Stone Rain"	4	--	--	11	7	--	--	--	--	Lymle	Earth Paint x 3, Attack Card x 1
Symbol Card "Stone Rain" +	7	--	7	9	10	--	11	--	10	Lymle	Earth Paint x 5, Attack Card + x 1
Symbol Card "Terra Hammer"	6	--	7	9	10	--	11	--	10	Lymle	Earth Paint x 4, Attack Card + x 1
Symbol Card "Terra Hammer" +	9	--	--	9	9	--	--	10	--	Lymle, Arumat	Earth Paint x 6, Fine Parchment x 1
Symbol Card "Ice Needles"	2	--	--	10	4	--	--	--	3	Lymle	Water Paint x 2, Attack Card x 1
Symbol Card "Ice Needles" +	5	--	--	4	7	--	--	5	8	Lymle	Water Paint x 4, Attack Card + x 1
Symbol Card "Deep Freeze"	4	--	--	10	4	--	--	--	3	Lymle	Water Paint x 4, Attack Card x 1
Symbol Card "Deep Freeze" +	7	--	--	4	7	--	--	5	8	Lymle	Water Paint x 5, Attack Card + x 1
Symbol Card "Arctic Impact"	6	--	--	4	7	--	--	5	8	Lymle	Water Paint x 4, Attack Card + x 1
Symbol Card "Arctic Impact" +	9	--	1	1	16	--	--	14	12	Lymle, Myuria	Water Paint x 6, Parchment x 1
Symbol Card "Fire Bolt"	1	--	--	--	10	--	--	6	6	Lymle	Fire Paint x 2, Attack Card x 1
Symbol Card "Fire Bolt" +	4	--	7	9	14	--	11	--	10	Lymle	Fire Paint x 4, Attack Card + x 1
Symbol Card "Explosion"	3	--	--	--	10	--	--	6	6	Lymle	Fire Paint x 3, Attack Card x 1
Symbol Card "Explosion" +	6	--	7	9	14	--	11	--	10	Lymle	Fire Paint x 5, Attack Card + x 1
Symbol Card "Volcanic Burst"	5	--	7	9	14	--	11	--	10	Lymle	Fire Paint x 4, Attack Card + x 1
Symbol Card "Volcanic Burst" +	8	--	--	9	9	--	--	10	3	Lymle, Arumat	Fire Paint x 6, Parchment x 1
Symbol Card "Wind Blade"	1	--	--	--	10	--	--	6	6	Lymle	Wind Paint x 2, Attack Card x 1
Symbol Card "Wind Blade" +	4	--	--	--	19	--	10	--	13	Lymle	Wind Paint x 4, Attack Card + x 1
Symbol Card "Blast Hurricane"	3	--	--	--	10	--	10	--	6	Lymle	Wind Paint x 3, Attack Card x 1
Symbol Card "Blast Hurricane" +	6	--	--	--	19	--	10	--	13	Lymle	Wind Paint x 5, Attack Card + x 1
Symbol Card "Tornado"	5	--	--	--	19	--	10	--	13	Lymle	Wind Paint x 4, Attack Card + x 1
Symbol Card "Tornado" +	8	--	--	--	19	--	--	--	17	Lymle, Sarah	Wind Paint x 6, Parchment x 1
Symbol Card "Lightning Blast"	1	--	--	--	10	--	--	6	6	Lymle	Thunder Paint x 2, Attack Card x 1
Symbol Card "Lightning Blast" +	4	--	--	--	15	--	22	--	8	Lymle	Thunder Paint x 4, Attack Card + x 1
Symbol Card "Thunder Flare"	3	--	--	--	10	--	16	--	8	Lymle	Thunder Paint x 3, Attack Card x 1
Symbol Card "Thunder Flare" +	6	--	--	--	15	--	22	--	8	Lymle	Thunder Paint x 5, Attack Card + x 1
Symbol Card "Plasma Cyclone"	5	--	--	--	15	--	22	--	8	Lymle	Thunder Paint x 4, Attack Card + x 1
Symbol Card "Plasma Cyclone" +	8	--	--	--	17	--	--	--	12	Lymle, Myuria	Thunder Paint x 6, Parchment x 1
Symbol Card "Radiant Lancer"	2	--	--	9	10	--	11	--	10	Lymle	Light Paint x 2, Attack Card x 1
Symbol Card "Radiant Lancer" +	5	--	--	9	10	--	11	--	10	Lymle	Light Paint, x 4, Attack Card + x 1
Symbol Card "Sunflare"	4	--	--	9	10	--	11	--	10	Lymle	Light Paint x 3, Attack Card x 1
Symbol Card "Sunflare" +	7	--	--	9	10	--	11	--	10	Lymle	Light Paint x 5, Attack Card + x 1
Symbol Card "Aurora Rings"	6	--	--	9	10	--	11	--	10	Lymle	Light Paint x 4, Attack Card + x 1
Symbol Card "Aurora Rings" +	9	--	1	3	16	--	11	--	13	Lymle, Sarah	Light Paint x 6, Parchment x 1
Symbol Card "Shadow Needles"	2	--	--	1	9	--	--	--	3	Lymle, Myuria	Dark Paint x 2, Attack Card x 1
Symbol Card "Shadow Needles" +	5	--	--	1	16	--	--	--	3	Lymle, Myuria	Dark Paint x 4, Attack Card + x 1
Symbol Card "Vampiric Blade"	4	--	--	1	9	--	--	--	3	Lymle, Myuria	Dark Paint x 3, Attack Card x 1
Symbol Card "Vampiric Blade" +	7	--	--	1	16	--	--	--	3	Lymle, Myuria	Dark Paint x 5, Attack Card + x 1
Symbol Card "Dark Devourer"	6	--	--	1	16	--	--	--	3	Lymle, Myuria	Dark Paint x 4, Attack Card + x 1
Symbol Card "Dark Devourer" +	9	--	--	1	19	--	--	--	3	Lymle, Myuria	Dark Paint x 6, Parchment x 1
Symbol Card "Divine Wave"	8	--	--	--	17	--	--	9	14	Lymle	Nil Paint x 2, Parchment x 1

Artistry (continued)

Recipe	S. Lvl	Smith	Cook	Alch	Art	Engine	Craft	Comp	Sense	Additional Flags	Ingredients
Symbol Card "Divine Wave" +	10	--	13	3	19	--	8	19	17	Lymle	Nil Paint x 4, Fine Parchment x 1
Symbol Card "Extinction"	7	--	--	--	17	--	11	5	14	Lymle	Nil Paint x 3, Parchment x 1
Symbol Card "Extinction" +	9	--	--	--	19	--	11	7	17	Lymle	Nil Paint x 5, Fine Parchment x 1
Symbol Card "Reaping Spark"	7	--	7	5	17	--	--	5	14	Lymle	Nil Paint x 4, Parchment x 1
Symbol Card "Reaping Spark" +	9	--	7	3	19	--	--	5	14	Lymle	Nil Paint x 6, Fine Parchment x 1
Symbol Card "Healing"	2	--	--	5	5	--	--	--	8	Lymle	Healing Paint x 2, Healing Card x 1
Symbol Card "Healing" +	5	--	--	5	10	--	--	--	11	Lymle	Healing Paint x 3, Healing Card+ x 1
Symbol Card "Ex Healing"	4	--	--	5	13	--	--	--	14	Lymle	Healing Paint x 4, Healing Card x 1
Symbol Card "Ex Healing" +	7	--	--	5	15	--	--	--	17	Lymle	Healing Paint x 5, Healing Card+ x 1
Symbol Card "Faerie Healing"	5	--	--	5	15	--	--	--	14	Lymle	Healing Paint x 4, Healing Card x 1
Symbol Card "Faerie Healing" +	8	--	--	5	17	--	--	--	14	Lymle	Healing Paint x 6, Healing Card+ x 1
Symbol Card "Faerie Light"	7	--	--	5	15	--	--	--	17	Lymle, Sarah	Healing Paint x 5, Healing Card+ x 1
Symbol Card "Faerie Light" +	10	--	--	5	19	--	--	--	17	Lymle, Sarah	Healing Paint x 7, Fine Parchment x 1
Symbol Card "Antidote"	3	--	--	5	10	--	--	--	10	Lymle	Healing Paint x 2, Healing Card x 1
Symbol Card "Cure Condition"	7	--	--	5	14	--	--	--	11	Lymle	Healing Paint x 4, Healing Card x 1
Symbol Card "Restoration"	6	--	--	5	15	--	--	--	14	Lymle	Healing Paint x 4, Healing Card x 1
Symbol Card "Restoration" +	9	--	--	5	17	--	--	--	19	Lymle, Sarah	Healing Paint x 6, Healing Card+ x 1
Symbol Card "Resurrection"	10	--	--	5	17	--	--	15	17	Lymle, Sarah	Healing Paint x 8, Fine Parchment x 1
Symbol Card "Enhance"	4	--	--	--	10	--	--	5	12	Lymle	Mysterious Paint x 2, Support Card x 1
Symbol Card "Enhance" +	6	--	--	--	11	--	--	5	14	Lymle	Mysterious Paint x 4, Support Card+ x 1
Symbol Card "Enlighten"	4	--	11	10	--	--	--	14	Lymle	Mysterious Paint x 2, Support Card x 1
Symbol Card "Enlighten" +	6	--	--	11	15	--	--	--	14	Lymle	Mysterious Paint x 4, Support Card+ x 1
Symbol Card "Angel Feather"	5	--	--	11	15	--	--	--	14	Lymle	Mysterious Paint x 3, Support Card+ x 1
Symbol Card "Angel Feather" +	8	--	--	11	17	--	--	--	19	Lymle, Sarah	Mysterious Paint x 5, Parchment x 1
Symbol Card "Enshelter"	4	--	--	--	10	--	--	5	12	Lymle	Mysterious Paint x 2, Support Card x 1
Symbol Card "Enshelter" +	6	--	--	--	11	--	--	5	14	Lymle	Mysterious Paint x 4, Support Card+ x 1
Symbol Card "Reflection"	5	--	--	11	10	--	--	--	14	Lymle	Mysterious Paint x 2, Support Card x 1
Symbol Card "Reflection" +	7	--	--	11	15	--	--	--	14	Lymle	Mysterious Paint x 4, Support Card+ x 1
Symbol Card "Sacred Pain"	3	--	--	--	10	--	--	5	12	Lymle	Mysterious Paint x 2, Support Card x 1
Symbol Card "Sacred Pain" +	6	--	--	--	14	--	--	5	14	Lymle	Mysterious Paint x 4, Support Card+ x 1
Symbol Card "Silence"	2	--	--	--	10	--	--	--	10	Edge, Lymle	Mysterious Paint x 2, Support Card x 1
Symbol Card "Silence" +	5	--	--	--	11	--	--	--	14	Edge, Lymle	Mysterious Paint x 4, Support Card+ x 1
Symbol Card "Void"	6	--	--	5	14	--	--	--	14	Lymle	Mysterious Paint x 4, Support Card+ x 1
Symbol Card "Void" +	9	--	--	3	19	--	--	19	17	Lymle, Myuria	Mysterious Paint x 6, Parchment x 1
Symbol Card "Symbolic Weapon"	5	1	--	--	4	--	--	--	3	Edge, Lymle	Mysterious Paint x 2, Support Card+ x 1
Symbol Card "Symbolic Weapon" +	9	5	--	--	10	--	--	--	10	Edge, Lymle	Mysterious Paint x 4, Fine Parchment x 1
Healing Sheet	6	--	--	--	--	--	--	--	--	Recipe Memo 13	Magical Brush x 1, Healing Paint x 4, Parchment x 2

Engineering

Recipe	S. Lvl	Smith	Cook	Alch	Art	Engine	Craft	Comp	Sense	Additional Flags	Ingredients
Homing Arc	7	10	--	3	--	10	--	--	--	Reimi, Bacchus	Carbon Fiber x 2, Mithril x 1, Aramid Fiber x 1, Sighting Unit x 1
Deadly Cannon	4	5	--	--	--	13	--	--	-6	Bacchus, Meracle	Steel x 4, Quantum Processor x 1, Micro Hadron Collider x 1, [PS3-only] Ancient Cannon x 1
Dragoon Blaster	6	10	--	--	--	16	--	--	--	Bacchus, Arumat	Mithril x 4, Mystery Electronic Circuit x 1, Micro Hadron Collider x 1, Dragonblood Crystal x 3, [PS3-only] Star Ruby x 2
Photonic Blaster	10	11	--	--	--	19	--	--	--	Bacchus, Arumat	Moonstone x 4, Mystery Electronic Circuit x 2, Micro Hadron Collider x 1, T08 Lightning Cannon x 1
Symbol Cannon "Tempest"	8	11	--	12	--	19	--	10	--	Bacchus, Arumat	Moonstone x 5, Mystery Electronic Circuit x 1, Micro Heavy Ion Collider x 2, Philosopher's Stone x 1, Thorstone x 3
Laser Scythe	7	--	--	--	--	12	--	--	--	Bacchus, Arumat	All--Purpose Ceramic x 2, Laser Oscillator x 5, [PS3-only] Citrine x 2
Quadplex Scythe	8	--	--	--	--	17	--	--	--	Bacchus, Arumat	Meteorite x 2, Laser Oscillator x 5, Star Sapphire x 1
Quake Scythe	10	--	--	--	--	21	--	--	--	Bacchus, Arumat	Moonstone x 2, Laser Oscillator x 5, Philosopher's Stone x 1, Gnomestone x 4
Mithril Protector	7	--	--	--	--	10	--	--	--	Bacchus, Meracle	Mithril x 3, Rivet x 8, Mystery Mobile Frame x 2, Star Protector x 1, [PS3-only] Mana Ribbon x 1
Volcanic Gear	4	--	--	--	--	--	--	--	--	Recipe Memo 14	Runic Metal x 3, Bracteate x 1, Rivet x 20, Quantum Processor x 1, Fire Gem x 8
Fully-Tuned Plate	6	9	--	6	--	16	--	--	--	Bacchus	Mithril x 6, Rivet x 12, Mystery Electronic Circuit x 1, [PS3-only] Star Sapphire x 1
Override Gear "Omega"	9	11	--	14	--	22	--	20	--	Bacchus	Moonstone x 4, Rivet x 12, Mystery Electronic Circuit x 2, Philosopher's Stone x 1
Laser Suit	10	--	--	14	--	21	--	--	2	Bacchus	Laser Oscillator x 4, [X360-only] Gnomestone x 2, [PS3-only] Thorstone x 4, Symbol Card "Aurora Rings" + x 1
Void Recovery Unit	6	--	--	--	--	--	--	--	--	Recipe Memo 15	Universal Device x 1, Ge Gen Tang x 1, Ginseng x 1, Caterpillar Fungus x 1
Poison Relief Unit	5	--	--	14	--	8	--	--	--	Bacchus	Universal Device x 1, Aquaberries x 1
Melting Unit	3	--	--	--	--	4	--	6	--	Lymle, Bacchus	Universal Device x 1, Hot Chocolate x 1
Mobilization Unit	4	--	4	--	--	10	--	4	--	Bacchus	Universal Device x 1, Basil x 1
Speech Restoration Unit	4	--	--	--	--	10	--	--	--	Bacchus, Meracle	Universal Device x 1, Red Herb x 1
Vision Enhancement Unit	3	--	--	--	--	20	--	10	--	Bacchus	Universal Device x 1, Glowstick x 1
Dispelling Unit	5	--	--	--	--	12	--	--	--	Bacchus, Meracle	Universal Device x 1, Holy Water x 1
Element Breaker	6	--	--	--	--	4	--	6	--	Bacchus	Resistance Potion x 1, Gunpowder x 1, Micro Circuit x 1
Attack Breaker	5	--	--	14	--	8	--	--	--	Bacchus	Strength Potion x 1, Gunpowder x 1, Micro Circuit x 1
Intelligence Breaker	5	--	--	--	--	4	--	--	--	Lymle, Bacchus	Mental Potion x 1, Gunpowder x 1, Micro Circuit x 1
Defense Breaker	3	--	--	--	--	8	--	6	--	Bacchus	Fortitude Potion x 1, Gunpowder x 1, Micro Circuit x 1
EM Bomb	2	--	--	--	--	10	--	4	--	Bacchus	Gunpowder x 1, Micro Circuit x 1, Fire Gem x 1
Wide-Range EM Bomb	5	--	--	--	--	--	--	--	--	Recipe Memo 16	Intensified Gunpowder x 2, Micro Circuit x 1, Fire Gem x 2
Self--Destructor 3000	1	--	--	--	--	2	--	--	--	Bacchus, Sarah	Gunpowder x 1, Micro Circuit x 1, DANGER! DO NOT DRINK! x 1
Compact Poison Bomb	4	--	--	14	--	8	--	--	--	Bacchus	Gunpowder x 1, Micro Circuit x 1, Poison Cider x 1
Compact Stun Bomb	3	--	--	--	--	4	--	6	--	Lymle, Bacchus	Gunpowder x 1, Micro Circuit x 1, Peryton Droppings x 1
Compact Freezing Bomb	4	--	4	--	--	10	--	4	--	Bacchus	Gunpowder x 1, Micro Circuit x 1, Frozen Cider x 1
Compact Silence Bomb	2	--	--	--	--	10	--	--	--	Bacchus, Meracle	Gunpowder x 1, Micro Circuit x 1, Silent Cider x 1
Deluxe Poison Bomb	6	--	--	4	--	12	--	6	--	Bacchus	Intensified Gunpowder x 1, Micro Circuit x 1, Poison Cider x 1
Deluxe Stun Bomb	5	5	--	4	--	15	--	10	--	Bacchus, Myuria	Intensified Gunpowder x 1, Micro Circuit x 1, Peryton Droppings x 1
Deluxe Freezing Bomb	6	--	--	11	--	4	--	6	1	Bacchus	Intensified Gunpowder x 1, Micro Circuit x 1, Frozen Cider x 1
Deluxe Silence Bomb	4	--	--	--	--	13	--	--	2	Edge, Bacchus	Intensified Gunpowder x 1, Micro Circuit x 1, Silent Cider x 1

engineering (continued)

Recipe	S. Lvl	Smith	Cook	Alch	Art	Engine	Craft	Comp	Sense	Additional Flags	Ingredients
HP Absorption Unit	7	--	--	10	--	5	--	6	1	Lymle, Bacchus	EM Bomb x 1, Laser Oscillator x 1, Micro Circuit x 1, tri-Emblum x 1
MP Absorption Unit	8	--	--	--	--	17	--	--	--	Bacchus, Myuria	Vile Goop x 1, Laser Oscillator x 1, Micro Circuit x 1, tri-Emblum x 1, Mental Stimulant x 1
Scrambling Unit	2	--	--	--	--	10	--	--	--	Bacchus	Universal Device x 1, Barrier Spiritwater x 1
Music Box	1	--	--	--	--	5	--	--	--	Bacchus, Meracle	Broken Music Box x 1, Repair Kit x 1
Li'l Vending Machine No. 2	10	--	--	--	--	6	--	--	5	Bacchus, Sarah	Micro Circuit x 2, Iron x 4, Scrambling Unit x 1, Universal Device x 2
Biorhythm Tester	6	--	--	--	--	13	--	--	--	Reimi, Bacchus	Crystal x 1, Micro Circuit x 2, Quantum Processor x 4
Jukebox	9	--	--	--	--	15	--	--	--	Bacchus	Micro Circuit x 2, Laser Oscillator x 1, Ebony x 4

crafting

Recipe	S. Lvl	Smith	Cook	Alch	Art	Engine	Craft	Comp	Sense	Additional Flags	Ingredients
Ruby Wand	3	--	--	1	--	--	11	--	--	Lymle, Meracle	Oak x 1, Taffeta Ribbon x 1, Ruby x 1
Rune Wand	5	--	--	1	--	--	14	--	--	Lymle, Meracle	Runic Metal x 1, Ash x 1, Bracteate x 1, Velvet Ribbon x 1
Crystal Wand	6	--	--	--	--	--	--	--	--	Recipe Memo 17	Oak x 1, Taffeta Ribbon x 1, Crystal x 1
Star Ruby Wand	7	--	--	--	--	--	--	--	--	Recipe Memo 18	Cane x 1, Satin Ribbon x 1, Star Ruby x 1
Wand of Resonance	8	--	--	7	--	--	14	2	10	Lymle, Meracle	Cane x 1, Satin Ribbon x 1, Star Sapphire x 1, Symbol Booster x 1
Ancient Sage's Wand	10	--	--	--	--	--	24	--	13	Lymle, Meracle	Cane x 1, Mana Ribbon x 1, Green Beryl x 1, Ethereal Queen's Feather x 1, Philosopher's Stone x 1
Ocean Claws	4	--	--	--	--	--	3	--	2	Meracle, Myuria	Runic Metal x 2, Bracteate x 2, Carbon Fiber x 2, Ice Gem x 2
Bigfoot's Claws	6	--	--	--	--	--	14	--	12	Meracle	Mithril x 2, Carbon Fiber x 2, Wool x 4, Red Dragon Scale x 2
Rumble Claws	9	--	--	--	--	--	24	--	13	Meracle	Moonstone x 2, Carbon Fiber x 2, Philosopher's Stone x 1, Shadow Rose x 2, Ethereal Queen's Feather x 1
Staff of Freezing	4	--	--	--	--	--	4	--	2	Meracle, Myuria	Ash x 2, Bracteate x 1, Magic Capacitor x 1, Ice Gem x 4
Wildfang Staff	5	--	--	--	--	--	9	--	5	Meracle, Myuria	Saber--Toothed Tiger Fang x 1, Magic Capacitor x 1
Calamity Staff	8	--	--	4	--	--	1	--	7	Meracle, Myuria	Cane x 2, Symbol Booster x 1, Star Sapphire x 2, Crystal Skull x 1
Wizard's Staff	10	--	--	--	--	--	11	3	10	Meracle, Myuria	Cane x 2, Symbol Booster x 1, Green Beryl x 1, Philosopher's Stone x 1
Lizard Guard	5	--	--	--	--	--	10	--	--	Meracle	Lizardskin x 12, Handspun Thread x 4
Dragon Guard	7	2	--	--	--	--	11	--	10	Meracle	Dragon Scale x 5, Handspun Thread x 4
Sorcerous Guard	9	4	--	--	--	--	14	--	12	Meracle	Dragon God Scale x 6, Handspun Thread x 4, Barrier Spiritwater x 3
Traveler's Cloak	1	--	--	--	--	--	11	--	5	Meracle	Wool x 4, Handspun Thread x 4
Protective Robe	3	--	--	--	--	--	14	--	8	Meracle	Silk x 4, Handspun Thread x 2, Dwarven Embroidery Thread x 2, [PS3-only] Velvet Ribbon x 1
Mirage Robe	4	--	--	--	--	--	9	--	5	Meracle, Myuria	Cashmere x 4, Handspun Thread x 1, Faerie Embroidery Thread x 1
Earthen Robe	6	--	--	4	--	--	6	--	7	Meracle	Biocloth x 4, Dwarven Embroidery Thread x 4, Earth Gem x 8
Lustrous Robe	7	--	--	--	14	--	11	--	8	Meracle	Biocloth x 3, Dwarven Embroidery Thread x 4, Mana Ribbon x 2, Angelstone x 2
Virtuous Robe	8	--	--	--	23	--	24	--	13	Meracle	Manacloth x 3, Faerie Embroidery Thread x 4, Mana Ribbon x 2, Dragon God Scale x 2
Energy Bracelet	2	--	--	--	--	2	10	--	--	Meracle	Oak x 1, Light Gem x 2
Magic Bracelet	4	--	--	--	--	--	11	--4	8	Meracle	Snakeskin x 2, Light Gem x 1
Power Bracelet	4	16	--	--	--	--	6	--	7	Edge, Meracle	All--Purpose Ceramic x 1, Silver x 1, Light Gem x 1, Darkness Gem x 1
Wisdom Bracelet	7	--	--	--	--	--	--	--	--	Recipe Memo 19	Silver x 2, Ice Gem x 1, Intelligence Seeds x 1
Attack Bracelet	7	16	--	--	--	--	14	--	7	Edge, Meracle	Gold x 2, Fire Gem x 1
Sturdy Bracelet	3	--	--	--	--	--	10	--	--	Meracle	Platinum x 2, Earth Gem x 1
Slayer's Bangle	9	6	--	--10	--	--	16	--	10	Edge, Meracle	Platinum x 4, Thunder Gem x 4, Bracteate x 1
Light Scarf	5	--	--	--	--	--	10	--	7	Meracle, Sarah	Manacloth x 1, Angelstone x 1, Mana Ribbon x 2
Darkness Scarf	5	--	--	--	--	--	12	--	7	Meracle, Arumat	Manacloth x 1, Shadestone x 1, Darkness Charm x 2
Berserker's Scarf	3	--	--	--	4	--	6	--	4	Meracle	Manacloth x 1, Pickled Pepper Potion x 8, Giant Bird Feather x 4
Healing Band	7	--	--	--	--	--	17	--	10	Meracle, Sarah	Velvet Ribbon x 2, Dwarven Embroidery Thread x 2
Faerie Band	8	--	--	--	--	--	11	--	8	Meracle, Myuria	Velvet Ribbon x 2, Faerie Embroidery Thread x 2, Biocloth x 1
Learning Gloves	9	--	--	--	--	--	14	--	7	Edge, Meracle	Snakeskin x 2, Dwarven Embroidery Thread x 4, Caterpillar Fungus x 1, Symbol Card "Enhance"+ x 1
Foal Snaps	8	--	--	--	--	--	14	--	12	Meracle	Gold x 2, Citrine x 8
Stallion Snaps	7	--	--	--	--	--	9	--	10	Meracle	Gold x 2, Green Beryl x 2, Riot Potion x 16
Fire Armlet	3	--	--	--	--	--	11	--	5	Lymle, Meracle	Silver x 3, Fire Gem x 4, Fire Paint x 2, Fire Charm x 1
Wind Armlet	4	--	--	--	--	--	14	--	5	Meracle	Silver x 3, Wind Gem x 4, Wind Paint x 2
Earth Armlet	3	--	--	--	--	--	--	--	---	Recipe Memo 20	Silver x 3, Earth Gem x 4, Earth Paint x 2, Earth Charm x 1
Water Armlet	4	--	--	--	--	--	9	--	5	Meracle, Myuria	Silver x 3, Ice Gem x 4, Water Paint x 2
Thunder Armlet	3	--	--	--	--	5	9	--	5	Meracle	Silver x 3, Thunder Gem x 4, Thunder Paint x 2
tri-Emblem	10	--	--	--	--	--	--	--	--	Recipe Memo 27	Ethereal Queen's Feather x 2, Gabriel Celeste's Feather x 2, Symbol Card "Divine Wave"+ x 1
Anti-Poison Amulet	7	--	--	--	--	--	15	--	10	Meracle	Ebony x 2, Light Gem x 1, Aquaberries x 4
Anti-Stun Amulet	5	--	--	--	--	--	--	--	--	Recipe Memo 21	Ebony x 2, Earth Gem x 1, Vinegar x 3
Anti-Freezing Amulet	6	--	--	--	--	--	11	--	8	Meracle, Myuria	Ebony x 2, Ice Gem x 1, Hot Chocolate x 4
Anti-Paralysis Amulet	7	--	--	--	--	--	4	--	8	Meracle, Myuria	Ebony x 2, Thunder Gem x 1, Basil x 4
Anti-Silence Amulet	5	--	--	--	--	--	9	--	8	Meracle	Ebony x 2, Wind Gem x 1, Red Herb x 4
Anti-Fog Amulet	5	--	--	--	--	--	--	--	--	Recipe Memo 22	Ebony x 2, Fire Gem x 1, Glowstick x 3
Anti-Curse Amulet	6	--	--	--	--	--	--	--	--	Recipe Memo 23	Ebony x 2, Darkness Gem x 1, Holy Water x 4
Anti-Pumpkin Amulet	6	--	--	--	--	--	16	--	10	Meracle	Ebony x 2, Earth Gem x 1, Pumpkin Extract x 3
Anti-Void Amulet	8	--	--	--	--	--	--	--	--	Recipe Memo 24	Ebony x 2, Light Gem x 1, Magical Brush x 4
Battler Amulet	7	--	--	--	--	--	10	--	5	Edge, Meracle	Mithril x 2, Holy Water x 4, Neck Chain x 1
Demon Amulet	6	--	--	--	10	--	14	--	10	Meracle	Runic Metal x 2, Holy Water x 4, Neck Chain x 1
Raven Amulet	6	--	--	--	--	--	14	--	10	Meracle	Platinum x 3, Holy Water x 4, Neck Chain x 1
Silver Amulet	7	--	--	--	--	2	10	--	--	Meracle	Silver x 4, Holy Water x 4, Neck Chain x 1
Green Talisman	6	--	--	--	--	--	17	--	5	Meracle	Green Beryl x 1, Meteorite x 1, Sacrificial Doll x 2
Red Talisman	6	--	--	--	--	--	12	--	4	Meracle, Arumat	Star Ruby x 1, Meteorite x 1, Bigberries x 4
Blue Talisman	4	--	--	--	--	--	--	--	--	Recipe Memo 25	Star Sapphire x 1, Meteorite x 1, Blackberries x 4
Regeneration Symbol	8	--	--	--	--	--	20	--	8	Lymle, Meracle	Light Gem x 2, Holy Water x 4, Neck Chain x 1, Light Paint x 4
Small Guitar	3	--	--	--	--	--	15	--	10	Meracle	Ebony x 2, Steel x 1, Guitar Parts x 1
Japonesque Vase	4	--	--	--	--	--	10	--	10	Meracle, Sarah	Magical Clay x 2, Mental Stimulant x 1
Vivid Vase	4	--	--	--	--	--	10	--	10	Meracle, Sarah	Magical Clay x 2, Mental Stimulant x 1
Coquettish Vase	4	--	--	--	--	--	10	--	10	Meracle, Sarah	Magical Clay x 2, Mental Stimulant x 1
Traditional Vase	4	--	--	--	--	--	10	--	10	Meracle, Sarah	Magical Clay x 2, Mental Stimulant x 1
Fang Flute	3	--	--	--	--	--	10	--	5	Meracle	Wolf Fang x 1, Lacquer x 1

crafting (continued)

Recipe	S. Lvl	Smith	Cook	Alch	Art	Engine	Craft	Comp	Sense	Additional Flags	Ingredients
Feathered Comb	2	--	--	--	--	--	7	--	5	Meracle, Myuria	Giant Bird Feather x 4, Lacquer x 1
Funereal Bouquet	6	--	--	--	--	--	--	--	--	Recipe Memo 26	Dendrobium x 1, Blue Rose x 2, Velvet Ribbon x 1
Boy's Gift Box	9	--	--	--	--	--	15	--	10	Meracle	Mystery Box x 1, Satin Ribbon x 1
Bunny Plush	7	--	--	--	--	--	15	--	7	Reimi, Meracle	Fur Pelt x 4, Star Ruby x 2, Dwarven Embroidery Thread x 4

compounding

Recipe	S. Lvl	Smith	Cook	Alch	Art	Engine	Craft	Comp	Sense	Additional Flags	Ingredients
Mixed Syrup	1	--	5	--	--	--	--	14	5	Myuria	Red Seed x 1, Blue Seed x 1
Ripe Berries	3	--	9	--	--	--	--	14	5	Myuria	Blueberries x 3, Holy Water x 1
Perfect Berries	5	--	9	--	--	--	--	15	5	Myuria	Bigberries x 4, Holy Water x 1
Physical Stimulant	5	--	18	--	--	--	--	11	--	Myuria	Blueberries x 2, Bigberries x 2, Empty Bottle x 1
Mental Stimulant	6	--	--	--	--	--	--	--	--	Recipe Memo 28	Blackberries x 4, Vinegar x 2, Empty Bottle x 1
Gambleberries	2	--	10	--	--	--	--	10	--	Myuria	Thornberries x 1, Holy Water x 1, Pumpkin Cider x 1
Resurrection Elixir	6	--	10	--	--	--	--	12	8	Myuria	Blueberries x 2, Fresh Sage x 1, Empty Bottle x 1
Resurrection Unit	8	--	10	5	--	--	--	16	8	Myuria	Ripe Berries x 2, Fresh Sage x 2, Universal Device x 1
Riot Potion	4	--	--	2	--	--	--	10	--	Myuria	Nectar x 1, Sweet Fruit x 1, Empty Bottle x 1
Fainting Potion	3	--	--	2	--	--	--	9	--	Myuria	Poison Hemlock x 1, Ginseng x 1, Empty Bottle x 1
DANGER! DO NOT DRINK!	1	--	5	--	--	--	--	11	5	Myuria	Empty Bottle x 1, Thornberries x 1
Poison Cider	1	--	--	--	--	--	2	11	5	Myuria	Empty Bottle x 1, Natural Water x 1, Poison Hemlock x 1
Frozen Cider	1	--	--	5	--	--	--	11	5	Myuria	Empty Bottle x 1, Natural Water x 1, Insect Leg x 1
Static Cider	1	--	5	--	--	--	--	11	5	Myuria	Empty Bottle x 1, Natural Water x 1, Gunpowder x 1
Silent Cider	1	--	--	--	--	--	5	11	5	Myuria	Empty Bottle x 1, Natural Water x 1, Lacquer x 1
Cloudy Cider	1	--	5	--	--	--	--	11	5	Myuria	Empty Bottle x 1, Natural Water x 1, Peryton Droppings x 1
Cursed Cider	1	--	--	--	--	--	--	--	--	Recipe Memo 29	Empty Bottle x 1, Natural Water x 1, Insect Egg x 1
Pumpkin Cider	1	--	--	--	--	--	--	11	5	Myuria	Empty Bottle x 1, Natural Water x 1, Bunny Feed x 1
Super Aphrodisiac	5	--	--	--	--	--	--	14	9	Lymle, Myuria	Tasty Mushroom? x 4, Ginseng x 2, Lemon x 1, Empty Bottle x 1
Love Potion No. 256	7	--	--	--	--	--	--	14	10	Myuria, Arumat	Tasty Mushroom x 4, Ginseng x 2, Vile Goop x 2, Empty Bottle x 1
Potent Attack Seeds	10	--	4	11	--	--	--	18	13	Edge, Myuria	Attack Seeds x 2, Natural Water x 3, Japonesque Vase x 1, Alchemist's Water x 1
Potent Defense Seeds	9	--	1	11	--	--	--	20	--	Bacchus, Myuria	Defense Seeds x 2, Natural Water x 3, Vivid Vase x 1, Alchemist's Water x 1
Potent Accuracy Seeds	9	--	19	3	--	--	--	14	11	Reimi, Myuria	Accuracy Seeds x 2, Natural Water x 3, Coquettish Vase x 1, Alchemist's Water x 1
Potent Protection Seeds	9	--	1	--	--	--	--	17	--	Bacchus, Myuria	Protection Seeds x 2, Natural Water x 3, Traditional Vase x 1, Alchemist's Water x 1
Potent Intelligence Seeds	10	--	13	5	--	--	--	19	16	Sarah, Myuria	Intelligence Seeds x 2, Natural Water x 3, Vivid Vase x 1, Alchemist's Water x 1
Potent Health Seeds	10	--	2	14	--	--	--	20	--	Bacchus, Myuria	Health Seeds x 2, Natural Water x 3, Coquettish Vase x 1, Alchemist's Water x 1
Potent Magic Seeds	10	--	13	5	--	--	--	19	16	Sarah, Myuria	Magic Seeds x 2, Natural Water x 3, Traditional Vase x 1, Alchemist's Water x 1
Intensified Gunpowder	4	--	--	--	--	--	--	12	9	Myuria	Gunpowder x 4, Thunder Gem x 1
Growth Stimulant Ampule	2	--	--	--	--	--	--	--	--	Recipe Memo 30	Ginseng x 4, Caterpillar Fungus x 2, Empty Bottle x 1
Aroma of Love	3	--	10	--	--	--	--	11	12	Myuria	Lemon x 8, Wind Gem x 2, Empty Bottle x 1

SYNTHESIS GUIDE

Synthesis allows the player to take a piece of equipment and combine it with a secondary item, acquiring some or all of the secondary item's effects. The base piece of equipment can be improved a specific number of times (Synth Limit), which is different for every weapon. The combinations of abilities and stats that can be added is virtually limitless, making Synthesis an especially powerful and cheap means of improving any piece of equipment you have, even pieces you may replace soon.

Though it may not be feasible to include an exhaustive list of the many possibilities Synthesis grants, this section contains suggestions and tips that are useful for effectively synthesizing items into equipment. Hopefully, it'll provide a few hints on how to handle your equipment during the later stages of the game.

SYNTHESIS RULES & NOTES

- Only equipment can be used as the base item. Usable items, food, and materials add special "Factors" to the base item. However, two pieces of equipment can be synthesized together to improve the stats of the base item.

- Even though Monster Jewels cannot be improved upon with Synthesis, they can be synthesized with other items to add their special effects. This is quite useful in a number of cases for taking advantage of their positive effects, while also laying waste to their negative effects.

- When both items are of the same type (weapon, armor, etc), you can move factors directly from the Synthesis item to the base item. Otherwise, the Synthesis item's factors may change during the transfer or disappear entirely.

- Up to four "Factors" can be attached to any one item (the special effects that some items carry). If multiple Factors with similar effects are attached, in most cases their effects will be added together.

- Defense-oriented Factors tend to give higher bonuses when synthesized to armor, while offensive Factors get higher bonuses on weapons. Some Factors may not appear at all when synthesized to a specific type of equipment. Since accessories take a backseat to the other two equipment types, they always get lower Factor and stat bonuses from an item.

RECOMMENDED ITEMS FOR SYNTHESIS

CHARACTER BUILDING SUGGESTIONS

Curry Rice

Weapon Synthesis: *+20% EXP after each battle, ATK +2.*
Accessory Synthesis: *+15% EXP after each battle, ATK +1.*

Adds a 15%~20% EXP increase after battles. This option comes with no disadvantages, unlike the ATK penalty the Learning Gloves come with. Use it in combination with EXP boosting bonus tile rewards for an even bigger effect.

Mille-feuille

Weapon Synthesis: *+40% Fol after each battle, INT +2.*
Accessory Synthesis: *+30% Fol after each battle, INT +1.*

Increases the amount of Fol received after battle by either 30% or 40%, depending on whether it's synthesized to a weapon or accessory. Use it in combination with Foal Snaps or the Metal Scumbag Jewel for an even bigger cash increase. Perfect for earning the Fol you need for expensive Santa Maria shop items.

OFFENSIVE SUGGESTIONS

Caesar Salad, Ratatouille, Vegetable Stir-fry

Accessory Synthesis: *MP cost -15% in battle. ATK +1.*
Weapon Synthesis: *MP cost -25% in battle. ATK +2.*

These items reduce MP costs by 25% when synthesized to a weapon. This is a vital method of decreasing casting costs for symbology users. However, outside of their bonus factors, these items alter the base item's ATK and INT in varying ways (depending on which of the 3 items is used). Caesar Salad grants +1 ATK/-2 INT, Ratatouille +2 ATK/+3 INT, and the Vegetable Stir-fry adds +3 ATK/+3 INT. Both Ratatouille and the Vegetable Stir-fry are superior to the Caesar Salad, though it still works well as a synthesis substitute for melee units (when your cooking ability is low).

Ultimate Bomb

Weapon Synthesis: *HP Damage +35%.*

Improves any HP damage dealt, whether it's a symbol or physical attack, by +35%. An extremely useful item for improving the overall damage output of both melee units and symbol users alike. This is also one of the few methods of bypassing ATK and INT damage caps; once either stat reaches 9999, this is the best means to further increase the damage dealt. Works well when synthesized to the same weapon the Spriggan or Arch Spellmaster Jewels are attached to.

Spriggan Jewel

Weapon Synthesis: *Increases critical hit chance, ATK doubled but maximum HP halved.*

The Spriggan Jewel is an accessory that increases a character's critical hit rate, grants immunity to the stun status, *and* doubles his or her ATK, but at the cost of reducing DEF by -40% and halving the person's HP. Though the defense penalties are too great to use the item normally, synthesizing it to a weapon negates the DEF penalty and stun immunity while retaining the remainder of its effects. Though the HP halving property is a problem, pairing this ability with the **HP Boost** skill can relieve the majority of the problems it causes. The doubled ATK property and improved critical hit rate can easily make any melee unit incredibly powerful, in some cases maxing out a character's potential damage output. Synthesize it to Reimi's Mediumistic Bow to make her one of the strongest damage-dealers in the game, or to Bacchus's Symbol Cannon "Tempest" to turn him into an army destroying tank.

Arch Spellmaster Jewel

Weapon Synthesis: *MP cost -25% in battle, INT doubled but maximum MP halved.*

When equipped as an accessory, this item reduces MP costs by -15% and doubles the character's current INT. The price for this buff is extremely heavy though: it reduces your DEF by -70% while also halving your MP pool. However, synthesizing the jewel to a weapon bypasses the massive DEF penalty entirely, improves the MP cost reduction up to -25%, and retains the doubled INT property. The end result is what is easily the best Synthesis option for aggressive symbologists. Though your character's MP amount is still halved by the remaining negative attribute, the doubled INT and reduced MP cost is more than enough to make up for the problem. This is the fastest means of maxing out your character's INT rating to 9999.

DEFENSIVE SUGGESTIONS

Potent Defense Seeds

Armor Synthesis: *DEF +20%.*
Accessory Synthesis: *DEF +12%.*

An effective way of improving your DEF substantially. It's much more effective when synthesized to a piece of armor, which grants a 20% DEF boost.

Potent Health Seeds

Armor Synthesis: *Maximum HP +20%.*
Accessory Synthesis: *Maximum HP +10%.*

Increases your maximum HP by 20% when synthesized to armor. Very useful for characters like Meracle and Sarah, who come with low HP ratings.

Blue Talisman

Armor Synthesis: *Nullifies HP damage 25% of the time.*
Accessory Synthesis: *Nullifies HP damage 15% of the time.*

When combined to armor, the Blue Talisman improves its own nullification effect by negating HP damage 25% of the time. This is one of the most important defensive additions you can add to a character's armor, as later enemies inflict near-fatal damage with almost every attack. Also acts as an important means of protecting a character when they've activated Rush Mode or Berserk. Pair it with the Energy Shield battle skill to make a character virtually indestructible.

Darkblood Chainmail

Armor Synthesis: *GRD +80, restores 2% of HP periodically in battle, nullifies HP damage 25% of the time.*
Accessory Synthesis: *GRD +40, restores 1% of HP periodically in battle, nullifies HP damage 15% of the time.*

A much more potent version of the Blue Talisman, the Darkblood Chainmail comes packed with the same HP damage nullification effect, while also adding a HP restoration effect and a GRD boost. Though the armor itself is quite powerful on its own, you can synthesize its effects to other pieces of armor that have a higher base DEF rating.

Damascus Fort Jewel

Armor Synthesis: *+2 to all elemental resistances, grants immunity to stun status.*

This Monster Jewel increases your armor's resistance to every elemental type by +2. It also increases the armor's DEF by +69 while granting immunity to the stun status. A basic, but effective, means of fortifying your armor against symbols.

Ashlay Bernbeldt

Armor Synthesis: *ATK +77, DEF +129, HIT +72, GRD +57, INT --23.*
Weapon Synthesis: *Adds one hit chance per attack, ATK +103, HIT +65, INT -12.*

Ashlay's Monster Jewel massively improves the base stats of armor, serving as the perfect Synthesis option when you don't have any Factor slots remaining. It also acts as a beefed up Slayer's Bangle when synthesized to weapons. Unfortunately, this item is not an ideal choice for symbol users because of the slight INT loss.

The crew of the Calnus encounters many alien dangers during their journey across the star system, all of which wield unimaginable strength and furor. To ensure nothing unexpected rains down on your party, take a gander at the following collection of monster statistics. Found here is an examination of each creature's vital weaknesses and potential strengths, a goldmine of data that will allow you prepare for any battle. You'll also find many uses for each monster's drop and Monster Jewel lists, which are quite useful for gathering needed materials and accessories. Hopefully, this information will provide all that you need before battle arrives at your doorstep.

MONSTER DATA EXPLANATION

① **HP:** The amount of hit points the monster has. This number goes down as the monster takes damage. The creature is defeated when this value reaches zero.

② **EXP:** The experience points your party gains after defeating the monster.

③ **Resistant To:** Illustrates the element types the enemy is strong against. Avoid using attack symbols with the element listed in this field.

④ **Race:** The species the monster belongs to. This field affects skills associated with a specific race. For example, the Botany skill acquired by Reimi increases the drop rate of items found off of only Plant enemies.

⑤ **Fol:** The amount of Fol acquired after defeating the monster.

⑥ **Weak Against:** Shows the element types the enemy is weak against. Symbols utilizing the elements in this field inflict additional damage to the enemy.

⑦ **Drops:** The types of items the monster drops when defeated. Items listed in this field drop at random, having only a very low chance of being acquired.

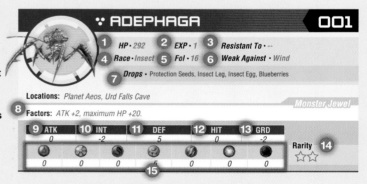

❖ ADEPHAGA		001
① HP · 292	**②** EXP · 1	**③** Resistant To · --
④ Race · Insect	**⑤** Fol · 16	**⑥** Weak Against · Wind
⑦ Drops · Protection Seeds, Insect Leg, Insect Egg, Blueberries		

Locations: *Planet Aeos, Urd Falls Cave*

Monster Jewel

⑧ **Factors:** *ATK +2, maximum HP +20.*

⑨ ATK	**⑩** INT	**⑪** DEF	**⑫** HIT	**⑬** GRD	
0	-2	5	0	-2	Rarity **⑭** ☆☆
0	0	0	5	0	0

⑮

ELEMENT KEY

= EARTH	= FIRE	= THUNDER	= DARKNESS
= WATER	= WIND	= LIGHT	

DIFFICULTY LEVEL MODIFIERS

This section of the guide contains the base attributes for each monster. These attributes decrease or increase in strength depending on the difficulty level that you're playing on. The following information shows the exact modifiers used to change each monster's statistics based on the difficulty selected. Use it to figure out an enemy's stats by multiplying its attribute with the shown modifier.

Earth Level

Enemy HP/MP x 0.7
Enemy ATK x 0.8
Enemy INT x 0.8
Enemy GRD x 0.8

Galaxy Level

Enemy HP/MP x 1.0
Enemy ATK x 1.0
Enemy INT x 1.0
Enemy GRD x 1.0

Universal Level

Enemy HP/MP x 1.3
Enemy ATK x 1.3
Enemy INT x 1.3
Enemy GRD x 1.3
Enemy Rush Gauge Increase
Rate x 1.5

Chaos Level

Enemy HP/MP x 1.7
Enemy ATK x 1.7
Enemy INT x 1.7
Enemy GRD x 1.7
Enemy Rush Gauge Increase
Rate x 2.0

MONSTER JEWEL DATA EXPLANATION

8 **Factors:** The jewel's latent abilities.

9 **ATK:** The attack rating of the item. This value combines with the character's base ATK rating to increase it. Helps determine the amount of damage dealt by the character's attacks.

10 **INT:** The intelligence rating of the item. This value combines with the character's base INT rating to increase it. This field determines the amount of damage dealt by the character's symbols.

11 **DEF:** The defense rating of the item. This value combines with the character's base DEF rating to increase it. Determines how resilient a character is to enemy attack.

12 **HIT:** The hit rating of the item. This value combines with the character's base HIT rating to increase it. Determines how easy it is for a character to smash through the enemy's defenses.

13 **GRD:** The item's guard rating. This value combines with the character's base GRD rating to increase it. Determines how often the character guards attacks.

14 **Rarity:** A general rating of the jewel's scarcity.

15 **Elemental Resistance:** How the item affects the character's elemental defense. Elements with a negative number show a weakened defense against that element, while positive numbers show an improvement.

Monster Data

MONSTER DATA

ADEPHAGA — 001

HP · 292	EXP · 1	Resistant To · --
Race · Insect	Fol · 16	Weak Against · Wind

Drops · Protection Seeds, Insect Leg, Insect Egg, Blueberries

Locations: Planet Aeos, Urd Falls Cave

Monster Jewel

Factors: ATK +2, maximum HP +20.

ATK	INT	DEF	HIT	GRD		
0	-2	5	0	-2		
0	0	0	-5	0	0	0

Rarity ☆☆

ADEPHAGA DRUS — 002

HP · 351	EXP · 2	Resistant To · --
Race · Insect	Fol · 33	Weak Against · Wind

Drops · Protection Seeds, Insect Leg, Insect Egg, Blueberries

Locations: Planet Aeos, Urd Falls Cave

Monster Jewel

Factors: ATK +5, maximum HP +100.

ATK	INT	DEF	HIT	GRD		
1	-2	5	0	-2		
0	0	0	-4	0	0	0

Rarity ☆☆

KILLER WASP — 003

HP · 228	EXP · 1	Resistant To · --
Race · Insect	Fol · 33	Weak Against · Earth

Drops · Accuracy Seeds, Aquaberries, Blueberries

Locations:

Monster Jewel

Factors: 30% immunity to poison.

ATK	INT	DEF	HIT	GRD		
2	-2	5	2	0		
-2	0	0	0	0	0	0

Rarity ☆☆

GIANT BAT — 004

HP · 259	EXP · 2	Resistant To · --
Race · Bird	Fol · 25	Weak Against · --

Drops · Accuracy Seeds, Blackberries

Locations: Urd Falls Cave

Monster Jewel

Factors: Maximum MP -50, maximum HP +20.

ATK	INT	DEF	HIT	GRD		
0	-2	6		0		
0	0	0	0	0	0	0

Rarity ☆☆

GEREL — 005

HP · 327	EXP · 1	Resistant To · Wind
Race · Plant	Fol · 27	Weak Against · Earth

Drops · Fresh Sage, Seaweed, Blackberries

Locations: Planet Aeos, Urd Falls Cave

Monster Jewel

Factors: ATK +5.

ATK	INT	DEF	HIT	GRD		
1	-2	5	0	0		
-3	0	0	8	0	0	0

Rarity ☆☆

POLYPHAGA — 006

HP · 447	EXP · 3	Resistant To · --
Race · Insect	Fol · 58	Weak Against · Earth

Drops · Protection Seeds, Insect Leg, Insect Egg, Fresh Sage, Iron

Locations: Planet Aeos

Monster Jewel

Factors: DEF +2, maximum HP +100.

ATK	INT	DEF	HIT	GRD		
1	-2	6	1	-2		
-2	0	0	0	0	0	0

Rarity ☆☆

KILLER CHELAE — 007

HP · 374	EXP · 4	Resistant To · Water
Race · Insect	Fol · 29	Weak Against · Thunder

Drops · Fresh Sage, Warped Carapace, Seaweed, White Rice

Locations: Planet Aeos

Monster Jewel

Factors: 30% immunity to stun status.

ATK	INT	DEF	HIT	GRD		
2	-2	6	0	-1		
0	5	0	0	-2	0	0

Rarity ☆☆

ARMAROS — 008

HP · ?????	EXP · 40	Resistant To · Water, Wind
Race · Other	Fol · 609	Weak Against · Earth

Drops · Warped Carapace

Locations: Planet Aeos

Monster Jewel

Factors: Maximum HP +100.

ATK	INT	DEF	HIT	GRD		
0	-3	17	0	0		
-5	5	0	-5	0	0	0

Rarity ☆☆☆☆☆

PERYTON — 009

HP · 355	EXP · 5	Resistant To · ---
Race · Bird	Fol · 58	Weak Against · ---

Drops · Giant Bird Feather, Peryton Droppings, Common Egg

Locations: Planet Lemuris: Thalia Plains

Monster Jewel

Factors: 30% immunity to stun status.

ATK	INT	DEF	HIT	GRD		
1	-2	7	-1	0		
0	0	0	0	0	0	0

Rarity ★☆☆

DRYAD — 010

HP · 341	EXP · 5	Resistant To · Earth
Race · Plant	Fol · 49	Weak Against · Fire

Drops · Magic Seeds, Nectar, Wooden Stick, Blueberries

Locations: Planet Lemuris: Thalia Plains

Monster Jewel

Factors: Restores 1% of HP periodically in battle, 30% immunity of stun status.

ATK	INT	DEF	HIT	GRD		
1	-3	7	-1	-3		
5	0	-2	0	0	0	0

Rarity ★★☆

KOBOLD — 011

HP · 576	EXP · 5	Resistant To · Ice
Race · Animal	Fol · 114	Weak Against · ---

Drops · Attack Seeds, Raw Animal Meat, Hot Chocolate

Locations: Alanaire Citadel, Planet Lemuris: Van Elm Region

Monster Jewel

Factors: Maximum HP +20.

ATK	INT	DEF	HIT	GRD		
0	-2	8	-2	-3		
0	5	0	0	0	0	0

Rarity ★★☆

LIZARD SOLDIER — 012

HP · 628	EXP · 7	Resistant To · ---
Race · Animal	Fol · 76	Weak Against · Fire

Drops · Lizardskin

Locations: Planet Lemuris: Thalia Plains, Alanaire Citadel, Celestial Ship

Monster Jewel

Factors: ATK +2%, maximum HP -50.

ATK	INT	DEF	HIT	GRD		
1	-1	7	1	-2		
0	0	-2	0	0	0	0

Rarity ★★☆

WISE LIZARDMAN — 013

HP · 628	EXP · 9	Resistant To · ---
Race · Animal	Fol · 68	Weak Against · Fire

Drops · Lizardskin, Attack Card, Support Card

Locations: Planet Lemuris: Thalia Plains, Alanaire Citadel, Celestial Shop

Monster Jewel

Factors: INT +10.

ATK	INT	DEF	HIT	GRD		
0	0	7	-1	-3		
0	0	-2	0	0	0	0

Rarity ★★☆

MIST GRAVE — 014

HP · 433	EXP · 6	Resistant To · Earth
Race · Plant	Fol · 61	Weak Against · Fire

Drops · Tasty Mushroom, Basil, Tasty Mushroom?

Locations: Planet Lemuris: Thalia Plains

Monster Jewel

Factors: 30% immunity to paralysis.

ATK	INT	DEF	HIT	GRD		
1	-1	7	-2	0		
5	0	-2	0	0	0	0

Rarity ★★☆

SKELETON SOLDIER — 015

HP · 728	EXP · 7	Resistant To · *Dark*
Race · *Undead*	Fol · 79	Weak Against · *Fire, Light*

Drops · Special Warishita Sauce, Rotten Fish, Darkness Gem, DANGER! DO NOT DRINK!

Locations: *Alanaire Citadel*

Monster Jewel

Factors: *Maximum MP -50, HIT +2.*

ATK	INT	DEF	HIT	GRD	
0	-3	8	0	-2	Rarity
0	0	-2	0	0	1	5	☆☆

STONE GOLEM — 016

HP · 1039	EXP · 13	Resistant To · *Earth*
Race · *Demon*	Fol · 160	Weak Against · *Wind*

Drops · Iron, Crystal, Silver, Earth Gem

Locations: *Planet Lemuris: Van Elm Region, Alanaire Citadel*

Monster Jewel

Factors: *Causes attacks to damage allies as well, nullifies earth symbols 20% of the time, 30% immunity to stun status.*

ATK	INT	DEF	HIT	GRD	
0	-2	8	2	-3	Rarity
5	0	0	-2	0	0	0	☆☆

DRAGON NEWT — 017

HP · 1700	EXP · 19	Resistant To · --
Race · *Demon*	Fol · 176	Weak Against · --

Drops · Lizardskin, Fire Gem, Attack Card, Support Card

Locations: *Alanaire Citadel, Celestial Ship, Cardianon Mothership, Biological Laboratory*

Monster Jewel

Factors: *Maximum HP +100.*

ATK	INT	DEF	HIT	GRD	
1	1	11	2	-3	Rarity
0	0	0	0	0	0	0	☆☆

MANA YETI — 018

HP · 1291	EXP · 17	Resistant To · *Ice*
Race · *Animal*	Fol · 86	Weak Against · *Fire*

Drops · Health Seeds, Ice Gem, Raw Animal Meat, Frozen Cider

Locations: *Planet Lemuris: Van Elm Region*

Monster Jewel

Factors: *Increases critical hit chance, 30% immunity to frozen status.*

ATK	INT	DEF	HIT	GRD	
2	-3	10	4	0	Rarity
0	8	-2	0	0	0	0	☆☆

HORNED TURTLE — 019

HP · 1124	EXP · 12	Resistant To · *Ice*
Race · *Animal*	Fol · 96	Weak Against · *Fire*

Drops · Mercury, Raw Fish, Rotten Fish

Locations: *Planet Lemuris: Van Elm Region*

Monster Jewel

Factors: *GRD +40.*

ATK	INT	DEF	HIT	GRD	
2	-3	9	-2	0	Rarity
0	5	-7	0	0	0	0	☆☆

APPRENTICE SCUMBAG — 020

HP · 651	EXP · 13	Resistant To · --
Race · *Humanoid*	Fol · 106	Weak Against · --

Drops · Support Card, Hot Chocolate, Special Warishita Sauce, Peryton Droppings, Tasty Mushroom?

Locations: *Planet Lemuris: Van Elm Region*

Monster Jewel

Factors: *+15% Fol after each battle.*

ATK	INT	DEF	HIT	GRD	
0	-2	9	5	0	Rarity
0	0	0	0	0	0	0	☆☆

MAN-EATING TREE — 021

HP · 1082	EXP · 18	Resistant To · *Earth*
Race · *Plant*	Fol · 83	Weak Against · *Fire*

Drops · Tasty Mushroom, Wooden Stick, Aquaberries, Blackberries, Fire Gem

Locations: *Planet Lemuris: Van Elm Region*

Monster Jewel

Factors: *Restores 1% of HP periodically in battle, 30% immunity to poison.*

ATK	INT	DEF	HIT	GRD	
0	-3	9	-2	-4	Rarity
5	0	-2	0	0	0	0	☆☆

GIANT FUNGUS — 022

HP · 756	EXP · 8	Resistant To · *Ice*
Race · *Plant*	Fol · 63	Weak Against · *Fire*

Drops · Tasty Mushroom, Basil, Tasty Mushroom?, Nectar

Locations: *Planet Lemuris: Van Elm Region*

Monster Jewel

Factors: *30% immunity to paralysis.*

ATK	INT	DEF	HIT	GRD	
1	-1	8	-1	0	Rarity
0	5	-2	0	0	0	0	☆☆

SABER-TOOTHED TIGER — 023

HP · 919	EXP · 6	Resistant To · *Ice*
Race · *Animal*	Fol · 102	Weak Against · *Fire, Water*

Drops · Saber-Toothed Tiger Fang, Wolf Fang, Wolf Oil, Raw Animal Meat

Locations: *Planet Lemuris: Thalia Plains, Celestial Ship*

Monster Jewel

Factors: *Nullifies water symbols 20% of the time.*

ATK	INT	DEF	HIT	GRD	
2	-4	10	0	-4	Rarity
0	8	-5	-2	0	0	0	☆☆

HARPYIA — 024

HP · 1220	EXP · 19	Resistant To · *Wind*
Race · *Bird*	Fol · 85	Weak Against · --

Drops · Giant Bird Feather, Static Cider, Blackberries

Locations: *Planet Lemuris: Thalia Plains, Celestial Ship*

Monster Jewel

Factors: *Nullifies wind symbols 20% of the time, 30% immunity to stun status.*

ATK	INT	DEF	HIT	GRD	
0	0	11	0	0	Rarity
0	0	0	5	0	0	0	☆☆

LIZARD COMMANDER — 025

HP • 1351	EXP • 15	Resistant To • ---			
Race • Animal	Fol • 99	Weak Against • Fire			

Drops • Lizardskin, Aquaberries

Locations: Celestial Ship

Monster Jewel

Factors: DEF +2%

ATK	INT	DEF	HIT	GRD
0	-2	11	2	3
0	0	-2	0	0

Rarity ☆

BARACHIEL — 026

HP • ???	EXP • 833	Resistant To • Earth, Ice			
Race • Other	Fol • 2403	Weak Against • Fire			

Drops • Monster Jewel

Locations: Celestial Ship

Monster Jewel

Factors: Increases chance of surviving incap via Fury, 60% immunity to frozen status.

ATK	INT	DEF	HIT	GRD
-5	0	23	18	0
3	0	-7	0	0

Rarity ☆☆☆☆☆

GUARD BOT "COMMANDO" — 027

HP • 969	EXP • 19	Resistant To • Wind			
Race • Mech	Fol • 102	Weak Against • Water, Thunder			

Drops • Compact Freezing Bomb, Universal Device, Electromagnetic Bomb, Micro Circuit, Silver

Locations: Cardianon Mothership, Biological Laboratory

Monster Jewel

Factors: 30% immunity to stun status.

ATK	INT	DEF	HIT	GRD
0	0	12	-2	0
0	-2	0	8	-5	0	0

Rarity ☆☆

GUARD BOT "ASSAULTER" — 028

HP • 1389	EXP • 23	Resistant To • Wind			
Race • Mech	Fol • 123	Weak Against • Water, Thunder			

Drops • Compact Poison Bomb, Universal Device, Electromagnetic Bomb, Micro Circuit, Quantum Processor

Locations: Cardianon Mothership, Biological Laboratory, Cardianon Subterranean City, Control Tower

Monster Jewel

Factors: 30% immunity to stun status.

ATK	INT	DEF	HIT	GRD
0	0	13	0	0
0	-2	0	8	-5	0	0

Rarity ☆☆

CARDIANON SOLDIER — 029

HP • 1706	EXP • 19	Resistant To • ---			
Race • Humanoid	Fol • 153	Weak Against • ---			

Drops • Strength Potion, Self-Destructor 3000, Gunpowder, Compact Silence Bomb

Locations: Cardianon Mothership, Biological Laboratory, Cardianon Subterranean City, Control Tower

Monster Jewel

Factors: GRD +2, INT +10.

ATK	INT	DEF	HIT	GRD
0	0	12	2	0
0	0	0	0	0

Rarity ☆☆

LIZARD WARRIOR — 030

HP • 1709	EXP • 39	Resistant To • Ice			
Race • Animal	Fol • 144	Weak Against • ---			

Drops • Iron, Frozen Cider

Locations: Cardianon Mothership, Biological Laboratory

Monster Jewel

Factors: GRD +40.

ATK	INT	DEF	HIT	GRD
0	-4	13	1	0
0	5	0	0	0

Rarity ☆☆

LIZARD SHAMAN — 031

HP • 1382	EXP • 30	Resistant To • ---			
Race • Animal	Fol • 148	Weak Against • ---			

Drops • Empty Bottle, Darkness Gem, Light Gem

Locations: Cardianon Mothership, Biological Laboratory, Cardianon Subterranean City, Control Tower

Monster Jewel

Factors: INT +15.

ATK	INT	DEF	HIT	GRD
-3	0	13	-5	-4
0	0	0	0	0

Rarity ☆☆

ARMED DRAGON NEWT — 032

HP • 2519	EXP • 68	Resistant To • ---			
Race • Demon	Fol • 159	Weak Against • ---			

Drops • Basil, Berserker's Scarf, Mercury, Alchemist's Water

Locations: Cardianon Subterranean City, Control Tower

Monster Jewel

Factors: Maximum HP +300.

ATK	INT	DEF	HIT	GRD
0	0	14	1	-3
0	0	0	0	0

Rarity ☆☆

CARDIANON GENERAL — 033

HP • 2048	EXP • 24	Resistant To • ---			
Race • Humanoid	Fol • 163	Weak Against • ---			

Drops • Ripe Berries, Basil, Electromagnetic Bomb, Barrier Spiritwater, Fortitude Potion

Locations: Biological Laboratory, Cardianon Subterranean City, Control Tower

Monster Jewel

Factors: 30% immunity to paralysis.

ATK	INT	DEF	HIT	GRD
0	4	14	7	4
0	0	0	0	0

Rarity ☆☆

ARMED DRAGOON — 034

HP • 5215	EXP • 57	Resistant To • Wind			
Race • Mech	Fol • 270	Weak Against • Water, Thunder			

Drops • Laser Oscillator, Compact Stun Bomb, Warning Brooch

Locations: Cardianon Subterranean City, Control Tower

Monster Jewel

Factors: Increases chance of surviving incap via Fury, 30% immunity to stun status.

ATK	INT	DEF	HIT	GRD
1	-5	15	-3	-5
0	-2	0	8	-5	0	0

Rarity ☆☆☆

✦ DRAGON GENERAL — 035

HP · 11157 · EXP · 135 · Resistant To · ---
Race · Demon · FoI · 191 · Weak Against · ---

Drops · Dragon Scale, Poison Cider

Locations: Control Tower

Monster Jewel

Factors: HIT +30, maximum HP +100.

ATK	INT	DEF	HIT	GRD	
0	0	15	0	-6	Rarity
0	0	0	0	0	0	0	★☆☆

✦ SAHARIEL — 036

HP · ??? · EXP · 10003 · Resistant To · Fire, Wind
Race · Other · FoI · 7,711 · Weak Against · Water, Thunder

Drops · --

Locations: Control Tower

Monster Jewel

Factors: Increases chances of surviving incap via Fury, ATL -40, maximum HP +10%.

ATK	INT	DEF	HIT	GRD	
0	0	29	0	0	Rarity
0	-5	5	10	-7	0	0	★★★★★

✦ GENOMIC BEAST — 037

HP · 32396 · EXP · 5156 · Resistant To · Fire
Race · Demon · FoI · 2,388 · Weak Against · Thunder

Drops · Iron Claws

Locations: Military Facility

Monster Jewel

Factors: Causes attacks to damage allies as well, 30% immunity to paralysis.

ATK	INT	DEF	HIT	GRD	
0	0	17	-3	0	Rarity
0	0	5	0	-2	0	0	★★★

✦ SOLDIER ZOMBIE — 038

HP · 3301 · EXP · 76 · Resistant To · ---
Race · Undead · FoI · 102 · Weak Against · Fire

Drops · Ripe Berries, Natto, Pickled Plum, Gunpowder, Aquaberries

Locations: Military Facility

Monster Jewel

Factors: 30% immunity to poison.

ATK	INT	DEF	HIT	GRD	
0	0	16	-5	0	Rarity
0	0	-2	0	0	0	0	★☆

✦ LITTLE ALIEN — 039

HP · 2267 · EXP · 64 · Resistant To · ---
Race · Humanoid · FoI · 81 · Weak Against · ---

Drops · Bizarre Fruit, Fresh Sage, Bigberries

Locations: Military Facility

Monster Jewel

Factors: 30% immunity to stun status.

ATK	INT	DEF	HIT	GRD	
-3	0	17	-3	-3	Rarity
0	0	0	0	0	0	0	★★★

✦ BIGFOOT SAM — 040

HP · 4030 · EXP · 144 · Resistant To · Thunder
Race · Mech · FoI · 134 · Weak Against · Water

Drops · Bigberries, Basil

Locations: Military Facility

Monster Jewel

Factors: Increases critical hit chance, 30% immunity to stun status.

ATK	INT	DEF	HIT	GRD	
3	-3	17	2	3	Rarity
0	-2	0	0	5	0	0	★★

✦ HONEYBEE — 041

HP · 2468 · EXP · 108 · Resistant To · ---
Race · Insect · FoI · 90 · Weak Against · Earth

Drops · Accuracy Seeds, Bee Stinger, Aquaberries

Locations: Planet Roak: Astralian Continent

Monster Jewel

Factors: 30% immunity to poison.

ATK	INT	DEF	HIT	GRD	
1	-7	18	3	0	Rarity
-3	0	0	0	0	0	0	★★

✦ UNICORN WOLF — 042

HP · 2776 · EXP · 108 · Resistant To · Fire
Race · Animal · FoI · 111 · Weak Against · Water

Drops · Saber-Toothed Tiger Fang, Wolf Fang, Blueberries

Locations: Planet Roak: Astralian Continent

Monster Jewel

Factors: ATK +10.

ATK	INT	DEF	HIT	GRD	
0	-7	18	4	-4	Rarity
0	-2	5	0	0	0	0	★★

✦ KOBOLD BANDIT — 043

HP · 3084 · EXP · 162 · Resistant To · Fire
Race · Animal · FoI · 189 · Weak Against · ---

Drops · All-Purpose Ceramic

Locations: Planet Roak: Astralian Continent

Monster Jewel

Factors: Maximum MP -50, maximum HP +100.

ATK	INT	DEF	HIT	GRD	
0	-5	18	2	-5	Rarity
0	0	5	0	0	0	0	★★

✦ WAVING PINCERS — 044

HP · 4510 · EXP · 162 · Resistant To · Water
Race · Insect · FoI · 163 · Weak Against · Thunder

Drops · Protection Seeds, Rotten Fish, Warped Carapace

Locations: Planet Roak: Astralian Continent

Monster Jewel

Factors: Maximum HP +100.

ATK	INT	DEF	HIT	GRD	
1	-5	18	-4	9	Rarity
0	5	0	0	-2	0	0	★★

▾ AXE BEAK — 045

HP · 3393 EXP · 189 **Resistant To** · Wind
Race · Bird **Fol** · 151 **Weak Against** · Earth

Drops · Rotten Fish, Basil, Giant Bird Feather, Common Egg, Peryton Droppings

Locations: Planet Roak: Astralian Continent

Monster Jewel

Factors: 30% immunity to stun status.

ATK	INT	DEF	HIT	GRD
1	-5	18	2	0

-2	0	0	5			0

Rarity ☆☆

▾ SKELETON ARMOR — 046

HP · 3930 EXP · 236 **Resistant To** · --
Race · Undead **Fol** · 179 **Weak Against** · Fire, Light

Drops · Defense Seeds, Vile Goop, Solid Protector

Locations: Planet Roak: Astralian Continent

Monster Jewel

Factors: Maximum MP -50, HIT +2, GRD +2, DEF +2.

ATK	INT	DEF	HIT	GRD
0	0	16	0	0

0	0	-2	0	0	1	5

Rarity ☆☆

▾ DESERT OGRE — 047

HP · 7205 EXP · 409 **Resistant To** · Wind
Race · Animal **Fol** · 949 **Weak Against** · Earth

Drops · Attack Seeds, Bigberries

Locations: Planet Roak: Astralian Continent

Monster Jewel

Factors: Increases critical hit chance, 30% immunity to stun status.

ATK	INT	DEF	HIT	GRD
3	-7	18	4	0

-2	0	0	5	0	0	0

Rarity ☆☆

▾ THIEVING SCUMBAG — 048

HP · 3275 EXP · 163 **Resistant To** · --
Race · Humanoid **Fol** · 237 **Weak Against** · --

Drops · tri-Emblum, Hot Chocolate, Natto

Locations: Planet Roak: Astralian Continent

Monster Jewel

Factors: 30% immunity to stun status, +15% Fol after each battle.

ATK	INT	DEF	HIT	GRD
0	-5	18	4	2

0	0	0	0	0	0	0

Rarity ☆☆☆

▾ ALBERO DI ANIMA — 049

HP · 6550 EXP · 354 **Resistant To** · Earth
Race · Plant **Fol** · 290 **Weak Against** · Fire

Drops · Bigberries, Aquaberries, Basil, Nectar

Locations: Planet Roak: Astralian Continent

Monster Jewel

Factors: Restores 1% of HP periodically in battle, 30% immunity to poison, 30% immunity to paralysis.

ATK	INT	DEF	HIT	GRD
0	-5	18	0	0

5	0	-2	0	0	0	0

Rarity ☆☆

▾ BLACK EAGLE — 050

HP · 37916 EXP · 871 **Resistant To** · Resistant Against:
Race · Humanoid **Fol** · 2,031 **Weak Against** · --

Drops · Attack Seeds

Locations: Planet Roak: Astralian Continent

Monster Jewel

Factors: 30% immunity to stun status.

ATK	INT	DEF	HIT	GRD
-2	-7	22	4	-4

0	0	0	0	0	0	0

Rarity ☆☆☆☆

▾ VOMITING GEL — 051

HP · 5119 EXP · 183 **Resistant To** · Water
Race · Plant **Fol** · 248 **Weak Against** · Earth, Fire

Drops · Natto, Vile Goop, Blackberries, Glowstick

Locations: Planet Roak: Astralian Continent, Astral Caves

Monster Jewel

Factors: 30% immunity to fog status.

ATK	INT	DEF	HIT	GRD
0	-4	19	-2	0

0	5	-2	0	0	0	0

Rarity ☆☆

▾ CORPSE BAT — 052

HP · 3890 EXP · 97 **Resistant To** · --
Race · Bird **Fol** · 165 **Weak Against** · Fire

Drops · Protection Seeds, Raw Animal Meat, Lizardskin

Locations: Planet Roak: Astralian Continent, Astral Caves

Monster Jewel

Factors: Maximum HP +20, 30% immunity to fog status.

ATK	INT	DEF	HIT	GRD
0	-4	19	4	0

0	0	-2	0	0	0	0

Rarity ☆☆

▾ HARPY — 053

HP · 4090 EXP · 226 **Resistant To** · Wind
Race · Bird **Fol** · 304 **Weak Against** · Thunder

Drops · Cashmere, Glowstick, Common Egg, Silk

Locations: Planet Roak: Astralian Continent

Monster Jewel

Factors: Nullifies win symbols 20% of the time, 30% immunity to fog status.

ATK	INT	DEF	HIT	GRD
1	-2	20	4	0

0	0	0	5	-2	0	0

Rarity ☆☆

▾ MANDRAGORA — 054

HP · 4648 EXP · 187 **Resistant To** · Earth
Race · Plant **Fol** · 241 **Weak Against** · Fire

Drops · Faerie Embroidery Thread, Nectar, Dwarven Embroidery Thread, Mixed Syrup

Locations: Planet Roak: Astralian Continent

Monster Jewel

Factors: Restores 1% of HP periodically in battle, 30% immunity to stun status.

ATK	INT	DEF	HIT	GRD
0	-4	20	0	0

5	0	-2	0	0	0	0

Rarity ☆☆

SPIRIT PRIEST — 055

- **HP** · 3230   **EXP** · 228
- **Race** · Humanoid   **Fol** · 304
- **Resistant To** · Resistant Against:
- **Weak Against** · --

Drops · Lezard's Flask, Glowstick, Pumpkin Extract, Healing Card, Pumpkin Cider

Locations: Planet Roak: Astralian Continent, Purgatorium

Monster Jewel

Factors: Recovers 1% of light-based damage as MP, 30% immunity to stun status, 30% immunity to pumpkin status.

ATK	INT	DEF	HIT	GRD
-6	3	21	-2	0
0	0	0	0	0	0	0

Rarity: ☆☆

SYDONAIST ALPHA — 056

- **HP** · 2513   **EXP** · 114
- **Race** · Humanoid   **Fol** · 117
- **Resistant To** · --
- **Weak Against** · --

Drops · Cloudy Cider, Aquaberries, DANGER! DO NOT DRINK!, Static Cider

Locations: Planet Roak: Astralian Continent, Purgatorium

Monster Jewel

Factors: 30% immunity to poison.

ATK	INT	DEF	HIT	GRD
-4	-4	21	-4	-8
0	0	0	0	0	0	0

Rarity: ☆☆

SYDONAIST BETA — 057

- **HP** · 2513   **EXP** · 125
- **Race** · Humanoid   **Fol** · 141
- **Resistant To** · --
- **Weak Against** · --

Drops · Intelligence Seeds, Aquaberries, Healing Card, Poison Cider, Frozen Cider

Locations: Planet Roak: Astralian Continent, Purgatorium

Monster Jewel

Factors: 30% immunity to poison.

ATK	INT	DEF	HIT	GRD
-3	-4	21	-2	-6
0	0	0	0	0	0	0

Rarity: ☆☆

MAGE CHIMERA — 058

- **HP** · 9646   **EXP** · 576
- **Race** · Demon   **Fol** · 532
- **Resistant To** · Earth
- **Weak Against** · Wind

Drops · Snakeskin, Aquaberries, Raw Animal Meat, Lizardskin

Locations: Purgatorium, Astral Caves

Monster Jewel

Factors: Causes attacks to damage allies as well, 30% immunity to poison.

ATK	INT	DEF	HIT	GRD
3	-6	21	-4	0
5	0	0	-2	0	0	0

Rarity: ☆☆☆

FIRE CORPSE — 059

- **HP** · 5527   **EXP** · 214
- **Race** · Undead   **Fol** · 156
- **Resistant To** · Fire
- **Weak Against** · Water

Drops · Fire Gem, Holy Water

Locations: Purgatorium

Monster Jewel

Factors: 30% immunity to curse status, nullifies fire symbols 20% of the time.

ATK	INT	DEF	HIT	GRD
-2	-4	21	3	0
0	-2	0	0	0	0	0

Rarity: ☆☆

SUCCUBUS — 060

- **HP** · 4523   **EXP** · 863
- **Race** · Demon   **Fol** · 299
- **Resistant To** · --
- **Weak Against** · --

Drops · Manacloth, Velvet Ribbon, Silent Cider

Locations: Purgatorium, Astral Caves

Monster Jewel

Factors: ATK +4%, DEF +5%, maximum MP +50.

ATK	INT	DEF	HIT	GRD
0	-2	21	6	4
0	0	0	0	0	0	0

Rarity: ☆☆

GUARDIAN BEAST — 061

- **HP** · 55733   **EXP** · 5,940
- **Race** · Demon   **Fol** · 4,626
- **Resistant To** · Light
- **Weak Against** · Water, Fire, Thunder, Dark

Drops · Lezard's Flask

Locations: Purgatorium

Monster Jewel

Factors: Increases chance of surviving incap via Fury.

ATK	INT	DEF	HIT	GRD
0	5	23	7	0
0	-2	-2	0	1	5	2

Rarity: ☆☆☆☆

TAMIEL — 062

- **HP** · 59099   **EXP** · 4,778
- **Race** · Other   **Fol** · 14,129
- **Resistant To** · Fire, Darkness
- **Weak Against** · Water, Thunder

Drops · Fanatic's Staff

Locations: Purgatorium

Monster Jewel

Factors: Increases chance of surviving incap via Fury, ATK -80, maximum HP +10%, INT +25.

ATK	INT	DEF	HIT	GRD
0	0	36	0	-11
0	-5	8	0	-2	0	0

Rarity: ☆☆☆☆☆

ROCK HERMIT — 063

- **HP** · 9474   **EXP** · 600
- **Race** · Demon   **Fol** · 993
- **Resistant To** · Earth
- **Weak Against** · Wind

Drops · Mystery Box, Thunder Gem

Locations: Astral Caves

Monster Jewel

Factors: Nullifies earth symbols 20% of the time, recovers 1% of earth-based damage as MP, grants immunity to stun status.

ATK	INT	DEF	HIT	GRD
3	-5	23	2	0
5	0	0	-2	0	0	0

Rarity: ☆☆

ICE CORPSE — 064

- **HP** · 11674   **EXP** · 448
- **Race** · Undead   **Fol** · 257
- **Resistant To** · Water
- **Weak Against** · Fire

Drops · Dwarven Embroidery Thread, Holy Water, Cursed Cider, Frozen Cider

Locations: Astral Caves

Monster Jewel

Factors: 30% immunity to curse status, nullifies water symbols 20% of the time.

ATK	INT	DEF	HIT	GRD
-2	-5	23	3	0
0	0	-2	0	0	0	0

Rarity: ☆☆

065 · CAVE GUARDIAN

HP · 120184 EXP · 25,623 Resistant To · Water, Thunder
Race · Mech Fol · 13.406 Weak Against · ---

Drops · Regeneration Symbol

Locations: Astral Caves

Monster Jewel

Factors: Increases chance of surviving incap via Fury, 60% immunity to stun status.

ATK	INT	DEF	HIT	GRD
-6	-8	28	-6	0

Symbols: 0 · 5 · 0 · 0 · 5 · 0

Rarity: ☆☆☆☆

---

066 · SAND BIRD

HP · 94798 EXP · 6,384 Resistant To · Earth, Wind
Race · Bird Fol · 15,893 Weak Against · ---

Drops · Bracteate

Locations: Astral Desert

Monster Jewel

Factors: Nullifies earth symbols 20% of the time, nullifies wind symbols 20% of the time.

ATK	INT	DEF	HIT	GRD
5	0	22	7	0

Symbols: 5 · 0 · 0 · 5 · 0 · 0 · 0

Rarity: ☆☆☆☆

---

067 · PHANTOM LEADER

HP · 5476 EXP · 470 Resistant To · ---
Race · Humanoid Fol · 232 Weak Against · Dark

Drops · Darkness Gem, Glowstick, Electromagnetic Bomb, Self-Destructor 3000

Locations: Planet Aeos: Southern Reaches

Monster Jewel

Factors: ATK/INT/DEF/HIT/GRD +10.

ATK	INT	DEF	HIT	GRD
-3	-5	25	13	0

Symbols: 0 · 0 · 0 · 0 · 0 · 0 · 0

Rarity: ☆☆

---

068 · PHANTOM SOLDIER

HP · 4648 EXP · 374 Resistant To · ---
Race · Humanoid Fol · 168 Weak Against · Dark

Drops · Healing Card+, Compact Stun Bomb, Self-Destructor 3000

Locations: Planet Aeos: Southern Reaches

Monster Jewel

Factors: 30% immunity to stun status.

ATK	INT	DEF	HIT	GRD
-5	-7	24	5	-5

Symbols: 0 · 0 · 0 · 0 · 0 · 0 · 5

Rarity: ☆☆

---

069 · ADEPHAGA VENOM

HP · 6370 EXP · 467 Resistant To · ---
Race · Insect Fol · 224 Weak Against · Wind

Drops · Fresh Sage, Aquaberries, Insect Egg

Locations: Planet Aeos: Southern Reaches, Undersea Tunnel, Miga Insect Warren

Monster Jewel

Factors: 30% immunity to poison.

ATK	INT	DEF	HIT	GRD
0	-5	24	5	-5

Symbols: 0 · 0 · 0 · -4 · 0 · 0 · 0

Rarity: ☆

---

070 · ADEPHAGA MILIES

HP · 8214 EXP · 431 Resistant To · ---
Race · Insect Fol · 155 Weak Against · Wind

Drops · Light Gem, Insect Egg, Blueberries, Fresh Sage

Locations: Planet Aeos: Southern Reaches, Undersea Tunnel, Miga Insect Warren

Monster Jewel

Factors: HIT +30.

ATK	INT	DEF	HIT	GRD
1	-8	25	5	-5

Symbols: 0 · 0 · 0 · -5 · 0 · 0 · 0

Rarity: ☆☆☆

---

071 · VAMPIRE BAT

HP · 6345 EXP · 236 Resistant To · ---
Race · Bird Fol · 105 Weak Against · Light

Drops · Biocloth, Blackberries, Bigberries

Locations: Undersea Tunnel, Miga Insect Warren

Monster Jewel

Factors: Maximum HP +100.

ATK	INT	DEF	HIT	GRD
-1	-5	25	13	-3

Symbols: 0 · 0 · 0 · 0 · 2 · 0

Rarity: ☆☆

---

072 · STINGER

HP · 6698 EXP · 266 Resistant To · ---
Race · Insect Fol · 128 Weak Against · Earth

Drops · Bigberries, Aquaberries, Bee Stinger

Locations: Planet Aeos: Southern Reaches

Monster Jewel

Factors: 30% immunity to poison.

ATK	INT	DEF	HIT	GRD
2	-5	25	8	0

Symbols: -2 · 0 · 0 · 0 · 0 · 0 · 0

Rarity: ☆☆

---

073 · LAMIA RADIX

HP · 6738 EXP · 512 Resistant To · Earth
Race · Plant Fol · 160 Weak Against · Fire

Drops · Ripe Berries, Glowstick, Nectar

Locations: Planet Aeos: Southern Reaches, Miga Insect Warren

Monster Jewel

Factors: Restores 1% of HP periodically in battle, 30% immunity to stun status.

ATK	INT	DEF	HIT	GRD
1	-3	25	5	-18

Symbols: 10 · 0 · -7 · 0 · 0 · 0 · 0

Rarity: ☆☆

---

074 · HORNED TORTOISE

HP · 9165 EXP · 1,477 Resistant To · ---
Race · Animal Fol · 361 Weak Against · Ice

Drops · Defense Seeds, Red Herbs

Locations: Planet Aeos: Southern Reaches

Monster Jewel

Factors: 30% immunity to stun status.

ATK	INT	DEF	HIT	GRD
1	-8	25	-5	0

Symbols: 0 · -7 · 0 · 0 · 0 · 0 · 0

Rarity: ☆☆

POLYPHAGA DRUS 075

HP · 7255	EXP · 1,030	Resistant To · ---
Race · Insect	Fol · 415	Weak Against · Earth

Drops · Health Seeds, Red Herb, Thornberries

Locations: Miga Insect Warren

Monster Jewel

Factors: Maximum HP +100.

ATK	INT	DEF	HIT	GRD
2	-3	26	-5	5
-3	0	0	0	0	0	0

Rarity ☆☆

DERMOPTERA 076

HP · 8707	EXP · 475	Resistant To · ---
Race · Insect	Fol · 311	Weak Against · Earth

Drops · Magick Emblem, Aquaberries, Basil, Earth Gem

Locations: Miga Insect Warren, Alternate Dimension

Monster Jewel

Factors: Nullifies earth symbols 20% of the time, 30% immunity to poison.

ATK	INT	DEF	HIT	GRD
0	-5	26	8	-3
5	0	0	-2	0	0	0

Rarity ☆☆

ARMAROS MANIFEST 077

HP · ?????	EXP · 34,147	Resistant To · Earth
Race · Other	Fol · 34,302	Weak Against · Wind

Drops · Monster Jewel

Locations: Miga Insect Warren

Monster Jewel

Factors: Increases chance of surviving incap via Fury, INT +10%, causes attacks to damage allies as well, 60% immunity to paralysis.

ATK	INT	DEF	HIT	GRD
-6	-8	41	0	0
10	0	0	-7	0	0	0

Rarity ☆☆☆☆☆

STROPER 078

HP · 13649	EXP · 629	Resistant To · Water
Race · Plant	Fol · 263	Weak Against · Fire

Drops · Intelligence Seeds, Aquaberries, Basil

Locations: Old Road to the Sanctuary

Monster Jewel

Factors: 30% immunity to poison, 30% immunity to paralysis.

ATK	INT	DEF	HIT	GRD
0	-6	28	-3	0
0	5	-2	0	0

Rarity ☆☆

CURSED HORROR 079

HP · 12242	EXP · 842	Resistant To · Dark
Race · Undead	Fol · 171	Weak Against · Light

Drops · Faerie Embroidery Thread, Red Herb, Lesser Demon's Fetish, Shadow Rose, Alchemist's Cloak

Locations: Old Road to the Sanctuary, En II: Sanctuary

Monster Jewel

Factors: Increases critical hit chance, maximum HP +300.

ATK	INT	DEF	HIT	GRD
1	-3	29	9	9
0	0	0	0	0	7	5

Rarity ☆☆

METAL GOLEM 080

HP · 15581	EXP · 1,474	Resistant To · Earth
Race · Mech	Fol · 2,351	Weak Against · Thunder

Drops · Bracteate, Void Recovery Unit

Locations: Old Road to the Sanctuary

Monster Jewel

Factors: Causes attacks to damage allies as well, 60% immunity to stun status.

ATK	INT	DEF	HIT	GRD
1	0	29	-6	-6
5	0	0	0	-7	0	0

Rarity ☆☆☆

LIGHTNING CORPSE 081

HP · 10651	EXP · 943	Resistant To · Thunder
Race · Undead	Fol · 269	Weak Against · Water

Drops · Thorstone, Disintegration Stone, Thunder Paint, Thunder Gem

Locations: Old Road to the Sanctuary, Palace of Creation

Monster Jewel

Factors: 30% immunity to curse status, nullifies thunder symbols 20% of the time.

ATK	INT	DEF	HIT	GRD
-1	-6	28	-9	0
0	-2	0	0	0	0	0

Rarity ☆☆

MASTER WIZARD 082

HP · 11524	EXP · 1,375	Resistant To · ---
Race · Undead	Fol · 270	Weak Against · ---

Drops · Dragonblood Crystal, Hot Chocolate, Mana Ribbon, Manacloth, Fine Parchment

Locations: Old Road to the Sanctuary, En II: Sanctuary

Monster Jewel

Factors: MP cost -5% in battle.

ATK	INT	DEF	HIT	GRD
-1	15	29	-1	0
0	0	0	0	0	0

Rarity ☆☆

ANCIENT CHIMERA 083

HP · 21955	EXP · 2,040	Resistant To · Fire, Wind
Race · Demon	Fol · 804	Weak Against · Earth, Water

Drops · Cane, Basil, Ebony, Snakeskin

Locations: En II: Sanctuary

Monster Jewel

Factors: Causes attack to damage allies as well, 30% immunity to stun status, 30% immunity to paralysis.

ATK	INT	DEF	HIT	GRD
1	-5	30	0	0
-2	-5	5	5	0	0	0

Rarity ☆☆☆

EARLY PSYNARD 084

HP · 25237	EXP · 4,500	Resistant To · Fire
Race · Bird	Fol · 419	Weak Against · Water

Drops · Psynard Egg, Holy Water, Barrier Spiritwater, Giant Bird Feather

Locations: En II: Sanctuary

Monster Jewel

Factors: Increases chance of surviving incap via Fury, nullifies fire symbols 20% of the time.

ATK	INT	DEF	HIT	GRD
1	1	30	0	0
0	-7	0	0	0	0	0

Rarity ☆☆☆

KOKABIEL 085

HP · ??? | EXP · 63,166 | Resistant To · Earth, Ice, Fire, Wind, Thunder, Light
Race · Other | Fol · 30,712
Drops · Potent Magic Seeds | Weak Against · Dark

Locations: En II: Sanctuary

Monster Jewel

Factors: Increases chance of surviving incap via Fury.

ATK	INT	DEF	HIT	GRD			
-2	4	43	9	0			
8	8	8	8	8	10	7	

Rarity ☆☆☆☆☆

KOKABIEL SPAWN 086

HP · ??? | EXP · 0 | Resistant To · Earth, Ice, Fire, Wind, Thunder, Light
Race · Other | Fol · 15
Drops · -- | Weak Against · Dark

Locations: En II: Sanctuary

Monster Jewel

Factors: Maximum HP -20%, INT +10%.

ATK	INT	DEF	HIT	GRD			
-20	0	39	0	0			
8	8	8	8	8	10	7	

Rarity ☆☆☆☆☆

PHANTOM BEETLE 087

HP · 19384 | EXP · 1,643 | Resistant To · Dark
Race · Insect | Fol · 311 | Weak Against · Earth
Drops · Biocloth, Insect Leg, Thornberries

Locations: Nox Obscurus

Monster Jewel

Factors: Maximum HP +300.

ATK	INT	DEF	HIT	GRD		
1	-10	32	6	-10		
-3	0	0	0	0	0	8

Rarity ☆☆☆

PHANTOM CHIMERA 088

HP · 23609 | EXP · 3,486 | Resistant To · Dark
Race · Demon | Fol · 965 | Weak Against · Earth
Drops · Bizarre Fruit, Red Herb, Holy Water, Snakeskin

Locations: Nox Obscurus

Monster Jewel

Factors: Causes attacks to damage allies as well, 30% immunity to poison, 30% immunity to curse status.

ATK	INT	DEF	HIT	GRD		
2	-5	32	0	0		
-2	0	0	0	0	0	5

Rarity ☆☆☆

SOUL REAPER 089

HP · 20017 | EXP · 1,419 | Resistant To · Dark
Race · Undead | Fol · 2,572 | Weak Against · Light
Drops · Lezard's Flask, Runic Metal, Attack Card

Locations: Nox Obscurus

Monster Jewel

Factors: Increases critical hit chance, maximum HP +2%.

ATK	INT	DEF	HIT	GRD		
-6	-3	32	10	10		
0	0	0	0	0	2	5

Rarity ☆☆☆

DARK PANZER 090

HP · 20017 | EXP · 1,878 | Resistant To · Dark
Race · Humanoid | Fol · 386 | Weak Against · --
Drops · Mercury, Blackberries, Thornberries

Locations: Nox Obscurus

Monster Jewel

Factors: ATK/INT/DEF/HIT/GRD +20.

ATK	INT	DEF	HIT	GRD		
0	-6	32	16	0		
0	0	0	0	0	0	5

Rarity ☆☆

DARK SOLDIER 091

HP · 17893 | EXP · 1,598 | Resistant To · Dark
Race · Humanoid | Fol · 280 | Weak Against · --
Drops · Shadestone, Blackberries, Bracteate

Locations: Nox Obscurus

Monster Jewel

Factors: 30% immunity to stun status.

ATK	INT	DEF	HIT	GRD		
-6	-10	32	6	-6		
0	0	0	0	0	0	5

Rarity ☆☆

PHANTOM LIZARD 092

HP · 17893 | EXP · 2,215 | Resistant To · Dark
Race · Animal | Fol · 467 | Weak Against · --
Drops · Physical Stimulant, Fresh Sage, Bigberries

Locations: Nox Obscurus, Palace of Creation

Monster Jewel

Factors: Maximum HP +300.

ATK	INT	DEF	HIT	GRD		
0	-10	32	3	3		
0	0	0	0	0	0	5

Rarity ☆☆

LITTLE PHANTOM 093

HP · 19384 | EXP · 3,930 | Resistant To · Dark
Race · Humanoid | Fol · 311 | Weak Against · --
Drops · Intelligence Seeds, Hot Chocolate, Red Herb, Silent Cider, Alien's Robe

Locations: Nox Obscurus

Monster Jewel

Factors: 60% immunity to frozen status.

ATK	INT	DEF	HIT	GRD		
1	-1	32	20	3		
0	0	0	0	0	0	5

Rarity ☆☆

DARK RAPTOR 094

HP · 28593 | EXP · 2,115 | Resistant To · Dark
Race · Humanoid | Fol · 331 | Weak Against · Light
Drops · Disintegration Stone, Cardianon Sword, Basil, Static Cider

Locations: Nox Obscurus, Palace of Creation

Monster Jewel

Factors: 30% immunity to paralysis.

ATK	INT	DEF	HIT	GRD		
-3	0	33	0	0		
0	0	0	0	0	0	5

Rarity ☆☆

❖ DARK BOT "STRIKER" — 095

HP · 15885	**EXP** · 1,538	**Resistant To** · Dark
Race · Mech	**Fol** · 497	**Weak Against** · Light

Drops · MP Absorption Unit, Poison Relief Unit, Scrambling Unit

Locations: Nox Obscurus

Monster Jewel

Factors: 60% immunity to stun status.

ATK	INT	DEF	HIT	GRD
1	0	33	7	0

0	-2	0	8	-2	0	5

Rarity ☆☆

❖ PHANTOM DRAGOON — 096

HP · 37159	**EXP** · 7,448	**Resistant To** · Wind, Thunder
Race · Mech	**Fol** · 819	**Weak Against** · Water

Drops · Symbol Booster, Cardianon Bow, Rivet

Locations: Nox Obscurus

Monster Jewel

Factors: Increases chance of surviving incap via Fury, 30% immunity to stun status.

ATK	INT	DEF	HIT	GRD
7	0	33	0	0

0	-2	0	8	5	0	0

Rarity ☆☆

❖ CHAOTIC LEADER — 097

HP · 21557	**EXP** · 1,878	**Resistant To** · Dark
Race · Undead	**Fol** · 386	**Weak Against** · Fire

Drops · Attack Seeds, Aquaberries, Vile Goop, DANGER! DO NOT DRINK!

Locations: Nox Obscurus, Palace of Creation

Monster Jewel

Factors: 30% immunity to poison.

ATK	INT	DEF	HIT	GRD
-1	-3	32	10	-5

0	0	-2	0	0	0	5

Rarity ☆☆

❖ PHANTOM DRAGON NEWT — 098

HP · 25069	**EXP** · 3,279	**Resistant To** · --
Race · Demon	**Fol** · 887	**Weak Against** · --

Drops · Red Dragon Scale, Dragon Scale

Locations: Nox Obscurus, Palace of Creation

Monster Jewel

Factors: Maximum HP +2%.

ATK	INT	DEF	HIT	GRD
1	0	33	3	-7

0	0	0	0	0	0	0

Rarity ☆☆

❖ DARK MATERIAL — 099

HP · 28593	**EXP** · 2,230	**Resistant To** · Dark
Race · Demon	**Fol** · 646	**Weak Against** · Light

Drops · Crystal Skull, Glowstick, Cloudy Cider, Darkness Gem, Shadestone

Locations: Nox Obscurus

Monster Jewel

Factors: Nullifies darkness symbols 20% of the time, recovers 1% of darkness-based damage as MP, 30% immunity to frozen status.

ATK	INT	DEF	HIT	GRD
1	-7	33	3	0

0	0	0	0	0	2	5

Rarity ☆

❖ CHAOTIC CELL — 100

HP · 18920	**EXP** · 1,551	**Resistant To** · Fire
Race · Plant	**Fol** · 396	**Weak Against** · Thunder

Drops · Accuracy Seeds, Aquaberries, Basil, Vile Goop, Poison Cider

Locations: Palace of Creation

Monster Jewel

Factors: 60% immunity to paralysis.

ATK	INT	DEF	HIT	GRD
1	-7	34	-3	0

0	0	5	0	-2	0	0

Rarity ☆☆

❖ LAVA GOLEM — 101

HP · 48224	**EXP** · 2,952	**Resistant To** · Fire
Race · Demon	**Fol** · 6,482	**Weak Against** · Water

Drops · Meteorite, Mithril, Coal

Locations: Palace of Creation

Monster Jewel

Factors: Causes attacks to damage allies as well, recovers 1% of fire-based damage as MP, shoots a blast of fire when guarding.

ATK	INT	DEF	HIT	GRD
0	0	34	-7	-7

0	-2	0	0	0	0	0

Rarity ☆☆☆

❖ DARK APE — 102

HP · 30967	**EXP** · 3,137	**Resistant To** · Dark
Race · Animal	**Fol** · 443	**Weak Against** · --

Drops · Health Seeds, Hot Chocolate, Frozen Cider, Bigberries

Locations: Palace of Creation

Monster Jewel

Factors: Increases critical hit chance, 30% immunity to stun status, 30% immunity to frozen status.

ATK	INT	DEF	HIT	GRD
7	-14	35	7	4

0	0	0	0	0	0	5

Rarity ☆☆

❖ DARK BISHOP — 103

HP · 21614	**EXP** · 1,895	**Resistant To** · Dark
Race · Humanoid	**Fol** · 456	**Weak Against** · --

Drops · Mental Stimulant, Pumpkin Extract, Parchment

Locations: Palace of Creation

Monster Jewel

Factors: Recovers 1% of darkness-based damage as MP, 30% immunity to stun status, 30% immunity to pumpkin status.

ATK	INT	DEF	HIT	GRD
-7	7	34	-3	0

0	0	0	0	0	0	5

Rarity ☆☆

❖ NECROMANCER — 104

HP · 33386	**EXP** · 2,776	**Resistant To** · Dark
Race · Undead	**Fol** · 378	**Weak Against** · --

Drops · Biocloth, Hot Chocolate, Holy Water, Void Recovery Unit

Locations: Palace of Creation

Monster Jewel

Factors: MP cost -5% in battle, INT +4%, 30% immunity to curse status, 30% immunity to void status.

ATK	INT	DEF	HIT	GRD
-10	17	34	-2	0

0	0	0	0	0	0	5

Rarity ☆☆☆

DARK CLOWN — 105

HP • 25673 EXP • 2,609 Resistant To • ---
Race • Demon Fol • 1,163 Weak Against • ---

Drops • Dragonblood Crystal, Pumpkin Extract, Pumpkin Cider

Locations: *Palace of Creation*

Monster Jewel

Factors: INT +4%, 30% immunity to pumpkin status.

ATK	INT	DEF	HIT	GRD		
-4	18	35	11	0		
0	0	0	0	0	0	0

Rarity ★★★☆

GUST HORNET — 110

HP • 95807 EXP • 4,193 Resistant To • ---
Race • Insect Fol • 382 Weak Against • Earth

Drops • Anti-Poison Amulet, Aquaberries, Darkness Gem

Locations: *Cave of the Seven Stars*

Monster Jewel

Factors: 60% immunity to poison.

ATK	INT	DEF	HIT	GRD		
-7	0	44	13	0		
-7	0	0	0	0	0	0

Rarity ★★★☆

FORSAKEN BEAST — 106

HP • 59815 EXP • 14,617 Resistant To • Dark
Race • Demon Fol • 3,404 Weak Against • Light

Drops • Star Sapphire, Star Ruby, Shadestone

Locations: *Palace of Creation*

Monster Jewel

Factors: Increases chance of surviving incap via Fury, 30% immunity to frozen status.

ATK	INT	DEF	HIT	GRD		
7	-4	35	-7	0		
0	0	0	0	0	5	10

Rarity ★★★☆

BONE KNIGHT — 111

HP • 94685 EXP • 6,695 Resistant To • Dark
Race • Undead Fol • 443 Weak Against • Fire, Light

Drops • Bracteate, Hyper Potion, Magical Clay

Locations: *Cave of the Seven Stars*

Monster Jewel

Factors: Maximum HP -200, HIT +30, GRD +40, DEF +10.

ATK	INT	DEF	HIT	GRD		
3	0	36	0	0		
0	0	-7	0	0	2	10

Rarity ★★☆

APOSTLE OF CREATION — 107

HP • ??? EXP • 63,052 Resistant To • Dark
Race • Other Fol • 7,984 Weak Against • Light

Drops • --

Locations: *Palace of Creation*

Monster Jewel

Factors: Increases chance of surviving incap via Fury, 60% immunity to void status, ATK +10%.

ATK	INT	DEF	HIT	GRD		
0	0	49	0	-10		
0	0	0	0	0	7	10

Rarity ★★★★★

WINGED NIGHTMARE — 112

HP • 97913 EXP • 7,151 Resistant To • Wind
Race • Bird Fol • 630 Weak Against • Fire

Drops • Gnomestone, Red Herb, Cashmere

Locations: *Cave of the Seven Stars*

Monster Jewel

Factors: Nullifies wind symbols 20% of the time, 30% immunity to fog status, 30% immunity to void status.

ATK	INT	DEF	HIT	GRD		
2	-5	46	9	0		
0	0	-7	5	0	0	0

Rarity ★★★☆

SATANAIL — 108

HP • ??? EXP • 0 Resistant To • Dark
Race • Other Fol • 0 Weak Against • Light

Drops • --

Locations: *Palace of Creation*

Monster Jewel

Factors: Increases chance of surviving incap via Fury, Rush Gauge charge rate +2, maximum HP/MP +3%.

ATK	INT	DEF	HIT	GRD		
-5	11	54	0	0		
0	0	0	0	0	5	5

Rarity ★★★★★

TREANT — 113

HP • 166288 EXP • 25,960 Resistant To • Earth
Race • Plant Fol • 871 Weak Against • Fire

Drops • Cane, Red Herb, Pumpkin Extract

Locations: *Cave of the Seven Stars*

Monster Jewel

Factors: Restores 1% of HP periodically in battle, 60% immunity to pumpkin status.

ATK	INT	DEF	HIT	GRD		
0	-12	47	0	0		
8	0	-7	0	0	0	0

Rarity ★★☆

UNDYING DRAGON — 109

HP • 1896572 EXP • 41,365 Resistant To • Fire
Race • Demon Fol • 35,867 Weak Against • Water

Drops • Darkness Ring

Locations: *Palace of Creation*

Monster Jewel

Factors: Hit +2%, maximum HP +10%, shoots blasts of dark energy when guarding.

ATK	INT	DEF	HIT	GRD		
2	0	41	25	-16		
0	-2	5	0	0	0	0

Rarity ★★★★★

GREATER PERYTON — 114

HP • 109943 EXP • 6,579 Resistant To • Wind
Race • Bird Fol • 532 Weak Against • Earth

Drops • Sylphstone, Basil, Peryton Droppings, Bunny Feed

Locations: *Cave of the Seven Stars*

Monster Jewel

Factors: 60% immunity to stun status.

ATK	INT	DEF	HIT	GRD		
2	-14	47	5	0		
-7	0	0	8	0	0	0

Rarity ★★☆

LEONBLADE — 115

HP · 116146 **EXP** · 4,967 **Resistant To** · --
Race · Demon **Fol** · 441 **Weak Against** · --

Drops · Protection Seeds, Saber-Toothed Tiger Fang, Gambleberries, Bigberries

Locations: *Cave of the Seven Stars*

Monster Jewel

Factors: ATK +10, 30% immunity to silence, 60% immunity to poison.

ATK	INT	DEF	HIT	GRD
1	-19	48	0	-19
0	0	0	0	0	0	0

Rarity ★★★☆

GUIAFAIRO — 116

HP · 104435 **EXP** · 4,657 **Resistant To** · --
Race · Bird **Fol** · 385 **Weak Against** · --

Drops · Anti-Fog Amulet, Glowstick, Barrier Spiritwater

Locations: *Cave of the Seven Stars*

Monster Jewel

Factors: Maximum HP +300, 60% immunity to fog status.

ATK	INT	DEF	HIT	GRD
-5	-7	45	9	0
0	0	0	0	0	0	0

Rarity ★★★☆

QUEEN MANDRAGORA — 117

HP · 141851 **EXP** · 7,758 **Resistant To** · Earth
Race · Plant **Fol** · 431 **Weak Against** · Fire

Drops · Shadow Rose, Basil, Nectar, Ripe Berries

Locations: *Cave of the Seven Stars*

Monster Jewel

Factors: Restores 1% of HP periodically in battle, 60% immunity to stun status.

ATK	INT	DEF	HIT	GRD
2	-5	48	10	-34
8	0	-7	0	0	0	0

Rarity ★★★☆

FLYING ICE — 118

HP · 145584 **EXP** · 8,695 **Resistant To** · Water
Race · Demon **Fol** · 9,752 **Weak Against** · Fire

Drops · Nereidstone, Gold, Platinum

Locations: *Cave of the Seven Stars*

Monster Jewel

Factors: Nullifies water symbols 20% of the time, 30% immunity to frozen status.

ATK	INT	DEF	HIT	GRD
6	-10	49	5	0
0	0	-7	0	0	0	0

Rarity ★★☆

SYDONAIST GAMMA — 119

HP · 115380 **EXP** · 4,923 **Resistant To** · --
Race · Humanoid **Fol** · 545 **Weak Against** · --

Drops · Healing Band, Aquaberries, Holy Water, Neck Chain

Locations: *Cave of the Seven Stars*

Monster Jewel

Factors: 30% immunity to curse status, 30% immunity to poison.

ATK	INT	DEF	HIT	GRD
0	0	49	0	0
0	0	0	0	0	0	0

Rarity ★★★☆

SYDONAIST DELTA — 120

HP · 99261 **EXP** · 4,678 **Resistant To** · --
Race · Humanoid **Fol** · 542 **Weak Against** · --

Drops · Sacrificial Doll, Aquaberries, Holy Water

Locations: *Cave of the Seven Stars*

Monster Jewel

Factors: 30% immunity to curse status, 30% immunity to poison.

ATK	INT	DEF	HIT	GRD
0	0	51	0	0
0	0	0	0	0	0	0

Rarity ★★★☆

MOONLIGHT LADY — 121

HP · 142527 **EXP** · 10,218 **Resistant To** · Dark
Race · Demon **Fol** · 827 **Weak Against** · Light

Drops · Mana Ribbon, Glowstick, Mental Potion

Locations: *Cave of the Seven Stars*

Monster Jewel

Factors: INT +4%, DEF +12%, maximum MP +150.

ATK	INT	DEF	HIT	GRD
-5	10	50	0	10
0	0	0	0	0	5	10

Rarity ★★★☆

SPRIGGAN — 122

HP · 145920 **EXP** · 8,900 **Resistant To** · --
Race · Demon **Fol** · 832 **Weak Against** · --

Drops · Anti-Freezing Amulet, Hot Chocolate, Bigberries

Locations: *Cave of the Seven Stars*

Monster Jewel

Factors: Increases critical hit chance, grants immunity to stun status, DEF -40%, ATK doubled but maximum HP halved.

ATK	INT	DEF	HIT	GRD
11	-26	51	15	15
0	0	0	0	0	0	0

Rarity ★★★☆

SPIRIT ARCHBISHOP — 123

HP · 137436 **EXP** · 8,616 **Resistant To** · --
Race · Humanoid **Fol** · 729 **Weak Against** · --

Drops · Symbol Booster, Pumpkin Extract, Faerie Embroidery Thread

Locations: *Cave of the Seven Stars*

Monster Jewel

Factors: Recovers 1% of light-based damage as MP, 30% immunity to stun status, 30% immunity to pumpkin status.

ATK	INT	DEF	HIT	GRD
-16	11	52	-5	0
0	0	0	0	0	0	0

Rarity ★★☆

METAL SCUMBAG — 124

HP · 149913 **EXP** · 82,184 **Resistant To** · --
Race · Mech **Fol** · 558 **Weak Against** · --

Drops · Thorstone, Hot Chocolate, Void Recovery Unit, Self-Destructor 3000

Locations: *Cave of the Seven Stars*

Monster Jewel

Factors: +25% Fol after each battle.

ATK	INT	DEF	HIT	GRD
-5	-13	-51	-8	-35
0	0	0	0	0	0	0

Rarity ★★★★☆

✧ HADES CRAB — 125

HP · 186754 EXP · 27,738 **Resistant To** · Water, Dark
Race · Insect **Fol** · 733 **Weak Against** · Thunder

Drops · Green Beryl, Vile Goop, Runic Metal

Locations: *Cave of the Seven Stars*

Monster Jewel

Factors: *60% immunity to stun status.*

ATK	INT	DEF	HIT	GRD
2	-16	52	-10	26
0	5	0	0	-7	0	3

Rarity ☆☆☆

✧ TEMPLE GUARDIAN — 126

HP · 958949 EXP · 110,000 **Resistant To** · Water
Race · Mech **Fol** · 3,270 **Weak Against** · Thunder

Drops · Basil, Void Recovery Unit, Poison Relief Unit

Locations: *Cave of the Seven Stars*

Monster Jewel

Factors: *Increases chance of surviving incap via Fury, 60% immunity to paralysis.*

ATK	INT	DEF	HIT	GRD
15	-10	49	0	0
0	5	0	0	-7	0	0

Rarity ☆☆☆☆

✧ BLUE EAGLE RANGER — 127

HP · 916237 EXP · 40,000 **Resistant To** · Water
Race · Humanoid **Fol** · 3,384 **Weak Against** · Fire

Drops · Ice Gem

Locations: *Cave of the Seven Stars*

Monster Jewel

Factors: *60% immunity to stun status, nullifies HP damage 15% of the time.*

ATK	INT	DEF	HIT	GRD
0	0	52	0	0
0	5	-2	0	0	0	0

Rarity ☆☆☆☆

✧ WHITE EAGLE RANGER — 128

HP · 839884 EXP · 40,000 **Resistant To** · Light
Race · Humanoid **Fol** · 3,364 **Weak Against** · Dark

Drops · Light Gem

Locations: *Cave of the Seven Stars*

Monster Jewel

Factors: *60% immunity to stun status, DEF +12%.*

ATK	INT	DEF	HIT	GRD
0	0	52	0	0
0	0	0	0	0	5	-2

Rarity ☆☆☆☆

✧ BLACK EAGLE RANGER — 129

HP · 839884 EXP · 40,000 **Resistant To** · Dark
Race · Humanoid **Fol** · 3,364 **Weak Against** · Light

Drops · tri-Emblum

Locations: *Cave of the Seven Stars*

Monster Jewel

Factors: *60% immunity to stun status, increases critical hit chance.*

ATK	INT	DEF	HIT	GRD
0	0	52	0	0
0	0	0	0	0	-2	5

Rarity ☆☆☆☆

✧ RED EAGLE RANGER — 130

HP · 763531 EXP · 40,000 **Resistant To** · Fire
Race · Humanoid **Fol** · 3,364 **Weak Against** · Water

Drops · Fire Gem

Locations: *Cave of the Seven Stars*

Monster Jewel

Factors: *60% immunity to stun status, ATK +10%.*

ATK	INT	DEF	HIT	GRD
0	0	52	0	0
0	-2	5	0	0	0	0

Rarity ☆☆☆☆

✧ GABRIEL CELESTE — 131

HP · ?????? EXP · 400,000 **Resistant To** · Earth, Water, Fire, Wind,
Race · Other **Fol** · 3,776 Thunder, Light, Dark

Drops · Gabriel Celeste's Feather

Locations: *Cave of the Seven Stars*

Monster Jewel

Factors: *Maximum HP +10%, shoots blasts of lightning when guarding.*

ATK	INT	DEF	HIT	GRD
0	-500	76	15	61
5	5	5	3	10	10	3

Rarity ☆☆☆☆☆☆

✧ ADEPHAGA PROX — 132

HP · 228692 EXP · 7,345 **Resistant To** · ---
Race · Insect **Fol** · 3,752 **Weak Against** · Wind

Drops · Geostone, Insect Leg, Bigberries

Locations: *Wandering Dungeon*

Monster Jewel

Factors: *30% immunity to paralysis.*

ATK	INT	DEF	HIT	GRD
-7	-33	65	0	13
0	0	0	-7	0	0	0

Rarity ☆☆

✧ ACID GEREL — 133

HP · 246264 EXP · 10,292 **Resistant To** · Dark
Race · Plant **Fol** · 627 **Weak Against** · Fire

Drops · Geostone, Red Herb, Vile Goop

Locations: *Wandering Dungeon*

Monster Jewel

Factors: *30% immunity to silence, 30% immunity to fog status, 30% immunity to pumpkin status.*

ATK	INT	DEF	HIT	GRD
0	-13	65	-16	0
0	0	-7	0	0	0	5

Rarity ☆☆☆

✧ TRINITY TUSK — 134

HP · 297160 EXP · 49,980 **Resistant To** · Earth, Fire, Wind
Race · Demon **Fol** · 1,259 **Weak Against** · Water

Drops · Geostone, Salamanderstone, Sylphstone, Snakeskin

Locations: *Wandering Dungeon*

Monster Jewel

Factors: *Causes attacks to damage allies as well, 60% immunity to poison.*

ATK	INT	DEF	HIT	GRD
7	0	65	8	-3
8	-5	8	8	0	0	0

Rarity ☆☆☆

MISFORTUNER — 135

HP · 232835 EXP · 10,368 Resistant To · Dark
Race · Undead Fol · 631 Weak Against · Light

Drops · Geostone, Greater Demon's Fetish, Lesser Demon's Fetish

Locations: Wandering Dungeon

Monster Jewel

Factors: Increases critical hit chance, maximum HP +5%.

ATK	INT	DEF	HIT	GRD
2	-3	66	33	-3

0	0	0	0	0	-7	8

Rarity ★☆☆

ARCH SPELLMASTER — 140

HP · 244732 EXP · 14,666 Resistant To · Earth, Water, Fire, Wind, Thunder, Light, Dark
Race · Undead Fol · 953

Drops · Geostone, Cane, Ash

Locations: Wandering Dungeon

Monster Jewel

Factors: MP cost -15% in battle, DEF -70%, INT doubled but maximum MP halved.

ATK	INT	DEF	HIT	GRD
-20	40	67	-7	34

5	5	5	5	5	5	5

Rarity ★★☆

JADE GOLEM — 136

HP · 314299 EXP · 19,652 Resistant To · Thunder
Race · Demon Fol · 19,000 Weak Against · Earth

Drops · Geostone, Shadestone, Darkness Gem, Moonstone, Disintegration Stone

Locations: Wandering Dungeon

Monster Jewel

Factors: Causes attacks to damage allies as well, grants immunity to stun status.

ATK	INT	DEF	HIT	GRD
13	0	67	-13	-13

-2	0	0	0	5	0	0

Rarity ★★☆

ANTLERED TORTOISE — 141

HP · 247795 EXP · 14,723 Resistant To · Earth, Fire, Wind, Thunder, Light, Dark
Race · Animal Fol · 956 Weak Against · Water

Drops · Geostone, Warped Carapace, Raw Fish

Locations: Wandering Dungeon

Monster Jewel

Factors: GRD +40.

ATK	INT	DEF	HIT	GRD
8	-14	68	7	21

5	-7	5	5	5	5	5

Rarity ★★☆

KOBOLD RANGER — 137

HP · 234537 EXP · 10,292 Resistant To · --
Race · Animal Fol · 627 Weak Against · --

Drops · Geostone, Tent, Fresh Sage

Locations: Wandering Dungeon

Monster Jewel

Factors: HIT +2%, maximum MP -200.

ATK	INT	DEF	HIT	GRD
-1	0	65	13	-1

0	0	0	0	0	0	0

Rarity ★☆☆

AUGMENTOID — 142

HP · 253623 EXP · 10,216 Resistant To · --
Race · Undead Fol · 923 Weak Against · --

Drops · Geostone, Aquaberries, Pickled Plum Rice

Locations: Wandering Dungeon

Monster Jewel

Factors: Nullifies fire symbols 20% of the time, 30% immunity to poison.

ATK	INT	DEF	HIT	GRD
0	0	69	21	0

0	0	0	0	0	0	0

Rarity ★★☆

MYCONID — 138

HP · 235841 EXP · 11,996 Resistant To · Earth, Water
Race · Plant Fol · 629 Weak Against · Fire

Drops · Geostone, Tasty Mushroom, Tasty Mushroom?

Locations: Wandering Dungeon

Monster Jewel

Factors: 60% immunity to paralysis.

ATK	INT	DEF	HIT	GRD
8	-13	66	-13	0

8	5	-7	0	0	0	0

Rarity ★★☆

LITTLE MUTANT — 143

HP · 241596 EXP · 8,999 Resistant To · --
Race · Demon Fol · 585 Weak Against · --

Drops · Geostone, Micro Heavy Ion Collider, Mixed Syrup

Locations: Wandering Dungeon

Monster Jewel

Factors: Grants immunity to fog status.

ATK	INT	DEF	HIT	GRD
-14	0	71	-14	-14

0	0	0	0	0	0	0

Rarity ★★☆

GHOSTKEEPER — 139

HP · 200527 EXP · 14,780 Resistant To · Dark
Race · Undead Fol · 959 Weak Against · Earth, Water, Fire, Wind, Thunder, Light

Drops · Geostone, Disintegration Stone, Parchment, Fine Parchment

Locations: Wandering Dungeon

Monster Jewel

Factors: 60% immunity to curse status, nullifies darkness symbols 20% of the time.

ATK	INT	DEF	HIT	GRD
-5	-14	68	10	0

-5	-5	-5	-5	-5	7	0

Rarity ★★☆

DAMASCUS FORT — 144

HP · 282245 EXP · 66,470 Resistant To · Earth, Water, Fire, Wind, Thunder, Light, Dark
Race · Demon Fol · 1,254

Drops · Geostone, Philosopher's Stone, Alchemist's Water, Disintegration Stone

Locations: Wandering Dungeon

Monster Jewel

Factors: Grants immunity to stun status.

ATK	INT	DEF	HIT	GRD
9	-14	69	7	0

5	5	5	5	5	5	5

Rarity ★★☆

LIZARD TYRANT — 145

HP · 262513   EXP · 17,610   Resistant To · --
Race · Animal   Fol · 2,133   Weak Against · Water

Drops · Geostone, Lizardskin, Dragon Scale

Locations: Wandering Dungeon

Monster Jewel

Factors: Maximum HP +5%.

ATK	INT	DEF	HIT	GRD
1	-7	70	0	-14
0	-2	0	0	0

Rarity ☆☆☆

BLOODTAIL — 146

HP · 259550   EXP · 10,634   Resistant To · Earth
Race · Insect   Fol · 645   Weak Against · Wind

Drops · Geostone, Insect Egg, Caterpillar Fungus, Disintegration Stone

Locations: Wandering Dungeon

Monster Jewel

Factors: Nullifies earth symbols 20% of the time, 60% immunity to poison.

ATK	INT	DEF	HIT	GRD
6	0	70	0	0
10	0	0	-7	0

Rarity ☆☆

GRIM REAPER — 147

HP · 286203   EXP · 12,644   Resistant To · Dark
Race · Undead   Fol · 660   Weak Against · Light

Drops · Geostone, Philosopher's Stone, Bracteate

Locations: Wandering Dungeon

Monster Jewel

Factors: Increases critical hit chance, maximum HP +10%, 30% immunity to curse status.

ATK	INT	DEF	HIT	GRD
9	0	74	0	0
0	0	0	0	7

Rarity ☆☆☆

HELL CLOWN — 148

HP · 271404   EXP · 17,679   Resistant To · --
Race · Demon   Fol · 978   Weak Against · --

Drops · Bizarre Fruit, Pumpkin Extract, Common Egg, Pie Crusts

Locations: Wandering Dungeon

Monster Jewel

Factors: INT +10%, Rush Gauge charge rate +2, 60% immunity to pumpkin status.

ATK	INT	DEF	HIT	GRD
14	14	72	29	0
0	0	0	0	0

Rarity ☆☆☆

DOMINATOR DRAGON — 149

HP · 477858   EXP · 41,197   Resistant To · Water
Race · Demon   Fol · 2,528   Weak Against · Fire

Drops · Valkyrie's Garb, Geostone, Dragonblood Crystal, Dragon God Scale

Locations: Wandering Dungeon

Monster Jewel

Factors: 60% immunity to frozen status.

ATK	INT	DEF	HIT	GRD
2	0	71	43	-28
0	10	-7	0	0

Rarity ☆☆☆☆

PREHISTORIC PSYNARD — 150

HP · 1504988   EXP · 230,000   Resistant To · Earth, Water, Fire, Wind, Thunder, Light, Dark
Race · Bird   Fol · 20,047   Weak Against · --

Drops · Seraphic Doll

Locations: Wandering Dungeon

Monster Jewel

Factors: Increases chances of surviving incap via Fury.

ATK	INT	DEF	HIT	GRD
9	23	77	15	0
5	5	5	5	5

Rarity ☆☆☆☆

RING BEAST — 151

HP · 1582849   EXP · 260,000   Resistant To · Light
Race · Demon   Fol · 12,164   Weak Against · Dark

Drops · Seraphic Doll

Locations: Wandering Dungeon

Monster Jewel

Factors: Increases chances of surviving incap via Fury, grants immunity to frozen status.

ATK	INT	DEF	HIT	GRD
0	0	79	0	0
0	0	0	0	10	-7

Rarity ☆☆☆☆

CHIMERA BEAST — 152

HP · 1994019   EXP · 290,000   Resistant To · Earth
Race · Demon   Fol · 8,195   Weak Against · --

Drops · Seraphic Doll

Locations: Wandering Dungeon

Monster Jewel

Factors: Causes attacks to hit allies as well, 30% immunity to poison, 30% immunity to frozen status.

ATK	INT	DEF	HIT	GRD
20	18	82	21	10
5	0	0	0	0	0

Rarity ☆☆☆

ETHEREAL QUEEN — 153

HP · ?????   EXP · 900,000   Resistant To · Earth, Water, Fire, Wind, Thunder, Light, Dark
Race · Other   Fol · 4,449   Weak Against · --

Drops · Seraphic Doll

Locations: Wandering Dungeon

Monster Jewel

Factors: MP cost -15% in battle, Rush Gauge charge rate +3, adds two hit chances per attack.

ATK	INT	DEF	HIT	GRD
-800	0	114	34	46
5	3	10	5	5	10	3

Rarity ☆☆☆☆☆

ASHLAY BERNBELDT — 154

HP · ?????   EXP · 45,383   Resistant To · --
Race · Humanoid   Fol · 5,664   Weak Against · --

Drops · --

Locations: Planet Roak: Tatroi Colosseum (Team Match)

Monster Jewel

Factors: Adds one hit chance per attack.

ATK	INT	DEF	HIT	GRD
77	-23	129	72	57
0	0	0	0	0

Rarity ☆☆☆☆☆

After completing the "Where's the Receptionist?" quest in Tatroi, the colosseum, a place where challengers come to fulfill their dreams of conquest and glory, opens its doors. A completely optional undertaking from the main story, this arena pits you against powerful competitors in the form of three different match types: Solo Mode, Team Mode, and Survival. The only goal in any of these modes is simple and to the point: slaughter the opposing team. Does the blood of a warrior boil through your veins?

FIGHT COIN EXCHANGE

For every battle won, Fight Coins are awarded. These coins act as currency at the Fight Coin Exchange, a special shop available only at the colosseum. The items available here are exceedingly rare, and are often good replacements for lesser armors and weapons during the main story. The Monster Jewel, Darkblood Chainmail, and Dark Elf's Robe are the best of the bunch, so work your way up to them whenever it is possible.

Exchange List		
Item	Type	Price
Ripe Berries	Usable Items	20
Monster Jewel	Other Items	200
Dragon Scale	Other Items	300
Wild Arc	Weapon	1,500
Mithril Rapier	Weapon	1,900
Crested Spear	Weapon	2,200
Mithril Sword	Weapon	2,500

Exchange List		
Item	Type	Price
Dragon Claws	Weapon	2,800
Earthcrest Guard	Armor	3,200
Crystal Armor	Armor	3,900
Mystic Robe	Armor	4,200
Inferno Sickle	Weapon	9,000
Darkblood Chainmail	Armor	11,000
Dark Elf's Robe	Armor	12,000

RANKS & COLOSSEUM POINTS

Both the Solo and Team modes of play are initiated by selecting a competitor from a ranking board of 100 enemies. You can challenge fighters up to three ranks ahead of you. The exception to this rule is the #1 ranked fighter or team, who can't be challenged initially. An invisible point system is used to tally your progress through both modes, and points go up after each fight. To fight the last match in each mode, you must earn 299 colosseum points. Since you can't actually see your score, your only choice is to keep fighting lower ranked battles until the top fighter becomes available. Be diligent and stick with it!

ITEM SELECTION

The only real rule in the colosseum is that you can't use your own items; you have to use specialized item sets provided for you. These sets come in three flavors: Offensive, Curative, and Strategic. The Curative set is the most useful of the bunch, since it offers a small selection of restorative items. The Offensive and Strategic sets are designed to help you get through special case scenarios where you may not be able to win with brute force. Look over the item sets listed under each match mode and consider the items they grant for troublesome fights.

❖ GENERAL COLOSSEUM TIPS

- All colosseum matches are winnable when your group is around level 110. You can shoot through almost 70 ranks at around level 50, however. Play cautiously and never take unnecessary risks.

- If you're trying to tackle harder battles at low levels, use Berserk on any melee unit you are personally controlling. Though it comes with some risk, this is the only reasonable way to effectively attack enemies above your level. Use a Riot Potion from the Strategic item set to boost your ATK even further.

- Stick with Edge in Solo mode. His well-rounded attributes, Berserk skill, and powerful combos make him effective during one-on-one fights. Use Berserk in combination with Celestial Sword-based combos to rack up giant amounts of damage.

- Bacchus and his incredible Black Hole Sphere are vital during team battles. Many of these matches come flooded with enemies that are difficult to manage, a problem that his Black Hole Sphere can fix. Give him Berserk and move out to a distance to make this strategy even more potent.

- When all else fails, try Reimi. Her potent ranged attacks make it easy to keep your distance and attack enemies while they are busy making an approach. Even if the remainder of your party is down, she can often make a comeback when all odds are against you.

- All battles containing Metal Scumbags are easily ended with the Scumbag Slayer, a weapon that carries a 20% chance of instantly killing them. Their high DEF rating means nothing against this weapon.

MATCH TYPES

SOLO MODE

Select any one of your party members to fight in a traditional one-on-one match. There are 100 ranks to climb through, each harder than the last. The ultimate goal is to reach the top spot and defeat the Lord of Dragons.

Take note that any character you use in Solo Mode immediately solidifies his/her spot in the ranking. This means that your own party members can become potential challengers for another character climbing the ranks.

1st Place Prize: Solo Champion Medal

SOLO ITEM SETS

Offensive Set	Compact Poison Bomb x 1, EM Bomb x 2, Compact Stun Bomb x 1, Mixed Syrup x 1.
Curative Set	Blueberries x 1, Bigberries x 1, Physical Stimulant x 1, Blackberries x 1.
Strategic Set	Hyper Potion x 1, Element Breaker x 1, Riot Potion x 1, Gambleberries x 2.

PROBLEMATIC CHALLENGERS

Rank 9 - Smashing Feet

This temple guardian copycat is resistant to the light element, so avoid using weapons like Edge's Holy Sword "Farewell". He's also prone to firing homing projectiles from long ranges, which are practically impossible to avoid with certain characters. Stay close and circle around him to lure out his leaping attack, which opens him up to punishment. Continue this pattern until he enters Rush Mode, in which case just continue to circle around him until it expires. He starts to use a powerful dashing attack when his HP drops below 25%, which may end the fight if it hits you. Perform a jump just as he starts to travel towards you in order to avoid it (this doesn't work if you're Myuria).

Rank 6 - Crusher Ape

The Crusher Ape is extremely vulnerable to Blindsides, making him easy pickings for melee characters like Edge. Despite this, it's extremely important to watch for his ice-based attacks, which all have a high chance of inflicting the Frozen status. Avoid being caught off guard by this status and equip an Anti-Freezing Amulet.

Rank 3 - Great Solar Phoenix

The Phoenix is resistant against the Light and Fire elements, so stay away from weapons and symbols that use them. Remain just outside of its stomp attack range and start charging a Blindside. If it begins to cast a symbol, move in and attack it to stop the charging period. If it starts to approach, Blindside it and perform your biggest combo. There's very little you can do if it enters Rush Mode; in that scenario, attempt to Blindside the monster to buy yourself a little time. If that doesn't work, run to the edge of the battlefield and keep your HP high enough to survive its Plasma Cyclone symbol.

Rank 1 - Lord of Dragons

This bad boy is slow and easy to avoid, but his massive DEF and HP rating make him difficult to slay. Base your attack strategy around landing big damage off of a Blindside. Stay at several character lengths away from him and begin charging your Rush Gauge. If he stops to perform his breath attack, Blindside him and perform the biggest combo you have. If he moves well into your attacking distance, back away and watch for his stomp attack; if he does it, perform a jump to avoid the shockwave. Do not perform a Blindside unless you visibly see him going for his breath attack; otherwise, he can counter your movement for giant damage. Bide your time and wait for the right moment to strike!

TEAM MODE

Take your entire party into battle and crush the opposing team. As with Solo Mode, there are 100 challengers to face to get to the top spot. Ashlay Bernbeldt is the final challenger, and he's a powerful swordsman with a particularly useful Monster Jewel. Fight him as many times as needed to fully analyze him and obtain his jewel.

1st Place Prize: Team Champion Medal

TEAM ITEM SETS

Offensive Set	Compact Poison Bomb x 12, Deluxe Freezing Bomb x 1, Compact Stun Bomb x 3, Mixed Syrup x 4.
Curative Set	Bigberries x 8, Physical Stimulant x 4, Blackberries x 8, Fresh Sage x 3.
Strategic Set	Hyper Potion x 4, Element Breaker x 8, Riot Potion x 6, Gambleberries x 8.

PROBLEMATIC CHALLENGERS

Rank 23 - Le Pierrot Assassinant

This group of clowns and the many other teams with clowns on them have extremely powerful attacks that generally incapacitate characters in a single hit. With their Rush Mode activated, these ingrates can move into striking range with little difficulty. With that said, the majority of this match is going to revolve around Reimi, as she's the only character that can effectively attack them without risking damage. Field Sarah in the party as well, who should start the battle by using Enhance on Reimi. Since you aren't going to survive many hits anyway, activate Berserk and start blasting the cretins with Hunter's Moon and Crimson Squall loops. Use Crescent Wings against them if several clowns approach you at a time. Whenever they activate Rush Mode, halt your attack and circle around the field until it deactivates.

Rank 19 - Symbol Liberation Front

A group of wizards with a bone to pick. The problem with this match up is their Faerie Star healing symbol, which rejuvenates 90% of the entire party's HP. This is difficult to stop when the enemy enters Rush Mode, which allows them to absorb hits without their symbol being canceled. Silence can be used against the Violent Wizards, though the hit rate is extremely low. It's recommended to form a team that consists of Bacchus, Reimi, Lymle, and Sarah. Make sure Sarah is only allowed to cast Faerie Light, Restoration, and Cure Condition. All AI character tactics should be set to "Fight freestyle with full force!" to ensure that they are always doing something. With Bacchus as your leader, initiate the Berserk status and start chaining Black Hole Sphere ➔ Irradiation ➔ Black Hole Sphere repeatedly. When the enemy activates Rush Mode, back away from them and start firing Bacchus's dash gunfire attack over and over again. This attack occasionally stuns the enemies, which may cancel their spell attempts when they're in Rush Mode. Lastly, Anti-Pumpkin Amulets should also be added to protect against the pumpkin status the priests inflict. It's a minor fix to a small problem, but it'll help in the long run.

Rank 18 - Beetlemania

The first problem is the paralysis status the insects inflict on hit. Equip the Anti-Paralysis Amulet to your entire party to counter this problem. The second problem, and probably the most irritating, is the Buster Whip's cure symbol that heals a massive amount of HP. Though the success rate is low, try using silence to seal their symbology away. Otherwise, they'll continue to heal themselves regardless of how much damage you deal. Finally, the Cannibal Insects have a latent defense improvement that you can remove with a void spell. This is just another reason to field Lymle in this battle.

Rank 1 – Wandering Swordsman

Ashlay Bernbeldt has no symbols to speak of, relying entirely on special arts and his incredible statistics to stage an offense. The only thing to worry about is the distance you are fighting him at; never let him approach you. Pilot Reimi and focus on pummeling him with chained attacks from a distance. He'll most likely defeat you in a single hit, so ignore Berserk's risks and use it as often as you like. If he activates Rush Mode, keep your distance until it runs out, and then return to your ranged attack strategy.

SURVIVAL MODE

The best method for earning Fight Coins, Survival Mode is a team-based endurance test against several back-to-back matches. The enemies in these matches are randomly chosen from the Team Mode ranking list, so you never know who you are up against. The prize money doubles with every victory, but losing a battle causes you to go home without a dime. You can end your romp through Survival by selecting to quit in between bouts, which allows you to walk away with the Fol you have. Gauge how well you're doing in matches and leave early if you're performing poorly.

Completing Every Survival Match: 512 Fight Coins

TEAM ITEM SETS

Offensive Set	Compact Poison Bomb x 20, Deluxe Freezing Bomb x 2, Wide-Range EM Bomb x 8, Mixed Syrup x 8.
Curative Set	Bigberries x 20, Physical Stimulant x 8, Blackberries x 16, Fresh Sage x 4.
Strategic Set	Hyper Potion x 10, Element Breaker x 12, Riot Potion x 20, Gambleberries x 20.

After acquiring a bunny by completing the "Listless Bunny" quest, you can take part in the cutest, fuzziest, most darling race that's ever been witnessed by Astralian eyes: the Bunny Races. Take control of your love-infused bunny and race him against four other competitors in a heart-pounding contest of passion. The ultimate goal is to win first place (or watch cute things hop, whichever you prefer), which earns either Fight Coins or the rare **Bunny Champion Medal** (in class 100 only).

Race Classes

Race Type	FC Cost	Difficulty
Class 5	5 Coins	Easy
Class 20	20 Coins	Moderate
Class 100	100 Coins	Hard

BUNNY CONTROLS

As the bunny's manager and loving owner, you surprisingly don't have any control over the bunny's movements during a race; you can only help them out by initiating one of two actions: the dash or the jump. The dash, performed by pressing ✕ or Ⓐ, is a quick burst of movement that drains some of the bunny's stamina. This is used as a general method of keeping the bunny from slowing down, and for making speedy turns around corners. The jump attack, done by pressing ⬤ or Ⓑ, stuns every grounded bunny in the area at random. This is used to halt the progression of the other bunnies on the track; however, the shockwave caused from the jump can be avoided if an opponent is airborne.

Since this is the case, use jumps mainly as a method of countering your opponent's jumps. If you hear a nearby opponent jump (listen for a delightful "boing" noise), immediately perform a jump yourself. Not only will your bunny's initial jump avoid the ground tremor, but the quake you produce when you land then hits the recovering opponent.

TRAINING YOUR BUNNY

Bunnies need more than just a good pilot; they require a strange diet of pies. Pressing ✕ or Ⓐ next to your bunny opens its status menu. From here, feeding them certain pies raises their various attributes, improving movement speed and acceleration, or increasing the recharge rate of their stamina bar. The maximum strength your bunny can have in any area is 200. You'll need a stamina and speed rating of at least 170 to complete the class 100 race, so spend a lot of time in Item Creation to make the pies you need. Refer to the table below for info on how pies improve each attribute.

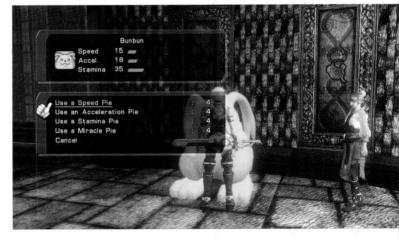

Pie Types and Effects

Pie	Effect
Speed Pie	Adds 3 points to the bunny's speed rating.
Acceleration Pie	Adds 3 points to the bunny's acceleration rating.
Stamina Pie	Adds 3 points to the bunny's stamina rating.
Miracle Pie	Adds 3 points to any one of the bunny's stats at random.

Bunny Races

① **Name:** The name of the skill.

② **Max Lv:** The maximum amount of skill levels the ability can be increased by. Skills with a 1 in this field cannot be leveled up. The number shown will always be 1 or 10. Leveling your skills up improves their effectiveness while also raising the MP needed to use them.

③ **Damage:** The amount of damage dealt by the symbol. The number value shown is multiplied by a character's INT to get the final damage amount. Symbols that inflict no damage have a "None" written here. Fields with two numbers represent the damage range between the level 1 and level 10 versions of the skill. For example, the damage calculation for Faize's Earth Glaive is listed as INT x195%~260%. The first number, 195, is the level 1 strength of the skill, while the second number is the level 10 value.

④ **MP Cost:** The amount of MP required to use the skill. Two values are listed here if the skill's MP cost increases at higher levels, the first number being the level 1 MP cost, while the second is the MP requirement at level 10.

⑤ **CP Cost:** The capacity points necessary to equip the skill in battle configuration.

⑥ **Used By:** Shows which characters are capable of learning the skill in question.

⑦ **Notes:** Various bits of information about the skill that range from specific effect properties to info about the inputs needed to use it.

① Name	② Max Lv	③ Damage	④ MP Cost	⑤ CP Cost	⑥ Used By	⑦ Notes
Earth Glaive	10	INT x195%~260%	5~14	3	Faize, Arumat	Attack symbol ⬤. Blades of stone burst forth from under the enemy's feet.
Stone Rain	10	INT x195%~430%	7~16	4	Faize, Arumat	Attack symbol ⬤. Countless rocks rain down upon the enemy.
Terra Hammer	10	INT x304%~672%	21~30	--	Faize, Arumat	Attack symbol ⬤. Digs up three giant boulders and smashes them into the ground.
Ice Needles	10	INT x312%~532%	5~14	2	Faize, Myuria	Attack symbol ⬤. Launches six needles of ice at the enemy.
Deep Freeze	10	INT x161%~281%	7~16	4	Faize, Myuria	Attack symbol ⬤. Cools the air surrounding the enemy, freezing it from the ground up.

Field Skills

Name	Max Lv	MP Cost	Used By	Notes
Smithery	10	--	Edge	Item Creation skill. Allows you to craft metallic weapons and armor. At higher levels, more types of items become available.
Cooking	10	--	Reimi	Item Creation skill. Allows you to prepare food items. At higher skill levels, more types of items become available.
Alchemy	10	--	Faize, Arumat	Item Creation skill. Allows you to forge metal into other materials. At higher skill levels, more types of items become available.
Artistry	10	--	Lymle	Item Creation skill. Allows you to create symbol cards and other symbology-related items. At higher levels, more types of items become available.
Engineering	10	--	Bacchus	Item Creation skill. Allows you to craft mechanical equipment and items such as bombs. At higher levels, more types of items become available.
Crafting	10	--	Meracle	Item Creation skill. Allows you to craft lightweight equipment and accessories. At higher skill levels, more types of items become available.
Compounding	10	--	Myuria	Item Creation skill. Allows you to create medicinal items. At higher skill levels, more types of items become available.
Synthesis	1	--	Sarah	Item Creation skill. Allows you to merge equipment with other items to synthesize even stronger equipment.
Anthropology	10	--	Edge	Increases chance of earning items after defeating humanoid enemies. At higher levels, the effect increases. Once the skill is learned, its effect is always active.
Botany	10	--	Reimi	Increases the chance of earning items after defeating plant enemies. At higher skill levels, the effect increases. Once the skill is learned, its effect is always active.
Entomology	10	--	Faize, Arumat	Increases the chance of earning items after defeating insect enemies. At higher skill levels, the effect increases. Once the skill is learned, its effect is always active.
Parapsychology	10	--	Lymle	Increases the chance of earning items after defeating undead enemies. At higher skill levels, the effect increases. Once the skill is learned, its effect is always active.
Robotics	10	--	Bacchus	Increases the chance of earning items after defeating mechanical enemies. At higher skill levels, the effect increases. Once the skill is learned, its effect is always active.
Ornithology	10	--	Meracle	Increases the chance of earning items after defeating avian enemies. At higher skill levels, the effect increases. Once the skill is learned, its effect is always active.
Demonology	10	--	Myuria	Increases the chance of earning items after defeating demon enemies. At higher skill levels, the effect increases. Once the skill is learned, its effect is always active.
Zoology	10	--	Sarah	Increases the chance of earning items after defeating animal enemies. At higher skill levels, the effect increases. Once the skill is learned, its effect is always active.
Appetite	10	--	Edge, Meracle	Adds a bonus to the effect of HP recovery items. At higher skill levels, the effect increases. Once the skill is learned, its effect level is always active.
Haggling	10	--	Myuria	Increases the amount of Fol received when selling items at shops by 5% over the original selling price at level 1. At level 10, the amount is increased by 30%. Once the skill is learned, its effect is always active.
Chain Combos	10	--	All	Allows you to assign multiple skills to a chain combo. At higher skill levels, the number of slots and the amount of damage dealt increases. Once the skill is learned, its effect is always active.
Pickpocketing	10	--	Edge	Allows you to steal items and Fol from others. At higher skill levels, the chance of success increases. To use this skill, press the ⬤ or Ⓑ button while wearing the Bandit's Gloves. Be careful not to steal too much…
Sprinting	1	--	Edge	Allows you to run faster on the field for a limited distance. Press the ⬤ or Ⓧ button while running to use.
Harvesting	10	--	Reimi	Allows you to harvest items at harvesting points. Press the ⬤ or Ⓑ button at a harvesting point to use. At higher skill levels, the number of items you can harvest increases.
Duplication	10	--	Faize, Arumat	Allows you to duplicate items using Magical Clay. At higher skill levels, the amount of clay needed decreases. Some items cannot be duplicated.
Treasure Sense	1	--	Lymle	Displays the locations of treasure chests and harvesting points on the minimap. Once the skill is learned, its effect is always active.
Recharge	10	--	Lymle	Allows you to use a Disintegration Stone to charge a Disintegration Ring. One use adds two charges.
Trap Evasion	10	--	Bacchus	Reduces the amount of damage taken from traps on the field. At higher levels, the effect increases. Once the skill is learned, its effect is always active.
Mining	10	--	Bacchus	Allows you to mine ores at mining points. Press the ⬤ or Ⓑ button at a mining point to use. At higher levels, the number of items you can mine increases.
Stealth	10	--	Bacchus	Allows you to hide from enemies on the field for a limited time. At higher levels, the duration of the stealth effect increases. If you touch an enemy, you'll enter into battle.
Ocarina	1	1	Meracle	Allows you to attract nearby enemies by playing an alluring melody with the ocarina.
Augury	10	--	Sarah	Allows you to listen to Eleyna's auguries anywhere you like. Auguries are special tips that come straight from Eleyna herself. There are 62 auguries in all, each appearing at random.
Bunny Call	1	--	Sarah	Allows you to summon a bunny to ride on the field. Requires Bunny Feed.

Battle Skills

Name	Max Lv	MP Cost	CP Cost	Use By	Notes
ATK Boost	10	--	1	Edge, Reimi, Bacchus, Meracle, Arumat	Adds 10 to your ATK at level 1. The ATK boost granted increases as the skill's level increases (granting +1000 ATK at level 10). The effect is only active when set as a battle skill.
INT Boost	10	--	1	Faize, Lymle, Sarah, Myuria	Adds 10 to your INT at level 1. The INT boost granted increases as the skill's level increases (granting +1000 INT at level 10). The effect is only active when set as a battle skill.
HP Boost	10	--	2	All	Adds 100 to your maximum HP at level 1. At level 10, your maximum HP increases by 10000. The effect is only active when set as a battle skill.
MP Boost	10	--	2	All	Adds 10 to your maximum MP at level 1. At level 10, your maximum MP increases by 1000. The effect is only active when set as a battle skill.
Fast Cast	10	--	2	Lymle, Myuria	Reduces the amount of time it takes to cast a symbol. At higher skill levels, the effect increases. The effect is only active when set as a battle skill.
Energy Shield	10	--	1	Reimi, Lymle, Sarah, Myuria	Occasionally nullifies physical attacks. At higher skill levels, the chance of success increases. The effect is only active when set as a battle skill.
Critical Hit	10	--	1	Edge, Reimi, Meracle, Arumat	Allows you to perform critical hits outside of Rush Mode. At higher skill levels, the chance of success and the amount of damage dealt increases. The effect is only active when set as a battle skill.
No Guard	10	--	3	Edge, Faize, Bacchus, Meracle, Arumat	Prevents you from being thrown off balance when taking damage less than 1% of your maximum HP (at level 1). At level 10, the effect increases to 10%. The effect is only active when set as a battle skill.
First Aid	10	--	2	All	When taking damage from an enemy, occasionally recovers 20% of damage taken as HP (at level 1). At level 10, 60% of the damage taken is converted. The effect is only active when set as a battle skill.
Auto Healing	10	--	1	All	Gradually restores HP during battle. At higher skill levels, HP is restored more frequently. The effect is only active when set as a battle skill.
Stun	10	--	2	Edge, Faize, Meracle, Arumat	Occasionally adds a stun effect when attacking enemies. At higher skill levels, the chance of success increases. The effect is only active when set as a battle skill.
Pride	10	--	--	Faize, Myuria, Arumat	Boosts status parameters when fighting weaker enemies. At higher skill levels, the effect increases. The effect is only active when set as a battle skill.
Fury Boost	10	--	1	All	Increases the chance of surviving via Fury when your HP hits 0. At higher skill levels, the effect increases. The effect is only active when set as a battle skill.
Elusion	10	--	--	Sarah, Lymle	Allows you to run away from battles quickly. At higher levels, the time needed to escape decreases. The effect is only active when set as a battle skill.
Rage	10	--	2	Reimi, Lymle, Myuria	Increases the chance of becoming enraged when an ally falls, and provides an ATK and INT bonus when enraged. At higher levels the effect increases. The effect is only active when set as a battle skill.
Steal	10	--	1	Meracle, Myuria	Occasionally steals an item when attacking enemies. At higher skill levels, the chance of success increases. The effect is only active when set as a battle skill.
Taunt	1	1	--	Edge, Reimi, Bacchus, Meracle, Arumat	Attracts the attention of enemies, making them target you more often. Use this skill from the battle menu.
Berserk	10	8	--	Edge, Reimi, Bacchus, Meracle, Arumat	Boosts ATK by 40% for 30 seconds (at level 1), but doubles the damage taken from attacks. At level 10, ATK is increased by 100%. Use this skill from the battle menu.
Scan Enemy	1	1	--	Faize, Bacchus, Arumat	Allows you to view information on the targeted enemy. Use this skill from the battle menu.
Convert	10	4	--	Edge, Faize, Bacchus, Myuria, Arumat	Converts some HP to MP over a period of 30 seconds. At higher skill levels, the effect increases. Use this skill from the battle menu.
Emergency Repairs	10	5	--	Bacchus	Recovers 30% of your maximum HP (at level 1). The effect increases to 55% at level 10. Use this skill from the battle menu.
Focus	10	6	--	Reimi, Sarah, Meracle	Boosts HIT and critical chance for 30 seconds. At higher skill levels, the effect increases. Use this skill from the battle menu.
Hide	1	1	--	Faize, Lymle, Sarah, Myuria	Diverts the attention of enemies, making them target you less often. Use this skill from the battle menu.
Mindflare	10	8	--	Faize, Lymle, Sarah, Myuria	Boosts INT by 40% for 30 seconds (at level 1), but triples MP costs. INT is boosted by 100% at level 10. Use this skill from the battle menu.

Symbol Data

Name	Max Lv	Damage	MP Cost	CP Cost	Used By	Notes
Earth Glaive	10	INT x195%~260%	5~14	3	Faize, Arumat	Attack symbol ●. Blades of stone burst forth from under the enemy's feet.
Stone Rain	10	INT x195%~430%	7~16	4	Faize, Arumat	Attack symbol ●. Countless rocks rain down upon the enemy.
Terra Hammer	10	INT x304%~672%	21~30	--	Faize, Arumat	Attack symbol ●. At level 1, digs up three giant boulders and smashes them into the ground. At level 10, six giant boulders are dug up.
Ice Needles	10	INT x312%~532%	5~14	2	Faize, Myuria	Attack symbol ●. At level 1, launches six needles of ice at the enemy. At level 10, nine needles of ice are launched.
Deep Freeze	10	INT x161%~281%	7~16	4	Faize, Myuria	Attack symbol ●. Cools the air surrounding the enemy, freezing it from the ground up.
Arctic Impact	10	INT x323%~430%	21~30	--	Myuria	Attack symbol ●. Encases the enemy in a giant pillar of ice, then shatters it to pieces.
Fire Bolt	10	INT x117%~390%	5~14	2	Lymle, Arumat	Attack symbol ●. At level 1, unleashes three enemy-seeking fireballs. At level 10, six balls of fire are unleashed.
Explosion	10	INT x272%~485%	21~30	--	Lymle, Arumat	Attack symbol ●. Sets off a large explosion centered around the enemy.
Volcanic Burst	10	INT x433%~721%	10~19	5	Lymle	Attack symbol ●. Summons a swirling torrent of fire from beneath the enemy.
Wind Blade	10	INT x156%~358%	5~14	3	Lymle, Sarah	Attack symbol ●. Fires swirling blades of wind at the enemy.
Tornado	10	INT x250%~464%	7~16	5	Lymle, Sarah	Attack symbol ●. Calls forth an enemy-seeking tornado that sweeps up any foe it touches.
Blast Hurricane	10	INT x225%~408%	10~19	4	Sarah	Attack symbol ●. Summons a great vortex that blows away any enemy caught in its grasp.
Lightning Blast	10	INT x198%~418%	5~14	3	Lymle, Sarah, Myuria	Attack symbol ●. Hurls lightning bolts at the enemy.
Thunder Flare	10	INT x195%~374%	7~16	4	Lymle, Sarah, Myuria	Attack symbol ●. Summons a ball of lightning that envelops and damages the enemy.
Plasma Cyclone	10	INT x355%~507%	21~30	--	Myuria	Attack symbol ●. Conjures up a storm of lightning bolts that streak across the battlefield.
Radiant Lancer	10	INT x169%~301%	5~14	2	Edge, Sarah	Attack symbol ○. At level 1, rains four spears of light down upon the enemy. At level 10, rains seven spears of light down upon the enemy.
Aurora Rings	10	INT x156%~260%	7~16	4	Edge, Sarah	Attack symbol ○. At level 1, erects three pillars of light, damaging any enemy that touches them. At level 10, six pillars of light are erected.
Sunflare	10	INT x478%~560%	10~19	7	Sarah	Attack symbol ○. Irradiates the enemy with a shower of light from above.
Shadow Needles	10	INT x162%~332%	5~14	2	Faize, Myuria	Attack symbol ●. At level 1, launches five needles of darkness at the enemy from behind. At level 10, eight needles of darkness are launched.
Vampiric Blade	10	INT x41%~131%	10~19	4	Faize	Attack symbol ●. Mows down the area surrounding the caster with dark blades that absorb MP.
Dark Devourer	10	INT x375%~646%	21~30	--	Faize, Myuria	Attack symbol ●. Summons a creature from the netherworld and sends it to feast upon the enemy.
Reaping Spark	10	INT x163%~311%	10~19	5	Faize	Attack symbol [non-elemental]. At level 1, creates four black spheres that slice up anything inside. At level 10, seven spheres are created.
Extinction	10	INT x269%~399%	7~16	6	Faize, Myuria	Attack symbol [non-elemental]. Encases the enemy in a ball of light, then releases the energy inside in an explosive blast.
Divine Wave	10	INT x447%~616%	21~30	--	Faize, Myuria	Attack symbol [non-elemental]. Summons a wall of light around the caster, damaging nearby enemies.
Healing	10	--	6	--	Edge, Lymle, Sarah, Myuria	HP recovery symbol. Recovers 31% of one ally's maximum HP (at level 1). The HP healed increases to 40% at level 10.
Ex Healing	10	--	10	--	Sarah	HP recovery symbol. Recovers at least 71% of one ally's HP (at level 1). Recovers 80% of their HP at level 10.
Faerie Healing	10	--	18	--	Lymle, Sarah, Myuria	HP recovery symbol. HP recovery symbol. Summons a faerie to recover at least 26% of all allies' maximum HP (at level 1). At level 10, it recovers 35% of their HP.
Faerie Light	10	--	30	--	Sarah	HP recovery symbol. Summons a faerie to recover at least 51% of all allies' maximum HP (at level 1). Recovers 60% of their HP at level 10.
Faerie Star	10	--	50	--	Edge, Lymle, Sarah, Myuria	HP recovery symbol. Summons a faerie to recover 81% of all allies' maximum HP (at level 1). At level 10, it recovers 90% of their HP.
Antidote	1	--	4	--	Faize	Curative symbol. Purifies one ally of poison.
Cure Condition	1	--	8	--	Edge, Sarah	Curative symbol. Purifies one ally of all status ailments.
Restoration	10	--	25	--	Sarah, Myuria	Resurrection symbol. Revives an incapacitated ally with 22% of their maximum HP (at level 1). Revives allies with 40% of their HP at level 10.
Resurrection	1	--	44	--	Sarah	Resurrection symbol. Revives an incapacitated ally with 100% of their maximum HP.
Enhance	10	--	18	--	Sarah	Support symbol. Temporarily boosts one ally's ATK by 30%. At higher skill levels, the effect duration increases.
Enlighten	10	--	16	--	Faize, Myuria	Support symbol. Temporarily boosts one ally's INT by 30%. At higher skill levels, the effect duration increases.
Angel Feather	10	--	14	--	Sarah	Support symbol. Temporarily boosts one ally's ATK, INT, HIT, GRD, and DEF by 15%. At higher skill levels, the effect duration increases.
Enshelter	10	--	16	--	Sarah	Support symbol. Temporarily boosts one ally's DEF by 30%. At higher skill levels, the effect duration increases.
Reflection	10	--	15	--	Lymle, Myuria	Support symbol. Temporarily boosts one ally's elemental resistance by 3. At higher skill level, the effect duration increases.
Sacred Pain	10	--	17	--	Sarah	Support symbol. Temporarily lowers one enemy's elemental resistance by 4. At higher skill levels, the effect duration increases.
Silence	10	--	22	--	Edge, Lymle	Support symbol. Places the target and nearby enemies in silence status, preventing them from using symbols. At higher skill levels, the chance of success increases.
Void	10	--	30	--	Lymle, Myuria	Support symbol. Places the target and nearby enemies in void status, canceling all support effects. At higher skill levels, the chance of success increases.
Symbolic Weapon	10	--	17	--	Edge	Support symbol. Allows one ally to absorb MP from the enemy with each attack. At higher skill levels, the effect duration increases.

Welcome to the Shop Appendix, a complete list of the stores encountered on your journey. These peddlers offer myriad products that range from life-restoring foods to creature-smashing weaponry. Many of these shops also need favors from your willing party, which come in the form of rare item requests that need to be delivered to them. Please refer to this section when you're looking for quick information on how to complete these quests, or to find materials that you can purchase for an Item Creation recipe.

PLANET: AEOS

LOCATION: EXPLORATION BASE

BASE SHOP: ALPHA

Item List

Item	Type	Price
Blueberries	Usable Items	40
Blackberries	Usable Items	60
Aquaberries	Usable Items	30
Fresh Sage	Usable Items	150
Uncooked Pasta	Other Items	100
Raw Animal Meat	Other Items	80
Common Egg	Other Items	40
Vegetables	Other Items	80
Seasonings	Other Items	40
Olive Oil	Other Items	120

ORDERS

WHITE RICE X 3

Reward	Rarity	From
300	☆	Marie, SRF-004 Crewwoman

You'll find White Rice at the harvesting points on Lemuris. It's also a rare item dropped from the Killer Chelae monster found on Aeos's beach.

PICKLED PLUM X 5

Reward	Rarity	From
500	☆	Marie, SRF-004 Crewwoman

Found at harvesting points on Lemuris.

SEAWEED X 5

Reward	Rarity	From
800	☆	Marie, SRF-004 Crewwoman

Seaweed is dropped off of the Gerels and Killer Chelae found in northern reaches of Aeos.

GAMBLEBERRIES X 3

Reward	Rarity	From
800	☆☆☆☆☆	Marie, SRF-004 Crewwoman

Gambleberries are found at harvesting points on Lemuris: Thalia Plains.

BASE SHOP: OMEGA

Item List

Item	Type	Price
Eldarian Bow	Weapon	500
Silver Bangle	Wrist Accessory	800
Anthropology	Skill	800
Botany	Skill	900
Entomology	Skill	600
First Aid	Skill	2000
Repair Kit	Other Items	100

ORDERS

IRON X 5

Reward	Rarity	From
700	☆	Felius, Eldarian Clerk

The majority of the Iron you'll need is found in treasure boxes throughout your first journey on Aeos. It's also dropped from the Polyphaga monster.

SILVER X 4

Reward	Rarity	From
700	☆	Felius, Eldarian Clerk

The earliest place to get Silver is from the Stone Golem enemy on Lemuris: Van Elm Region. It's also obtainable from the mining points on Aeos, but you'll need Bacchus to get it, who doesn't join your party until well after you've received this order.

LIZARDSKIN X 5

Reward	Rarity	From
900	☆	Felius, Eldarian Clerk

This item is dropped from the Lizard Soldiers and Wise Lizardmen found on planet Lemuris: Thalia Plains.

LEMON X 5

Reward	Rarity	From
300	☆☆	Felius, Eldarian Clerk

Three Lemons can be found in a concealed box just outside of the Exploration Base. You'll find more within any harvest point on planet Aeos.

PLANET: LEMURIS

LOCATION: **TRIOM**

REFLECTED MOON WEAPONS   *SHOP*

Item List

Item	Type	Price
Blessed Sword	Weapon	700
Mystic Chainmail	Armor	1000
Sniper's Bangle	Wrist Accessory	800
Silver Bangle	Wrist Accessory	800
Sacrificial Doll	Neck Accessory	500
Bowstring	Other Items	100

 ## ORDERS

FLAME SWORD X 1

Reward	Rarity	From
600	☆☆☆	Taciturn Old Man

The Flame Sword, a level 1 Smithery item, must be made with Item Creation. It requires a Blessed Sword and Fire Gems (2) to make. Purchase the Blessed Sword from the order's very own Reflected Moon Weapons shop, and find the Fire Gem from the Man-Eating Trees on Planet Lemuris: Van Elm Region.

HUNTING BOW X 1

Reward	Rarity	From
700	☆☆☆	Taciturn Old Man

This level 2 Smithery item requires the Eldarian Bow, Bowstring, and Iron (2) items to make. The Eldarian Bow is bought in the Omega shop on Exploration Base, while the Bowstring can be obtained here at the Reflected Moon Weapons shop. You'll have to get Iron from the Stone Golems in the Van Elm Region.

OYAKODON X 2

Reward	Rarity	From
900	☆☆	Taciturn Old Man

This delicious item is a level 3 Cooking recipe. The Can-Can General Goods store sells the White Rice (2) and Common Egg needed for the recipe. The Raw Animal Meat and the Special Warishita Sauce are found in the Thousand Gods General Store in Woodley.

CAN-CAN GENERAL GOODS   *SHOP*

Item List

Item	Type	Price
Blueberries	Usable Items	40
Blackberries	Usable Items	60
Aquaberries	Usable Items	30
Basil	Usable Items	30
Fresh Sage	Usable Items	150
Hot Chocolate	Usable Items	50
Vile Goop	Usable Items	300
Ge Gen Tang	Other Items	400
Empty Bottle	Other Items	40
Natural Water	Other Items	120
Magical Brush	Other Items	200
Earth Paint	Other Items	80
Fire Paint	Other Items	80
Attack Card	Other Items	60
Support Card	Other Items	40
Alchemist's Water	Other Items	300
Vinegar	Other Items	40
White Rice	Other Items	60
Common Egg	Other Items	30
Vegetables	Other Items	60
Fresh Cream	Other Items	100
Pie Crusts	Other Items	60

 ## ORDERS

CUSTARD PIE X 2

Reward	Rarity	From
700	☆☆☆	Lively Youth

The Custard Pie is a level 4 Cooking recipe that requires the Fresh Cream and Pie Crusts items. You'll find both ingredients right here at Can-Can General Goods.

GINSENG X 5

Reward	Rarity	From
400	☆☆☆	Lively Youth

Ginseng is harvested from the glowing points on Planet Lemuris: Van Elm Region.

CRYSTAL X 1

Reward	Rarity	From
1,000	☆☆☆	Lively Youth

The Crystal material is dropped from the Stone Golem wandering around the Van Elm Region (Lemuris).

TIGER DOJO

Item List

Item	Type	Price
Skill Manual "Botany"	Usable Items	900
Skill Manual "Parapsychology"	Usable Items	1000
Skill Manual "First Aid"	Usable Items	2000
Skill Manual "Elusion"	Usable Items	1000

LOCATION: WOODLEY

THREE LEAF BOOKS

Item List

Item	Type	Price
Skill Manual "Botany"	Usable Items	900
Skill Manual "Parapsychology"	Usable Items	1000
Skill Manual "Chain Combos"	Usable Items	3000
Skill Manual "Pickpocketing"	Usable Items	200
Skill Manual "First Aid"	Usable Items	2000
Skill Manual "Elusion"	Usable Items	1000
Skill Manual "Taunt"	Usable Items	800

WOODLEY WEAPON SHOP VIII

Item List

Item	Type	Price
Blessed Sword	Weapon	700
Torch Bow	Weapon	800
Flame Wand	Weapon	1500
Mystic Chainmail	Armor	1000
Bandit's Gloves	Wrist Accessory	3300
Sniper's Bangle	Wrist Accessory	800
Silver Bangle	Wrist Accessory	800
Sacrificial Doll	Neck Accessory	500
Iron	Other Items	400
Bowstring	Other Items	100

ORDERS

FIRE GEM X 4

Reward	Rarity	From
2,400	☆☆	Wise Old Woman

Fire Gems are a rare drop from the Man-Eating Tree monster in the Silent Forest and the Dragon Newts in the celestial ship.

WOLF FANG X 3

Reward	Rarity	From
300	☆	Wise Old Woman

Saber-Toothed Tigers drop the Wolf Fang. They're found in the Thalia Plains region of Lemuris.

LACQUER X 5

Reward	Rarity	From
200	☆	Wise Old Woman

This item is found at harvesting points in the Van Elm Region. It's fairly difficult to come by, so it might be worth waiting until you can go to the Black Cat Material Shop in Tatroi (Planet Roak), where it can be bought.

IRON SABER X 1

Reward	Rarity	From
600	☆☆	Wise Old Woman

The Iron Saber is a level 2 Smithery recipe. Make it with the Sharkskin (2) material found in the Thousand Gods General Store, and the Iron (3) and Silver materials dropped from the Stone Golem.

THOUSAND GODS GENERAL STORE

Item List

Item	Type	Price
Blueberries	Usable Items	40
Blackberries	Usable Items	60
Mixed Syrup	Usable Items	100
Aquaberries	Usable Items	30
Basil	Usable Items	30
Fresh Sage	Usable Items	150
Hot Chocolate	Usable Items	50
Vile Goop	Usable Items	300
Rich Cheese	Food	180
Ge Gen Tang	Other Items	400
Sharkskin	Other Items	80
Empty Bottle	Other Items	40
Natural Water	Other Items	120
Magical Brush	Other Items	200
Earth Paint	Other Items	80
Water Paint	Other Items	80
Fire Paint	Other Items	80
Mysterious Paint	Other Items	60
Support Card	Other Items	40
Rivet	Other Items	20
Alchemist's Water	Other Items	300
Vinegar	Other Items	40
White Rice	Other Items	60
Raw Animal Meat	Other Items	60
Raw Fish	Other Items	80
Common Egg	Other Items	30
Vegetables	Other Items	60
Olive Oil	Other Items	80
Special Warishita Sauce	Other Items	120
Fresh Cream	Other Items	100
Pie Crusts	Other Items	60

ORDERS

SHORTCAKE X 2

Reward	Rarity	From
800	☆☆	Harried Mother

This level 5 Cooking recipe is made with a Common Egg, Fresh Cream (2), and Blueberries. You'll find all of these items in this very same shop, the Thousand Gods store.

CATERPILLAR FUNGUS X 2

Reward	Rarity	From
400	☆☆☆	Harried Mother

Caterpillar Fungus is acquired from the harvesting points in the Van Elm Region (Planet Lemuris).

MERCURY X 3

Reward	Rarity	From
600	☆☆	Harried Mother

Obtain Mercury from the Horned Turtle monster found on Lemuris: Van Elm Region.

CARDIANON MOTHERSHIP

LOCATION: COMPACT VENDOR UNIT 003

VENDING MACHINE

Item List

Item	Type	Price
Blueberries	Usable Items	40
Blackberries	Usable Items	60
Ripe Berries	Usable Items	200
Basil	Usable Items	30
Fresh Sage	Usable Items	150
Compact Poison Bomb	Usable Items	800
Compact Stun Bomb	Usable Items	800
Compact Freezing Bomb	Usable Items	800
Compact Silence Bomb	Usable Items	700
Scrambling Unit	Usable Items	300
Gunpowder	Other Items	80
Micro Circuit	Other Items	400

LOCATION: COMPACT VENDOR UNIT 050

VENDING MACHINE

Item List

Item	Type	Price
Blueberries	Usable Items	40
Blackberries	Usable Items	60
Ripe Berries	Usable Items	200
Basil	Usable Items	30
Fresh Sage	Usable Items	150
Compact Poison Bomb	Usable Items	800
Compact Stun Bomb	Usable Items	800
Compact Freezing Bomb	Usable Items	800
Compact Silence Bomb	Usable Items	700
Scrambling Unit	Usable Items	300
Gunpowder	Other Items	80
Micro Circuit	Other Items	400

LOCATION: COMPACT VENDOR UNIT 025

VENDING MACHINE

Item List

Item	Type	Price	Item	Type	Price	Item	Type	Price
Blueberries	Usable Items	40	Fresh Sage	Usable Items	150	Compact Silence Bomb	Usable Items	700
Blackberries	Usable Items	60	Compact Poison Bomb	Usable Items	800	Scrambling Unit	Usable Items	300
Ripe Berries	Usable Items	200	Compact Stun Bomb	Usable Items	800	Gunpowder	Other Items	80
Basil	Usable Items	30	Compact Freezing Bomb	Usable Items	800	Micro Circuit	Other Items	400

PLANET: ROAK

LOCATION: TATROI

TOOLS 'R' US

Item List

Item	Type	Price
Tent	Usable Items	4,000
Gunpowder	Other Items	80
Magical Brush	Other Items	200
Fire Paint	Other Items	80
Wind Paint	Other Items	80
Thunder Paint	Other Items	80
Light Paint	Other Items	100
Healing Paint	Other Items	80
Parchment	Other Items	400
Repair Kit	Other Items	100
Alchemist's Water	Other Items	300

ORDERS

OAK X 5

Reward	Rarity	From
700	☆	Elder Who Can See Through People

Gather Oak at harvesting points in the Tropp Area or (in the PS3 version) the Northeast Astralian Continent.

ANTI-SILENCE AMULET X 1

Reward	Rarity	From
4,000	☆☆☆	Elder Who Can See Through People

The Anti-Silence Amulet is made from a level 5 Crafting recipe. The ingredients consist of Ebony (harvest 2 in the Tatroi area), Wind Gem (which is found in various chests on Roak), and Red Herb (buy 4 at Morgan's Weapons in Tropp)

SILVER AMULET X 1

Reward	Rarity	From
1,200	☆☆	Elder Who Can See Through People

This level 7 Crafting recipe requires three ingredients: Silver, Holy Water, and Neck Chain. Find Silver (4) at the harvesting points in the Tatroi and Northern Astralian Continent areas. Holy Water (4) is obtained from defeated Fire Corpses and various boxes in the Purgatorium. Buy a Neck Chain from the Black Cat Material Shop in Tatroi.

FIRE CHARM X 1

Reward	Rarity	From
2,000	☆☆☆	Elder Who Can See Through People

Create this level 4 Artistry recipe with Parchment (2), a Magical Brush, and Fire Gems (4). Get Parchment from the Tool 'R' Us store, the Magical Brush from the Can-Can General Goods store on Lemuris, and Fire Gems from the Fire Corpses in the Purgatorium.

BLACK CAT MATERIAL SHOP

Item List

Item	Type	Price
Lacquer	Other Items	200
Aramid Fiber	Other Items	800
Carbon Fiber	Other Items	1,000
Fur Pelt	Other Items	2,000
Taffeta Ribbon	Other Items	200
Handspun Thread	Other Items	100
Empty Bottle	Other Items	40
Rivet	Other Items	20
Neck Chain	Other Items	80

ORDERS

HOLY WATER X 4

Reward	Rarity	From
800	☆☆	Business-Savvy Shopkeeper

Obtain Holy Water from the Fire Corpses in the Purgatorium.

PUMPKIN CIDER X 5

Reward	Rarity	From
500	☆☆☆	Business-Savvy Shopkeeper

The Spirit Priests in the Purgatorium drop Pumpkin Cider, but it does have a fairly low appearance rate. You can try making it in Item Creation instead, as it's a level 1 Compounding item. Buy the Empty Bottle and Natural Water ingredients at the Can-Can General Goods Store, and purchase Bunny Feed at Ruddle's Place (this store is unlocked by completing the "Ruddle Strikes Again" quest).

SILK X 10

Reward	Rarity	From
10,000	☆	Business-Savvy Shopkeeper

The Harpy monster flying around the Astralian Continent section of Roak drops Silk. It's also easily bought from Mobius's One-Stop Shop in Astral City.

CASHMERE X 8

Reward	Rarity	From
7,000	☆☆	Business-Savvy Shopkeeper

Cashmere is found off of the defeated Harpy, a commonly seen enemy in the Astralian Continent area on Roak.

ROOMY FOODS

Item List

Item	Type	Price
Rich Cheese	Food	180
Natural Water	Other Items	120
Vinegar	Other Items	40
Uncooked Pasta	Other Items	100
Raw Animal Meat	Other Items	60
Raw Fish	Other Items	80
Common Egg	Other Items	30
Vegetables	Other Items	60
Seasonings	Other Items	20
Special Warishita Sauce	Other Items	120
Fresh Cream	Other Items	100

ORDERS

RED HERB X 3

Reward	Rarity	From
300	☆	Peppita, Girl Who Loves to Help

Red Herb is collected from the harvest points directly next to the Calnus's landing spot on Roak. You'll also find it at Morgan's Weapons in Tropp.

MIXED SYRUP X 5

Reward	Rarity	From
200	☆	Peppita, Girl Who Loves to Help

Mixed Syrup is found at the Thousand Gods General Store on Lemuris, but that's pretty far if you're on Roak. Instead, fashion the item with Item Creation. It's a level 1 Compounding item that requires the Blue Seed and Red Seed ingredients. Harvest both ingredients in the Tatroi area.

PICKLED PEPPER POTION X 10

Reward	Rarity	From
1,200	☆☆	Peppita, Girl Who Loves to Help

This level 3 Cooking recipe requires the use of Seasonings, Vinegar, and an Empty Bottle. Get Seasonings at the Roomy Foods store, while Vinegar and the Empty Bottle are found at Can-Can General Goods.

CAESAR SALAD X 3

Reward	Rarity	From
300	☆☆	Peppita, Girl Who Loves to Help

Vegetables (2), Olive Oil, Lemon, and Rich Cheese are needed to make this level 3 Cooking recipe. You'll find Vegetables, Olive Oil, and Rich Cheese at the Thousand Gods General Store on Lemuris. Lemon is only found at harvesting points on Lemuris.

ED'S WEAPONS SHOP

Item List

Item	Type	Price
Blessed Sword	Weapon	700
Silvance	Weapon	5,000
Bastard Sword	Weapon	11,000
Torch Bow	Weapon	800
Icicle Rapier	Weapon	4,000
Flame Wand	Weapon	1,500
Dragonscale Armor	Armor	3,500
Mystic Chainmail	Armor	1,000
Blizzard Protector	Armor	1,200
Comet Robe	Armor	2,400

ORDERS

GOLD X 5

Reward	Rarity	From
7,000	☆	Shopkeeper Obsessed with Knights

Obtain Gold from the mining points in the Tropp area. This includes the Cave to the Purgatorium.

RUNIC METAL X 2

Reward	Rarity	From
2,000	☆☆☆	Shopkeeper Obsessed with Knights

Runic Metal is procured from the mining points in Astral Caves. It's also found in a few boxes within the Purgatorium (B1).

VENOM SWORD X 1

Reward	Rarity	From
1,500	☆☆☆	Shopkeeper Obsessed with Knights

To create the Venom Sword (a level 3 Smithery recipe), Steel (3), Aluminum, Carbon Fiber, and Poison Hemlock (2) are needed as ingredients. Steel is the most difficult to make, since it must be made with Item Creation (level 3 Smithery recipe). Get the Coal needed for the Steel recipe in the Cave to the Purgatorium (or, in the PS3 version, in the Purgatorium Area). Acquire Aluminum from the mining points in the Purgatorium Area, and buy Carbon Fiber in the Black Cat Materials shop in Tatroi. Poison Hemlock is found at the harvesting points in the Astral Desert and the Tropp Area.

MITHRIL X 1

Reward	Rarity	From
1,200	☆☆☆	Shopkeeper Obsessed with Knights

Mithril is a level 9 Alchemy recipe. To make it, obtain Platinum (8), Alchemist's Water (2), and the Symbol Card "Angel Feather." Platinum is mined in Astral Desert, and Alchemist's Water is bought at the Tools 'R' Us store in Tatroi. Unfortunately, the Support Card+ that you need to make Symbol Card "Angel Feather" is sold only in En II's Masterful Materials shop.

NEREIDSTONE X 2

Reward	Rarity	From
6,000	☆☆☆☆	Shopkeeper Obsessed with Knights

If you want to complete this level 7 Alchemy recipe now, you'll have to make Mythril again like the previous order. Ice Gems (4) are mined on Lemuris, and Lezard's Flask is an extremely rare item dropped from the Spirit Priests in the Purgatorium. You can always wait until you arrive at En II's Sanctuary, where it's possible to mine Nereidstone.

LOVESONG ACCESSORIES SHOP

Item List

Item	Type	Price
Bandit's Gloves	Wrist Accessory	3,300
Sniper's Bangle	Wrist Accessory	800
Silver Bangle	Wrist Accessory	800
Earth Armlet	Wrist Accessory	15,000
Anti-Freezing Amulet	Neck Accessory	5,000
Sacrificial Doll	Neck Accessory	500
Warning Brooch	Neck Accessory	1,000

ORDERS

GREEN BERYL X 3

Reward	Rarity	From
9,000	☆☆☆☆	Handmade Craftsman

Green Beryl is found at mining points within the Astral Caves.

SALAMANDERSTONE X 3

Reward	Rarity	From
26,000	☆☆☆☆	Handmade Craftsman

Obtain Salamanderstone from the mining points in Astral Desert.

SHADESTONE X 2

Reward	Rarity	From
20,000	☆☆☆☆	Handmade Craftsman

Mine the Shadestone in the Astral Caves or the Cave to the Purgatorium.

STALLION SNAPS X 1

Reward	Rarity	From
2,100	☆☆☆	Handmade Craftsman

This level 7 Crafting recipe requires Gold (2), Green Beryl (2), and Riot Potions (16). Procure Gold from the mining points in the Tatroi and Tropp Areas on Roak, and snag Green Beryl from the mining points in the Astral Caves. There are several places on Roak where Riot Potions appear in dungeons but, if you still don't have the amount you need, make it by means of a level 4 Compounding recipe. You'll need Nectar (kill Mandragoras), Sweet Fruit (bought in Tatroi shops), and an Empty Bottle (also bought in Tatroi shops) to create it.

GOOD GROCERS

Item List

Item	Type	Price
Blueberries	Usable Items	40
Bigberries	Usable Items	100
Blackberries	Usable Items	60
Aquaberries	Usable Items	30
Basil	Usable Items	30
Fresh Sage	Usable Items	150
Hot Chocolate	Usable Items	50
Glowstick	Usable Items	90
Vile Goop	Usable Items	300
Pickled Plum	Food	20

ORDERS

THORNBERRIES X 3

Reward	Rarity	From
100	☆	Cheerfully-Working Girl

Find Thornberries at the harvesting points in Astral Desert.

RIPE BERRIES X 5

Reward	Rarity	From
200	☆☆	Cheerfully-Working Girl

Purchase Ripe Berries at the Fight Coin Exchange in Tatroi's colosseum, or harvest them in the Purgatorium area.

PHYSICAL STIMULANT X 3

Reward	Rarity	From
300	☆☆	Cheerfully-Working Girl

This item is a level 5 Compounding recipe. The ingredients needed to make it (Blueberries (2), Bigberries (2), and the Empty Bottle) can all be found in Tatroi's shops.

TASTY MUSHROOM X 8

Reward	Rarity	From
200	☆	Cheerfully-Working Girl

Tasty Mushrooms are found off of most fungus-like monsters, like the Mist Grave and Giant Fungus. Both monster types are on planet Lemuris.

FEZ'S BOOKS

Item List

Item	Type	Price
Skill Manual "Entomology"	Usable Items	600
Skill Manual "Ornithology"	Usable Items	1,100
Skill Manual "Chain Combos"	Usable Items	3,000
Skill Manual "First Aid"	Usable Items	2,000
Skill Manual "Fury Boost"	Usable Items	4,000
Skill Manual "Elusion"	Usable Items	1,000
Skill Manual "Taunt"	Usable Items	800
Skill Manual "Hide"	Usable Items	1,200

CHAZ'S BOOKS

Note: this shop is only available after completing the "Missing Brother" quest.

Item List

Item	Type	Price
Skill Manual "Anthropology"	Usable Items	800
Skill Manual "Botany"	Usable Items	900
Skill Manual "Parapsychology"	Usable Items	1,000
Skill Manual "HP Boost"	Usable Items	8,000
Skill Manual "MP Boost"	Usable Items	8,000
Skill Manual "No Guard"	Usable Items	3,000
Skill Manual "Auto Healing"	Usable Items	4,200

RUDDLE'S PLACE

Note: this shop is available only after completing the "Ruddle Strikes Again" quest.

Item List

Item	Type	Price
Sylph's Saber	Weapon	19,800
Resurrection Elixir	Usable Items	2,000
Skill Manual "Energy Shield"	Usable Items	3,000
Skill Manual "Convert"	Usable Items	2,500
Sweet Fruit	Food	200
Quantum Processor	Other Items	1,600
Laser Oscillator	Other Items	3,000
Bunny Feed	Other Items	80

ORDERS

CATERPILLAR FUNGUS X 2

Reward	Rarity	From
5,000	☆☆☆	Ruddle the Traveler

Caterpillar Fungus is acquired from the harvesting points in the Astralian Continent region of Roak.

LIZARD GUARD X 1

Reward	Rarity	From
3,000	☆☆	Ruddle the Traveler

Create this level 5 Crafting recipe with Lizardskin and Handspun thread. Lizardskin (12) is dropped from the ever grotesque Corpse Bat (Astralian Continent area), and Handspun Thread (4) can be bought from the Black Cat Material Shop in Tatroi.

WATER ARMLET X 1

Reward	Rarity	From
2,500	☆☆☆	Ruddle the Traveler

The Water Armlet is a level 4 Crafting recipe that requires Silver (3), Ice Gems (4), and Water Paint (2) to complete. Unfortunately, both Ice Gems and Water Paint are found on planet Lemuris. Acquire Water Paint from the Thousand Gods General Store in Woodley, and mine the Ice Gems from the points in the Thalia Plains and Van Elm Regions. Obtain Silver from almost any mining point on Roak.

MENTAL POTION X 1

Reward	Rarity	From
400	☆☆	Ruddle the Traveler

Mental Potions are made via a level 4 Item Creation recipe. To make it, procure the Ge Gen Tang, Ice Gem, and Empty Bottle items. As with the previous order, Ice Gems are found on Lemuris mining points. Ge Gen Tang is obtained from the Whole Heart Foods store in Astral City. Finally, get the Empty Bottle from the Black Cat Material shop.

FIGHT COIN EXCHANGE SHOP

Item List

Item	Type	Price
Ripe Berries	Usable Items	20
Monster Jewel	Other Items	200
Dragon Scale	Other Items	300
Wild Arc	Weapon	1,500
Mithril Rapier	Weapon	1,900
Crested Spear	Weapon	2,200
Mithril Sword	Weapon	2,500
Dragon Claws	Weapon	2,800
Earthcrest Guard	Armor	3,200
Crystal Armor	Armor	3,900
Mystic Robe	Armor	4,200
Inferno Sickle	Weapon	9,000
Darkblood Chainmail	Armor	11,000
Dark Elf's Robe	Armor	12,000

LOCATION: ASTRAL CITY

MOBIUS'S ONE-STOP SHOP SHOP

Item List

Item	Type	Price
Anti-Paralysis Amulet	Neck Accessory	8,000
Sacrificial Doll	Neck Accessory	500
Warning Brooch	Neck Accessory	1,000
Tent	Usable Items	4,000
Skill Manual "HP Boost"	Neck Accessory	8,000
Skill Manual "Critical Hit"	Neck Accessory	4,400
Skill Manual "Fury Boost"	Neck Accessory	4,000
Skill Manual "Hide"	Neck Accessory	1,200
Iron	Other Items	400
Wool	Other Items	200
Silk	Other Items	400
Satin Ribbon	Other Items	400
Parchment	Other Items	400
Map of Astral	Other Items	1,000

ORDERS

COAL X 10

Reward	Rarity	From
3,000	☆	Jack-of-All-Trades

Mine Coal in the Cave to the Purgatorium and Astral Caves. In the PS3 version, it can also be found in the Purgatorium Area.

LIGHT GEM X 4

Reward	Rarity	From
8,000	☆☆	Jack-of-All-Trades

Light Gems can be obtained from any mining point in Astral Desert.

ASH X 3

Reward	Rarity	From
500	☆☆	Jack-of-All-Trades

Ash is obtained from the harvesting points in the Tropp Area.

THUNDER CHARM X 1

Reward	Rarity	From
2,000	☆☆☆	Jack-of-All-Trades

The Thunder Charm is a level 4 Artistry recipe that requires Parchment (2), a Magical Brush, and Thunder Gems (4). Both the Parchment and Magical Brush are bought at the Tools 'R' Us store in Tatroi. Get Thunder Gems from the mining point in the Tropp or the Tatroi Areas.

WHOLE HEART FOODS SHOP

Item List

Item	Type	Price
Pumpkin Extract	Usable Items	200
Sweet Fruit	Food	200
Natto	Food	300
Ge Gen Tang	Other Items	400
Natural Water	Other Items	120
Uncooked Pasta	Other Items	100
Raw Animal Meat	Other Items	60
Raw Fish	Other Items	80
Common Egg	Other Items	30
Vegetables	Other Items	60
Seasonings	Other Items	20
Special Warishita Sauce	Other Items	120
Fresh Cream	Other Items	100

ORDERS

POISON HEMLOCK X 10

Reward	Rarity	From
3,000	☆☆	Madonna of the Greengrocer's

Gather Poison Hemlock from the harvesting points in the Tatroi and Astral Desert areas.

DENDROBIUM X 2

Reward	Rarity	From
1,000	☆☆☆	Madonna of the Greengrocer's

The beautiful Dendrobium is obtained from the harvesting points in the Tatroi Area.

CURRY RICE X 4

Reward	Rarity	From
500	☆☆	Madonna of the Greengrocer's

This level 4 Cooking recipe requires White Rice (2), Raw Animal Meat, Vegetables, and Seasonings to make. You'll find the Raw Animal Meat, Vegetables, and Seasonings right here at the Whole Heart Foods shop. White Rice is harvested from the Cave to the Purgatorium or from the Purgatorium Area.

NECTAR X 8

Reward	Rarity	From
300	☆	Madonna of the Greengrocer's

Obtain Nectar from the Mandragoras in the Purgatorium Area.

THE HAPPY SKIP GROCERY

SHOP

Item List

Item	Type	Price
Blueberries	Usable Items	40
Bigberries	Usable Items	100
Blackberries	Usable Items	60
Aquaberries	Usable Items	30
Basil	Usable Items	30
Fresh Sage	Usable Items	150
Hot Chocolate	Usable Items	50
Glowstick	Usable Items	90
Vile Goop	Usable Items	300

ORDERS

RED SEED X 5

Reward	Rarity	From
500	☆	High-Spirited Girl

Harvest the Red Seed at the points in the Tatroi area.

BLUE SEED X 5

Reward	Rarity	From
600	☆	High-Spirited Girl

Like the Red Seed, procure the Blue Seed at the harvesting points in the Tatroi Area.

BIZARRE FRUIT X 1

Reward	Rarity	From
2,000	☆☆	High-Spirited Girl

The Bizarre Fruit is a rare harvesting point item in the Astral Desert.

PERFECT BERRIES X 4

Reward	Rarity	From
400	☆☆	High-Spirited Girl

Making Perfect Berries (level 5 Compounding recipe) entails the use of Blueberries (4), an item found at almost any shop, and Holy Water, which is dropped from the Fire Corpses in the Purgatorium.

TREASURE HUNTER WEAPONS

SHOP

Note: this shop is available after completing the "Locked Out" quest.

Item List

Item	Type	Price
Blessed Sword	Weapon	700
Bastard Sword	Weapon	11,000
Torch Bow	Weapon	600
Sylph's Saber	Weapon	19,800
Dragonscale Armor	Weapon	3,500
Bronto Armor	Armor	3,800
Astral Armor	Armor	6,000
Mystic Chainmail	Armor	1,000
Blizzard Protector	Armor	1,200
Streaked Chainmail	Armor	2,400

ORDERS

PLATINUM X 4

Reward	Rarity	From
5,000	☆☆	Careless Shopkeeper

Acquire Platinum from the mining points in Astral Desert. In the PS3 version, it can also be mined in the Tatroi Area.

METEORITE X 2

Reward	Rarity	From
3,000	☆☆☆	Careless Shopkeeper

Meteorite is a level 8 Alchemy recipe. The Runic Metal (4) ingredient is located in mining points within Astral Caves. You'll find Lezard's Flask on the Spirit Priests in the Purgatorium.

RUBY X 2

Reward	Rarity	From
4,000	☆☆	Careless Shopkeeper

This item is found at the mining points in the Tatroi Area and Astral Desert.

ICECRUSHER SWORD X 1

Reward	Rarity	From
3,000	☆☆	Careless Shopkeeper

The Icecrusher Sword is a level 5 Smithery recipe that requires a ton of ingredients. Runic Metal (2) is only obtained at mining points in Astral Caves, while Ash is a common item at harvesting within the Tropp Area. You'll have to fly out to Lemuris's Van Elm Region for Ice Gems (3). Unfortunately, Bracteate is very difficult to obtain at this point of the game, only appearing after the special "The Sand Bird Strikes Back" quest, or within boxes in the Purgatorium. Players of the PS3 version will find plenty of Bracteate in the Astral Caves. But players of the Xbox 360 version may have to wait until the Old Road to the Sanctuary in En II, where the Bracteate-dropping Metal Golem resides.

LOCATION: TROPP

MORGAN'S WEAPONS SHOP

Item List

Item	Type	Price
Silvance	Weapon	5,000
Icicle Rapier	Weapon	4,000
Sylph's Saber	Weapon	19,800
Wand of Wonder	Weapon	5,800
Vermilion Claws	Weapon	5,800
Bronto Armor	Armor	3,800
Streaked Chainmail	Armor	2,400
Volcanic Chainmail	Armor	7,700
Comet Robe	Armor	2,400
Blueberries	Usable Items	40
Red Herb	Usable Items	100

○ ORDERS

ALUMINUM X 5

Reward	Rarity	From
1,300	☆	Sharp-Eyed Man

Mine this item from the points in the Purgatorium area.

THUNDER GEM X 5

Reward	Rarity	From
9,000	☆☆	Sharp-Eyed Man

Thunder Gems are obtained from the mining points around the Astralian Continent, Tatroi, and Tropp areas.

SYLPHSTONE X 3

Reward	Rarity	From
18,000	☆☆☆☆	Sharp-Eyed Man

Acquire Sylphstones from the mining points in the Astral Desert and the Cave to the Purgatorium.

COMPOSITE BOW X 1

Reward	Rarity	From
2,000	☆☆☆	Sharp-Eyed Man

The Composite Bow is a level 6 Smithery recipe created with Carbon Fiber (3), Aluminum, and Aramid Fiber (2). Players of the PS3 version will also have to throw in the Alien Arc bow they found on Alternate Earth, which means they'll only be able to complete this recipe once. Obtain Aramid and Carbon Fiber from the Black Cat Material Shop. Aluminum is found at Purgatorium Area mining points.

RUBY WAND X 1

Reward	Rarity	From
2,000	☆☆	Sharp-Eyed Man

This level 3 Crafting recipe is made with Oak, Taffeta Ribbon, and Ruby. Procure Oak from the harvesting points in the Tropp area, grab the Taffeta Ribbon from the Black Cat Material Shop, and find the Ruby in the mining points in the Tropp Area and the Astral Desert.

RASCAL'S GUILD SHOP

Item List

Item	Type	Price
Skill Manual "Anthropology"	Usable Items	800
Skill Manual "Botany"	Usable Items	900
Skill Manual "Entomology"	Usable Items	600
Skill Manual "Parapsychology"	Usable Items	1,000
Skill Manual "Ornithology"	Usable Items	1,100
Skill Manual "Demonology"	Usable Items	2,200
Skill Manual "Appetite"	Usable Items	1,800
Skill Manual "Chain Combos"	Usable Items	3,000
Skill Manual "HP Boost"	Usable Items	8,000
Skill Manual "Critical Hit"	Usable Items	4,400
Skill Manual "First Aid"	Usable Items	2,000
Skill Manual "Auto Healing"	Usable Items	4,200
Skill Manual "Stun"	Usable Items	3,500
Skill Manual "Fury Boost"	Usable Items	4,000
Skill Manual "Elusion"	Usable Items	1,000
Skill Manual "Taunt"	Usable Items	800
Skill Manual "Convert"	Usable Items	2,500
Skill Manual "Hide"	Usable Items	1,200

⬡ EN II

LOCATION: CENTROPOLIS

IMITATION GALLERY SHOP

Note: this shop does not appear on the Centropolis map. To find it, proceed to the small area on the east side of the map and walk around the shiny building. Move up to the metal chamber to find a hidden door.

Item List

Item	Type	Price
Mysterious Scepter	Weapon	48,000
Grim Reaper	Weapon	39,000
Holy Chainmail	Armor	58,000
Mighty Varigear	Armor	41,000
Sorceress's Robe	Armor	32,000
Sighting Unit	Other Items	500
Bunny Feed	Other Items	80

○ ORDERS

OTHERWORLDLY CUISINE X 3

Reward	Rarity	From
5,000	☆	Shifty Guy

Otherworldly Cuisine is a level 2 Cooking recipe. The 4 ingredients needed to make the recipe are as follows: Insect Leg (2), Insect Egg (4), Rotten Fish, and Vinegar (2). Get both the Insect Leg and Insect Egg from most insect enemies (try the Adephaga on Aeos). Rotten Fish is obtained from the Waving Pincers and Axe Beaks on Planet Roak. Buy Vinegar at the Magical Foods shop right here at the Centropolis.

MYSTERY BOX X 2

Reward	Rarity	From
10	☆☆	Shifty Guy

The Mystery Box is dropped from the Rock Hermit enemy in Roak's Astral Caves.

TRI-EMBLUM X 9

Reward	Rarity	From
2,700	☆	Shifty Guy

Tri-Emblums are found off of defeated Thieving Scumbags, a common enemy in Roak's Astral Desert. Use Edge's Anthropology ability to improve your chances of seeing the drop.

GREEN'S SKILL GUILD

SHOP

Item List

Item	Type	Price
Skill Manual "Anthropology"	Usable Items	800
Skill Manual "Botany"	Usable Items	900
Skill Manual "Entomology"	Usable Items	600
Skill Manual "Parapsychology"	Usable Items	1,000
Skill Manual "Ornithology"	Usable Items	1,100
Skill Manual "Demonology"	Usable Items	2,200
Skill Manual "Zoology"	Usable Items	1,500
Skill Manual "Appetite"	Usable Items	1,800
Skill Manual "Chain Combos"	Usable Items	3,000
Skill Manual "HP Boost"	Usable Items	8,000
Skill Manual "MP Boost"	Usable Items	8,000
Skill Manual "Fast Cast"	Usable Items	8,000
Skill Manual "Critical Hit"	Usable Items	4,400
Skill Manual "No Guard"	Usable Items	3,000
Skill Manual "First Aid"	Usable Items	2,000
Skill Manual "Auto Healing"	Usable Items	4,200
Skill Manual "Stun"	Usable Items	3,500
Skill Manual "Fury Boost"	Usable Items	4,000
Skill Manual "Elusion"	Usable Items	1,000
Skill Manual "Rage"	Usable Items	3,000
Skill Manual "Steal"	Usable Items	19,800
Skill Manual "Taunt"	Usable Items	800
Skill Manual "Berserk"	Usable Items	2,500
Skill Manual "Scan Enemy"	Usable Items	1,500
Skill Manual "Convert"	Usable Items	2,500
Skill Manual "Hide"	Usable Items	1,200
Skill Manual "Mindflare"	Usable Items	3,000

FRONT DESK

SHOP

Item List

Item	Type	Price
Thornberries	Usable Items	100
Basil	Usable Items	30
Red Herb	Usable Items	100
Pumpkin Extract	Usable Items	200
Seaweed	Food	30

ORDERS

BEE STINGER X 15

Reward	Rarity	From
1,000	☆	Nimahl, Flora/Fauna Laboratory Chief

Acquire Bee Stingers from any bee-like enemy. Try the Honeybees buzzing around Roak's Tatroi.

SABER-TOOTHED TIGER FANG X 15

Reward	Rarity	From
4,000	☆☆	Nimahl, Flora/Fauna Laboratory Chief

Obtain this item from the Unicorn Wolf on Roak. You'll find them in the Astralian Continent area.

PERYTON DROPPINGS X 15

Reward	Rarity	From
300	☆	Nimahl, Flora/Fauna Laboratory Chief

Axe Beaks drop this strangely sought-after item. Hunt them in the Astralian Continent area on Roak.

INSECT EGG X 15

Reward	Rarity	From
500	☆	Nimahl, Flora/Fauna Laboratory Chief

Gather Insect Eggs from the Adephaga creatures on Aeos. All versions of the creature drop the item, so slay them all.

TASTY MUSHROOM? X 15

Reward	Rarity	From
600	☆	Nimahl, Flora/Fauna Laboratory Chief

Find this item at the harvesting points in Lemuris's Van Elm Region. It's also a rare drop from the Apprentice Scumbag and Giant Fungus enemies.

VILE GOOP X 15

Reward	Rarity	From
500	☆☆	Nimahl, Flora/Fauna Laboratory Chief

Buy Vile Goop from the Happy Skip Grocery Store in Roak's Tatroi.

ROTTEN FISH X 15

Reward	Rarity	From
1,000	☆	Nimahl, Flora/Fauna Laboratory Chief

Rotten Fish is dropped from the Waving Pincer and Axe Beak monsters found on Roak.

SANDFISH X 1

Reward	Rarity	From
9,000	☆☆☆	Nimahl, Flora/Fauna Laboratory Chief

The Sandfish resides in Astral Desert, just on the shore of the southernmost oasis. It's difficult to see, so walk around the water's edge until the examine button appears.

RAW FISH X 15

Reward	Rarity	From
1,000	☆	Nimahl, Flora/Fauna Laboratory Chief

Buy Raw Fish from Roomy Foods in Tatroi.

WOLF OIL X 15

Reward	Rarity	From
600	☆	Nimahl, Flora/Fauna Laboratory Chief

Wolf Oil is an item that drops from the Saber-Toothed Tigers on Lemuris. They're found prancing around the Woodley Area.

MELTINA JEWELERS

SHOP

Item List

Item	Type	Price
Magic Bracelet	Wrist Accessory	900
Stallion Snaps	Wrist Accessory	3,000
Fire Armlet	Wrist Accessory	15,000
Wind Armlet	Wrist Accessory	15,000
Earth Armlet	Wrist Accessory	15,000
Water Armlet	Wrist Accessory	15,000
Thunder Amulet	Wrist Accessory	15,000
Anti-Poison Amulet	Neck Accessory	8,000
Anti-Stun Amulet	Neck Accessory	4,000
Anti-Silence Amulet	Neck Accessory	4,000
Anti-Pumpkin Amulet	Neck Accessory	5,000
Raven Amulet	Neck Accessory	4,000
Green Talisman	Neck Accessory	4,800
Earth Charm	Neck Accessory	9,000
Water Charm	Neck Accessory	9,000
Fire Charm	Neck Accessory	9,000
Wind Charm	Neck Accessory	9,000
Thunder Charm	Neck Accessory	9,000

ORDERS

SLAYER'S BANGLE X 2

Reward	Rarity	From
10,000	☆☆☆☆	Dazzling Woman

The Slayer's Bangle is a level 9 Crafting recipe with three ingredients: Platinum (4), Thunder Gems (4), and Bracteate. Mine Platinum at Astral Desert, and Thunder Gems on Roak's Astralian Continent. Bracteate is obtained from the Metal Golem, an enemy in the Old Road to the Sanctuary. In the PS3 version, it can also be found in chests throughout the Astral Caves.

DARKNESS SCARF X 3

Reward	Rarity	From
30,000	☆☆	Dazzling Woman

This level 5 Crafting item is comprised of Manacloth, Shadestone, and a Darkness Charm (2). Manacloth is dropped off of the Master Wizards in En II's Sanctuary. Acquire Shadestone from mining points within the Cave to the Purgatorium and the Purgatorium area. A Darkness Charm can be found on Nox Obscurus, but you'll probably need to make a copy (the recipe is also found on Nox Obscurus). It requires Parchment (2), a Magical Brush, and Darkness Gems (5). Obtain Parchment and the Magical Brush from the Masterful Materials store in the shopping mall, and Darkness Gems from mining points on Nox Obscurus.

ANTI-CURSE AMULET X 3

Reward	Rarity	From
12,000	☆☆☆☆	Dazzling Woman

Anti-Curse Amulets are a level 6 Crafting recipe with three ingredients: Ebony (2), a Darkness Gem, and Holy Water (4). Ebony is harvested in the Tatroi and Tropp areas, while Darkness Gems are obtained from mining points in the Miga Insect Warren, a cave on Aeos. Acquire Holy Water from Min Min's Rejuvenation Shop right here on Aeos.

DEMON AMULET X 3

Reward	Rarity	From
2,000	☆☆☆	Dazzling Woman

To make this level 6 Crafting recipe, procure Runic Metal (2) from the mining points in Astral Caves, Holy Water (4) from Min Min's Rejuvenation Shop, and a Neck Chain from Tatroi's Black Cat Material Shop.

LIGHT CHARM X 2

Reward	Rarity	From
6,000	☆☆☆☆	Dazzling Woman

Create this level 8 Artistry recipe with the Parchment, Magical Brush, and Fire Gem items. Acquire the Parchment (2) and Magical Brush from the Masterful Materials shop in the Centropolis. Light Gems are mined from points on Roak, most notably the Tatroi Area and the Astral Desert. They're also found in the Miga Insect Warren.

SILKWORM'S RETRO SHOP

Item List

Item	Type	Price
Blessed Sword	Weapon	700
Silvance	Weapon	5,000
Bastard Sword	Weapon	11,000
Eldarian Bow	Weapon	500
Torch Bow	Weapon	800
Alien Arc	Weapon	5,400
Icicle Rapier	Weapon	4,000
Flame Wand	Weapon	1,500
Wand of Wonder	Weapon	5,800
Vermilion Claws	Weapon	5,800
Dragonscale Armor	Armor	3,500
Bronto Armor	Armor	3,800
Mystic Chainmail	Armor	1,000
Blizzard Protector	Armor	1,200
Streaked Chainmail	Armor	2,400
Aqua Robe	Armor	800
Comet Robe	Armor	2,400
Bandit's Gloves	Wrist Accessory	3,300
Sniper's Bangle	Wrist Accessory	800
Silver Bangle	Wrist Accessory	800
Sacrificial Doll	Neck Accessory	500
Warning Brooch	Neck Accessory	1,000
Alchemist's Water	Other Items	300

ORDERS

EARTHSOUL BOW X 1

Reward	Rarity	From
3,000	☆☆☆	Hardcore Collector

A Torch Bow, Earth Gems (2), and Iron (2) are needed to make this level 4 Smithery recipe. Buy the Torch Bow right here at Silkworm's Retro Shop. Take a trip out to Aeos for Earth Gems and Iron, which are excavated from mining points in the Southern Reaches area.

RUNE WAND X 1

Reward	Rarity	From
12,000	☆☆☆	Hardcore Collector

The Rune Wand is a level 5 Crafting recipe that requires Runic Metal, Ash, Bracteate, and a Velvet Ribbon to make. Obtain Runic Metal and Ash from the mining and harvesting points on Nox Obscurus: Pulsating Bog. Bracteate is a rare drop from the Dark Soldiers occupying the same area. Finally, purchase the Velvet Ribbon from the Masterful Materials shop right here on En II.

STAFF OF FREEZING X 2

Reward	Rarity	From
30,000	☆☆☆	Hardcore Collector

The Staff of Freezing is a level 4 Crafting recipe that requires Ash (2), Bracteate, a Magic Capacitor, and Ice Gems (4). Acquire Ash from the Pulsating Bog on Nox Obscurus. Bracteate can be obtained in the same area from Dark Soldiers. The Magic Capacitor is bought from the Flaming Fist Explosives shop right here in the shopping mall. Unfortunately, Ice Gems can only be gathered from mining points on Planet Lemuris. Try the snowy Woodley Area for the best results.

SHELL ARMOR X 2

Reward	Rarity	From
800	☆☆	Hardcore Collector

To create Shell Armor, a level 1 Smithery recipe, gather Iron (4) and a Warped Carapace (2). You can buy all of the Iron you need at Mobius's One-Stop Shop in Astral City (Planet Roak). Procure the Warped Carapace from the Waving Pincers along the way (Astralian Continent region).

IRON PROTECTOR X 3

Reward	Rarity	From
500	☆☆	Hardcore Collector

Four pieces of Iron and a single SRF Protector are needed for this level 2 Smithery recipe. Reimi starts with the SRF Protector, so all you need is the Iron. Get it from Mobius's One-Stop Shop on Roak.

PROTECTIVE ROBE X 2

Reward	Rarity	From
9,000	☆☆☆	Hardcore Collector

The Protective Robe is a level 3 Crafting recipe made with Silk, Handspun Thread, and Dwarven Embroidery Thread. Buy Silk from Mobius's One-Stop Shop in Astral City, and Handspun Thread from the Black Cat Material Shop in Tatroi. Get the Dwarven Embroidery Thread at the Masterful Materials store right here in the shopping mall.

STURDY BRACELET X 10

Reward	Rarity	From
12,000	☆	Hardcore Collector

You need two ingredients to make this level 3 Crafting recipe: (2) Platinum and an Earth Gem. Acquire Platinum from the mining points in Astral Desert. The Earth Gem is a common material mined on Aeos: Southern Reaches.

RED CLAW WEAPONS

Item List

Item	Type	Price
Watcher's Sword	Weapon	36,000
Saint's Bow	Weapon	33,000
Sylph's Saber	Weapon	19,800
Booster Wand	Weapon	3,000
Plasma Cannon	Weapon	4,000
TO8 Lightning Cannon	Weapon	36,000
Slasher Claws	Weapon	48,000
Watcher's Spear	Weapon	51,000

◯ ORDERS

SPIRIT BOW "DARKSTRIKER" X 1

Reward	Rarity	From
20,000	☆☆☆☆	Man Who Knows Too Much

The Spirit Bow is a level 9 Smithery recipe that initially doesn't have a name (appearing only as question marks in the menu). To make it, you need Carbon Fiber (4), All-Purpose Ceramic (3), Aramid Fiber (2), and Darkness Gems (6). In the PS3 version of the game, you'll also need a Darkness Charm.

Acquire Carbon Fiber and Aramid Fiber from the Black Cat Materials shop in Tatroi, nab All-Purpose Ceramic from the Masterful Materials store at the Centropolis, and harvest Darkness Gems from mining points on Nox Obscurus. A Darkness Charm and the recipe to make more can also be found on Nox Obscurus.

WAND OF RESONANCE X 1

Reward	Rarity	From
30,000	☆☆☆	Man Who Knows Too Much

This level 8 Crafting recipe is made with Cane, a Satin Ribbon, Star Sapphire, and a Symbol Booster. Cane is best found in the harvesting points on Aeos (Southern Reaches), while the Satin Ribbon can be bought from Mobius's One-Stop Shop. The Star Sapphire is mined from the points in Nox Obscurus's Halls of Termination. The final ingredient, the Symbol Booster, is a rare item drop from the Phantom Dragoon. They're also found in the Halls of Termination.

DRAGOON BLASTER X 1

Reward	Rarity	From
25,000	☆☆☆☆	Man Who Knows Too Much

The powerful Dragoon Blaster, a level 6 Engineering recipe, consists of four ingredients: Mithril (4), Mystery Electronic Circuit (4), Micro Hadron Collider(1), and Dragonblood Crystals (3). Masterful Materials also sells the Velvet Ribbon you'll need to complete this recipe in the PS3 version of the game. Mithril is obtained from mining points in En II's Sanctuary. The Electronic Circuit and Micro Hadron Collider are acquired at the Flaming Fist Explosives store at the Centropolis. You'll find Dragonblood Crystals by defeating Master Wizards in the Old Road to the Sanctuary. Star Rubies can be mined throughout Nox Obscurus.

SACRED SPEAR X 1

Reward	Rarity	From
30,000	☆☆☆	Man Who Knows Too Much

Sacred Spears are made via a level 7 Smithery recipe. Obtain the Meteorite (2) needed for it by mining it in the Miga Insect Warren, or by defeating Lava Golems in the Palace of Creation. Carbon Fiber is sold at the Black Cat Material Shop in Tatroi, and Angelstone can be found at mining points in En II's Sanctuary. In the PS3 version, you'll also need one of the Crystal Skulls that can be mined at the Pulsating Bog or Halls of Termination in Nox Obscurus.

QUADPLEX SCYTHE X 1

Reward	Rarity	From
40,000	☆☆☆	Man Who Knows Too Much

The Quadplex Scythe is a level 8 Engineering recipe that needs Meteorite (2), Laser Oscillators (5), and a Star Sapphire to build. Meteorite is found at mining points in the Miga Insect Warren, or acquired by defeating Lava Golems in the Palace of Creation. The Laser Oscillator is found at Ruddle's Place, a store in Tatroi that only opens up after completing the "Ruddle Strikes Again" quest. The final material, Star Sapphire, is mined at the points in Nox Obscurus's Halls of Termination.

D. FENSE'S DEFENSIVE TOOLS

SHOP

Item List

Item	Type	Price
Astral Armor	Armor	6,000
Majestic Armor	Armor	8,000
Earthrock Mail	Armor	10,800
Duel Armor	Armor	36,000
Volcanic Chainmail	Armor	7,700
Star Protector	Armor	34,500
Alien's Robe	Armor	3,300
Flare Robe	Armor	10,000
Feathered Robe	Armor	12,000

ORDERS

OGRE'S ARMOR X 2

Reward	Rarity	From
12,000	☆☆☆	Armor Shopkeeper

The ingredient-heavy Ogre's Armor is a level 7 Smithery recipe. Forging the item requires the use of All-Purpose Ceramic (2), Rivets (8), Gold, Aluminum, and Steel (12). All-Purpose Ceramic is bought at the Masterful Materials store here in the shopping mall, along with the Rivets, which are found at the Flaming Fist Explosives shop. Obtain Gold by mining almost anywhere on Roak, while Aluminum can only be mined specifically in the Purgatorium Area. Steel can only be acquired by combining Coal and Iron in Item Creation.

DRAGON GUARD X 1

Reward	Rarity	From
11,000	☆☆☆	Armor Shopkeeper

This level 7 Crafting recipe only needs two ingredients: Dragon Scale (5) and Handspun Thread (4). Pick up Dragon Scale at the Fight Coin Exchange in the colosseum, or from the Phantom Dragon Newts on Nox Obscurus. Handspun Thread is an item easily bought from the Black Cat Materials shop in Tatroi.

MITHRIL PROTECTOR X 1

Reward	Rarity	From
15,000	☆☆☆	Armor Shopkeeper

The Mithril Protector is created with a level 7 Engineering recipe, which contains three ingredients in the Xbox 360 version: Mithril (3), Rivets (8), and Mystery Mobile Frames (2). Mithril is obtained from mining areas in En II's Sanctuary. Rivets and the Mystery Mobile Frames can both be bought at the Masterful Materials store. In the PS3 version, you'll also need a suit of Star Protector armor, sold at this very shop, and a Mana Ribbon, which can be found in chests or by defeating Master Wizards.

FULLY-TUNED PLATE X 1

Reward	Rarity	From
15,000	☆☆☆	Armor Shopkeeper

The Fully-Tuned Plate is made with a level 6 Engineering recipe. Acquire the Mithril (3) from mining points at the Sanctuary, and buy Rivets (8) and the Mystery Electronic Circuit at the Masterful Materials shop. In the PS3 version, you'll also need a Star Sapphire, which can be mined in the Halls of Termination or dropped by Forsaken Beasts.

EARTHEN ROBE X 2

Reward	Rarity	From
20,000	☆☆☆☆	Armor Shopkeeper

The Earthen Robe is made with a level 6 Crafting recipe that consists of Biocloth (4), Dwarven Embroidery Thread (4), and Earth Gems (8). Biocloth is dropped off of defeated Phantom Beetles, a common enemy in Nox Obscurus. Dwarven Embroidery Thread can be bought from the Masterful Materials store, and Earth Gems are located in the mines on Aeos: Southern Reaches.

MASTERFUL MATERIALS

SHOP

Item List

Item	Type	Price
Tent	Usable Items	4,000
Ash	Other Items	800
Cashmere	Other Items	600
Velvet Ribbon	Other Items	800
Dwarven Embroidery Thread	Other Items	400
All-Purpose Ceramic	Other Items	2,400
Magical Brush	Other Items	200
Earth Paint	Other Items	80
Water Paint	Other Items	80
Fire Paint	Other Items	80
Wind paint	Other Items	80
Thunder Paint	Other Items	80
Light Paint	Other Items	100
Dark Paint	Other Items	100
Nil Paint	Other Items	160
Healing Paint	Other Items	80
Mysterious Paint	Other Items	60
Attack Card	Other Items	60
Attack Card+	Other Items	400
Healing Card	Other Items	60
Healing Card+	Other Items	400
Support Card	Other Items	40
Support Card+	Other Items	300
Parchment	Other Items	400
Fine Parchment	Other Items	600
Repair Kit	Other Items	100
Swept Hilt	Other Items	200
Guitar Parts	Other Items	200

ORDERS

FUR PELT X 6

Reward	Rarity	From
11,000	☆☆	Creative Warrior

Fur Pelt can be bought from the Black Cat Material Shop in Tatroi.

MANACLOTH X 1

Reward	Rarity	From
2,000	☆☆☆	Creative Warrior

Acquire Manacloth from the Master Wizards in the Old Road to the Sanctuary.

MANA RIBBON X 2

Reward	Rarity	From
1,000	✳✳✳✳	Creative Warrior

Acquire Mana Ribbon from the Master Wizards in the Old Road to the Sanctuary.

CITRINE X 2

Reward	Rarity	From
9,900	☆☆☆☆	Creative Warrior

Citrine is a strangely rare stone that's very difficult to come by. The easiest place to get it is from the mining points in En II's Sanctuary, though it's very rare. Another option is to use Pickpocketing on the Psychic Girl in the En II hotel, who also has it. From there, you can use Arumat's Duplication skill to make more of it. Unfortunately, Duplication isn't received until you reach the very bottom floor in the Cave of the Seven Stars.

FAERIE EMBROIDERY THREAD X 4

Reward	Rarity	From
3,000	☆☆☆☆	Creative Warrior

The Cursed Horror, an enemy lurking around the Old Road to the Sanctuary, drops Faerie Embroidery Thread.

MIN MIN'S REJUVENATION SHOP

SHOP

Item List

Item	Type	Price
Blueberries	Usable Items	40
Bigberries	Usable Items	100
Blackberries	Usable Items	60
Mixed Syrup	Usable Items	100
Perfect Berries	Usable Items	1,200
Physical Stimulant	Usable Items	800
Mental Stimulant	Usable Items	1,000
Aquaberries	Usable Items	30
Basil	Usable Items	30
Fresh Sage	Usable Items	150
Hot Chocolate	Usable Items	50
Red Herb	Usable Items	100
Glowstick	Usable Items	90
Holy Water	Usable Items	120
Resurrection Elixir	Usable Items	2,000

ORDERS

SUPER APHRODISIAC X 6

Reward	Rarity	From
10,000	☆☆	Soothing Girl

This delightfully awkward potion is a level 5 Compounding recipe with several components. Find the Tasty Mushroom? (4), Ginseng (2), and Lemon at the harvesting points in Lemuris's Van Elm Region. The Empty Bottle is bought at the Black Cat Material Shop in Tatroi.

GROWTH STIMULANT AMPULE X 3

Reward	Rarity	From
6,000	☆☆☆	Soothing Girl

The Growth Stimulant Ampule is a level 2 Compounding recipe acquired during the Sanctuary's Trial of Love side quest. To produce it, find Ginseng (4) and Caterpillar Fungus (2) at harvesting points on Lemuris (Van Elm Region), and get the Empty Bottle at the Thousand Gods General Store.

HYPER POTION X 5

Reward	Rarity	From
1,000	☆☆	Soothing Girl

The Hyper Potion recipe (level 5 Alchemy) requires an Earth Gem, Ice Gem, Fire Gem, Wind Gem, and an Empty Bottle to make. Earth, Fire, and Ice Gems are all found at mining points on Lemuris,

while the Wind Gem can only be mined at En II's Sanctuary. Grab an Empty Bottle from the Thousand Gods General Store while you're on Lemuris.

LOVE POTION NO. 256 X 5

Reward	Rarity	From
11,000	☆☆	Soothing Girl

The arousing Love Potion is a level 7 Compounding recipe. Find the Tasty Mushroom (4) and Ginseng (2) at mining points within the Van Elm Region of Lemuris. The Vile Goop and Empty Bottle are bought at the Thousand Gods General Store in Woodley.

SYMBOL CARD "HEALING"+ X 8

Reward	Rarity	From
10,000	☆☆☆☆	Soothing Girl

Healing+ Symbol Cards are a level 2 Artistry recipe. Obtain its ingredients, the Healing Paint (3) and a Healing Card+, from the Masterful Materials store at the Centropolis shopping mall.

SYMBOL CARD "EX HEALING"+ X 6

Reward	Rarity	From
12,000	☆☆☆☆	Soothing Girl

The Ex Healing Symbol Card is a level 4 Artistry recipe with two ingredients: Healing Paint (5) and a Healing Card+. Get both items from the Masterful Materials store in the shopping mall.

SYMBOL CARD "FAERIE HEALING"+ X 6

Reward	Rarity	From
12,000	☆☆☆☆	Soothing Girl

As with the last two orders, the Faerie Healing Symbol Card (level 8 Artistry) requires Healing Paint (6) and a Healing Card+ to make. Get both items from the Masterful Materials store in the shopping mall.

SYMBOL CARD "FAERIE LIGHT"+ X 4

Reward	Rarity	From
16,000	☆☆☆☆	Soothing Girl

This Symbol Card is a level 10 Artistry recipe. Obtain both of its ingredients, Healing Paint (7) and Fine Parchment, from the Masterful Materials store.

SYMBOL CARD "ANTIDOTE" X 10

Reward	Rarity	From
1,000	☆☆☆	Soothing Girl

Min Min's shop is certainly giving the Masterful Materials store plenty of business. The ingredients for this level 3 Artistry recipe are again found at the Masterful Materials store. Pick up 2 Healing Paints and a Healing Card while you're there.

SYMBOL CARD "CURE CONDITION" X 5

Reward	Rarity	From
2,000	☆☆☆	Soothing Girl

The Cure Condition Symbol Card is a level 7 Artistry recipe with two ingredients: Healing Paint (4) and a Healing Card+. Get both items from the Masterful Materials store in the shopping mall.

SYMBOL CARD "RESTORATION"+ X 5

Reward	Rarity	From
3,000	☆☆☆☆	Soothing Girl

The Restoration Symbol Card is a level 6 Artistry recipe with two ingredients: Healing Paint (4) and a Healing Card+. As always, get these items from the Masterful Materials store in the shopping mall.

FLAMING FIST EXPLOSIVES

SHOP

Item List

Item	Type	Price
Poison Relief Unit	Usable Items	300
Melting Unit	Usable Items	500
Mobilization Unit	Usable Items	300
Speech Restoration Unit	Usable Items	1,000
Vision Enhancement Unit	Usable Items	900
Dispelling Unit	Usable Items	1,200
Intelligence Breaker	Usable Items	500
Defense Breaker	Usable Items	400
EM Bomb	Usable Items	400
Wide-Range EM Bomb	Usable Items	1,200
Compact Poison Bomb	Usable Items	800
Compact Stun Bomb	Usable Items	800
Compact Freezing Bomb	Usable Items	800
Compact Silence Bomb	Usable Items	700
Scrambling Unit	Usable Items	300
Rivet	Other Items	20
Magic Capacitor	Other Items	800
Universal Device	Other Items	100
Micro Circuit	Other Items	400
Micro Hadron Collider	Other Items	3,200
Laser Oscillator	Other Items	3,000
Mystery Electronic Circuit	Other Items	1,300
Mystery Mobile Frame	Other Items	1,800

◯ ORDERS

PLASTIC EXPLOSIVE X 15

Reward	Rarity	From
3,000	☆☆	Symbologist Woman

Plastic Explosives are found inside the Celestial Ship on Lemuris. Look for shining glimmers of light amongst the ship's ravaged interior.

INTENSIFIED GUNPOWDER X 12

Reward	Rarity	From
2,000	☆☆	Symbologist Woman

Intensified Gunpowder is a level 4 Compounding recipe. Mine for the Thunder Gems in the Astral Desert and Tatroi Area, and buy the Gunpowder in Tatroi. If you have it, you can also get Gunpowder from your ship's Li'l Vending Machine No. 2.

DISINTEGRATION STONE X 8

Reward	Rarity	From
5,000	☆☆☆	Symbologist Woman

The useful Disintegration Stone can be mined from the Southern Reaches of Aeos, but it's much easier to get it from Lightning Corpses. Make your way to the Old Road to the Sanctuary to find these electrified terrors.

STEEL X 4

Reward	Rarity	From
2,000	☆☆	Symbologist Woman

Steel is made with a level 3 Smithery recipe in Item Creation. Get the Coal needed in the Cave to the Purgatorium, and Iron from Mobius's One-Stop Shop in Astral City.

ELEMENT BREAKER X 10

Reward	Rarity	From
1,200	☆☆	Symbologist Woman

A level 6 Engineering recipe, the Element Breaker requires a Resistance Potion, Gunpowder, and a Micro Circuit. The Resistance Potion is the toughest to get, as it needs to be made in Item Creation with the following ingredients: Ge Gen Tang, Light Gem, Darkness Gem, and an Empty Bottle. You can buy Gunpowder in Tatroi, or at your ship's Li'l Vending Machine No. 2 (if you have it). Lastly, pick up the Micro Circuit at Flaming Fist Explosives, this very shop.

MAGICAL FOODS

SHOP

Note: this shop is only available after completing the "Where's the Recipe?" quest.

Item List

Item	Type	Price
Riot Potion	Usable Items	600
Fainting Potion	Usable Items	200
Natto	Food	300
Natural Water	Other Items	120
Vinegar	Other Items	40
White Rice	Other Items	60
Uncooked Pasta	Other Items	100
Common Egg	Other Items	30
Vegetables	Other Items	60
Seasonings	Other Items	20
Olive Oil	Other Items	80
Special Warishita Sauce	Other Items	120
Fresh Cream	Other Items	100
Pie Crusts	Other Items	60

◯ ORDERS

RAW ANIMAL MEAT X 14

Reward	Rarity	From
500	☆	Magical Chef

Raw Animal Meat can be bought from a number of stores, including Whole Heart Foods and Roomy Foods in Astral City and Tatroi.

SHARKSKIN X 12

Reward	Rarity	From
800	☆	Magical Chef

Purchase this item at the Thousand Gods General store in Woodley (Planet Lemuris).

HAMBURG STEAK X 4

Reward	Rarity	From
800	☆☆	Magical Chef

All four of the components for this level 4 Cooking recipe are obtained at Whole Heart Foods, a store in Astral City.

LOCATION: CALNUS: RECREATION ROOM

LI'L VENDING MACHINE NO. 1

SHOP

Item List

Item	Type	Price
Blueberries	Usable Items	40
Bigberries	Usable Items	100
Blackberries	Usable Items	60
Thornberries	Usable Items	100
Mixed Syrup	Usable Items	100
Gambleberries	Usable Items	200
Aquaberries	Usable Items	30
Basil	Usable Items	30
Fresh Sage	Usable Items	150
Hot Chocolate	Usable Items	50
Red Herb	Usable Items	100
Glowstick	Usable Items	90
Pumpkin Extract	Usable Items	200
Holy Water	Usable Items	120
Void Recovery unit	Usable Items	300
Micro Circuit	Other Items	400

LOCATION: CALNUS: RECREATION ROOM

LI'L VENDING MACHINE NO. 2

SHOP

Item List

Item	Type	Price
DANGER! DO NOT DRINK!	Usable Items	100
Poison Cider	Usable Items	100
Frozen Cider	Usable Items	100
Static Cider	Usable Items	100
Silent Cider	Usable Items	100
Cloudy Cider	Usable Items	100
Cursed Cider	Usable Items	100
Pumpkin Cider	Usable Items	120
Gunpowder	Other Items	80
Empty Bottle	Other Items	40
Rivet	Other Items	20
Bowstring	Other Items	100
Swept Hilt	Other Items	200
Neck Chain	Other Items	80
Universal Device	Other Items	100
White Rice	Other Items	60
Uncooked Pasta	Other Items	100
Olive Oil	Other Items	80
Special Warishita Sauce	Other Items	120
Fresh Cream	Other Items	100
Pie Crusts	Other Items	60

LOCATION: CALNUS: RECREATION ROOM

LI'L VENDING MACHINE NO. 3

SHOP

Item List

Item	Type	Price
Magical Brush	Other Items	200
Earth Paint	Other Items	80
Water Paint	Other Items	80
Fire Paint	Other Items	80
Wind Paint	Other Items	80
Thunder Paint	Other Items	80
Light Paint	Other Items	100
Dark Paint	Other Items	100
Nil Paint	Other Items	160
Healing Paint	Other Items	80
Mysterious Paint	Other Items	60
Attack Card	Other Items	60
Attack Card+	Other Items	400
Healing Card	Other Items	60
Healing Card+	Other Items	400
Support Card	Other Items	40
Support Card+	Other Items	300
Parchment	Other Items	400
Fine Parchment	Other Items	600

WANDERING DUNGEON

LOCATION: **WANDERING DUNGEON**

THE SANTA MARIA

Item List

Item	Type	Price
Binding Sword "Shiho Murasame"	Weapon	1,200,000
Fierce Bow "Reppu Shingetsu"	Weapon	980,000
Sky Sword "Ama-no-Murakumo"	Weapon	1,500,000
Nightmare Wand	Weapon	30,000
Divine Wand "Empyreal Reverie"	Weapon	2,000,000
Ogre Cannon "Legion's Howl"	Weapon	1,000,000
Conqueror Scythe "Asura Vajra"	Weapon	1,200,000
Battle Armor "God of Hellfire"	Armor	800,000
Electroshock Gear "War Deity"	Armor	1,300,000
tri-Emblem	Neck Accessory	2,000,000
Skill Manual "ATK Boost"	Usable Items	6,000
Skill Manual "INT Boost"	Usable Items	6,000
Skill Manual "Divine Wave"	Usable Items	1,000,000
Natto	Food	300
Disintegration Stone	Other Items	30,000
Aramid Fiber	Other Items	800
Carbon Fiber	Other Items	1,000
Rivet	Other Items	20
Laser Oscillator	Other Items	3,000
Sighting Unit	Other Items	500
Mystery Electronic Circuit	Other Items	1,300

* This shop only appears on floor 8F and higher — randomly.

ORDERS

ATTACK SEEDS X 1

Reward	Rarity	From
2	☆☆☆☆	Santa, Mercantilean

Dropped off of Kobolds in the Alanaire Citadel, Desert Ogres in Astral Desert, and various boxes on many planets.

INTELLIGENCE SEEDS X 1

Reward	Rarity	From
2	☆☆☆☆	Santa, Mercantilean

Dropped off of the Sydonaist Beta enemy in the Purgatorium, or the Stroper lurking in the Old Road to the Purgatorium.

DEFENSE SEEDS X 1

Reward	Rarity	From
5	☆☆☆☆	Santa, Mercantilean

Harvested in the Northern Coast area of Aeos, or found off of the defeated Horned Tortoise in the Southern Reaches area.

ACCURACY SEEDS X 1

Reward	Rarity	From
1	☆☆☆☆	Santa, Mercantilean

Drops off of the Killer Wasp on Aeos, or the Honeybee on Roak. Can also be Pickpocketed from the Shadowy Dollmaker in Tatroi.

PROTECTION SEEDS X 1

Reward	Rarity	From
3	☆☆☆☆	Santa, Mercantilean

Drops off of defeated Adephaga and Adephaga Drus monsters on Aeos, and off of the Waving Pincers on planet Roak. Also found in harvesting points on Lemuris: Van Elm Region.

HEALTH SEEDS X 1

Reward	Rarity	From
10	☆☆☆☆	Santa, Mercantilean

Obtained from the Mana Yeti and Mist Grave on planet Lemuris. Also harvested from points on Nox Obscurus: Halls of Termination.

MAGIC SEEDS X 1

Reward	Rarity	From
5	☆☆☆☆	Santa, Mercantilean

Dropped from the Dryad monster on planet Lemuris. Can also be harvested in planet Roak's Cave to the Purgatorium.

FERMENTED SUSHI X 10

Reward	Rarity	From
2,000	☆☆☆	Santa, Mercantilean

This level 7 cooking recipe requires White Rice (2) and Raw Fish (2). Buy White Rice at the Magical Foods store in En II's shopping mall. Raw Fish is bought at Whole Heart Foods in Astral City.

Each member of the *Star Ocean* crew member has 100 tasks to complete. These tasks are called Battle Trophies. Each of the 100 undertakings is entirely unique to each character, and range from meaninglessly performing a jump 3,000 times to defeating Ashlay in under five minutes. The rewards for completing Battle Trophies come in the form of additional voice types for each character, the removal of the maximum level cap, and a Capacity Point bonus. If you're the type that loves to complete every facet of a game, this is the job for you.

COLLECTION BONUSES

Extra Battle Voices, Set 1	Extra Battle Voices, Set 2
Level Cap Removal	CP Bonus

EDGE

OBJECTIVES

001 Defeat 100 enemies
002 Attack first five times in a row
003 Attack first with a special art
004 Defeat an enemy using a special art
005 Register 10 preemptive attacks
006 Deal at least 100 points of damage
007 Pull off five Blindsides
008 Defeat an enemy using a wake-up attack
009 Land 1,000 hits in total
010 Deal exactly 55 points of damage
011 Defeat 200 enemies
012 Land 20 hits during Rush Mode
013 Win a battle with nothing equipped
014 Land 10 consecutive hits unassisted
015 Register 30 preemptive attacks
016 Deal at least 500 points of damage
017 Pull off 20 Blindsides
018 Survive three ambushes in one battle
019 Fight as battle leader for 60 minutes
020 Defeat an enemy with a knockdown attack
021 Defeat 400 enemies
022 Attack first 10 times in a row
023 Recover HP to the exact maximum capacity
024 Stay in Rush Mode for 20 seconds
025 Deal exactly 555 points of damage
026 Register 50 preemptive attacks
027 Deal at least 1,000 points of damage
028 Defeat a poisoned enemy
029 Land 10 consecutive hits from in front
030 Land 3,000 hits in total
031 Defeat 100 enemies with Aura Spark
032 Obtain 20 Anthropology item drops
033 Defeat 700 enemies
034 Win 20 colosseum solo battles
035 Land 20 consecutive hits unassisted
036 Defeat an enemy using only leg-based attacks
037 Register 100 preemptive attacks
038 Deal at least 4,000 points of damage
039 Pull off 50 Blindsides
040 Land a 5-hit Rush Combo
041 Survive four ambushes in one battle
042 Win 50 colosseum solo battles
043 Defeat 1,000 enemies
044 Attack first 20 times in a row
045 Deal exactly 5,555 points of damage
046 Land 30 consecutive hits from in front
047 Register 200 preemptive attacks
048 Deal at least 10,000 points of damage
049 Land 10,000 hits in total
050 Land a 6-hit Rush Combo
051 Press 10,000 buttons
052 Squat 200 times
053 Obtain 50 Anthropology item drops
054 Defeat a Grigori with a Rush Combo
055 Defeat 2,000 enemies
056 Land 50 hits during Rush Mode
057 Fight as battle leader for 120 minutes
058 Defeat 200 humanoid enemies
059 Register 300 preemptive attacks
060 Deal at least 30,000 points of damage
061 Pull off 200 Blindsides
062 Complete a perfect Rush Combo
063 Win 100 colosseum solo battles
064 Survive five ambushes in one battle
065 Defeat 4,000 enemies
066 Attack first 30 times in a row
067 Stay in Rush Mode for 30 seconds
068 Deal at least 50,000 points of damage
069 Defeat 500 humanoid enemies
070 Land 30,000 hits in total
071 Obtain 100 Anthropology item drops
072 Defeat 8,000 enemies
073 Survive six ambushes in one battle
074 Deal exactly 55,555 points of damage
075 Land 30 consecutive hits unassisted
076 Defeat 100 enemies with Raging Strike
077 Defeat 100 poisoned enemies
078 Deal at least 70,000 points of damage
079 Pull off 1,000 Blindsides
080 Win 200 colosseum solo battles
081 Land 50 consecutive hits from in front
082 Jump for a total height of 3,776 meters
083 Defeat Ashlay
084 Defeat 15,000 enemies
085 Attack first 50 times in a row
086 Land 100 hits during Rush Mode
087 Fight as battle leader for 180 minutes
088 Deal at least 99,999 points of damage
089 Win 50 consecutive colosseum solo battles
090 Land 99,999 hits in total
091 Press 100,000 buttons
092 Obtain two Anthropology item drops in a row
093 Defeat 30,000 enemies
094 Stay in Rush Mode for 60 seconds
095 Jump for a total height of 8,848 meters
096 Defeat 999 humanoid enemies
097 Defeat own shadow
98. Obtain 255 Anthropology item drops
99. Deal 99,999 points of damage without a weapon
100. Defeat Ashlay within five minutes

REIMI

OBJECTIVES

001 Win without being targeted
002 Land three critical hits in a row
003 Avoid getting a status ailment
004 Recover from poison 10 times
005 Survive incapacitation via Fury
006 Deal at least 100 points of damage
007 Defeat an enemy using only jump attacks
008 Land four consecutive long-range attacks
009 Deal exactly 111 points of damage
010 Win with the Rush Gauge maxed out
011 Take no damage five times in a row
012 Defeat an enemy using a close-quarters attack
013 Land four critical hits in a row
014 Win 20 battles without using MP
015 Strike two airborne enemies at once
016 Land 20 hits during Rush Mode
017 Survive incapacitation via Fury 10 times
018 Deal at least 500 points of damage
019 Recover from paralysis 10 times
020 Land nine consecutive long-range attacks
021 Defeat an enemy using only leg-based attacks
022 Recover from incapacitation three times in one battle
023 Take no damage 10 times in a row
024 Defeat 200 plant enemies
025 Land five critical hits in a row
026 Interrupt an enemy's casting
027 Defeat 20 enemies using only jump attacks
028 Survive incapacitation via Fury 30 times
029 Deal at least 1,000 points of damage
030 Defeat a paralyzed enemy
031 Land 15 consecutive long-range attacks
032 Obtain 20 Botany item drops
033 Defeat an enemy in exactly one minute
034 Land a critical hit from behind
035 Deal exactly 1,111 points of damage
036 Land six critical hits in a row
037 Interrupt an enemy's casting 10 times
038 Win 20 colosseum solo battles
039 Survive incapacitation via Fury 50 times
040 Defeat 100 enemies with Chaotic Blossoms
041 Deal at least 4,000 points of damage
042 Recover from cursed status 10 times
043 Land 22 consecutive long-range attacks
044 Avoid status ailments five times in a row
045 Defeat 300 plant enemies
046 Take no damage 20 times in a row
047 Land a critical hit on an enemy's weak point
048 Land seven critical hits in a row
049 Interrupt an enemy's casting 44 times
050 Win 50 colosseum solo battles
051 Survive incapacitation via Fury 5 times in a row
052 Deal at least 10,000 points of damage
053 Absorb a total of 5,000 MP
054 Land 30 consecutive long-range attacks
055 Obtain 50 Botany item drops
056 Deal exactly 11,111 points of damage
057 Recover from poison 99 times
058 Interrupt an enemy's casting 99 times
059 Land 50 hits during Rush Mode
060 Survive incapacitation via Fury 10 times in a row
061 Deal at least 30,000 points of damage
062 Land 39 consecutive long-range attacks
063 Recover from incapacitation 10 times in one battle
064 Take no damage 30 times in a row
065 Recover from paralysis 99 times
066 Win 100 colosseum solo battles
067 Get three status ailments at once
068 Interrupt an enemy's casting 144 times
069 Absorb a total of 20,000 MP
070 Survive incapacitation via Fury 15 times in a row
071 Deal at least 50,000 points of damage
072 Defeat 500 plant enemies
073 Land 49 consecutive long-range attacks
074 Obtain 100 Botany item drops
075 Defeat an enemy in exactly three minutes
076 Win without ever moving
077 Interrupt an enemy's casting 200 times
078 Recover from cursed status 99 times
079 Defeat 100 paralyzed enemies
080 Defeat 100 enemies using only jump attacks
081 Win 100 battles without using MP
082 Land 60 consecutive long-range attacks
083 Take no damage 40 times in a row
084 Win 200 colosseum solo battles
085 Defeat 100 enemies with Heavenly Flight
086 Interrupt an enemy's casting 255 times
087 Absorb a total of 30,000 MP
088 Land 100 hits during Rush Mode
089 Deal at least 70,000 points of damage
090 Get four status ailments at once
091 Win 50 consecutive colosseum solo battles
092 Land 72 consecutive long-range attacks
093 Obtain two Botany item drops in a row
094 Take no damage 50 times in a row
095 Defeat 999 plant enemies
096 Interrupt an enemy's casting 500 times
097 Obtain 255 Botany item drops
098 Deal at least 99,999 points of damage
099 Land 85 consecutive long-range attacks
100 Defeat own shadow

FAIZE

OBJECTIVES

001 Defeat 10 types of enemies
002 Fight 50 battles
003 Defeat an enemy using only weapon attacks
004 Deal at least 100 points of damage
005 Use an earth symbol on an enemy weak to earth
006 Defeat 100 insect enemies
007 Defeat an enemy using only symbols
008 Get three Bonus Board tiles in one battle
009 Reduce an enemy's HP to 9
010 Cure a poisoned ally
011 Land 10 consecutive hits unassisted
012 Fight 100 battles
013 Get enraged 10 times
014 Deal at least 500 points at damage
015 Defeat an enemy using a close-quarters attack
016 Stun two enemies in a row
017 Blindside two enemies at once
018 Use Antidote within five seconds of poisoning
019 Scan 10 enemies
020 Land 10 critical hits during Rush Mode
021 Defeat 20 types of enemies
022 Fight 200 battles
023 Reduce an enemy's HP to 7
024 Deal at least 1,000 points of damage
025 Defeat 200 insect enemies
026 Stun three enemies in a row
027 Defeat an enemy while in Berserk status
028 Freeze an enemy with Ice Needles
029 Spend a total of 30 minutes airborne
030 Blindside three enemies at once
031 Reduce an enemy's HP to 5
032 Defeat a frozen enemy
033 Fight 333 battles
034 Get enraged 20 times
035 Deal at least 4,000 points of damage
036 Win 20 colosseum solo battles
037 Stun five enemies in a row
038 Get four Bonus Board tiles in one battle
039 Win while poisoned
040 Land 20 consecutive hits unassisted
041 Stab enemies 1,000 times with a rapier
042 Reduce an enemy's HP to 4
043 Defeat 40 types of enemies

044 Fight 500 battles
045 Use a water symbol on an enemy weak to water
046 Deal at least 10,000 points of damage
047 Win 50 colosseum solo battles
048 Stun seven enemies in a row
049 Defeat 100 enemies using only symbols
050 Blindside four enemies at once
051 Reduce an enemy's HP to 3
052 Defeat 300 insect enemies
053 Land a hit on an enemy's weak point
054 Fight 777 battles
055 Get enraged 30 times
056 Deal at least 30,000 points of damage
057 Stay in Berserk status for two minutes
058 Fail to recover stolen Fol
059 Win without ever moving
060 Use a darkness symbol on an enemy weak to darkness
061 Land eight hits with Stone Rain
062 Blindside five enemies at once
063 Reduce an enemy's HP to 2
064 Defeat 60 types of enemies
065 Fight 1,000 battles
066 Win 100 colosseum solo battles
067 Deal at least 50,000 points of damage
068 Get five Bonus Board tiles in one battle
069 Cast Enlighten on one character four times
070 Use Antidote within one second of poisoning
071 Reduce an enemy's HP to 1
072 Stab enemies 2,000 times with a rapier
073 Absorb an earth-based attack
074 Defeat 100 enemies with Terra Hammer
075 Fight 1,500 battles
076 Get enraged 40 times
077 Absorb a water-based attack
078 Deal at least 70,000 points of damage
079 Defeat 500 insect enemies
080 Land 50 critical hits in Rush Mode
081 Defeat 50 consecutive enemies of the same type
082 Land 30 consecutive hits unassisted
083 Absorb a darkness-based attack
084 Defeat 100 types of enemies
085 Fight 2,000 battles
086 Win 200 colosseum solo battles
087 Stay in Berserk status for five minutes
088 Defeat 100 enemies with Reaping Spark
089 Defeat 255 enemies using only symbols
090 Get eight Bonus Board tiles in one battle
091 Win 50 consecutive colosseum solo battles
092 Defeat 130 types of enemies
093 Fight 3,000 battles
094 Blindside six enemies at once
095 Get enraged three times in one battle
096 Deal at least 99,999 points of damage
097 Defeat 999 insect enemies
098 Defeat own shadow
099 Stab enemies 3,000 times with a rapier
100 Defeat 55 Grigori

✦ LYMLE

OBJECTIVES

001 Use a fire symbol on an enemy weak to fire
002 Obtain a Bonus Board tile
003 Defeat 10 enemies with Cerberus
004 Become incapacitated 10 times
005 Defeat an enemy using a close-quarters attack
006 Defeat an enemy using only Fire Bolt
007 Get knocked down 40 times
008 Win without being targeted
009 Keep the Rush Gauge maxed out for one minute
010 Allow all enemies to escape from battle
011 Deal at least 100 points of damage
012 Use a thunder symbol on an enemy weak to thunder
013 Defeat 30 enemies with Cerberus
014 Win with 0 MP remaining
015 Silence three enemies in a row
016 Defeat an enemy using only Wind Blade
017 Deal exactly 123 points of damage
018 Make a Mandragora cry
019 Earn a total of 10,000 Fol
020 Hide 20 times
021 Defeat a silenced enemy
022 Deal at least 500 points of damage
023 Run one kilometer in battle
024 Defeat 80 enemies with Cerberus
025 Become incapacitated 30 times
026 Use a wind symbol on an enemy weak to wind
027 Use Energy Shield twice in a row
028 Get knocked down 100 times
029 Roll forward a total of 10km
030 Strike three enemies with Lightning Blast
031 Obtain 20 Parapsychology item drops
032 Deal at least 1,000 points of damage
033 Get knocked down 20 times in one battle
034 Defeat 100 undead enemies
035 Defeat 100 enemies with Cerberus
036 Absorb a fire-based attack
037 Silence five enemies in a row
038 Win 20 colosseum solo battles
039 Get knocked down 200 times
040 Deal exactly 1,234 points of damage
041 Defeat 200 enemies with Cerberus
042 Defeat 100 "Scumbag" enemies
043 Deal at least 4,000 points of damage
044 Hide 50 times
045 Defeat 10 consecutive enemies with Cerberus
046 Become incapacitated 50 times
047 Defeat 100 enemies with Scorching Star
048 Absorb a thunder-based attack
049 Use Energy Shield three times in a row
050 Get knocked down 333 times
051 Win 50 colosseum solo battles
052 Defeat 300 undead enemies
053 Obtain 50 Parapsychology item drops
054 Deal at least 10,000 points of damage
055 Defeat 20 consecutive enemies with Cerberus
056 Absorb a wind-based attack
057 Roll forward 123 times
058 Summon Cerberus 10 times in one battle
059 Win without ever moving
060 Silence 10 enemies in a row
061 Deal exactly 12,345 points of damage
062 Defeat 300 "Scumbag" enemies
063 Deal at least 30,000 points of damage
064 Defeat 30 consecutive enemies with Cerberus
065 Become incapacitated 70 times
066 Get knocked down 40 times in one battle
067 Win 100 colosseum solo battles
068 Earn a total of 100,000 Fol
069 Get turned into a pumpkin in battle
070 Win while pumpkined
071 Obtain 100 Parapsychology item drops
072 Deal at least 50,000 points of damage
073 Defeat 40 consecutive enemies with Cerberus
074 Hide 100 times
075 Defeat 500 undead enemies
076 Use Energy Shield four times in a row
077 Obtain two Parapsychology item drops in a row
078 Land 10 hits with Explosion
079 Deal at least 70,000 points of damage
080 Defeat 999 "Scumbag" enemies
081 Roll forward 456 times
082 Land 12 hits with Scorching Star
083 Defeat 50 consecutive enemies with Cerberus
084 Become incapacitated 100 times
085 Defeat 100 silenced enemies
086 Win with 1 MP remaining
087 Win 200 colosseum solo battles
088 Defeat the Ethereal Queen
089 Defeat 100 enemies with Trinity Blaze
090 Obtain 255 Parapsychology item drops
091 Deal at least 99,999 points of damage
092 Earn a total of 1,000,000 Fol
093 Defeat 60 consecutive enemies with Cerberus
094 Win 50 consecutive colosseum solo battles
095 Defeat 999 undead enemies
096 Land 16 hits with Scorching Star
097 Defeat own shadow
098 Defeat 99 Metal Scumbags
099 Deal 99,999 points of damage with Fire Bolt
100 Defeat the Ethereal Queen within 10 minutes

✦ BACCHUS

OBJECTIVES

001 Land four consecutive long-range attacks
002 Guard against five consecutive attacks
003 Defeat an enemy with exact damage
004 Land the battle-winning blow 10 times
005 Win in 90 seconds or less
006 Deal at least 500 points of damage
007 Defeat 10 enemies using jump attacks
008 Defeat 100 mechanical enemies
009 Use Emergency Repairs 16 times
010 Defeat an enemy using a close-quarters attack
011 Win a battle in exactly one minute
012 Guard against eight consecutive attacks
013 Defeat an enemy using only melee attacks
014 Land the battle-winning blow 30 times
015 Deal exactly 512 points of damage
016 Deal at least 1,000 points of damage
017 Land eight consecutive long-range attacks
018 Activate Rush Mode 30 times
019 Defeat an enemy while in fog status
020 Defeat 30 enemies without being knocked down
021 Land eight hits with Galvanic Shock
022 Take no damage 15 times in a row
023 Defeat 55 enemies using jump attacks
024 Deal exactly 1,024 points of damage
025 Land the battle-winning blow 60 times
026 Win in 70 seconds or less
027 Deal at least 4,000 points of damage
028 Defeat 300 mechanical enemies
029 Land 12 consecutive long-range attacks
030 Use Emergency Repairs 32 times
031 Obtain 20 Robotics item drops
032 Deal exactly 4,096 points of damage
033 Guard against 11 consecutive attacks
034 Defeat an enemy in one hit with exact damage
035 Land the battle-winning blow 100 times
036 Win a battle in exactly two minutes
037 Deal at least 10,000 points of damage
038 Win 20 colosseum solo battles
039 Activate Rush Mode 60 times
040 Defeat 255 enemies using jump attacks
041 Defeat 100 enemies without being knocked down
042 Stay in Rush Mode for 15 seconds
043 Deal exactly 16,384 points of damage
044 Land 16 consecutive long-range attacks
045 Land the battle-winning blow 10 times in a row
046 Win in 50 seconds or less
047 Deal at least 30,000 points of damage
048 Strike three enemies with Black Hole Sphere
049 Win 50 colosseum solo battles
050 Deal exactly 32,768 points of damage
051 Obtain 50 Robotics item drops
052 Guard against 14 consecutive attacks
053 Land a long-range hit while in fog status
054 Land the battle-winning blow 15 times in a row
055 Defeat 500 mechanical enemies
056 Land 30 consecutive long-range attacks
057 Defeat an enemy using only support mechs
058 Activate Rush Mode 99 times
059 Use Emergency Repairs 64 times
060 Defeat 32 consecutive enemies without being knocked down
061 Win a battle in exactly three minutes
062 Take no damage 25 times in a row
063 Win 100 colosseum solo battles
064 Land the battle-winning blow 20 minutes in a row
065 Win in 30 seconds or less
066 Deal at least 50,000 points of damage
067 Stay in Rush Mode for 20 seconds
068 Land 50 consecutive long-range attacks
069 Obtain 100 Robotics item drops
070 Defeat 100 Kokabiel Spawn
071 Guard against 17 consecutive attacks
072 Defeat 100 enemies while in fog status
073 Land the battle-winning blow 30 times in a row
074 Deal exactly 65,536 points of damage
075 Deal at least 70,000 points of damage
076 Obtain two Robotics item drops in a row
077 Activate Rush Mode 150 times
078 Use Emergency Repairs 256 items
079 Defeat 64 consecutive enemies without being knocked down
080 Win a battle in exactly five minutes
081 Stay in Rush Mode for 30 seconds
082 Win without any player-controlled actions
083 Win 200 colosseum solo battles
084 Land the battle-winning blow 40 times in a row
085 Win in 20 seconds or less
086 Deal at least 99,999 points of damage
087 Take no damage 35 times in a row
088 Land 80 consecutive long-range attacks
089 Win 50 consecutive colosseum solo battles
090 Defeat own shadow
091 Defeat two enemies in a row with exact damage
092 Guard against 20 consecutive attacks
093 Defeat 999 mechanical enemies
094 Land the battle-winning blow 50 times in a row
095 Win in 10 seconds or less
096 Obtain 255 Robotics item drops
097 Activate Rush Mode 255 times
098 Defeat 100 enemies with Godslayer
099 Defeat 128 consecutive enemies without being knocked down
100 Stay in Rush Mode for 120 seconds

BattleTrophies

MERACLE

OBJECTIVES

001 Deal at least 500 points of damage
002 Defeat an enemy using only special arts
003 Land 10 consecutive hits unassisted
004 Defeat an enemy using a wake-up attack
005 Land 1,000 hits in total
006 Fight a single battle for five minutes
007 Defeat 100 avian enemies
008 Attack first with a special art
009 Steal food
010 Deal exactly 777 points of damage
011 Deal at least 1,000 points of damage
012 Defeat an enemy from behind
013 Land 25 hits during Rush Mode
014 Recover HP with items 20 items in a row
015 Land 20 critical hits during Rush Mode
016 Survive incapacitation via Fury
017 Earn 10 consecutive Bonus Board bonuses
018 Defeat an enemy using only leg-based attacks
019 Steal successfully 10 times
020 Land 15 consecutive hits unassisted
021 Land a critical hit from behind
022 Deal at least 4,000 points of damage
023 Defeat 20 enemies using only special arts
024 Land a hit on an enemy's weak point
025 Defeat an enemy while in Berserk status
026 Defeat 200 avian enemies
027 Land 3,000 hits in total
028 Steal an accessory
029 Deal exactly 7,777 points of damage
030 Steal successfully 20 times
031 Obtain 20 Ornithology item drops
032 Deal at least 10,000 points of damage
033 Survive incapacitation via Fury 10 times
034 Prevent an enemy from escaping battle
035 Win 20 colosseum solo battles
036 Win without ever standing still
037 Earn 20 consecutive Bonus Board bonuses
038 Defeat an enemy using only wake-up attacks
039 Land 20 consecutive hits unassisted
040 Steal successfully 30 times
041 Hit a falling enemy with Claws of Fury
042 Deal at least 30,000 points of damage
043 Defeat 70 enemies using only special arts
044 Win 50 colosseum solo battles
045 Land 10,00 hits in total
046 Fight a single battle for 10 minutes
047 Recover HP with items 30 times in a row
048 Defeat 100 enemies with Acrobatic Vault
049 Land 20,000 hits in total
050 Survive incapacitation via Fury 30 times
051 Steal successfully 40 times
052 Obtain 50 Ornithology item drops
053 Steal armor
054 Defeat 300 avian enemies
055 Land 25 consecutive hits unassisted
056 Run 42.195 kilometers in battle
057 Jump 55 times in a row
058 Land 55 hits during Rush Mode
059 Recover stolen Fol
060 Earn 30 consecutive Bonus Board bonuses
061 Steal successfully 50 times
062 Win 100 colosseum solo battles
063 Deal at least 50,000 points of damage
064 Defeat 200 enemies using only special arts
065 Defeat a pumpkined enemy
066 Strike three enemies with Max Shockwave
067 Blindside one enemy 10 times
068 Land 30,000 hits in total
069 Steal a weapon

070 Survive incapacitation via Fury 5 times in a row
071 Pull off 20 Blindsides
072 Obtain 100 Ornithology item drops
073 Deal at least 70,000 points of damage
074 Obtain two Ornithology item drops in a row
075 Spend a total of 60 minutes airborne
076 Land 30 consecutive hits unassisted
077 Defeat 500 avian enemies
078 Survive incapacitation via Fury 10 times in a row
079 Strike five enemies with Max Shockwave
080 Deal exactly 77,777 points of damage
081 Pull off 50 Blindsides
082 Win 200 colosseum solo battles
083 Deal at least 99,999 points of damage
084 Defeat 500 enemies using only special arts
085 Earn 40 consecutive Bonus Board bonuses
086 Defeat Gabriel Celeste
087 Defeat 100 enemies with Drill Spike
088 Land 99,999 hits in total
089 Win 50 consecutive colosseum solo battles
090 Fight a single battle for 15 minutes
091 Pull off 200 Blindsides
092 Blindside one enemy 30 times
093 Obtain 255 Ornithology item drops
094 Land 35 consecutive hits unassisted
095 Land 999 avian enemies
096 Land 120 hits during Rush Mode
097 Earn 50 consecutive Bonus Board bonuses
098 Defeat own shadow
099 Pull off 1,000 Blindsides
100 Defeat Gabriel Celeste within 10 minutes

SARAH

OBJECTIVES

001 Recover exactly 777 HP
002 Defeat an enemy using only weapon attacks
003 Escape from battle 20 times
004 Jump 100 times
005 Land a hit on an enemy's weak point
006 Absorb a total of 3,000 HP
007 Use a wind symbol on an enemy weak to wind
008 Deal at least 1,000 points of damage
009 Cure a paralyzed ally
010 Strike three enemies with Wind Blade
011 Defeat 10 airborne enemies
012 Defeat an enemy using a close-quarters attack
013 Escape from battle 40 times
014 Jump 300 times
015 Defeat 100 animal enemies
016 Absorb a total of 4,000 HP
017 Use a light symbol on an enemy weak to light
018 Deal at least 4,000 points of damage
019 Cure a poisoned ally
020 Win while in the middle of casting a symbol
021 Defeat an enemy using only Radiant Lancer
022 Absorb a wind-based attack
023 Escape from battle 60 times
024 Jump 500 times
025 Absorb a light-based attack
026 Use a thunder symbol on an enemy weak to thunder
027 Cure a silenced ally
028 Deal at least 10,000 points of damage
029 Absorb a total of 5,000 HP
030 Obtain 20 Zoology item drops
031 Defeat 100 airborne enemies
032 Absorb a total of 200 MP
033 Escape from battle 100 times
034 Defeat a frozen enemy
035 Jump 777 times

036 Win 20 colosseum solo battles
037 Absorb a thunder-based attack
038 Revive an incapacitated ally 20 times
039 Cure a cursed ally
040 Deal at least 30,000 points of damage
041 Use 10 healing symbols in one battle
042 Absorb a total of 8,000 HP
043 Cast Faerie Heal on an entire party with critical HP
044 Recover exactly 7,777 HP
045 Spend a total of 30 minutes airborne
046 Absorb a total of 1,000 MP
047 Escape from battle 10 times in a row
048 Jump 1,000 times
049 Get turned into a pumpkin in battle
050 Win 50 colosseum solo battles
051 Cure a pumpkined ally
052 Deal at least 50,000 points of damage
053 Absorb a total of 12,000 HP
054 Obtained 50 Zoology item drops
055 Defeat 500 airborne enemies
056 Absorb a total of 5,000 MP
057 Escape from battle 20 times in a row
058 Jump 1,500 times
059 Defeat 300 animal enemies
060 Revive an incapacitated ally 99 times
061 Cure a frozen ally
062 Deal at least 70,000 points of damage
063 Absorb a total of 20,000 HP
064 Strike two enemies with Tornado
065 Cast Enhance on one character four times
066 Spend a total of 60 minutes airborne
067 Absorb a total of 10,000 MP
068 Escape from battle 30 times in a row
069 Jump 2,000 times
070 Fail to survive incapacitation via Fury 10 times in a row
071 Use Restoration within one second of incapacitation
072 Cure stun status with a symbol
073 Win 100 colosseum solo battles
074 Deal at least 99,999 points of damage
075 Absorb a total of 30,000 HP
076 Obtain 100 Zoology item drops
077 Defeat 1,000 airborne enemies
078 Absorb a total of 30,000 MP
079 Defeat 500 animal enemies
080 Jump 3,333 times
081 Revive an incapacitated ally 300 times
082 Obtain two Zoology item drops in a row
083 Win 200 colosseum solo battles
084 Absorb a total of 50,000 HP
085 Defeat 100 enemies with Blast Hurricane
086 Recover exactly 77,777 HP
087 Absorb a total of 50,000 MP
088 Defeat Satanail
089 Jump 4,444 times
090 Win 50 consecutive colosseum solo battles
091 Strike three enemies with Aurora Rings
092 Spend a total of 90 minutes airborne
093 Obtain 255 Zoology item drops
094 Get turned into a pumpkin in battle 100 times
095 Absorb a total of 99,999 MP
096 Defeat own shadow
097 Jump 5,555 times
098 Revive an incapacitated ally 999 times
099 Defeat 999 animal enemies
100 Defeat Satanail within five minutes

MYURIA

OBJECTIVES

001 Win without being targeted
002 Use a thunder symbol on an enemy weak to thunder
003 Cast a symbol within close range of an enemy
004 Absorb a total of 200 MP
005 Defeat an enemy using only close-quarters attacks
006 Get enraged 10 times
007 Fight for over one hour in total
008 Activate Rush Mode 30 times
009 Defeat 100 demon enemies
010 Defeat an enemy using only items
011 Take no damage five times in a row
012 Defeat an enemy using only symbols
013 Absorb a total of 1,000 MP
014 Successfully cast a symbol 10 times in a row
015 Deal at least 1,000 points of damage
016 Use a water symbol on an enemy weak to water
017 Fight for over two hours in total
018 Defeat an enemy while in Berserk status
019 Defeat a frozen enemy
020 Defeat an enemy over 20 meters away
021 Defeat an enemy via damage from poison
022 Use MP in 10 consecutive victorious battles
023 Recover HP to the exact maximum capacity
024 Strike three enemies with Lightning Blast
025 Absorb a total of 5,000 MP
026 Defeat 10 enemies using only symbols
027 Deal at least 4,000 points of damage
028 Win 20 colosseum solo battles
029 Fight for over three hours in total
030 Activate Rush Mode 60 times
031 Defeat an enemy using three elements
032 Obtain 20 Demonology item drops
033 Successfully cast a symbol 20 times in a row
034 Cast a symbol with no casting time
035 Get enraged 20 times
036 Absorb a total of 10,000 MP
037 Take no damage 10 times in a row
038 Deal at least 10,000 points of damage
039 Use a darkness symbol on an enemy weak to darkness
040 Fight for over four hours in total
041 Win 50 colosseum solo battles
042 Defeat 100 enemies with Shadow Needles
043 Absorb a thunder-based attack
044 Cast 200 symbols
045 Successfully cast a symbol 50 times in a row
046 Absorb a total of 30,000 MP
047 Take no damage 20 times in a row
048 Deal at least 30,000 points of damage
049 Use MP in 30 consecutive victorious battles
050 Defeat 300 demon enemies
051 Fight for over five hours in total
052 Activate Rush Mode 99 times
053 Obtain 50 Demonology item drops
054 Freeze two enemies with Deep Freeze
055 Absorb a total of 50,000 MP
056 Defeat 100 enemies using only symbols
057 Cast Faerie Heal on an entire party with critical HP
058 Deal at least 50,000 points of damage
059 Win 100 colosseum solo battles
060 Fight for over six hours in total
061 Get enraged 30 times
062 Absorb a water-based attack
063 Defeat 50 enemies using only items
064 Get enraged twice in one battle

065 Recover HP with First Aid twice in a row
066 Absorb a total of 70,000 MP
067 Use MP in 50 consecutive victorious battles
068 Take no damage 30 times in a row
069 Defeat an enemy using four elements
070 Deal at least 70,000 points of damage
071 Absorb a darkness-based attack
072 Fight for over seven hours in total
073 Activate Rush Mode 150 times
074 Obtain 10 Demonology item drops
075 Defeat an enemy via damage from poison only
076 Survive incapacitation via Fury 10 times in a row
077 Get enraged 40 times
078 Defeat 100 enemies with Plasma Cyclone
079 Absorb a total of 99,999 MP
080 Obtain two Demonology item drops in a row
081 Defeat 500 demon enemies
082 Take no damage 40 times in a row
083 Win 200 colosseum solo battles
084 Fight for over eight hours in total
085 Defeat 100 enemies with Dark Devourer
086 Defeat 100 frozen enemies
087 Take no damage 50 times in a row
088 Win 50 consecutive colosseum solo battles
089 Freeze three enemies with Deep Freeze
090 Successfully cast a symbol 100 times in a row
091 Deal at least 99,999 points of damage
092 Fight for over nine hours in total
093 Activate Rush Mode 255 times
094 Defeat own shadow
095 Get enraged three times in one battle
096 Cast 999 symbols
097 Use MP in 100 consecutive victorious battles
098 Obtain 255 Demonology item drops
099 Fight for over 100 hours in total
100 Defeat 999 demon enemies

ARUMAT

OBJECTIVES

001 Use Taunt 20 times
002 Deal exactly 999 points of damage
003 Deal at least 1,000 points of damage
004 Win with 5 MP remaining
005 Defeat an enemy in one hit 10 times
006 Defeat 100 insect enemies
007 Pull off 20 Blindsides
008 Defeat an enemy with a knockdown attack
009 Defeat 108 enemies
010 Attack first 30 times
011 Win 30 consecutive battles
012 Defeat an enemy while in Berserk status
013 Deal at least 4,000 points of damage
014 Bury a Scumbag with a single swipe
015 Defeat an enemy in one hit 40 times
016 Deal exactly 4,444 points of damage
017 Defeat an enemy using only symbols
018 Pull off 50 Blindsides
019 Stay in Berserk status for two minutes
020 Defeat an enemy during Rush Mode
021 Deal at least 10,000 points of damage
022 Survive 30 surprise attacks
023 Win 20 colosseum solo battles
024 Deal at least 20,000 points of damage
025 Win with 4 HP remaining
026 Defeat an enemy in one hit 100 times
027 Defeat a cursed enemy
028 Defeat 200 enemies
029 Deal exactly 9,999 points of damage
030 Defeat 400 enemies
031 Obtain 20 Entomology item drops
032 Win 10 battles in a row without taking damage
033 Use Taunt 100 times

034 Deal at least 30,000 points of damage
035 Defeat an enemy in one hit 300 times
036 Defeat an enemy in one hit 300 times
037 Bury a Scumbag with a single swipe 50 times
038 Pull off 200 Blindsides
039 Win 50 colosseum solo battles
040 Defeat an enemy from behind
041 Defeat 666 enemies
042 Deal exactly 44,4444 points of damage
043 Defeat 300 insect enemies
044 Deal at least 50,000 points of damage
045 Survive 60 surprise attacks
046 Defeat an enemy in one hit 10 times in a row
047 Allow all enemies to escape from battle
048 Win with 3 HP remaining
049 Stay in Berserk status for five minutes
050 Land eight hits with Stone Rain
051 Obtain 50 Entomology item drops
052 Win 20 battles in a row without taking damage
053 Defeat 1,000 enemies
054 Guard against 15 consecutive attacks
055 Defeat an enemy in one hit 20 times in a row
056 Deal at least 70,000 points of damage
057 Win 10 consecutive battles with no item drops
058 Pull off 1,000 Blindsides
059 Deal the same amount of damage twice in a row
060 Defeat 2,000 enemies
061 Win 100 colosseum solo battles
062 Attack first 200 times
063 Use taunt 200 times
064 Deal at least 99,999 points of damage
065 Deal at least 30,000 points of overkill damage
066 Defeat an enemy in one hit 30 times in a row
067 Defeat 4,444 enemies
068 Win with 2 HP remaining
069 Defeat 500 insect enemies
070 Fight as battle leader for 120 minutes
071 Obtain 100 Entomology item drops
072 Survive 100 surprise attacks
073 Win 150 colosseum solo battles
074 Bury a scumbag with a single swipe 100 times
075 Defeat an enemy in one hit 40 times in a row
076 Attack first 300 times
077 Defeat 100 cursed enemies
078 Guard against 20 consecutive attacks
079 Defeat 8,000 enemies
080 Win 50 consecutive battles without healing
081 Win 200 colosseum solo battles
082 Obtain two Entomology item drops in a row
083 Win 20 consecutive battles with no item drops
084 Guard against 30 consecutive attacks
085 Defeat an enemy in one hit 50 times in a row
086 Defeat 999 insect enemies
087 Win with 1 HP remaining
088 Defeat own shadow
089 Defeat 15,000 enemies
090 Deal at least 90,000 points of overkill damage
091 Win 50 consecutive colosseum solo battles
092 Use Taunt 300 times
093 Attack first 500 times
094 Use Taunt on Gabriel Celeste 10 times
095 Defeat an enemy in one hit 60 times in a row
096 Obtain 255 Entomology item drops
097 Use Taunt on the Ethereal Queen 10 times
098 Defeat 30,000 enemies
099 Win 100 consecutive battles without healing
100 Defeat 100 enemies while HP is at 5% or less

In addition to the in-game Battle Trophy system, owners of the PlayStation 3 version of *Star Ocean: The Last Hope* can earn 46 Bronze and Silver Trophies to unlock the game's Platinum Trophy. Xbox 360 players can unlock 50 Achievements to earn 1,000 Gamerscore Points.

Achievements and Trophies	GP	Trophy Color	Requirement
Abolished Armaros	20	Bronze	Defeated Armaros on the northern coast of Aeos.
Butchered Barachiel	20	Bronze	Defeated Barachiel in the engine room of the celestial ship.
Rookie Battler	10	Bronze	Obtained 10% of all battle trophies. (15% in PS3 version)
Novice Battler	10	–	Obtained 20% of all battle trophies.
Practiced Battler	10	–	Obtained 30% of all battle trophies.
Skilled Battler	10	Bronze	Obtained 40% of all battle trophies. (45% in PS3 version)
Accomplished Battler	10	–	Obtained 50% of all battle trophies.
Seasoned Battler	10	Bronze	Obtained 60% of all battle trophies.
Advanced Battler	10	Bronze	Obtained 70% of all battle trophies. (75% in PS3 version)
Expert Battler	10	–	Obtained 80% of all battle trophies.
Master Battler	10	Silver	Obtained 90% of all battle trophies.
Ultimate Battler	10	Silver	Obtained 100% of all battle trophies.
Ship Savant	20	Bronze	Collected 100% 0f all spaceship data.
Arms Addict	30	Bronze	Collected 100% of all weapon data.
Creature Collector	20	Bronze	Collected 50% of all monster data.
Monster Master	30	Silver	Collected 100% of all monster data.
Escaped from Earth	20	Bronze	Narrowly escaped from the alternate Earth before its untimely demise…
Squelched Sahariel	30	Bronze	Defeated Sahariel in the Cardianon control tower's central isolation chamber.
Trounced Tamiel	30	Bronze	Defeated Tamiel and his Sydonaist henchmen in the hallowed halls of the Purgatorium.
Treasure Hunter	20	Bronze	Opened 50% of all treasure chests.
Massacred Manifest	30	Silver	Defeated Armaros Manifest in the grimy depths of the Miga Insect Warren.
Quelled Kokabiel	30	Silver	Defeated Kokabiel and her spawn in the sacred En II Sanctuary.
Colosseum Charter	10	Bronze	Broke into the top 30 in solo or team battle rankings.
Silenced Satanail	40	Silver	Defeated Satanail in the Palace of Creation on Nox Obscurus.
Lymle's Ending	10	Bronze	Viewed Lymle's ending sequence.
Bacchus's Ending	10	Bronze	Viewed Bacchus's ending sequence.
Sarah's Ending	10	Bronze	Viewed Sarah's ending sequence.
Myuria's Ending	10	Bronze	Viewed Myuria's ending sequence.
Reimi's Ending	10	Bronze	Viewed Reimi's ending sequence.
Errand Boy	20	Bronze	Completed 30% of all quests. (50% in PS3 version)
Colosseum Challenger	20	Bronze	Broke into the top 10 in solo or team battle rankings.
Celestial Slayer	40	Silver	Defeated Gabriel Celeste.
Colosseum Champion	30	Silver	Took over the top spot in solo or team battle rankings.
Rapid Rabbit Wrangler	20	Silver	Earned 100 victories in class 100 bunny racing.
Universal Victor	30	Silver	Completed the game on the Universe difficulty level.
Chaotic Conqueror	70	Silver	Completed the game on the Chaos difficulty level.
Faize's Ending	10	Silver	Viewed Faize's ending sequence.
Meracle's Ending	10	Bronze	Viewed Meracle's ending sequence.
Arumat's Ending	10	Bronze	Viewed Arumat's ending sequence.
Crowe's Ending	10	Bronze	Viewed Crowe's ending sequence.
Dilettante Designer	20	Bronze	Created 20% of all possible items.
Aspiring Architect	20	Bronze	Created 40% of all possible items.
Creative Craftsman	20	Bronze	Created 60% of all possible items.
Inspired Inventor	20	Bronze	Created 80% of all possible items.
World's Biggest Welch Fan	20	Silver	Created 100% of all possible items.
Treasure Hoarder	30	Silver	Opened 100% of all treasure chests.
Potential Postman	20	–	Completed 60% of all quests.
Dutiful Deliverer	30	Silver	Completed 100% of all quests.
Hasty Hare Handler	10	Bronze	Earned 50 victories in class 100 bunny racing.
Ethereal Executioner	40	Silver	Defeated the Ethereal Queen.

Achievements and Trophies

006

SRF-002 BALENA

Found on a console at the north end of Exploration Base (where G
resides).

SRF-004 DENTDELION

Found on a console at the north end of the Exploration Base
(where Grafton resides).

007

008

SRF-005 EREMIA

Found on a console at the north end of the Exploration Base
(where Grafton resides).

PHANTOM CRAFT

[SRF-STYLE]

Found on a console within En II's Monitoring Room B (only available
after your arrival on Nox Obscurus).

009

010

USTA WARPSHIP

Found on a console within En II's Monitoring Room B (only availa
after your arrival on Nox Obscurus).

091 OBSERVER'S SPEAR

Bought at Red Claw Weapons.

092 SACRED SPEAR

Must be made with Item Creation (Recipe Memo 03).

093 SEA SERPENT HARPOON

Acquired from the Palace of Creation (Area 2).

094 UNICORN LANCE

Acquired from the Cave of the Seven Stars (B5).

095 TRIDENT HARPOON

Acquired in the Wandering Dungeon (9F).

096 VICTORY LANCE

Must be made with Item Creation.

097 SYMBOL STAFF

Initially equipped to Myuria.

098 FANATIC'S STAFF

Obtained after defeating Tamiel in the Purgatorium.

099 STAFF OF FREEZING

Must be made with Item Creation.

100 SACRED SCEPTER

Acquired in the Alanaire Citadel

101 WILDFANG STAFF

Must be made with Item Creation.

102 MYSTERIOUS SCEPTER

Bought at the Imitation Gallery.

103 RAVEN STAFF

Acquired from the Old Road to the Sanctuary (En II)

104 CALAMITY STAFF

Must be made with Item Creation.

105 BLOOD SCEPTER

Acquired from the Wandering Dungeon (14F, 15F).

106 WIZARD'S STAFF

Must be made with Item Creation.

107 ELDARIAN SCYTHE

Initially equipped to Arumat.

108 INFERNO SICKLE

Bought at the Colosseum Fight Coin Exchange.

109 LASER SCYTHE

Must be made with Item Creation.

110 GRIM REAPER

Bought at the Imitation Gallery.

111 QUADPLEX SCYTHE

Must be made with Item Creation.

112 CONQUEROR SCYTHE "ASURA VAJRA"

Bought at the Santa Maria shop.

113 QUAKE SCYTHE

Must be made with Item Creation.

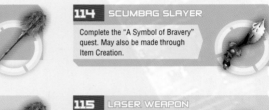

114 SCUMBAG SLAYER

Complete the "A Symbol of Bravery" quest. May also be made through Item Creation.

115 LASER WEAPON

Complete the "Trial of Might" quest.

116 FLZ01 BEAM SABER

Reunite with Crowe in chapter 6.

117 ELD7X PLASMA CANNON

Reunite with Crowe in chapter 6.

118 GESTURE ROD

Speak to Welch when she has her wand.

119 ORACLE'S STAFF

When on Lemuris, speak to Lutea in the Alanaire Citadel after saving Sarah for the first time. She's waiting at the very top of the tower.

120 MAIDEN'S STAFF

While on Roak, examine Lady Eleyna while she's sleeping (the scene just before raid on the Purgatorium).

121 ASTRAL SWORD

Speak to Lias, the Astralian Royal Knight in Astral City.

122 SRF-ISSUE F98 ASSAULT RIFLE

Found on a box within the Calnus's storage room.

123 SMG103U SUBMACHINE GUN

Obtained after meeting Mila on Alternate Earth.

124 S&T-M010 SECURITY PISTOL

Obtained after meeting Mila on Alternate Earth.

125 BOUNCER'S SWORD

Speak to Jarvis, Hot-Blooded Bouncer in Tatroi (Roak).

126 DONZEL'S SWORD

Speak to any knight in Astral City.

127 GUARDSMAN'S LANCE

Found after speaking to the Fiercely Resolute Guard in Tatroi (Roak).

128 ND003 HANDBLASTER

Speak to the Hopeful Man on En II.

129 NDS002 SYMBOLIC ROD

Speak to the Smiling Woman on En II

130 F98X ASSAULT RIFLE

Obtained during your first encounter with the Phantoms.

131 SKULLBREAKER

Obtained after your first encounter with a Lizardman.

132 KOBOLD'S SCIMITAR

Obtained after your first encounter with a Kobold.

133 DRACONIC JAMADHARS

Obtained after your first encounter with the Dragon Newt.

134 DRACONIC SMASHER

Obtained after your first encounter with the Cardianon.

135 M26 HAND GRENADE

Obtained after your first encounter with a Soldier Zombie.

136 COMET HAMMER

Found after defeating the Spirit Priest (planet Roak) for the first time.

137 SWORD OF PUNISHMENT

Obtained after your first encounter with any Skeleton monster.

138 CRESCENT MOON

Obtained after your first encounter with any Succubus.

139 DEMONHEAD STAFF

Defeat the Master Wizard enemy located in the **Old Road to the Sanctuary** (En II).

140 CHEAP DAGGER

Obtained after your first encounter with a Scumbag.

141 MOONFALX

Defeat Ashlay in the Tatroi Colosseum (the #1 ranked fighter in Team Mode).

142 BUSHRIPPER

Defeat the Sydonaist Alpha enemy located in the **Purgatorium** (planet Roak).

143 NIGHTSLASHER

Fight against the Black Eagle in Tatroi's Colosseum for the first time.

144 STAFF OF THE VALIANT EYE

Defeat Tamiel, the boss of the Purgatorium.

145 WICKED BLADE "AMEZU-JACULA"

Defeat the Apostle of Creation, an enemy located in the Palace of Creation.

146 LANCE OF TRUTH

Defeat Gabriel Celeste in the Cave of the Seven Stars.

147 CRESCENT OF PLUTO

Defeat the Ethereal Queen.

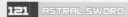

SRF-003 CALNUS

Found on an empty control panel within the New Calnus.

001

002

CALNUS-II
[W/ELDARIAN UPGRADES]

Found on Exploration Base control panel (where Grafton resides).

CALNUS-III
[W/ENHANCED ARMAMENTS]

Found on a spinning dish within En II's Monitoring Room B (only available after your arrival on Nox Obscurus).

003

004

SRF-001 AQUILA

Found on an empty control panel on the Calnus.

AQUILA-B
[HIGH-SPEED CRUISER]

Found on a spinning dish within En II's Monitoring Room B (only available after your arrival on Nox Obscurus).

005

CALNUS
[USTA TRANSPORT]

Found on a console within En II's Monitoring Room B (only available after your arrival on Nox Obscurus).

011

012

ZAGZAGEL
(ELDARIAN CRUISER)

Found on a console near the south-end of the Exploration Base.

ZAMZAGIEL
[ELDARIAN DESTROYER]

Found on a console within En II's Monitoring Room B (only available after your arrival on Nox Obscurus).

013

014

DOMINION
[ELDARIAN COLONY SHIP]

Found on a spinning dish within En II's Monitoring Room B (only available after your arrival on Nox Obscurus).

061 BLAZING WAND

Found in the Wandering Dungeon (7F, 8F).

062 DIVINE WAND "EMPYREAL REVERIE"

Bought at the Santa Maria shop.

063 ANCIENT SAGE'S WAND

Must be made with Item Creation.

064 MASER CANNON

Initially equipped to Bacchus.

065 PLASMA CANNON

Found on Alternate Earth.

066 ANCIENT CANNON

Found in the Purgatorium (B3).

067 DEADLY CANNON

Must be made with Item Creation.

068 TOB LIGHTNING CANNON

Bought at the Red Claw Weapons store.

069 DRAGOON BLASTER

Must be made with Item Creation.

070 IMMORTAL SMASHER

Acquired on the Celestial Ship.

071 VULCAN DISCHARGER

Acquired in the Palace of Creation (Area 4).

072 PHOTONIC BLASTER

Must be made with Item Creation.

073 ULTIMATE CANNON

Acquired in the Wandering Dungeon (16F, 18F).

074 OGRE CANNON "LEGION'S HOWL"

Bought at the Santa Maria shop.

075 SYMBOL CANNON "TEMPEST"

Must be made with Item Creation.

076 IRON CLAWS

Initially equipped to Meracle.

077 VERMILLION CLAWS

Bought at Morgan's Weapons.

078 OCEAN CLAWS

Must be made with Item Creation.

079 DRAGON CLAWS

Bought from the Colosseum Fight Coin Exchange.

080 HURRICANE CLAWS

Acquired in the Miga Insect Warren.

081 SLASHER CLAWS

Bought from Red Claw Weapons.

082 BIGFOOT'S CLAWS

Must be made with Item Creation.

083 BURNING CLAWS

Found in Astral Caves (B3).

084 HIDDEN CLAWS "CRIMSON FALCONS"

Found in the Wandering Dungeon (10F, 12F).

085 RUMBLE CLAWS

Must be made with Item Creation.

086 CEREMONIAL SPEAR

Initially equipped to Sarah.

087 SEAFARER'S HARPOON

Complete "The Seafarer's Treasure" quest.

088 CRESTED SPEAR

Bought at the Colosseum Fight Coin Exchange.

089 CYCLONE SPEAR

Must be made with Item Creation.

090 JUDGMENT SPEAR

Must be made with Item Creation.

MORPHUS ESCAPE POD

Found on a spinning dish in En II's Monitoring Room B.

019

020

CARDIANON LANDING SHIP

Found on a console within the deepest section of the celestial ship (control area).

CARDIANON MOTHERSHIP

Acquired from a console in the Cardianon Mothership (B1), at the opposite end of the room from chest 14.

021

022

CARDIANON BATTLECRAFT

Found on a spinning dish in En II's Monitoring Room B.

Weapon Collection Data

001 WORKMAN'S BLADE
Automatically obtained during first event on planet Aeos.

002 STORM BLADE
Item Creation only (Recipe Memo 05).

003 BLESSED SWORD
Acquire the weapon from shop on Lemuris.

004 FLAME SWORD
Must be made with Item Creation.

005 CARDIANON SWORD
Found within a box on the celestial ship.

006 SILVANCE
Found within a box on the Cardianon Mothership.

007 VENOM SWORD
Must be made with Item Creation.

008 BASTARD SWORD
Obtained from the Edis Weapons shop.

009 ICECRUSHER SWORD
Must be made with Item Creation.

010 FAMED SWORD "VEINSLAY"
Found in a box behind the King of Astral's throne.

011 MITHRIL SWORD
Bought at the Colosseum Fight Coin Exchange.

012 OBSERVER'S SWORD
Bought at the Red Claw Weapons store.

013 ARCANA SWORD
Item Creation only (Recipe Memo 01).

014 HOLY SWORD "FAREWELL"
Acquired from within the Palace of Creation (Area 6).

015 LIGHTNING SWORD
Found in a box within the Purgatorium (B1).

016 MOONSTONE SWORD
Must be made with Item Creation.

017 DEMON SWORD "LEVANTINE"
Obtained within the Wandering Dungeon (17F, 19F).

018 BINDING SWORD "SHIHO MURASAME"
Bought from the Santa Maria shop.

019 IMPERIAL SWORD
Must be made with Item Creation.

020 SHORT BOW
Initially equipped to Reimi.

021 ELDARIAN BOW
Bought from the Base Shop: Omega in the Exploration Base.

022 TORCH BOW
Bought at Woodley Weapon Shop VIII.

023 HUNTING BOW
Must be made with Item Creation.

024 EARTHSOUL BOW
Must be made with Item Creation.

025 CARDIANON BOW
Obtained from a box on the Cardianon Mothership.

026 ALIEN ARC
Obtained from a box on Alternate Earth.

027 COMPOSITE BOW
Must be made with Item Creation.

028 BELLWETHER'S BOW
Located within black tribeswoman's tent on Roak.

029 MYSTIC BOW
Must be made with Item Creation.

030 BOW OF WISDOM
Must be made with Item Creation.

031 WILD ARC

Acquired from the Colosseum Fight Coin Exchange.

032 SPIRIT BOW "DARKSTRIKER"

Must be made with Item Creation.

033 SAINT'S BOW

Bought at the Red Claw Weapons shop.

034 HOMING ARC

Must be made with Item Creation.

035 EVIL SPIRIT'S BOW

Found in the Cave of the Seven Stars (B2).

036 ARTIFACT BOW

Found in the Wandering Dungeon (4F, 6F).

037 FIERCE BOW "REPPU SHINGETSU"

Bought from the Santa Maria shop.

038 MEDIUMISTIC BOW

Must be made with Item Creation.

039 ELDARIAN RAPIER

Initially equipped to Faize.

040 GUARDIAN'S RAPIER

Found in the Alanaire Citadel.

041 IRON SABER

Must be made with Item Creation.

042 ICICLE RAPIER

Found in the Cardianon Mothership.

043 ELASTIC RAPIER

Must be made with Item Creation.

044 RUNE SABER

Must be made with Item Creation.

045 MITHRIL RAPIER

Acquired from the Colosseum Fight Coin Exchange.

046 SYLPH'S SABER

Bought from Ruddle's Place.

047 INFINITY SABER

Obtained in the Wandering Dungeon (7F, 11F).

048 SKY SWORD "AMA-NO-MURAKUMO"

Bought in the Santa Maria shop.

049 ONYX SABER

Must be made with Item Creation.

050 CANDY WAND

Initially equipped to Lymle.

051 FLAME WAND

Obtained from the Woodley Weapon Shop.

052 BOOSTER WAND

Obtained on the Cardianon Mothership.

053 RUBY WAND

Must be made with Item Creation.

054 WAND OF WONDER

Bought at Morgan's Weapons.

055 RUNE WAND

Must be made with Item Creation.

056 CRYSTAL WAND

Must be made with Item Creation.

057 NATURE WAND

Found in the Miga Insect Warren.

058 STAR RUBY WAND

Must be made with Item Creation.

059 NIGHTMARE WAND

Acquired on Nox Obscurus (Pulsating Bog). May also be bought from the Santa Maria shop.

060 WAND OF RESONANCE

Must be made with Item Creation.

REDNUHT
(ELDARIAN BATTLESHIP)

Found on a spinning dish within En II's Monitoring Room B.

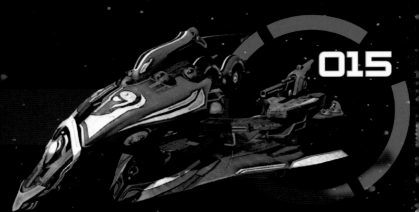

015

016

SOL
[ELDARIAN SHUTTLECRAFT]

Found on a console near the south end of the Exploration Base.

MORPHUS BATTLESHIP

Found on a spinning dish in En II's Monitoring Room B.

017

018

MORPHUS EXPLORATION CRAFT

Found on a spinning dish in En II's Monitoring Room B.